Lecture Notes in Computer Science 6905

Commenced Publication in 1973
Founding and Former Series Editors:
Gerhard Goos, Juris Hartmanis, and Jan van Leeuwen

Editorial Board

W0225678

Ching-Hsien Hsu   Laurence T. Yang
Jianhua Ma   Chunsheng Zhu (Eds.)

Ubiquitous Intelligence and Computing

8th International Conference, UIC 2011
Banff, Canada, September 2-4, 2011
Proceedings

 Springer

Volume Editors

Ching-Hsien Hsu
Chung Hua University
Department of Computer Science and Information Engineering
Hsinchu 300, Taiwan
E-mail: chh@chu.edu.tw

Laurence T. Yang
St. Francis Xavier University, Department of Computer Science
Antigonish, NS, B2G 2W5, Canada
E-mail: ltyang@stfx.ca

Jianhua Ma
Hosei University, Faculty of Computer and Information Sciences
Tokyo 184-8584, Japan
E-mail: jianhua@hosei.ac.jp

Chunsheng Zhu
St. Francis Xavier University, Department of Computer Science
Antigonish, NS, B2G 2W5, Canada
E-mail: chunsheng.tom.zhu@gmail.com

ISSN 0302-9743   e-ISSN 1611-3349
ISBN 978-3-642-23640-2   ISBN 978-3-642-23641-9 (eBook)
DOI 10.1007/978-3-642-23641-9
Springer Heidelberg Dordrecht London New York

Library of Congress Control Number: 2011934962

CR Subject Classification (1998): C.2, H.4, I.2, H.5, C.2.4, I.2.11, D.2.8, J.4

LNCS Sublibrary: SL 3 – Information Systems and Application, incl. Internet/Web
and HCI

Typesetting: Camera-ready by author, data conversion by Scientific Publishing Services, Chennai, India

Printed on acid-free paper

Springer is part of Springer Science+Business Media (www.springer.com)

Preface

It is our great pleasure to welcome you to the eighth annual event of the International Conference on Ubiquitous Intelligence and Computing (UIC 2011).

This volume contains the proceedings of UIC 2011, the 8th International Conference on Ubiquitous Intelligence and Computing: Building Smart Worlds in Real and Cyber Spaces. The conference was held in Banff, Canada, during September 2–4, 2011. The event was the eighth meeting of this conference series, following USW 2005 (Taiwan), UISW 2005 (Japan), UIC 2006 (Wuhan, China), UIC 2007 (Hong Kong), UIC 2008 (Oslo, Norway), UIC 2009 (Brisbane, Australia) and UIC 2010 (Xian, China).

UIC is recognized as the main regular event in the world that covers many dimensions of ubiquitous intelligent computing, smart environment and systems, smart objects and personal, social or physical aspects. UIC 2011 played an important role for researchers and industry practitioners to exchange information regarding advancements in the state of art and practice of IT-driven services and applications, as well as to identify emerging research topics and define the future directions of ubiquitous intelligence and computing.

We received a large amount of submissions this year, showing by both quantity and quality that UIC is a premier conference on ubiquitous intelligence computing. In the first stage, all papers submitted were screened for their relevance and general submission requirements. These manuscripts then underwent a rigorous peer-review process with at least three reviewers per paper. At the end, 44 papers were accepted for presentation and included in the main proceedings. To encourage and promote the work presented at UIC 2011, we were delighted to inform the authors that some of the papers will be accepted in special issues of several reputable international journals. All of these journals have played a prominent role in promoting the development and use of ubiquitous intelligence and computing.

An international conference of this scale requires the support of many people. First of all, we would like to thank the Steering Chairs, Jianhua Ma and Laurence T. Yang, for nourishing the conference and guiding its course. We appreciate the participation of the keynote speakers, Han-Chieh Chao and Victor C. M. Leung; their speeches greatly benefited the audience. We are also indebted to the members of the Program Committee, who put in hard work and long hours to review each paper in a professional way. Thanks to them all for their valuable time and effort in reviewing the papers. Without their help, this program would not be possible. Special thanks go to Chunsheng Zhu for his help with the conference website, paper submission and reviewing system and a lot of detailed work, which facilitated the overall process. Thanks also go to the entire local

Arrangements Committee for their help in making the conference a wonderful success. We take this opportunity to thank all the authors, participants and Session Chairs for their valuable efforts, many of whom traveled long distances to attend this conference and make their valuable contributions. Last but not least, we would like express our gratitude to all of the organizations that supported our efforts to bring the conference to fruition. We are grateful to Springer for publishing the proceedings.

The conference was held in the beautiful town of Banff, was an area with ample scenic spots. We trust that our guests enjoyed the academic side of the conference as well as the venue and magnificent natural beauty of the area.

September 2011

Ching-Hsien Hsu
Laurence T. Yang
Jianhua Ma
Chunsheng Zhu

Organization

Executive Committee

Honorary Chair

Stephen S. Yau   Arizona State University, USA

General Chairs

M. Jamal Deen   McMaster University, Canada
Witold Pedrycz   University of Alberta, Canada
Ying Zhang   Palo Alto Research Center, USA

Program Chairs

Robert C. Hsu   Chung Hua University, Taiwan
Torben Weis   University of Duisburg, Germany
Woontack Woo   GIST, Korea

Program Vice Chairs

Ren-Hung Hwang   National Chung Cheng University, Taiwan
Minkyong Kim   IBM, USA

Workshop Chairs

Bernady O. Apduhan   Kyushu Sangyo University, Japan
Waltenegus Dargie   Technical University of Dresden, Germany

Steering Committee

Jianhua Ma (Chair)   Hosei University, Japan
Laurence T. Yang (Chair)   St. Francis Xavier University, Canada
Hai Jin   Huazhong University of Science and
      Technology, China
Theo Ungerer   University of Augsburg, Germany
Jadwiga Indulska   University of Queensland, Australia
Daqing Zhang   Institute TELECOM SudParis, France

Advisory Committee

Sumi Helal (Chair)   University of Florida, USA
Norio Shiratori   Tohoku University, Japan
Jeffrey J.P. Tsai   University of Illinois at Chicago, USA
Mohan Kumar   University of Texas at Arlington, USA
Max Muehlhaeuser   Darmstadt University of Technology, Germany
Yuanchun Shi   Tsinghua University, China

Zhaohui Wu	Zhejiang University, China
Xingshe Zhou	Northwest Polytechnic University, China
Ahhwee Tan	Nanyang Technological University, Singapore
Christian Becker	University of Mannheim, Germany

Publicity Chairs

Carlos Westphall	Federal University of Santa Catarina, Brazil
Wenbin Jiang	Huazhong University of Science and Technology, China
Damien Sauveron	University of Limoges, France
Xingang Liu	Yonsei University, Korea
Mianxiong Dong	University of Aizu, Japan
Chao Chen	University of Florida, USA
Jiehan Zhou	University of Oulu, Finland
Agustinus Borgy Waluyo	Monash University, Australia
Senol Z. Erdogan	Maltepe University, Turkey
Weiwei Fang	Beijing Jiaotong University, China
Xu Li	University of Waterloo, Canada

International Liaison Chairs

Bessam Abdulrazak	Sherbrooke University, Canada
Frode Eika Sandnes	Oslo University College, Norway
Marius Portmann	University of Queensland, Australia
Jiannong Cao	Hong Kong Polytechnic University, Hong Kong
Yo-Ping Huang	National Taipei University of Technology, Taiwan

Industrial Liaison Chairs

Nagula Sangary	RIM, Canada
Alvin Chin	Nokia Research Centre Beijing, China

Demo/Exhibition Chairs

Gang Pan	Zhejiang University, China
Itiro Siio	Ochanomizu University, Japan

Award Chairs

Judith Symonds	Auckland University of Technology, New Zealand
Jong Hyuk Park	Kyungnam University, Korea

Panel Chairs

Daqing Zhang	Institute TELECOM SudParis, France
Ramiro Liscano	University of Ontario Institute of Technology, Canada

Special Track Chairs

Zheng Yan   Nokia Research Center, Finland
Yan Wang   Macquarie University, Australia

Web Chair

Chunsheng Zhu   St. Francis Xavier University, Canada

Local Chairs

Andy Yongwen Pan   St. Francis Xavier University, Canada
Alice Ying Huang   St. Francis Xavier University, Canada
Shizheng Jiang   St. Francis Xavier University, Canada

Program Committee

Rafael 'Tico' Ballagas   Nokia Research, USA
Martin Bauer   NEC Laboratories Europe, Germany
Rachid Benamri   Lakehead University, Canada
Neil Bergmann   The University of Queensland, Australia
Miriam Capretz   The University of Western Ontario, Canada
Lin-huang Chang   National Taichung University, Taiwan
Yue-Shan Chang   National Taipei University, Taiwan
Alvin Chin   Nokia Research Center Beijing, China
Antonio Coronato   ICAR-CNR, Italy
Babak Esfandiari   Carleton University, Canada
Dingyi Fang   Northwest University, China
Raghu K. Ganti   IBM T.J. Watson Research Center, USA
Jinhua Guo   University of Michigan-Dearborn, USA
Song Guo   University of Aizu, Japan
Jessica Heesen   Tübingen University, Germany
Didier Hoareau   University of La Réunion, France
Hui-Huang Hsu   Tamkang University, Taiwan
Peizhao Hu   NICTA, Australia
Chung-Ming Huang   National Cheng Kung University, Taiwan
Runhe Huang   Hosei University, Japan
Yo-Ping Huang   National Taipei University of Technology,
                              Taiwan
Yu Huang   Nanjing University, China
Fuyuki Ishikawa   National Institute of Informatics, Japan
Beihong Jin   Chinese Academy of Sciences, China
Yasuharu Katsuno   IBM Research-Tokyo, Japan
Sehwan Kim   WorldViz, USA
Youngho Lee   Mokpo National University, Korea

Table of Contents

Smart Objects and Environments

Cloud and Services Computing

Security, Privacy and Trustworthy

P2P, WSN and Ad Hoc Networks

Ubiquitous Intelligent Algorithms and Applications

Internet of Things and Cloud Computing for Future Internet

Han-Chieh Chao

President of National Ilan University
Director of the Computer Center for Ministry of Education (2008-2010)
Joint appointed Full Professor of the Department of Electronic Engineering and Institute of
Computer Science & Information Engineering, National Ilan University, I-Lan, Taiwan, R.O.C
hcc@niu.edu.tw

In recent years, Internet of Things (IoT) and Cloud Computing are the hottest issues of Future Internet. The IoT is the most important concept of Future Internet for providing a common global IT Platform to combine seamless networks and networked things. Cloud Computing provides backend solution for processing huge data streams and computations while facing the challenges of everything will be connected with seamless networks in the future. However, there is a lack of common fabric for integrating IoT and Cloud. In telecommunications, the IMS (IP Multimedia Subsystem) based on the All-IP and Open Services Architecture has been regarded as the trend for Next Generation Network (NGN). We believe that the IMS communication platform is the most suitable fabric for integrating IoT and Cloud. In this study, we will provide the discussion of open challenges and possible solutions for Future Internet.

C.-H. Hsu et al. (Eds.): UIC 2011, LNCS 6905, p. 1, 2011.

Networking of Vehicles - Applications, Challenges and Some Recent Results

Victor C.M. Leung

Fellow of IEEE
Fellow of the Engineering Institute of Canada
Fellow of the Canadian Academy of Engineering
Distinguished Lecturer of the IEEE Communications Society
Professional Engineer in the Province of British Columbia, Canada
Professor and Holder of the TELUS Mobility Research Chair in Advanced Telecommunications
Engineering in the Department of Electrical and Computer Engineering, University of British
Columbia, Vancouver, BC, Canada vleung@ece.ubc.ca

Recent advances in wireless communication technologies are making it possible for automobiles to be integrated into the global network. Intelligent Transportation Systems with vehicles in the loop are expected to significantly improve road safety, reduce traffic congestion and cut greenhouse gas emissions. This is made possible in the USA by Dedicated Short Range Communications (DSRC), which employs the IEEE 802.11p standard over the 75MHz of spectrum in the 5.9 GHz band allocated by the FCC for vehicle-to-vehicle (V2V) and vehicle-to-infrastructure (V2I) communications. DSRC is expected to revolutionize road transportation by making possible many real-time safety applications. However, global deployment of DSRC is not expected to materialize in the near term due to regulatory and financial challenges. In the meantime, vehicles and their passengers are increasingly equipped with different forms of wireless networking capabilities, e.g., cellular, WiFi and WiMAX. Thus there is also a growing interest in supporting applications like infotainment, travel advisory, route planning, etc., using heterogeneous wireless networks. In this presentation, I shall describe several applications that leverage the wireless communications to put vehicles in the loop. Different applicants impose different requirements on the wireless network for data routing, transfer latency, etc. I shall review the technical challenges that need to be overcome to meet some of these requirements, and describe solutions developed in our recent research to meet these challenges. I shall conclude the presentation by discussing some future research directions.

C.-H. Hsu et al. (Eds.): UIC 2011, LNCS 6905, p. 2, 2011.
© Springer-Verlag Berlin Heidelberg 2011

Ubiquitous Meeting Facilitator with Playful Real-Time User Interface

Ying Zhang[1], Marshall Bern[1], Juan Liu[1], Kurt Partridge[1],
Bo Begole[1], Bob Moore[1], Jim Reich[1], and Koji Kishimoto[2]

[1] Palo Alto Research Center Inc.
3333 Coyote Hill Rd
Palo Alto, CA 94304, USA
yzhang@parc.com
[2] Fujitsu
Tokyo, Japan
Koji.koshimoto@jp.fujitsu.com

Abstract. Effective group meetings are important for the productivity of corporations. But many meetings do not achieve their goals because some people are too shy to speak while others are too dominant. To avoid the cost and intrusiveness of human meeting facilitation and to increase self-awareness of conversation behaviors, various types of meeting facilitators have been developed over the past couple of years. We present a prototype that is unique because it captures both individual and group behaviors and provides *real time* playful feedback. The portable prototype includes a set of table-top microphones with an audio interface to a laptop PC, where audio data are processed and an avatar-based UI displays the shared state of individual and group behaviors during a meeting. The interface reveals not only level of participation, but also several other meaningful but harder to detect behaviors such as turn taking, interruptions, and group laughter. The presentation's design is deliberately playful to keep participants monitor, self-estimate and improve their meeting behavior.

1 Introduction

In meetings, as in most forms of verbal interaction, the right to talk is a limited resource [11]. The participants must manage who will speak next locally and on a turn-by-turn basis [11]. We argue that one key part of poor communication in meetings is the ineffective and inefficient allocation of speaking turns. Some meeting participants talk too much, or at inappropriate times, while others may need encouragement to contribute, or are interrupted or blocked from speaking by more vocal participants [1].

One of the roles of a human meeting facilitator is to help the participants allocate turns-at-talk. Facilitators draw attention to participants who have not contributed and explicitly invite them to participate, at times shutting down other participants who are dominating the floor. In our research, we ask the

C.-H. Hsu et al. (Eds.): UIC 2011, LNCS 6905, pp. 3–11, 2011.
© Springer-Verlag Berlin Heidelberg 2011

Fig. 1. The Ubiquitous Meeting Facilitator (UMF)

question: Can an automated system detect turn-taking behavior in meetings and how can it help facilitate the allocation of turns-at-talk more effectively?

We designed and implemented a prototype of the "Ubiquitous Meeting Facilitator" (UMF) that monitors the level of participation, detects turn-taking and various types of interruptions, and shows the individual behaviors and group states visually in a shared display (Fig. 1). We intend to make the display not too personal or serious – such a system could seem threatening or insulting. We use avatars to represent participants, sizes of avatars to represent level of participation, and facial expressions to represent individual behaviors, etc. Simultaneously, group states, such as prolonged silence, interruptions, overlapping conversation, and group laughter, are captured with background colors and icons. Note that laughter detection provides not only information about emotion, but it also reduces false alarms of overlapping speech (if laughters were identified as speech). Meeting events are detected and recorded, so that the effectiveness of the meeting can be analyzed offline. The system is portable with table-top microphones connecting through an audio interface to a laptop. In addition to real-time facilitation, the system can also use recorded audio files to analyze past meetings.

There has been ample previous work on capturing meetings for offline analysis. For example, the AMI and AMIDA projects [10] addressed the recognition and interpretation of multiparty meetings. The VACE project [12] developed systems and tools to automatically detect, extract, and report high interest people, patterns, and trends in visual content from foreign news, using video information capture, indexing, and retrieval technology. The CALO Meeting Assistant [9] is an integrated, multimodal system that captures speech and gestures and uses machine learning and robust discourse processing to provide a rich, browsable record of a meeting. Our system, UMF, which uses only audio, is simpler and lighter weight than these offline systems, yet it retains the core functionality of capturing meeting events and conversational status.

There has also been work on real-time GUIs for meeting participation. Conversation Clock [2] displays a visualization of each speaker's activity over time, however the shared display only shows level of participation from individuals, while conversational behaviors such as turn-taking and interruptions are not clearly depicted. DiMicco et. al. [3] describe a shared display for influencing group participation by exposing each speaker's total speech time. Again, no conversational behaviors are shown other than the total amount of speech time from individuals. The MIT Media Lab's Meeting Mediator (MM) [7] consists of portable sociometric badges for capturing data and cellphones for displaying meeting status. MM emphasizes balance, using the position of a colored circle to depict the dominating behavior intuitively. However, there are no visual highlights for interruptions, common laughter or group behaviors. UMF, on the other hand, displays a rich set of high-level features based on Conversation Analysis, including turn-taking, domination, interrupts, laughter, and other group behaviors such as long overlapping or silence. UMF can be used for both online facilitation and offline meeting analysis. In addition, such a system would be more useful for tele-conferences, where turn-taking becomes more important due to delays of communication and lack of direct facial expressions. Although the current system is implemented for a shared display, it should adapt easily to individual displays on cellphones [5].

2   UMF System Design

The design objective for UMF was to build a prototype of a meeting facilitator for group brainstorming meetings, with at most 12 participants. At the outset, we determined that the system should:

- be portable, and cheap and easy to install;
- be humorous, non-intrusive, and not too personal;
- provide real-time feedback of meeting progress;
- detect over- and under-participation;
- detect and display interruptions;
- distinguish laughter from speech;
- detect and display group state and individual behavior; and
- enable after-meeting statistics and meeting quality analysis.

The software components of UMF are depicted in Fig. 2. It consists of a microphone input component, speech and laughter detection component, conversation behavior detection and a GUI component. The components will be described in detail in the rest of this section.

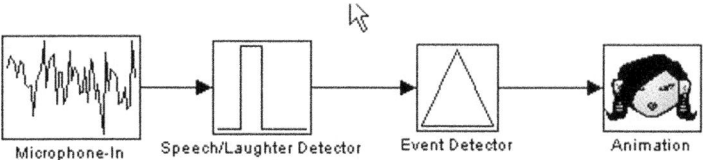

Fig. 2. UMF software components, consisting of speech/laughter detection, conversation behavior detection and avatar-based animation

2.1   Speech and Laughter Detection

The low-level signal processing algorithms perform simple detection and classification operations. The system breaks down a raw audio stream into short segments, and classifies each segment into a category (silence vs. utterance and speech vs. laughter). The classified segments are then fed to the event detection mechanism to detect high-level events such as turn-taking and interruptions. The low-level signal processing and classification algorithms that we implemented in the UMF prototype were built on the state of the art in speech [8] and laughter detection [6], and were chosen for simplicity and speed. The algorithms work in real-time, enabling the overall system to give real-time feedback to meeting participants.

In our prototype implementation, each meeting participant uses his/her own microphone, set on the shared conference table and pointed roughly in the direction of the person. The UMF system issues a silence/utterance classification 32 times per second for each microphone. For silence/utterance differentiation, we use two features, each reflecting integration over the last 1/8 second: the total broadband energy (30–2000 Hz), and the total narrowband energy in the strongest harmonic series of spectrum peaks. In order to capture speech formants, attention is limited to harmonic series with fundamental frequency 70 to 440 Hz. Both features must exceed threshold values for a time segment to be classified as utterance (speech or laughter). The thresholds are set adaptively in order to compensate for noise baselines varying in both time and space, due to fans, computers, open doors, and so forth. The narrowband feature is quite successful at distinguishing speech and laughter from typical meeting-room noises such as rustling paper, banging coffee cups, and squeaking chairs.

The UMF system handles crosstalk, which arises when one person speaks the signal is detected by all the nearby microphones. To suppress the utterance detection from crosstalk, we correlate the time-series power across different microphones. If a microphone has higher power than all its correlates, it is considered the "primary channel", and its detection suppresses the detections from all other channels with sufficiently high correlation coefficients. In this way, we ensure that each speaker is detected by only one microphone.

The UMF system distinguishes laughter from speech. This classification is especially important for distinguishing impolite interruptions, which should be discouraged, from collegial laugher, which should be encouraged (at least up to a point). For speech/laughter classification, we used features proposed in [6], along with some newly devised features. A number of features are extracted from the audio segments, such as the first and sixth cepstrum coefficients, which measure the relative energies in speech formants (stripes in the spectrogram Fig.3). One of our newly devised features measures time periodicity, because laughter is often characterized by "hah-hah-hah-hah" sounds with a period of 100-300 miliseconds. Another new feature simultaneously measures both time and frequency periodicity (a checkerboard pattern in the spectrogram), because each "hah" resembles a voiced sound, with strong formants. We used

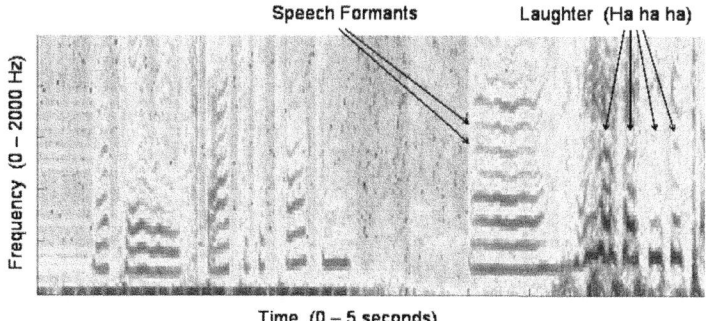

Fig. 3. Spectrogram showing distinct features of speech and laughter

quadratic discriminant analysis (QDA) to combine these features into a binary classifier for distinguishing speech and laughter. The classifier's performance (approximately 80% correct classifications) is comparable to that reported [6].

2.2 Conversation Behavior Specification and Detection

We have used a formal specification approach for meeting behaviors and designed and implemented timed-automata-based detection algorithms. As we described in the previous section, a speech sequence S_i from a channel i is a mapping from time to a tri-state: 0, 1, or 2 where 0 means silence, 1 means normal speech, and 2 means laughter. Given speech sequences from two channels, properties of the sequence or the relationship between the two sequences can be formally specified. In the following specification, we use $S(t-1)$ to represent the previous state of S before time t. Let $S^+(t) \triangleq (S(t) > 0) \wedge (S(t-1) = 0)$ and $S^-(t) \triangleq (S(t) = 0) \wedge (S(t-1) > 0)$. Also we use $t_l(S,t) \triangleq \max_t\{S(\mathbf{t}) > 0 \wedge \mathbf{t} \leq t\}$ to represent the last time S is not silence and $t_f(S,t) \triangleq \max_t\{S^+(\mathbf{t}) \wedge \mathbf{t} \leq t\}$ to represent the most recent time S starts speech. A continuous speech segment starts at t, if and only if $S^+(t) \wedge (t - t_l(S,t) > \tau_t)$, where τ_t is a minimum turn separation time. We use continuous segments as the input sequences for other event detection, rather than using the original sequences detected by the speech detection algorithm. Some major conversation events are defined as follows (Fig. 4).

Competes are defined for two sequences S_1 and S_2, as occasions when two individuals try to speak at the same time. A compete happens at t, if and only if $S_1^+(t) \wedge (S_2 = 1) \wedge (t - t_f(S_2,t) < \tau_c)$ where τ_c is the maximum interval for competes. S_1 loses compete with S_2 at t, if and only if, $S_1^-(t) \wedge (S_2(t) > 0) \wedge (|t_f(S_1,t) - t_f(S_2,t)| < \tau_c)$. *Interrupts* are defined as occasions when two segments S_1 and S_2 overlap for an extended period of time. There are two possibilities: successful interrupt and unsuccessful interrupt. Let τ_o be the minimum time of overlap for interrupts, S_1 successfully interrupts S_2 at time t, if and only if, $S_2^-(t) \wedge (t - t_f(S_1,t) > \tau_o) \wedge (t_f(S_1,t) - t_f(S_2,t) > \tau_c)$, and S_1 unsuccessfully interrupts S_2 at time t, if and only if, $S_1^-(t) \wedge (t - t_f(S_1,t) > \tau_o) \wedge (t_f(S_1,t) - t_f(S_2,t) > \tau_c)$. We also define that S starts to *hold the floor* at t,

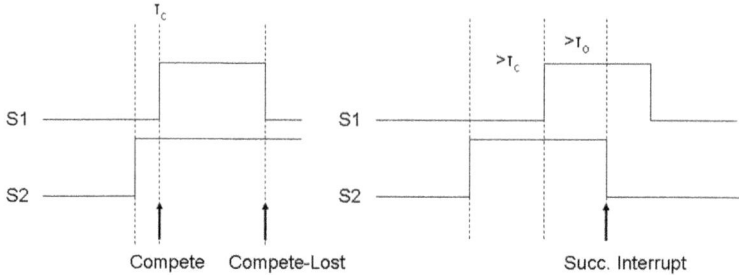

Fig. 4. Formal event specification: Left - compete, Right - successful interrupt

if $S(t) > 0$ and $t - \max_{S_i \neq S} t_l(S_i, t) > \tau_t$. The person stops holding the floor after silence for more than τ_t. At any time, there is only one person holding the floor.

Each specification corresponds to a timed-automaton in which the time entering and leaving a state is used in conditions of state transitions.

2.3   Avatar-Based GUI

The main display is a clock face with a maximum of 12 avatars, each representing a participant (Fig. 5). There is an extendable set of different styles of avatars (ours are designed using [4]) to choose from for a meeting, and each participant can choose his/her avatars. Each avatar has four types of faces: normal, talking, laughter and frown. The size of an avatar represents the relative value of the exponentially weighted moving average $H_i(t) = \lambda S_i(t) + (1 - \lambda)H_i(t - 1)$ where $0 < \lambda < 1$ can be set accordingly. The hand of the clock points to the current floor holder. A face is talking or laughing if its corresponding participant is talking or laughing, respectively. A face frowns if its corresponding participant was successfully interrupted by someone or lost a compete to speak; a hat displayed on the head of a face indicates the seriousness of offensive behaviors, i.e., successfully interrupting others many times. There are currently two levels of the repeated interruption indicator, represented by two types of hats. The level of interruption fades with time, and hats change or disappear as the level falls below its threshold. The background of the clock has five colors: gray, red, blue, green and white. Gray represents one speaker at a time, red means there were overlapping conversations, blue means there are people being interrupted or lost in a compete, green means there is group laughter, and white means there is an overly long period of silence. In practice, laughter played an important role in the meetings we studied when designing the system. Laughter frequently occurs concurrently with speech, but must be prevented from counting as an interruption or change of turn. In cases of group laughter, where multiple people laugh nearly simultaneously, we consider this to be a positive sign of group cohesion, and these group laughs are counted and indicated in our UI by a "smiley" token

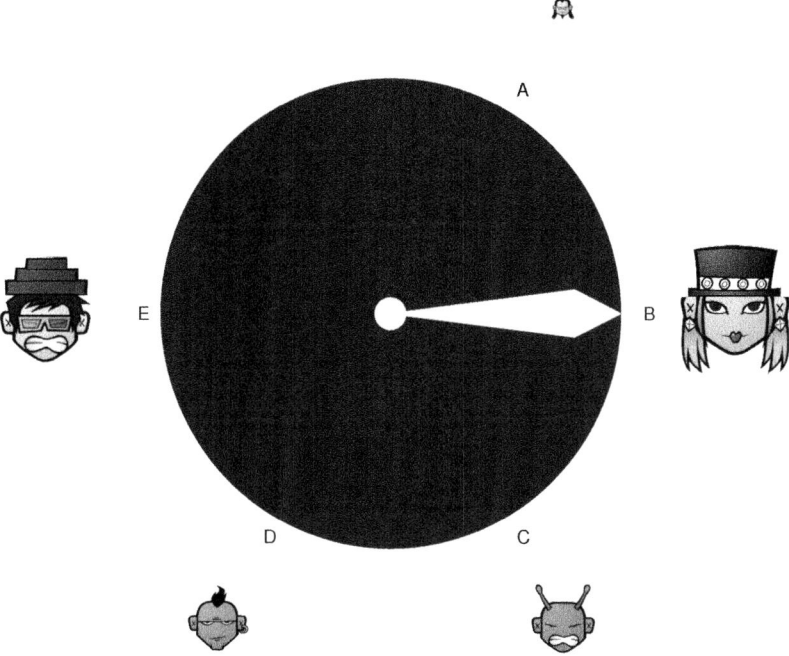

Fig. 5. UMF Avatar-based GUI: head size represents the level of participation, red (E) and black (B) hats represent level-1 and level-2 aggressive behaviors, respectively. Frown faces (C and E) indicate lost competition or being interrupted. The white arrow indicates the current floor holder.

that is added to a tally at the top of the screen. Meetings with too few of these tokens may be overly serious and one could hypothesize that effort to lighten up the meeting might increase creativity.

2.4 Meeting Quality Analysis

Events such as turns, race/competition, overlaps and interrupts are detected and recorded over time. Meeting quality metrics are calculated based on statistics of events. Number of turns, total length of turns, and average length of turns are obtained for each participant. Interactive behaviors, such as interrupts and competes, are represented by interaction matrices. These statistical data can be displayed (e.g. Fig. 6 shows the number of turns of individual speakers and competition among speakers).

One can also define overall meeting quality based on the statistical data. For example, let N_i be the total number of turns for participant i, $std\{N_i\}$ and $max\{N_i\}$ be standard deviation and maximum the set of values $\{N_i\}$, respectively, $std\{N_i\}/max\{N_i\}$ measures the distribution of speech among participants; this value is between 0 and 1. The smaller the value, the more even the distribution, or meeting attendees are more equally participated in discussions.

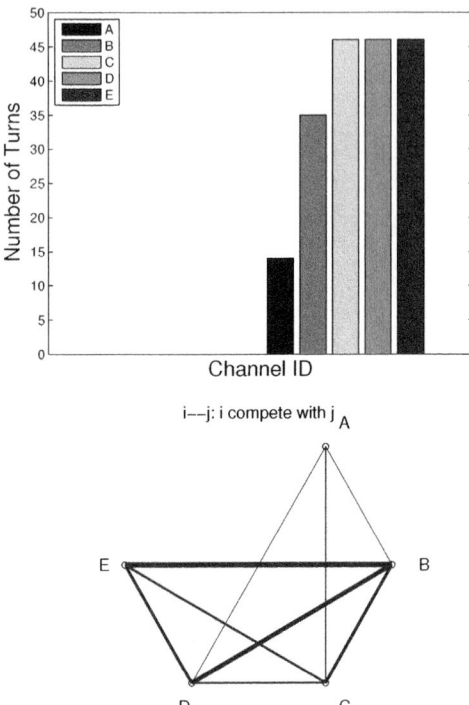

Fig. 6. Statistics graphs for offline meeting analysis. It has 5 participants, with channel ID A, B, C, D and E. Top – number of turns for each participant, Bottom - competes among participants.

If the distribution is skewed, the chances are someone dominates the floor while others are shy to enter the conversations. For a brain-storming meeting, the former is better.

3   Implementation and Evaluation

The hardware of this system includes Sony ECM-CZ10 directional microphones with table stands, one microphone per person, and PreSonus FirePod (8 ports) with FireWire audio interface to a host PC or laptop. The system is portable and easy to set up. The software was implemented using Matlab/Simulink.

The system has been demonstrated at various meetings. Although neither speech/laughter detection is 100% accurate, most people said they enjoyed the humorous display. The recorded meeting data suggest that the quality of the meeting has been reflected in the statistics.

4   Conclusion

UMF is a meeting facilitator with a playful GUI presenting a wide varity of conversational metrics. The idea is to encouraging good meeting behaviors such as turn taking and laughter, and discouraging domination and shyness. UMF does not only provide real time feedback, but can also be used to analyze meetings offline.

References

1. Barsade, S.: The Ripple Effect: Emotional Contagion and Its Influence on Group Behavior Administrative. Science Quarterly 47, 644–675 (2002)
2. Bergstrom, T., Karahalios, K.: Conversation Clock: Visualizing Audio Patterns in Co-located Groups. In: Proceedings of the 40th Annual Hawaii international Conference on System Sciences (January 2007)
3. DiMicco, J.M., Pandolfo, A., Bender, W.: Influencing Group Participation with a Shared Display. In: Proceedings of the 2004 ACM Conference on Computer Supported Cooperative Work (November 2004)
4. Dookyweb. Avatar creation (2007),
   http://www.buscarmessenger.com/avatars.swf
5. Kass, A.: Transforming the cell phone into a personal performance coach. In: Fogg, B.J., Eckles, D. (eds.) Mobile Persuasion: 20 Perspectives on the Future of Influence, Stanford University (2007)
6. Kennedy, L., Ellis, D.: Laughter Detection in Meetings. In: Notebook Paper. NIST ICASSP 2004 Meeting Recognition Workshop, Montreal, Canada, pp. 118–121 (May 2004)
7. Kim, T., Chang, A., Holland, L., Pentland, A.: Meeting Mediator: Enhancing Group Collaboration using Sociometric Feedback. In: Proceedings of ACM Computer Supported Cooperative Work, CSCW 2008 (2008)
8. Lu, L., Jiang, H., Zhang, H.J.: A Robust Audio Classification and Segmentation Method. In: Proceedings of the 9th ACM International Conference on Multimedia (MM 2001), pp. 203–211 (2001)
9. Niekrasz, J., Ehlen, P.: Multimodal Meeting Capture and Understanding with the CALO Meeting Assistant Demo. In: Popescu-Belis, A., Renals, S., Bourlard, H. (eds.) MLMI 2007. LNCS, vol. 4892, Springer, Heidelberg (2008)
10. Renals, S., Hain, T., Bourlard, H.: Recognition and Understanding of Meetings The AMI and AMIDA Projects. In: Proc. of the IEEE Workshop on Automatic Speech Recognition and Understanding, ASRU 2007, Kyoto (December 9, 2007) IDIAP-RR 07-46
11. Sacks, H., Schegloff, E.A., Jefferson, G.: A Simplest Systematics for the Organization of Turn-Taking for Conversation. Language 50(4), 696–735 (1974)
12. Wactlar, H., Stevens, S., Hauptmann, A., Christel, M., Bharucha, A.J.: A System of Video Information Capture, Indexing and Retrieval for Interpreting Human Activity. In: IEEE International Symposium on Image and Signal Processing and Analysis (ISPA 2003), Special Session on System Perspectives on Information Retrieval (September 2003)

An Application of the Wireless Sensor Network Technology for Foehn Monitoring in Real Time

Chih-Yang Tsai[1], Yu-Fan Chen[1], Hsu-Cheng Lu[1], Chi-Hung Lin[1],
Jyh-Cherng Shieh[1], Chung-Wei Yen[1], Jeng-Lung Huang[2], Yung-Shun Lin[2],
Ching-Lu Hsieh[3], and Joe-Air Jiang[1,*]

[1] Department of Bio-Industrial Mechatronics Engineering,
National Taiwan University, 10617 Taipei, Taiwan
[2] Taitung District Agricultural Research and Extension Station, COA,
Executive Yuan, 950 Taitung County, Taiwan
[3] Department of Biomechatronics Engineering,
National Pingtung University of Science and Technology
912 Pingtung County, Taiwan
*jajiang@ntu.edu.tw

Abstract. Foehn is one of the common climate phenomena in Taiwan because of geographical factors. The foehn is associated with high temperature and low humidity, which often leads to plant death and even causes serious forest fires. The natural disaster relief fund in Taiwan has covered the loss caused by the foehn. However, no monitoring system has been developed for the foehn, so farmers are not able to immediately obtain foehn-related information and activate necessary schemes for disaster reduction. The research aims at foehn detection and uses the wireless sensor network technology to build a real-time system to monitor foehn. Since the characteristics of wireless sensor networks are low costs, unmanned control and transmission distance up to 80 meters, it is feasible to apply the networks to environmental monitoring. When foehn occurs, the wireless communication devices in the proposed monitoring system will transmit the temperature and humidity information collected by monitoring stations to the gateway module, and sprinkler module action immediately for cooling and increasing humidity to protect the plants from pericarp damage or fruit drop phenomenon caused by foehn.

Keywords: wireless communication, foehn monitoring, environmental parameter monitoring.

1 Introduction

Taiwan is located at the Western Pacific, midway between Japan and the Philippines, and the area is often struck by typhoons in summer and autumn every year, resulting in a huge loss of life and property damage, even greatly affecting agricultural production.

---

* Corresponding author.

C.-H. Hsu et al. (Eds.): UIC 2011, LNCS 6905, pp. 12–24, 2011.
© Springer-Verlag Berlin Heidelberg 2011

Typhoons not only bring strong winds and heavy rainfall but also cause the foehn when winds blow over mountains. The foehn occurs because the warm and moist air travels up the windward side of a mountain and drops most of its moisture, which is caused by the decrease of atmospheric pressure. As the air flow crests the mountain top, it becomes dry and cold with all of moisture rained out of the air. Thus, the air on the downside slope of the mountain becomes warmer than equivalent elevation on the windward slope since the atmospheric pressure increases. In Taiwan, the foehn is often found in the Taitung area famous for sugar apple production, because the air mass coming from the north brings a southwesterly wind across the Central Mountain Range to the Taitung area. Temperature and humidity affect crop growth and pollination timing; a sudden drop in humidity will result in reducing fruit production while a sharp increase in temperature will also affect pollen vitality. Therefore, the hot and dry weather which characterizes the foehn will seriously affect the growth of local crops [1].

In this study, we use the wireless sensor network technology to build a system which consists of various monitoring modules, gateway modules and sprinkler devices to detect the foehn all day in real time, since it is hard to carry out it for man. The monitoring module that includes temperature/humidity sensors and an Octopus II sensor node is used to monitor temperature and humidity, and send the sensed data to the gateway modules. The sensing information will then be sent to a database and cellular phones through which farmers can check foehn-related information via the global mobile communications system. The Octopus II sensor node will trigger automatic sprinklers to reduce or avoid crop losses, when it detects that temperature and humidity have reached certain thresholds.

2   Material and Method

The system architecture is shown in Fig. 1. It includes monitoring modules, gateway modules, and sprinkler systems.

2.1   Monitoring Module

In the foehn detection system, each monitoring module is equipped with a wireless communications device, temperature and humidity sensors and a power supply module, as shown in Fig. 2.

Wireless Communication Device. The wireless communication device, the Octopus II, is designed by the Department of Computer Science at National Tsing Hua University [2]. It is capable of communication and transmission. In this study, the sensors originally attached to the Octopus II are replaced by new temperature and humidity sensors. In addition, compatible with the IEEE 802.15.4 wireless Radio frequency transceiver, the wireless communication chip CC2420, manufactured by the Texas Instruments (TI), is responsible for the task of communication. The microcontroller MSP430F1611 [3], also from TI, is charged with the task of transmission through its analog-to-digital converter function after a sensor receives surrounding signals. It will send the sensing information to the gateway module via 2.4 GHz band. Figure 3 shows the physical image of Octopus II.

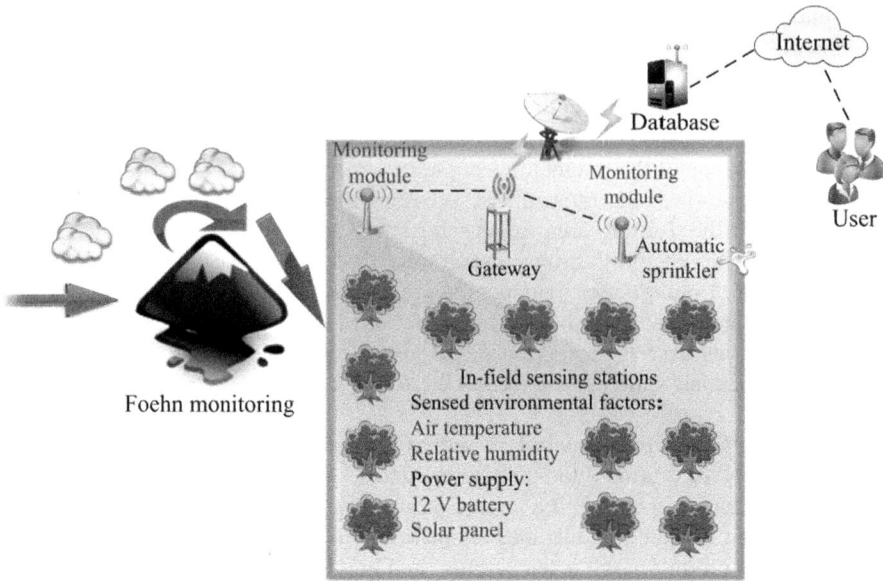

Fig. 1. System architecture of the proposed monitoring system

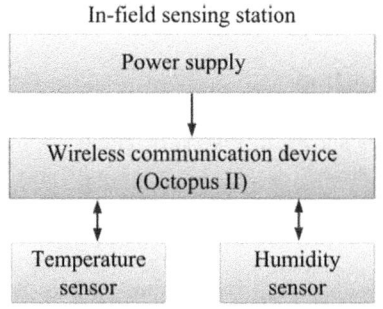

Fig. 2. Architecture of the monitoring module

Temperature and Humidity Sensors. The main task of this system is to collect environmental information, so temperature and humidity sensors are the most important devices in the system. The sensors must be the ones with high sensing accuracy and can be integrated with wireless sensors. In order to meet these demands, this study uses Sensirion SHT75[4]. Its temperature operating range is – 40 °C ~ 120 °C, and the humidity operating range is 0 ~ 100 %RH. A micro-processing chip is built in this sensor to measure temperature and relative humidity, and the error is ± 0.3 °C and ± 1.8% RH, respectively. The greatest advantage of using the sensor is that the output signals are digital signals, so no additional signal processing circuit is required. Figure 4 shows the SHT75.

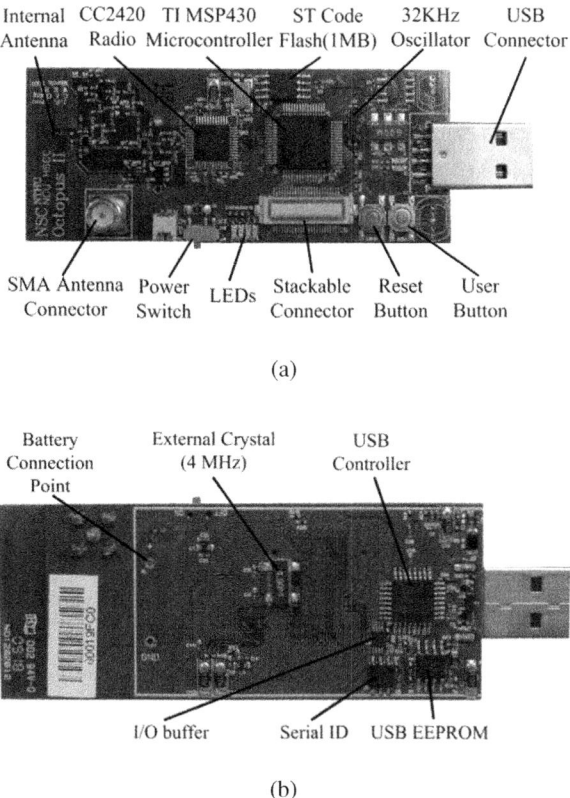

(a)

(b)

Fig. 3. Wireless communication device used in this study, (a) Octopus II (front), and (b) Octopus II (back) [2]

Power Supply Module. The power supply module is mainly composed of three parts, including a solar panel, a solar controller, and a rechargeable 12-V 36 Ah battery. We put the solar controller and the battery in a water-proofed box. In order to monitor weather conditions without any interruption, the system recharges the battery through the solar panel. This module can continue to provide power to the system. The solar panel connects with the solar charge controller CE-SLC05 developed by Clenergy company to recharge the battery [5]. The CE-SLC05 charge controller comes with

Fig. 4. SHT75 temperature and humidity sensors [4]

low-voltage discharge protection and over-charge protection; the former can avoid excessive battery discharge, preventing solar panels from being not recharged, while the latter can secure the battery voltage to avoid deformation.

2.2   Gateway Module

The gateway module consists of a Global System for Mobile Communications (GSM) [6], a Liquid Crystal Display module and a Global Positioning System receiver (GPS) [7]. The wireless communication devices in the monitoring system will transmit the temperature and humidity information collected by monitoring stations to the gateway module. Figure 5 shows the architecture of the gateway module.

In order to transmit real-time information to users or the database, the system will send SMS messages through the GSM module to inform the users, providing the most recent real-time information that allows the users to take necessary action.

2.3   Operations of the Monitoring System

Monitoring modules collect environmental data and are capable of being programmed, computing and wireless communication. In this study, after the monitoring modules complete a sensing task, the sensing data will be sent back to the gateway through RF with 2.4 GHz. This study focuses on the changes of temperature and humidity. Thus, it is very important to find the best timing for the proposed system to start the sprinkler in order to achieve the maximum utilization of the sprinkler system. Figure 6 shows the flow chart of operations of the monitoring system.

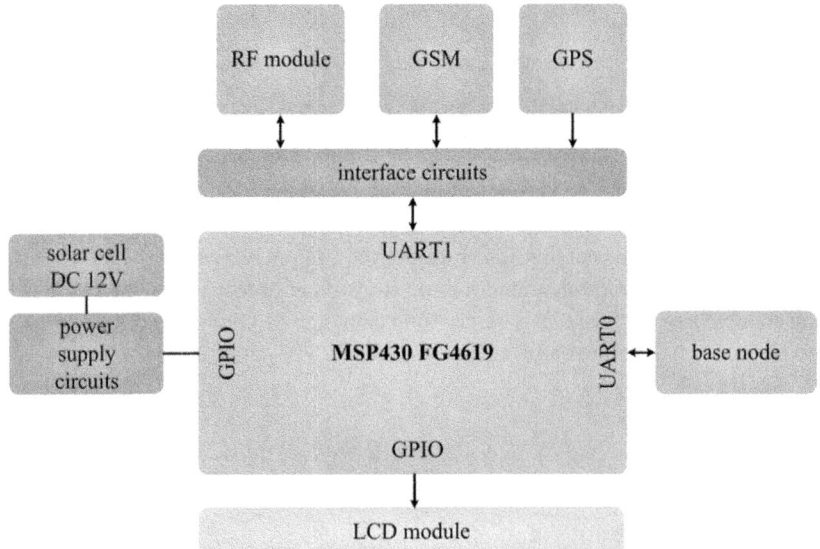

Fig. 5. The architecture of the gateway module

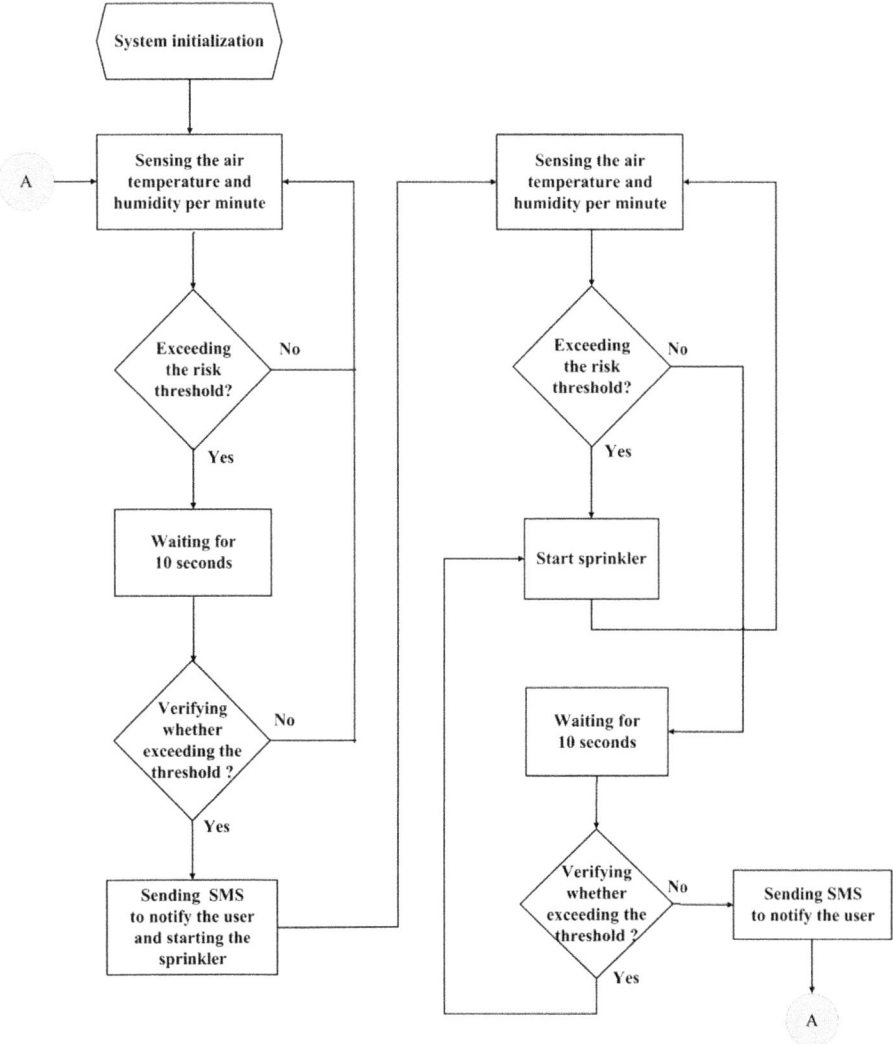

Fig. 6. Flow chart of operations of the proposed monitoring system

The program that controls the monitoring module is written in the nesC [8], and it determines when to activate the sprinkler. The sprinkler module includes a circuit board and a sprinkler and is controlled by the Octopus II sensor, and the sprinkler will start when the monitoring readings reach a dangerous threshold. How to determine the threshold will be discussed in the next section.

2.4 Online Inquiry System

The proposed monitoring system provides a user-friendly online inquiry system that enables users to quickly acquire critical foehn information. The online inquiry system

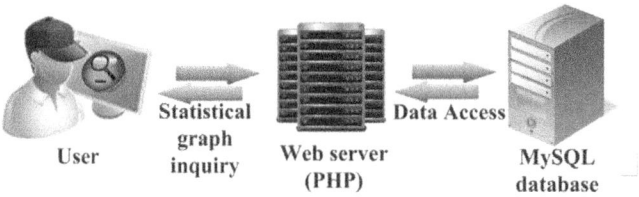

Fig. 7. The architecture of the online inquiry system

is mainly composed of two parts, including a MySQL database [9] and a dynamic PHP [10] website conducted on a web server.   Parameters and charts required by users can be shown on the website after data retrieving from the database. Finally, users can browse web pages with the searched results of charts at any time. Figure 7 depicts this online inquiry system that users can find important foehn data through the website.

3   Experimental Results

The proposed system has been deployed at the Agricultural Research and Extension Station located in the Taitung area (E 121°09'03", N 22°44'45") where foehn winds are frequently struck. Foehn is found in this area from February to November each year. When foehn occurs, the temperature rises sharply, and can be as high as 35 ~ 39 ° C while the humidity will drop down to 30 ~ 40 %RH. In the foehn period, the temperature and humidity change rapidly which is the main factor that lead to crop damages [1]. In order to effectively prevent the foehn disaster, the threshold can be set when the temperature hits 30 ° C and the relative humidity reaches 42 %RH. In this study, temperature and humidity sensors conduct auto-sensing each minute. If the readings exceed the threshold that we set, the Octopus II sensor node will trigger the sprinkler to spray water to lower the temperature and raise the relative humidity in the orchard. Thus, the risk brought by foehn is expected to be reduced.

The proposed system started to collect environmental parameters on 2011/03/03. In order to obtain a complete 24-hour data which is necessary for foehn monitoring, this system did not include a design for the sensors to enter a sleeping mode. With a consideration of energy efficiency, some corresponding sleeping strategies for sensors can be used to save more energy in the future design.

3.1   Verification of the Temperature/Humidity Sensor

Up until the end of April, 2011, the Taitung area has not witnessed any foehn. In order to validate the proposed system, the temperature and humidity data coming from the weather station under the Central Weather Bureau of Taiwan (E 121°08'48", N 22°45'15") was compared with the sensing data collected by the proposed system. The comparisons of temperature and relative humidity are shown in Fig. 8 and Fig. 9.

From fig. 8 (a) and (b), we can see that the system temperature and weather station comparison, the curve shows almost the same trend. During the invasion of foehn, there is a sudden rise in temperature and a rapid decline in humidity, so humidity is also an important observation parameter in environmental by system.

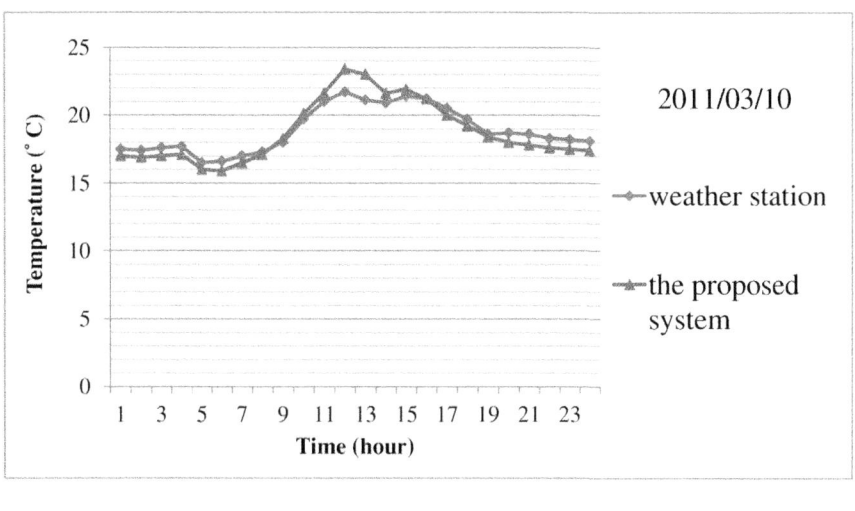

(a)

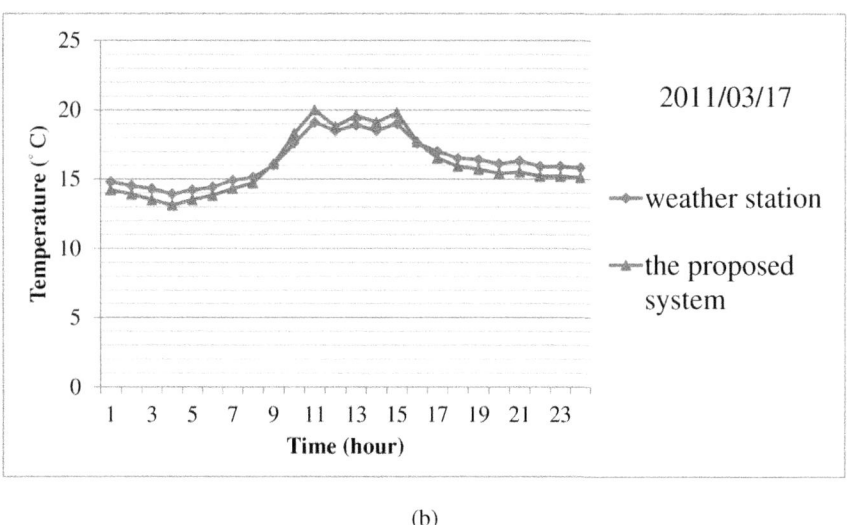

(b)

Fig. 8. Temperature comparison between the weather station and the proposed system on (a) 2011/03/10 and (b) 2011/03/17

The weather station is about 1.5 km away from the place where the proposed system is located, as shown in Fig. 10, so a small difference in temperature and relative humidity may exist. However, the curves of temperature and relative humidity in Fig. 8 and 9 generally share similar trends, which suggests that the environmental parameters provided by the proposed system are reliable.

Another critical element of the proposed system is sprinkler activation after the wireless sensors detect that temperature and relative humidity have reached the dangerous threshold. To test whether the sensor node is able to activate the sprinkler system, a number of experiments have been conducted and the experimental results are discussed in the following section.

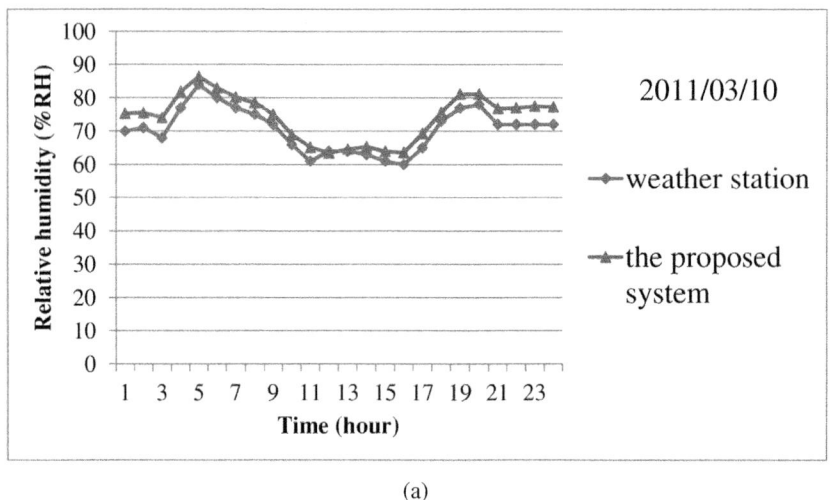

(a)

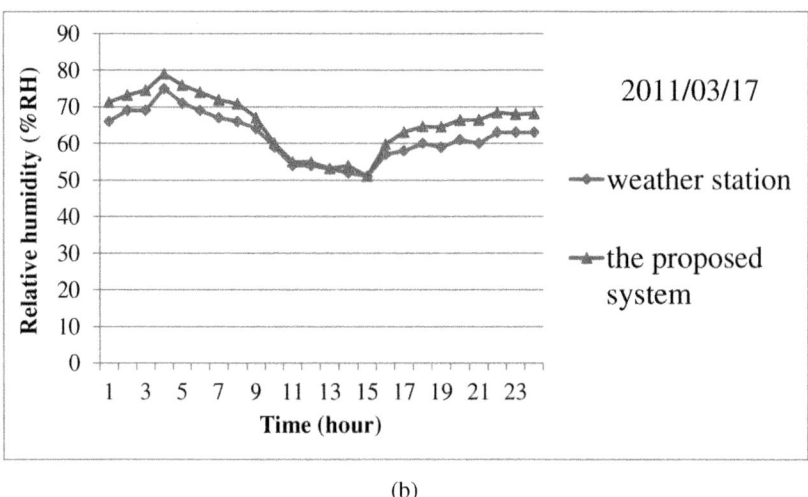

(b)

Fig. 9. Humidity comparison between the weather station and the proposed system on (a) 2011/03/10 and (b) 2011/03/17

500 m

Fig. 10. Relative position of the proposed system (Point A) and the weather station (Point B)

3.2   Sensing Devices and Sprinkler Testing

In order to test whether the sprinkler was activated exactly, a hairdryer was used to simulate foehn situation. In the experiment, we supposed that only when the temperature was higher than 30 °C or the humidity was lower than 42 %RH, the

Fig. 11. The actual settings of the monitoring module and the sprinkler

sprinkler would be initiated. In the experiment, the sprinkler was roughly two meters away from the monitoring modules, as shown in Fig. 11. The proposed system was tested under three different scenarios: 1) the temperature above 30 °C, 2) the relative humidity below 42 %RH, and 3) the temperature above 30 °C and the relative humidity below 42 %RH. Figure 12 shows the results of the temperature testing, while Fig. 13 demonstrates the result of the humidity testing.

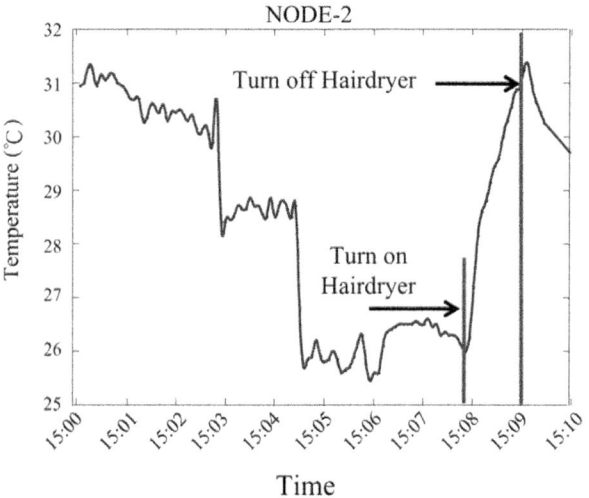

Fig. 12. Temperature variation under scenario 1 (the temperature above 30 °C)

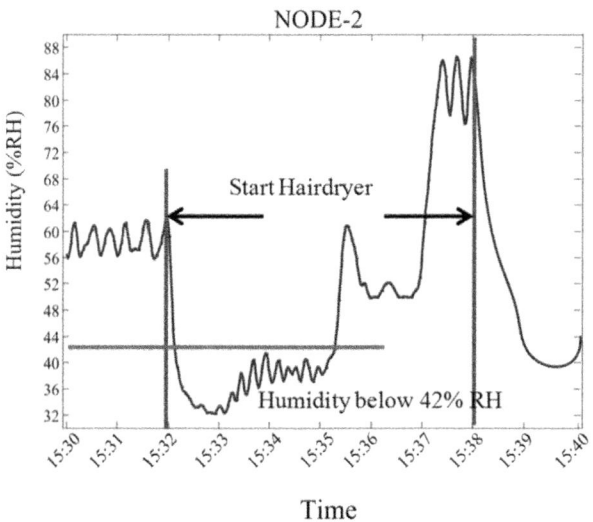

Fig. 13. Relative humidity variation under scenario 2 (the relative humidity below 42 %RH)

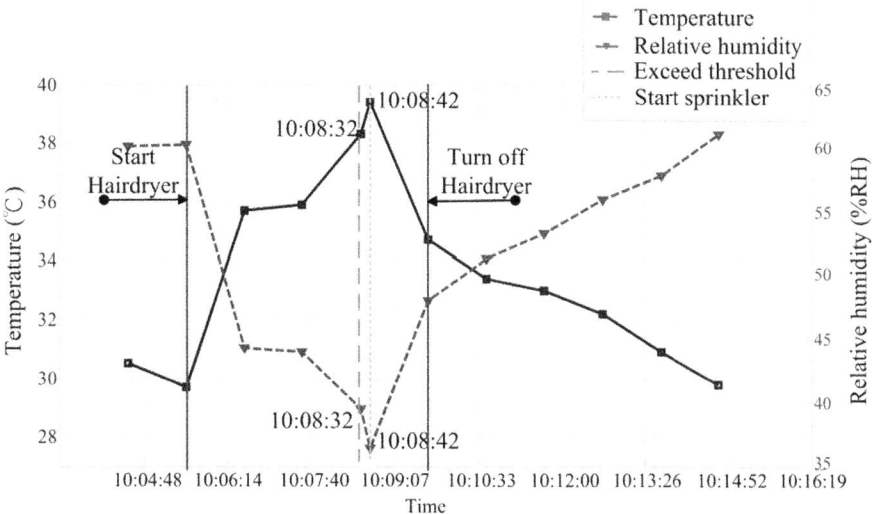

Fig. 14. Both temperature and relative humidity variations under scenario 3 (the temperature above 30 °C and the relative humidity below 42 %RH)

The temperature testing was conducted at three o'clock in the afternoon. Initially, the ambient temperature by then exceeded 30 °C, so the sprinkler was activated. In Fig. 12, the curve shows a marked decline in temperature. Then, the hairdryer was turning on at 15:08, and turning off at 15:09. Since the temperature was over 30 °C, higher than the temperature threshold, the sprinkler started to spray water. Moreover, the hairdryer was turning on at 15:32 (Fig. 13), causing the relative humidity dropped below 42 %RH. The sprinkler was triggered, because the threshold of low humidity was reached. After the water was sprayed, the relative humidity went up. The hairdryer was turning on again at 15:38, which also led to low relative humidity.

Under the third scenario, the sprinkler would be initiated when the temperature was above 30 °C and the relative humidity is below 42 %RH simultaneously. The hairdryer was turned on at about 10:04:48. Then, from Fig. 14, is can be observed that both temperature and relative humidity reaches the dangerous threshold at the time point of data return (10:08:32). After ten seconds (10:08:42), the system checked whether both the dangerous values still remain in order to prevent sensors from misreading. The sprinkler would be triggered if the dangerous condition remained. It is obvious that the temperature went down and the humidity went up after the water was sprayed at 10:08:42.

Although the field experiments were carried out based on fewer sensors deployed in a small orchard, these experimental results show that the proposed system is feasible. When densely applied to a wide area, the proposed WSN-based system is able to provide a more comprehensive and effective protection for corps. We leave this to the future works.

4   Conclusions and Future Works

The experimental results from the field tests show that the proposed foehn monitoring system is able to accurately and stably collect environmental data and trigger the sprinkler if temperature and relative humidity reach the predefining threshold. Since the deployment, the system has operated stably for nearly three weeks. During the three weeks, the system was disconnected for six hours due to the electricity shortage caused by deficiency of sunlight. As soon as the sunlight reappeared, and the solar panel was able to recharge the battery, the gateway was able to collect environmental parameters and send data to the database.

In the future works, the ADC functions of wireless sensors will be used to obtain the latest battery status. It will be very helpful to know the status of power supply for the gateway and the monitoring module when the proposed system is deployed to a remote location.

Acknowledgement. This work was financially supported in part by the National Science Council, Taiwan, under contract no. NSC 99-2218-E-002-015, NSC 100-3113-E-002-005, NSC 99-2218-E-002-005, and NSC 99-2218-E-002 -016. The authors would also like to thank Council of Agriculture of the Executive Yuan, Taiwan, for their financial supporting under contracts no.: 100AS-6.1.2-BQ-B1, and 100AS-6.1.2-BQ-B2.

References

1. Lin, Y.-S.: Foehn Sensing System and Orchard Irrigation. In: Huang, D.-C. (ed.) Sugar Apple (Annona sqwamosa) Production Management, pp. 30–31. Taitung District Agricultural Research and Extension Station, COA, Executive Yuan (2010)
2. Octopus II Manual, `http://hscc.cs.nthu.edu.tw/project` (access date: June 25, 2011)
3. TI MSP430 microcontroller, `http://focus.ti.com/mcu/docs/mcumspoverview.tsp?sectionId=95&tabId=140&familyId=342&DCMP=MCU_other&HQS=Other+IL+msp430` (access at: June 1, 2011)
4. Sensirion SHT7x Manual, `http://www.sensirion.com/en/pdf/product_information/-Datasheet-humidity-sensor-SHT7x.pdf` (access date: June 28, 2011)
5. CatalystLight Solar Light Controller Manual (CE-SLC05), `http://www.clenergy.com-.au/product-detail.php?id=32` (access date: June 30, 2011)
6. Wavecom Fastrack Supreme Manual, `http://www.mobitek.-com.my/Wavecom/-Fastrack_Supreme10.pdf` (access date: June 30, 2011)
7. GPS Receiver (GM-44) Manual, `http://www.sanav.com/gps_receivers/gps_locators/gm-44_FB.htm` (access date: June 30, 2011)
8. Gay, D., Levis, P., Behren, R.V., Welsh, M., Brewer, E., Guller, D.: The nesC Language: A Holistic Approach to Networked Embedded Systems. In: Proceedings of the ACM SIGPLAN 2003 Conference on Programming Language Design and Implementation (2003)
9. Kofler, M.: MySQL. Apress, Berkeley, CA, USA (2001)
10. Brown, M.C.: XML Processing with Perl, Python, and PHP. Sybex, San Francisco, USA (2002)

Proactive Ambient Social Media for Supporting Human Decision Making[*]

Tatsuo Nakajima, Tetsuo Yamabe, and Mizuki Sakamoto

Department of Computer Science and Engineering,
Waseda University
tatsuo@dcl.info.waseda.ac.jp

Abstract. Since our daily life is becoming more and more complex, it is difficult to make a decision for a variety of occurrences in our daily life. Of course, the Internet gives us a possibility to reactively find necessary information through search engines or browsing hyperlinks among Web pages. But, it requires users understand what they like to know and what they should do for finding the currently necessary information. Also, they need great efforts to collect a set of necessary information reactively for making their decisions. It requires us always continue to be rational to think consciously with heavy cognitive load. If users receive necessary information proactively using information technologies, it is helpful to make reasonable decisions without heavy cognition, and their daily lives will become less stressful and more pleasurable due to desirable decision making.

We are developing several case studies to support the user's decision making in our daily life by returning necessary information proactively, and the information is embodied into our daily environment to avoid information overload. This paper shows two case studies and analyzes them to make our daily life more desirable. The purpose of the analysis is to understand the current status of proactive ambient social media and to identify a set of future challenges.

Keywords: Persuasive Technologies, Decision Making, Interaction Design, Ambient Social Media, Design Methodology, Psychological and Design Theories, Harmonizing Virtual and Real World.

1 Introduction

Information technologies are changing our daily life dramatically. Everyday, we are using various Web services to find necessary information for a variety of decision making. For example, we use a search engine to know detailed information about a keyword that we found everyday in our daily life. Also, we use a train transfer guidance service to know how to reach at the destination place with minimum time. Although these services are very useful for supporting decision making in our daily life, they require reactive interaction with a service, where the user needs to make an

---

[*] This research was supported by Waseda University Global COE Program 'International Research and Education Center for Ambient SoC' sponsored by MEXT, Japan.

C.-H. Hsu et al. (Eds.): UIC 2011, LNCS 6905, pp. 25–39, 2011.

attention explicitly what he/she likes to do and know. This requires us to keep heavy conscious cognition for a long time, and needs to concentrate on thinking what they want to do explicitly. However, our daily life becomes busier and busier, and we sometimes do not have enough time to find necessary information in a reactive way. Also, we usually become lazy to behave desirable activities if we require more efforts to concentrate on the activities. Moreover, in some cases, it is not easy to find necessary information if the user does not have enough skills to search the information.

In our recent daily life, our heuristics may make mistake making a decision that may damage our lifestyle seriously. It is helpful to return appropriate information proactively to be aware of the bias in our thinking for choosing a better decision [30]. Future information technologies should help human to make better decisions without heavy cognitive thinking, and various information services that return useful information to help their decision making will be pervasive and ambient into their daily lives. Of course, context-aware proactive information feedback systems [7, 13] have been popular researches, but most of researches focused on offering advertising information for users to spend more money. Our approach uses *proactive ambient social media* for helping more general decision making. To reduce the cognitive overload, feedback information should be embodied in their daily lives. Also, the media need to take into account human factors when feedback is returned and what kinds of ambient information are desirable. In this paper, we discuss these questions through our experiences with building two prototype *proactive ambient social media* to return ambient and proactive feedback information.

The *proactive ambient social media* that help human decision making need to proactively return necessary information to us because the traditional media require us to find the necessary information reactively with extra efforts. We have developed two types of the *proactive ambient social media*.

The first type of media superimposes necessary information on the real world. We call this type of proactive ambient social media *decision making ambient social media*. The basic technology behind the media is the augmented reality. The media make hidden information visible to the user for making a decision more rationally. Especially, less skillful users do not have enough abilities to find useful information embedded in our environment. If information technologies can make more useful information explicitly visible to users, it is helpful for them to make more desirable decisions. In Section 2.1, we show *Augmented GO* as an example of the media. When using the media, a user's decision making becomes explicit via projected information to choose a better decision. Since the explicitly visible information is embedded in our daily objects in an ambient way, a user does not require heavy conscious cognition to find necessary information explicitly. Although skillful users can construct their thinking by augmenting information automatically through their past experiences, but non skillful users cannot find the information by themselves, and they sometimes give up to gain more skills for making their future daily lives better. If hidden information is ambiently appeared to the less skillful users, their decision making will become more desirable and it increases their knowledge and skills for future decision making because the user can concentrate on one medium and not to divert the user's attention for making a better decision.

The second *proactive ambient social media* persuade the user to encourage desirable behavior. The media are called *persuasive ambient social media*. The basic question is how to change the user's behavior with information technologies [3]. The media proactively return appropriate information that affects the user's behavior according to him/her current situation. In Section 2.2, we show *Virtual Aquarium* as an example. The media are embodied in our lavatory ambiently. The user's current behavior is reflected into information shown in the user' environment ambiently. Also, the environment returns appropriate information according to the user's current behavior. This means that it does not require conscious thought, and the user is forced to choose desirable behavior with emotional heuristic thinking.

This paper shows case studies of *persuasive ambient social media* and *decision making ambient social media* in Section 2. Then, we analyze the case studies based on several psychological and design theories in Section 3. We discuss the essential differences between the two types of *proactive ambient social media* and the theoretical backgrounds behind them. The analysis can be used in the two ways. The first is to integrate the two types of media into one unified framework. For developing better *proactive ambient social media*, we believe that the system should choose the two types of media according to the user's current attitude and belief. The second is to show some experiences for identifying potential issues that we need to challenge in the near future. Section 4 shows a framework to design *proactive ambient social media*. The *proactive ambient social media* need to harmonize virtual worlds into the real world. The discussion described in the section will become the meaningful first step towards developing a comprehensive framework to increase the reality of *proactive ambient social media*. In Section 5, we conclude the paper and present future research possibilities.

2   Case Studies

In this section, we show two *proactive ambient social media* developed in our project as case studies.

2.1   Decision Making Ambient Social Media: Augmented Board Gaming

Go is a traditional board game for two players, where the goal is to occupy a larger portion in the board than another player. Black and white stones are used to control the territory and a board with a grid of 19 x 19 lines is used as the game field. The rules of Go are relatively simple, but the underlying strategies are extremely complex and rich. As in chess and reversi, a numerous set of strategies have been invented to reduce the complexity, but studying them requires the player to actually understand the strategic concepts. Thus it takes a long time for a beginner to play well with an experienced player and to feel pleasure during the play. *Augmented Go* [10] supports several gaming modes to play a game. The basic idea is to offer useful information to beginners without extra interactions and devices that they need to operate as shown in Figure 1. In this *decision making ambient social media*, proactive feedback information is offered visually by superimposing guidance information onto the Go board by a projector. A web camera connected to a personal computer is used to detect the position of each Go stone. The OpenCV library is used for visual analysis and the core logic of the ambient social media generates information presented to the players according to the current game situation.

The system supports several gaming modes. As shown in Figure 2-(a), players can interact with the media by placing Go stones on a menu that is projected onto a board. We explain some of the modes and how players interact with *Augmented Go*.

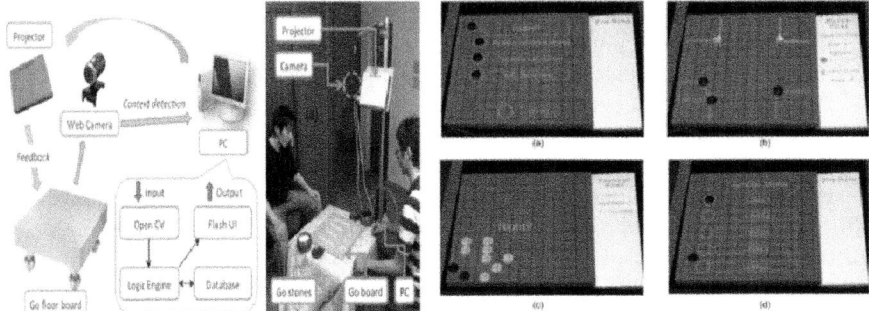

Fig. 1. Augmented Go System   **Fig. 2.** Proactive Information Feedback in the Augmented Go System

Normal Play Mode: The normal play mode represents the original concept of the Go augmentation. In this mode, two players play Go as usual, but useful information is projected on the board to help beginners recognize the situation and make better decisions. The rules of Go are simple, but the vast number of possible moves in each turn makes it hard for beginners to make decisions. Moreover, on the large 19x19 board, beginners tend to concentrate on localized fighting in a narrow region and lose the big picture. It is difficult to recognize invaded areas, since an invasion process gradually progresses as new stones are put on the board. For choosing good offense and defense strategies, recognizing the links between the Go stones is important, but it requires some skills. Moreover, the normal play mode visualizes the strength of links between the Go stones. As shown in Figure 2-(b), same-colored stones are connected with lines. If a dangerous situation occurs somewhere on the board, a warning message appears for the players to avoid losing the area. The sequence of stone moves is also recorded into the database, which facilitates replaying the game for self-training. Replaying allows us to review and analyze the play by projecting the stones on the board later.

Tsumego Mode: Tsumego is a type of exercise where the player is given a game board situation. The aim is to find the best sequence of stones' placement in a given board situation. In this mode, the positions of the stones are visualized on the board. Players can try different moves by placing stones on the board, whereas the results and comments explaining key important points are displayed as visual feedback (Figure 2-(c)). The Tsumego mode prepares questions for a player with different skill levels, and the level of difficulty can be selected in the menu. (Figure 2-(d)).

The advantage of our approach is to allow players to receive information through the normal interaction with the Go board and the stones. By superimposing information onto the board, players can concentrate on the normal play or self-training without fragmenting their attention by taking an instructional book and etc. into their hands. This is important to make it possible for the players to allocate enough cognitive resources for understanding the current situations in the game.

2.2   Persuasive Ambient Social Media: Virtual Aquarium

Virtual Aquarium [20] has the objective of improving users' dental hygiene by promoting correct toothbrushing practices. It is set up in the lavatory where it turns a mirror into a simulated aquarium as shown in Figure 3. Fish living in the aquarium are affected by the users' toothbrushing activity. If users brush their teeth properly, the fish prosper and procreate. If not, they are weakened and may even perish.

In this media, we used a 3-axis accelerometer sensor that is attached to each toothbrush in a household. Since toothbrushes are usually not shared and each sensor has a unique identification number, we are able to infer which user is using the media at a given time. Toothbrushing patterns are recognized by analyzing the acceleration data. A user brushes his teeth in front of the *Virtual Aquarium* using a brush with a sensor attached. The toothbrush is able to observe how the user brushes his/her teeth passively. This is the only interaction needed to use this media.

The objective of *Virtual Aquarium* is to promote good toothbrushing practices. In this media, the ideal behavior was defined as follows: 1) users should brush their teeth at least twice per day; 2) one session should involve at least three minutes of brushing; and 3) brushing should involve patterns that ensure the teeth are properly cleaned. User behavior is compared to this ideal and translated to feedback as described below. We believe that the existence of an aquarium is in-artificial in a lavatory, but the aquarium enriches our daily life.

Fig. 3. Virtual Aquarium System   **Fig. 4.** Proactive Information Feedback in the Virtual Aquarium System

As shown in Figure 4, when a user begins to brush him/her teeth, a scrub inside the aquarium starts cleaning algae off the aquarium wall. At the same time, a set of fish associated with the user starts moving in the aquarium in a playful manner. When the user has brushed for a sufficient time, the scrub finishes cleaning and the fishes' dance turns to a more elegant pattern. When the user finishes brushing, the fish end their dance and resume their normal activities. Both the activity of the fish and the movement of the scrub are designed in such a way as to give the user hints regarding the correct method of toothbrushing. However, if a user does not brush his/her teeth sufficiently, the aquarium becomes dirty, and the fishes in the aquarium become sick. The feedback information is returned immediately according to the movement of a user's toothbrush. We call the feedback *immediate feedback*.

The fish's health is visibly affected by how clean the aquarium is. If the user neglects to brush her teeth, some fish fall ill and may even die. In contrast, faithful brushing may result in the fish laying eggs as shown in the right pictures in Figure 2. At first, the eggs are not very likely to hatch. If the user continues to brush consistently for a number of days in row, the incubation ratio increases. This way, the long-term feedback gives clues to the correct behavior and attempts to maintain motivation over a period of time. The long-term feedback is called *accumulated feedback*.

While designing the media, we consider the association between a user's healthy lifestyle and the cleanness of the aquarium. Also, our design takes into account that the user feels empathy by using virtual fishes.

In our daily lives, a mirror reflects our figure to show our appearance. Using a mirror allows us to know whether we are well or not, and whether our makeup and clothes are fit or not. A mirror has a power to make what are invisible from us visible. We believe that mirrors are adequate devices to reflect our current behavior to return feedback because we sometimes remind ourselves in front of a mirror. *Virtual Aquarium* is a new type of mirrors that reflect a user's current situation, and encourage him/her to change his/her lazy behavior to motivate desirable lifestyle.

3   Design Implications

3.1   The Elaboration Likelihood Model

In *proactive ambient social media*, design strategies for presenting information to support human decision making are important. The *elaboration likelihood model* [23] explains the importance for the dual routes to persuasion. The central route offers heavily cognitive information to change the user's attitude, and the peripheral route enables the user to change his/her attitude through emotionally influential information. The theory provides a basic design strategy for designing *proactive ambient social media*. The central route offers enough information for decision making. If we can have a confidence to believe the importance of the information, our current attitude is changed according to the information. Also, the information is useful to understand whether the current strategy is good or bad, and gives hints for making a decision for the next step. The central route requires users not to focus on peripheral routes or other central routes. They distribute the user's current attention and increase the possibility to rely on heuristics to investigate the given information for decision making.

Augmented Go provides superimposed information on a real game board to make better decisions. A user will be able to think rationally by using the information because the user can concentrate on only the current situation of the board without losing his/her current attention. A beginner does not need to search necessary information from books or search engines reactively. In traditional approaches to use the central route, enough information needs to be offered to users to think rationally to make a better decision. The amount of information needs to be increased to let users have strong confidence for making a decision, but increasing information also causes information overload and requires heavy cognitive overload.

Our approach offers an alternative way that represents information ambiently on daily objects. Of course, we sometimes need detailed information to make a better decision. If the media allow the user to manipulate any superimposed information in a tangible way like [9], it is possible to present necessary detailed information for making a better decision according to the user's requirements and background knowledge. We believe that tangible information is a promising approach to offer the central route with avoiding extra cognitive overload. It is also a key to offer good affordances indicating how to manipulate given tangible information naturally.

The *persuasive ambient social media* usually use a peripheral route to change the user's behavior towards desirable lifestyle. In *Virtual Aquarium*, a user feels empathy to virtual fish because the user considers the fish as virtual pets, and feels attached to them emotionally. The positive or negative reaction of the fish to a user has a great influence on him or her, and the social incentive to change his/her behavior while the reaction continues. The media offer *extrinsic motivation* [31] to persuade a user's current intention. There are several types of incentives to be used to increase *extrinsic motivation*: physical incentive, social incentive, psychological incentives and economic incentives. These incentives provide pleasurable experiences to users, but *extrinsic motivation* does not enable users to continue their desirable behavior for a long time.

In *Virtual Aquarium*, the cleanness of an aquarium is a metaphor to the cleanness of users' teeth. The metaphor makes users to be aware of the importance of the toothbrushing. The wellness of fishes is also the metaphor of the wellness of users' teeth. The users finally recognize that toothbrushing is important to keep the wellness of their teeth. This kind of motivation is called *intrinsic motivation* [31]. The motivation can change a user's attitude, then change his/her behavior. The effect continues for a long time because he/she believes the importance of the current habits. The metaphor is an important tool in *persuasive ambient social media* because metaphors usually represent some meaning that can be understood without too much information. Using metaphors in *persuasive ambient social media* is a key to support *intrinsic motivation* when we like to offer persuasive information in an ambient way.

3.2 The Transtheoretical Model

The returned information needs to be changed according to the current stage of the user's attitude, skills and knowledge. The *transtheoretical model* proposes the five stages as a process involving the progress to change the user's undesirable behavior [33]. In earlier stages, the user prefers emotional reinforcement not to give up his current efforts. This is the same as the peripheral route to persuasion. On the other hand, for the user who is in a near final stage, enough information for making a better decision through rational thinking is more suitable. This is the same as the central route to persuasion. This means that *persuasive ambient social media* are suitable in near the first stages, and *decision making ambient social media* are appropriate in near the last stages. The user will not continue using *Virtual Aquarium* if it cannot fascinate him for a long time. On the other hand, in *Augmented GO*, a very beginner cannot understand the meaning of the information projected on the board. Thus, the augmented information is not useful for him/her to motivate to play the Go game. The type of *proactive ambient social media* should be changed according to the current stage.

When designing *proactive ambient social media*, a beginner may not have an interest to continue the target activity. This is a reason that most of people give up many interesting activities quickly. Especially, if the activity requires some efforts to do, it is not easy to continue the activity since the curiosity is not stronger than the extra effort. It is important to offer *extrinsic motivation* like joy, comfort or reward in the early stage.

In the next stage, self-efficacy is a key to raise the stage. A user feels self-efficacy when he/she has a confidence to continue the target activity. The confidence comes from the evidence that he/she has an ability to do the activity well. The user needs to be offered enough information showing what he/she should do to construct the evidence to do the activity well. Of course, using a metaphor is a key to raise the current stage in the next stage without offering too much information to users as described in the previous section.

When designing the proactive ambient social media that can be used from a beginner to a skillful user, the two types of the ambient social media should be integrated. For example, *Virtual Aquarium* will add a functionality to show the detailed current condition of the user's teeth for their better tooth maintenance. In a similar way, *Augmented Go* will add playful interaction to give a good sound if a player chooses a good movement of a stone. The feedback strategy should be changed according to a user's current skills and knowledge.

The presentation of information is a key issue for designing *proactive ambient social media*. The information should be appeared in an ambient way. For example, a metaphor is a useful tool for the purpose. However, the information should be tangibly manipulated to show more detailed information as described in the previous section. The basic idea is proposed in *AwareMirror* [5]. *AwareMirror* offers useful information on a mirror in an abstract way not to disturb washing a user's teeth. However, *AwareMirror* has a zipper to offer an affordance to open abstract information for showing concrete information. After a user can choose one of ambient images, detailed and concrete information is appeared on a mirror to make a better decision. This style of information design is effective to show enough information in *proactive ambient social media*. A skillful user chooses several necessary abstract information and opens the information to show more detailed information. Choosing how much necessary information depends on the user's current stage. As described at the beginning of the section, the *proactive ambient social media* require us to choose an appropriate feedback strategy according to a user's current stage, but it is not easy to detect the user's current stage with the current sensing technologies. The interaction design enables the users to explicitly retrieve necessary information according to his/her current stage because a more skillful user has a strong incentive to know more detailed information for raising up the current level to the next stage.

3.3 Semiotics of Feedback Information

When designing *persuasive ambient social media*, a designer needs to consider how to evoke the user's emotion to persuade his/her using the peripheral route. Empathetic expression is effective to evoke the user's emotion. Empathy is a strong social incentive to change the user's behavior. Empathy engages the user to feel close to the empathetic expression. Virtual pets are typical empathic expression and they are very popular in many online services. Social robot pets also make our daily lives happier. The pets evoke the user's empathetic emotion and encourage him/her to change undesirable behavior with negative emotions. The emotional impact is very effective in making the user keep desirable habits. One interesting theoretical result is *media equation* [24]. A user feels empathy to even non-living things like a personal computer. The result indicates that there is a possibility to use various expressions or products that do not represent living or animated characters. On the other hand, if the expression showing a pet is too realistic, a user may feel uncanny although she feels empathy for unrealistic characters. The phenomenon is called the uncanny valley [18]. When the user considers that something expressed by information services have a personality, the user feels empathy. If the personality fits the user's personality or he/she feels altruism on the personality, he/she feels close relationship [11]. Therefore, designing a good personality is an important topic for designing *persuasive ambient social media*

When designing a *decision making ambient social media*, it is important to consider how much information should be offered. The information offered by the media should be ambiently and naturally integrated into our daily environment. The user needs to feel that the information is a part of our real world. Attaching the meaning on information is an important issue when designing *decision making ambient social media*. In *Augmented GO*, extra information is projected on the physical GO board. The user can still use normal stones and a board without attaching any artificial objects like visual tags. Also, the user does not need to equip special devices like a head mounted display.

The meaning of the information should be easily understandable by the user [15]. If the user needs to learn the meaning of information, the *persuasive ambient social media* should offer an easy instruction before starting to use it. Our daily life becomes busier and busier, so it is not a good idea to assume that the user reads a manual. One of the solutions is to use a metaphor. Understanding a metaphor relies on the user's prior knowledge. Therefore, the user can understand the media without learning the meaning of the information offered by it if the information represents an appropriate metaphor. A metaphor does not require too much information for making a better decision. For example, as described before, in *Virtual Aquarium*, the cleanness of an aquarium is a metaphor of the cleanness of the user's teeth.

3.4 The Feeling as Information Theory

The *feeling as information theory* is useful to consider how proactive ambient social media evoke the user's emotion [27]. The theory indicates that it is difficult to think rationally during a positive feeling. On the other hand, the user tends to think rationally when she feels to be in a negative situation. The results indicate that positive stimuli are effective in early stages, but in latter stages, negative stimuli are desirable under the transtheoretical model. *Virtual Aquarium* provides positive stimulus when the user's current behavior is desirable, but negative stimulus is returned when she behaves undesirably. One of the findings is that negative stimulus alone are not effective, because the user becomes rational, and he/she considers the effectiveness of his behavior. He/she needs enough information to think the importance of the activity in a rational way. In *decision making ambient social media*, if the purpose is better decision making, the media should not evoke a user's positive emotion too much. It may lead heuristic thinking to make a wrong decision.

In the positive psychology, thinking positively makes people to feel a self-efficacy and to try to challenge hard tasks [4]. The fact tells us to use negative stimulus carefully because strong negative stimulus offer a possibility to lose self-efficacy from the user, and he/she gives up to change his/her current undesirable behavior. However, the weak negative stimulus can be effective, if the user is already believing that a target activity is useful for the user. The negative stimulus act as a kind of a reminder to encourage continuing his/her current efforts. Social pressure is also a kind of negative stimulus, but it works well in *EcoIsland*, which is another *persuasive ambient social media* [28]. In this media, negative stimuli based on empathy are effective to increase the user's eco-friendly behavior. In *Virtual Aquarium*, when the user neglects to wash his teeth, negative stimulus, ex. virtual fish's sickness, are returned. We found that negative stimuli that punishes the user do not work well to increase the user's motivation. Therefore, in *Virtual Aquarium*, instead of a virtual fish's sickness, it may be better to present a fish's sad emotion when the user neglects his/her efforts.

3.5 Conscious and Unconscious Thought

The bias on decision making is an important aspect to design *proactive ambient social media*. A user makes a different decision when a giving frame is changed because there is usually some uncertainty in most of our daily situations [12]. The fact shows that right feedback information is important to make a right decision. Especially, as described in the previous section, the mood has a strong effect on the human decision making. In many cases, a user uses heuristics when making a decision. If available information is not enough to think in a rational way, we need to use heavy heuristics, and there is a risk that our thinking is significantly biased [12]. Adequate feedback information can reduce the bias by making users to be aware of the bias and giving enough information to think in a rational way [30].

Of course, a bias is useful when designing *persuasive ambient social media* because a user may feel a small effort as a big effort. For example, in [34], a model to use the economic incentive is proposed. The *ubipay model* and the *ubirebate model* should be chosen according to the current situation. If human think rationally, the both models are the same, but they usually feel the models differently when giving a different frame.

A theory of unconscious thought [2] shows that heuristic thinking is not always bad. Giving more information may lead a wrong decision. When we become conscious, our heuristics is biased according to the current frame. However, as describe in the theory, when our thought is unconscious, heuristic thinking may lead to a right decision. The result leads a new problem whether a *proactive ambient social media* should make a user conscious or not when making a decision. An alternative approach is to offer information in a subliminal way. This topic is a promising new research direction for designing *proactive ambient social media*. In traditional approaches, all ambient information systems assume that users need to understand the meaning of the expression in the media consciously. However, most of people may not understand the meaning of the expression that is offered to the user, but there is a subliminal impact on their thinking. The lighting effect is also a similar impact on our thinking. The combination of colors has a strong relationship with our feelings. We believe that investigating unconscious thought will be fruitful for future researches on designing *proactive ambient social media.*

Our daily behavior becomes a habit by repeating the behavior frequently. In the *transtheoretical model*, reaching to the final stage means that the behavior becomes a habit, and a user sustains his/her behavior. In the earlier stage, ambient information feedback is used to motivate him/her to change his behavior. The original behavior is a current habit and the current behavior is unconscious to the user. Therefore, we need to understand what is his current automatic and unconscious behavior. By repeating the same new behavior, the behavior becomes gradually a new habit, and the new habit is performed mindlessly. When the behavior becomes automatic and unconscious, a user is not aware of the degradation of the current behavior's performance. In this case, a user needs feedback information to know the performance of the new behavior is degraded. However, if the user wants to change the behavior, he needs to escape from the automatic behavior in a mindfully [16]. *Proactive ambient social media* can be used to design human habit, but we also need to consider ethics or morals to design human habits.

3.6 Customizing Ambient Information

Media are used for a long time when a user feels the empathy on the media as described in Section 3.3. However, it is not easy to offer empathetic experiences to users. One of promising ways to solve the problem is make it possible for a user to customize the experiences with *proactive ambient social media*. For example, decorating a mobile phone is very typical for Japanese ladies. Japanese people attach something to their daily belongings to differentiate them from others. It is also very typical to customize their avatars in online games. They change their avatars' accessories, clothes, shoes, and hair styles even by paying extra money.

The *product attachment theory* [32] explains why people like more customized things than uncustomized things. In the theory, people prefer a product whose personality is matched to a user's personality. The customization is a process to make the products more preferable to a user. This means that the product's personality is customized to match to its user's personality.

Our current studies do not offer a mechanism to customize the *proactive ambient social media*. In [14], Kawsar et. al. proposes a computing infrastructure to customize the *proactive ambient social media* in a tangible way. The approach is effective to change the media's personality to be matched to its user's personality.

4 Digital-Physical Hybrid Design: Harmonizing Virtual World and Real World

Information technologies can enhance our real world by embedding computers and networks everywhere. The Internet makes it possible to extend our social communication even if people live in different places. For example, Facebook enables a large number of people to create their social networks and make it easy to expand the number of friends. Niconico Douga, which is a popular social TV service in Japan[1], can increase the pleasurability to watch streaming videos by adding respective

---

[1] Social TV enhances the sociality among people when watching TV programs [22].

audiences' comments on the same video. Also, crowdsourcing [8] enables us to use the power of a large number of people on the Internet by dividing a task into small micro-tasks, and assign the tasks to the people.

Context-awareness [25] allows us to develop a variety of adaptive services that change their behavior according to the current surrounding situation. The world model implemented in the services defines a model of the real world, and can be accessed by the services to know when the surrounding situation is changed. Moreover, virtual world services such as Second Life have becoming popular recently. Each person has an avatar that is his agent in the virtual world, and creates his social networks where avatars meet at the same place virtually.

The above technologies make it possible to enhance our daily live significantly because various physical constraints are removed by replacing some real items in the real world to virtual items.

On the other hand, modern computer graphics techniques enable the virtual world to add the sense of the real world. Actually, some of recent movies and video games use the techniques to create virtual worlds that cannot be distinguished from the real world. Also, tangle interfaces [9] allow us to manipulate information in the virtual world in a more tangible way. These above techniques recover the feeling of the real world by removing the feeling of virtualness introduced by information technologies.

In social ambient media described in this paper, we also add some kinds of reality to the ambient social media. For example, in Virtual Aquarium, our design aims that a user feels the virtual aquarium as the real aquarium. Also, in Augmented Go, projected information are seamlessly integrated into the real Go board. This means that our current *proactive ambient social media* aim to increase the reality by removing the feeling of virtualness in order to integrate the virtual media into our real world in a natural way.

However, increasing the reality may decrease the attractiveness to use the media because these media are truly blended into the real world. One reason is the uncanny valley effect [19]. If the virtual media become to close to the real, people feel uncanny on the media. The second reason is that the pure reality does not make people to feel values on the media because the media are too unremarkable. The real goal is to add values on the media, where people feel the media attractive. This means that seeking the true reality is not a good idea. It may be better to remain some kinds of virtualness to avoid the uncanny valley problem. Thus, it is desirable to consider how to add some values on the media instead of seeking the true reality. In [17], a framework to add values on the virtual items is presented, and these values make people to buy and possess the items. The framework is based on economic concepts, but adding values is also possible to use psychological or ideological concepts. We are considering three approaches to add values based on the psychological and ideological concepts.

The first approach is to add some kinds of metaphor on the media. In Virtual Aquarium, the approach is considered to be important to be used by users for a long time. Cleaning the aquarium becomes a metaphor of cleaning a user's teeth. If a user is aware of the importance to clear his teeth, he will consider to feel some values to use the virtual aquarium. The second approach is to exploit the aesthetics of virtual items. We usually feel aesthetical beauty when the forms of the items have consistent structure. Beauty makes the items attractive, and we want to own the beautiful items to decorate our daily life. The third approach is to increase to feel empathy on the media [21]. Currently, we are discussing the following three possibilities currently. The first possibility is to use virtual creatures on the media. If a user grows the virtual creatures, he feels empathy on the creatures, and he is willing to use the media. The second possibility is to add something related to a user on the media. For example, if the media contain the landscape of the city where a user or his friend is currently living, he feels more empathy on the media. In a similar way, if the media contain some people who a user likes, he feels more empathy on the media. The third possibility is to add the personality on the media. If the personality of the media is close to a user's personality, he feels strong empathy on the media [32]. The customizing something in the media is the most popular way to add the personality on the media. For example, a decorated mobile phone is popular in Japan, and a user is willing to use the phone for longer time than undecorated phone because he feels more empathy on the decorated phone.

We consider that the above approaches are very promising to extend the current *proactive ambient social media*. In the future, we are planning to develop more *proactive ambient social media*, and a framework to design *proactive ambient social media*, based on the discussions in this section.

5 Conclusion and Future Direction

This paper showed two case studies of *proactive ambient social media*: *Virtual Aquarium* and *Augmented Go*. Supporting human decision making will become more important in one future daily lives because our life will become more and more complex and our time that can be used for our decision making become shorter and shorter.

We believe that proper supports of decision making will become more important and proactive ambient social media should be incorporated in various future media and products. We hope the experiences described in the paper are useful to design future digitally augmented media and products.

In the near future, our daily life will become more nomad and we often stay at different places for personal or business reasons. Thus, *proactive ambient social media* embedded in our daily objects and environments will be installed in any place to enhance our daily experiences. We can use *proactive ambient social media* as a design material to build new smart daily digital lifestyle. Internet of Things(IoT) are objects that are connected to the Internet to sense the real world and to offer the information to the Internet. IoT can integrate *proactive ambient social media*, and make it possible to pervasively support human decision making anytime, anywhere. The *proactive ambient social media* can be blended into our daily life, but we also need to consider whether this is our dream or just a nightmare. Is this really a better lifestyle for the future? Also, using *proactive ambient social media* everywhere may take control of our attitude, which may cause serious ethical problems.

Ethical issues should be taken into account designing proactive ambient social media. The media offer a possibility to change a user's behavior and attitude. Preparing many selections may solve the problem because users can choose their favorite one by themselves, but this causes the paradox of choice problem [26], and the approach contradicts the goal of the proactive ambient social media.

When designing *proactive ambient social media*, it is important to consider how much information is needed to make better decisions. First, if there are too many choices, the user tends to choose no choice [10]. A large amount of information also requires heavy cognitive efforts, and it is important not to give too much information to make a decision. Also, too much information is not effective to think rationally. In some cases, heuristics is dangerous to make a mistake in decision making [1], and the bias in heuristic thinking may cause the user to make a wrong decision. However, heuristics is necessary to make better decision from many choices within a reasonable time [29]. The amount of information should be carefully designed for better decision making.

In *persuasive ambient social media*, our current case study basically uses a social incentive based on empathy. However, the effect sometimes does not have enough power for the media used for a long time. In this case, we may use other incentive like an economic incentive or an ideological incentive. As the ideological incentive, we may use public policies and ethics. Electric money is a promising candidate to use the economic incentive in our computer-mediated daily environment [28]. In future research, we need to work how to use an economic incentive and an ideological incentive in designing *proactive ambient social media*.

References

1. Ariely, D.: Predictably Irrational: The Hidden Forces That Shape Our Decisions. HarperCollins Publishers Ltd., New York (2008)
2. Dijksterhuis, A., Nordgren, L.F.: A Theory of Unconscious Thought. Perspectives on Psychological Science 1(2) (2006)
3. Fogg, B.J.: Persuasive technology: using to change what we think and do. Morgan Kaufmann, San Francisco (2002)
4. Fredrikson, B.L.: The Value of Positive Emotions: The Emerging Science of Positive Psychology is Coming to Understand Why It's Good to Feel Good. American Scientist 91 (2003)
5. Fujinami, K., Kawsar, F., Nakajima, T.: AwareMirror: A Personalized Display using a Mirror. In: Proceedings of the 3rd International Conference on Pervasive Computing (2005)
6. Hallnas, L., Redstrom, J.: Slow Technology - Designing for Reflection. In: Personal and Ubiquitous Computing, vol. 5(3) (2001)
7. Hosio, S., Kawsar, F., Riekki, J., Nakajima, T.: DroPicks – A Tool for Collaborative Content Sharing Exploiting Everyday Artefacts. In: Ichikawa, H., Cho, W.-D., Chen, Y., Youn, H.Y. (eds.) UCS 2007. LNCS, vol. 4836, pp. 258–265. Springer, Heidelberg (2007)
8. Howe, J.: The Rise of Crowdsourcing. Wired (2006), http://www.wired.com/wired/archive/14.06/crowds.html (retrieved 2007-03-17)
9. Ishii, H., Ullmer, B.: Tangible Bits: Towards Seamless Interfaces between People, Bits, and Atoms. In: Proceedings of the CHI 1997 (1997)
10. Iwata, T., Yamabe, T., Nakajima, T.: Augmented Reality Go: Extending Traditional Game Play with Interactive Self-Learning Support. In: Proceedings of the 17th IEEEE Conference on Embedded and Real-Tie Computing Systems ad Applications (2011)
11. Jordan, P.: The Personalities of Products. In: Volume Pleasure With Products: Beyond Usability. Taylor & Francis, Abington (2002)
12. Kahneman, D., Slovic, P., Tversky, A.: Judgment Under Uncertainty: Heuristics and Biases. Cambridge University Press, New York (1982)
13. Kawsar, F., Fujinami, K., Pirttikangas, S., Hayashi, K., Nakajima, T.: RoonRoon: A Wearable Teddy as Social Interface for Contextual Notification. In: Proceedings of NGMAST 2007 (2007)

14. Kawsar, F., Fujinami, K., Nakajima, T.: Deploy Spontaneously: Supporting End-Users in Building and Enhancing a Smart Home. In: Proceedings of Ubicomp 2008 (2008)
15. Krippendorff, K.: The Semantic Turn: A New Foundation for Design. CRC Press, Boca Raton (2005)
16. Langer, E.J.: Mindfulness. Da Capo Press, Philadelphia (1990)
17. Lehdonvirta, V.: Virtual Item Sales as a Revenue Model: Identifying Attributes that Drive Purchase Decisions. Electronic Commerce Research 9(1) (2009)
18. MacDorman, K.F.: Androids as an experimental apparatus: Why is there an uncanny valley and can we exploit it? In: CogSci 2005 Workshop: Toward Social Mechanisms of Android Science, pp. 106–118 (2005)
19. Mori, M.: On the Uncanny Valley. In: Proceedings of the Humanoids 2005 Workshop (2005)
20. Nakajima, T., Lehdonvirta, V., Tokunaga, E., Kimura, H.: Reflecting Human Behavior to Motivate Desirable Lifestyle. In: Proceedings of ACM Designing Interactive Systems 2008 (2008)
21. Nakajima, T., Kimura, H., Yamabe, T., Lehdonvirta, V., Takayama, C., Shiraishi, M., Washio, Y.: Using aesthetic and empathetic expressions to motivate desirable lifestyle. In: Roggen, D., Lombriser, C., Tröster, G., Kortuem, G., Havinga, P. (eds.) EuroSSC 2008. LNCS, vol. 5279, pp. 220–234. Springer, Heidelberg (2008)
22. Oehlberg, L., Ducheneaut, N., Thornton, J.D., Moore, R.J., Nickell, E.: Social TV: Designing for distributed, sociable television viewing. In: EuroITV (2006)
23. Petty, R.E., Wegner, D.T.: The Elaboration Likelihood Model: Current Status and Controversies. In: Chaiken, S., Trope, Y. (eds.) Dual-Process Theories in Social Psychology. Guilfond Press, New York (1999)
24. Reeves, B., Nass, C.: The Media Equation: How People Treat Computers, Television, and New Media like Real People and Places. Cambridge University Press, Cambridge (1998)
25. Salber, D., Dey, A.K., Abowd, G.D.: The Context Toolkit: Aiding the Development of Context-Enabled Applications. In: The Proceedings of CHI 1999 (1999)
26. Schwartz, B.: The Paradox of Choice: Why More Is Less. Harper Perennial (2005)
27. Schwarz, N., Clore, G.L.: Feelings and phenomenal experiences. In: Higgins, E.T., Kruglanski, A.W. (eds.) Social Psychology: Handbook of Basic Principles (2006)
28. Shiraishi, M., Washio, Y., Takayama, C., Lehdonvirta, V., Kimura, H., Nakajima, T.: Using Individual, Social and Economic Persuasion Techniques to Reduce CO2 Emissions in a Family Setting. In: Persuasive Technologies 2009 (2009)
29. Todd, P.M.: How much information do we need? European Journal of Operational Research 177, 1332–1417 (2007)
30. Thaler, R.H., Sunstein, C.R.: Nudge: Improving Decisions About Health, Wealth, and Happiness. Yale University Press, New Haven and London (2008)
31. Reeve, J.: Understanding Motivation and Emotion, 4th edn. Wiley, Chichester (2005)
32. Ruth, M., Schoormans, J.P.L., Schifferstein, H.N.J.: Product Attachment: Design Strategies to Stimulate the Emotional Bonding with Products. In: Product Experience. Elsevier, Amsterdam (2007)
33. Velicer, W.F., Prochaska, J.O., Fava, J.L., Norman, G.J., Redding, C.A.: Smoking cessation and stress management: applications of the transtheoretical Model of behavior change. Homeostasis 38 (1998)
34. Yamabe, T., Lehdonvirta, V., Ito, H., Soma, H., Kimura, H., Nakajima, T.: Applying Pervasive Technologies to Create Economic Incentives that Alter Consumer Behavior. In: Proceedings of ACM Ubicomp 2009 (2009)

Social Interaction Mining in Small Group Discussion Using a Smart Meeting System

Zhiwen Yu[1], Xingshe Zhou[1], Zhiyong Yu[2], Christian Becker[3], and Yuichi Nakamura[4]

[1] School of Computer Science, Northwestern Polytechnical University, P.R. China
{Zhiwenyu,zhouxs}@nwpu.edu.cn
[2] College of Mathematics and Computer Science, Fuzhou University, P.R. China
yuzhiy@gmail.com
[3] Chair for Information Systems II, Mannheim University, Germany
christian.becker@uni-mannheim.de
[4] Academic Center for Computing and Media Studies, Kyoto University, Japan
yuichi@media.kyoto-u.ac.jp

Abstract. In this paper, we propose a mining method to discover high-level semantic knowledge about human social interactions in small group discussion, such as frequent interaction patterns, the role of an individual (e.g., the "centrality" or "power"), subgroup interactions (e.g., two persons often interact with each other), and hot sessions. A smart meeting system is developed for capturing and recognizing social interactions. Interaction network in a discussion session is represented as a graph. Interaction graph mining algorithms are designed to analyze the structure of the networks and extract social interaction patterns. Preliminary results show that we can extract several interesting patterns that are useful for interpretation of human behavior in small group discussion.

Keywords: social interaction; interaction mining; smart meeting; graph mining.

1 Introduction

Small group discussion is very common in our daily work and lives for purposes of problem solving, information exchange, and knowledge creation. Understanding how people interact in a discussion is important to make it more productive and creative. Compared with physical behaviors such as speaking and gesturing, high-level semantic knowledge about human social interaction is more meaningful for deeply learning social rules in discussion, such as usually how many people from a group are involved in a discussion session, how many interactions occur in a discussion session, and whether any subgroup interactions occur (e.g., two persons often interact with each other, or one person often responds to another one). Understanding how people are interacting can also be used to support a variety of pervasive applications, such as accomplishing social awareness in intelligent environments [1].

This knowledge can be extracted as important patterns of human interaction from group discussion. Discovering such knowledge consists of two steps: first interaction identification, and second pattern mining. One ordinary solution for interaction identification is to take notes during the discussion. However, note-taking is insufficient

C.-H. Hsu et al. (Eds.): UIC 2011, LNCS 6905, pp. 40–51, 2011.

to store all relevant activities and distracts the participants. Furthermore, it is subjective and inaccurate. An automatic system, e.g., a smart meeting room might be helpful in this task. Meeting is intrinsically a human group discussion process that encapsulates a large amount of social and communication information. A smart meeting system aims at archiving, analyzing and summarizing a meeting discussion so as to make the discussion more efficient in its organization and viewing.

In this paper, we propose a pattern mining method to discover high-level semantic knowledge about human social interaction in small group discussion. A smart meeting system is developed for capturing and recognizing social interactions, such as proposing an idea, giving comments, expressing a positive opinion, and requesting information [2]. Interaction network in a discussion session is represented as a graph. Inspired by graph mining [3, 4, 5], we designed interaction graph pattern mining algorithms to analyze the structure and density of a network, and extract interaction patterns among meeting participants, such as centrality and cliques.

The remainder of this paper is structured as follows. In Section 2, previous studies related to this paper are discussed. Section 3 gives the overview of our smart meeting system. The social interaction mining method is described in Section 4. Section 5 presents the experimental results. Finally, we present the conclusions in Section 6.

2   Related Work

Many smart meeting systems have been implemented in the past decade (see [6] for a full review). They can be roughly divided into two main categories. One is about providing adaptive services and relevant information in a meeting room by using ubiquitous sensors and context-awareness techniques. The other class aims at meeting capture and view. Unlike these systems, our study focuses on detecting human interactions and discovering higher-level semantic knowledge in meeting discussion.

A number of studies have been conducted on discovering knowledge about human actions by applying the concept of data mining. Casas-Garriga [7] proposed algorithms to mine unbounded episodes (those with unfixed window width or interval) from a sequence of events on a time line. The work is generally used to extract frequent episodes, i.e., collections of events occurring frequently together. Morita et al [8] proposed a pattern mining method for the interpretation of human interactions in a poster exhibition. It extracts simultaneously occurring patterns of primitive actions such as gaze and speech. Sawamoto et al [9] presented a method for extracting important interaction patterns in medical interviews (i.e., doctor–patient communication) using nonverbal information. The patterns are defined as a set of concurrently occurring primitives, e.g., utterance, gazing, and gesture. Liu et al [10] applied data mining techniques to detect and analyze frequent trajectory patterns for activity monitoring from RFID (Radio frequency Identification) tag data. Cao et al [11] proposed models and algorithms for mining frequent periodic human trajectories from historical spatio-temporal data, such as mobile phone tracing. In [12], the authors presented approaches to discover impact-targeted activity patterns, i.e., identifying those activities that are likely to lead to the targeted impact. The Discussion Ontology [13], which forms the basis of discussion methodology, was proposed for discovering semantic information such as a statement's intention and the discussion flow in meetings.

Unlike mining patterns of actions occurring together [7, 8, 9], patterns of trajectories [10, 11], patterns of activities [12], and discussion flow [13], our study focuses on discovering interaction *network* patterns among a group of persons, such as centrality and cliques in small group discussion.

3   Smart Meeting System

We developed a prototype smart meeting system for capture, recognition, and visualization of human social interactions during a discussion. We use multiple devices such as video cameras, microphones, and motion sensors for capturing human interactions. Fig. 1 shows the overview of our smart meeting system setup.

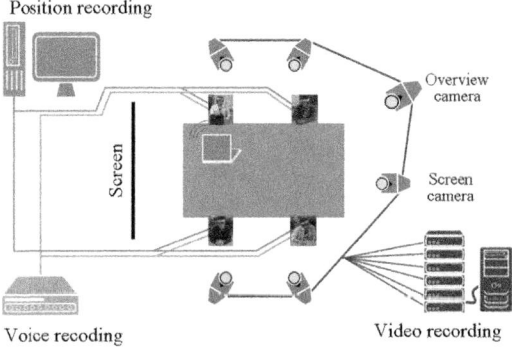

Fig. 1. Smart meeting system overview

Six video cameras (SONY EVI-D30) are deployed in our smart meeting system. Four of them capture the upper-body motions of four participants (breast shot), one records presentation slides (screen shot), and the other captures an overview of the meeting including all participants (overview shot). A head-mounted microphone (SHURE WH30XLR) is attached to each participant for recording audio data. An optical motion capture system (PhaseSpace IMPULSE) [14] is adopted for head tracking (i.e., position recording). It has three main parts: a light-emitting diode (LED) module, camera, and server. The tracking system uses multiple charge-coupled device (CCD) cameras for three-dimensional measurement of LED tags, and obtains their exact position. We placed six LED tags around each person's head. The tags are scanned 30 times per second, and position data can be obtained in real time with less than 10-ms latency. Through the three-dimensional position data, head gestures (e.g., nodding) and face orientation can be detected.

We adopt a multimodal method to detect human social interactions based on a variety of features, such as gestures, attention, speech tone, and speaking time. Four kinds of classification models, Support Vector Machine (SVM), Bayesian Net, Naïve Bayes, and Decision Tree, are selected to infer the type of each interaction. The interaction types include *propose, comment, acknowledgement, requestInfo, askOpinion*, *posOpinion*, and *negOpinion*. The results show that SVM outperforms the others and achieves a recognition rate of approximately 80%. Please refer to our earlier papers [2, 15] for details about social interaction definition and recognition.

4   Interaction Mining

4.1   Interaction Network Construction and Representation

Based on the interaction recognition result derived from the smart meeting system, we need to construct the interaction network in a discussion session.

Definition 1 (Session). A session is a unit of a meeting that begins with a spontaneous interaction and ends with an interaction that is not followed by any reactive interactions.

Here, spontaneous interactions are those interactions initiated by a person spontaneously (e.g., proposing an idea or asking a question are usually spontaneous interactions), and reactive interactions are triggered in response to another interaction (e.g., acknowledgement). Hence, a session contains at least *one* interaction (i.e., a spontaneous interaction). A meeting discussion consists of a sequence of sessions in which participants discuss topics continuously. Sessions are identified based on the manual annotations in our current system. Automatic segmentation method will be explored in our future research.

During the process of session identification, we also manually specify which interaction (or which person) a reactive interaction really responds to. Thus an interaction network among the participants in a discussion session could be formed.

We first use a graph structure to represent an interaction network and then adopt a string for encoding the graph formally.

Definition 2 (Interaction Graph). A graph is used to represent an interaction network in a session. In this paper, interaction graphs are directed and labeled, but may be unconnected. An interaction graph is denoted as $G = (V, E)$. $V = \{P_1, P_2, ..., P_n\}$ is the set of vertices representing a total of n persons participating in the meeting. A distinguished vertex $P_i \in V$ is designated the initiator of the session (see Fig. 2). $E = \{(P_i, P_j) \mid P_i, P_j \in V \wedge P_i \neq P_j\}$ is the set of edges representing interaction responses. For any $(P_i, P_j) \in E$, it means P_i responds to P_j. Edges are labeled with numbers denoting how many times a person responds to another in the session. An isolated node means that the person has no interactions with others.

Two examples of interaction graphs are shown in Fig. 2. In this case, a total of four persons participate in the meeting. In Fig. 2a, P_1 initiates the session, P_2 and P_3 respond to him, and then P_1 responds to P_2. In Fig. 2b, P_2 is the initiator of the session, and P_1 responds to him two times.

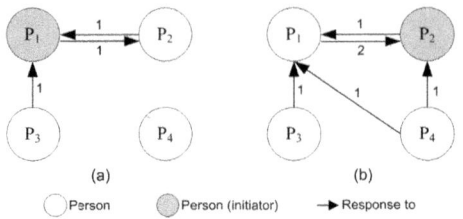

Fig. 2. Graph representation of the interaction network

This graph is represented by an adjacency matrix that is widely adopted in mathematical graph theory [16].

Definition 3 (Adjacency Matrix). Given an interaction graph $G = (V, E)$, the adjacency matrix X has the following (i, j)-element, x_{ij},

$$x_{ij} = \begin{cases} label((P_i, P_j)) & (P_i, P_j) \in E \\ A & i = j \text{ AND } P_i \text{ is the initiator} \cdot \\ 0 & else \end{cases}$$

The graphs in Fig. 2a and 2b can be represented as X_a and X_b, respectively:

$$X_a = \begin{pmatrix} A & 1 & 0 & 0 \\ 1 & 0 & 0 & 0 \\ 1 & 0 & 0 & 0 \\ 0 & 0 & 0 & 0 \end{pmatrix} \quad X_b = \begin{pmatrix} 0 & 2 & 0 & 0 \\ 1 & A & 0 & 0 \\ 1 & 0 & 0 & 0 \\ 1 & 1 & 0 & 0 \end{pmatrix} \cdot$$

For efficient processing, we use a string coding method for the adjacency matrices.

Definition 4 (Graph String Code). An interaction graph G is represented by its string encoding, denoted as gsc. The code of an interaction graph with adjacency matrix,

$$X = \begin{pmatrix} x_{11} & x_{12} & x_{13} & \cdots & x_{1n} \\ x_{21} & x_{22} & x_{23} & \cdots & x_{2n} \\ \vdots & \vdots & \vdots & \ddots & \vdots \\ x_{n1} & x_{n2} & x_{n3} & \cdots & x_{nn} \end{pmatrix},$$

is defined as

$$gsc(G) = x_{11}, x_{12}, x_{13}, \cdots, x_{1n}, x_{21}, x_{22}, x_{23}, \cdots, x_{2n}, \cdots, x_{n1}, x_{n2}, x_{n3}, \cdots, x_{nn} \cdot$$

According to this definition, the string codes of the interaction graphs in Fig. 2a and 2b are "A,1,0,0,1,0,0,0,1,0,0,0,0,0,0,0" and "0,2,0,0,1,A,0,0,1,0,0,0,1,1,0,0" respectively.

Now we introduce the definition of an interaction subgraph and a non-initiator-label (NIL) graph string code for the purpose of subgraph mining.

Definition 5 (Interaction Subgraph). Given an interaction graph $G = (V, E)$, graph $G' = (V', E')$ is called a subgraph of G, denoted as $G' \subseteq G$, if (1) $V' \subseteq V$; (2) $E' \subseteq E$ ($E' \neq \phi$); and (3) $\forall P_i, P_j \in V'$, there is a path between P_i and P_j with all edges in E' regarded as undirected.

An interaction subgraph is a *connected* graph. In this subgraph definition, the initiator and edge label are not considered; in other words, we focus only on how many people interact and who interacts with whom, not on who is the initiator and how many times a person responds to another. The purpose is to find potential subgroups in a discussion. Fig. 3 shows all subgraphs of the interaction graph depicted in Fig. 2a.

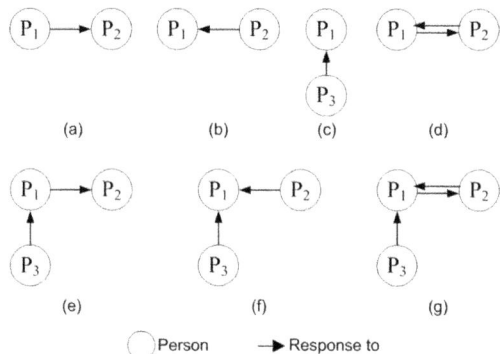

Fig. 3. Interaction subgraph examples

Definition 6 (NIL Graph String Code). The NIL (Non-Initiator-Label) graph string code, denoted as *n-gsc*, is a revised version of the graph string code (*gsc*) formed by omitting the features of the initiator and edge labels, specifically, replacing "A" with "0" and changing numbers that are larger than 1 to "1".

According to this definition, the NIL graph string codes of the interaction graphs in Fig. 2a and 2b are "0,1,0,0,1,0,0,0,1,0,0,0,0,0,0,0" and "0,1,0,0,1,0,0,0,1,0,0,0,1, 1,0,0" respectively.

4.2 Pattern Discovery

Graph mining techniques are adopted to extract patterns of interaction. By analyzing the structure and density of the network, we can identify the role of an individual in the meeting (e.g., the "centrality" or "power" in the interaction network), detect cliques (i.e., groups of connected individuals), and determine hot sessions (i.e., interaction networks with a lot of edges).

   We first provide the definitions of a pattern and support for determining patterns.

Definition 7 (Pattern). Patterns are frequent interaction graphs or subgraphs in the graph database.

Definition 8 (Support). Given an interaction graph or subgraph g and a dataset of graphs GD, the support of g is defined as

$$sup(g) = \frac{number\ of\ occurrences\ of\ g}{total\ number\ of\ graphs\ in\ GD}.$$

If the value of $sup(g)$ is larger than a threshold value σ (e.g., 5%), g is an interaction pattern, i.e., a frequent interaction graph or frequent interaction subgraph.

In our problem setting, we have a dataset of interaction graphs GD. Given a minimum support σ, we would like to find all interaction graphs and subgraphs that appear at least $\sigma \times |GD|$ times in the dataset. Table 1 shows the notations we use.

Table 1. Notations

Notation	Description
GD	A dataset of interaction graphs with gsc string encoding
NGD	The non-initiator-label string encoding (n-gsc) of GD
g	An interaction graph
g^k	A subgraph with k edges
C^k	A set of candidates with k edges
F^k	A set of frequent subgraphs with k edges
σ	A support threshold

Algorithm 1 shows the procedure of frequent interaction graph pattern mining. It scans the graph database, calculates the support of each graph, and outputs frequently occurring graphs.

Algorithm 1. figm (GD, σ) (Frequent interaction graph pattern mining)

Input: a graph database GD and a support threshold σ
Output: all frequent graph patterns with respect to σ
Procedure:
(1)   scan database GD, count the number of occurrences for each graph g
(2)   calculate the support of each graph
(3)   output the graphs whose supports are larger than σ

Our frequent interaction subgraph mining algorithm is inspired by Apriori (a well-known association rule mining algorithm) [17]: *every non-empty subtree of a frequent tree pattern is also frequent*. Algorithm 2 outlines the pseudocode of frequent subgraph mining. It first generates an n-gsc database NGD, calculates the support of each edge, and selects the edges whose supports are larger than σ to form the set of frequent edges, F^1 (Steps 2–4). It then adds a frequent edge to the existing frequent subgraphs with i edges to generate the set of candidates with $i+1$ edges (Steps 5–9). If any graphs exist with supports larger than σ, it selects them to form F^{i+1} and repeats the procedure from Step 5; otherwise, it stops to output frequent subgraphs. In Step 7, "$(g^1 \notin g^i)$ AND $(\exists P_i \in g^1, P_i \in g^i)$" is used to guarantee that g^1 is not an edge of g^i and they can be connected.

Algorithm 2. fisgm (GD, σ) (Frequent interaction subgraph pattern mining)

Input: a graph database GD and a support threshold σ

Output: all frequent subgraph patterns with respect to σ

Procedure:

(1)　$i \leftarrow 0$

(2)　scan database GD, generate its n-gsc database NGD

(3)　scan database NGD, calculate the support of each edge

(4)　select the edges whose supports are larger than σ to form F^1

(5)　$i \leftarrow i + 1$

(6)　for each graph g^i in F^i, do

(7)　　for each edge g^1 in F^1 satisfying $(g^1 \notin g^i)$ AND $(\exists P_i \in g^1, P_i \in g^i)$, do

(8)　　　combine g^i and g^1 to generate C^{i+1}

(9)　　calculate the support of each graph in C^{i+1}

(10)　if there are any graphs whose supports are larger than σ, then select them to form F^{i+1} and return to Step (5)

(11)　else output the frequent subgraphs whose supports are larger than σ

---

5 Experiments

The experimental data includes two captured meetings, one trip planning meeting (18 min, discussing time, place, activities, and transportation for a summer trip) and one soccer preparation meeting (23 min, talking about the players and their roles and positions in an upcoming soccer match). Both meetings had the same four participants. Human social interactions were detected by using a multimodal automatic approach [15]. For the purpose of mining, we tuned the interaction types manually after applying the recognition method. We ultimately got a data set comprising a total of 926 interactions and 251 sessions. Hence, the graph dataset contains 251 interaction graphs.

Fig. 4 shows the session distribution according to the number of interactions in one session. We observe that sessions consisting of 3 interactions are the most numerous. The longest sessions (those with the maximum interactions) are composed of 12 interactions. Sessions containing 1 to 5 interactions, which account for 83.7% of all sessions, could be regarded as ordinary sessions. Other sessions, with 6 to 12 interactions, are special sessions. They might be hot sessions in which participants engaged in an emphatic and heated discussion. The three longest (or hottest) sessions, with 12 interactions, are depicted in Fig. 5. Their string encoding are "0,2,0,0,1,0,2,1, 0,3,0,1,0,1,0,A"; "0,0,0,0,0,0,1,1,0,1,A,2,0,1,5,0"; and "A,1,0,0,1,0,0,1,2,1,0,1,1,3,0, 0" respectively. In Fig. 5a, P_4 initiates the session, and then all persons participate. P_2 might be the center of this session because he interacts three times with P_1, five times with P_3, and two times with P_4. In Fig. 5b, P_3 initiates the session, and then P_2, P_3, and P_4 interact. P_3 and P_4 interact many times, while P_1 is isolated from the others in the session. He might be not interested in the current discussion topic. In Fig. 5c, P_1 initiates the session and all persons interact with each other. It seems in this session that the persons are balanced in participation.

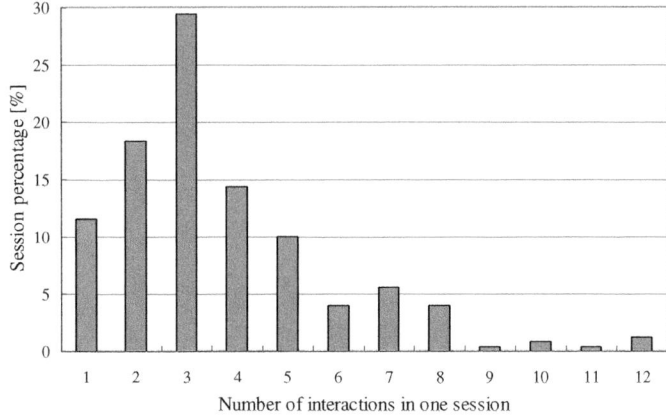

Fig. 4. Session distribution

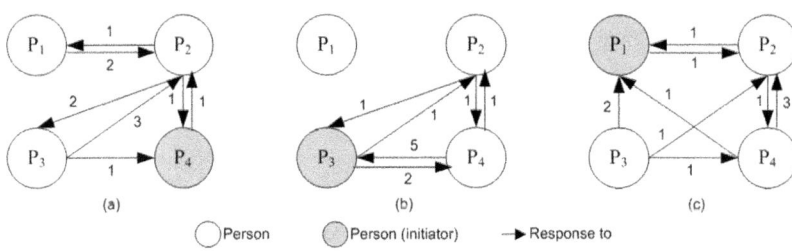

Fig. 5. Three sessions with 12 interactions

In frequent interaction graph mining, we set the support threshold σ at 3% and obtained six patterns. They are presented in Fig. 6, ranked by the value of support. Fig. 6a shows the most frequent graph, which denotes P_3 launching the session and P_4 responding to him. The patterns shown in Fig. 6b and 6c represent one-interaction sessions. The pattern of Fig. 6d represents P_4 initiating the session and P_3 responding to him, and those of Fig. 6e and 6f represent three-interaction sessions. From these patterns, we can conclude that sessions were often launched by P_3 or P_4. They were active in the meetings and might be central in the group. P_1 was the least active.

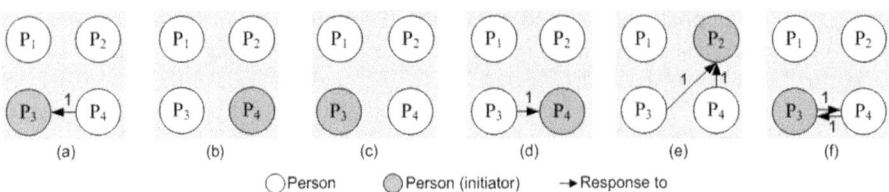

Fig. 6. Frequent graph patterns

The experimental results for finding frequent interaction subgraphs are shown in Figs. 7 and 8. Fig. 7 shows the running time required for different values of support threshold. Fig. 8 displays the number of discovered frequent subgraphs on those support levels. With σ =1%, the running time for pattern discovery takes around 3.8 seconds, a total of 173 frequent subgraphs are discovered, and the largest frequent subgraph has five edges. Both the running time and the number of frequent subgraphs decrease as the support threshold increases. In particular, with the support threshold increasing from 1% to 2%, both the running time and the number of frequent subgraphs decrease dramatically.

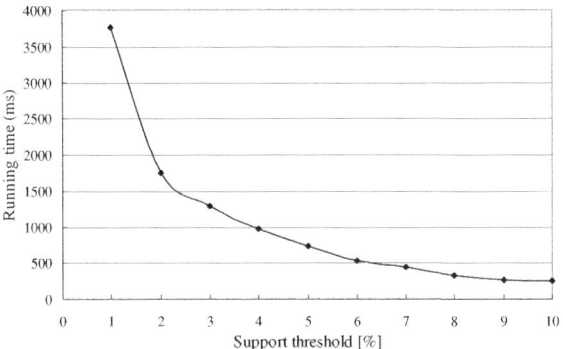

Fig. 7. Support threshold and running time

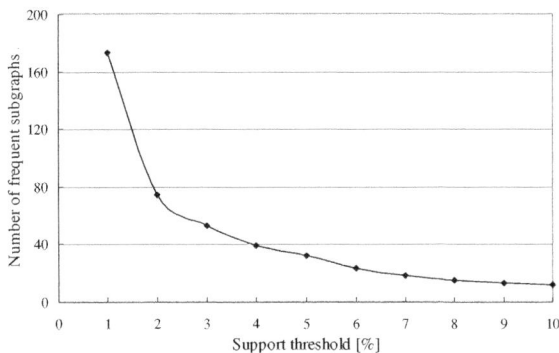

Fig. 8. Support threshold and the number of discovered frequent subgraphs

If the support threshold σ is set as 3%, 53 frequent subgraphs are obtained, in which 12 graphs have one edge, 38 have two edges, and 11 have three edges. The top five patterns for each number of edges ranked by the value of support are presented in Fig. 9.

The one-edge patterns represent the most primitive patterns of interaction. The patterns of two edges are basically combinations of one-edge patterns. For instance, pattern 2-1 is a combination of 1-1 and 1-2. Pattern 2-2 is obtained from 1-3 and 1-4.

The patterns of three edges are combinations of one-edge and two-edge patterns. For example, pattern 3-1 is a combination of 1-4 and 2-3. It also can be obtained from 1-3 and 2-5.

From the patterns discovered with subgraphs, we can conclude that P_3 and P_4 are likely to form a clique in a discussion, i.e., they often respond to each other. Besides this clique, P_2 often connects with P_3 or P_4 and forms less frequent subgroups. These extracted patterns can be used for interpretation of human interaction in small group discussion.

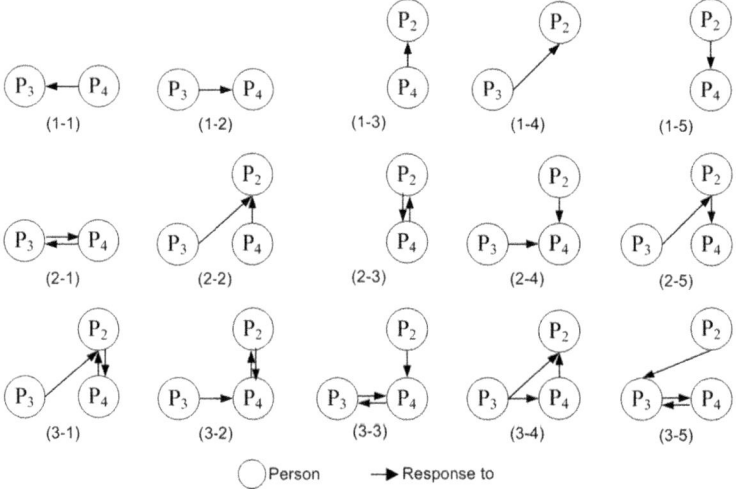

Fig. 9. Top five patterns for one, two, and three edges (The numbers under the pattern indicate the number of edges and the rank, e.g., pattern 3-2 is the second rank of three-edge patterns.)

6   Conclusion and Future Work

We proposed an approach for mining patterns of human social interactions in small group discussion by using a smart meeting system. Our work is crucial for understanding how people are interacting in a meeting discussion. For future work, we plan to investigate sequential interaction mining to extract interaction flow pattern. An interaction flow that appears frequently reveals relationships between different types of interactions, such as proposing an idea, giving comments, expressing a positive opinion, and requesting information. For instance, if one type of interaction appears, what is the probability of another type following it?

Acknowledgments. This work was partially supported by the National Natural Science Foundation of China (No. 60903125), the Program for New Century Excellent Talents in University (No. NCET-09-0079), the Natural Science Basic Research Plan in Shaanxi Province of China (No. 2010JM8033), and the Science and Technology Research Plan in Shaanxi Province of China (No. 2011KJXX38).

References

1. Pentland, A.: Socially Aware Computation and Communication. IEEE Computer 38(3), 33–40 (2005)
2. Yu, Z., et al.: Capture, Recognition, and Visualization of Human Semantic Interactions in Meetings. In: The 8th IEEE International Conference on Pervasive Computing and Communications (PerCom 2010), pp. 107–115 (2010)
3. Chakrabarti, D., Faloutsos, C.: Graph Mining: Laws, Generators, and Algorithms. ACM Computing Surveys 38(1), Article No. 2 (2006)
4. Yan, X., Han, J.: gSpan: Graph-Based Substructure Pattern Mining. In: Proceedings of 2002 IEEE International Conference on Data Mining ICDM, pp. 721–724 (2002)
5. Kuramochi, M., Karypis, G.: Frequent Subgraph Discovery. In: Proceedings of 2001 IEEE International Conference on Data Mining (ICDM), pp. 313–320 (2001)
6. Yu, Z., Nakamura, Y.: Smart Meeting Systems: A Survey of State-of-the-Art and Open Issues. ACM Computing Surveys 42(2) (2010)
7. Casas-Garriga, G.: Discovering unbounded episodes in sequential data. In: Lavrač, N., Gamberger, D., Todorovski, L., Blockeel, H. (eds.) PKDD 2003. LNCS (LNAI), vol. 2838, pp. 83–94. Springer, Heidelberg (2003)
8. Morita, T., et al.: A Pattern Mining Method for Interpretation of Interaction. In: Proc. of ICMI 2005, pp. 267–273 (2005)
9. Sawamoto, Y., et al.: Extraction of Important Interactions in Medical Interviews Using Nonverbal Information. In: Proc. of ICMI 2007, pp. 82–85 (2007)
10. Liu, Y., Chen, L., Pei, J., Chen, Q., Zhao, Y.: Mining Frequent Trajectory Patterns for Activity Monitoring Using Radio Frequency Tag Arrays. In: Proc. of PerCom 2007, pp. 37–46 (2007)
11. Cao, H., Mamoulis, N., Cheung, D.W.: Mining Frequent Spatio-Temporal Sequential Patterns. In: Proc. Fifth IEEE Int'l. Conf. Data Mining (ICDM 2005), pp. 82–89 (2005)
12. Cao, L., Zhao, Y., Zhang, C.: Mining Impact-Targeted Activity Patterns in Imbalanced Data. IEEE Transactions on Knowledge and Data Engineering 20(8), 1053–1065 (2008)
13. Tomobe, H., Nagao, K.: Discussion Ontology: Knowledge Discovery from Human Activities in Meetings. In: Washio, T., Satoh, K., Takeda, H., Inokuchi, A. (eds.) JSAI 2006. LNCS (LNAI), vol. 4384, pp. 33–41. Springer, Heidelberg (2007)
14. PhaseSpace IMPULSE system (2008), http://www.phasespace.com/
15. Yu, Z., Yu, Z., Ko, Y., Zhou, X., Nakamura, Y.: Inferring Human Interactions in Meetings: A Multimodal Approach. In: Zhang, D., Portmann, M., Tan, A.-H., Indulska, J. (eds.) UIC 2009. LNCS, vol. 5585, pp. 14–24. Springer, Heidelberg (2009)
16. Fortin, S.: The graph isomorphism problem. Technical Report 96-20, University of Alberta, Canada (1996)
17. Agrawal, R., Srikant, R.: Fast algorithms for mining association rules. In: Proc. Of the 20th Int. Conf. on Very Large Databases (VLDB), pp. 487–499 (1994)

Probabilistic Path Selection in Mobile Wireless Sensor Networks for Stochastic Events Detection

Xiwei Zhang[1] and Jia Yu[2]

[1] Department of Computer and Information, Hohai University
Nanjing, Jiangsu, China
zxw@hhu.edu.cn
[2] Department of Modern Science, Administrative College of JiangSu Province
Nanjing, Jiangsu, China
yuj@sdx.js.cn

Abstract. Mobile sensors cover more area over a fixed period of time than the same number of stationary sensors. With the combination of communication and mobility capabilities, we can envision a new class of proactive networks that are able to adapt themselves, via physical movement, to meet the need of different applications. In this paper we consider the following event capture problem: The stochastic events arrive at certain points, called points of interesting (PoIs), in the sensor field with a long enough duration time. Mobile sensors visit all PoIs start from Base Station (BS) with a fixed velocity and finally return to BS. An event is said to be captured if it is sensed by one of the mobile sensors before it fades away. Due to the over-detection problem when ever mobile sensors blindly visit every PoIs with the same interval time, we propose a general event detection framework (EDF) for mobile sensors using probabilistic path selection (PPS) protocol to reduce detection latency, and employ less number mobile nodes at the same time. A distinctive feature is that the system ensures that the detection delay of any event occurring at PoIs is statistically bounded, and mobile sensor framework (MSF) reduces transmitting delay from the time mobile sensor detecting event to return to BS simultaneously. Extensive experiments have been conducted and the results demonstrate that our algorithm allows us use less number mobile nodes within the delay bound and reduce the transmitting delay significantly.

1 Introduction

During the past several years, great progresses were made in both the capabilities and miniaturization of wireless sensors. The wireless sensor networks have been deployed in a class of mission-critical applications such as environmental monitoring [1], event detection [2] and security surveillance [3]. These advances herald the development of systems that can gather and harness information in ways previously unexplored. Equipped with sensing and wireless communication capabilities, the nodes can form a network to detect intruders or observe environment in their interesting region.

For many envisioned applications, a non-mobile wireless sensor network is usually adequate to meet the application requirements. However, this approach has several

C.-H. Hsu et al. (Eds.): UIC 2011, LNCS 6905, pp. 52–63, 2011.
© Springer-Verlag Berlin Heidelberg 2011

disadvantages. First, in order to satisfy coverage and connection demand, a large amount of sensor nodes are needed, it raises a serious over-detection problem in some areas. Second, stationary sensor networks cause "hot spot" problem, i.e., the energy of some sensor nodes will be depleted quickly due to frequently data relaying. Third, the lifetime of the networks is short for the nodes not only have to sense the physical events but also transmit the sensed data. In short, because of absence of mobility, a dense network may often be infeasible, due to financial constraints, or undesirable, due to the negative effects a dense network may have on the sensor field or the environment.

With recent advances in robotics and low power embedded systems, mobile nodes [4] are becoming a viable choice for the sensing applications mentioned above. These mobile nodes may be mobile data ferries, or mobile data relays, which responsible to collect data from the sensor nodes or relay data from the sensor nodes to base station. In this approach, a small number of mobile devices referred to as data ferry roam about sensing fields and collect data from sensors. As a result, significant network energy saving can be achieved by reducing or completely avoiding costly multi-hop wireless transmissions. On the other hand, if the mobile node has sense ability, called *mobile sensor*, it can cover more area than a stationary sensor over a period of time because it can move to anywhere to capture the event. However mobile sensors have their own drawbacks. Although the energy consumption of mobile sensors is less constrained as they can replenish their energy supplies because of the mobility, the primary disadvantage of this approach is the increased latency. Mobile sensor need a lot of time to move to the interesting position for speed constraint. The other problem is some area may not be covered for the unstable trajectory of the mobile sensor. So without proper motion planning, a substantial portion of the sensor field may not be covered by mobile sensors for a long time period. This problem is severe if the phenomenon being covered is highly dynamic (either spatially or temporally) in nature.

In this paper, we propose an event detection framework (EDF) for mobile sensors. The EDF is a general framework which allows arbitrary number of mobile sensors with fixed velocity to satisfy user's delay constraint, including detection delay and transmitting delay together. The EDF uses probabilistic path selection protocol (PPS) for stochastic events capture efficiently. The central idea is the mobile nodes dynamically select different path through setting their visiting probability according to the required delay constraint of PoIs. For we find in most event detection scenario, different events need different delay constraint. For instance, it may be desirable for the user that 80% of events are detected within 10s, 15% are within 20s and 5% are within 30s, which is shorter than event duration. If the mobile sensors visit PoIs with the same interval time, which will cause over detection problem at some PoIs, and the transmitting delay will be prolonged.

We consider a scenario where events appear and disappear at certain points within a sensor field and the events have to be *captured* using mobile sensors (Figure 1). An event is said to be captured if a mobile sensor senses it before it disappears. The points where the event may occur are assumed to be known a priori and are referred to as *Points of Interest (PoIs)*. An event should be captured before user's *delay constraint*, and the sensors move back to BS to report the result. We call this the *Bounded Delay Constraint Problem (BDCP)*. As the name suggest, the goal of the BDCP is to plan the sensor motion such that the delay constraint is bounded from above. We consider two versions of BDCP: i) The detectability of a PoI is fixed and the visit probability of sensors is identical, we named this *non-adaptive schema (NAS)*; ii)

Each mobile node works adaptively and reduce its visit probability according to detectability of other nodes to transmit data quickly, which is called *probabilistic adaptation schema (PAS)*.

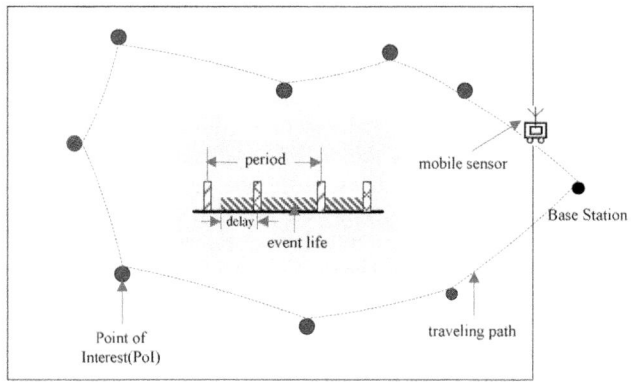

Fig. 1. Event capture using mobile sensors

This paper makes the following contributions:

1) We define a general event detection framework for mobile sensor networks, and then formulate a soft bound for access delay specification and devise a simple but effective metric to realize such a statistical soft bound.

2) We formulate a bounded delay constraint problem (BDCP) to satisfy the delay constraint. A probabilistic path selection (PPS) algorithm is proposed, which select the traveling path of mobile sensors according to the PoI's visit probability. PPS can reduce the data transmitting time for selecting a shorten path and satisfy the delay constraint at the same time.

3) Two kinds of PPS scheme are proposed named NAS and PAS. The difference between them is whether can adjust the PoIs' visit probability of mobile sensors. In PAS, the sensor's visit probability of a PoI will be reduced according to detectability of other nodes.

The rest of the paper is organized as follows. Section II reviews the related works and compares other different mobile sensor networks. Section III formulate the problem and define the EDF. The PPS algorithms are described in section IV, section V presents simulation experiment results and section VI concludes the paper.

2   Related Works

More recently, there has been interest in understanding how the coverage properties of a sensor network may be improved by introducing mobility to the sensor devices. We know for a random deployment in static sensor networks, the sensor density should increase as $O(\log l + k \log \log l)$ to provide k-coverage in a network with size of l. In [5], authors prove an all mobile sensor network can provide k-coverage over the field with a constant density of $O(K)$, independent of network size l.

Chellappan et al. introduce flip-based sensors for network coverage improvement in [6]. The flip-based sensors can only move once, over a limited distance, therefore the costs of such sensors are quite low. In [7] and [8], the authors propose virtual force based algorithms in order to guide sensor movements for improving the coverage properties after random deployment. In [9], the authors propose algorithms to detect the vacancies in a sensor field and use them to guide sensor motion in order to increase coverage.

[10] analyzed the impact of mobility on detection delay and area coverage. Their study is based on random mobility model and do not address the issue of actively controlling the movement of sensors. Bisnik et al. [11] analyzed the performance of detecting stochastic events using mobile sensors. Different from these works, we take detection delay and transmitting delay together into consideration to study efficient sensor collaboration and movement scheduling strategies.

Mobile nodes are often used as data collectors which named Data Mules or Data Ferries [12, 13, 14]. In order to reduce the data transmitting delay, path selection problem are elaborately studied in these papers. In [12], authors studied path selection problem, assuming that each sensor generates data at a certain rate and that the data mule needs to collect data before the buffer of each sensor overflows. Gandham et al. [13] used multiple mobile base stations to prolong the lifetime of the sensor networks. Xing et al. [14] presented path selection algorithms for rendezvous based approach. In these works, mobile nodes visit part of static nodes to collect data, but they did not use probabilistic method. In our work, we employ a fuzzy mobility control model with delay constraint and also realize a more optimized path selection where every mobile node only needs to visit subset of PoIs which makes a shorten traveling path to reduce the data transmitting time.

3 Problem Formulation

It is intuitive that there is an intrinsic tradeoff between the number of mobile sensor nodes and the event detection delay. In this section we present an analysis of delay quality of mobile sensor networks for a simplistic scenario. We consider a PoIs, numbered 1 through a, randomly scattered in the monitoring field F. We consider mobile sensor set S, which conclude m mobile sensors, visit the PoIs with fixed velocity v. The process that a mobile sensor starts from base station to visit PoIs once time and return to base station is called a *period*. The mobile sensors can detect the event at a PoI (the PoI is *visible* to the sensor) if the distance between the sensor and the PoI along the trajectory is less than the sensing range r.

We focus on persistent events which exist for a certain duration time before they disappear. The event life is long enough and we assume that the event is always be detected. Each mobile sensor knows the position of PoIs and the interval time between the PoI's consecutive visits of one mobile sensor is τ_{period}.

3.1 Full Visiting Period

At first, we consider a simple approach that the mobile sensors move along a fixed path and visit each PoI once time in such a period.

Definition 1 (Full Visiting): *Suppose all the PoIs are connected by a simple closed curve of length L. The mobile sensors move from BS to visit every PoI once only along the closed curve before return to BS. Such a period is called a full visiting period.*

In a full visiting period, the traveling path of mobile sensors is the closed curve, all sensors move along the curve one by one. The distance between two adjacent sensors is assumed to be the same and equal to L/m. The case where distance between adjacent mobile sensors is less than $2r$, i.e., $L/m \leq 2r$, is trivial since in this case each PoI would always be seen by one of the mobile sensors and hence all the events would be captured with no duration, as shown in Figure 2(a). Now we focus on the case where $L/m > 2r$, i.e. $m < L/2r$.

Theorem 1. *In a full visiting period, if the constraint event detection delay is t, then the number of mobile sensors must satisfy*

$$m \geq \lceil L/ (vt + 2r) \rceil. \tag{1}$$

Proof. As shown in Figure 2(b), in order to satisfy the user's delay constraint, the distance between two adjacent sensors should not greater than $vt + 2r$. The mobile sensors visit PoI on by one, so the number of sensors must not less than $\lceil L/ (vt + 2r) \rceil$.   ∎

In order to reduce the data transmitting time after the mobile sensor capture the event, we need find a trajectory whose length L is minimized. This is similar to Traveling Salesman Problem (TSP). For the events occur at PoIs is randomly, so the average transmitting time is $L/2v$.

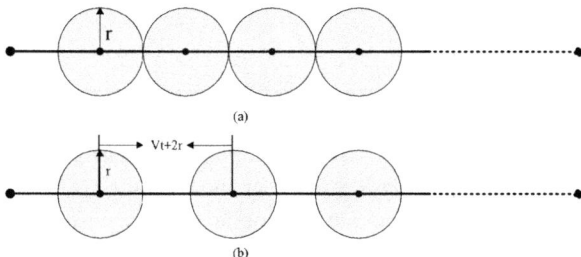

Fig. 2. Moving mode of sensors in full visiting: (a) Distance between adjacent mobile sensors is less than $2r$. (b) Distance between two adjacent sensors should not greater than $vt + 2r$.

3.2 Soft Bound for Detection Delay

The detection delay of an event is a random variable dependent on the arrival time of the event, the number of sensors visit the PoI, and the time of period. It is ideal that the system provides a hard bound for detection delay, i.e., any detection delay is less than a given value. However, this compels mobile sensors to visit PoIs at least once in every period, which will cause the serious over-detection problem.

Providing soft bound for event detection is also very valuable for uses. More specially, the user specifies a longest delay (D_r) that is characterized by a cumulative distribution function (*cdf*). Note that this longest delay specified by the user is actually a random variable. The system should then ensure that the detection delay at any point is less than D_r.

To specify the requirement on detection latency, the users can simply set the *cdf* of D_r. The objective of the system then becomes to ensure that the detection delay of any event is less than D_r. However, we have to address a new critical issue, i.e., how to realize such a soft bound. To address this, we devise a simple yet effective metric, detectability in one period (*DoP*).

Definition 2 (*DoP*): *The DoP of Point p (denoted by γ_p) is the probability that any event at p is detected by at least one sensor, within a visiting period since its occurrence.*

In fact, an event is detected at point p also characterize the detection delay of this event, denoted by D_p. We drive the *cdf* of the D_p which reveals the relationship between D_p and γ_p.

Theorem 2. *The cdf of D_p is given by*

$$F_{D_p}(d) = 1 - (1 - \gamma_p)^k \left(1 - \frac{d - \kappa \tau_{period}}{\tau_{period}} \gamma_p\right), \tag{2}$$

where $k = \lfloor d/\tau_{period} \rfloor$.
Proof. By definition, the *cdf* of D_p is

$$F_{D_p}(d) = Pr(D_p \leq d) = 1 - Pr(D_p > d).$$

This implies that there is no mobile sensor visit the PoI in duration of d since the emergence of event. There are κ full interval and an additional length of $d - \kappa \tau_{period}$. The probability that the mobile sensor does not visit the PoI is $1 - \gamma_p$, and that within the duration of $d - \kappa \tau_{period}$ is $1 - \gamma_p (d/\tau_{period} - \kappa)$. ∎

With this metric, it becomes possible to realize the soft bond on detection latency. We determine such a *DoP* γ_0 is the minimum *DoP* that the corresponding D_0 is less than D_r, we have

$$D_0 \leq D_r. \tag{3}$$

It is apparent that a higher *DoP* at a point implies a shorter latency of event detection at this point. So we have

$$D_p \leq D_0, \forall \gamma_p \geq \gamma_0 \tag{4}$$

By combining (3) and (4), we can conclude that

$$D_p \leq D_r, \forall p \in F \tag{5}$$

Thus, by guaranteeing that the *DoP* of any point is larger than γ_0, we are able to ensure that the detection delay of any event is less than the user's requirement D_r. Note that a more rigid requirement on real-time detection needs a higher γ_0. In the following, we derive the expected value of D_0, which follows a theorem.

Theorem 3. *The expected value of D_0 is*

$$E(D_0) = (1 - 0.5\gamma_0)\,\tau_{period}/\gamma_0 \qquad (6)$$

Proof. The expected delay is $\tau_{period}/2$ if the event is detected within the first interval. If it is detected in j period, $j > 1$, then the additional $(j-1)\,\tau_{period}$ latency is introduced. Let N denote the number of full periods that an event undergoes before it is detected. The probability mass function (*pdf*) of N is given by

$$Pr(N = k) = (1 - \gamma_0)^{k-1}\gamma_0, k \ge 0 \qquad (7)$$

We derive the expect delay by condition on N,

$$E(D_0) = \sum_{i=0}^{\infty}(\tau_{period}/2 \times Pr(M = i)) = (1 - 0.5\gamma_0)\,\tau_{period}/\gamma_0 \qquad (8)$$

For any individual node, the expected delay is a function of γ_0, and is inversely proportional to γ_0. ∎

4   Probabilisitic Path Selection Protocol

4.1   Shortest Path Selection Based on Visit Probability

The design goals of MSF are: 1) to ensure that the detection latency of any event is statistically bounded by the requirement posed the users; 2) to minimize the transmission time before the mobile sensor return to BS. As discussed previously, the first goal is achieved by ensuring that the DoP of any point is larger than γ_0. Now we focus on the second goal.

Following the probabilistic approach, a mobile sensor Q visits a PoI in one period with probability β_Q, and ignore this point with the probability $1 - \beta_Q$. The key issue is clearly the determination of the visit probability. To minimize the transmission time, the visit probability should be as small as possible for shorten the length of path. At the same time, however, it ought to be sufficiently large to guarantee the DoP of all points in the field.

For the mobile node to detect the event of each PoI, a path connect all PoIs in the field should be constructed. Here we assume the mobile node should go to the accurate position of PoI to detect event, as shown in Figure 3(a). This assumption does not affect the mobile node move along the path for the PoI must within its sensing range. The objective is to find a path such that the shortest travel time of mobile node by that path is minimized. However, finding a "smooth" path as shown in the figure is computationally expensive. In addition, controlling the mobile node along such a smooth path is often difficult in practice. From these reasons, we have designed a simplified problem to analyze in the following.

As shown in Figure 3(b), we consider a complete graph having vertices at PoIs' locations and assume the mobile nodes move between vertices along a straight line. Each edge is associated with a value which represents the visit probability to this vertex. In this way, while traveling alone an edge, the mobile node can visit the PoI according to the probability and find the shortest path at the same time. We use Euclidean distance as the metric, since we have observed in the experiments that it has a strong positive correlation with the shortest travel time in the induced MSF problem.

Here we solve the shortest path problem through combining the visit probability and metric. Our objective is to find the set μ including BS and part of PoIs, and the existence probability of the path composed by these PoIs is maximized and the metric is minimized. We construct the Integer Linear Programming (ILP) model as follows:

$$\text{Minimize} \sum_{v_i, v_j \in \mu} (1 - p_{ij}) \, w_{ij} \tag{9}$$

Subject to

$$p_{ij} = p_{sj} \tag{10}$$

$$1 - (1 - p_{sj})^m \geq \gamma_0. \tag{11}$$

In (9), v_i, v_j are two vertexes on μ, p_{ij} is the visit probability from v_i to v_j, p_{sj} means the probability from base station to vertex v_j. w_{ij} is the metric. The objective function (10) requires the visit probability assigned to v_j is identical. Function (11) ensures the visit probability of PoI is larger than the minimum value.

This probabilistic shortest path selection problem by be simply solved by using Dijkstra algorithm.

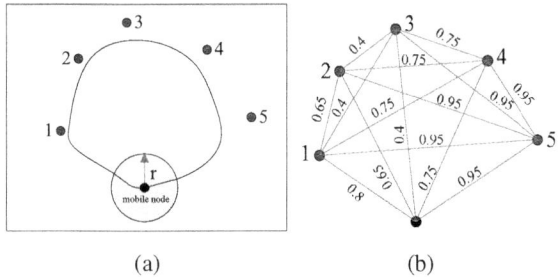

(a)   (b)

Fig. 3. Probability path selection problem: (a) Original problem with an example path. (b) Simplified problem, in which the objective is to find the shortest path with connection probablility.

4.2 Non-adaptive Schema

At first, we focus on the general case that every mobile sensor node visits the PoI with identical probability, i.e., not adaptive to its neighborhood. To guarantee that the DoP of any point is greater than γ_0, this schema simply sets the visit probability in each cycle of every sensor to γ_0. The problem is that when the number of mobile sensor visiting the PoI is great, resulting in unnecessary waste of time.

We analyze the detection delay achieved by identical probability schema.

Theorem 4. *With identical probability schema, the expected detection delay of an event that happens at any point is given by*

$$E(D) = \frac{3(1-\beta)^m - (1-\beta)^{2m}}{2(1-(1-\beta)^m)} \tau_{period} \tag{12}$$

Proof. Let N denote the number of full periods that elapsed before an event is detected. The pdf of N is

$$Pr\left(N = i\right) = \left(1 - \theta\right)^{i-1}\theta. \tag{13}$$

where θ is the probability that an event is detected within one period. It is apparent that

$$\theta = 1 - \left(1 - \beta\right)^{m}. \tag{14}$$

Substituting the value of θ into (13), we get

$$Pr\left(N = i\right) = \left(1 - \beta\right)^{m(i-1)}\left(1 - \left(1 - \beta\right)^{m}\right). \tag{15}$$

If an event is detected in the ith period, an additional latency of $(i - 1)\tau_{period}$ is introduced. Thus, we compute the expectation by conditioning on N,

$$E\left(D\right) = \sum_{i=1}^{\infty}\left(\frac{\tau_{period}}{2} + (i - 1)\tau_{period}\right) \times Pr\left(N = i\right)$$
$$= \frac{3(1-\beta)^{m} - (1-\beta)^{2m}}{2(1-(1-\beta)^{m})}\tau_{period}. \qquad\blacksquare$$

4.3 Probabilistic Adaptation Schema

At the beginning, each mobile sensor should be set visit probability for all PoIs. The initial probability guarantees that the DoP of any point is greater than γ_0. All mobile sensors visiting the PoI are supposed to play an equally important role in detection event at this point. Take sensor Q for example, to meet the constraint (4), its necessary probability for a PoI p is

$$\beta_Q\left(p\right) > 1 - \sqrt[m]{1 - \gamma_0}. \tag{16}$$

Obviously, the initial visit probability is larger than the probability which ensure the delay constraint. So sensors exchange their visit probabilities by local broadcast. Each sensor recalculates a feasible visit probability based on the visit probability of other sensors. The new feasible visit probability for point p is given by

$$\beta_Q\left(p\right) = \begin{cases} 0 & \text{if } \prod_{B \in S-Q}\left(1 - \beta_B\right) > 1 - \gamma_0 \\ 1 - \frac{1 - \gamma_0}{\prod_{B \in S-Q} 1 - \beta_B} & \text{otherwise} \end{cases} \tag{17}$$

If the new probability is smaller than the original one, the sensor will update the probability to the new on for reducing the transmitting time. Thus, any sensor that obtains a smaller new probability makes an update attempt, trying to reduce its probability.

5   Performance Evaluation

To compare the proposed solution, we simulated a sensor network of 20 PoIs evenly distributed in 40×40 meter square sensor field. A maximum of 10 mobile sensors were available. Each sensor was equipped with four AA rechargeable batteries which can typically provide about 4×10^4J power. The velocity of sensor is 2m/s. The sense range of node is set to 2 meter. Base station is on the edge of the field. The results presents in this section are averaged over 20 independent experiments with different event occurring frequency.

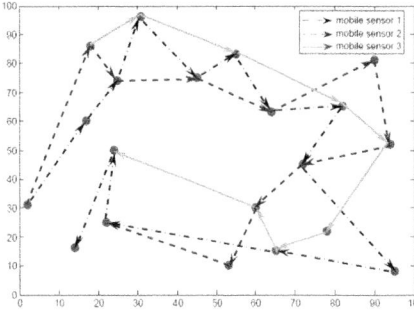
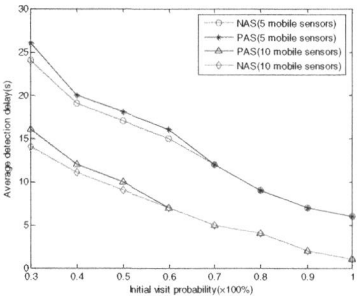

Fig. 4. A path selection profile with 3 mobile nodes in one period

Fig. 5. Detection delay vs. initial visit probability

In the full visiting schema, we should find the shortest closed curve that connects all PoIs, i.e., the traveling path that the sensor along which visit PoIs once is minimized. We get the length of path is 98 meter through solving the TSP problem. So a mobile sensor visits all nodes in one period need 49s.

In NAS or PAS, the mobile sensors visit the PoIs with different probability according to the events which require various DoP for PoIs. Mobile sensors will select different path based on the visit probability. In each period, some nodes will be visited by different sensors. Figure 4 shows the path selection process when we use 3 mobile sensors with the visit probability of 80% for all PoIs in one period.

The first set of experiments investigates the relationship between average detection delay and initial visit probability. We vary the number of mobile sensors to study the difference between NAS and PAS. At first we calculate detection delay in full visiting period. We get the delay is 7.8s when using 5 sensors and the delay is 2.9s using 10 sensors. As we can see in Figure 5, when the initial visit probability is less than 90%, the detection delay of NAS and PAS both greater than 7.8s, this means the NAS and PAS will increase the detection delay with a low visit probability. However, when the initial visit probability is greater than 90%, the detection delay is decreased well for the mobile nodes visit the PoIs frequently. If the event occurring frequency is low at the PoIs, the delay is less than 7.8s. From Figure 4 we also can see that the detection delay of NAS is less than PAS if the initial probability is greater than a certain value regardless the number of sensors. This is because in PAS, some mobile sensors were set a low visit probability on the basis of satisfying the delay constraint.

In this set of experiments we also can observe the relationship between average transmitting delay and initial visit probability, which is described in Figure 6. We can see that PAS has a lower transmitting delay than NAS with the same initial probability, for in PAS some sensors will reduce the visit probability according the detectability of their neighbors so the length of traveling path will be shorten.

In the second set of experiments, we explore how many mobile sensors are needed to satisfy the required detection delay constraint for different schemas, in other words, with the same number of sensors, whose delay is minimized. In these experiments we suppose that the visit probabilities of all sensors are 90% for all PoIs. From Figure 7

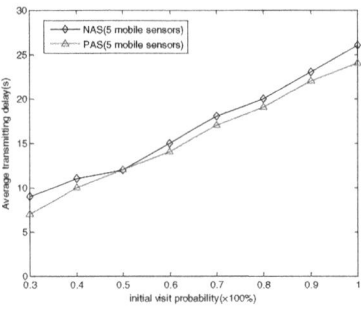
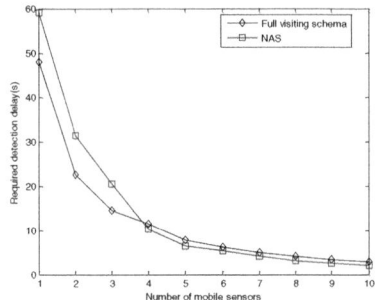

Fig. 6. Transmitting delay vs. initial visit probability

Fig. 7. Detection delay vs. number of mobile sensors

we can see that when the number is greater than 4, the detection delay of NAS is less than full visiting schema. We also can see that when the number of sensors is 8, the delay of full visiting schema is 4.25, which is greater than the delay of NAS whose only need 7 sensors. So for the same required detection delay, NAS need less number of mobile sensors.

6   Conclusions

In this paper, we have investigated the the probabilistic approach to distributed event detection in mobile sensor networks. We proposed an event detection framework which allows the mobile sensors visit the PoIs with different probabilities. Due to the various events capture demands, different PoIs have different probabilities. Mobile sensors select various trajectories according the visit probabilities in every period under the user's delay constraint. Two schemas named NAS and PAS are presented. Comprehensive simulation experiments demonstrate that the algorithm allows us use less number mobile nodes within the delay bound and reduce the transmitting delay significantly.

Acknowledgments. The work is supported by the Fundamental Research Funds for the Central Universities and Hohai Science Fund grants (2009424211).

References

1. Tolle, G., Polastre, J., Szewczyk, R., Culler, D., et al.: Amacroscope in the redwoods. In: ACM SenSys, pp. 51–63 (2005)
2. Xue, W., Luo, Q., Chen, L., Liu, Y.H.: Contour mapmatching for event detection in sensor networks. In: ACM SIGMOD (2006)
3. Arora, A., Dutta, P., Bapat, S., et al.: Aline in the sand: A wireless sensor network for targetdetection, classification, and tracking. Computer Net-works 46(5), 605–634 (2004)
4. Zhang, X., Zhang, L., Chen, G.: Probabilistic Path Selection in Wireless Sensor Networks with Controlled Mobility. In: WCSP (2009)

5. Srinivasan, W.W.V., Chua, K.-C.: Trade-offs between mobility and density for coverage in wireless sensor networks. In: MobiCom (2007)
6. Chellappan, S., Bai, X., Ma, B., Xuan, D.: Sensor Networks Deployment Using Flip-Based Sensors. In: Proceedings of IEEE MASS (2005)
7. Howard, A., Mataric, M.J., Sukhatme, G.S.: Mobile sensor network deployment using potential fields: A distributed, scalable solution to the area coverage problem. In: International Symposium on Distributed Autonomous Robotic Systems (DARS 2004), pp. 299–308 (2002)
8. Zou, Y., Chakrabarty, K.: Sensor deployment and target localization based on virtual forces. In: 22nd Annual IEEE Conference on Computer Communications (INFOCOM), pp. 1293–1303 (2003)
9. Wang, G., Cao, G., Porta, T.L.: Movement-assisted sensor deployment. In: 23rd Annual IEEE Conference on Computer Communications (INFOCOM), pp. 2469–2479 (2004)
10. Liu, B., Brass, P., Dousse, O., Nain, P., Towsley, D.: Mobility improves coverage of sensor networks. In: MobiHoc (2005)
11. Bisnik, N., Abouzeid, A., Isler, V.: Stochastic event capture using mobile sensors subject to a quality metric. In: MOBICOM (2006)
12. Somasundara, A.A., Ramamoorthy, A., Srivastava, M.B.: Mobile element scheduling with dynamic deadlines. IEEE Trans. on Mobile Computing 6(4), 395–410 (2007)
13. Gandham, S.R., Dawande, M., Prakash, R., Venkatesan, S.: Energy efficient schemes for wireless sensor networks with multiple mobile base stations. In: Globecom (2003)
14. Xing, G., Wang, T., Jia, W., Li, M.: Rendezvous design algorithms for wireless sensor networks with a mobile base station. In: MobiHoc (2008)

Distributed Road Surface Condition Monitoring Using Mobile Phones

Mikko Perttunen[1], Oleksiy Mazhelis[2], Fengyu Cong[2],
Mikko Kauppila[1], Teemu Leppänen[1], Jouni Kantola[3],
Jussi Collin[3], Susanna Pirttikangas[1], Janne Haverinen[1],
Tapani Ristaniemi[2], and Jukka Riekki[1]

[1] Computer Science and Engineering Laboratory, University of Oulu
P.O. BOX 4500, Oulu, Finland
[2] Faculty of Information Technology, University of Jyväskylä
P.O. BOX 35, Jyvaskyla, Finland
[3] Department of Computer Systems, Tampere University of Technology
P.O. BOX 553, Tampere, Finland

Abstract. The objective of this research is to improve traffic safety
through collecting and distributing up-to-date road surface condition information using mobile phones. Road surface condition information is
seen useful for both travellers and for the road network maintenance.
The problem we consider is to detect road surface anomalies that, when
left unreported, can cause wear of vehicles, lesser driving comfort and vehicle controllability, or an accident. In this work we developed a pattern
recognition system for detecting road condition from accelerometer and
GPS readings. We present experimental results from real urban driving
data that demonstrate the usefulness of the system. Our contributions
are: 1) Performing a throughout spectral analysis of tri-axis acceleration
signals in order to get reliable road surface anomaly labels. 2) Comprehensive preprocessing of GPS and acceleration signals. 3) Proposing a
speed dependence removal approach for feature extraction and demonstrating its positive effect in multiple feature sets for the road surface
anomaly detection task. 4) A framework for visually analyzing the classifier predictions over the validation data and labels.

Keywords: accelerometer, signal processing, pattern recognition, support vector machine, classification, road roughness, GPS.

1 Introduction

The need to reduce fuel consumption, traffic accidents, congestion as well as
making public transportation more efficient are some of the problems faced
worldwide. Aside from developing more efficient motors and more ecological
fuels, making traffic infrastructure and vehicles more efficient through the use of
advanced information technology is being studied widely.

Friction of the road surface is the most important environmental factor affecting safety. Road surface quality can be characterized using microtexture and

C.-H. Hsu et al. (Eds.): UIC 2011, LNCS 6905, pp. 64–78, 2011.

macrotexture, which contribute to friction, and megatexture and roughness that are formed by the combination of stone particle surfaces and by the gaps between stones used in the surfacing material, respectively [5]. Megatexture refers to potholes, joints, patching, cracks and other small surface defects that cause increased noise levels and rolling resistance. Roughness refers to large surface unevenness that increases vehicle operating costs and decreases driving comfort. In the nordic countries, frost heave causes both seasonal variation in road surface condition as well as permanent cracks and bumps [7].

To manage the quality of the road condition, administrators use special instrumented vehicles to measure the road roughness periodically [4]. To cope with the burden of dedicated condition monitoring, researchers have proposed the use of built-in sensor systems of new passenger vehicles [12] to detect road condition. However, the penetration of vehicles with such integrated sensors will be low at least for the next decade [3] and there is no standard interface to access onboard sensors, rendering it difficult to implement a generic solution using these sensors. Mobile devices with integrated or external sensors provide an alternative traffic sensing and communication system [16]. We envision collecting information about all traffic using mobile phones, for example, pedestrians, bicyclers, and passenger cars.

In the present research, we focus on developing a pattern recognition system for recognizing road surface anomalies that contribute to road roughness, using data from mobile phones installed in vehicles. The problem we consider is to detect road surface anomalies that, when left unreported, can cause wear of vehicles, lesser driving comfort and vehicle controllability, or an accident. It should be noted that this goal is complementary to the usual road roughness evaluation [4], since we consider it important to recognize also individual severe anomalies, not only to categorize the road segments according to average roughness. This work sheds light on the feasibility of the road condition monitoring using sensor-enabled mobile phones and low sampling rates.

The rest of this paper is organized as follows: In the next section we summarize related work. In section 3 we describe data collection setup and initial analysis. Section 4 describes the anomaly recognition system and in section 5 we present the results. In section 6 we discuss and conclude the paper.

2 Related Work

Road roughness is typically measured using special instrumented vehicles [4]. In [12] the authors studied, through simulation, the use of vehicle integrated accelerometers to analyze road roughness. Mobile devices with integrated or external sensors have been proposed as a surrogate traffic sensing and communication system [16]. The suitability of tri-axis accelerometers in an embedded system [11] and integrated in a mobile phone [16] have been experimented together with GPS receivers to recognize road surface anomalies, such as potholes and bumps. In [2] GPS-enabled mobile phones were used to collect traffic information and to estimate the traffic situation.

Traffic conditions monitoring of Google Maps for Mobile [1] is based on using GPS data on mobile phones to estimate vehicle speed. Similarly, in TJam [17], congestions were predicted using estimated vehicle speeds. VTrack [20] utilized location tracks of mobile phones to estimate travel times in real time. In [21] a system was presented to detect car accidents using on-board mobile phones and attemps at filtering out false positives such as high accelerations due to dropping the phone were described.

Using mobile phones makes a large set of sensors readily available, enabling more reliable and exact information, with larger coverage. This kind of setting where citizens contribute to collecting data about the environment has been called participatory sensing [6].

The previous work [16] has identified labeling the road surface condition accurately as a difficult task. We tried to overcome this problem by spectral analysis of the 3D acceleration signals. In the literature, multiple classifiers have been applied as an attempt to solve the problem of speed dependency of accelerometer readings, that is, the fact that driving over the same road surface anomaly with different speeds results in different signal patterns [16]. We propose a robust feature extraction approach which removes speeds dependency of the features. Moreover, while in previous work simple thresholds on various features have been used in anomaly detectors, we use support vector machines [9] to classify road segments. We present also a visualization framework for the classification results to enable visual inspection of, for instance, examples close to the class border.

3   Data Collection

3.1   Data Collection Hardware and Software

The Nokia N95 8GB mobile phone was used to collected data. Accelerometer samples were recorded at 38Hz and GPS readings stored at 1Hz. The GPS readings included only latitude, longitude and timestamp. The data collection tool was written in Java, with a native component for accessing the accelerometer.

3.2   Data Collection Setup

Data was collected using a mobile phone that was attached to a rack on the windshield of a vehicle. The rack was carefully positioned and secured to maintain approximately the same accelerometer coordinates across data collection drives. Camcorder was attached to the head rest of passenger's seat. Fig.1b shows the view of the camcorder, including the phone rack. The accelerometer orientation is shown in Fig.1a.

We have used several vehicles for data collection, however, in this paper we report results on using a single passenger car, for which an accurate - and hence laborous - labeling has been carried out.

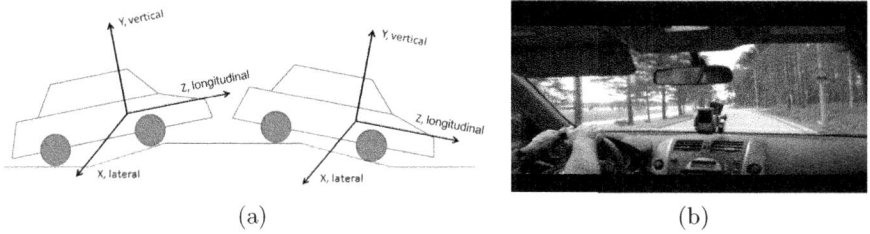

(a)   (b)

Fig. 1. a) Accelerometer orientation. b) Mobile phone setup.

3.3   Collected Data Sets and Labeling

Several data collection drives were performed. For the work reported in this paper, a drive of about 40 minutes in length (25km) was selected among the drives, as it seemed to contain the most diverse anomalies based on a quick route review.

Two label files were produced by two labelers independently, using the figures (described below) and video. One label file contains the anomalies on the road surface and the other contains the surface types. Two examples of the plots used for labeling and the created labels are shown in Fig.2. However, in the real setup, multiple segments of the full spectrogram were plotted in the same figure (page) to make it easier for the labellers to compare the magnitudes of signals and spectral energies across longer periods. Labeling process was as follows: first, preprocessing for the GPS and acceleration signals was done. Second, a spectrogram of the sum of the band energies of accelerometer signals was plotted and the preprocessed accelerometer signals were plotted on top of the spectrogram. Also speed was superimposed in the same figure. Most of the labelled anomalies were confirmed from the video, but there very a few clear signal artifacts that were not confirmed from video. For each labelled anomaly, also a textual description was added. After the independent labelling, the label sets were merged.

When labeling, the anomalies were categorized into two classes according to their severity. Type 1 represents small potholes, rail road crossings and other road surface roughness. Type 2 represents a) man-made speed bumps and other road surface artifacts directing drivers to slow down and b) severe anomalies that might cause accidents or vehicle breakdown when driven on at a high speed. In this we focus on detecting Type 2 anomalies from asphalt roads. Note that man-made artifacts are included for two reasons: Firstly, their automatic recognition enables adding them to digital maps and thus, warning other drivers. Secondly, they cause signal patterns that are very similar to anomalies caused by worn down road surface, or damage by frost. For these reasons, they represent useful data to build a recognition system. However, type 1 anomalies were also labelled as accurately as possible to enable assessing their contribution to the detection accuracy.

Cobblestone segments from the data set were discarded. This is justified by the fact that the road surface type is available from road databases and having

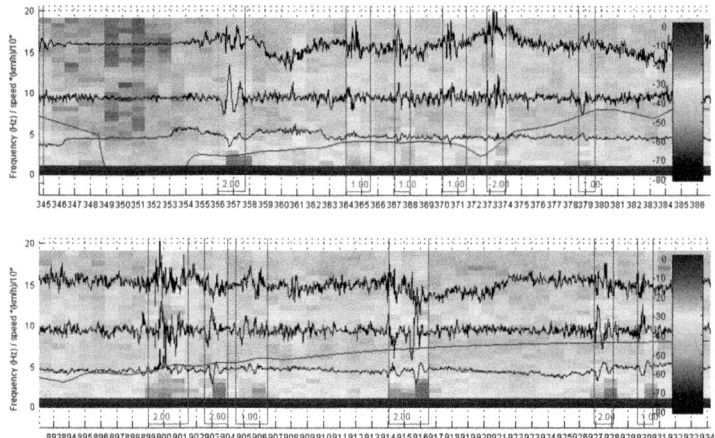

Fig. 2. Two example segments with labels. The sum spectrograms of 3D acceleration signals are plotted with original acceleration signals and speed.

Table 1. Anomaly statistics

Category	Example types	Count	Total length (s)
Type 1	railroad crossing, small pothole, roughness	184	613.9
Type 2	speed bump, bump, pedestrian crossing with cobblestones, large pothole	42	81.6

cobblestone in the data can bias the results, since there can be an unusual proportion of "'anomalous"' road surface.

Information about the data sets are shown in Table 1. The mean length of Type 2 anomaly was 1.94s, the maximum and minimum being 5.0s and 1.0s, respectively.

4   Anomaly Recognition

The proposed road surface anomaly recognition system is part of our cooperative traffic sensor network middleware [15] and is based on tri-axis acceleration and GPS data. In brief, GPS was used to estimate speed and several other features were extracted from the acceleration signals. Positioning data was also used to visualize the results on a map. The feature set was used to recognize road surface anomalies and to filter out other similar signal artifacts caused by door slams and jerks at the end of braking, for example.

To put the system into a context, in comparison to [11], we propose an additional preprocessing step: before running the anomaly detection algorithm, our

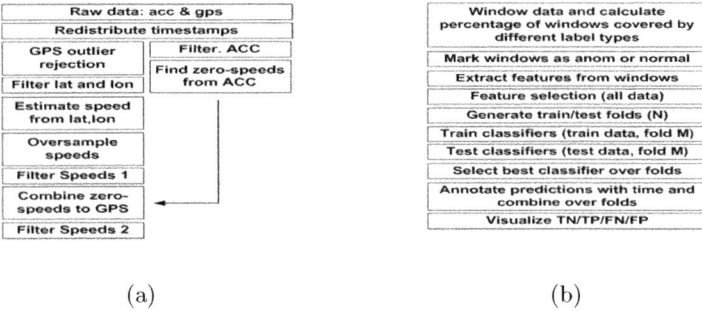

(a)   (b)

Fig. 3. a) Preprocessing flowchart. b) Windowing and classification flowchart.

(a)   (b)

Fig. 4. a) A Segment of raw GPS signal on a map. b) A segment of preprocessed GPS on a map.

system aims to recognize the means of travel of the user [13], [15]. Based on recognizing the means of travel, the system aims to recognize and report road surface anomalies only when the phone is in a car.

4.1   Preprocessing

Using mobile phone sensors was reflected in the signals in two ways: Firstly, the GPS signal of the used phone was very noisy. Secondly, both the GPS measurements and the acceleration measurements were contaminated by bursts, which are measurements recorded with the same timestamp. We believe the reason for such bursts is the way that process switches and priorities are handled in the phone.

Fig.3 shows an overview of the anomaly recognition system as a block diagram. As shown in the figure the timestamps of the acceleration and GPS measurements were first redistributed evenly within short time segments. Next, GPS outlier rejection was done and Kalman filter was applied to latitude and longitude to further reduce noise. Example segment of the raw and preprocessed latitude and longitude are shown in Figs. 4a and 4b. In this example, the vehicle was momentarily stopped on a parking lot on the left side of the road.

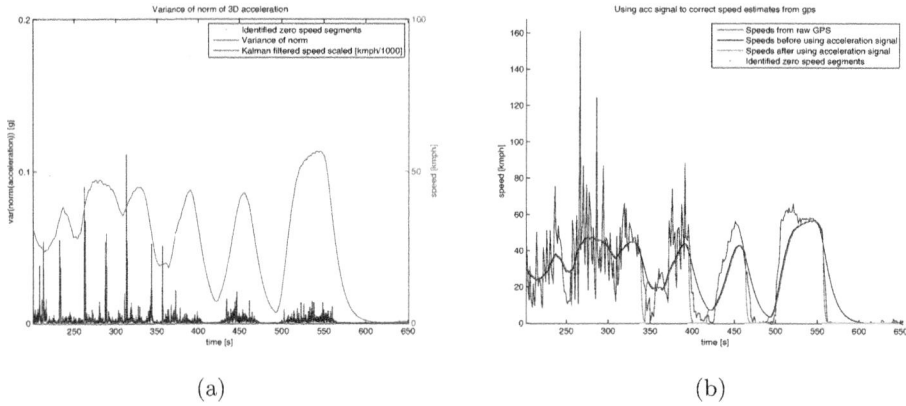

(a)   (b)

Fig. 5. Data collection. a) Fusion of acceleration signals and latitude and longitude based speed estimation through identifying zero speed segments from the acceleration signal. b) Estimated speed signal after applying the identified zero speed segments.

Next, speed was estimated from each consequtive latitude and longitude pairs. The resulting speed signal was oversampled and filtered using reasonable physical limits for acceleration of the vehicle. We used as limits for maximum acceleration 3.5 m/s^2 and for maximum deceleration -11 m/s^2.

While experimenting with the previous steps we noticed that regardless of tuning the filters, we could not reach satisfactory speed estimates. When speed estimates seemed smooth enough, the signal was often contaminated by large latency compared to original (noisy) speed estimate and the speed failed to reach zero on vehicle stops, see Fig.5a. To alleviate the problem, we used two corrections. First, we removed a visually determined latency from the filtered speed estimate. Second, we applied a very simple fusion of the acceleration and GPS signal: the variance of the norm of the acceleration was calculated for the whole acceleration signal and visually examined, see Fig.5b. By simple thresholding, we were able to detect segments of the signal, where speed of the vehicle was zero, or very close to zero. Next, we set the corresponding segments of the speed signal to zero and smoothed the speed signal by applying a Kalman filter. The correctness of the speed estimate was checked to the extent possible from the video. The temporal accuracy of the stops were the easiest to confirm. We recognize a more careful analysis of the preprocessing approach as future work.

4.2   Windowing

As shown in Fig. 3b, the data was framed using a sliding window. We experimented with multiple frame lengths from 0.5s to 2s, a scale we assumed suitable for the anomaly recognition task, as the mean anomaly length was around 2s. For each window, we determined the percentage of the window covered by anomalies (one or more together). In the experiments reported in this paper, we marked the window as representing anomalous road, when it was covered by more than 50% by anomalies. Temporal order of the windows was kept throughout the processing.

4.3 Feature Extraction and Selection

Feature extraction was done using sliding windows of 2.0s in length, the slide being 0.5s. Several features were extracted from acceleration signals: standard deviation, mean, variance, peak-to-peak, signal magnitude area, 3-order autoregressive coefficients, tilt angles and root mean square for each dimension. Absolute value of correlations of signals between all dimensions were used as well, since it was visually observed that often all the acceleration signals showed similar waveforms in the anomaly segments. This can be seen, for example, in the first anomaly in Fig.2. However, this is not the case when only one side of the car hits a pothole.

Fast Fourier Transformation (FFT) based features were used in order to incorporate information from specific frequencies. This was based on the assumption that bumps and potholes would produce lower frequency components in comparison to vibration originating from the motor and normal road surface. FFT energy was extracted from 17 frequency bands for each acceleration direction (as shown in Fig.2) and mel frequency cepstral coefficients in 4 bands.

We utilized the backwards feature selection algorithm of PRTools [10] to select the optimal feature sets for both the speed scaled and non-speed scaled feature sets.

4.4 Removing Speed Dependence of Features

Most of the features vary as a function of speed. As an example, Fig.6 shows the speed-dependency of the peak of the Y signal. This dependency is considered harmful for classification, because data points at a slow speed may look much different than points at a high speed. However, it is clear that speed cannot by itself be used to classify road surface anomalies, since ideally anomalies can occur equally likely at any speed. Thus, to remove linear dependency on speed, we first fit a line

$$y = ax + b_0 \tag{1}$$

to each feature of the data. Then, we form a new linearly (speed) independent data set

$$\varepsilon_i = y_i - b_0 - ax_i. \tag{2}$$

This method for removing linear dependence is described in the general case in [19].

Fig.6 shows the effect of removing speed dependency for the y-peak feature. This is further illustrated in Fig.7 where both speed dependent (a) and speed independent (b) versions of y-peak and energy of y signal on band 3 (from 2.2Hz

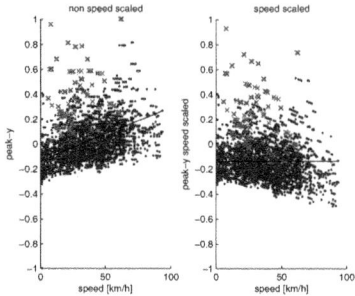

Fig. 6. Peak of y acceleration as a function of time in normal and anomalous windows with a line fitted to the data points. Anomalies are shown as red crosses and normals as blue dots.

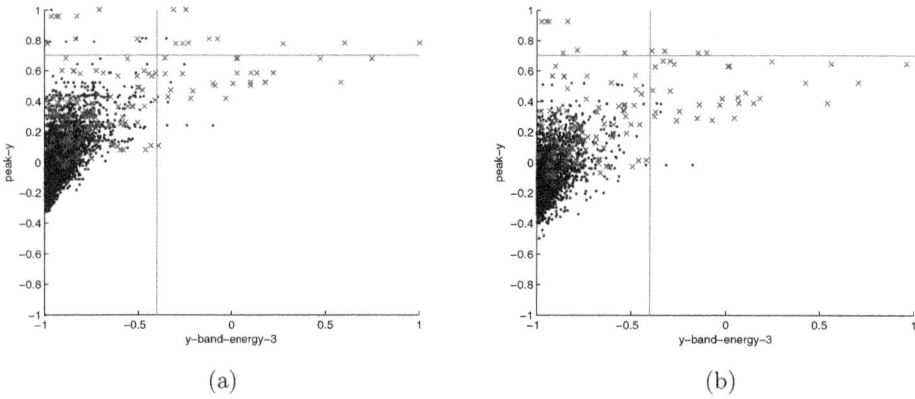

Fig. 7. Peak of y signal plotted against signal energy of y on band 3. Anomalies are shown as red crosses and normals as blue dots. a) Speed dependent. b) Speed independent. The vertical and horizontal lines help illustrating the discrimination improvement due to speed independence removal. Note that there are no normals above the horizontal line in b).

to 3.6Hz) are plotted against each other. The horizontal and vertical lines were added to make it easier to read the figure, that is, to see that more anomalies become linearly separable from the normal road after removing speed dependency.

4.5 Cross-Validation and Evaluation Criteria

All experiments were performed using 5-fold cross-validation, where the training set of each fold contains 4/5 of the total anomaly windows and 4/5 of the normal windows (1/5 for the test set). The folds were created from consequtive windows. We did not use random selection, because then examples from the same anomaly (or same normal) segment could end up in both test and training sets.

Because the datasets are skewed, accuracy is not a reliable measure of model goodness. Instead, we use the geometric mean of accuracies on positive and negative examples, the G-means metric, suggested in [14]. The metric is defined as

$$g = \sqrt{sensitivity \cdot specificity}. \tag{3}$$

Models producing a high G-means have balanced sensitivity and specificity, thus the effect of dataset skew is diminished when using G-means as evaluation criteria. To further illustrate the classification performance, we report also relative sensitivity (RS), a measure proposed by Su and Hsiao [18] to evaluate the relative accuracy on positive and negative examples; the relative sensitivity is defined as

$$RS = \frac{sensitivity}{specificity}. \tag{4}$$

The RS value should be around one for the classification accuracy to be of similar order for the positive and negative classes.

4.6   Classifier Training and Evaluation

To classify the windows representing short road segments we use support vector machines [9], one of the most widely applied classification method. To train a soft margin support vector machine for N input vectors $\mathbf{x}_1...\mathbf{x}_n$ with labels $t_n \in \{-1, 1\}$, generally the quadratic optimization problem

$$C \sum_{n=1}^{N} \varepsilon_n + \frac{1}{2} \parallel \mathbf{w} \parallel^2 \tag{5}$$

has to be solved. Here, the slack variables $\varepsilon_n \geq 0$ and $t_n y(\mathbf{x}_n) \geq 1 - \varepsilon_n$ for n = 1,...N. The parameter C controls the cost of misclassification - the larger its value, the more the SVM fits to training data. To enable nonlinear classification boundaries, kernels are used. We utilize the radial basis kernel,

$$k(\mathbf{x}_i, \mathbf{x}_j) = \exp\left(-\gamma \parallel (\mathbf{x}_i - \mathbf{x}_j) \parallel^2\right), \tag{6}$$

where $\gamma > 0$.

As the data sets were dominated by normal road surface with no anomalies, the resulting sets of examples were heavily biased. To improve the recognition results we used a different misclassification weight for the normal and anomaly classes. The misclassification weight for the normal and anomaly classes were set according to their counts in the train dataset, that is,

$$\frac{c_-}{c_+} = \frac{n_+}{n_-}, \tag{7}$$

where c_- is the weight for normal class, c_+ is the weight for the anomaly class, and n_- and n_+ are the corresponding class counts in the training set.

The classifier training and testing procedure is illustrated as a part of the whole process in Fig 3a. Using the test data, we determined the area under ROC curve (AUC) for each classifier. The classifier with the best average G-means over folds was selected. We evaluated 49 SVM parameter combinations using radial basis function kernels (RBF) in LIBSVM [8], corresponding to a grid of values of the parameters γ and C. The parameter γ controls the width of the RBF kernel.

5   Results and Analysis

The classification results for different feature sets are shown in Table 2. Two observations were be done: speed dependence removal improves the classification performance significantly and the feature subset selected by using the backward search procedure worked at least as well as the full feature set.

5.1   Visualization of Recognition Results

Fig. 8 shows the labeled anomalies of two segments of the test set with the predictions superimposed. To avoid clutter, true negatives are not shown. The probability of an anomaly according to the classifier is shown as a continuous red signal.

To further illustrate the results, the predictions are shown on a map in Fig.9. It should be noted from Fig.9c that many of the predictions marked as false positives aren't, strictly speaking, false positives but represent an anomaly of Type 1 or a window partially overlapping with an anomaly of Type 2.

5.2   Result Analysis

The confusion matrix for the best result of Table 2 is shown in Table 3. Note that some of the false positives were a 'natural' consequent of the sliding window approach - some of the windows were overlapped by part of Type 1 anomaly or Type 2 anomaly (see Table 1), but overlapping less than 50% of the window (recall that a window was labelled as anomalous when 50% of it was covered by a labelled anomaly). In this case, there were 127 such false positives, the mean

Table 2. Evaluated feature sets

Name	G-means	AUC	Sens.	Spec.	FPR	FNR	RS
all features	0.68	0.96	0.49	0.99	0.01	0.51	0.49
norm-based features	0.54	0.90	0.32	0.99	0.01	0.68	0.31
95 backward selected	0.67	0.97	0.48	0.99	0.01	0.52	0.49
all features, speed scaled	0.77	0.98	0.61	0.99	0.01	0.39	0.61
norm-based features, speed scaled	0.67	0.96	0.47	0.99	0.01	0.53	0.47
95 backward selected, speed scaled	**0.89**	0.97	**0.82**	0.97	0.03	**0.18**	**0.84**
20 backward selected, speed scaled	0.79	0.98	0.63	0.99	0.01	0.63	0.64

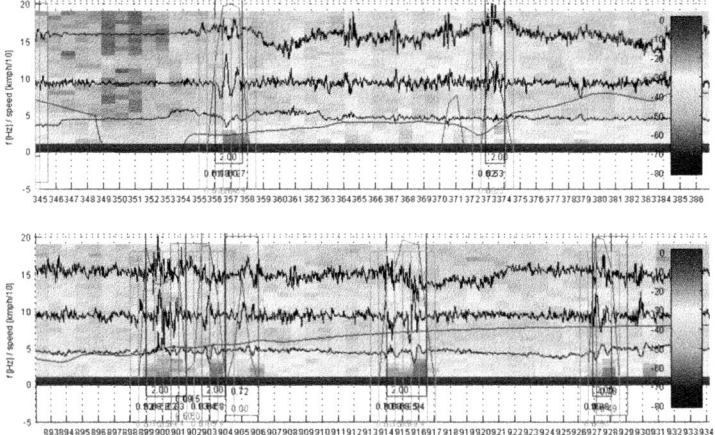

Fig. 8. Two example segments with predictions shown on top of original spectrograms, signals and labels. The original labels are shown as blue rectangles, the true positive windows as green, false positives as red and false negatives as magenta rectangles, correspondingly. The probability of an anomaly according to the classifier is shown as a continuous red signal.

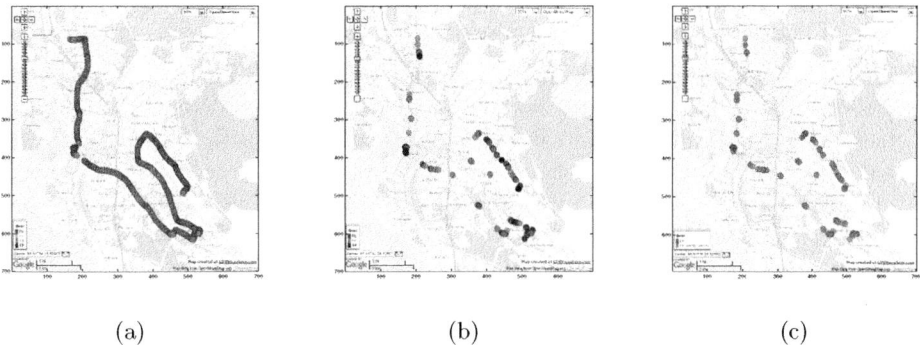

(a)   (b)   (c)

Fig. 9. Predictions on map. a) All predictions. The breaks represent the removed cobblestone segments. b) False negatives (red), false positives (green) and true positives (blue). c) False positives. The proportion of them overlapping with a Type 1 or Type 2 anomaly are shown in green and the windows not overlapping with an anomaly in magenta.

overlap being 59%. An example can be seen in the bottom of Fig.8, where a false positive prediction occurs after the first labelled anomaly; this is a Type 1 anomaly, as can be seen from Fig.2.

In Table 3 the number in parenthesis after FP signifies the number of false positives after removing the 127 windows that overlapped with an anomaly.

Table 3. Confusion matrix of anomaly detection using 95 features selected by backward search (γ : 1.0 and C : 0.1). The number in parenthesis after FP signifies the number of false positives after removing the (127) windows that overlapped with an anomaly.

	Anomaly	Normal
Anomaly	139	140 (13)
Normal	31	4440

In total, 1623 windows in the normal data overlapped to some extend with a labelled anomaly of Type 1 or Type 2. The mean overlap of the false negatives with the Type 2 anomalies was 71%, while for true positives this was 82%.

The results indicate that Type 2 anomalies could be quite accurately be distinguished from good condition road surface, but the Type 1 and Type 2 anomalies could not be well discriminated. However, this result suggests that locations where a significant amount of both Type 1 and Type 2 anomalies occur will be easy to point out. This is important for road administrators, because maintenance resources can be allocated to where they have the largest effect. It should also be noted that when deployed in practice, the classifier can be followed by a filter that, using a database, removes known speed bumps, cobblestone roads and other segments that are not actually in need of repair but do cause very similar signal patterns to actual road surface anomalies.

5.3   Comparison to Related Work

Similar results were reported in [11] and [16], although exact comparison is not possible due to different data sets and test setups. In [16], dedicated bump detectors were trained for two different speed categories using both known and unknown orientation of the phone. The authors rated as one of their best performing systems a bump detector with FPR=3% and FNR=51%, whereas our best result in terms of those statistics was FPR=3% and FNR=18% – a large reduction in false negatives. In [16], the test setup was not fully described; for example, it was not told whether locations of predictions were compared to locations of labeled bumps, or if time based labels and predictions were used. The data sets were compatible in length, in [16] around 30km and in our data around 25km.

It should also be mentioned that the results on labeled data in [11] were not comparable to ours, because in their data set, unrealistically, the number of examples from normal road surface roughly equalled the number of pothole examples, and they did not report the number of examples from normal road surface predicted as potholes or other anomalies. We used all examples from a continuous drive in the testing.

6   Conclusion

This work deals with monitoring road condition using sensors embedded in mobile phones. We have performed initial data collection and analysis, and developed road surface condition monitoring system that includes preprocessing, classification and visualization stages. The system was demonstrated to perform favourably when evaluated against a data set which is comparable in size to previously published results in the literature [16].

In this paper we utilized spectral analysis of 3-dimensional acceleration signals in order to get reliable road surface anomaly labels. Preprocessing of GPS and acceleration signals were used to estimate speed and to reduce sampling errors. Moreover, we proposed a speed dependence removal approach to the feature extraction in order to get more robust features. We demonstrated that the speed dependence removal improves the performance of several feature sets for the road surface anomaly detection task. A framework for visually analyzing the classifier predictions over the validation data and labels was presented. Compared to earlier work [11], [16], where only final detections were presented on a map, the framework is clearly advantageous as it allows analyzing what kind of waveforms were falsely classified.

The current recognition performance is not completely satisfactory, but as suggested in [11], collecting data from multiple drivers and clustering the suspected anomalies based on location and requiring an anomaly to be detected a number of times improve the performance. With limited data, we were unable to repeat the suggested clustering experiment, but we plan this as future work.

A practical lesson learned is that labelling driving data from video is time consuming and error prone work. Thus, alternative ways of developing surface anomaly detectors should be studied. For example, unsupervised learning could be experimented with.

Due to the inadequate quality of the data, we plan to experiment with other mobile phones to study the variance of sensor quality between devices and to confirm the results on new datasets. Future work will also address recognizing overall road condition from multiple vehicles of unknown types. This requires robustness against the different dampers and chassis of vehicles. Should this be achievable, the mobile phones based sensors could be carried in any vehicles, producing useful data without pre-configuration.

Acknowledgment. This work was supported by TEKES as part of the Co-operative Traffic ICT program of TIVIT (Finnish Strategic Centre for Science, Technology and Innovation in the field of ICT). The first author would also like to thank the Nokia Foundation.

References

1. Google maps for mobile (2009), http://www.google.com/mobile/maps
2. The mobile millenium project (2009), http://traffic.berkeley.edu/
3. Final report and integration of results and perspectives for market introduction of ivss, eimpact consortium (August 11, 2008)
4. Comparative performance measurement: Pavement smoothness. NCHRP 20-24(37B), American Association of State Highwayand Transportation Officials (AASHTO) (May 18, 2008)

5. Alauddin, M., Tighe, S.L.: Incorporation of surface texture, skid resistance and noise into pms. In: Proc: 7th International Conference on Managing Pavement Assets. Calgary, Canada (June 24-28, 2008)
6. Burke, J., Estrin, D., Hansen, M., Parker, A., Ramanathan, N., Reddy, S., Srivastava, M.B.: Participatory sensing. In: Workshop on World-Sensor-Web (WSW 2006), pp. 117–134 (2006)
7. Byrne, M., Albrecht, D., Sanjayan, J.G., Kodikara, J.: Recognizing patterns in seasonal variation of pavement roughness using minimum message length inference. Computer-Aided Civil and Infrastructure Engineering 24(2), 120–129 (2009)
8. Chang, C.C., Lin, C.J.: LIBSVM: a library for support vector machines (2001), software http://www.csie.ntu.edu.tw/~cjlin/libsvm
9. Cortes, C., Vapnik, V.: Support-vector networks. Machine Learning 20, 273–297 (1995)
10. Duin, R.P.W., Juszczak, P., de Ridder, D., Paclik, P., Pekalska, E., Tax, D.: Prtools, a matlab toolbox for pattern recognition (2004), http://www.prtools.org
11. Eriksson, J., Girod, L., Hull, B., Newton, R., Madden, S., Balakrishnan, H.: The pothole patrol: using a mobile sensor network for road surface monitoring. In: MobiSys 2008: Proceeding of the 6th International Conference on Mobile Systems, Applications, and Services, pp. 29–39. ACM, New York (2008)
12. Gonzlez, A., O'brien, E.J., Li, Y.Y., Cashell, K.: The use of vehicle acceleration measurements to estimate road roughness. Vehicle System Dynamics: International Journal of Vehicle Mechanics and Mobility 46, 483–499 (2008)
13. Kantola, J., Perttunen, M., Leppänen, T., Collin, J., Riekki, J.: Context awareness for gps-enabled phones. In: ION 2010 Technical Meeting (January 25-27, 2010)
14. Kubat, M., Matwin, S.: Addressing the curse of imbalanced training sets: One-sided selection. In: Proceedings of the Fourteenth International Conference on Machine Learning, pp. 179–186 (1997)
15. Leppänen, T., Perttunen, M., Riekki, J., Kaipio, P.: Sensor network architecture for cooperative traffic applications. In: 6th International Conference on Wireless and Mobile Communications, September 20-25, pp. 400–403. IEEE, Los Alamitos (2010)
16. Mohan, P., Padmanabhan, V.N., Ramjee, R.: Nericell: rich monitoring of road and traffic conditions using mobile smartphones. In: Proc. ACM SenSys 2008, pp. 323–336. ACM, New York (2008)
17. Riva, O., Nadeem, T., Borcea, C., Iftode, L.: Context-aware migratory services in ad hoc networks. IEEE Trans. Mobile Comput. 6(12), 1313–1328 (2007)
18. Su, C.T., Hsiao, Y.H.: An evaluation of the robustness of mts for imbalanced data. IEEE Trans. Knowl. Data Eng. 19, 1321–1332 (2007)
19. Tanaka, N., Okamoto, H., Naito, M.: Detecting and evaluating intrinsic nonlinearity present in the mutual dependence between two variables. Physica D: Nonlinear Phenomena 147(1-2), 1–11 (2000)
20. Thiagarajan, A., Ravindranath, L.S., LaCurts, K., Toledo, S., Eriksson, J., Madden, S., Balakrishnan, H.: VTrack: Accurate, Energy-Aware Traffic Delay Estimation Using Mobile Phones. In: ACM SenSys 2009, Berkeley, CA (November 2009)
21. Thompson, C., White, J., Dougherty, B., Albright, A., Schmidt, D.C.: Using smartphones to detect car accidents and provide situational awareness to emergency responders. In: Mobile Wireless Middleware, Operating Systems, and Applications. LNICST, vol. 48, pp. 29–42. Springer, Heidelberg (2010)

Verifiable and Lossless Distributed Media Content Sharing

Pei-Yu Lin

Department of Information Communication, Yuan Ze University,
135 Yuan-Tung Rd., Chung-Li 32003, Taiwan
linpy@cs.ccu.edu.tw

Abstract. For digital communication, distributed storage and management of media content over system holders is a critical issue. In this article, an efficient verifiable sharing scheme is proposed that can satisfy the significant essentials of distribution sharing and can achieve the lossless property of the host media. Verifiability allows holders to detect and identify the counterfeited shadows during cooperation in order to prevent cheaters. Only authorized holders can reveal the lossless shared content and then reconstruct the original host image. The shared media capacity is adjustable and proportional to the increase of t. The more distributed holders, the larger the shared media capacity. Moreover, the ability to reconstruct the image preserves the fidelity of valuable host media, such as military and medical images. According to the results, the proposed approach can achieve superior performance to that of related sharing schemes in order to effectively provide distributed media management and storage.

Keywords: Secret sharing, verifiable, lossless, cheater, steganography.

1 Introduction

To reduce the risk lost, distorted, and stolen secret keys by a single holder, the secret sharing mechanism [1-4] splits the secret key into several shadows and then distributes the shadows to corresponding participants. The concept of secret key sharing mechanism was first introduced by Blakley [1] and Shamir [2] with the (t, n)-threshold system. A dealer is responsible for encoding and dividing the secret key into n shadows. The derived shadows then dispatch to n corresponding participants; that is, each participant has a private shadow. In the extraction process, any t out of n shadows provided by the involved participants can cooperate to reveal the secret key.

One assumption in Shamir's sharing system is that all shadows are genuine and are provided by honest participants during cooperation. In the real world, however, this assumption is impractical. Tompa and Woll [5] indicate that Shamir's system is insecure to resist the attack of fraudulent participants. A fraudulent participant can provide a fake shadow to cheat the other participants out of their shadows. With the collected shadows, only the fraudulent participant can reveal the original secret key.

Instead of sharing a secret key, Thien and Lin [6] developed a specific method for sharing a secret image based on Shamir's (t, n)-threshold system. Because the capacity of secret image is usually large and the pixel value is bounded within [0, 255], sharing

C.-H. Hsu et al. (Eds.): UIC 2011, LNCS 6905, pp. 79–93, 2011.

a image content using Shamir's approach can easily cause shadow expansion and distortion. The derived shadow in [6] can reduce the size of shadows in order to avoid shadow expansion. Nevertheless, their derived shadows are meaningless (random-like) from visual perception and incapable of resisting cheaters. Delivering and storing meaningless shadows over an insecure channel and storage may attract the attention of malicious intruders. Besides, their scheme truncates all of the secret gray pixels within [251-255] to 250, and thereby distorts the content of the revealed secret image. To reveal a lossless secret image, the approach in [6] needs to extra record the exceeding pixel values.

To generate a meaningful shadow, the steganography technique [7] is utilized to camouflage shadows into a meaning host image [8-12]. The host image with the embedded shadows is called a stego image. The schemes [9-13] divide the host image into non-overlapping blocks with size 2×2 pixels. In [9, 10], the shadows and a parity check bit subsequently are embedded into each host block to form the stego image. By verifying the parity check bit, the involved participants can confirm the validity of the provided stego image. Hence, the schemes in [9, 10] can satisfy the requirements of meaningful stego image and verifiability.

To improve the verifiability and the embeddable shadow capacity in [9, 10], Chang et al. [11] embed four parity check bits and t secret digits into each block. For lossless secret image sharing, their scheme needs to represent the secret pixels in two digits, 250 and the value of the difference between the pixel value and 250. Recently, Eslami et al. [12] proposed a secret image sharing scheme based on cellular automata and steganography. This scheme embeds the shadows into each block by altering fewer bits of each block pixel in order to achieve better stego image quality than that of [9-11]. In [13], the scheme allows the participants to repair the tampered regions of the secret image. Nevertheless, the capacity of the sharable secret image is limited to one-quarter of the host image size as in [9, 10].

Apart from the requirements of meaningful stego image, lossless secret image, and verifiability, reconstruction of the distorted host image is a practical essential for preserving the fidelity of valuable host image, such as military, medical, and artistic images. That is, authorized participants can remove the embedded shadows from the stego image to restore the host image losslessly. The reconstruction of the lossless host image can be widely applied to the e-commerce, communications, and multimedia fields [14, 15]. However, the methods [6, 8-13] are incapable of restoring the lossless host image.

To satisfy the essential of lossless host image, Lin et al. [16] proposed a sharing scheme using a modulus operator. Their scheme permits the authorized participants to reveal the lossless secret image and to reconstruct the lossless host image. Moreover, they utilize Rabin's signature algorithm [17] to generate a certificate for the purpose of verifiability. Using the certificate mechanism ing [16], Ulutas et al. [18] present a medical image sharing scheme. However, the generation of the certificate [12, 16, 18] is computationally complex and time-consuming.

To achieve the essentials of meaningful stego image, verifiability, lossless secret image, lossless host image, and maximum sharable capacity, we propose a new media sharing approach. The proposed verifiable media sharing scheme allows for the protection and sharing of confidential multimedia among the distributed system holders. The shared media capacity is adjustable and proportional to the increase of t. That is, the more distributed holders, the larger the media capacity.

The rest of this article is organized as follows. The related works of Shamir's (t, n)-threshold method is briefly introduced in Section 2. The proposed verifiable and recoverable image sharing scheme is discussed in Section 3, followed by the experimental results in Section 4. Finally, we make conclusions in Section 5.

2 Shamir's (t, n)-Threshold System

The concept of Shamir's (t, n)-threshold sharing approach [2] is described in this section. Given a shared secret s, a dealer determines a prime m and generates a $(t-1)$-degree polynomial as

$$F(x) = (s + a_1x^1 + \ldots + a_{t-1}x^{t-1}) \bmod m, \tag{1}$$

where the coefficients $a_1, a_2, \ldots, a_{t-1}$ are randomly determined from integers within $[0, m-1]$. The dealer then computes the shadows as

$$y_1 = F(1), y_2 = F(2), \ldots, y_n = F(n) . \tag{2}$$

Eventually, the dealer issues shadows y_i's to involved participants.

Generally, we label a shadow set as a *forbidden set* if there are fewer than t participants. No one in the forbidden set can correctly reconstruct $F(x)$ using the Lagrange interpolation polynomial. A shadow set is called a *qualified set* if the number of participants is greater than or equal to t. Authorized participants in a qualified set can cooperate to reconstruct $F(x)$. That is, authorized participants can construct $F(x)$ to recover all coefficients $s, a_1, a_2, \ldots, a_{t-1}$. In this way, the secret s can be obtained.

Note that the values of generated shadows y_i range within $[0, m-1]$. While forming those y_i, it appears meaningless (random-like). To conceal the shadows from intruders, our proposed secret image sharing scheme produces n meaningful stego images by camouflaging the shadows in a host image. Besides, Shamir's scheme is insecure against the cheating attacks. To prevent such malicious attempts, the new approach can detect the dishonest participants by verifying the contents of their shadows, as explained in Section 3.

3 Paper Preparation

Given a shared media S and a host image O with $H \times W$ pixels, the dealer can derive shadows from S and then generate n stego images by O in the (t, n)-threshold system, where $2 < t \leq n$. The n stego images subsequently dispatch to the corresponding system holders for the purpose of media distributed management and storage. The stego image generation procedure is introduced in subsection 3.1. To extract the shared media S, any t out of n system holders can first verify the contents of the provided stego images with one another. The authorized holders can then cooperate to extract the S and restore the O without distortion. The verification and extraction procedure is discussed in subsection 3.2.

3.1 The (t, n) VSS Procedure

In the (t, n) verifiable secret sharing (VSS) system, the dealer must select a prime number m and unique key K_i for the n system holders, where $i = 1, 2, ..., n$, and K_i is unequal to a multiple of m. In the preliminary step, the dealer convers the shared media S into m-ary notation system and generates the verification bit stream V.

Shadow Derivation Phase
The shadow derivation process generates shadows from S by the $(t–1)$-degree polynomial $F(x)$. Instant of sharing one secret pixel in $F(x)$ [9, 10, 13], the new approach shares $t–2$ secret digits to increase the shared media capacity. For convenience, let the $t–2$ shared digits from S be $s_1, s_2, ..., s_{t-2}$, and the corresponding host pixel from O be p. To generate the shadows as well as satisfy restorability of the host image, the feature of p must be preserved by computing the value r as

$$r = p \bmod m . \tag{3}$$

The quantization value Q is calculated as

$$Q = \lfloor p/m \rfloor \times m . \tag{4}$$

From the value Q, a check bit c can bedetermined as

$$c = lsb(Q) . \tag{5}$$

Here, the $lsb(Q)$ indicates the least significant bit (LSB) of the value Q.

Consequently, with the $t–2$ shared digits s1, s2, ..., st-2, the shared polynomial $F(x)$ can be formulated as

$$F(x) = (c + rx + s_1 x^2 + s_2 x^3 + ... + s_{t-2} x^{t-1}) \bmod m . \tag{6}$$

The dealer can derive n shadows y_i by feeding the key K_i into $F(x)$, where

$$y_1 = F(K_1), \quad y_2 = F(K_2), \quad ..., \text{ and } \quad y_n = F(K_n) . \tag{7}$$

Shadow Camouflage Phase
To conceal the derived shadows with verifiability and camouflage, the y_i's are embedded into the host pixel p in order to generate stego pixel p_i, for $i = 1, 2, ..., n$. The n stego pixels p_i for y_i can be formed as

$$p_i = Q + y_i . \tag{8}$$

Let the verification bit from V be v. To achieve verifiability, the stego pixels p_i are adjusted by

$$p_i = \begin{cases} p_i & , \text{if } v = lsb(p_i) \\ p_i + m & , \text{if } v \neq lsb(p_i) \end{cases} . \tag{9}$$

According to the shadow derivation and camouflage phases, the dealer can share the remaining secret digits to generate the corresponding stego pixels and then obtain the n stego images O_i. Here, the stego images are meaningful and similar to the original host image O. Subsequently, the dealer can distribute the stego images O_i along with the key K_i to the corresponding i-th system holders to achieve distributed management and storage.

3.2 Additional Information Required by the Volume Editor

To reveal the secret media S during the distributed system, any t out of n authorized system holders should provide stego image O_j' and key K_j', where $j = 1, 2, ..., t$. Verifiability of VSS allows the involved system holders to detect fraudulent holders by checking the content of the O_j' with the verification bit stream V. That is, the holders can validate each other without revealing the secret key K_i and shadows.

Shadow Verification Phase
Let p_j' be a stego pixel of O_j' and v be corresponding verification bit of V. Compare the least significant bit of p_j' with v, if $lsb(p_j')$ equals to v, and then indicate p_j' as "pass", otherwise, indicate p_j' as "fail".

$$p_j' = \begin{cases} pass & , \text{if } v = lsb(p_j') \\ fail & , \text{if } v \neq lsb(p_j') \end{cases} . \tag{10}$$

Repeating Equation (10) for all pixels in O_j', if all pixels pass, then the content of the stego image O_j' is authentic. On the other hand, if one of the pixels fails, the stego image can be considered counterfeit. The extraction procedure halts to prevent the dishonest holders.

Reveal and Restoration Phase
With any t out of n authorized O_j', key K_j, and the prime number m, the system holders can cooperate to extract the lossless secret media S and to reconstruct the original host image O. For the t stego pixels p_j' corresponding to the O_j', $j = 1, 2, ..., t$, the holders can compute the shadow value of y_j by

$$y_j = p_j' \bmod m . \tag{11}$$

With t pairs of shadows y_j and key K_j, the $(t-1)$-degree polynomial $F(x)$ can be formulated as

$$F(x) = (c + rx + s_1x^2 + s_2x^3 + ... + s_{t-2}x^{t-1}) \bmod m . \tag{12}$$

Subsequently, the shared digits $s_1, s_2, ..., s_{t-2}$, can be obtained by extracting the last $t-2$ coefficients of $F(x)$.

To restore the original host pixel p, assign the first and second coefficients of $F(x)$ as the feature values c and r, respectively. Calculate the Q_j value, where $j = 1, 2, ..., t$.

$$Q_j = \lfloor p_j'/m \rfloor \times m . \tag{13}$$

Adjust Q_j if the value of the least significant bit of Q_j is different from the value of c:

$$Q_j = \begin{cases} Q_j & , \text{if } c = lsb(Q_j) \\ Q_j - m & , \text{if } c \neq lsb(Q_j) \end{cases} . \tag{14}$$

Finally, the holders can losslessly reconstruct their stego pixel p_j by

$$p_j = Q_j + r . \tag{15}$$

By repeating the above phases until all secret digits are extracted, authorized holders can obtain all secret digits and restore the original host image O without distortion. The holders eventually transform the secret digits from m-ary notation system to the binary system to reveal the lossless secret media S.

Consider the luminous pixel of host image that approximates to 255. The stego pixel generated by Equations (8) and (9) may exceed the pixel value boundary and cause distortion of the recovered host pixel. To prevent the overflow situation, the host pixel within $[(\lfloor 255/m \rfloor - 1] \times m, 255]$ is excluded from embedding in the shadow derivation and camouflage phases. Similarly, in the extraction procedure, if the stego pixel is within the range $[(\lfloor 255/m \rfloor - 1] \times m, 255]$, this means that the stego pixel is innocent and equals to the original host pixel.

| (a) Airplane | (b) Baboon | (c) Barb | (d) Butterfly | (e)Cameraman |

| (f) Clown | (g) Couple | (h) Elaine | (i) Fruits | (j) Girl |

| (k) Goldhill | (l) House | (m) Lena | (n) Peppers | (o) Sailboat |

| (p) Splash | (q) Tiffany | (r) Toys | (s) Watch | (t) Zelda |

Fig. 1. Test host images with 512×512 pixels

4   Experimental Results and Analysis

In the simulations, different types of natural images are used as the host images shown in Fig. 1. The size of the grayscale host images is 512×512 pixels. Fig. 2 shows the shared image with 256×256 pixels. The prime number $m = 7$. The peak signal-to-noise rate (PSNR) is utilized to evaluate the quality of the derived stego images,

$$PSNR = 10\log_{10}\left(\frac{255^2}{MSE}\right) \text{dB} \ . \tag{16}$$

The mean square error (*MSE*) of an image with $H \times W$ pixels is defined as

$$MSE = \frac{1}{H \times W} \sum_{u=1}^{H} \sum_{v=1}^{W} (p_{uv} - p'_{uv})^2 \ , \tag{17}$$

where p_{uv} is the host pixel value, and p'_{uv} is the stego pixel value.

Fig. 2. The shared image with 256×256 pixels

Table 1. The qualities of the derived stego images for various natural images, $t=3$

Host images	PSNR (dB)		
	Stego image1	Stego image2	Stego image3
Airplane	34.19	34.28	34.26
Baboon	34.19	34.26	34.25
Barb	34.20	34.17	34.13
Butterfly	34.19	34.28	34.22
Cameraman	34.16	34.22	34.20
Clown	34.23	34.33	34.26
Couple	34.25	34.30	34.28
Elaine	34.23	34.32	34.29
Fruits	34.18	34.25	34.25
Girl	34.16	34.26	34.23
Goldhill	34.19	34.27	34.25
House	33.91	33.95	33.99
Lena	34.20	34.29	34.25
Peppers	34.21	34.26	34.24
Sailboat	34.21	34.30	34.26
Splash	34.20	34.29	34.28
Tiffany	34.21	34.26	34.24
Toys	34.20	34.30	34.26
Watch	34.19	34.28	34.23
Zelda	34.18	34.25	34.25
Average	34.19	34.26	34.23

4.1 Simulation Results

To evaluate the practicability of the distributed sharing approach, the quality of the derived stego image, lossless property, verifiability, and shared media capacity are the major concerns. Table 1 displays the quality of the derived stego images while sharing Fig. 2 with various host images in the (3, 3)-threshold system. The average PSNR value of the stego images is around 34.2 dB no matter what host image is the carrier. That is, the new VSS approach is practical for normally distributed natural images and satisfies the purpose of steganography. Figs. 3(b) through (d) demonstrate the corresponding stego images of the host image Lena (Fig. 3(a)). The stego images can be dispatched to individual system holders for distributed management and storage. According to the extraction procedure, the authorized holders can cooperate to extract the shared image losslessly as shown in Fig. 3(e) and then recover the original host image without distortion as shown in Fig. 3(f). Hence, the new scheme can satisfy the lossless essential to protect the shared media and preserve the valuable host image.

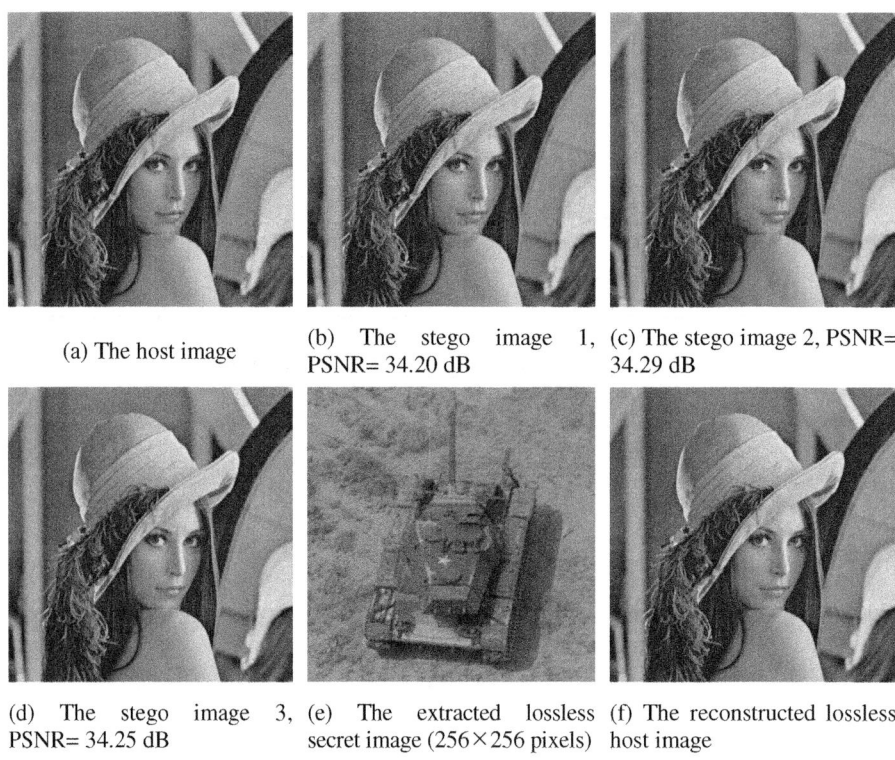

(a) The host image

(b) The stego image 1, PSNR= 34.20 dB

(c) The stego image 2, PSNR= 34.29 dB

(d) The stego image 3, PSNR= 34.25 dB

(e) The extracted lossless secret image (256×256 pixels)

(f) The reconstructed lossless host image

Fig. 3. The results of host image Lena

Fig. 4(a) presents the original enlarged image of Lena. After embedding 512×512 sharing digits into the host images, Fig. 4(b) shows the corresponding enlarged stego images. Since the proposed scheme embeds the shadows into the host pixels by

Equations (8) and (9), the pixel value increases and may lead to brightness as shown in Fig. 4(f). Comparing the difference between the original images and the stego images, the alteration is slight, and the visual quality is acceptable.

(a) The original enlarged image, *Lena*   (b) The stego image of (a), PSNR=33.03 dB

Fig. 4. The enlarged image with secret capacity=512×512 digits, t=3

The ability to detect and identify fraudulent participants during cooperation is critical in the VSS approach. That is, an efficient VSS scheme should allow system holders to first verify the content of the provided stego images with one another. With sufficient stego images, authorized holders can subsequently reveal the shared media without distortion. Fig. 5(a) displays the common counterfeit attack by adding the tampered text and a logo. According to the proposed shadow verification phase, a holder can detect and identify the tampered shadows as shown in the white dots of Fig. 5(b).

(a) The tampered stego image, PSNR=16.06 dB   (b) The verification results

Fig. 5. The tampering attack and the verification result

Table 2. The capacity of the shared media and the qualities of the corresponding stego images under different setting of t with Lena, $m=7$

t	Capacity		PSNR		
	Digits	Pixels	Stego image 1	Stego image 2	Stego image 3
3	262,144	87,381	33.02	33.03	33.04
4	524,288	174,763	33.02	33.02	33.01
5	786,432	262,144	33.03	33.04	33.03
6	1,048,576	349,525	33.03	33.04	33.02
7	1,310,720	436,907	33.02	33.04	33.02
8	1,572,864	524,288	33.03	33.01	33.02
9	1,835,008	611,669	33.04	33.02	33.02
10	2,097,152	699,051	33.02	33.01	33.03
11	2,359,296	786,432	33.04	33.02	33.03
12	2,621,440	873,813	33.02	33.03	33.02
13	2,883,584	961,195	33.02	33.02	33.01
14	3,145,728	1,048,576	33.03	33.02	33.03
15	3,407,872	1,135,957	33.02	33.04	33.04

Table 3. The percentage of the host pixels within [245, 255], $m=7$

Host images	Excluded from embedding	
	Pixels	Percentage (%)
Airplane	-	0.000%
Baboon	-	0.000%
Barb	6	0.002%
Butterfly	-	0.000%
Cameraman	316	0.121%
Clown	416	0.159%
Couple	11	0.004%
Elaine	5,507	2.101%
Fruits	6,378	2.433%
Girl	-	0.000%
Goldhill	-	0.000%
House	-	0.000%
Lena	-	0.000%
Peppers	-	0.000%
Sailboat	-	0.000%
Splash	-	0.000%
Tiffany	-	0.000%
Toys	8	0.003%
Watch	155	0.059%
Zelda	-	0.000%
Average	1,600	0.244%

Because the proposed VSS scheme embeds $t-2$ shared digits for each polynomial $F(x)$ in Equation (6), the capacity of the shared media can be increased according to t. For a $H \times W$ pixels host image, the sharable media capacity is $(H \times W) \times (t-2)$ digits. Since a shared digit is in the m-ary notation system, the shared media capacity is equal to $(H \times W) \times (t-2)/\lceil \log_m 255 \rceil$ pixels. That is, the larger the setting of threshold t, the greater the media capacity that system holders can share. Table 2 illustrates the maximum capacity of the shared media and the qualities of three derived stego images under different settings of t. The new VSS scheme is capable of sharing a larger amount of media among the distributed system holders for a host image. The qualities of the derived stego images are around 33 dB, without respect to how many media digits are shared. Thus, the new approach is efficient for sharing large media quantity with considerable distributed system holders.

4.2 Analysis and Discussion

In the proposed system, a host pixel within $[(\lfloor 255/m \rfloor - 1] \times m, 255]$ is excluded for shadow embedding and extracting to prevent overflow. To analyze the exceeding pixels of the natural host images, Table 3 lists the percentages of the pixels within [245, 255] for various host images, where $m = 7$. The average percentage of the exceeding pixels is 0.244%. The corresponding histogram of the pixel distribution is shown in Fig. 6. The red bar charts indicate the exceeding pixels. Although a few of the host pixels are restricted and excluded from shadow embedding, most of the pixels are feasible for a natural image.

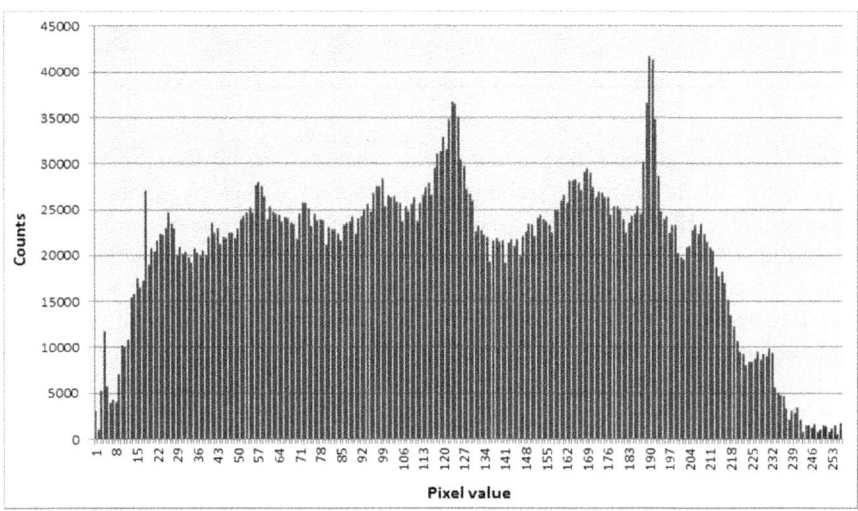

Fig. 6. The statistic histogram of the natural host images

Table 4 compares the functionalities between related sharing schemes and the proposed scheme. Form visual perception, the derived stego image of [8-13, 16, 18] and the proposed scheme can satisfy the meaningful stego image to reduce the risk of the intruders' attention.

Table 4. Comparisons to related secret image sharing mechanisms

Schemes	Functionalities					
	Meaningful stego image	Extra expansion/ storage	Verifiability	Lossless shared image	Lossless host image	Maximum capacity (pixels)
[6]	No	No	No	No	-	-
[8]	Yes	No	No	No	No	-
[9]	Yes	No	$1-(1/2)^{H\times W/4}$	No	No	$\dfrac{H\times W}{4}$
[10]	Yes	Yes	$1-(1/2)^{H\times W/4}$	Yes	No	$\dfrac{H\times W}{4}$
[11]	Yes	No	$1-(1/2)^{H\times W}$	Yes	No	$\dfrac{H\times W\times t}{4\times\lceil\log_{251}255\rceil}$
[12]	Yes	Yes	Certificate	Yes	No	$\dfrac{H\times W\times(t-1)}{4\times\lceil\log_{251}255\rceil}$
[13]	Yes	No	$1-(1/2)^{H\times W}$	Yes	No	$\dfrac{H\times W}{4}$
[16]	Yes	Yes	Certificate	Yes	Yes	$\dfrac{H\times W\times(t-3)}{\lceil\log_7255\rceil}$
[18]	Yes	Yes	Certificate	Yes	No	$\dfrac{H\times W\times t}{4\times\lceil\log_{251}255\rceil}$
Ours	Yes	No	$1-(1/2)^{H\times W}$	Yes	Yes	$\dfrac{H\times W\times(t-2)}{\lceil\log_7255\rceil}$

The sensitivity of detecting a cheater is a critical essential for estimating the performance of a sharing mechanism. To achieve cheater detection, several approaches [10, 12, 16, 18] apply the secret information to generate a hashed result and certification. The approaches can efficiently detect the counterfeited shadows. However, they require extra to record the corresponding secret information, such as block IDs, sequence numbers, and certifications. Proving the validity of the shadows using the certificate system is computationally complex and time-consuming. The sharing schemes [9-11, 13] and the proposed scheme can validate the shadow integrity by embedding the authentication code into the host image. The participants can directly verify the shadows by comparing the extracted authentication code with the original one.

Consider the probability that a cheater can successful forge a counterfeit shadow (stego image) to pass the verification process. The probability should be as small as possible. The column of verifiability in Table 4 shows the corresponding probabilities. The schemes [9-11, 13] divide an $H\times W$ host image into non-overlapping blocks with size 2×2 pixels. In [9, 10], a parity check bit is embedded into each block. Hence, the probability is $(1/2)^{H\times W/4}$. To improve the probability, Chang et al.'s scheme [11] embeds four parity check bits into each bock, enhancing the probability to $(1/16)^{H \times W/4}$ $= (1/2)^{H \times W}$. One authentication digit in [0, 15] is embedded into a block in [13]. Thus, the corresponding probability is $(1/16)^{H \times W/4} = (1/2)^{H \times W}$.

The proposed manner adjusts each stego pixel according to the verification bit by Equation (9). That is, a verification bit is embedded for each pixel, and the probability is $(1/2)^{H \times W}$. Unlike block-based sharing schemes [9-13], the new scheme is a pixel-based sharing approach. The false positive and false negative probabilities of our scheme are reduced [19, 20]. The false negative probability means that the pixel suffers from forgery, but some tampered pixels are not detected. The false positive probability means that the pixels are judged as maliciously tampered, but some pixels are not. The block-based authentication approach with one check bit can lead to false positive and false negative probabilities.

Sharing media without distortion is important to reveal the original media content. Moreover, to preserve the fidelity of the valuable host image is significant for medical, artistic, and military media, where any slight distortion is unacceptable. The scheme in [16] and the proposed approach not only allow authenticated participants to reveal the lossless shared image but also to reconstruct the lossless host image.

The capacity of the sharable media among system holders should as large as possible in order to reduce the storage space and the communication bandwidth. Instant of embedding one shared pixel into $F(x)$ with a 2×2 block [9, 10, 13], the new approach shares $t-2$ secret digits into $F(x)$ for each pixel. The maximum capacity of the proposed scheme can be increased to $H \times W \times (t-2) / \lceil \log_7 255 \rceil$, where $m=7$. The capacities of the schemes [11, 18] and [12] are $H \times W \times t / (4 \times \lceil \log_{251} 255 \rceil)$ and $H \times W \times (t-1) / (4 \times \lceil \log_{251} 255 \rceil)$ pixels, respectively. They split the shared pixels into 251-ary notation system for the lossless purpose. Here, the block size is 2×2 pixels in [11, 12], and 8 pixels in [18].

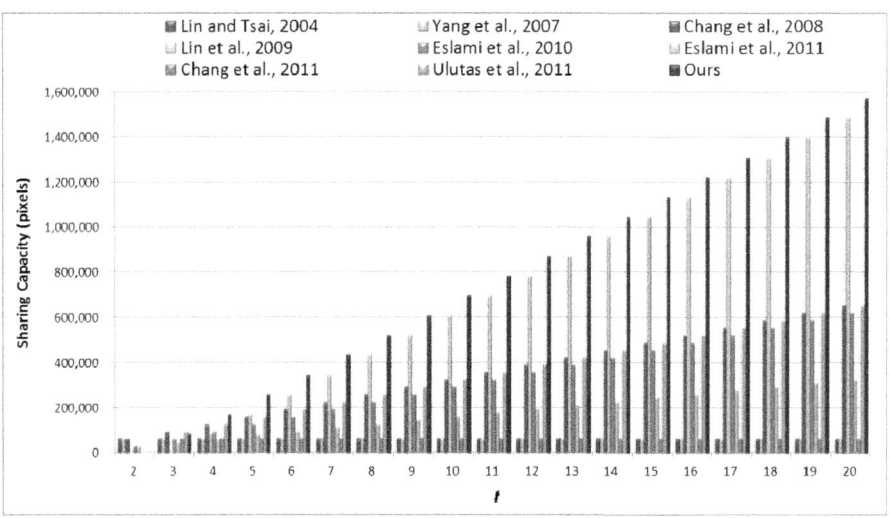

Fig. 7. The maximum capacity of the sharable media under different t setting

More precisely, Fig. 7 compares the corresponding capacity of the shared media for related schemes and the new scheme under different settings of t. The maximum capacity of [11, 12, 16, 18] is proportional to the increase of t. It is obvious that the proposed approach can share more media than related schemes in most cases. The more distributed holders, the larger the shared media capacity. That is, the new algorithm is quite suitable for sharing and managing the large media content among distributed system holders.

5 Conclusions

In this article, we propose a verifiable media sharing approach that allows the system holders to distributively manage and store media content. The new VSS approach can achieve the sharing essentials of verifiability, camouflage, lossless shared media, lossless host image, and maximum sharable capacity. Compared with related sharing schemes, the new method can share superior media capacity in a host image and efficiently reduce the storage space and the communication bandwidth. According to the results, the verifiability essential permits the system holders to detect and identify the dishonest participants with satisfying probability. Only the authorized holders can reveal the shared media content and restore the host image without distortion. The reconstruction of host image offers significant practicability to preserve the fidelity of the valuable host media.

References

1. Blakley, G.R.: Safeguarding cryptographic keys. In: Proceedings of AFIPS National Computer Conference, vol. 48, pp. 313–317 (1979)
2. Shamir, A.: How to share a secret. Communications of the ACM 22(11), 612–613 (1979)
3. Naor, M., Shamir, A.: Visual cryptography. In: De Santis, A. (ed.) EUROCRYPT 1994. LNCS, vol. 950, pp. 1–12. Springer, Heidelberg (1995)
4. Beimel, A., Chor, B.: Secret sharing with public reconstruction. IEEE Transactions on Information Theory 44(5), 1887–1896 (1998)
5. Tompa, M., Woll, H.: How to share a secret with cheaters. Journal of Cryptology 1(2), 133–138 (1988)
6. Thien, C.C., Lin, J.C.: Secret image sharing. Computer & Graphics 26(1), 765–770 (2002)
7. Lee, C.C., Wu, H.C., Tsai, C.S., Chu, Y.P.: Adaptive lossless steganographic scheme with centralized difference expansion. Pattern Recognition 41(6), 2097–2106 (2008)
8. Wu, Y.S., Thien, C.C., Lin, J.C.: Sharing and hiding secret images with size constraint. Pattern Recognition 37(7), 1377–1385 (2004)
9. Lin, C.C., Tsai, W.H.: Secret image sharing with steganography and authentication. The Journal of Systems and Software 73(3), 405–414 (2004)
10. Yang, C.N., Chen, T.S., Yu, K.H., Wang, C.C.: Improvements of image sharing with steganography and authentication. The Journal of Systems and Software 80(7), 1070–1076 (2007)
11. Chang, C.C., Hsieh, Y.P., Lin, C.H.: Sharing secrets in stego images with authentication. Pattern Recognition 41(10), 3130–3137 (2008)
12. Eslami, Z., Razzaghi, S.H., Ahmadabadi, J.Z.: Secret image sharing based on cellular automata and steganography. Pattern Recognition 43(1), 397–404 (2010)

13. Chang, C.C., Chen, Y.H., Wang, H.C.: Meaningful secret sharing technique with authentication and remedy abilities. Information Sciences 181(14), 3073–3084 (2011)
14. Liu, T.Y., Tsai, W.H.: Generic lossless visible watermarking - a new approach. IEEE Transactions on Image Processing 19(5), 1224–1235 (2010)
15. Zeng, X.T., Ping, L.D., Pan, X.Z.: A lossless robust data hiding scheme. Pattern Recognition 43(4), 1656–1667 (2010)
16. Lin, P.Y., Lee, J.S., Chang, C.C.: Distortion-free secret image sharing mechanism using modulus operator. Pattern Recognition 42(5), 886–895 (2009)
17. Stinson, D.R.: Cryptography – Theory and Practice, 2nd edn. CRC Press Inc., New York (2002)
18. Ulutas, M., Ulutas, G., Nabiyev, V.V.: Medical image security and EPR hiding using Shamir's secret sharing scheme. Journal of Systems and Software 84(3), 341–353 (2011)
19. Kundur, D., Hatzinakos, D.: Digital watermarking for telltale tamper proofing and authentication. IEEE Proceedings 87(7), 1167–1180 (1999)
20. Lu, C.S., Liao, H.Y.: Structural digital signature for image authentication: an incidental distortion resistant scheme. IEEE Transactions on Multimedia 5(2), 161–173 (2003)

NuNote: An Augmented Reality Social Note Posting Service

Chun-Yi Lin, Cheng-Ting Chang, Meng-Tsen Chen, Zoeh Ruan, Alan Hsueh, Yi-Yang Chang, and Ren-Hung Hwang[*]

Dept. of Computer Science and Information Engineering,
National Chung-Cheng University, Taiwan, R.O.C
rhhwang@cs.ccu.edu.tw

Abstract. Equipping with feature rich sensors, smart phone are able to run many interesting applications utilizing these sensors. For example, many location based services are based on GPS sensor. In this paper, we present a new note posting service on mobile phones which delivers location based service, social network service, and Augmented Reality (AR). The new service is named NuNote; a new way of posting notes. NuNote offers many interesting features; include multimedia notes associated with location tags, viewing cyberspace notes in physical world based on the AR technology, sharing notes with friends through Facebook website, etc. We also present how NuNote could be used in commercial advertisement and situated learning.

Keywords: Augmented Reality (AR), Location Based Service (LBS), Note Posting Service, Android Smart Phone.

1 Introduction

Full featured smart mobile application service has become a niche in the market due to the feature rich sensors, such as compass, accelerometer, and GPS, embedded in smart phones. Features of these applications include location based services (LBS), maps, mails, calendar, social media interface buttons, etc. Among them, location based service seems to attract most of attentions.

By utilizing geographical position information, e.g., GPS, the mobile device could provide a variety of smart services, such as social service, entertainment, location or object search, route planning, discovering nearest place of interest or the whereabouts of a friend. Furthermore, most of these applications are built on top of map service, such as Google Map [1,2]. While geographical position information of a mobile device is the essential to enable location based service, collecting this information together with other sensing data also provides "digital footprints" to be further utilized or analyzed by other applications [3], such as social network service [4] or urban sensing [5,6].

An interesting new application on mobile phones is Augmented Reality (AR) [7]. Most of mobile phones are equipped with camera nowadays. Therefore, an easy way to

---

[*] Corresponding author.

C.-H. Hsu et al. (Eds.): UIC 2011, LNCS 6905, pp. 94–108, 2011.

provide AR is to overlay some virtual entities on the live view of a mobile device's camera. Combining with location based service, the virtual entity could be location data. For example, Wikitude Drive has provided an application which overlays video captured through the camera with driving instructions [8]. This allows users to literally drive and watch the road while they are looking at directions through mobile phones.

In this paper, we present a new note posting service on mobile phones which delivers location based service, social network service, and Augmented Reality (AR). The new service is named NuNote; a new way of posting notes. NuNote has three unique features. First, users can post a multimedia note at any location. The content of the note could include text, picture, video clip, and audio clip. Each note is associated with geographical position information when it is posted. Second, users can view notes on Google map through Web interface. Furthermore, users can view notes in AR mode. That is, by choosing AR mode, users can view notes overlaid on the live view of the mobile phone's camera. A note will appear at the exact location according to its geographical position information. Range-adjustable radar will also appear on the screen to indicate nearby notes. Users could use notes to store any kind of information. For example, when looking at a tree through the camera, a note overlaid on top of it could show the detail information of the tree, such as its name, species, variety, and cultivar. Finally, NuNote is integrated with Facebook such that notes could be shared among friends through Facebook. As a user posts a note on NuNote, he could also choose the option to post to its Facebook wall. His friends could comment on the note which will become notes on NuNote too. With NuNote, we extend the notation of posting notes to more fun and functionality.

The remainder of the paper is organized as follows. Section 2 sketches the overview of our system. Section 3 illustrates the way we implement it in detail. In Section 4, we show some demonstration of some possible scenarios in our daily lives. Section 5 compares some software related to location based services. Lastly, section 6 is our conclusion.

2   System Architecture Overview

2.1   Design Motivation

People take notes on several occasions. For example, we take notes to remind us something to do or to record some wonderful memories. Sometimes, we also use notes to communicate with each other. Recently, several web sites, such as atlaspost, provide users to associate notes with location information in a way that users can see notes, posted by themselves or others, on a map. With the advance of technology, these services are also available on smart phones. However, the interface of leaving notes is not that handy on smart phones. For example, we just pass by a fantastic restaurant and we would like to take a note of it so that we can come back for dinner in the future. Therefore, taking notes with smart phone would be better if it can automatically associate the note location information, such the information of GPS.

However, showing notes on a map is not intuitive. Augmented reality could further enhance the service interface by overlaying the notes on the live view of the mobile phone's camera. Recall the scenario of having a note of a fantastic restaurant, it becomes more convenient and intuitive if the note is overlaid with the live street view.

Users would be able to locate the restaurant easier than looking at the map. With the AR, more creative applications of notes could be created. For example, it is immoral for tourists to leave their names on famous scenery spot. However, their names could be left on the cyberspace and shown in the physical space through the AR technology. That is, image that many friends' names of a tourist overlaid with the live view of a scenery spot through his smart phone. It also becomes vivid to read stories about a historic spot on top of the live view of the location. Clearly, integrating notes with location information and augmented reality on smart phones creates a novel and interesting service.

The note posting service could be even further enhanced if it is integrated with social networking sites, such as Facebook. Nowadays people like to share their thoughts or stories through social networking sites. Notes posted on a location could be interested to friends in the social community. Therefore, it would be very convenient to integrate the note posting service with social networking sites through APIs provided by these sites.

Therefore, in this work, we design and develop the NuNote system. NuNote is based on a client-server model which integrates location service, augmented reality, and social networking service. Design goals of NuNote include handy for use, easy for search, intuitive interface and interaction, rich multimedia information. The main client software is run on Android smart phones, but a web-based interface is also provided for general clients. The server runs on FreeBSD system and provides notes repository and network connectivity service, includes implementation of Facebook APIs to access the data on behalf of users [9].

2.2   Design of NuNote Client and Server

Fig. 1 shows the functions of NuNote on a smart phone. The user interface provides three major interfaces, namely, menu, browsing mode, and toolbar. The menu interface is invoked by pressing the menu button on the bottom of smart phone. The browsing mode and toolbar are shown on the upper portion of the screen, as shown in Fig. 2. Meanwhile, current version of NuNote is implemented on smart phones running Android OS version 2.2 or later.

The browsing modes include map mode, reality mode, and list mode. Fig. 2 shows the screenshot of the map mode. When NuNote is in the map mode, notes are shown as pins on the map. Click on a pin will display the detail of the note. Secondly, when in the reality mode, the camera of the smart phone is activated and the screen shows the live video captured through the camera. In addition, pinned notes with title are overlaid on the live video as shown in Fig. 3. Notes in reality mode are displayed in 3-D (horizontal angel and vertical angel) centered at the user so that notes could be separated better than in the map mode. Lastly, when in the list mode, notes nearby the location are shown as a list, as shown in Fig. 4. If the list is too long, users can use the "filter" function to add constraints on which notes shall be listed. The filter function will be introduced later. In any mode, the detail of the note could be displayed by clicking on the note as shown in Fig. 5. A note consists following information: author, title, note context, picture, video or audio clip, referred URLs. When browsing the content of a note, a user can tag the note as one of his favorite notes, modify or delete his own note, and comment on other user's note (also see the function list on the top row of Fig. 1).

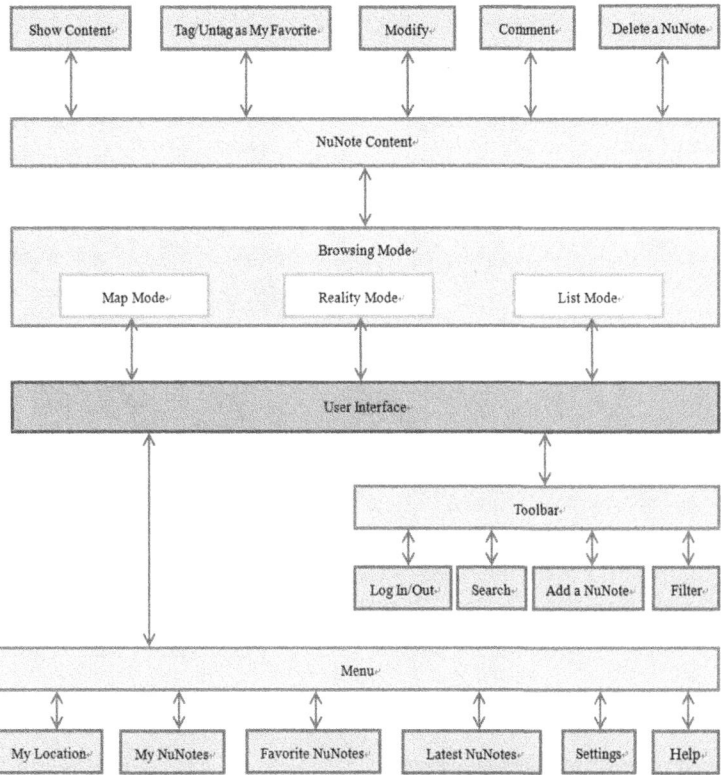

Fig. 1. Design of NuNote functions

The toolbar has four buttons. The first button is to integrate users account with Facebook. This log in/out button allows users to log in/out of Facebook. Functions such as posting notes to Facebook walls, follow friends' NuNotes, etc, require users log into Facebook first. The search button is designed for searching a NuNote by a keyword. Clicking on the add button allows users to publish a new note in NuNote, and if users logged into Facebook, on the user's Facebook wall. Finally, the filter function is used to add constraints on which notes shall be displayed. It is useful when the screen is crowded with notes. The filter could limit NuNote to only show notes of the users' friends or new posted notes. Again, the list of users' friends is obtained through Facebook's API.

Six functions are provided in the menu interface, namely my location, my NuNotes, my favorite NuNotes, latest NuNotes, settings, and help. The "my location" function will center the map to where the user located. "My NuNotes" and "my favorite NuNotes" display the lists of the user's NuNotes and favorite NuNotes, respectively. "Latest NuNotes" display the most recent posted NuNotes. By pressing "settings", users could adjust their preferences, such as the range for searching/displaying notes. (This range is called search range which is displayed as radar on the right bottom corner). Finally, "help" provides the help manual.

Fig. 2. Map mode of NuNote

Fig. 3. Reality mode of NuNote

Fig. 4. List mode of NuNote

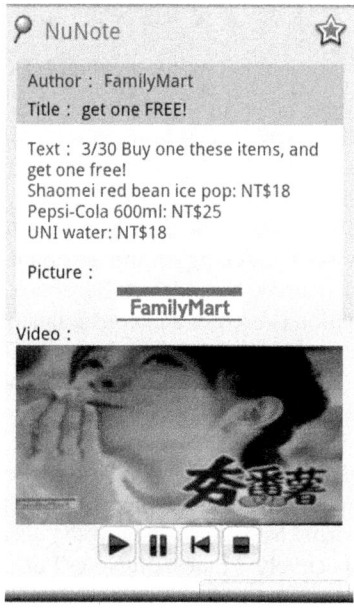

Fig. 5. Content of a NuNote

Besides the client software on Android phones, we also provide NuNote website for general users using browsers on any kind of devices. The website has almost the same functions as the Android counterpart. For example, a user can leave a note on a location through the Web interface using the map mode just like he adds a note through the android phone.

Currently, NuNote server runs on FreeBSD 7.1-RELEASE. It also runs an Apache server with PHP extension, as the communication interface for Android clients and the back end of the Facebook application. In addition, MySQL server is also installed on the server to manage data of multimedia notes.

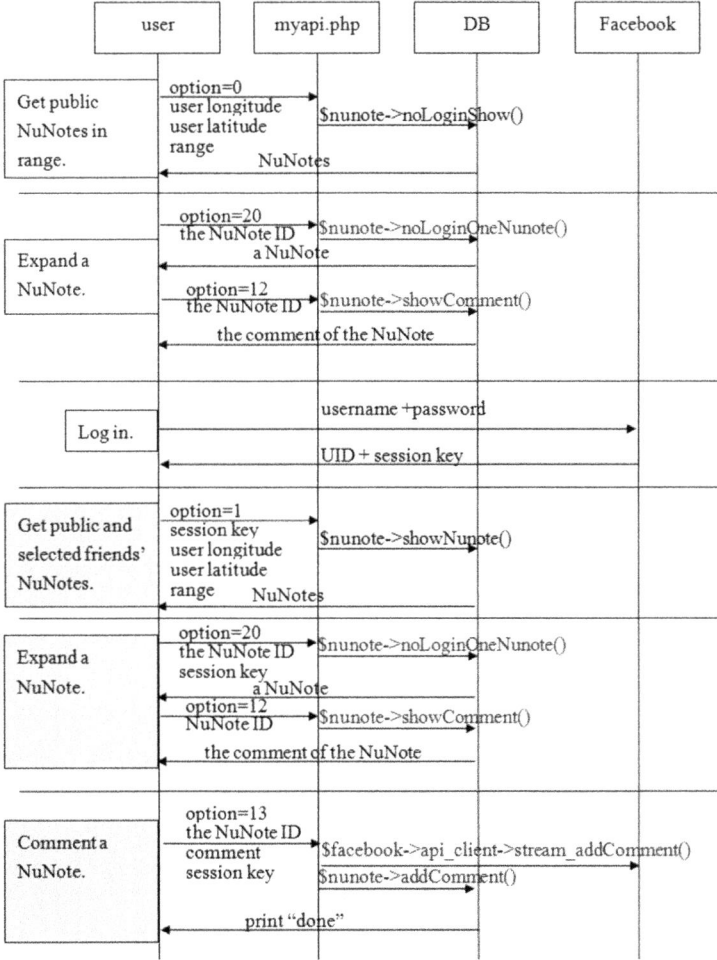

Fig. 6. Data communication between NuNote clients and server

The communication between a client and the server is through APIs. In general, there are two types of APIs: NuNote and Facebook. NuNote APIs deal with requests that are processed by the server alone while Facebook APIs deal with requests that need to be forwarded to Facebook server (API) on behalf of the user. For the objects communicated between client and server, NuNote encodes text object JavaScript Object Notation (JSON) [10] and returned the result as a web page to clients. On the other hand, for file objects, the standard http request and response method is adopted with the help of PHP forms.

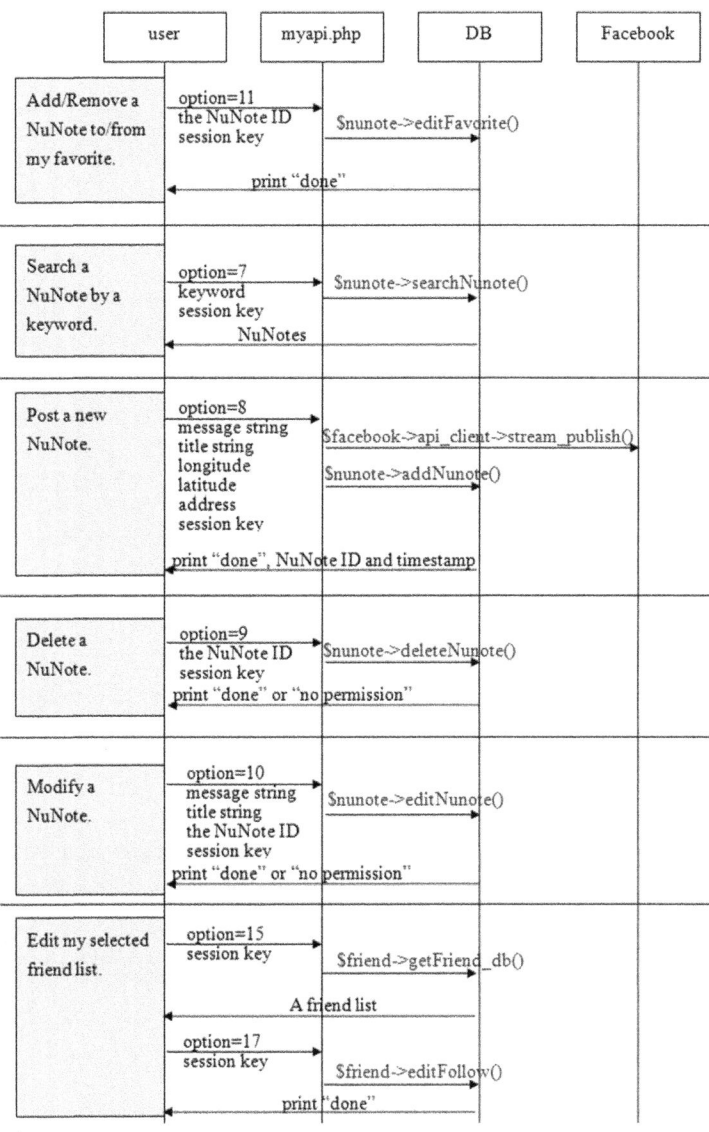

Fig. 7. Data communication between NuNote clients and server (cont.)

2.3 Social Network Integration

We believe that interaction of NuNotes through existing social networking site will promote the use of NuNote. Therefore, as stated above, NuNote integrate user accounts with Facebook, one of the most popular social networking sites on the Internet. There are three main functions provided through Facebook APIs. First, users can choose log in to NuNote using existing account on Facebook. Second, social relationship, namely friends, on Facebook is transferred to NuNote. Finally, users can decide to have notes posted in NuNote also posted on his Facebook wall. Similar, comments replied on Facebook can be posted on NuNote also.

Privacy is an important issue when integrating NuNote with Facebook. NuNote gives uses the rights to set their access control option. When posting note in NuNote as well as Facebook, the user can choose whether the post is to be public, private, or only viewable to his friends. A user can also follow, i.e., subscribe, notes posted by his friends. Recall that the "filter" button allows users to set constraints on which notes to display to avoid too many notes appear on the smart phone.

2.4 Communication

Data transfer between clients and NuNote server is through the HTTP protocol. Fig. 6-8 show the diagrams of detailed transfer sequences between client and server for different tasks. According to different option that client sends to Server, server responses different data. Functions with a session key are shown with green background. Most of the tasks were done on the server to decrease latency.

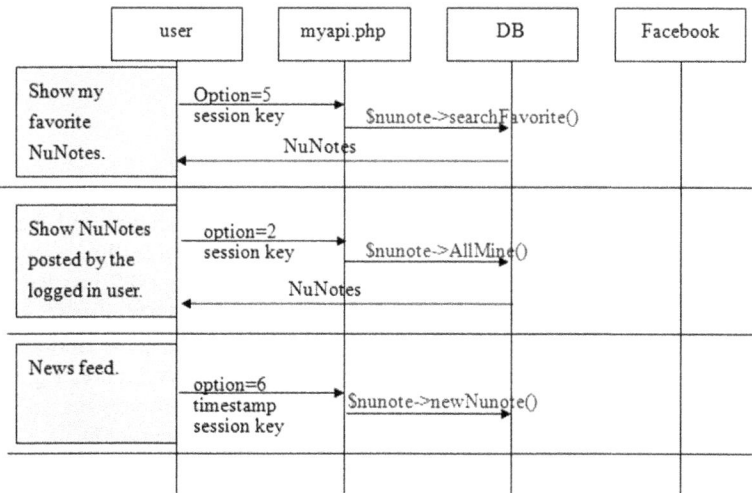

Fig. 8. Data communication between NuNote clients and server (cont.)

3   System Implementation

3.1   Database Design

Current version of NuNote server adopts MySQL as its database system; we are now porting the database to Hadoop system to test for large scalability. Fig. 9 shows the database schema. Five tables are created for storing users' data. The NuNote Table is the main table for storing notes. Fields in the table are self-explanatory. Comments on posted notes are stored in the Comment Table. When a user adds a note to his favorite list, the relation is recorded in the Favorite Table. When a user logged into Facebook through the NuNote login button, a tuple in the user table would be created or updated with the data imported from Facebook. The friend list table would also be loaded or updated from Facebook.

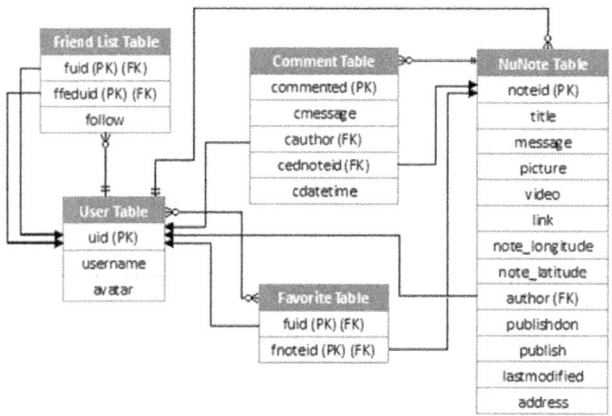

Fig. 9. Database schema for NuNote

3.2   Augmented Reality (AR)

As aforementioned, AR is achieved by overlaying notes on the live video captured by the smart phone's camera according to the user's current location and the location information associated with notes in NuNote. NuNote adopts three ways to get location information: GPS, AGPS or specified by users. Using GPS was the best way but it might consume more energy. If GPS is not available, AGPS might help. If both are not available, users could specify their location by tapping on Google Maps in map mode. The map has a layer translating the point to the corresponding longitude and latitude information. As location information is known to NuNote, when a user post a NuNote, his location will be tagged on the NuNote automatically.

When displaying notes on the screen, NuNote needs to which direction the user (camera) faces to, in addition to the user's location. This information can be obtained from the compass built in the smart phone. By adopting Android SDK version 1.5 (API Level 3) or later, the Sensor class in android hardware package has provided APIs for developers to read sensors [11]. In NuNote, we use the orientation sensor in the Sensor class. The orientation sensor class returns three values as arguments: azimuth, pitch and roll. By calculating the differences between the user's and a note's locations, a note's icon is then overlaid on the live video. Specifically, given the user's and a note's location and the Earth's radius, a triangular function is used to compute the angle difference between azimuth and magnetic north direction. If the difference approaches zero and a note is within the visible angle of the camera, the note is shown on the screen. Otherwise, the note is not displayed.

3.3 Facebook

When a user uses the login button to login, NuNote forwards the username and password to Facebook site using its authentication API for authentication. If the login is successful, an access token is returned which can be used to access the user's information. NuNote uses the access token to obtain the user's friend list or post a note to his Facebook wall.

4 Demonstration

In this section, we present two scenarios of using NuNote. The first scenario describes how NuNote could be used for commercial advertisements for stores. The second scenario demonstrates how NuNote could be used for situated learning in outdoor environment.

4.1 Commercial Advertisement

Have you seen stores hire works to deliver flyers on the street or put coupons in local newspapers? NuNote provides a more effective way for delivering flyers or coupons. First of all, a store manager uses the map mode to show his store location using his

Fig. 10. Store manager uses map mode to locate his store

smart phone or PC, as shown in Fig. 10. He then uses the add function to add a NuNote which contains the sale information (flyer or coupon), similar the one shown in Fig. 5. There are two ways for consumers to see the NuNote. First, the store manager could form a Facebook group such that the posted NuNote will also be posted on the group's Facebook wall and all members of the group will be able to see it. In this way, consumers could see the advertisement on the Internet. What is even better is to attract window shoppers. They usually go on the street with no target stores to shop. If they use the reality mode of NuNote, their shopping will be enriched with many vivid flyers and coupons displayed as NuNotes, as shown in Fig. 3. Image that a window shopper stands at the front of a store and see the NuNote that contains the sale information of the store, isn't it very attractive to the shopper? The reality mode provides a novel but interesting way for vivid advertising on the street.

4.2 Situated Learning

Situated learning has been one of the main applications of ubiquitous learning research. In the past, situated learning is made possible through the RFID technology. For example, students learn English by seeing objects in the real world. RFID tag is embedded to the learning objects and smart phone with RFID reader is used to know a learner is approaching a learning object such that learning activities can be evoked. However, the deployment of RFID tags and readers is tedious and expensive such that this kind of learning cannot be widespread around the world. NuNote provides an easy approach for situated learning. Let us use learning the plants on campus as an example.

Fig. 11. Instructor uses NuNote to add teaching material

Fig. 12. A NuNote contains teaching material

First of all, the instructor makes his instruction plan by collecting all the information of plants to be learned. He then carries a smart phone and walks to each plant to be learned. He uses NuNote map mode to locate the plant and add a NuNote for each plant, as shown in Fig. 11. The content of the note is the learning material or activities (quizzes, group discussion, etc), as shown in Fig. 12. It can consist of multimedia content, such as picture or video clip. The "comment" function when browsing a note provides students a basic tool for discussion. Besides, the integration of NuNote with Facebook further provides the interface for group discussion among students in a designated group. Students can also have further discussion after class through the Web interface of NuNote. The instructor could prepare an instructional design to group students or arrange the learning path.

After the preparation of teaching material and activities, the instructor can take the students outdoor for field teaching. Depends on the instructional design, students will be guided by the instructor or search for learning objects (plants) by themselves based on the notes shown on the map using the map mode, as shown in Fig. 13. When near a learning object, students can change NuNote to the reality mode which shows the real environment and notes to be learned, as shown in Fig. 14. For each plant to be learned, the students can click on the note to see the teaching material and instructions.

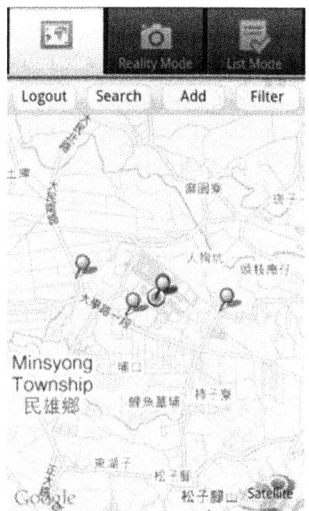

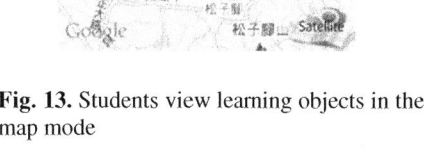

Fig. 13. Students view learning objects in the map mode

Fig. 14. Students view learning objects in the reality mode

5 Related Work and Software

5.1 Related Work

There are some studies on note posting service. GeoNotes provides posting text message and location-based information [12]. Place-Its is a reminder application that can post text note and set the note to be triggered upon arrival/departure of the associated place [13]. Either GeoNotes or Place-Its can only provide functions of posting text note and viewing the text of a note on the screen. In addition, NuNote also integrates with social network community.

Unlike previous studies, NuNote can post multimedia note. Furthermore, notes can be viewed in the augmented reality mode, map mode, or list mode. TABLE I shows the differences among NuNote, GeoNotes, and Place-Its.

Table 1. Difference between related works

	Viewing Note		MultiMedia Note	Integrated with Social Network
	AR	Nearby note		
GeoNotes	No	Yes	No	No
Place-Its	No	No	No	No
NuNote	Yes	Yes	Yes	Yes

5.2   Related Software

A. AirPainter [14]

AirPainter allows users to leave messages at a place. It is like daubing graffiti but it is fulfilled by AR. Messages can be deleted by the author or automatically by AirPainter after it expires. They can be seen by all users using it. Users can bind their preferences with a username or an e-mail address but it does not integrate social networking sites. Users can also limit the message detecting range through system settings. AirPainter detects messages by distance and sorts it by distance but is unable to search a message by title.

B. Layar [15]

Layar supports searching spots by keywords and divides information into a wide variety of categories. In its AR mode, brief information will show up on the screen automatically if it is related to the selected category. Besides, it can also trigger alerts when a user is around to get more details. However, it does not have manual locating function when GPS or AGPS is not available. As a consequence, it could keep waiting for location information. It also lacks integration with social networking sites and does not support users to publish a message or share with others.

C. hiPageSogo! [16]

It is a local service provided by Hinet in Taiwan. It also integrates AR with map and provides quite rich information about stores, tourist attractions and Wi-Fi hotspots. In addition, it allows a user to search an attraction with Google, and then provide route planning to guide the user his way to the destination. It also provides the user to make a phone call if a contact number of the attraction is available. The user can add an attraction to his favorite list or share it with friends via social networking site.

6 Conclusion and Future Works

In this paper, we present a novel Augmented Reality note posting service, referred to as NuNote, on Android smart phones. By integrating note posting service with location, map, AR, and social networking, NuNote offers many interesting features include multimedia notes associated with location, viewing cyberspace notes in physical world, sharing notes with friends, etc. NuNote is a service framework that could be applied to many interesting applications, such as leaving cyberspace notes on historic/scenery spots, flyers/coupons of stores, and situated learning as we described in this paper. NuNote is handy to use and well-designed such that it was selected as the best mobile service in a national contest with more than 600 competitive teams and won the best popularity prize in our department's senior project contest.

We are currently extending the features of NuNote. For example, it can now show friends nearby the user, positioning by taking pictures when the user is indoor, automatically identify cyberspace friends in reality, etc.

References

1. Wang, S., Min, J., Yi, B.K.: Location Based Services for Mobiles: Technologies and Standards. In: IEEE International Conference on Communication, ICC 2008, Beijing, China (2008)
2. Ma, X., Wei, Z., Chai, Y., Xie, K.: Integrating Map Services and Location-based Services for Geo-Referenced Individual Data Collection. In: Geoscience and Remote Sensing Symposium, Boston, MA, July 7-11 (2008)
3. Zhang, D., Guo, B., Li, B., Yu, Z.: Extracting Social and Community Intelligence from Digital Footprints: An Emerging Research Area. In: Yu, Z., Liscano, R., Chen, G., Zhang, D., Zhou, X. (eds.) UIC 2010. LNCS, vol. 6406, pp. 4–18. Springer, Heidelberg (2010)
4. Quercia, D., Ellis, J., Capra, L.: Nurturing Social Networks Using Mobile Phones. IEEE Pervasive Computing (2010)
5. Campbell, A.T., et al.: The Rise of People-Centric Sensing. IEEE Internet Computing 12(4), 12–21 (2008)
6. Murty, R., et al.: CitySense: A Vision for an Urban-Scale Wireless Networking Testbed. In: Proc. 2008 IEEE Int'l. Conf. Technologies for Homeland Security, pp. 583–588. IEEE Press, Los Alamitos (2008)
7. Chang, S.Y., Shih, Z.C.: Rendering Virtual Objects in Augmented Reality. In: Computer Graphics Workshop, December 6-7, pp. 50–54 (1996)
8. http://www.wikitude.org/en/drive
9. Facebook developers, http://developers.facebook.com/
10. JSON, http://www.json.org/
11. Access online at, http://developer.android.com/reference/android/hardware/Sensor.html
12. Espinoza, F., et al.: GeoNotes: Social and Navigational Aspects of Location-Based Information Systems. In: Abowd, G.D., Brumitt, B., Shafer, S. (eds.) UbiComp 2001. LNCS, vol. 2201, pp. 2–17. Springer, Heidelberg (2001)

13. Sohn, T., Li, K.A., Lee, G., Smith, I., Scott, J., Griswold, W.G.: Place-its: A study of location-based reminders on mobile phones. In: Beigl, M., Intille, S.S., Rekimoto, J., Tokuda, H. (eds.) UbiComp 2005. LNCS, vol. 3660, pp. 232–250. Springer, Heidelberg (2005)
14. Access online at, http://air.iwillnow.org/airpainter/index.htm
15. Access online at, http://layar.com/
16. Access online at,
    https://sites.google.com/a/myp.com.tw/hipagesogo/

A Context-Aware Seamless Handover Mechanism for Mass Rapid Transit System

Hung-Yi Teng, Ren-Hung Hwang, and Chang-Fu Tsai

Dept. of Computer Science and Information Engineering,
National Chung-Cheng University, Taiwan, R.O.C
{thy95p,rhhwang,tcf96m}@cs.ccu.edu.tw

Abstract. Internet users are now able to connect to the Internet anywhere at any time for the provision of ubiquitous wireless network. Furthermore, as IEEE 802.11 wireless networks have deployed widely, passengers of Mass Rapid Transit (MRT), one of the most popular transportation systems in modern cities nowadays, can access to the Internet through their mobile devices easily. However, MRT passengers bring massive simultaneous handovers to the system while they are getting on and off MRT coaches. Hence, mobility management becomes a challenging problem for ubiquitous Internet service in a MRT system. Although Mobile IPv6 (MIPv6) is designed to support IP mobility, several drawbacks of MIPv6 are reported and result in unacceptable handover latency. As a consequence, many proposals, such as Fast handovers for Mobile IPv6, Hierarchical Mobile IPv6 (HMIPv6), Fast Handover for Hierarchical MIPv6 (F-HMIPv6), and Proxy Mobile IPv6, have been proposed to tackle these drawbacks. Nevertheless, none of these proposals are adequate to cope with the large-number-simultaneous-handovers challenge. In this paper, we propose a context-aware seamless handover mechanism (C-HMIPv6) which solves the massive simultaneous handover problem based on the concept of context-awareness. C-HMIPv6 is based on HMIPv6 with following special designs. Firstly, distributed mobility anchor points (MAPs) are deployed to separate the loading of forwarding traffic. Secondly, every access router (AR) periodically exchanges mobile nodes (MNs') context with adjacent ARs and periodically broadcasts the network configuration of adjacent ARs to its MNs. Thus, all MNs and ARs are fully context-awareness in the MRT system. The MN is able to generate its new CoA prior to the actual handover and skip IEEE 802.11 channel scanning, which alleviate the majority of the handover latency. The old AR can notify the MN's MAP to take care of the MN's packets during the handover procedure while the new AR can perform binding update on behalf of the MNs. In C-HMIPv6, MNs do not need to participate in sending any related IP mobility signaling. As a result, seamless handover can be achieved even when a large number of MNs perform handover simultaneously. The performance of C-HMIPv6 and F-HMIPv6 is evaluated via simulations. The simulation results show that C-HMIPv6 is able to provide better performance in terms of handoff delay, packet delay and packet loss rate than F-HMIPv6.

Keywords: Mass Rapid Transit, Mobility Management, Context-aware, Massive Simultaneous Handover, Hierarchical Mobile IPv6.

C.-H. Hsu et al. (Eds.): UIC 2011, LNCS 6905, pp. 109–123, 2011.
© Springer-Verlag Berlin Heidelberg 2011

1 Introduction

One of the key technologies to support ubiquitous computing is ubiquitous network by which users can connect to the network and enjoy context-aware services anywhere at any time. Although wired networks provide better network bandwidth, they cannot provide network service to mobile users anywhere at any time. On the other hand, with the support of mobility, wireless networks become the key technology to achieve ubiquitous network service. However, ubiquitous network service is still difficult to provide for some daily activities in our life by current wireless technology. For example, Mass Rapid Transit (MRT) system has become one of the most important transportation systems in modern cities nowadays. With wireless networks, MRT passengers can access to the Internet any time they want through their mobile devices. However, MRT system has its unique working scenario and its own user behavior patterns which create obstacles in providing ubiquitous network service.

First of all, parts of the MRT system are built underground and the speed of a MRT train is averagely between 70 to 100 km/h. Consequently, the quality of large-coverage wireless access technologies such as IEEE 802.16 or 3.5G/3G would be varied significantly according to the location of the mobile nodes, which may cause unstable service quality. In order to deal with these challenges, deploying IEEE 802.11 wireless networks within a MRT system has becoming a practical solution to the current situation. The IEEE 802.11 access points are deployed elaborately in every MRT station and MRT train. The connections of the mobile nodes can remain stable regardless the mobile nodes are at a MRT station or on a running MRT train. Thus, we assume IEEE 802.11 wireless LAN is adopted as the access wireless network technology in this study.

Secondly, on a MRT system, massive simultaneous handovers frequently occur because of a large number of MRT passengers getting on and off coaches simultaneously. There is often a short period of time that a mobile node cannot send or receive any packets during handover. This time period is defined as handover latency. Longer handover latency will lead to intolerable service quality, particularly in real-time services. The large-number-simultaneous-handovers phenomenon will lead to significant increment of the handover latency due to the limited capacity, as well as contention, of the wireless media. Moreover, it is possible that MRT passengers may switch MRT trains several times until they reach their destination. Then the mobile nodes may frequently experience such handovers as mentioned above and their connections would be seriously interrupted or disconnected. Therefore, how to reduce the handover latency for the mobile nodes within a MRT system is a critical issue.

Managing handover at the IP layer has been well studied in the research community in order to support end-to-end connectivity for mobile nodes. Mobile IPv6 (MIPv6) [1], an IETF RFC, is the basic protocol which provides IP mobility. With MIPv6, each mobile node has a static home network address which is obtained from its home network. While a mobile node roams to a visiting network, it updates its home agent with information about its current IP address (Care-of-Address, CoA). The home agent is responsible for intercepting all packets destined to the mobile node and tunneling intercepted packets to the mobile node's current address. Thus, the connections of the mobile node can be kept alive wherever it roams to. Unfortunately, the flaws in MIPv6 are reported and result in unacceptable handover latency. As a consequence, many proposals, such as Fast handovers for Mobile IPv6 [2], Hierarchical Mobile IPv6 [3] (HMIPv6), Fast Handover for Hierarchical MIPv6 [4] (F-HMIPv6), and Proxy Mobile IPv6 [5], have been proposed to tackle these drawbacks. However, none of these proposals are adequate to cope with the large-number-simultaneous-handovers phenomenon.

In this paper, we present C-HMIPv6, a context-aware seamless handover mechanism, which is capable of dealing the large-number-simultaneous-handovers phenomenon in a MRT system. C-HMIPv6 is based on HMIPv6 with two special designs: distributed MAPs and context-awareness. Firstly, mobile nodes register with the MAP at their entrance station as its local home agent. As a result, packet forwarding loads are distributed among MAPs of all MRT stations. Secondly, each access router periodically exchanges its mobile nodes' context with adjacent access routers and periodically broadcasts the network configuration of the adjacent access routers to its mobile nodes. Based on the announced or exchanged context, the mobile nodes and the access routers can be fully aware of the context and then can react properly to the handover procedure. In C-HMIPv6, the mobile nodes do not need to participate in sending any related IP mobility signaling. Therefore, seamless handover can be achieved even when massive simultaneous handovers occur. The performance of C-HMIPv6 and F-HMIPv6 is evaluated via simulations. The simulation results show that C-HMIPv6 provides better performance in terms of handoff delay, packet delay, and packet loss rate than F-HMIPv6.

The rest of this paper is organized as follows. Section 2 provides the related work. Our approach is presented in Section 3. Section 4 evaluates performance of the proposed approach via simulations. Conclusions are finally drawn in Section 5.

2   Related Work

2.1   Fast Handovers for Mobile IPv6 (FMIPv6)

The main idea of FMIPv6 is providing a mobile node (MN) with IP layer (L3) information of the subnet it is about to move to. The basic operation of FMIPv6 is illustrated in Figure 1. The previous access router (PAR) is defined as the router to which the MN is currently attached while the new access router (NAR) as the router to which the MN is going to visit. FMIPv6 is launched by a link-layer (L2) trigger indicating the MN will execute handover soon. Upon receiving the L2 trigger, the MN sends a *RtSolPr* message to the PAR. The *RtSolPr* contains the MAC address of the new attachment points. In response, the PAR will send the MN a *PrRtAdv* message indicating the status of the new attachment points (unknown, known or known but connected through the same access router). Furthermore, it may specify the network prefix of the NAR in the message. Based on the response, the MN generates a new CoA by the stateless address configuration [6]. Subsequently, the MN sends the PAR a *FBU* message to bind the current CoA to the new CoA. The MN then receives a *FBack* message either via the oAR or the nAR to indicate a successful binding. The PAR also sends a duplicated *FBack* message to the NAR in order to ensure that the MN receives the *FBack* message. Finally, the MN sends a *UNA* message to initiate the data flow at the NAR. In addition to the message exchange with the MN, the PAR sends a *HI* message to the NAR. The *HI* message contains MN's new CoA and the MN's current CoA. If the new CoA is accepted by the NAR, the PAR sets up a temporary tunnel to the new CoA. Otherwise, the PAR will tunnel packets destined for the MN to the NAR. The NAR will temporarily buffer the forwarding packets for the MN. FMIPv6 aims to eliminate the movement detection latency and the CoA acquisition latency. This is made possible for the MN announces actively of its attachment after attaching the new link and configures new CoA before the handover actually occurs. Unfortunately, FMIPv6 yields an unacceptable handover latency when the massive simultaneous handovers take place. It is because each MN has to send signaling messages such as *RtSolPr*, *FBU* and *UNA*. Therefore the wireless media will be very congested. Moreover, MNs may not have enough time to perform the so called *"predictive"* fast handover due to MRT passengers getting on and off coaches very quickly.

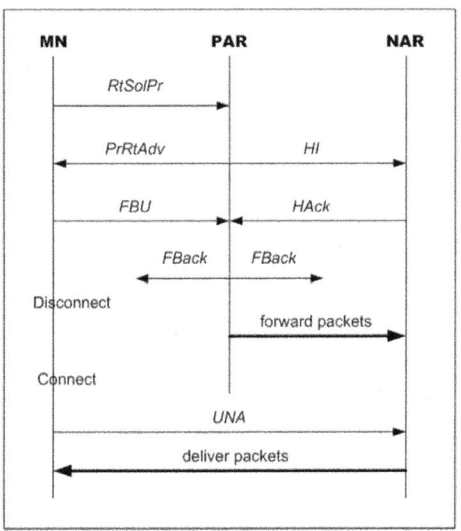

Fig. 1. Handover operation of FMIP

2.2   Hierarchical Mobile IPv6 (HMIPv6)

HMIPv6 [3] is another extension of MIPv6 that aims to reduce the binding update latency. HMIPv6 introduces a hierarchy of Mobility Anchor Points (MAPs) to separate mobility into intra-domain mobility and inter-domain mobility. The MAP is normally placed at the edge of a network, above a set of access routers, which constitute its network domain. It could be a router or a set of routers that maintains a binding between itself and MNs within its network domain. Thus, when a MN attaches itself to a new network, it is required to register with the MAP. The MAP intercepts all the packets addressed to the MN and tunnels them to the MN's on-link care-of-address (LCoA). If the MN roams to other access routers within the same MAP domain, only a local binding with the MAP is required. Thus, the binding update latency can be reduced significantly. If a MN roams into a separate MAP domain, it needs to acquire a new regional address (RCoA) as well as LCoA. After obtaining these addresses, the MN sends a regular MIPv6 binding update to the MAP, which will bind the MN's RCoA to the LCoA. In response, the MAP will return a *BAck* message to the MN. Moreover, the MN must also register its new RCoA with its home agent by sending another binding update that specifies the binding between its home address and the new RCoA. Finally, it may send a binding update to its current corresponding nodes. When HMIPv6 is employed in a MRT system, the boundary of a MAP domain needs to be defined carefully. If the entire MRT system is defined as a MAP domain and only a MAP is deployed, the MAP will become the performance bottleneck for it requires intercepting and forwarding all packets to all mobile nodes. If each MRT station is defined as a MAP domain, mobile nodes need to perform the registration procedure frequently during its journey. As a result, the mobile nodes' connections would likely to be interrupted because of their frequent handover.

Later on, Fast Handover for Hierarchical MIPv6 (F-HMIPv6) [4] that incorporates the concepts of HMIPv6 and FMIPv6 has proposed. Hsieh and Seneviratne [7] show that F-HMIPv6 significantly reduces the overall handoff latency to around 300 to 400 milliseconds. However, similar to FMIPv6, each MN has to send signaling messages so the handover latency increased greatly when the massive simultaneous handovers occur.

2.3 Proxy Mobile IPv6 (PMIPv6)

PMIPv6 [5] is another approach to provide IP mobility support. This approach supports mobility without requiring the MN to participate in any IP mobility related signaling. The mobility entities in the network will track the MN's movements and perform the mobility signaling on behalf of the MN. The core entities of PMIPv6 are the Local Mobility Anchor (LMA) and the Mobile Access Gateway (MAG). The LMA is responsible for maintaining the MN's binding and routing state while the MAG is responsible for tracking the MN's movements and initiating binding registrations to the MN's LMA. When a MN enters the PMIPv6 domain, it sends the MAG a Router Solicitation (*RtSol*) message. For updating the current location of the MN, the MAG sends a *PBU* message to the MN's LMA. Upon receiving the message, the LMA sends a *PBA* message including the MN's home network prefix(es). Meanwhile, a bi-directional tunnel between the LMA and the MAG is set up. Subsequently, the MAG sends Router Advertisement messages to the MN for advertising the MN's home network prefix(es). Based on these messages, the MN is able to generate its home address (HoA) using either stateful or stateless address configuration.

When the MN changes its point of attachment, the MAG on the previous link (p-MAG) will detect the MN's detachment from the link. It then sends the LMA a *DeReg PBU* message to remove the binding and routing state for the MN. In response, the LMA will send a *PBA* message back to the p-MAG. Upon detecting the MN on its access link, the MAG on the new link (n-MAG) will signal the LMA to update the binding and routing state. MN will perform a router discovery by sending *RtSol* message to n-MAG. Subsequently, the MAG replies a Router Advertisement message containing the MN's home network prefix(es) and this will ensure the MN does not aware of any layer 3 changes. However, when a large number of MNs perform handover simultaneously, the n-MAG must send the Router Advertisement message one by one to the all MNs because each MN's home network prefix is unique. Therefore, the n-MAG would have to send the Router Advertisement massage a thousand times if there is a thousand MNs perform handover simultaneously, which may greatly increase the handover latency. Furthermore, the operation of sending *RtSol* to n-MAG may also cause wireless media congestion. And, detection of detachment and attachment of the MN is not defined in PMIPv6. A number of the packets will lose if the detached event of the p-MAG is triggered slowly.

Clearly, up to date, there is relatively little research work conducted on handover management for MRT system.

3   Context-Aware Seamless Handover Mechanism

3.1   Network Architecture of A MRT system

Figure 2 depicts the proposed network architecture for a MRT system. In the network architecture, each MRT station and each MRT train is equipped with a MAP and an access router (AR). The number of ARs that each MRT station and each MRT train should be deployed according to the traffic demand and is outside the scope of this paper. We assume that all ARs are equipped with a module that allows ARs to perform IEEE 802.11 access point (AP) functions. The AR in a MRT train is connected with the backbone network via fiber network or power-line network which is deployed on rails [6]. Mobile nodes (MN), regardless at a MRT station or in a MRT train, are able to access the Internet after associating with the AR. Every MN only registers with the MAP located in its entrance station. The registration procedure is described in Section 3.4 in detail. This MAP acts as the MN's local home agent (LHA) in the MRT system, which intercepts the MN's packets and forwards them to the MN. In other words, for each MN, the MAP hierarchy of the MRT system is a two-level hierarchy with its LHA as the root of the hierarchy and all other MAPs as the children of the LHA. The MN's RCoA is obtained from the router advertisement of the LHA and will remain

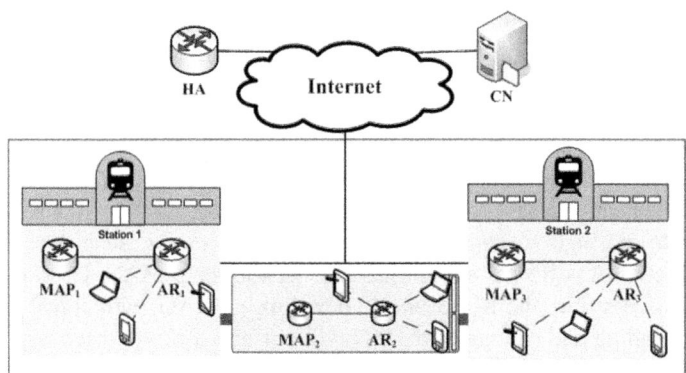

Fig. 2. The proposed network architecture for a MRT system

unchanged as long as it is in the MRT system. When the MN moves and is associated to another MAP, it only changes its LCoA. With route optimization, packets from corresponding nodes will send to the LHA first and then be forwarded via tunneling to the MN. As a consequence, different MNs entering the MRT system from different entrance stations will have different view of the MAP hierarchy.

3.2 Context Dissemination and Management

C-HMIPv6 aims to eliminate most of the handover latencies for the MNs within the MRT system by emphasizing the concept of context-awareness. Each AR has the responsibility to periodically exchange its context to all neighbor ARs via the neighbor advertisement message. The number of neighbor ARs is small because the adjacent ARs only include the ARs in the incoming MRT trains and the ARs in the nearby MRT stations. Thus, the amount of traffic caused by exchange of context brings a limited influence to the data traffic. All received contexts are maintained by the context tables (router table and node table). The context table can be implemented as a hash table over a sorted linked list which gives time complexity of $O(1)$ of a record lookup. Each record of the context table has a predefined lifetime. The record will be removed from the table when its timer expired. The context exchanged among ARs includes:

- **Router Context (c_{router})**: Router context consists of network prefix, global address of the corresponding AR, the current QoS status, etc. Based on our assumption, ARs are able to perform IEEE 802.11 access point functions, so IEEE 802.11 channel frequency and Service Set Identifier (SSID) are included.
- **Node Context (c_{node})**: Information related to the MN such as the MAC address, the LCoA, the LHA's IP address, and the user's preference profile are included.

Moreover, each AR periodically broadcasts the router context which includes all adjacent ARs' context to its MNs via the router advertisement message. Thus, the MNs can obtain the context of the ARs in the incoming MRT trains and the ARs in the nearby MRT stations prior to the actual handover. Each MN also has a router table to maintain the received context.

3.3 Handover Operation

When a MN enters its entrance station, the router advertisement message containing information about the MAP can be received. Upon receiving the router advertisement message, the MN configures its care-of-addresses (RCoA and LCoA) and registers with the MAP by sending a registration message. In C-HMIPv6, RCoA and LCoA, which are addresses on the MAP's subnet based on the prefix in the router advertisement message from the MAP, could be the same and formed in a stateless manner [6]. (LCoA will be changed later on when the MN moves to the range of other ARs.) A binding cache entry at the MAP and a bi-directional tunnel between the MN and the MAP are established after a successful registration. Acting as the MN's LHA, the MAP will forward all packets sent by MN to the CNs and vice versa. The MN's LHA is fixed to the MAP at the entrance station until the MN leaves the MRT system. In other words, the MN does not need to change its RCoA as it travels to other MRT stations.

Figure 3 depicts the handover operations of C-HMIPv6 in detail. Recall that before the MN actually handovers to the new AR (nAR), the nAR will periodically receive the context of adjacent ARs which includes the old AR (oAR) via the neighbor advertisement messages. The MN periodically receives the context of adjacent ARs sent by the old AR (oAR) via the router advertisement messages. The handover operations are described as follows.

1. When a MN disassociated with the oAR (trigger by layer 2), the oAR locates the MN's LHA IP address by looking up its router context table and sends a handover notification message to the MN's LHA. Upon accepting the handover notification, the MN's LHA sends a notification-ACK message to the oAR and then stops forwarding the MN's packets to the oAR. Subsequently, the MN's packets are buffered at the LHA for a predefined time period. If the LHA does not receive any Local Binding Update message within the given amount of time, it will delete the MN's binding cache entry and the MN's packets.

2. Based on the latest received router context, the MN uses the channel frequency and SSID to perform IEEE 802.11 association procedure with the new AR (nAR) without the channel scanning overhead. Without the procedure of scanning all channels, a significant IEEE 802.11 handover latency is thus reduced. In general, the IEEE 802.11 channel scanning takes about 400ms~800ms, depending on the channel conditions and the wireless NIC manufacturer 8. After associating with the nAR, the MN uses nAR's network prefix and its MAC address to generate its new LCoA by EUI-64 [6]. Since the nAR maintains context of all MNs, it is able to decide whether the formed LCoA of the coming MN is duplicated or not. In case of duplications, the nAR will assign a new IP address to the MN. Therefore, the MN is allowed to use the new LCoA immediately in most of cases.

3. Meanwhile, the nAR also uses its prefix and the MN's MAC address to generate the MN's new LCoA. It then looks for the MN's LHA IP address in the node table using the MN's MAC address. Lastly, the nAR sends a Local Binding Update (*LBU*) on behalf of the MN to the MN's LHA. In response, the MN's LHA will send a *LBU-ACK* message to the nAR, which indicates the binding between the MN's RCoA and the MN's new LCoA is successful updated.

4. The nAR notifies the MN that the handover is completed by sending a welcome message via a router advertisement message. In case of address duplications, this router advertisement message will include a new LCoA generated by the nAR. The MN resumes sending/receiving packets normally. Finally, the nAR sends the MN's context (MAC address, LCoA, and IP address of LHA) to the adjacent ARs via the neighbor advertisement message. Therefore, the adjacent ARs can be aware of the MN's context prior to the actual handover.

In C-HMIPv6, the ARs and the MNs are fully aware of the context. Therefore, the MNs do not participate in sending any related IP mobility signaling and do not require IEEE 802.11 scanning channels. When massive simultaneous handovers take place, every MN's handover procedure is able to be seamless.

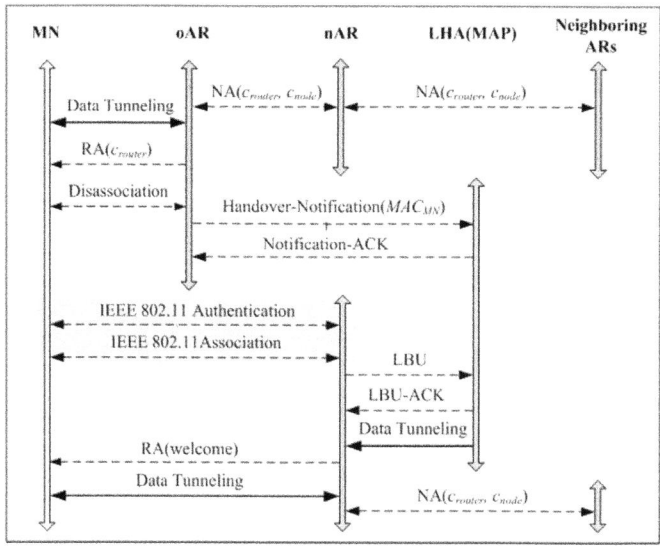

Fig. 3. Handover operation of C-HMIPv6

4 Performance Evaluation

In this section, we evaluate the performance of C-HMIPv6 and F-HMIPv6 via simulations. We used the Network Simulator (NS2) [10] as the simulator. We implemented C-HMIPv6 protocol for NS2 and incorporated F-HMIPv6 implementations [11] to support the simulation comparison. Figure 4 shows the simulated MRT system that consists of five MRT stations and four MRT trains. Figure 5 show the network topology used for the experiments of C-HMIPv6 and F-HMIPv6 respectively. There are five MAPs deployed in the simulation of C-HMIPv6 while only a MAP is deployed in the simulation of F-HMIPv6. Every MRT station and MRT train deploys an AR. Train 1 (AR 6) and train 4 (AR 7) move between the station 1 (AR 1), station 3 (AR 3), and station 5 (AR 5) while the train 2 (AR 8) and train 3 (AR 9) moves between the station 2 (AR 2), station 3, and station 4 (AR 4). All of the trains are scheduled to depart the source station and move to the destination station every 10 seconds. The travel time between two stations is 60 seconds. The link characteristics (bandwidth and delay) are shown on the link. The source station and destination station of each passenger is randomly selected. A pair of CBR source and sink agents are attached to the CN and MN respectively. Although the simulated MRT system is simplified, it does capture all moving patterns that we are interested to observe. For example, large number of passengers will change trains at station 3.

Our simulations are divided into two scenarios. The first scenario is that the passengers (MNs) arrive at the stations of the MRT system according to a Poisson process (scenario 1). Each passenger randomly chooses one of the stations, except the entrance station, as his destination. Passengers may need to change train at station 3 in order to get to his destination. For example, a passenger may take train 1 first and then train 3 if his entrance station and destination station are station 1 and station 2, respectively. The other scenario is that passengers simultaneously arrive at four randomly selected stations and all travel to the same destination station which is the station other than the four entrance stations (scenario 2). In both scenarios, the number of simultaneous handovers is significantly large for the purpose of this study. The performance metrics that we are interested are handoff delay, packet delay, and packet loss rate.

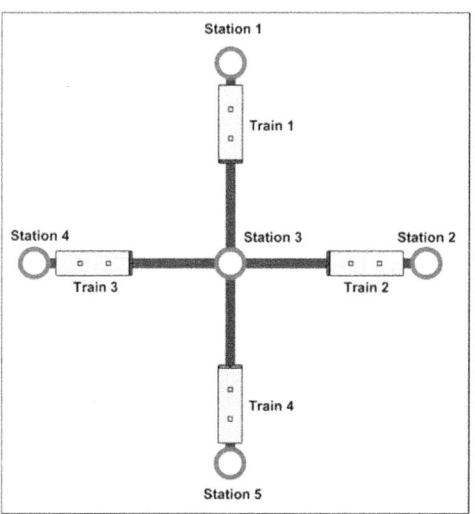

Fig. 4. Scenario of the simulated MRT system

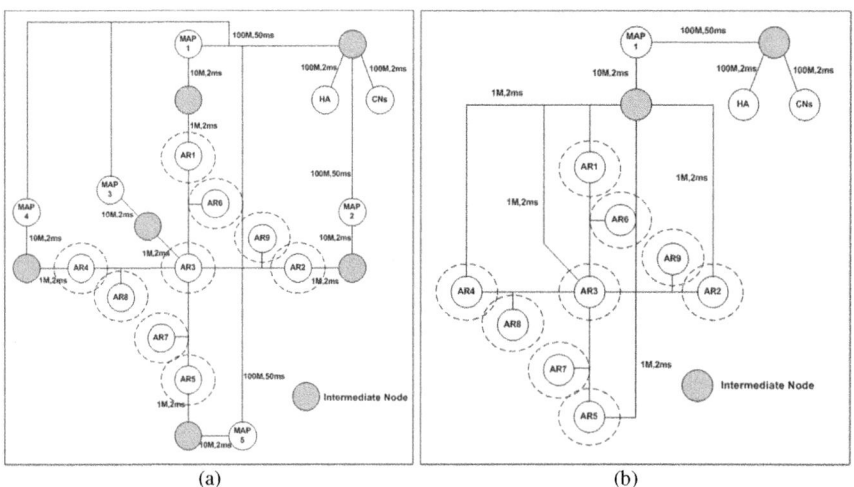

Fig. 5. Simulation Network topology of C-HMIPv6 (a) and F-HMIPv6 (b)

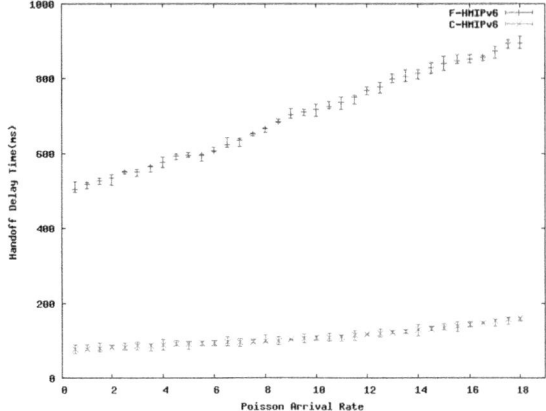

Fig. 6. Handoff delay with Poisson arrival

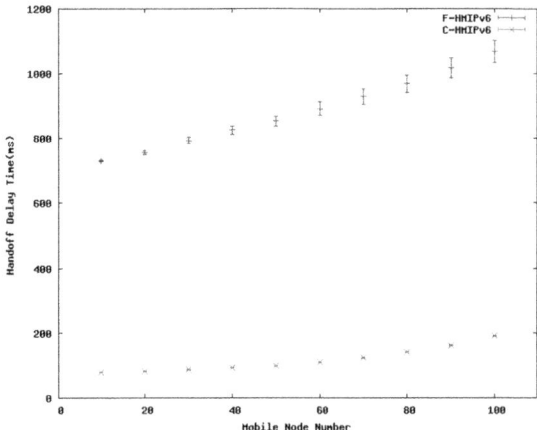

Fig. 7. Handoff delay with simultaneous arrival

4.1 Handoff Delay

Firstly, we observe and compare the handoff delay of C-HMIPv6 and F-HMIPv6. Long handoff delay will seriously interrupt the services of the MNs. Figure 6 and Figure 7 show the handoff delay of C-HMIPv6 and F-HMIPv6 with the Poisson arrival scenario and the simultaneous arrival scenario respectively. Apparently, the handoff delay of C-HMIPv6 is far less than that of F-HMIPv6 in both scenarios. In the Poisson arrival scenario, the average handoff delay of C-HMIPv6 and F-HMIPv6 are 80ms and 502ms respectively when the arrival rate is 1 MN per second (MN/s). In other words, the average handoff delay of C-HMIPv6 is approximately only 16% of F-HMIPv6. Similarly, the average handoff delay of C-HMIPv6 is approximately 11% of F-HMIPv6 (79ms and 718ms) when there are 10 MNs simultaneously arrivals. The rationale is as follows. Firstly, based on the received context, the MNs are able to avoid channel scanning latency and generate the new CoA prior to the actual handover. Secondly, the nAR is designed to send binding update on behalf of the MNs by using the received node context. Therefore, C-HMIPv6 can provide very low handoff delay for the MNs when they travel within the MRT system. But, in F-HMIPv6, the MNs have to perform two round-trip signaling (*RtsolPr/PrRtAdv* and *FBU/FBack*) with its MAP during the handover procedure. So, the F-HMIPv6 causes a significant handoff delay. Furthermore, the average handoff delay of F-HMIPv6 significantly increases as the arrival rate increases to 18 MN/s in scenario 1 (886ms) or the number of the MNs increases to 100 in scenario 2 (1174ms). It is because the MNs are difficult to obtain the wireless resource when the number of signaling messages significantly increases. However, the average handoff delay of C-HMIPv6 slightly increases due to the fact that MNs do not need to participate in any IP-related signaling during the handovers.

4.2   Packet Delay

Real-time applications are sensitive to the packet delay. Next, we observe the packet delays of the two protocols. Figure 8 and Figure 9 show the packet delay of C-HMIPv6 and F-HMIPv6 with the Poisson arrival scenario and the simultaneous arrival scenario, respectively. In the Poisson arrival scenario, the packet delay of F-HMIPv6 significantly increases from 80ms to 202ms as the arrival rate increases from 1 MN/s to 18 MN/s. Since only one MAP is set for the whole MRT system in F-HMIPv6, the MAP easily becomes the performance bottleneck. The packet delay of C-HMIPv6 is between 75ms and 105ms in the same scenario. It is because the distributed MAP deployment of C-HMIPv6 and each MN only needs to register with the MAP at its source station which acts as its LHA. We obtain the similar result in the simultaneous arrival scenario. The packet delay of F-HMIPv6 rapidly increases from 108ms to 248ms when the number of MNs is increased from 10 to 100. However, the packet delay of C-HMIPv6 is around 100ms regardless the number of the MNs. It shows that C-HMIPv6 is more scalable than the F-HMIPv6 and can provide better quality for real-time applications.

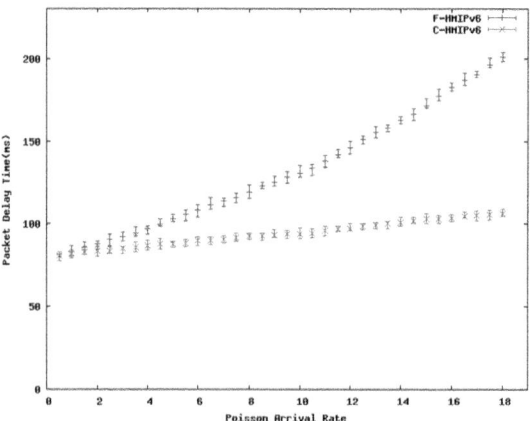

Fig. 8. Packet delay with Poisson arrival

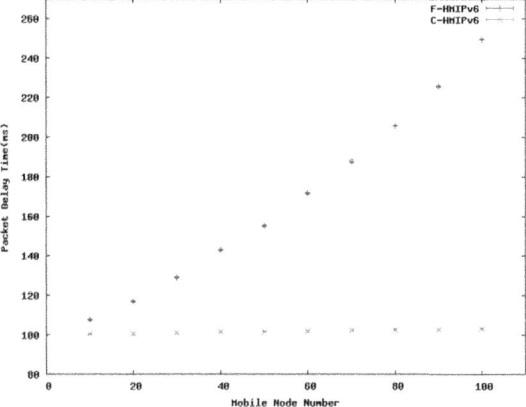

Fig. 9. Packet delay with simultaneous arrival

4.3 Packet Loss Rate

Lastly, we observe the packet loss rate. Figure 10 and Figure 11 show the packet loss rate of C-HMIPv6 and F-HMIPv6 under different buffer size of the MAP with the Poisson arrival scenario and the simultaneous arrival scenario respectively. Results in both scenarios still exhibit similar trend. Due to the handover delay of C-HMIPv6 is less than that of F-HMIPv6, the packet loss rate of C-HMIPv6 is also less than that of F-HMIPv6 in the both scenarios. Another factor that influences the packet loss rate is the buffer size of the MAP. Obviously, the packet loss rate is significantly decreased when the buffer size of the MAP increases. However, the MAPs do not require a large buffer to provide lower packet loss rate in C-HMIPv6.

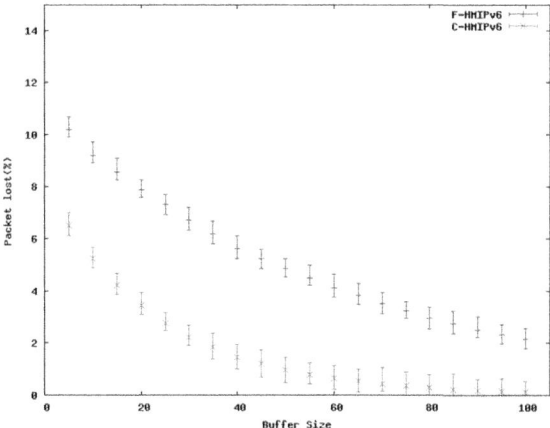

Fig. 10. Packet loss rate with Poisson arrival

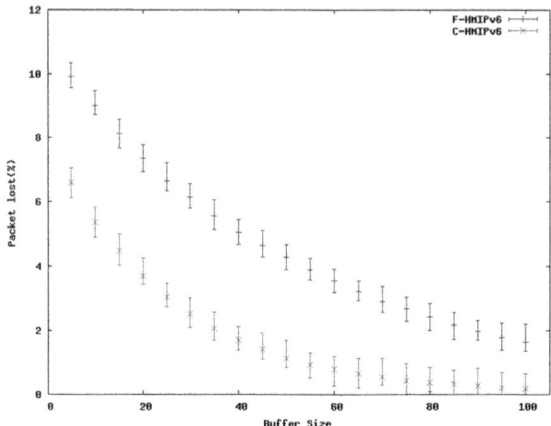

Fig. 11. Packet loss rate with simultaneous arrival

5 Conclusion

In this paper, we proposed a context-aware handover mechanism (C-HMIPv6) for MRT system, which emphasizes on the concept of context-awareness to support a large number of simultaneous handovers. Following approaches are adopted for the above purpose. Firstly, the loading of forwarding traffic of the MAP is scattered by the distributed MAP deployment. Secondly, every AR periodically exchanges the context with adjacent ARs and periodically broadcasts the context to its MN. All MNs and ARs are able to be fully aware of the context. The MN is able to generate its new CoA prior to the actual handover and skip IEEE 802.11 channel scanning, which alleviate the majority of the handover latency. The old AR can notify the MN's MAP to cache the MN's packets during the handover while the new AR can perform binding update on behalf of MNs. Moreover, MNs do not participate in sending any related IP mobility signaling. Therefore, seamless handover can be achieved even with a large number of MRT passengers perform handover simultaneously. The performance of C-HMIPv6 and F-HMIPv6 is demonstrated via simulations, which indicates that the handover delay of C-HMIPv6 is much less than that of F-HMIPv6. So is the packet delay. Moreover, C-HMIPv6 is capable of providing lower packet loss rate than F-HMIPv6 under the same size of MAP buffer.

References

1. Johnson, Perkins, C., Arkko, J.: Mobility Support in IPv6. RFC 3775, IETF (June 2004)
2. Koodli, R. (ed.): Mobile IPv6 Fast Handovers. RFC 5568, IETF (July 2005)
3. Soliman, H., El Malki, K., Bellier, L.: Hierarchical Mobile IPv6 (HMIPv6) Mobility Management (HMIPv6). RFC 5380, IETF (October 2008)
4. Jung, H.-Y., et al.: Fast Handover for Hierarchical MIPv6. Draft draft-jung-mobopts-fhmipv6-00.txt, IETF (April 2005)
5. Gundavelli, S., et al.: Proxy Mobile IP. RFC 5213, IETF (August 2008)

6. Thomson, S., Narten, T.: IPv6 Stateless Address Autoconfiguration, RFC 4862, IETF (September 2007)
7. Hsieh, R., Seneviratne, A.: Performance analysis on Hierarchical Mobile IPv6 with Fast-handoff over TCP. In: IEEE Global Telecommunications Conference, pp. 2488–2492. IEEE Press, New York (2002)
8. WLAN Enables Constant Connectivity Between Moving Trains and Trackside, http://www.moxa.com/applications/WLAN_Enables_Constant_ Connectivity_between_Moving_Trains_and_Trackside.htm
9. Mishra, A., Shin, M., Arbaugh, W.: An Empirical Analysis of the IEEE 802.11 MAC Layer Handover Process. ACM Computer Communication Review 33(2), 93–102 (2002)
10. The Network Simulator - ns-2, http://www.isi.edu/nsnam/ns/
11. Hsieh, R., Seneviratne, A.: A comparison of mechanisms for improving Mobile IP handoff latency for end-to-end TCP. In: 9th Annual International Conference on Mobile Computing and Networking, pp. 29–41. ACM, New York (2003)

Individual Activity Data Mining and Appropriate Advice Giving towards Greener Lifestyles and Routines

Toshihiro Tamura[1], Runhe Huang[2], Jianhua Ma[2], and Shiqin Yang[1]

[1] Graduate School of Computer and Information Sciences, Hosei University,
3-7-2 Kajino-cho, Koganei-shi, Tokyo 184-8584, Japan
{toshihiro.tamura.3k,shiqin.yang.jk}@stu.hosei.ac.jp
[2] Faculty of Computer and Information Sciences, Hosei University, 3-7-2 Kajino-cho,
Koganei-shi, Tokyo 184-8584, Japan
{rhuang,jianhua}@hosei.ac.jp

Abstract. Energy conservation and CO2 emission reduction have both recently become critical environmental issues. Despite the considerable efforts of governments and technological developments by private enterprise, such as energy saving appliances and solar power systems, CO2 emissions per household are still increasing. Continued effort not only from companies, but also from each household and individuals is necessary. This paper describes a smart home system that is aware of household situations, performs automatic energy conservation when necessary, mines data on individual activities and gives advice and suggestions to individuals. Initially, the system records related objects and domestic human activities and structures and places the recorded data into three data logs: a space log, a device log, and a person log. Secondly, the system recognizes a device- or appliance-related situation and deduces individual activities by applying data mining techniques to the structured data logs. Finally, the system automatically conserves energy according to situation and gives appropriate advice to individuals by making them aware of their activities. A long-term objective of this system is to build a perception-influence relational model with which the system can adopt personalized presentation styles to give personalized advice to different individuals. It is expected that people's behavior under this system will shift imperceptibly towards lifestyles and domestic routines that conserve energy and reduce CO2 emissions.

Keywords: data mining, multi-agents, personalized advice, green life style, activity log.

1   Introduction

Energy conservation and CO2 emission reduction are environmental issues which have increasingly become a concern worldwide. In fact, many organizations and companies have put a great deal of effort into developing ecological systems; for example, energy saving home appliances, hybrid cars and solar lighting systems. Taking air conditioners as an example, the amount of CO2 emissions per hour for comparable types of air-conditioners in 2009 is about 2/3rds that in 1995 [1], which

C.-H. Hsu et al. (Eds.): UIC 2011, LNCS 6905, pp. 124–136, 2011.

shows a significant decrease. However, in Japan annual CO2 emissions from households are still increasing. Therefore, efforts not only from companies, but also from each household and each individual are important and necessary. It is a fact that Japanese people have little knowledge of the concrete details on which actions, activities, or habits lead to energy waste or how much energy particular actions waste. It would be a positive development if there were a smart system that could remind or warn one if an action tends to lead to wasting energy, and advised one on how to avoid this energy waste.

This paper presents such a system in which each individual's daily life is monitored. Three structured data logs; a space log, a device log, and a person log sort and store data according to categories of space, device, and person. Details of situations and human activities are extracted with data mining techniques. A multi-agent system becomes aware of situations and makes inferences about individual activities. As a result, the system gives individuals appropriate advice, reminders or warnings. This system is actually aimed at imperceptibly influencing people toward greener lifestyles and habits as its final goal.

2   Related Work

With advances in wireless communication and sensor device technologies, ubiquitous computing has come into its own. In particular, smart home or space systems have been attracting a great deal of attention. Since building a real world home or space is expensive, there are many technologies that simulate these in so-called virtual homes or spaces. Ubiquitous Home [2] and GAIA [3] are two test platforms for virtual homes. UbiWise [4] and UbiREAL [5] are two simulators of smart virtual spaces.

Multi-agent systems are not a new development, but have been designed for practical use in many applications, such as providing smart functionalities in a smart environment and providing personalized services in a cyber system. No matter what applications it is used for, a multi-agent system requires a platform on top of which multiple agents can work smoothly, efficiently and effectively. MABS is a multi-agent based simulation [6], which has to be implemented on a multi-agent platform. Java Agent Development Framework (JADE) [7], and Universal Description Discovery and Integration (UDDI) [8] are examples of representative multi-agent platforms for agent management, communication and information services.

One of the problems in the processing of situation awareness is handling huge amounts of recorded data like classifying, clustering, or grouping data, which are involved with calculating so-called "distances" between a new item and items or collections of items. Three main approaches are Euclidean distance-based like K-Means [9], K-Modes [10], and Fuzzy C-Mean (FCM) [11], Mahalanobis distance-based [12], and kernel-based. Each of them has pros and cons. Euclidean distance has a straightforward geometric interpretation, but is blind to correlated variables. The kernel-based approach is sophisticated but too complex. This research adopted Mahalanobis distance, which takes into account the covariance among the variables in calculating distances, without using too complex a model.

3   Simulation and Visualization of Energy and CO_2

3.1   A Simulated Home

To build a physical home is too expensive, so this research uses a simulated home. To make people aware of the amount of energy consumption and CO_2 emission, the simulated home simulates the performance of each device or appliance and calculates its energy consumption and CO_2 emission. The left side of Fig.1 is an example of a home layout. The right side shows the dynamic information about the simulated devices, appliances, and humans, and displays energy consumption and CO_2 emission calculated in real time.

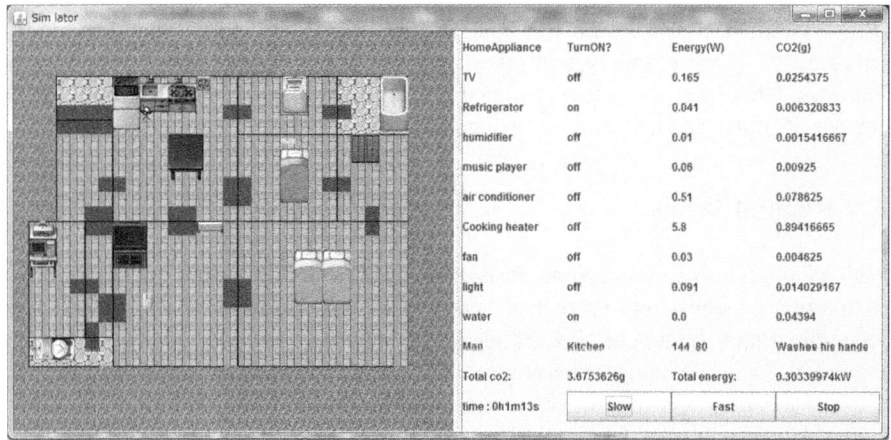

Fig. 1. A simulated home

3.2   Calculation of Energy Consumption

Each device or appliance consumes energy while it is either in operation mode (E_o) or in stand-by mode (E_s). The total amount of energy consumption in an interval of time is the sum of them (E_t). If we denote E_{ho} as the hourly energy consumption rate (kw/h) in operation mode and E_{hs} as the hourly energy consumption rate (kw/h) in stand-by mode, we have the following formulae for calculating energy consumption of a simulated device or appliance in an interval time, T.

$$E_o = E_{ho} \times T \tag{1}$$

$$E_s = E_{hs} \times (24 - T) \tag{2}$$

$$E_t = E_o + E_s \tag{3}$$

3.3   Calculation of CO_2 Emission

The energy consumption of each device or appliance can be correlated to the emission of CO_2 gas. Let us denote it as G_e (kg). If we use the emission factor, 0.555 (kg/kw) [13], the amount of CO_2 emission per kilowatt of energy consumption, we can calculate

$$G_e = E_t \times 0.555 \qquad (4)$$

Water use can also be correlated to CO_2 gas emission. Let us denote it as G_w (kg), which can be calculated using the following formula.

$$G_w = W \times 0.2197 \qquad (5)$$

Where, W is the amount of water (m^3) consumed and 0.2197 [14] is the emission factor (kg/m^3).

4   Multi-agents System

A number of agents are designed for and reside in the system. Each device or appliance has an agent attached for decision-making in certain contexts, such as automatic energy saving and CO_2 reduction. Agents communicate and cooperate with each other on top of a multi-agent framework to provide appropriate advice to individuals.

4.1   Multi Agents Platform

The platform is configured in three layers. Each agent is registered and can be discovered via UDDI. An agent attached with a device or appliance manipulates its associated device or appliance via the device access program as shown in Fig. 2. The registry access, service server, client server, and RuleBase system are in the top layer. The agent can register its information to UDDI registry and also search for any other agent's information from UDDI registry. The service server provides the service for accessing the agent. Communication between agents is performed by calling the services in the service server using RPC (Remote Procedure Call) on top of SOAP protocol. A Java method as a service is open and ready for accessing, i.e. it is called by a service client from any other agent. A RuleBase system is a rule-based reasoning system that contains a collection of rules, working memory, and an inference engine. It is regarded as a service and collected in the RuleBasePool. When the RuleBasePool agent registers its service method in UDDI registry, each RuleBase system as a service method is open to all other agents. Any agent can search for the service method and receive the package of the service from UDDI registry by calling the method, getRuleBase(). For details, please refer to our previous work [15].

4.2   Virtual Devices and Appliances

For collecting context information and data on individual activities, a variety of sensor devices is necessary. In the simulated home virtual devices are adopted instead of physical sensor devices. A simulated virtual sensor system is developed for various purposes to research ubiquitous intelligent computing. A virtual sensor or appliance can be simulated by a third party and plugged into the system. The virtual sensors can be shared by anyone for different applications. In this research, a number of virtual sensors such as a thermometer, a luminance meter, a surveillance camera, an RFID reader, an RFID tag and appliances such as a TV, an air conditioner, a refrigerator, water taps, are simulated and plugged into the simulated sensor system. These virtual sensors and appliances are shared in the simulated home system application.

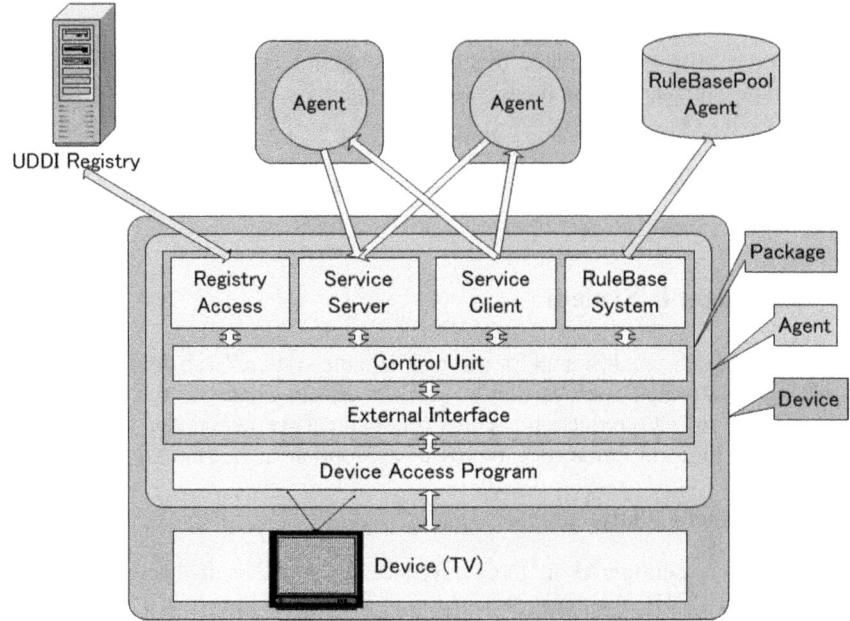

Fig. 2. The 3-layers multi-agents platform

5   Discriminant Analysis

As there is obviously a huge amount of recorded data in an environment space from all the different sensor devices and appliances associated with different objects and entities, including human inhabitants, it is necessary to pre-process this amount of data with a certain structure or structures.

5.1   Three Structured Data Logs

When we try to describe a person's activity, we may use a basic pattern, coined as 5W pattern, such as who is doing what with which object when and where. For instance, "Andy is watching TV from 2:00pm to 5:00pm in living room". Moreover, an activity is, in principle, related to three entities: person, device, and space. Therefore, three structured data logs are proposed to pre-process the huge amount of recorded data.

- Person Log
  This data log is built with person-centric data as shown in Table 1.

Table 1. An example: person data log

Person	Device	Time
TOM	TV	13:18:00
MIKE	LIGHT	13:26:12

● Device Log
  This data log is built with device- or appliance- oriented data as shown in Table 2.

Table 2. An example: device data log

Device	State	Detail	Time
TV	ON	CH 1	13:18:00
LIGHT	OFF	NULL	13:26:12

● Space Log
  This data log is built with space-oriented data as shown in Table 3.

Table 3. An example: space data log

Room	Person	Device	Time
LIVING ROOM	TOM	TV, LIGHT	13:18:00
KITCHEN	MIKE	LIGHT	13:26:12

5.2   Hayashi's Quantification Method

Some data are presented with qualitative variables. However, most discriminant methods work with quantitative data. Hayashi's quantification method is for converting qualitative data to quantitative using dummy variables [16]. A dummy variable is one that takes the values 0 or 1 (e.g. switch on=1, switch off=0) to indicate the absence or presence of some categorical effect that may be expected to shift the outcome [17]. By Hayashi's quantification method, all of the qualitative data can be converted to quantitative data. However the number of variables is large, which increases the computational complexity and computational time. The number of variables can be reduced by grouping them together.

5.3   Mahalanobis Distance and Activity Awareness

Further, it is necessary to figure out a person's activity from the structured data logs. Discriminant analysis is one method used to classify sample data into a number of clusters [18] and allocate new data to a certain cluster based on a form of distance calculation. In this research, Mahalanobis distance [19] was adopted. A new data set is extracted from the three logs and quantified by Hayashi's quantification methods. Then the Mahalanobis distance of the new data set to each cluster is calculated using the formula below.

$$D_j(X,Y_j) = \sqrt{\sum_{i=1}^{n} \frac{(x_i - y_{ji})^2}{\sigma_i^2}} \quad (j = 1, 2, ..., M) \tag{6}$$

Where X and Y_j are the feature vectors of a new unknown activity and a number of predefined clusters, having X=(x_1, x_2, ..., x_n), Y_j= (y_{j1}, y_{j2}, ... , y_{jn}). σ_i^2 is the standard deviation of the X over sample set Y_j. M is the number of predefined activity clusters.

5.4   Activity Clusters

The discriminant analysis is based on the Mahalanobis distance, which is calculated between the center point of a new activity and the centers of a number of the predefined activities. Therefore, it is necessary to cluster individual activities into a number of categories using a number of sample activity data sets in advance. In this research, the sample activity data sets are collected by observing and recording an individual's activities during a certain period, such as one week, ten days, or one month, between a start time and an end time. For example, a boy goes home from school and stays at home until his parents come back from work. The activities the boy performs everyday during this period can be concluded from one week's recording and observation. Below is an example of concluding the boy's activity: if the boy is in the living room, turns on the TV, and is sitting in front of the TV, then it may be concluded one of the boy's activities during this specified period of time is "watching TV".

All possible activities are defined and stored in a database, named "activity database". The activity database is organized in a hierarchical structure of sub-databases according to different time periods and locations for the efficient retrieval. Elements which are relevant to an activity are bound together. The correlations between each two elements associated with a location are represented in a matrix-like form with a coefficient, i.e., a value ranging from 0.0 (not related) to 1.0 (very closely related). For example, regarding the activity, "washing your hands", water tap, water, hand, and kitchen are relevant elements and they are bound together attached to the activity. In this example, apart from water tap, water, hand, there are other elements, such as table, refrigerator, cooker, etc. in a kitchen. If we use a matrix with coefficients to represent correlations of each pair of elements regarding an activity, a subset of the matrix in which their coefficient values are greater than a defined threshold is associated with an activity. A set of elements in a subset matrix are relevant elements bound to an activity. Therefore, for each location, there are a number of matrixes which correspond to a number of possible activities in this location.

For an individual, the possible activities conducted are a subset of the activities in the activity database referring to each location during a period. The possible activities are obtained from observing one's activities in each location during a certain period, collecting enough data in three logs, and identify each possible activity using the coefficient matrix based clustering approach from the activity database.

6   Advice to Individuals

Once individual activities have been extracted from the structured data logs as described above, the system should be able to make conclusions, such as what a person is doing, whether his/her activity leads to energy waste or not, or what advice can be provided to direct him/her to conserve energy. There are two approaches as follows.

- The Intuitive method

  Intuitive thinking is based on common sense. If a device or appliance is on, which does not benefit to any entity, it is regarded as wasting energy. The multi-agent system will automatically switch off it. Common sense and knowledge are written as a set of rules for such decision-making and reasoning.

- The statistics based inference

  This is a method to work out abnormal cases. When one is performing some activities that are exceptional and lead to abnormal energy consumption, the system can infer this by using statistical analysis method, which compares the normal or regular pattern with the current pattern of energy consumption. The system is also able to trace the reason for the abnormal situation by finding the related activities which were conducted by individual or individuals through the structured data logs and statistical data logs. The system then provides advice to them accordingly.

7   Two Simulated Scenarios

This system runs through two simulated scenarios. Assume that there is a family, a working couple with a child called Tom.

7.1   Scenario-I: "A Child At Home Alone"

Tom comes home and is at home alone until his parents come back from work. He is a careless boy and always forgets to switch off lights. A list of his activities is given in Table 4.

Table 4. The detail of scenario-I

No.	Time	Activity	Appliances
1	13:30	Wash hands	Water tap
2	13:32	Get something to drink	Refrigerator (leave the door open)
3	13:42	Watch TV	Light(Living room), TV, Air-conditioner, Humidifier
4	14:12	Study	Lights(Living room, His room), TV, Air-conditioner, Humidifier
5	15:12	Cook	Lights(Living room, Kitchen), Air-conditioner, IH, Fan
6	15:17	Eat	Lights(Living room, Kitchen), Air-conditioner, Music-player
7	15:27	Play outside	Light(Living room), Air-conditioner, Humidifier
8	15:57	Falls asleep while TV is on	Light(Living room), TV, Air-conditioner, Humidifier
9	17:30	End	

7.2   Scenario-II: "A Busy Morning"

On a busy morning, people tend to forget things and do not pay attention to eco-behavior. A list of Tom, his father (Mike) and his mother (Mary) activities is given in Table 5.

Table 5. The detail of scenario-II

No.	Time	Actor	Activity	Appliances
1	6:45	Mary	Cook	Light(Kitchen) IH, Fan
2	7:00	Mary	Wake up Tom and Mike	Light(Kitchen) IH, Fan
3	7:15	Tom and Mike	Wash face	Water tap Light(washroom)
4	7:20	Everyone	Eat	Light(Kitchen), TV
5	7:25	Tom	Get drinks from Refrigerator	Light(Kitchen), TV, Refrigerator (leave door opened)
6	7:40	Mary	Help Tom get dressed	Light, TV
7	7:50	Mary	See Tom and Mike off	Light, TV
8	8:00	End		

The sentences highlighted in red are related to his energy wasting activities.

7.3   Implementation and Result Analysis

Two simulated scenarios are implemented and the results are analyzed to check if our approaches are reasonable for extracting individual activities and making advice and suggestions to individuals.

The results from Scenario-I and Scenario- II are shown in Fig. 3 and Fig. 4. In scenario-I, about 1188kW of energy was consumed and 1864g of CO_2 was emitted as a result of Tom's activity, "Tom falls asleep while the TV is on in living room". It shows the system is able to detect the abnormal and find out where is the problem. In scenario- II, about 2698kW of energy was consumed and 4174g of CO_2 was emitted as a result of Tom's family's activity, "While Mary sees Tom and Mike off, the light and TV remain on".

water	off	0.0	0.04394
Total co2:	1864.5658g	Total energy:	1188.096kW
Human	Place	Purpose	
TOM	Living room	Falls in sleep while ...	
time : 4h0m0s	Slow	Fast	Stop

Fig. 3. The amount of energy consumption and CO2 emission in scenario-I

Total co2:	4173.573g	Total energy:	2698.2544kW
Human	Place	Activity	
Mary	Door room	sending them off	
Tom	Door room	going to school	
Mike	Door room	going to work	
time : 1h15m0s	Slow	Fast	Stop

Fig. 4. The amount of energy consumption and CO2 emission in scenario-II

The related devices and appliances are recorded. Fig.5. gives an example of TV state recorded in a certain period and stored in the device log. Data in the log are used to analyze human activity and detect dynamic changes in circumstances during the simulation.

Person	Device	State	Time
Tom	TV	Off	13:30:00
Tom	TV	On	13:42:00
Tom	TV	Off	15:12:00
Tom	TV	On	15:57:00
Tom	TV	Off	17:30:00

Fig. 5. An example of TV state in the device log

From Tom's history activity sample data, Tom's activities after school can be classified into 9 clusters as shown in Table 4. In a simulated scenario, for example, in Scenario-I, to recognize a Tom's current activity from a new activity data set, it is to calculate Mahalanobis distance between the new data set and each activity cluster center. The calculation results are shown in Fig. 6. From the calculation results, the new activity may be concluded as "Washing his hands" since the Mahalanobis distance between the new activity data set and the activity cluster, "Washing his hands", is the shortest one.

```
The activities                    Mahalanobis distance
Mah to Watching TV : 645.8652462348938
Mah to Cooking in the kitchen : 216.46008303299658
Mah to Getting foods from Refrigerator : 134.08363910279346
Mah to Studying his room : 19.004604408558066
Mah to Washing his hands : 15.629095709090207
Mah to Eating in the kitchen : 63.09014059219334
Mah to In the rest room : 128.32821472335738
Mah to In the bath : 403.0529349255299
Mah to Not in home : 423.52956648998287
This case may be [ Washing his hands ]
```

Fig. 6. Mahalanobis distance between new data and each activity cluster

The system can detect a problem, perform energy conservation automatically, or make an advice upon it is aware of the situation and individual's activity. Therefore, situation awareness and individual activity extraction are the premises of a rule for making a decision or taking an action. Fig. 7 and Fig. 8 show partial examples of two rules: a "camera.rule" and a "watertap.rule". These rules are related to watertap state and room situation in a RuleBase system and are used in the inference process. These rules dictate that if the light in a room is on but there is no one in the room, since the camera cannot detect anyone, the system switches off the watertap automatically.

Of course, the performance of the system with the advice function and without the advice function are different. Fig. 9 shows the comparisons of energy consumption in cases without the advice function and with the advice function.

```
📄 camera.rule ⊠
1 rule     "CameraRule1"
2 if       "DetectPeople==Null"
3 then     "Room(NoPeople())"
```

Fig. 7. A example of partial rules related to camera state

```
📄 watertap.rule ⊠
1 rule     "WaterTapRule1"
2 if       "Room(NoPeople())"
3          "WaterTap(DevicePower==ON)"
4 then     "WaterTap(DevicePower==OFF)"
-
```

Fig. 8. A example of partial rules related to watertap state

The blue color bars give the amount of energy consumed in scenario 1 and scenario 2 without the advice function, respectively. The red color bars give the amount of energy consumed in scenario 1 and scenario 2 with applying the advice function, respectively. As the results shown in Fig. 9, the eco-home system with the advice function has significant energy conservation comparing to the system without it.

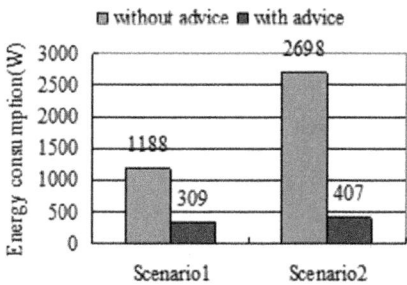

Fig. 9. The comparison of energy consumption in each scenario

8   Conclusion and Future Work

This research focuses on worldwide concern with the environmental problems of energy waste and $CO2$ emission, and adds to the effort in developing a smart eco-home system. This paper mainly describes how to collect data on an individual's daily life using virtual sensors in a simulated sensor system, storing them in three structured logs; a space log, a device log, and a person log, concluding what activities an individual is performing by exploiting data mining techniques, and further creating advice together with the person's accumulated profile by using a rule-based reasoning mechanism. Each device is attached to an agent while multi-agents work on top of a web server based service platform.

As we have addressed, this system's final goal is not only having an automatic energy saving mechanism and advising people who are wasting energy, but also providing each individual with personalized advice using appropriate presentation so as to imperceptibly influence people towards energy conservation and lifestyles which reduce CO_2 emissions. This requires a perception-influence relational model with which the system combines a personal profile, and works out how to appropriately present advice. Building such a perception-influence relational model will be our future work.

References

1. Online replacement navigator "Sinkyusan", http://shinkyusan.com/
2. Yamazaki, T., Ubiquitous Home: Real-Life Testbed for Home Context-Aware Service. In: Proceedings of the First International Conference on Testbeds and Research Infrastructures, for the Development of NeTworks and COMmunities (TRIDENTCOM 2005), February 23-25, pp. 54–59 (2005)
3. Manuel, R., Christopher, K.H., Renato, C., Anand, R., Gaia, R.H.: A middleware infrastructure to enable active spaces. In: IEEE Pervasive Computing, October-December, pp. 74–83 (October-December 2002)
4. Barton, J.J., Vijayaraghavan, V.: UBIWISE, A Simulator for Ubiquitous Computing Systems Design, Technical Report HPL-2003-93, HP Laboratories (2003)
5. Nishikawa, H., Yamamoto, S., Tamai, M., Nishigaki, K., Kitani, T., Shibata, N., Yasumoto, K., Ito, M.: UbiREAL: Realistic Smartspace Simulator for Systematic Testing. In: Dourish, P., Friday, A. (eds.) UbiComp 2006. LNCS, vol. 4206, pp. 459–476. Springer, Heidelberg (2006)
6. Drogoul, A., Vanbergue, D., Meurisse, T.: Multi-agent based simulation: Where are the agents? In: Sichman, J.S., Bousquet, F., Davidsson, P. (eds.) MABS 2002. LNCS (LNAI), vol. 2581, pp. 1–15. Springer, Heidelberg (2003)
7. Bellifemine, F., Caire, G., Poggi, A., Rimassa, G.: JADE: A software framework for developing multi-agent applications. Lessons learned, Information and Software Technology 50, 10–21 (2008)
8. Ort, E.: Service-oriented architecture and web services: Concepts, technologies, and tools, Sun Developer Network, http://java.sun.com/developer/technicalArticles/WebServices/soa2/index.html
9. Bradley, P.S., Fayyad, U.M.: Refining Initial Points for K–Means Clustering. In: Proc. of 15th ICML, pp. 91–99 (1998)
10. Chaturvedi, P.G., Carroll, J.: K-Modes Clustering. J. Classification 18, 35–55 (2001)
11. Bezdek, J.C.: Pattern Recognition with Fuzzy Objective Function Algorithms, Plenum, NY (1981)
12. Ito, Y., Srinivasan, C., Izumi, H.: Discriminant Analysis by a Neural Network with Mahalanobis Distance. In: Kollias, S.D., Stafylopatis, A., Duch, W., Oja, E. (eds.) ICANN 2006. LNCS, vol. 4132, pp. 350–360. Springer, Heidelberg (2006)
13. Environment Department, Calculation and Coefficient Table, http://www.env.go.jp/earth/ghgsanteikohyo/material/itiran.pdf
14. Bureau of Waterworks Tokyo Metropolitan Government, http://www.waterworks.metro.tokyo.jp/water/jigyo/hyouka/pdf/guideline_result.pdf

15. Huang, R., Ito, M., Tamura, T., Ma, J.: Agents based approach for smart eco-home environments. In: Proceedings of 2010 IEEE World Congress on Computational Intelligence (WCCI 2010), Barcelona, Spain, July 18-23, pp. 641–648 (2010)
16. Hayashi, C.: On the quantification of qualitative data from mathematic statistical point of view. Ann. Inst. Statistical Math. 2, 35–47 (1950)
17. Daniel, B.S.: Use of Dummy Variables in Regression Equations. Journal of the American Statistical Association 52(280), 548–551 (1957)
18. Ishimura, S., Kato, C., Chen, L., Ishimura, Y.: Data mining by multivariate analysis. Kyoritsu publisher (2010)
19. Moghaddam, B., Pentland, A.: Probalistic vi-sual learning for object detection. IEEE Transac-tions on Pattern Analysis and Machine Intelligence 17(7), 696–710 (1997)

Adaptive Context Oriented Component-Based Application Middleware (COCA-Middleware)

Basel Magableh and Stephen Barrett

Distributed Systems Group
Department of Computer Science and Statistics
Trinity College Dublin, Ireland
magablb@cs.tcd.ie, stephen.barrett@tcd.ie

Abstract. The cognitively impaired population is very sensitive to issues of abstraction, which presents the application designer with the challenge of tailoring navigational information to each specific user and context. COCA-middleware anticipating the users needs and the context environment. The self-adaptive application reduces the cognitive load and increases the user's ability to realize the desired route. COCA-middleware is performing the adaptation processes including context monitoring and detecting and dynamic decision making; and maintaining the architecture quality attributes during the adaptation.

Keywords: adaptive middleware, context-aware middleware, design patterns, context-oriented programming.

1 Introduction

There is a growing demand for developing applications with aspects such as context awareness and self-adaptive behaviors. Context awareness [1] means that the system is aware of its context, which is its operational environment. Hirschfeld et al. [2] considered context to be any information that is computationally accessible and upon which behavioral variations depend. A context-dependent application adjusts its behavior according to context conditions arising during execution. A self-adaptive application modifies its own structure and behavior in response to changes in its operating environment [3]. Mobile computing environments are heterogeneous and dynamic. Everything from the devices used and resources available to network bandwidths and user context can change drastically at runtime [4]. This presents the adaptation mechanism with the challenge of tailoring behavioural variations dynamical to both each specific user need and to the context information. Implementing an adaptable middleware in a resource secrecy environment must consider the adaptation cost/impact and the trade-off between the architecture quality attributes.

Context changes are the causes of adaptation. A context-driven adaptation requires the self-adaptive software to anticipate its context-dependent variations among its operational environment. The use of middleware in adopting the suitable adaptation approach provides a lead to achieving the adaptation results

C.-H. Hsu et al. (Eds.): UIC 2011, LNCS 6905, pp. 137–151, 2011.

with less cost and several levels of granularity [5]. In addition, the middleware can adapt its own functionality to the device resources and the architecture quality attributes. Context-Oriented Component-based Applications Model-Driven Architecture (COCA-MDA) emerged as a development paradigm which facilitates the development of self-adaptive context-oriented software [6,7]. A context oriented component model (COCA-component) [8] is used to encapsulate behavioural variations and decouple them from the application's core functionality. A COCA-component refers to any subpart of the software system that encapsulates a specific context-dependent behavior in a unit of behavior contractually specified by interfaces and explicit dependences. The result from this methodology is a component-based application described by an architecture description language, COCA-ADL [7]. Such employment of the COCA-ADL decouples the application's architecture design from the target platform implementation. In this way, dynamic adaptation is achieved through the recomposition of the COCA-component among the context changes. This paper focuses on describing the COCA-middleware design approach in terms of its main components and functionalities illustrated using a self-adaptive application for indoor navigation (IWayFinder) for individuals with cognitive impairments.

The rest of the article is structured as follows. Section 2 provides a comparative analysis of the related works. The design requirements for the adaptive middleware are discussed in Section 3. Section 4 provides information on the COCA-middleware components and their functions. In addition, it discusses composition and decomposition mechanisms. Section 5 demonstrating a case study implemented with the aid of COCA-middleware.

2   Related Works

Mukhija et al. [9] CASA middleware, which provides a framework for enabling the development and operation of adaptive applications by separating the adaptation concern from the business concern. CASA uses static Aspect-Oriented Programming (AOP) technique for enabling behavioural variation at the compile time. Capra et al. [10] proposes a mobile computing middleware CARISMA that enhances the construction of adaptive and context-aware applications. CARISMA based on aspectual weaving of functional concerns, which does not suit the context-driven adaptation. In such adaptation the context-dependent behaviours are entangled with other behaviours, and are likely to be included in multiple parts (scattered) of the software modules. In addition, the context handling mechanism is a concern that spans the whole software modules. However, existing AOP techniques tend to add a substantial overhead in both adaptation/-configuration time and code size, which restricts their practicality for hand-held devices with limited resources [11].

MADAM (Mobility and Adaptation-Enabling Middleware) aims to build adaptive applications for mobile devices using architecture models [12]. The middleware is responsible for constructing and analysing several variability models at runtime, which adds an intensive overhead over the mobile device. MUSIC is an extension of the MADAM component-based planning framework that optimizes the overall utility of applications when context-related conditions occur [13]. In MADAM and MUSIC the dynamic decision making is supported by a utility functions. The utility function is defined as the weighted sum of the different objectives based on user preferences and QoS. However, this approach suffers from a number of drawbacks. First, it is well known that correct identification of the weight of each goal is a major difficulty. Second, the approach hides conflicts among multiple goals in a single, aggregate objective function, rather than exposing the conflicts and reasoning about them. At runtime, a utility function is used to select the best application variant; this is the so-called 'adaptation plan'. In addition, mobile computing devices have limited resources for evaluating the many application variations at runtime and can consume significant amounts of device resources. As an outcome, the benefit gained from the adaptation is negated by the overhead required to achieve the adaptation. Because of the above issue, it is impossible to use MUSIC to provide unanticipated adaptation in a self-adaptive application.

3   Requirments for Middleware Design

Implementing an adaptable middleware in a resource secrecy environment presents a set of challenge dimensions, which capture the systems reaction towards context changes, meaning that they are related to the adaptation process itself. The dimensions associated with this group refers to the type of self-adaptation that is expected, the level of autonomy of the self-adaptation, how self-adaptation is controlled, the impact of self-adaptation in terms of space and time, how responsive is the self-adaptation, and how self-adaptation reacts to change. The middleware approaches support the adaptation process to solve the heterogeneity of context information. The middleware performs adaptation processes, including context monitoring and detecting, and dynamic decision making, and maintains the architecture quality attributes during the adaptation. This is achieved by utilising the middleware operations among the devices resources and considering the interoperability between the architecture components. This observation leads to the first requirement:

R1: The middleware should also be able to satisfy one or more self-* properties, including self-healing, self-organizing, self-optimizing, and self-protecting [14]. The middleware must be able to switch autonomously between weak adaptation and strong adaptation types. Considering the trade-off between cost/impact attributes during the adaptation action.

In addition, the middleware should be able to verify the adaptation output among the available resources and the trade-off between the quality attributes of the architecture. The proposed middleware in the literature [15,12,16,9,13] does not consider the effects of context monitoring on the devices resources. The second aspect of context detection is the need to detect these changes and notify the interested context consumer about them. Such enhancements of context monitoring and detecting can improve the efficiency of adaptation processes. The context manager in the COCA-middleware is designed to use the devices resources during context monitoring and detecting. This observation leads to the second requirement:

R2: The middleware should enhance the context binding mechanism. Specifically, the context monitoring and detecting processes.

Another aspect which the middleware must consider is the deciding process. Decision making determines which parts need to be changed and how to change them to achieve the best output. Some middleware, such as MADAM [12] and CASA [9], and CARISMA [10], has used static decision-making, where the deciding process is hard-coded and its modification requires recompiling and re-deploying the system or some of its components. Dynamic decision-making is externally defined and managed, so it can be changed during runtime to create or adjust the behaviour of both functional and behavioural adaptations. [16] used policies for maintaining and evaluating the adaptation results at runtime. This policy framework is managed by the policy manager, which verifies the policies among contradictions and evaluates the architecture evolution among constraints specified by the policy. However, dynamic decisions can be used not only for tuning the adaptation process, but also for assuring the adaptation and verifying its results. This observation leads to the third requirement:

R3: The middlware should be able to maintain and evaluates the architecture evolution by tuning the adaptation process. In the sense that the middleware should be able to adapt its own functionality and verify the adaptation results dynamically by means of dynamic decision making.

4   Overview of the Coca Architecture

The COCA-platform offers a context-aware middleware environment for adjusting an applications behaviour dynamically. The platform integrates the component-based context-ware application with an ADL and runtime infrastructure. The platform architecture, described in Figure 1, is divided into four major layers. Each layer provides an abstraction of the underlying technology. Each layer is totally technology independent.

The top layer represents the context-aware application generated by the COCA-MDA. The application is componentised into two major component types: the base-component and the COCA-component. The application base-component provides the user with UI views and context-free functions. The second component is the COCA-component, which provides context-dependent behaviour, providing multiple divisions of the implementation. Hereafter, these COCA-components are handled by the COCA-middleware for application composition and adaption. The second layer in the platform represents the COCA-middleware. Fuller details of the individual components and subcomponents can be found in Figure 1. The COCA-middleware is responsible for performing the adaptation dynamically. The third layer in the platform represents the resources and services layer. It provides information about the devices resources, physical sensors, and remote service to the middleware. The context information is retrieved from the OS, resources, and physical sensors.

In the following sections, each component of the COCA-middleware is discussed. The design principles are supported by showing the motivations behind

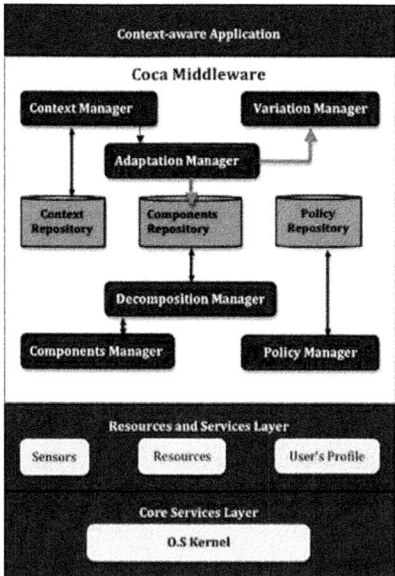

Fig. 1. COCA Platform Architecture

adopting the design patterns. In software engineering, a design pattern is a general reusable solution to a commonly occurring problem in software design. It is a description or template that can be used in many different situations for solving problems [17].

4.1   Context Manager

The context manager gathers and detects context information from the sensors. If the context is changed, the context manager notifies the adaptation manager and the observer COCA-component about the changes. Each COCA-component is designed to be an observer for one or more context entities. This type of interaction is called context binding. To achieve this integration, developers have to consider the following two aspects in the application design: how to notify the adaptation manager about context changes and how the component manager can identify the parts of the architecture which have to respond to these changes. These aspects can be achieved by adopting observer (notification) design patterns [17] in designing the context manager. The main function of the context manager is to provide a mechanism for context binding between the context entity and the COCA-component.

The observer pattern reduces the tight coupling between the context provider (context entity) and the context consumer (COCA-component). In addition, it enables the middleware to identify which COCA-component has to be manipulated in response to context changes. Figure 2 demonstrates the observer design pattern with one context entity and two observers. At runtime, the COCA-component registers itself as an observer for the context entity by sending a

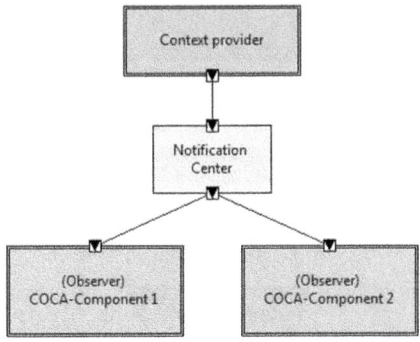

Fig. 2. Context Manager Observer Model

registration request to the context manager. The context-change event is sent to the context manager notification center instead of the COCA-component, then the context manager broadcasts the context changes, and only the registered component receives the notification.

4.2 Component Manager

The COCA-component model was proposed in [8], based on the concept of a primitive component introduced by Khattak et al. in [18] and context-oriented programming (COP) [2]. COP provides several features that fit the requirements of Context-aware application, such as behavioural composition, dynamic layers activation, and scoping. This component model dynamically composes adaptable context-dependent applications based on specific context-dependent functionality. The author developed the component model by designing components as compositions of behaviours, embedding decision points in the component at design time to determine the component behaviours, and supporting reconfiguration of decision policies at runtime to adapt behaviours.

The COCA-component has three major parts: a static part, a dynamic part, and ports. The component itself provides information about its implementation to the middleware. The COCA-component has the following attributes: ID, name, context entity, creation time, location, and remote variable. The Boolean attribute remote indicates whether or not the components are located on the distributed environment. The decision policy and decision points are attributes with getter and setter methods. These methods are used by the middleware to read the attached PolicyID and manipulate the application behaviour by manipulating the decision policy.

Each COCA-component handles the implementation of a context-dependent functionality, so the adaptation manager invokes these components whenever the COCA-component is notified by the context manager. At this stage, each COCA-component must adopt the COCA-component model design. A sample COCA-component is shown in Figure 3, it is modelled as a control class with the required attributes and operations. Each layer entity must implement two

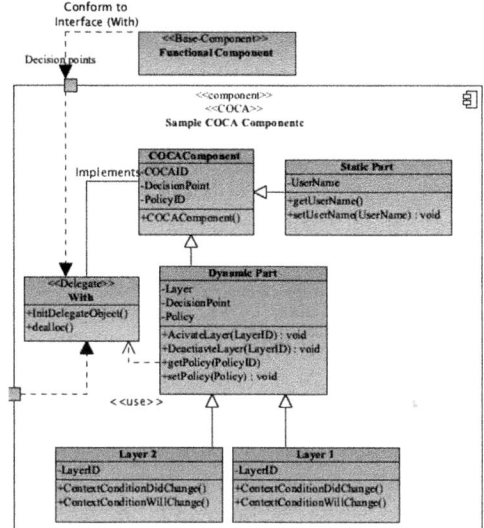

Fig. 3. COCA-component Conceptual Diagram

methods that collaborate with the context manager. Two methods inside the layer class, namely *ContextEntityDidchanged* and *ContextEntityWillChanged*, are called when the context manager posts the notifications in the form *[Notifi-cationCeneter Post:ContextConditionDidChanged]*. This triggers the class layer to invoke its method *ContextEntityDidchanged*, which embeds a subdivision of the COCA-component implementation.

4.3   Policy Manager

Self-adaptive systems have multiple context-sensitive parts, which are highly context dependent. Whenever a change in the context is captured, the software has to decide the need for adaptation based on three major factors: (1) the extra functionality that the software is providing, (2) the quality attributes that are affected by the change and their related self-* properties, and (3) the user's perspectives and/or the application goals. All of these factors prompt the need for verification activities to provide continual assessment. Deciding the fitness of the adaptation results requires the verification activities to be embedded in the adaptation mechanism. The COCA-MDA provides the developer with the ability to specify the adaptation goals, actions, causes with several context conditions using a policy-based framework. For each COCA-components the developers can embed one or more decision polices that specifies the adaptation goals, actions and context changes.

Each COCA-component embeds one or more decision points; each decision point realizes one or more decision policies. The decision policy described by a state-machine model based on a set of internal and external variables and conditional rules. The rules determine the true action or else an action based on the variable values. The action part of the state diagrams usually involves invoking one or more of the components layers. The policy framework implements the policy-definition language proposed in the AGILE framework [16].

At runtime, when a decision point (DP) is reached by the execution, the adaptation manager reads the policy ID from the attached DP to the COCA-component. The policy syntax is retrieved by the policy manager from the policy repository. The policy is evaluated to true or false action among architecture constraints and the predefined variables in the policy syntax. Afterwards, The decision is returned to the adaptation manager to execute it.

4.4   Decomposition Manager

When the application is lunched the COCA-middleware components are executed first. Afterwards, the adaptation manager calls the decomposition manager to build the application composition plan and the application graph. For each COCA-component, all layers are added to the graph node. In the same manner, decision points in each components dynamic parts are listed in the dispatch table. The decision policies are also extracted and stored in the policy repository. The policyID is attached to the associated component node. The decomposition manager pars the COCA-ADL XML file for the components' elements. The composition manager add the components to the graph and the component repository. We use a decomposition mechanism based on two main concepts: 1) separation of decision making from the application logic, and 2) building a component-dependences graph that reflects the context-condition dependences. The dependence graph contains information about components, layers, variation points, policies, and services. The composition plan is a runtime architecture representation of the application that used by the adaptation manger to add or reduce the components or even tuns specific components methods. A reasonable approach to pars the COCA-ADL XML file with less impact on the quality attributes is the use of the Flyweight design pattern [17]. The Flyweight pattern enables instance sharing to reduce the number of instances needed while preserving the advantages of using objects. In addition the Associative Storage pattern [17] is employed to organize the decision policies into data and keys, so that data can be quickly and easily accessed using the corresponding keys.

4.5   Adaptation Manager

Once the decomposition is finished. The adaptation manager asks the context manager for the context state. In the same time, the adaptation manager runs the component instance for the base-component type. Each base component is a sub class from the super class (Base-component). The adaptation manager checks each class by parsing the graph. The adaptation manager performs the following operations: 1) creating the application singleton. 2) adding the base-components to singleton. 3) construct the primary composition plan. In addition, the base-component and COCA-component both adopt the delegate design pattern [17]. A delegate is a component that is given an opportunity to react to changes in another component or influence the behaviour of another component. The delegate is typically a unique custom object within the controller subsystem of an application [17]. Moreover, the adaptation manager adopts the adaptor design pattern [17]. The adaptor is used to convert the interface of a class into another interface client expect. The adaptor lets classes work together, even if they have incompatible interfaces. Assume a base-component needs to communicate with a COCA-component, but its interfaces make that unachievable. To solve this problem, the base-component defines a protocol, which is essentially a series of method declarations unassociated with the component. The COCA-component then formally adopts the protocol and confirms this by implementing one or more of the methods of the protocol. The protocol may have mandatory or optional methods. The base-component can then send a message to the protocol interface [17]. This pattern verifies if the component can respond to the method call before calling the method using the responder pattern, which avoids coupling between the sender of a request and its receiver by giving more than one COCA-component a chance to handle the request.

The adaptation manager introspects the application's structure. The component sub layers are activated by redirecting the COCA-component delegate to the desired layer. In some cases, A COCA-component is loaded into the application. This require the adaptation manager to confirm to the bundle pattern [17]. The bundle pattern achieves the following goals: 1) Keep executable code and related resources together even when there are multiple versions and multiple files involved in the underlying storage. 2) Implement a flexible plug-in mechanism that enables dynamic loading of executable code and resources. In addition, the Invocations design pattern is used to provide a means of capturing runtime messages so that they can be stored, rerouted, or treated and manipulated as objects. 3) Allow new messages to be constructed and sent at runtime without requiring the compiler [17].

The adaptation process starts the adaptation action, including two types of composition mechanism: internal composition and external composition. In internal composition, the adaptation manager use the delegation pattern mechanism to switch a components layers on or off, based on the composition plan. In external composition, the adaptation manger use the bundle pattern to add or replace components from the application structure, based on the composition plan. The decomposition component builds the application graph by reading the COCA-ADL. The decision manager retrieves the decision policies described by the developers at the design stage from the policy storage; policy evaluation, selection, and conflict resolution are the main functions of the policy component, as described above.

4.6   Verification Manager

A context-aware application is self-assurable if it can adapt autonomously its own adaptation output to changing environmental conditions and its internal parts status. From a middleware perspective, such a feature relies on the following key characteristics: A) the middlewares ability to monitor and define its internal status and external conditions (e.g. Application modes, CPU and memory use, and attachment of external devices); B) its built-in knowledge of configuration variability and related policies/rules for deciding and planning changes; and C) its ability to conduce dynamic configuration changes without violating the constraints relating to overall system functionality, performance, and dependability.

The verification manager design adopted the adaptation assurance framework proposed by Cheng et al. [19]. Whenever the application execution reaches the decision points and/or the context manager has notified the adaptation manager for context changes. The adaptive software operates through a series of substates (modes). The substates are represented by j, and j might represent a known or unknown conditional state. Examples of known states in the generic form include detecting context changes in a reactive or proactive manner.

In the presence of uncertainty and unforeseen context changes, the self-adaptive application might be notified about an unknown condition prior to the software design. Such adaptation is reflected in a series of context-system states. $(C + S)_{ji}$ denotes the ith combination of context-dependent behavior, which is related to the decision points j by the notion mode M_{jk}. In this way, the development methodology decomposes the software into a set of context-driven and context-free states. At runtime, the middleware transforms the self-adaptive software form $state_i$ into $state_{i+1}$, considering a specific context condition t_{jk}, as shown in Figure 4. This enables the developer to clearly decide which part of the architecture should respond to the context changes t_{jk}, and provides the verification manager with sufficient information to consider a subset of the architecture during the adaptation assurance.

As long as the COCA-middleware is aware about the architecture configuration, which is supported by the COCA-ADL configuration element. The COCA-middleware can anticipate the associated configuration with specific context changes. In each decision point the COCA-middleware transforming the software from $state_i$ into $state_{i+1}$ considering the properties of the self-adaptive

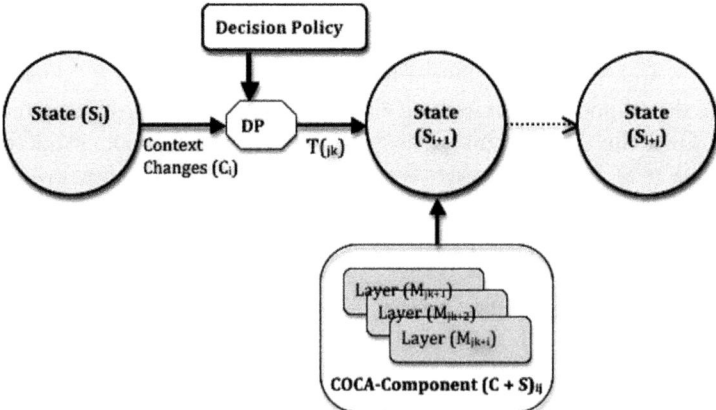

Fig. 4. Behavioral Decomposition Model

software . These properties include: 1) The set of decision policies attached to the COCA-components that participate in the adaptation. 2) The architecture configuration elements in the COCA-ADL, that include the description of the decision polices and the behavioural model of the architecture. The external and internal variables specified in the decision polices that associated to the COCA-components which are evolving through the adaptation process. 3) The adaptation goals, actions, rules and causes specified by the decision policies.

5   Self-adaptive Indoor Wayfinding Application for Individuals with Cognitive Impairments

IWayFinder provides distributed cognition support for indoor navigation to persons with cognitive disabilities. RFID tags and QR-codes are placed at decision points such as hallway intersections, exits, elevators, and entrances to stairways. After reading the encoded URL in the QR-codes, the Cisco engine provides the required navigation information and instructs the user. The proposed self-adaptive application uses an augmented reality browser (ARB) to display the navigation directions. The browser displays the directions on the physical display of the tool's camera. The application is able to provide the user with time-based events such as the opening hours of the building, lunch time, closing hours of the offices, location access rights which control the entrance of users to certain locations, and any real-time alarm events. Moreover, the infrastructure support allows several persons to monitor and collaborate with the user en route. Assuming that the context information is delivered by the Cisco infrastructure, we propose the following anticipation scenarios:

A1: Self-tuning. The application must track the user's path inside the building. When decision points (DPs) are reached, the application places a marker for each DP the user passed. If the user is unable to locate a decision point in the building, the application must be able to guide the user towards a safe exit. The route directions can be delivered to the user in several output formats: video, still images, and voice commands. The application should change the direction output while also adapting to the device resources and the level of cognitive impairment of the individual.

A2: Self-recovering. Assuming that the user is trapped in a lift with no GPRS connection (or in the case of a fire), the fire alarm is raised, the application is notified, and the application adopts the shortest path to the nearest fire exit. In both cases, the application submits the user's current coordinates and an emergency help message to the emergency number, parents, career team, and security staff. The communication is achieved using the available connection, regardless of the resource cost, to alert any nearby devices to the emergent need for help. If no connection is made, the device emits an alarm sound and increases the device volume to maximum. The security staff or fire fighters receive the emergency message and can view the CCTV video to identify the floor on which the user is trapped. When the CCTV system locates the user, full information about the user is displayed, including a personal and health profile. At the same time, the application guides the user to a safe exit using a preloaded path (in case the CCTV camera is disabled and the services engine is off). Fire fighters can use the received message to locate the user within the building.

The use of COCA-MDA for developing self-adaptive applications for indoor wayfinding for individuals with cognitive impairments was proposed in [6]. Evaluating the COCA-MDA productivity among the development effort was demonstrated in [20]. This article focuses on describing in detail the COCA-middleware design principles and evaluates the impact of the adaptation process over the device's resources. For example, the development approach enables the developer to specify the following policy to anticipate the proposed scenarios A1. **Policy 1:** This policy is attached to the COCA-component that adapt the resources when delivering the direction output, this policy is attached to direction output COCA-component. The policy syntax can be explained as the code shown in Listing 1.1. **Policy 2:** This policy is attached to the COCA-component, that anticipate the condition of fire. The policy syntax is shown in Listing 1.2.

Listing 1.1. Decision Policy 1: Self-tuning

```
If ( direction is Provided && Available memory >= 50
&& CPU throughput <= 89 && light level >= 50
 && BatteryLevel >= 50)
  then {PlayVideo(); displayImage(); VoiceCommand();}
  Else If ( BatteryLevel < 50
 || memory level < 50 || CPU >92)
  then {displayImage(); VoiceCommand();}
  else If( Available Memory level < 20
 && CPU > 92 && light level > 88)
  then VoiceCommand();
```

Listing 1.2. Decision Policy 2: Self-recovering

```
If ( FireAlaramRasied && HumidityLevel < 10
&& Body_Temperature > 38 &&
 BloodPressure between 120 and 180
  && LowOxygenLevel
  && RoomTemperature >= 40 )
  then {
if(connection = GPRS)
{HelpMessage(); GetEmergencyNumber();}
else if (connection = WIFI) {WebToSMS();
    SendEmail(); BroadcastNotification();}
else if (connection = bluetooth)
{ OpenBluetooth(); Add_Bonjour_Service();
HelpMessage(); BroadcastAlert(); }
  PlayAlarmSound(); FindFireExit(); DisplayRoute(); }
```

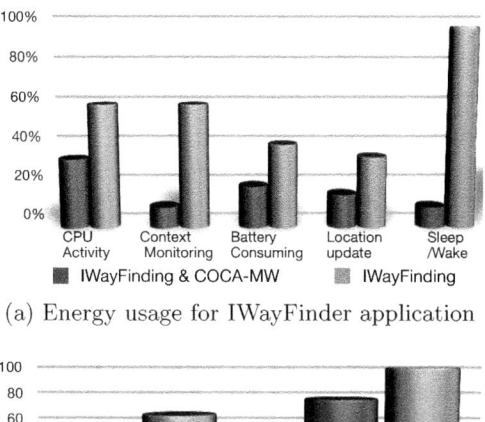

(a) Energy usage for IWayFinder application

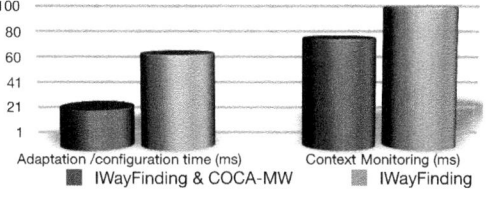

(b) Adaptation time (ms)

Fig. 5. Experiments Evaluation Results

The 'direction output' COCA-component registers itself with the context manager to be notified when the *BatteryLevelDidChanged, CPULevelDidChanged and/or MemoryLevelDidChanged*. When the context manager notifies *[PostNotfication:BatteryLevelDidChanged]* to the 'direction output' component, the adaptation manager reads the attached decision policy in list 1.1. Based on the policy action, the adaptation manager calls the delegate object *DisplayDirection* which forwards the method invocation to the desired sub layer, based on the battery level. If the battery level < 20%, then the adaptation manager activates the sub layer VoiceCommand to adapt this context condition.

The IWayFinder application has been implemented in two distinct versions, i.e. with and without the COCA-middleware. The Instruments is a tool application for dynamically tracing and profiling IPhone devices. The battery life has been measured by Energy Diagnostics Instruments running on the device [21]. The energy Diagnostic used to measure the battery while the device is not connected to external power supply. The experiments show that the COCA IPetra application saved the battery-consuming level by 13% in addition to its self-tuning adaptability. Fig. 5a shows the experimental results for energy usage. The IPetra implementation without adopting the COCA-platform consumes more energy during context monitoring, draining the battery faster. On the other hand, when the same application adopts the COCA-middleware, the application is able to adapt its behaviour and use less energy. The adaptation time for handling low and high battery-levels are shown in Table 5b. It is worth mentioning here that when the battery level is low, the COCA-middleware allocates less memory because of the size of the COCA-component, which is small compared to its implementation.

6   Conclusions

Supporting context-binding mechanisms with observer patterns was impossible before the introduction of COCA-MDA methodology. The dynamic decision is used for tuning the adaptation process and assuring the adaptation and verifying its results. In the sense, that the COCA-middlewre is be able to switch autonomously between week adaptation and strong adaptation types. The evaluation verifies the COCA middleware's ability to perform dynamic assurance and verification of the adaptation output. Employing the design patterns in the COCA-middleware design enhances the adaptation processes and improves the performance of the middleware.

References

1. Parashar, M., Hariri, S.: Autonomic computing: An overview. Unconventional Programming Paradigms, 257–269 (2005)
2. Hirschfeld, R., Costanza, P., Nierstrasz, O.: Context-oriented programming. Journal of Object Technology 7, 125–151 (2008)
3. Oreizy, P., Gorlick, M., Taylor, R., Heimhigner, D., Johnson, G., Medvidovic, N., Quilici, A., Rosenblum, D., Wolf, A.: An architecture-based approach to self-adaptive software. IEEE Intelligent Systems and Their Applications 14, 54–62 (1999)
4. Belaramani, N.M., Wang, C.L., Lau, F.C.M.: Dynamic component composition for functionality adaptation in pervasive environments. In: Proceedings of the Ninth IEEE Workshop on Future Trends of Distributed Computing Systems, FTDCS 2003, pp. 226–232. IEEE Computer Society, Los Alamitos (2003)
5. Salehie, M., Tahvildari, L.: Self-adaptive software: Landscape and research challenges. ACM Trans. Auton. Adapt. Syst. 4, 14:1–14:42 (2009)
6. Magableh, B., Barrett, S.: Self-adaptive application for indoor wayfinding for individuals with cognitive impairments. In: The 24th IEEE International Symposium on Computer-Based Medical Systems, CBMS 2011, Lancaster, UK, pp. 45–49 (in press, 2011)
7. Magableh, B., Barrett, S.: Context oriented software development (special issue). Journal of Emerging Technologies in Web Intelligence (JETWI) 3, 1–14 (2011)
8. Magableh, B., Barrett, S.: Pcoms: A component model for building context-dependent applications. In: Proceedings of the 2009 Computation World: Future Computing, Service Computation, Cognitive, Adaptive, Content, Patterns. COMPUTATIONWORLD 2009, pp. 44–48. IEEE Computer Society, Washington, DC (2009)
9. Mukhija, A., Glinz, M.: The casa approach to autonomic applications. In: Proceedings of the 5th IEEE Workshop on Applications and Services in Wireless Networks (ASWN 2005), pp. 173–182 (2005)
10. Capra, L., Emmerich, W., Mascolo, C.: Carisma: Context-aware reflective middleware system for mobile applications. IEEE Transactions on Software Engineering 29, 929–945 (2003)

11. Hundt, C., Stöhr, D., Glesner, S.: Optimizing aspect-oriented mechanisms for embedded applications. In: Vitek, J. (ed.) TOOLS 2010. LNCS(LNAI/LNB), vol. 6141, pp. 137–153. Springer, Heidelberg (2010)
12. Floch, J., Hallsteinsen, S., Stav, E., Eliassen, F., Lund, K., Gjorven, E.: Using architecture models for runtime adaptability. IEEE Software 23, 62–70 (2006)
13. Rouvoy, R., Eliassen, F., Floch, J., Hallsteinsen, S., Stav, E.: Composing components and services using a planning-based adaptation middleware. Software Composition, 52–67 (2008)
14. Horn, P.: Autonomic computing: IBM's Perspective on the State of Information Technology. Technical report, IBM (2001)
15. Capra, L.: Reflective mobile middleware for context-aware applications. PhD thesis, University of London (2003)
16. Anthony, R., Chen, D., Pelc, M., Perssonn, M., Torngren, M.: Context-aware adaptation in dyscas. In: Proceedings of the Context-aware Adaptation Mechanisms for Pervasive and Ubiquitous Services (CAMPUS 2009), vol. 15 (2009)
17. Buck, E., Yacktman, D.: Cocoa design patterns, 2nd edn. Developer's Library (2010)
18. Khattak, Y., Barrett, S.: Primitive components: towards more flexible black box aop. In: Proceedings of the 1st International Workshop on Context-Aware Middleware and Services: Affiliated with the 4th International Conference on Communication System Software and Middleware (COMSWARE 2009). CAMS 2009, pp. 24–30. ACM, New York (2009)
19. Cheng, B., de Lemos, R., Giese, H., Inverardi, P., Magee, J., Andersson, J., Becker, B., Bencomo, N., Brun, Y., Cukic, B.: Software engineering for self-adaptive systems: A research roadmap. Software Engineering for Self-Adaptive Systems, 1–26 (2009)
20. Magableh, B.: Model-Driven productivity evaluation for self-adaptive Context-Oriented software development. In: 5th International Conference and Exhibition on Next Generation Mobile Applications, Services, and Technologies (NGMAST 2011), Cardiff, Wales, United Kingdom (in press, 2011)
21. Ios 4.0 apple developer library (2010) , http://developer.apple.com/library/ios/navigation/ (Online; accessed April 1, 2011)

Intelligent Toilet System for Health Screening

Thomas Schlebusch and Steffen Leonhardt

RWTH Aachen University, Pauwelsstr. 20, 52074 Aachen, Germany
schlebusch@hia.rwth-aachen.de
http://www.medit.hia.rwth-aachen.de

Abstract. Home monitoring is a promising technology to deal with the increasing amount of chronically ill patients while ensuring quality of medical care. Most systems available today depend on a high degree of interaction between the user and the device. Especially for people relying on advanced levels of care, this scheme is impracticable. In this paper we are presenting an "intelligent toilet" performing an extensive health check while being as simple to use as a conventional toilet. Main focus of the system is to support the treatment of diabetes and chronic heart failure, but additional applications are possible.

Keywords: personal healthcare, toilet seat, vital parameters.

1 Introduction

Although healthcare technologies have been rapidly developed in the last years, the treatment of chronic diseases still is a problem. Today, 78 % of healthcare expenses in the USA are already related to chronic diseases [2], and this is expected to grow further for any ageing societies. As an example, in about thirty years around one third of the German population is expected to be over 65 years old. Since today's healthcare systems are optimized for treatment of emergencies, they have to be extended to also efficiently treat chronical diseases. Early diagnosis and frequent check-ups may be powerful contributions of telemedicine technology to this goal.

Current commercial telemedicine systems, as *Philips Telehealth Solutions*[TM] or *Bosch Telemedizin Plus*[TM], consist of a set of wireless measurement devices and a base station that receives sensor data and forwards them to a medical datacenter. This relies on a high degree of interaction with and compliance of the patient, who has to step onto the body scaling or stick electrodes for electrocardiogram measurements and press some buttons on the respective device. While this might be acceptable for the "Silver Generation" or "Golden Agers", the scheme of manual measurements is impracticable for elderly who suffer from dementia or otherwise are strongly dependent on care.

For latter, automatic measurements during daily life without any need of interaction with the measurement device is necessary. One possibility is to use implants, as *Biotronik Home Monitoring*[TM] uses their implantable cardiac

C.-H. Hsu et al. (Eds.): UIC 2011, LNCS 6905, pp. 152–160, 2011.

defibrillators to monitor patients suffering from chronic heart disease. Implants have the advantage of providing continuous monitoring but are not applicable for all patients.

An alternative is to embed measurement electronics in objects of daily life, enabling unobtrusive measurements on a daily basis. Objects taken into account in the last years have been beds [15, 14], chairs [1], bath tubs [7] or toilet seats [6, 3, 5]. While measurements in a bed or on a chair have to deal with measurement problems resulting from clothing between the body and the electrodes [13], measurements on a toilet seat provide direct contact to the skin and "the call of nature" is ensuring regular use of the system even for patients with dementia.

The system presented in this paper is focused on patients suffering from diabetes or chronic heart failure. It is intended for early detection of decompensation of a patient and to provide a physician with a powerful tool for assessment of therapy efficacy. A key attribute is the completely unobtrusive measurement during normal use of the toilet.

2   Medical Background

Diabetes mellitus (DM) is a chronic dysfunction of glucose utilization in the metabolism [9]. It is based either on an insulin deficiency or a dysfunction of the effect normally caused by insulin in the organs. Consequence of diabetes mellitus is an increased level of blood sugar. When the blood sugar level exceeds roughly $200\,\mathrm{mg/dl}$, blood sugar is rinsed by the kidneys. This leads to polyuria combined with glucosuria – the patient is using the toilet more frequently than healthy subjects and glucose is detectable in the urine. Together with the loss of water a dehydration and a loss of weight may occur. On longer periods of time, arteriosclerosis may develop which can lead to a decrease of perfusion in the extremities [9].

Chronic heart failure (CHF) is defined as the heart being too weak to supply the blood flow required by the human body [9]. In most cases, the heart failure affects only one side of the heart. If the left heart is affected, pulmonary edema is a major sign since the pulmonary vasculature is congested. In the other case, if the right heart is affected, congestion occurs in the venous system and leads to a swelling of abdomen, ankles and legs due to fluid accommodation. Furthermore, patients with chronic heart failure have reduced heart rate variability.

To account for the mentioned symptoms of diabetes and chronic heart failure, the "intelligent toilet" is monitoring nine parameters listed in Fig. 1. The figure shows which parameters are influenced by the two diseases and which sensor devices are used. Urine sugar is detected by an urine analysis unit presented earlier [4].

The second parameter, body weight, is of importance for both DM and CHF. For DM patients the weight will decrease as mentioned earlier while for CHF patients the weight will increase due to fluid accommodations. To consider the complete weight of the patient including the weight of the legs, sensors are used both in the toilet seat and in a foot rest in front of the toilet.

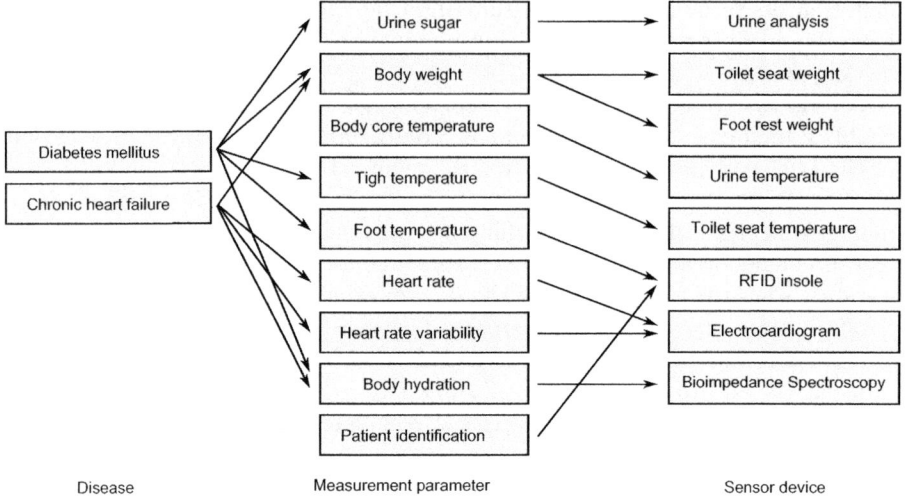

Fig. 1. Measureable parameters influenced by diabetes and heart failure and the respective sensor used

The three temperature values (body core temperature, thigh temperature and foot temperature) are used to create a perfusion analysis of the extremities for DM patients, since arteriosclerosis reduces the tissue perfusion and it is known that tissue temperature in the extremities correlates with tissue perfusion. Additionally, body core temperature alone is used to detect fever and the foot temperature could also be used to account for the diabetic foot syndrome [12]. Thigh temperature is measured by a Pt1000-sensor embedded in the toilet seat, while foot temperature measurement uses an RFID insole presented in sec. 3.4. This insole is also used to identify the user if the toilet is used by several people, as for example in a home for elderly. Body core temperature can not be measured directly on a toilet seat, so urine temperature is used instead.

Heart rate measurements address CHF patients. By the electrocardiogram electronics, bradycardia (unusually low beat rate), tachycardia (unusually high beat rate) and heart rate variability can be detected, all being important parameters for CHF patients.

The last parameter, body hydration, is intended for both DM and CHF patients. While for DM patients a dehydration resulting from polyuria can be discovered, for CHF patients fluid accommodations in the legs can be detected. Bioimpedance spectroscopy (BIS) is used for this task. Usually bioimpedance is measured between wrist and ankle and well defined formulas to calculate body composition from these whole-body bioimpedance measurements are available. However, if we are only interested in the hydration status, it has been shown that segmental knee-to-knee measurements are also applicable [8], because the thighs are very muscular and muscles are the main water reservoir in the human body.

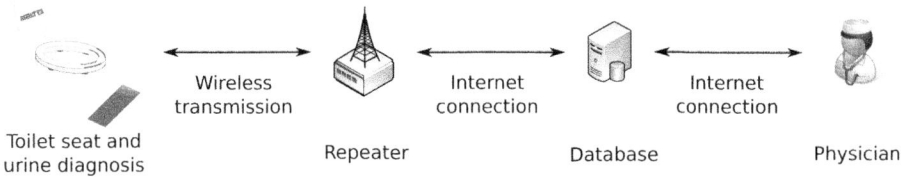

Fig. 2. System overview of the data transmission from the intelligent toilet to a physician

3 Measurement System

3.1 System Structure

The "intelligent toilet" consists of three parts, as shown in Fig. 2. In direct contact to the user is the toilet itself equipped with all sensors and a box with measurement and control electronics. The measurement results are then transmitted via an RF link to a repeater that forwards it via an internet connection to a medical database. By using a repeater, only a water supply and power outlet are required in the bathroom itself. The repeater can be placed several metres apart where either an internet connection or 3G mobile network are available. Further, if using several "intelligent toilets", for example in an apartment house for elderly, only one repeater is necessary for all toilets in range of the RF link.

3.2 Toilet Seat Design

For ECG and BIS measurements, electrodes with good contact to the human skin are necessary. Usually silver/silver-chloride or aluminium hydro-gel electrodes are used for the measurements, featuring low contact impedances and low movement artefacts. Since hydro-gel electrodes are disposables and not intended for a long-term use, it is advisable to use dry electrodes in the toilet seat. It was decided to use gold-plated copper printed circuit boards since they were easy to manufacture in our laboratory. The gold surface ensures good biocompatibility and a low contact impedance.

The electrodes have been integrated in the toilet seat where the contact pressure is the highest. For this, a pressure sensor matress (XSENSOR Technology Corporation, Canada) was placed on a toilet seat and ten voluntary students (seven male and three female) have been asked to sit on the experimental toilet seat in the same way as they usually do when they go to the toilet. The resulting average pressure distribution plot is shown in Fig. 3. Afterwards, the electrodes have been integrated at the sides of the toilet seat where good contact was guaranteed for all ten subjects.

Since for BIS four electrodes (two for current injection, two for voltage measurement) and for a one-channel ECG measurement three electrodes are necessary, a total of four electrodes have been integrated to the toilet seat shared

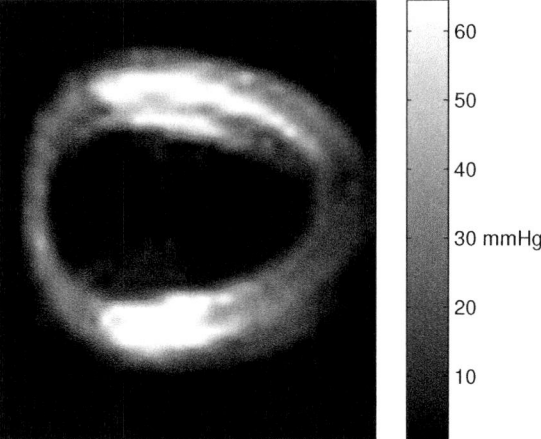

Fig. 3. Average pressure distribution obtained from ten voluntary students sitting on the experimental toilet seat

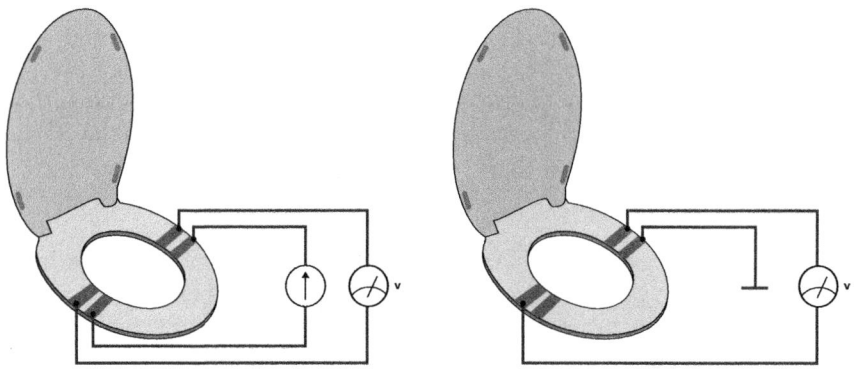

Fig. 4. BIS measurement   **Fig. 5.** ECG measurement

between ECG and BIS electronics. In the case of a BIS measurement, the two distal electrodes are used for current injection and the two proximal electrodes for voltage measurement, as shown in Fig. 4. For the case of an ECG measurement, the two proximal electrodes are used to connect the differential input channel of the biosignal amplifier and one distal electrode is used as the driven right leg reference potential, as shown in Fig. 5.

3.3   Electrocardiogram Measurement

The electrocardiogram (ECG) is the electric potential measurable at the surface of the human body resulting from the electric activity of the heart over time. Since the heart can be seen as an electric dipole during contraction, we can

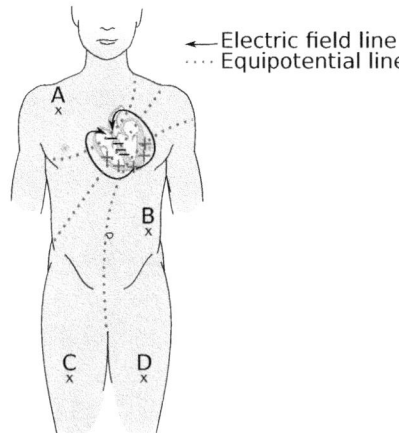

←—Electric field line
···· Equipotential line

Fig. 6. Thigh ECG measurement   **Fig. 7.** Foot temperature sensor

assume the electric equipotential lines shown in principle in Fig. 6 (data for the simplified illustration taken from [10, 11]). Usually the ECG is measured at the human chest (between points A and B for Einthoven II, for example), resulting in signal amplitudes in the magnitude of 1 mV. From the equipotential lines, it is plausible that also between the legs (points C and D) a potential difference caused by the activity of the human heart will be measurable, but with significant lower amplitude. For our thigh ECG measurements, a biosignal amplifier with an overall gain of 12.000 was built.

3.4   RFID Insole for Foot Temperature Measurement

The RFID insole developed for this project has two main purposes: On one hand, it provides the foot temperature to assess the foot perfusion and on the other hand it helps identifying the person using the toilet by its unique ID number. To keep the system free of maintenance, the insole uses energy harvesting from the electromagnetic field of the RFID base station mounted in the foot rest in front of the toilet. A 12-bit temperature sensor TMP275 from Texas Instruments is used in the insole. In the temperature range of interest, this sensor provides a temperature error of $\pm 0.14°$C, getting very close to the accuracy of commercial clinical thermometers of around $\pm 0.1°$C. The board shown in Fig. 7 is mounted in the front part of the slipper, the coil is embedded in the heel. The insole around the electronics is removed in the picture.

4   Results

So far, due to legal issues of patient safety in Germany, the system has only been tested by the author itself. For a detailed assessment of the clinical use of the

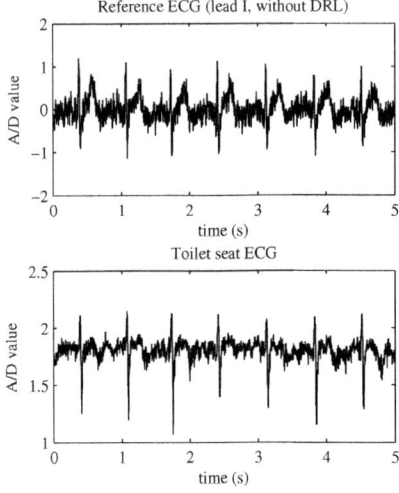

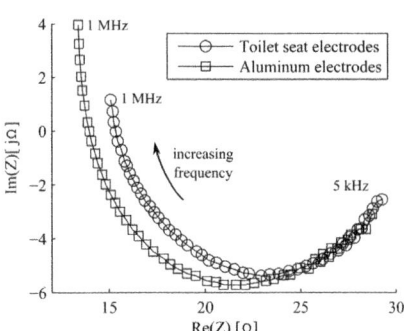

Fig. 8. ECG performance   **Fig. 9.** BIS performance

system, long term measurement data of patients suffering from DM or CHF are necessary. A clinical evaluation providing these results is in preparation at the moment.

For evaluation of the sensor system itself, measurements using the toilet seat and a reference device have been performed. In the case of the ECG electronics, the thigh biosignal amplifier has been connected to the toilet seat electrodes and a reference device (G.BSamp, g.tek, Austria) has been connected using standard silver/silver-chloride ECG electrodes placed on the chest. The outputs of both amplifiers have been connected to a National Instruments USB data acquisition card for simultaneous recording of both ECG signals. Electrical security was guaranteed since the USB acquisition card was only connected to a battery powered laptop and both amplifiers have been supplied by a medical approved power supply. The resulting ECG plot is shown in Fig. 8. The upper plot shows the reference chest ECG, the lower plot the ECG from the thighs. The R-peaks required for calculation of heart rate and heart rate variability are clearly visible in both plots. The reference ECG is very noisy here, since the amplifier's driven right leg electrode was not connected for this measurement. If the ground electrodes of both amplifiers were connected, this led to interferences.

The BIS measurements shown in Fig. 9 have both been taken with a commercial BIS device (Hydra 4200, Xitron Technologies, USA). The plot shows one measurement using the dry gold electrodes in the toilet seat and as a reference normal BIS aluminium hydro-gel electrodes (Fresenius, Germany). As can be seen here, the Hydra 4200 shows a strong dependence on the electrodes used, while the measurement with the toilet seat electrodes shows better results especially for high frequencies. This can be explained by a problem of the current source used in the Hydra 4200 when testing very small impedances. The Hydra

4200 is intended for whole body BIS measurements with impedance ranges in the magnitude of 800 Ω. Consequently, for the clinical evaluation a BIS device for the low segmental impedance range is needed and under development at the moment.

5   Conclusion

An "intelligent toilet" for unobtrusive measurements has been developed. The system is capable of measuring nine different parameters of clinical importance to patients suffering from Diabetes Mellitus or Chronic Heart Failure. Emphasis of the system is the autonomous measurement: while performing an extensive health check on one hand, the system is kept as simple in use as a conventional toilet.

It has been shown that it is practicable to measure a wide variety of vital parameters on a toilet seat without requiring any interaction of the patient with the system. This eliminates the burden of regular measurements present in most telemedicine systems available on the market today.

From a technical point of view, for electrocardiogram and bioimpedance spectroscopy measurements, devices optimized for the thigh region are required. The electrocardiogram signal measurable between the thighs requires an amplification of at least ten times higher than for conventional chest ECG amplifiers. For tigh-to-thigh bioimpedance spectroscopy measurements, a device optimized for low impedance ranges in the magnitude of 30 Ω is necessary.

For evaluation of clinical relevance of the overall system, a clinical evaluation is scheduled for this year.

References

[1] Aleksandrowicz, A., Walter, M., Leonhardt, S.: Wireless ECG measurement system with capacitive coupling. Biomed. Tech (Berl) 52, 185–192 (2007)

[2] Anderson, G., Horvath, J.: The growing burden of chronic disease in America. Public Health Reports 119(3), 263 (2004)

[3] Baek, H.J., Kim, J.S., Kim, K.K., Park, K.S.: System for unconstrained ECG measurement on a toilet seat using capacitive coupled electrodes: the efficacy and practicality. In: Conf. Proc. IEEE Eng. Med. Biol. Soc., pp. 2326–2328 (2008)

[4] Fichtner, W., Schlebusch, T., Leonhardt, S., Mertig, M.: Photometrische Urinanalyse als Baustein für ein mobiles Patientenmonitoring mit der Intelligenten Toilette. In: 3. Dresdner Medizintechnik-Symposium, Dresden, December 6th-9th (2010)

[5] Kim, J.S., Chee, Y.J., Park, J.W., Choi, J.W., Park, K.S.: A new approach for non-intrusive monitoring of blood pressure on a toilet seat. Physiol. Meas. 27, 203–211 (2006)

[6] Kim, K., Lim, Y., Park, K.: The electrically noncontacting ECG measurement on the toilet seat using the capacitively-coupled insulated electrodes. In: 26th Annual International Conference of the IEEE Engineering in Medicine and Biology Society, IEMBS 2004, vol. 1, pp. 2375–2378. IEEE, Los Alamitos (2004)

[7] Lim, Y.K., Kim, K.K., Park, K.S.: The ECG measurement in the bathtub using the insulated electrodes. In: Conf. Proc. IEEE Eng. Med. Biol. Soc., vol. 4, pp. 2383–2385 (2004)

[8] Medrano, G.: Continuous Monitoring of Body Fluids using Bioimpedance Measurements. Ph.D. thesis, Aachen University of Technology, Aachen (2011)

[9] Reuter, P.: Springer Taschenwörterbuch Medizin (Springer-Wörterbuch) (German Edition). Springer, 2., vollst. überarb. u. erw. aufl. edn (2001)

[10] Sachse, F., Werner, C., Meyer-Waarden, K., Dössel, O.: Applications of the visible man dataset in electrocardiology: calculation and visualization of body surface potential maps of a complete heart cycle. In: Second Users Conference of the National Libray of Medicine's Visible Human Project, pp. 47–48 (1998)

[11] Schneider, F., Dössel, O., Müller, M.: Optimierung von Elektrodenpositionen zur Lösung des inversen Problems der Elektrokardiographie. Biomedizinische Technik/Biomedical Engineering 43, 58–59 (1998)

[12] Unspecified: Thermografie zur frühzeitigen Entdeckung von Fußproblemen bei Diabetikern. Podojournal, 10–11 (July 2010)

[13] Wartzek, T., Lammersen, T., Eilebrecht, B., Walter, M., Leonhardt, S.: Triboelectricity in capacitive biopotential measurements. IEEE Transactions on Biomedical Engineering 58(5), 1268–1277 (2011)

[14] Watanabe, K., Watanabe, T., Watanabe, H., Ando, H., Ishikawa, T., Kobayashi, K.: Noninvasive measurement of heartbeat, respiration, snoring and body movements of a subject in bed via a pneumatic method. IEEE Transactions on Biomedical Engineering 52(12), 2100–2107 (2005)

[15] Zhu, X., Chen, W., Nemoto, T., Kanemitsu, Y., Kitamura, K., Yamakoshi, K., Woi, D.: Real-time monitoring of respiration rhythm and pulse rate during sleep. IEEE Transactions on Biomedical Engineering 53(12), 2553–2563 (2006)

An Efficient Earthquake Early Warning Message Delivery Algorithm Using an in Time Control-Theoretic Approach

Ting-Yun Chi[1], Chun-Hao Chen[2], Han-Chieh Chao[2], and Sy-Yen Kuo[1]

[1] Electrical Engineering, National Taiwan University, Taiepi 10617 Taiwan(R.O.C)
Louk.chi@gmail.com, sykuo@cc.ee.ntu.edu.tw
[2] Institute of Computer Science & Information Engineering,
National Ilan University, ILan 260 Taiwan (R.O.C)
alack02@hotmail.com, hcc@niu.edu.tw

Abstract. Earthquake is a fatal disaster in the world, and it is expected to occur in Taiwan with high probability. The Central Weather Bureau of Taiwan develops the early earthquake warning system as other countries. In this paper, we introduce the current development status for the earthquake early warning system. To integrate the various smart devices, we adopt SIP page-mode as the next generation earthquake early warning alert protocol. Due to the lack of multicast support in the general IP network, we try to deliver the warning message to multiple receivers in time base on SIP architecture, location information, priority with IoT devices and in time control-theoretic algorithm. With the proposed algorithm, we can not only reduce the burst message traffic for network but also send the message in time.

Keywords: Earthquake, IM/SIP, emergency message, location information, control-theoretic.

1 Introduction

Earthquake is the fatal disasters in earth. In the early 2011, a major earthquake hit Japan, which calculated to be at the Micron Log 9. According to official estimates, there are 10000 missed and 6000 people killed by the tsunami in the same area. Haiti also hit by earthquake in 2010, which calculated to be at the Micron Log 7. According to official estimates, 222,570 people killed, 300,000 injured, 1.3 million displaced, 97,294 houses destroyed and 188,383 damaged in the Port-au-Prince area and in much of southern Haiti. In Taiwan, the Chi-Chi Earthquake is in 1999 and made the serious damage.

By the recent developing of communication network, real-time earthquake information can be detected and calculate the predictive Micron Log for nation-wide locations. In today's technology, the earthquake early warning system announces the warning message 10 seconds before the earthquake arrives. There are theree major components for early earthquake warning system – (1)Real time eqrthquake information collection from the sensor nodes (2) Earthquake estimation with predictive result (3) Efficient earthquake early warning message delivery

C.-H. Hsu et al. (Eds.): UIC 2011, LNCS 6905, pp. 161–173, 2011.
© Springer-Verlag Berlin Heidelberg 2011

algorithm. In the paper, we will introduce the related researches and then focus on the algorithm to deliver the warning messages.

To collect the real time earthquake information from the sensor nodes, most of the projects [1][2] use digital seismometers or customized sensors. One of the innovated ideas in [3], the author tries to use the three-axis acceleration information in Hard disk or smart phones as a collaborative sensor system. The other researches [4] [5] [6] try to use wireless mesh network, wireless sensor network, P2P technology to collect the data rapidly. The data from sensor nodes is as the input for calculating the predictive Micron Log in nation-wide locations. There are a lot of studies [7][8][9][10] try to estimate earthquake in seconds. In Japan, several studies about earthquake early warning system are carried out. UrEDAS(Urgent Earthquake Detection and Alarm System) [11] service was lunched in 1992. The Japan Meteorological Agency (JMA) started providing the earthquake early warning service by several means such as TV and radio on Oct 2007. There are some works in [12][13][14][15][16][17] try to provide the information to the mobile users, Home automated systems and vehicles.

Warning message delivery is the most important issue for early earthquake warning system. Compare to information collection from hundreds of nodes, delivery the alert to millions of clients is much difficult. Although the japan mobile handset alert system proves itself with successful result, the same architecture cannot work in Taiwan. The telecom service providers do not enable Multimedia Broadcast Multicast Services (MBMS) in their network. Due to the price and performance issue for SMS system, it is also a bad idea to use SMS to delivery warning messages. There are more and more works in [18] [19] [20] [21] try to use SIP or IMS based message delivery mechanism. In this paper we introduce the earthquake early warning system in this section and analysis the related works and status of current SIP/IMS based message delivery mechanism in next section. We will purpose our system architecture and message delivery algorithm to reduce the useless message traffic issue in section 3. Finally we will verify our algorithm by simulating with MATLAB in section4 and make a conclusion in section5.

2   Related Work

2.1   SMS Messaging

Even the SMS messaging may beat out other technologies in terms of popularity, it suffers two disadvantages. First, the cost is relatively high – if we would like to send the message to large number of users. Secondly, although SMS message delivery is usually rapid, the receipt time and reliability can't be guaranteed, which is the fatal issue of SMS system. In [22], the article found approximately 5.1 % messages was not delivered at all. It is a large amount compared to the end to end message loss for e-mail, which was only 1.6%. In the general case, the SMS server only can handle two million messages per hour (around 500 messages per second). So it is a bad idea to use SMS to delivery warning messages.

2.2   SIP / IMS Messaging

SIP is the most popular communication protocol today. The general SIP message flow shows in Fig1. In the ALL IP cellular network, the IMS is also based on SIP protocol.

A lot of studies[23][24][25] try to deliver the emergency message on SIP/IMS.Compare with SMS, SIP/IMS clients provide much more multimedia capacity[26]. They usually use Session Initiation Protocol for Instant Messaging and Presence Leveraging Extension (SIMPLE) as the message format. SIP has a number of benefits over SMS, such as explicit rendezvous, tighter integration with other media-types, direct client to client operation. By RFC3428 page-mode message is enabled in SIP as a much simple way via the SIP MESSAGE method. The general SIP Page-Mode message flow shows in Fig2. However the messages will delivery by unicast when the sender sends the message to the group or updates the presence information. The burst message traffic will influence the low bandwidth network and may be blocked by the firewall.

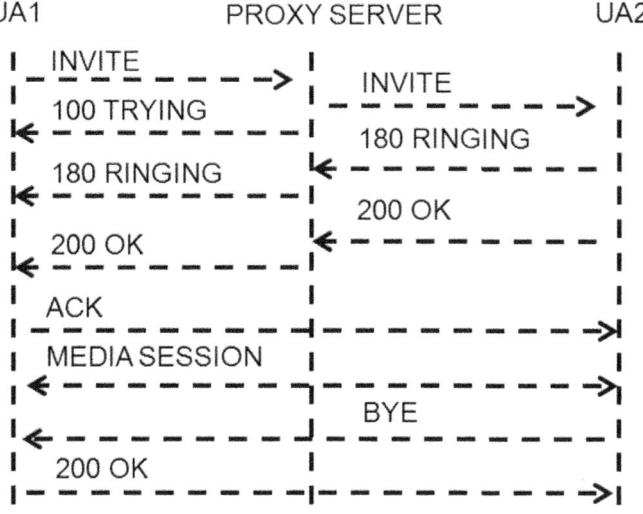

Fig. 1. IM Message Flow for RFC3261

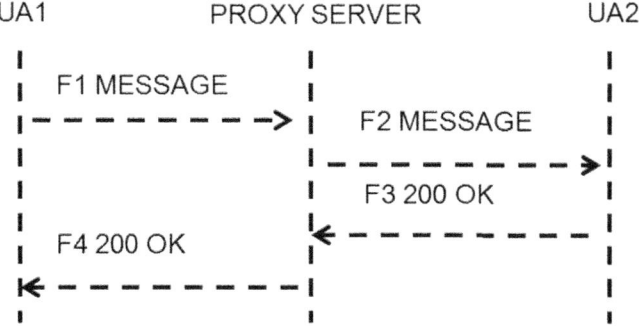

Fig. 2. IM Message Flow for RFC3428 (Page Mode)

2.3   Multimedia Broadcast Multicast Service (MBMS) Messaging

Multimedia Broadcast and Multicast Services (MBMS) [27] is a broadcasting service offered via existing GSM and UMTS cellular networks. The main application is mobile TV. MBMS uses multicast distribution in the core network instead of unicast links for each end device. The broadcast capability enables to reach unlimited number of users with constant network load. It also enables the possibility to broadcast information simultaneously to many cellular subscribers for example emergency alerts. However, the multicast network only work in the particular network. The message flow shows in Fig3 and Fig4.

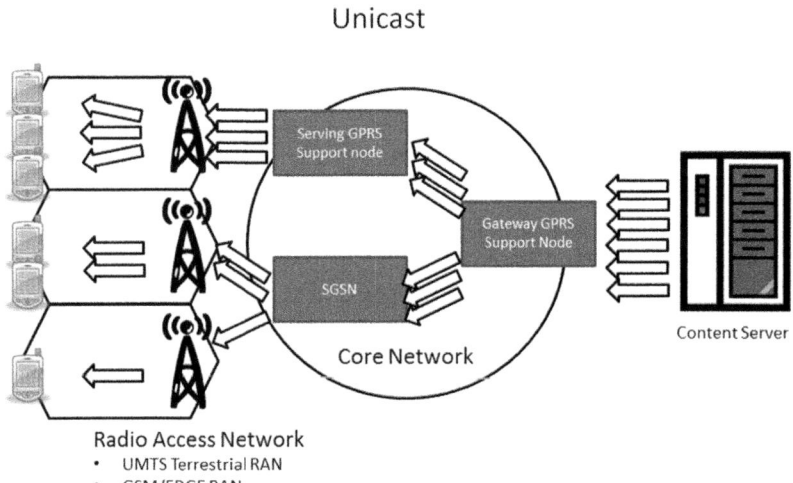

Fig. 3. Without MBMS, unicast transmissions consume more network resources as usage grows

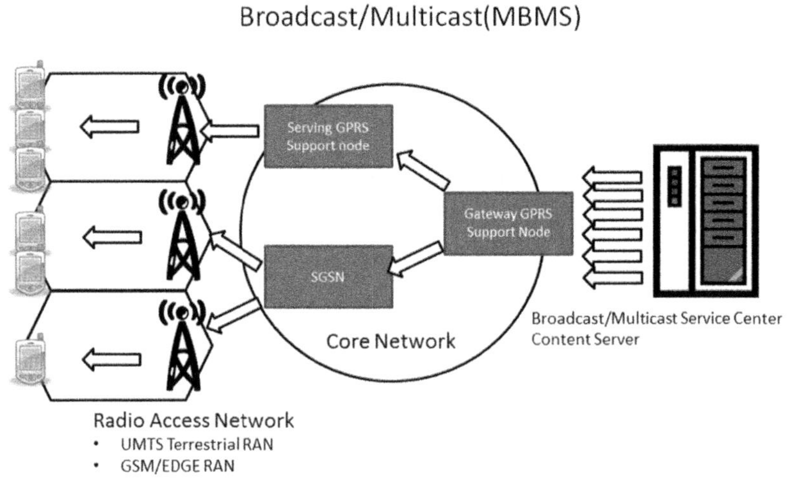

Fig. 4. With MBMS, broadcast transmissions efficiently use network resources at all usage levels

2.4   Mitigating SIP Overload Using a Control-Theoretic Approach

SIP (Session Initiation Protocol) is becoming the dominant signaling protocol for Internet-based communication services and it maintains its reliability by retransmission mechanism. The redundant retransmissions increase the CPU loads of both the overloaded server and its upstream servers. In [30] demonstrates that without overload control algorithm applied, the overload at the downstream server may propagate or migrate to its upstream servers eventually without protocol modification. The author proposes an overload control algorithm that can mitigate the overload effectively and prevent the overload propagation.

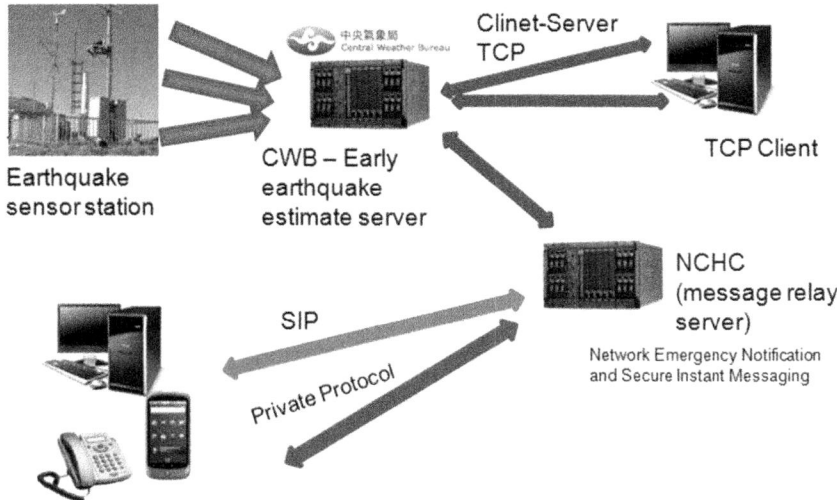

Fig. 5. Early earthquake warning system in Taiwan

Table 1. Comparison for the different delivered mechanisms

	SMS	Private TCP (client-server)	SIP	MBMS
Reliability	Low (without Ack)	High (with Ack)	High (with Ack)	Low (without Ack)
Message deliver efficiency	Low	Middle	Middle	High(multicast)
Advantage	It can be used without IP network	The design is simple	The most simple protocol in the IP network	High message deliver efficiency
Disadvantage	Low message deliver efficiency but expensive	It's hard to extend the protocol	Work with unicast in the real world	Only work in particular cellular network

2.5   Earthquake Early Warning System in Taiwan

In Taiwan, the movement of earthquake will take 30sec from Taichung to Taipei. CWB can receive the data form the sensors and finish the simulation in 10sec. currently they use Client-Server TCP software to deliver the message.

The CWB looks for a reliable and efficient solution to deliver the emergency message. By the comparison in Table 1, we can understand SIP will be the most appropriate solution for NGN(All IP) emergency message delivery system. The system is designed for general network – without multicast funcation. How to deliver the unicast SIP message efficiency is the most important issue[28][29].

3   An Efficient Earthquake Early Alert Message Delivery Algorithm Using an In Time Control-Theoretic Approach

Our purpose is to use the SIP page-mode as the next generation earthquake warning system protocol. But it still needs to send message to the users individually because multicast cannot work in the general network. Fig6 shows when a new user register with the service, the system will save the following information :(1) network subnet prefix (with C class) (2) Human or IoT Client. (3)location information. Fig7 shows the message delivery flow when CWB server send the alerts to clients.

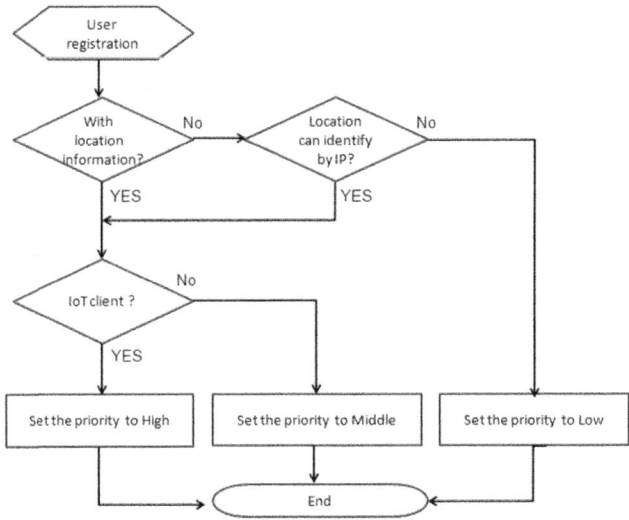

Fig. 6. User registration flow

We set the time for earthquake simulation as t_{cal}, CWB has α message servers and each server can handle β messages per second. There are N cities in the system and the earthquake will arrive on t_1.....t_N. In the cities with the IoT and human clients that mark as IoT_i+ $USER_i$. If the message in the queue can't be sent on time, it will be dropped from the delivery queue. The message delivery failure will mark as equation 1 for each city.

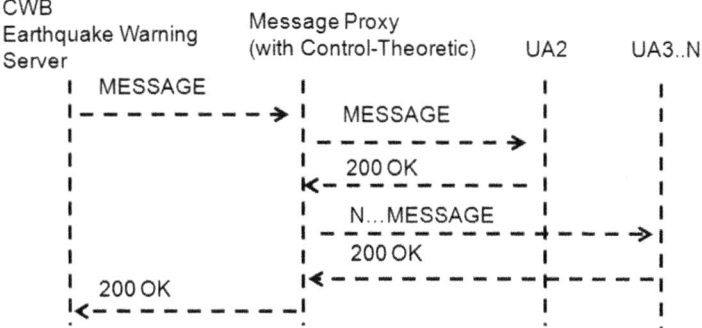

Fig. 7. Message delivery flow

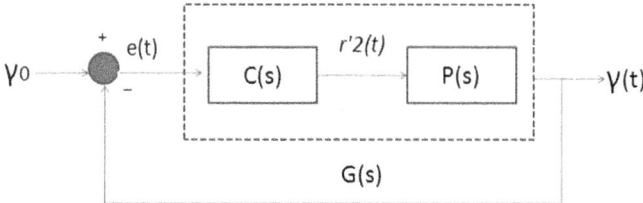

Fig. 8. Feedback control for SIP overload control system

$$LOSSIoT_i + LOSSUSER_i = LOSS_i \qquad (1)$$

The message delivery model reference from [30] and use the feedback control for SIP retransmission overload . Fig 8 and the equation (2) to (4) show how the feedback control work. The overload control plant $P(s)$ represents the interaction between a receiving server and a sending server, the transfer function is given by

$$P(s) = \gamma(t) / r'(t) \qquad (2)$$

And adaptive PI controller $C(s)$ is designed for mitigating the overload and achieving a desirable target redundant message ratio γ_0, when the overload is anticipated at the downstream server .The transfer function $C(s)$ is

$$C(s) = K_P + K_I / s \qquad (3)$$

By the following PI control algorithm expressed via, we can obtain the equation 4. We use the PI control to mitigate the overload and achieve a satisfactory target redundant message ratio by controlling retransmission rate.

$$r'(t) = K_P e(t) + K_I \int_0^t e(x)dx = K_P(\gamma_0 - \gamma(t)) + K_I \int_0^t (\gamma_0 - \gamma(x))dx \qquad (4)$$

Table 2. Control-Theoretic Parameters

Varying Parameters :	Fixed Parameters :
$\gamma(t)$: Redundant message ratio	$\gamma 0(t)$:Target redundant message ratio
r' (t): Message Retransmission rate	e(t): redundant message ratio deviation
Kp: Proportional gain	KI: Integral gain

As the pseudo code in Fig.9, we use the greedy algorithm try to process the most urgent event. Also we apply the in time limitation for the algorithm. If the message can't be sent in time, it will be skipped. The messages for IoT devices will get higher priority than human users in the same city. The message delivery model reference from [30] and use the feedback control for SIP retransmission overload . Fig 8 and Table 2 show how the feedback control work. Based on our algorithm, we reduce the message traffic as equation 5.

For(i=1;i<=N;i++) //deliver the message from City to CityN

{

if(t_i<=t_{cal})

 {

  //before the simulation finish, we can't send the alert nessages

  $LOSS_i = IoT_i + USER_i$

 }

 else

  {

  /*If the message can't be sent in time ,

  the messages for IoT devices will get higher priority than human users,

  and we calculate the number of loss users*/

  if($\alpha * \beta * (t_i-t_{cal}) < \sum_1^i[(IoT_x + USER_x) - LOSS_x])$

   LOSSi=$\sum_1^i[(IoT_x + USER_x) - LOS_x] - \alpha * \beta * (t_i-t_{cal})$;

  if($LOSS_i <= USER_i$)

   {$LOSSUSER_i = LOSS_i$}

  else

   {$LOSSUSER_i = USER_i$;

    $LOSSIoT_i=LOSS_i - LOSSUSER_i$ }

  }

}

Fig. 9. Pseudo code for the number of loss users by message delivery algorithm

$$\frac{\sum_{1}^{N}[(IoT_x + USER_x) - LOSS_x]}{\sum_{1}^{N}(IoT_x + USER_x)} = MessageTraffic \qquad (5)$$

4   Simulation

We use the data comes from 1999 Chi-Chi Earthquake in Taiwan, table3 show there are 23 mojor sensor stations in Taiwan(N=23). We assume there are 1000 IoT clients and 10000 human users in each city(IoT$_i$=1000, USER$_i$=10000). The system will take 10 sec to finish the simulation(Tcal=10). CWB have one message server that can handle 5000 message/sec (α=1, β=5000)

Table 3. Earthquake Historical data comes from 1999 Chi-Chi Earthquake

Station ID	Distance/ time	Station ID	Distance/ time
City01	5.53KM/1.38s	City13	109.6KM/27.4s
City02	21.42KM/5.35s	City14	109.9KM/27.4s
City03	26.13KM/6.53s	City15	123.7KM/30.9s
City04	38.32KM/9.58s	City16	129.1KM/32.2s
City05	41.61KM/10.4s	City17	132.3KM/33.1s
City06	55.97KM/13.9s	City18	137.3KM/34.3s
City07	62.64KM/15.6s	City19	142.5KM/35.6s
City08	64.52KM/16.1s	City20	154.6KM/38.6s
City09	66.02KM/16.5s	City21	156.7KM/39.1s
City10	78.89KM/19.7s	City22	171.2KM/42.8s
City11	99.10KM/24.7s	City23	214.5KM/53.6s
City12	103.8KM/25.9s		

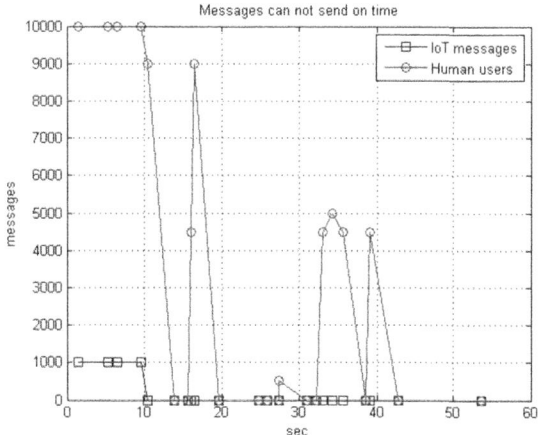

Fig. 10. Total number of dropped messages(without proposed algorithm)

From the result in Fig10, it shows the messages that should be sent before t_{cal} is identified as useless message. When the system can't delivery all of the messages, it will drop the messages for human user first. By this way, the IoT devices can be severed as many as possible. The delivery algorithm tries to send the emergency messages to IoT devices as many as possible. The system delivers 167500 useful messages with only one message server.

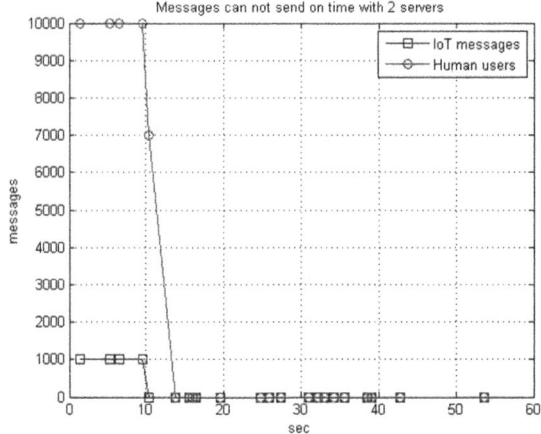

Fig. 11. Total number of dropped messages(with proposed algorithm)

Fig. 12. Earthquake warning UA detect the location information

If we add one server for the system(α=2), most of the message will be deliveried. However it can not reduce the dropped messages before t_{cal}. The system delivers 202000 useful messages with two message servers.

For the best case in our scenario, there are 253000 messages should be delivered without the location information; however the number of useful messages is 209000. If the system tries to send all of the messages in 1 sec, it will need around 50 servers. The useful message delivery rate with one server can be calculated by equation 3. The useful message delivery rate with two servers can be calculated by equation 4.

Fig 12 show the user interface for alert message service client, the location information can be obtain by GPS, IP lookup and manual control. When the UA receive the alert message, it will look like Fig 13.

$$\frac{the\_num\_sent\_message}{the\_num\_message} = \frac{167500}{209000} = 80.14\% \tag{3}$$

$$\frac{the\_num\_sent\_message}{the\_num\_message} = \frac{202000}{209000} = 96.65\% \tag{4}$$

Fig. 13. Earthquake warning message with An Efficient Early Earthquake Alert Message Delivery Algorithm Using an In Time Control-Theoretic Approach

5   Conclusion

In this paper, we propose an innovative alarm notification algorithm with Instant Message (IM) base on Session Initiation Protocol (SIP) replacing current proprietary Client-Server protocol. By improving the alarm notification algorithm considering with location information, higher priority for IoT devices and control-theoretic approach, we can both reduce the burst message traffic for network and send the message in time with fewer servers.

Acknowledgment
NSC 99-2219-E-007-007
MOTC-DPT-100-03。

References

1. Chin, J.-C., Rautenberg, J.M., Ma, C.Y.T., Pujol, S., Yau, D.K.Y.: An Experimental Low-Cost, Low-Data-Rate Rapid Structural Assessment Network. IEEE Sensors Journal 9(11), 1361–1369 (2009)
2. Basha, E., Rus, D.: Design of early warning flood detection systems for developing countries. In: ICTD 2007, December 15-16, pp. 1–10 (2007)
3. Heindl, E.: Peer-to-peer (P2P) earthquake warning system based on collaborative sensing. In: DEST 2009, June 1-3, pp. 174–176 (2009)
4. Nachtigall, J., Zubow, A., Sombrutzki, R., Picozzi, M.: The Challenges of Using Wireless Mesh Networks for Earthquake Early Warning Systems. In: MESH 2009, June 18-23, pp. 155–162 (2009)
5. Wenjun, W., Shun, Y.: Study of the TDM of the GPS Timing in Earthquake Early-Warning Information Transfer. In: ICICTA 2010, May 11-12, vol. 3, pp. 455–457 (2010)
6. Rajarapollu, P., Sharma, V.K.: Design and analysis of satellite based disaster warning system - II. In: TENCON 2007, October 30, pp. 1–4 (November 2007)
7. Gupta, D., Shahani, D.T., Khan, S.: Fast Fourier Transform based Earthquake Precursor Analysis of Radon in N-W Himalayas. In: ICEMI 2007, August 16, pp. 3-1–3-4 (2007)
8. Aminzadeh, F., Katz, S., Aki, K.: Adaptive neural nets for generation of artificial earthquake precursors. IEEE Transactions on Geoscience and Remote Sensing 32(6), 1139–1143 (1994)
9. Huang, C.-J., Chang, C.-H., Chang, K.-Y.: Uncertainty propagation of Earthquake Loss Estimation System on the early seismic damage evaluation. In: 17th International Conference on Geoinformatics, August 12-14, pp. 1–6 (2009)
10. Plag, H.-P., Blewitt, G., Hammond, W., Kreemer, C., Bar-Sever, Y.: Rapid GPS-based determination of earthquake displacement field and magnitude for tsunami propagation modeling and warning. In: IGARSS 2010, July 25-30, pp. 3039–3042 (2010)
11. Nakamura, Y.: Urgent Earthquake Detection and Alarm System, Now and Futire. In: Proc. 13th World Conference on Earthquake Engineering (paper no.908) (August 2004)
12. Nagaosa, T., Moriya, S.: An emergency Earthquake warning system for land mobile vehicles using the earthquake early warning. In: ICVES 2008, September 22-24, pp. 309–311 (2008)
13. Koike, N.: Catching the wave: real-time tsunami warning systems. IEEE Potentials 28(5), 14–17 (2009)
14. Teshirogi, Y., Sawamoto, J., Segawa, N., Sugino, E.: A Proposal of Tsunami Warning System Using Area Mail Disaster Information Service on Mobile Phones. In: WAINA 2009, May 26-29, pp. 890–895 (2009)
15. Kun, X., Zhihui, Z., Li, Q.: Research on earthquake alarm system in high speed railway. In: ICCTD 2010, November 2-4, pp. 744–748 (2010)
16. Wang, J., Su, M., Zhao, G., Liu, C., Zhang, M., Wang, D., Gao, X.: Design and Implementation of the Earthquake Precursor Network Running Monitoring Software Based on C/S Structure. In: WiCOM 2010, September 23-25, pp. 1–4 (2010)
17. Kokawa, T., Takeuchi, Y., Sakamoto, R., Ogawa, H., Kryssanov, V.V.: An Agent-Based System for the Prevention of Earthquake-Induced Disasters. In: ICTAI 2007, October 29-31, pp. 55–62 (2007)

18. Park, S.O., Huh, M.-Y., Han, J.C., Kang, S.G.: Enhanced 911 Mechanism for Internet Telephony Service. In: Portland International Center for Management of Engineering and Technology, August 5-9, pp. 899–902 (2007)
19. Costa-Requena, J., Haitao, T.: Enhancing SIP with spatial location for emergency call services. In: Tenth International Conference on Computer Communications and Networks Proceedings 2001, pp. 326–333 (2001)
20. Maes, S.H.: SDP-based IP and Multimedia real time communications integration with vehicle remote monitoring, monitoring and emergency systems. In: ITST 2008, October 24-24, pp. 328–333 (2008)
21. Waraporn, N., Triyason, T., Angsuchotmetee, C., Tilkanont, P.: Emergency service warning system using SIP for integrated media. In: NCM 2010, August 16-18, pp. 312–317 (2010)
22. Latimer, D.: Text Messaging as Emergency Communication Superstar? Nt so gr8. Educause Review 43(3), 84–85 (2008)
23. Song, W., Kim, J.Y., Schulzrinne, H., Boni, P., Armstrong, M.: Using IM and SMS for emergency text communications. In: IPTComm 2009, Article 4, pages 7 (2009)
24. Lakay, E.T., Agbinya, J.I.: SIP-based content development for wireless mobile devices. In: CCSP 2005, November 14-16, pp. 130–134 (2005)
25. Henry, K., Qunkai, L., Pasquereau, S.: Rich Communication Suite. In: 13th International Conference on ICIN 2009, October 26-29, pp. 1–6 (2009)
26. Han, J.C., Park, S.O., Kang, S.G., Lee, H.H.: A Study on SIP-based Instant Message and Presence. In: The 9th International Conference on Advanced Communication Technology, February 12-14, vol. 2, pp. 1298–1301 (2007)
27. Gomez-Barquero, D., Fernandez-Aguilella, A., Cardona, N.: Multicast Delivery of File Download Services in Evolved 3G Mobile Networks With HSDPA and MBMS. IEEE Transactions on Broadcasting 55(4), 742–751 (2009); Appendix: Springer-Author Discount
28. Chi, T.-Y., Chao, H.-C., Kuo, S.-Y.: An efficient emergency message delivery algorithm for early earthquake warning system. In: ICET 2011, Phuket (2011)
29. Chi, T.-Y., Che, C.-H., Chao, H.-C.: An efficient early earthquake alert message delivery algorithm with multi-ISP channels. In: ITAOI 2011, Taiwan, (2011)
30. Hong, Y., Huang, C., Yan, J.: Mitigating SIP Overload Using a Control-Theoretic Approach. In: Globecom 2010, Canada, (2011)

Dynamic Resource Management for a Cell-Based Distributed Mobile Computing Environment

Sung Il Kim, Jae Young Jun, Jong-Kook Kim[*], Kyung-Chan Lee,
Gyu Seong Kang, Taek-Soo Kim, Hee Kyoung Moon,
Hye Chan Yoon, Hyungmin Kim, and Sang Hoon Lee

School of Electrical Engineering, Korea University, Anam Dong, Seoul, Korea
jongkook@korea.ac.kr

Abstract. In a distributed mobile computing environment (DMC), managing resources is an important problem. If it is not done in an intelligent manner, many devices may die early because of the limited energy capacity of the devices thus overall system may fail to complete tasks/work by their deadline and failing to satisfy users. This research assumes a cell-based environment and the mobile devices in this environment are heterogeneous (i.e., different CPU speed, different limited battery capacity, different mobility), and different tasks have affinity to different devices and have deadlines that must be met. To use the devices' energy efficiently, dynamic voltage scaling and variable-range transmission power control techniques are applied. This paper will provide an insight on how to utilize a cell-based environment for distributed mobile computing purposes and discuss methods of resource management techniques crucial to the operation of such system.

Keywords: distributed mobile computing, cell-based environment, dynamic resource allocation/management, dynamic voltage scaling, energy-aware computing.

1   Introduction

As more and more powerful mobile devices are introduced to the users, the users will be carrying a mobile device that is as powerful as a desktop computer in the future. Also, there are a lot more mobile devices than desktops and the number of such devices carried by users are growing. In the future, it may be profitable to the users/system administrators to utilize these mobile devices for more computing power. One such environment can be the distributed mobile computing (DMC) environment, where the environment consists of mobile devices that communicate via wireless methods thus limited energy battery capacity is constraint on the device usage and energy management are a critical issue for the overall system. The devices in this environment may be heterogeneous (e.g., computing performance, battery capacity) and tasks must be completed by their deadline and tasks may have affinity to different devices.

---

[*] Corresponding author.

C.-H. Hsu et al. (Eds.): UIC 2011, LNCS 6905, pp. 174–184, 2011.

The heterogeneity of resources and tasks in a heterogeneous DMC system should be exploited to maximize the performance or the cost-effectiveness of the system. Hence, the important problem is how to allocate the resources to tasks or schedule tasks onto devices to maximize the performance criterion of the system. This mapping of resource to task or tasks to resources is generally known as the NP-Complete problem. A resource management system (RMS) maps tasks to devices and manages the system resources such that a given performance metric can be maximized with limited knowledge. In this research, the DMC environment changes dynamically, therefore dynamic resource management or dynamic mapping is performed.

This research provides insights on how to utilize a cell-based environment for distributed mobile computing purposes and discuss methods of resource management techniques crucial to the operation of such system. Five heuristics are extended and designed from previous methods (e.g., [1], [10], [11]) and four basic methods such as the Originator, Estimated Minimum Total Energy (EMTE), Minimum Execution Time (MET), and Minimum Completion Time (MCT) methods are included for performance comparison.

The goal of this paper is to complete as many tasks as possible within their deadlines while using limited energy of system efficiently.Because it is important to allow methods to save energy while trying to complete as many tasks as possible for system longevity, the modeled cell-based environment uses dynamic voltage scaling (DVS) [2] for the computation energy saving and variable transmission power control (VTPC) [3] for the communication energy saving.

The modeling of the environment and the evaluation of the heuristics for this research is done utilizing a distributed mobile computing simulator EarDruM (Energy-Aware Distributed Mobile Computing Simulator) [12], which is based on the network simulator 2(NS-2) [5].

A cell-based DMC environment is introduced in Section 2.

Section 3 contains five proposed heuristic methods. In Section 4, 5 describes the simulation model and shows simulation result. The last section concludes the research.

2   Cell-Based Distributed Mobile Computing Environment

In this paper, a single hop cell-based DMC model include devices that are mobile and communicate by wireless means.

Each device has a different battery capacity, different mobility, different CPU speed, and uses the dynamic voltage scaling (DVS) [2] method with different number of voltage levels. The DVS technique makes it possible to save the energy by means of controlling the CPU supply voltage (clock speed). The energy saving using DVS is based on exploiting the relationship between the power consumption and the CPU supply voltage of a device which is represented by a polynomial of at least second degree [4]. However, there is a tradeoff, i.e., the DVS method reduces the power consumption of CPU at the expense of increasing a task's execution time. The variable-range transmission power control (VTPC) [3] technique is used for the efficient use of communication power/energy. The number and value of discrete voltage levels differ in all devices while the number and value of VTPC power levels are same for all devices. The DVS and VTPC method is managed by the resource manager, and are not shown to the user. All devices can request tasks, send data, and receive data.

The operation of procedure of a cell-based RMS is as follows:

1. A task is requested from the source device.
2. The RMS picks a destination device to execute a given task considering task's deadline, task's execution time, energy usage, communication possibility, etc. The RMS decides whether inputs are needed or not. If the input is needed to execute the task, the RMS will send a command to the device which has the input. After RMS selects a destination device, decision information is sent to the task requester (source device).
3. The task requester sends the task to the RMS and if necessary, inputs are sent to the RMS. When the RMS receives the task and the inputs, the RMS sends them to the destination device.
4. When the destination device receives the task and input (if needed), the destination device executes the task. After executing the task, the result is sent back to the RMS and then the result is sent to the task requester.

The resource management system (RMS) is assumed to be in the center (it can be assumed that the base station has the capability in this environment). The RMS is assumed to be fixed in this location, have infinite computation energy, and has all the status information of all the tasks within its communication range. It is assumed that the task's execution time on a the devices is known however, it is not known which

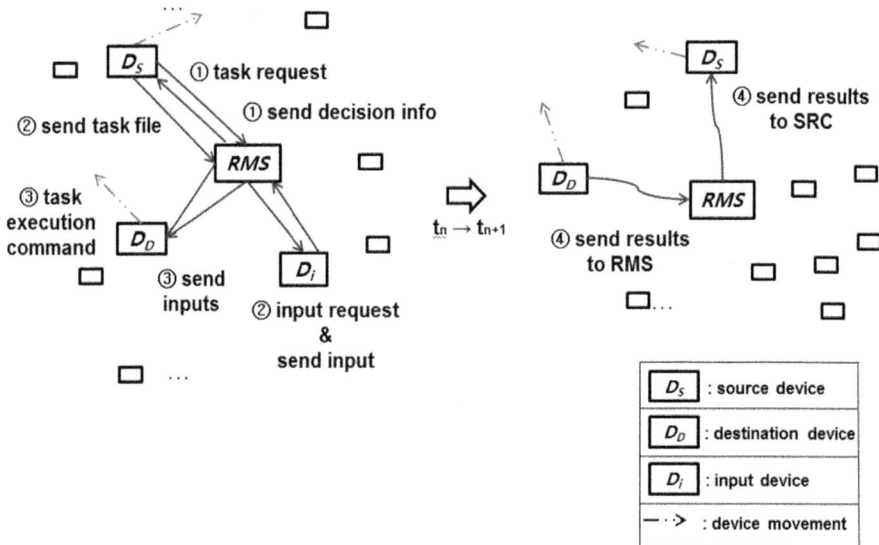

Fig. 1. The cell-based resource management system for a distributed mobile computing environment

task will be requested for execution and when the task will be requested. Expected time to complete for a task on each device can be calculated by the execution time, status of the devices, voltage levels used, and the heuristic method used for resource management. Each task has its own deadline, a task will be failed even if it is completed execution on a device if the reception of the results violates the deadline of the requested task.

3   Heuristic Description

3.1   Overview

The goal of this research is to complete as many tasks as possible within their deadline. A mapping event occurs when a new task arrives into the DMC system. The tasks must be assigned to try and achieve the goal. All heuristics choose the "best" device among the selectable devices, which in this particular scenario are devices that are still active and have battery capacity to execute tasks, according to their fitness function or method. If no selectable device can meet a task's deadline, the task will be dropped. Four basic methods for resource management is compared to the five that are designed in this research. The four basic methods are Originator, Estimated Minimum Total Energy (EMTE), Minimum Execution Time (MET), and Minimum Completion Time (MCT) methods. The originator tries to complete tasks on the source device without communicating with other devices. EMTE assigns each task to the device with the minimum total energy consumption without time consideration. MET assigns each task to the device with best expected execution time without energy consideration. MCT is a load balancing method where tasks are mapped to devices that will complete the task fastest.

3.2   Minimum Sum of Total Energy and Execution Time

Minimum Sum of Total Energy and Execution Time (MSET) assigns each task to the device that has minimum sum of total energy and execution time. This heuristic is designed to make up for the disadvantages of EMTE and MET. The EMTE does not consider execution time whereas MET does not consider energy consumption. The MSET considers both energy and execution time in an attempt to balance between these two criteria.

The total energy consumption is determined by adding the estimated energy consumption of the computation and the communication that must be done to complete a task. The execution time only includes the computational time. The procedure is as follows:

1. At a mapping event, calculate the estimated total energy consumption of all selectable devices.
2. For all selectable devices, calculate the sum of total energy consumption and execution time.
3. Assign a task to the device with minimum sum of total energy consumption and execution time.

3.3   Normalized Minimum Sum of Total Energy and Execution Time

Normalized Minimum Sum of Total Energy and Execution Time (N-MSET) assigns each task to the device using a similar method to MSET. MSET can be biased such that if the energy has a much larger average value than the execution time, the result of the sum will only be affected by the energy. N-MSET is designed to prevent this biased metric by normalizing each of the value. After normalization, the energy and execution time will have the similar average and variance. The relative importance of the values is indicated by inserting weights for each of the values. After preliminary experiments to get the best results, the weighting factors are determined.

3.4   K-Percent Best Energy with Minimum Completion Time

The KPE (K-Percent Best Energy) assigns each task to the device with minimum execution time, among the K-percent best energy consuming devices [11]. Unlike KPE, K-Percent Best Energy with Minimum Completion Time (KPE-MCT) assigns each task to the device with minimum completion time, among the K-percent best energy consuming devices. The procedure is as follows:

1. At the mapping event, calculate the energy consumption of each device.
2. Calculate the task completion time of each device among K percent devices that consume energy the least.
3. Assign a task to the device with minimum completion time.

3.5   MET-Originator

The advantage of using the originator method is as follows:

1. The originator has minimal communication time and uses almost no communication energy. This is because tasks are always assigned to the requested device and the originator does not have to send results back.
2. The originator reduces the work-load of the RMS.

However, because it does not consider other devices for execution of tasks, it cannot run tasks on devices that may be better suited for the tasks.

The MET-Originator is designed to improve the disadvantage of the originator by first trying to assign the tasks using the originator method then if the task cannot be completed then using some fitness function, try to find a suitable device for the task. The fitness function of the MET-Originator is as follows:

$$T_{req} \times N_{decice} \geq T_{exec} : function\ 1$$

$$T_{req} \times N_{decice} < T_{exec} : function\ 2$$

T_{Req}: calculated average interval of task request time.
N_{device}: total number of devices that is alive in the system
T_{exec}: execution time

The process of the MET-Originator is as follows:

1. If the source device is able to complete a task within the deadline, the task is assigned to the source device.

2. For any device which satisfies function 1, the task is assigned to maximum energy remaining device.

3. For any device satisfies function 2, the task is assigned to the device with minimum execution time.

3.6 Load-Balanced Minimum Execution Time

The MET only considers the execution time and does not consider the load balance or deadline. Therefore, it is possible that the tasks might be assigned to certain devices all the time, which leads to early death of some of the mobile devices.

The Load-Balanced Minimum Execution Time (LBMET) is designed to make up for the disadvantage of the MET method. LBMET uses two factors, DAT (Device Available Time) which is the time that the device becomes idle and the E-threshold which is determined by a percentage of the initial starting energy of each device.

A device is regarded as "crossed the E-threshold" when the energy of a certain device falls down 80% of its initial energy (for this environment and it was determined experimentally). The intuition behind setting the E-threshold is to prevent premature load-imbalance which will cause inefficient mapping of the tasks. The LBMET blocks the best 10% devices based on DAT assuming these devices are best suited for some of the future tasks. After blocking, LBMET assigns the task to the device with minimum execution time on other devices. The procedure is as follows:

1. For all devices, calculate DAT and the E-threshold.

2. Among the devices that have crossed the E-threshold, block the best 10% devices based on DAT.

3. For non-blocked devices, the task is assigned to the device with minimum execution time.

4   Simulation Model

Most of the simulation model is similar to [12]. For the simulation, six types of wireless devices modeled from the PXA270 processors in [6] are used and each device has any one of the three different number of voltage levels (2, 4, and 8 levels). Thus, eighteen combinations of device heterogeneity take simulation into consideration. And the maximum battery capacity of each device is set to the sum of maximum CPU energy consumption ratio and transmission energy ratio, multiplied by the maximum operation time. The maximum operation time is determined using a gamma distribution with a range of two hours. This means that if the CPU and wireless module use the maximum level (CPU energy consumption plus transmission energy), then the battery capacity will be only enough to operate the device for two hours.

To simplify DVS, this research assumes that each voltage level of a processor corresponds to a clock speed level for the processor. Each device has 2, 4, or 8 discrete speed levels with equal probability and the speed level of 2 is the highest speed level. The active power is considered as the maximum power for each of the six device types of frequency mode. After the decision of the level, the relative speed of each level is determined. The lowest speed level of a device is assumed to be one third of the maximum speed level (e.g., if the maximum speed level is 624MHz, then the lowest speed level would be 208MHz). The rest of the levels are determined dividing the gap between the maximum and lowest speed level equally according to the number of levels in each device. In order to determine the power usage at each of the levels, using the simplified relationship of power being proportional to voltage squared, a constant is calculated using the voltage and the active power in [6].

The power consumption for each level is determined by this constant and the fractions. We make the simplified assumption that task execution time varies linearly with the discrete speed level. It is assumed that the voltage switching is done dynamically and that the overhead associated with the switching is negligible (20 μs ~ 150 μs). Table 1 shows the maximum frequency (mode), maximum power consumption (active power), idle/sleep state power consumption (idle power), maximum voltage (voltage) on each device.

In each simulation of a system, 20, 30, 40 and 50 devices among the eighteen combinations are picked with equal probability. The arrival (request) of tasks is simulated by mean inter-task arrival times using a Poisson distribution. The mean inter-task arrival time of 6 seconds is used for the experiment.

For all tasks, the ETC values on 18 types of devices taking heterogeneity into consideration is randomly generated using the gamma distribution method described in [7]. The mean execution time of 200 seconds is used for the ETC matrix. The mean execution time is chosen to represent applications such as processing data (such as maps or weather reports), generating strategies, etc.

The size of the task and output (result to the source) data was calculated using 100 Kbytes as the mean and a COV of 0.7 using a Gamma distribution. The size of the input and the other communication data was calculated using 1 Kbytes as the mean and a COV of 0.7 using a Gamma distribution.

This research assumes that when the task arrives, the deadline of the task is given. For our simulation studies, the deadline of task i was equal to its arrival time plus the overall mean execution time of all tasks using Gamma distribution plus the median execution time of task i on all devices plus the expected communication time of task and result.

IEEE 802.11b standard is applied for wireless communication and communication power consumption value is based on specification in [8] and [9]. Based on the two-ray ground reflection model [5] in NS-2, whenever communication is occurred, the transmission power and the discrete transmission power level are determined according to the transmission range (for 10, 50, 100, 150, 200, 250 and 500 meters) by using VTPC. Because the two-ray ground model does not consider the interference influence, our simulation model also does not consider the interference influence. Therefore, to determine the appropriate transmission power level, we add an additional transmission power empirically. And only one way communication is available (i.e., only the communication of one source/destination device pair is possible at a moment).

A trial is defined as one such simulation of the system. For each of the eight scenarios (inter-task arrival time × execution times × four types of device number), 30 trials are run for 28800 seconds (i.e., 8 hours) for each heuristic. More details are shown in Table 2. As shown in Table 1, we use DSDV [13] for the routing protocol. The reason for using DSDV is that it provides the routing information before a decision is made because it periodically updates the routing table.

Table 1. Parameter setting for the simulations

simulation parameter	value
network area	1400 × 1400 meters
maximum transmission range	1500 meters
data / header packet size	1000 / 40 bytes
simulation time	28800 seconds
data rate	1 Mbps
maximum device's speed	6 meter/sec
traffic model	application/FTP
ad hoc routing protocol	AODV

5   Results

The experimental evaluation of the nine heuristics is performed in this research. In order to compare purposed heuristics, the four of the ten heuristics (Originator, EMTE, MET, MCT) are run in this simulation. Four out of nine heuristics (i.e., EMTE, MSET, N-MSET, KPE-MCT) apply DVS and the rest (i.e., Originator, MET, MCT, MET-Originator, LBMET) do not apply DVS. The results of average percentage of 30 trials shown in Figure 2.

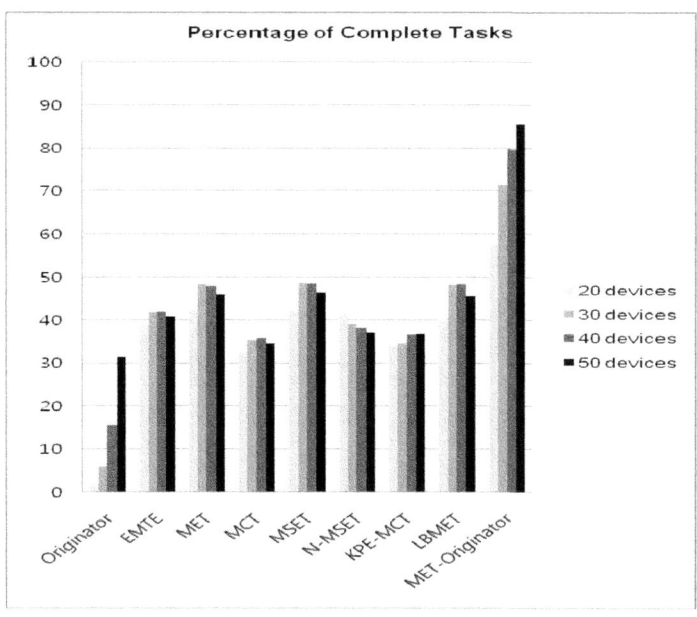

(a)

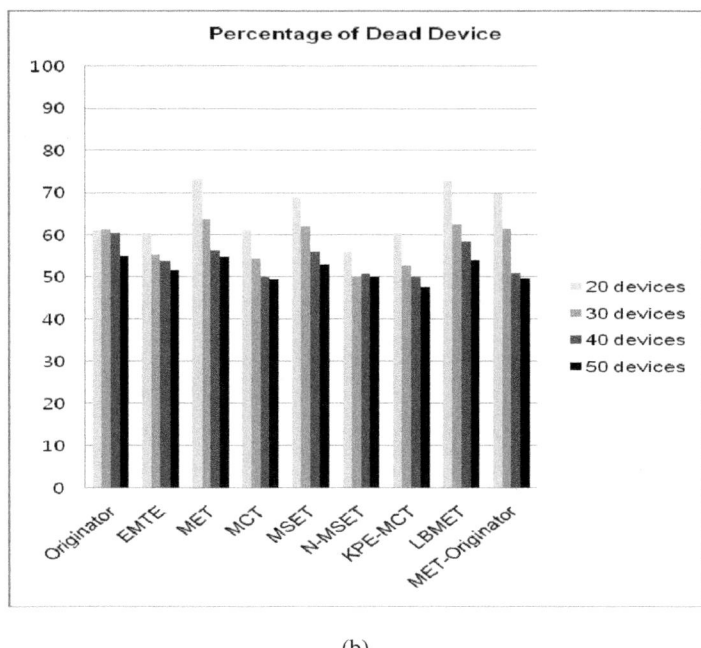

(b)

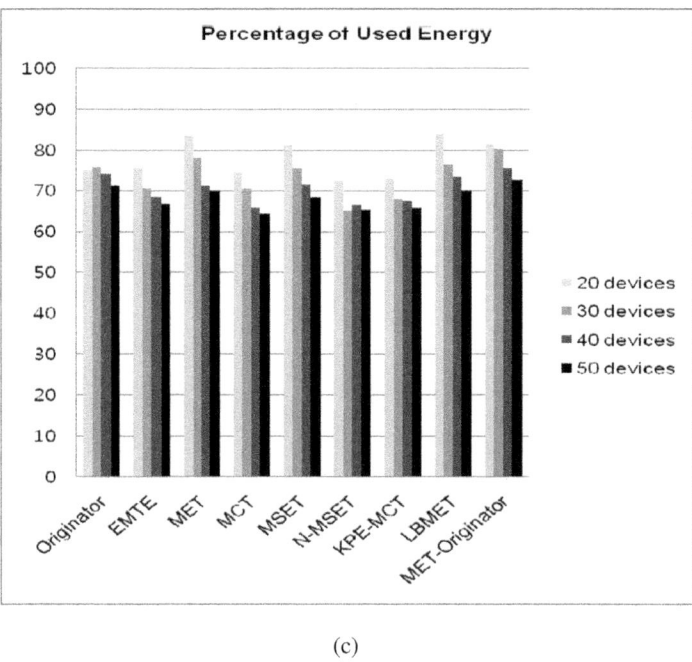

(c)

Fig. 2. The simulation result using the mean execution time of 200 seconds and mean inter-task arrival of 6 seconds for (a), (b), and (c)

Figure 2(a) shows the percentage of tasks completed by their deadline performance of the heuristics when the mean task arrival time is 6 seconds and the mean task execution time is 200 seconds. MET-Originator performed the best in this scenario.The effect of DVS seemed to be lost as all methods used a lot of the energy (shown in Figure 2(b)) even though some heuristic's peformance was not good. All of the proposed methods was better than originator and the simple MET method did pretty well. The reason may be that the task to device affinity was inconsistent, meaning that tasks preference of devices may be spread out. As the results show with completion percentage and energy used, there are lot of tasks that started to be sent to a destination device, start to execute on the destination device, or start to send back the results to the source device and failed to complete or failed to complete by the tasks' deadline.

6   Conclusion

In this paper, a cell-based distributed mobile computing environment was modeled and simulated using EArDruM. Five dynamic heuristics were designed and four basic methods are tested and evaluated the environment. The devices are heterogeneous in the sense that they have different compuation speed, battery capacity, different dynamic voltage scaling (DVS) levels, etc. The tasks are heterogeneous as they have affinity to different devices, they arrive randomly, and have deadlines. All status information about devices is given to the centralized resource management system (RMS). The RMS assigns each task to the best suited device based on the resource allocation method using various information about the system and status of the system (e.g., expected execution time, energy consumption). The main goal of this paper is to complete as many tasks as possible by their deadline under the constraint of available system energy and during a given interval of time. The MET-Originator performed the best and the percentage of tasks completed was around 2.7 times that of the originator.

Acknowledgement. This research is supported in part by the National Research Foundation of Korea grant no. 2009-0076378 and 331-2008-1-D00444.

References

1. Kim, J.-K., Siegel, H.J., Maciejewski, A.A., Eigenmann, R.: Dynamic Resource Management in Energy Constrained Heterogeneous Computing Systems Using Voltage Scaling. IEEE Trans. Parallel and Distributed Systems 19(11), 1445–1457 (2008)
2. Weiser, M., Welch, B., Demers, A., Shenker, S.: Scheduling for Reduced CPU Energy. In: Proc. Usenix Symp. Operating Systems Design and Implementation (OSDI 1994), pp. 13–23 (November 1994)
3. Gomez, J., Campbell, A.T.: A Case for variable-range transmission power control in wireless multihop networks. In: Proc. IEEE INFOCOM 2004, pp. 1425–1436 (March 2004)
4. Hong, I., Qu, G., Potkonjak, M., Srivastava, M.: Synthesis techniques for low-power hard real-time systems on variable voltage processors. In: Proc. 19th IEEE Real-Time Systems Symp (RTSS 1998), December 1998, pp. 95–105 (1998)

5. Fall, K., Varadhan, K.: The ns manual, http://www.isi.edu/nsnam/ns/
6. Intel PXA270 Processor Datasheet (2010),
    http://www.phytec.com/pdf/datasheets/PXA270_DS.pdf (accessed)
7. Ali, S., Siegel, H.J., Maheswaran, M., Hensgen, D., Ali, S.: Representing Task and
    Machine Heterogeneities for Heterogeneous Computing Systems. Tamkang J. Science and
    Eng., Special 50th Anniversary Issue 3(3), 195–207 (2000) (invited)
8. Nokia Mobile Phones, Nokia C110/C111 wireless LAN card, User guide, (2009),
    http://nds1.nokia.com/phones/files/guides/
    C110-C111_usersguide_en.pdf
9. Socket Communications, Low Power Wireless LAN Card, Datasheet (2009),
    http://www.quad.de/Datashe/Socket_WLAN.pdf
10. Braun, T.D., Siegel, H.J., Beck, N., Boloni, L., Freund, R.F., Hensgen, D., Maheswaran,
    M., Reuther, A.I., Robertson, J.P., Theys, M.D., Yao, B.: A Comparison of Eleven Static
    Heuristics for Mapping a Class of Independent Tasks onto Heterogeneous Distributed
    Computing Systems. J. Parallel and Distributed Computing 61(6), 810–837 (2001)
11. Kim, J.-K., Shivle, S., Siegel, H.J., Maciejewski, A.A., Braun, T.D., Schneider, M.,
    Tideman, S., Chitta, R., Dilmaghani, R.B., Joshi, R., Kaul, A., Sharma, A., Sripada, S.,
    Vangari, P., Yellampalli, S.S.: Dynamically Mapping Tasks with Priorities and Multiple
    Deadlines in a Heterogeneous Environment. J. Parallel and Distributed Computing 67(2),
    154–169 (2007)
12. Kim, J.S.: Energy-Aware Distributed Mobile Computing for Real-time Single-hop Ad hoc
    Mobile Environments., Korea University, Master's thesis, p. 60 (February 2010)
13. Perkins, C.E., Bhagwat, P.: Highly dynamic Destination-Sequenced Distance-Vector
    routing (DSDV) for mobile computers. In: Proceedings of the SIGCOMM 1994 Conference
    on Communications Architectures, Protocols and Applications, pp. 234–244 (August 1994)

Automatic Birdsong Recognition with MFCC Based Syllable Feature Extraction

Chih-Hsun Chou and Hui-Yu Ko

Department of Computer Science and Information Engineering,
Chung Hua University, No. 707, Sec. 2, WuFu Rd.,
Hsinchu, 30067 Taiwan, R.O.C
chc@chu.edu.tw

Abstract. In this study, an automatic birdsong recognition system based on syllable features was developed. In this system, after syllable segmentation, three syllable features, namely mean, QI and QE, were computed from the MFCCs of each syllable aims at capturing variations in time as well as amplitude transitions of the MFCC sequences. With the advantages of the fuzzy c-mean (FCM) clustering algorithm and the linear discriminant analysis (LDA), the presented feature vector was used to construct an automatic birdsong recognition system applied to a birdsong database with 420 bird species.

Keywords: MFCC, syllable, linear discriminant analysis, transition matrix.

1 Introduction

The vocalization types of bird species include birdsong and birdcall. Birdsong being complicated, varied, agreeable and pleasant to listen to, is usually generated by a male bird and is used to declare his turf or attract a mate. Birdcall, on the other hand, is monotonous, brief, repeated, fixed and sexless and is used to contact or alert companions. The time duration and acoustic structure of a birdcall are usually short and simple while the duration of a birdsong is longer and is composed of a succession of melodious musical notes.

One feature that has been successfully applied in human voice recognition is the cepstral of the voice waveform, of which the Mel-Frequency Cepstral Coefficients (MFCCs) were obtained based on the fact that the hearing perception of the human being performs better performance than the Linear Prediction Cepstral Coefficients (LPCCs) [1], [2], [3]. Although MFCCs have been well-applied in bird species recognition, further study on this feature is necessary to increase the recognition rate. In [1], [2], [3], [4], [5] optimal theories were used to obtain the center frequencies and bandwidths of the triangular filters. The discrete cosine transform (DCT) was replaced with the wavelet transform in [6]. Filter weighting was applied in [7] to assign a weight for each order of MFCCs. In [8] the MFCCs as well as their first-order and second-order differences were used to form the feature vector. Combination of MFCCs with a lot of low-level descriptive parameters such as zero-crossing rate, short time energy, syllable length, spectrum centroid, bandwidth and so on was applied in [9] for recognizing 14 bird species.

C.-H. Hsu et al. (Eds.): UIC 2011, LNCS 6905, pp. 185–196, 2011.

In this study, neither modifying the steps for computing the MFCCs nor combining the MFCCs with other types of features, three features were computed from the MFCCs of a syllable to form the syllable feature vector. The proposed method aimed at easy computation and small time complexity. Integrating with the advantages of FCM clustering algorithm and the LDA, the proposed system was applied for recognizing the birdsongs of 420 bird species. The remaining of this paper is as follows: Section 2 describes the structure of the proposed system. Experimental results are shown in Section 3. Section 4 is the conclusion.

2   The Proposed System

The block diagram of the proposed system containing the training part and the testing (recognition) part is shown in Fig. 1. Three terms named mean, QI and QE were computed to form the feature vectors of each syllable for recognition. Each step is described in detail in the following.

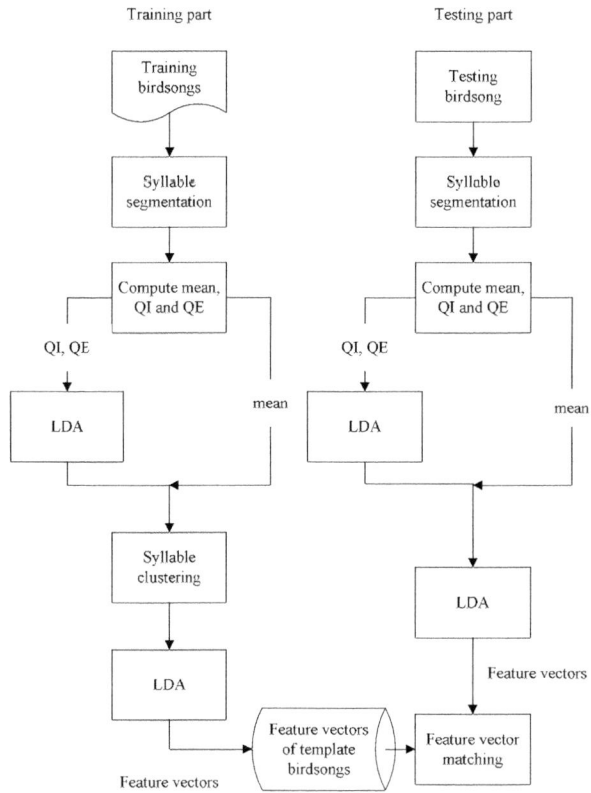

Fig. 1. Block diagram of the proposed system

2.1   Syllable Segmentation

Endpoint detection detects the waveform boundaries of a voice signal so as to extract the voice parts and ignore the noise parts of the signal. Due to the resistance to signal fading and echoing, the frequency domain analysis of the birdsong signal is better than in the time domain approach [15]. So the frequency domain approach was utilized in this study. The segmentation process applied in this study is as follows:

Step 1. Compute the short time Fourier transform of $x(t)$ with frame size $N = 512$, and form the spectrogram of the signal. The Hamming window for short time analysis has the form of

$$w[n] = \begin{cases} 0.54 - 0.46\cos\left(\dfrac{2\pi n}{N-1}\right), 0 \le n \le N-1 \\ 0 \qquad\qquad\qquad , \text{otherwise} \end{cases} \tag{1}$$

Step 2. For each frame m, find the frequency Bin bin_m with the greatest magnitude.
Step 3. Initialize the syllable index j, $j = 1$.
Step 4. Compute the frame t at which the maximum magnitude occurs

$$t = \arg \max_{1 \le m \le M} \left(\left|X[bin_m]\right|\right) \tag{2}$$

and set the amplitude of syllable j as

$$A_j = 20 \cdot \log_{10}\left|X[bin_t]\right| (\text{dB}) \tag{3}$$

in which M is the number of frames of $x(t)$, and $X[\cdot]$ denotes the spectrum of $x(t)$.
Step 5. Start from frame t and move backward and forward up to frames h_j and t_j such that both $20 \cdot \log_{10}\left|X[bin_{h_j}]\right|$ and $20 \cdot \log_{10}\left|X[bin_{t_j}]\right|$ are smaller than $(A_j - 20)$ (dB).
Step 6. Start from frames h_j and t_j, find frames $h_j - \alpha$ and $t_j + \beta$ $(\alpha, \beta > 0)$ such that both $20 \cdot \log_{10}\left|X[bin_{h_j-\alpha-1}]\right|$ and $20 \cdot \log_{10}\left|X[bin_{t_j+\beta+1}]\right|$ are greater than $(A_j - 20)$. Then $h_j - \alpha$ and $t_j + \beta$ are called the head frame and tail frame of syllable j.
Step 7. Set

$$\left|X[bin_m]\right| = 0, m = h_j - \alpha, h_j - \alpha + 1, \cdots, t_j + \beta - 1, t_j + \beta \tag{4}$$

Step 8. Let $j = j + 1$.
Step 9. Repeat Step 4 to Step 8 until $A_j < A_1 - 20$.

2.2   Feature Extraction

After syllable segmentation, three features named mean, QI and QE were computed to form the feature vector of the syllable as described in the following.

2.2.1   Compute the MFCCs of Each Frame

The steps for computing the MFCCs of each frame are as follows:

Step 1. Compute the fast Fourier transform (FFT) of each framed signal.

$$X[k] = \sum_{n=0}^{N-1} x[n]w[n]e^{-j2\pi nk/N}, 0 \le k < N \tag{5}$$

Step 2. Compute the energy of each triangular filter band

$$E_j = \sum_{k=0}^{N/2-1} \phi_j[k]|X[k]|^2, 0 \le j < J \tag{6}$$

where $\phi_j[k]$ denotes the amplitude(weight) of the jth triangular filter at frequency bin k as shown in Fig. 2, E_j denotes the energy of jth filter band, and J is the number of triangular filters.

Step 3. Compute the MFCCs by Cosine transformation

$$c_i(m) = \sum_{j=0}^{J-1} \cos\left(m\frac{\pi}{J}(j+0.5)\right)\log_{10}(E_j), 0 \le m < 15 \tag{7}$$

where $c_i(m)$ denotes the mth order MFCC of the ith frame.

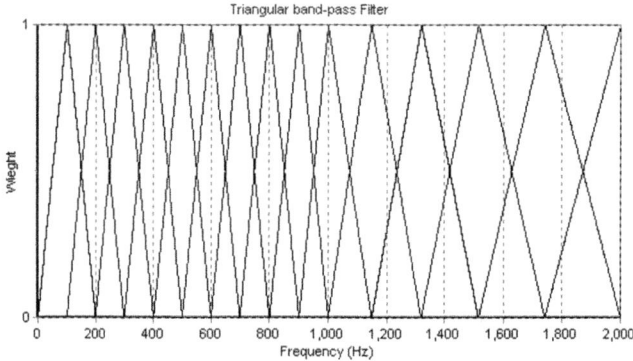

Fig. 2. Applied triangular filters for computing the MFCCs

2.2.2   Computing the Mean, QI, and QE

Although MFCCs have been well-applied in human voice recognition, the process for birdsong recognition needs to be improved because there is a greater diversity in the vocalizations of different bird species. In the following, three features named mean, QI and QE computed from the MFCCs were used to form the feature vector of a syllable.

Feature 1: mean of MFCCs

After computing the first 15 (order) MFCCs of each frame, the coefficients of the same order of all frames were averaged. The average of mth order MFCCs $a(m)$ was obtained by the following equation:

$$a(m) = \frac{1}{W} \sum_{i=1}^{W} c_i(m), \ 0 \le m < L \tag{8}$$

where W is the number of frames and $L = 15$ is the order of MFCCs applied in this study. Due to the scale diversity between different orders of MFCCs, a normalization process for $a(m)$ is required. The normalization equation is

$$\hat{a}(m) = \frac{a(m) - a_{min}(m)}{a_{max}(m) - a_{min}(m)}, 0 \le m < L \tag{9}$$

where $a_{max}(m)$ and $a_{min}(m)$ denote the maximum and minimum values of the mth order MFCCs of all frames.

Feature 2: QI of MFCCs

The second feature QI was used to capture variations in time of the MFCCs. For saving on computation complexity, consecutive frames were used as a time unit to compute QI. The process for computing QI is described in the following.

Step 1. Quantize the MFCCs of each order in all frames ($c_1(m), c_2(m),...,c_W(m)$) into Q levels (from level 0 to level $Q-1$).

$$v(m) = \frac{c_{max}(m) - c_{min}(m)}{Q} \tag{10}$$

where $\ \ max = \arg \max_{i=1,2,...,W} c_i(m) \ , \quad min = \arg \min_{i=1,2,...,W} c_i(m) \quad$ and $\quad v(m) \quad$ is the

quantization interval of the mth order MFCCs.

Step 2. Segment the W frames into S equal sections, then compute the mean of each order of MFCCs in every section.

$$\tilde{a}_s(m) = \frac{S}{W} \sum_{k=(s-1)W/S+1}^{s \cdot W/S} c_k(m), 0 \le m < L, \ 1 \le s \le S \tag{11}$$

where s is the section index.

Step 3. Find the level $I_s(m)$ at which the value $\tilde{a}_s(m)$ locates, where

$$I_s(m) \cdot v(m) \le \tilde{a}_s(m) - a_{min}(m) < (I_s(m) + 1) \cdot v(m),$$
$$0 \le m < L, \ 1 \le s \le S \tag{12}$$

Step 4. Form the sequence $I_1(m), I_2(m),...,I_S(m)$ for each order of MFCCs.

Step 5. Those sequences obtained in Step 4 for all the 15 orders of MFCCs form the second feature QI.

$$QI = I_1(0),...,I_S(0), I_1(1),...,I_S(1),...,I_1(L-1),...,I_S(L-1) \tag{13}$$

Feature 3: QE of MFCCs

The third feature QE aims at capturing the amplitude transition properties of MFCCs between frames. The process for obtaining QE is described in the following.

Step 1. Perform the same quantization process (Step 1) used in computing feature 2.

Step 2. Find the level $I_i(m)$ at which the value $c_i(m)$ locates, where

$$I_i(m) \cdot v(m) \le c_i(m) - c_{\min}(m) < (I_i(m)+1) \cdot v(m),$$
$$0 \le m < L, \; 1 \le i \le W \tag{14}$$

Step 3. For each order of MFCCs, record the frames that transit from level x to level y, $0 \le x, y \le Q-1$, and denote it as $G_m(x, y)$. That is

$$G_m(x, y) = \{i \big| x \cdot v(m) \le c_i(m) - c_{\min}(m) < (x+1) \cdot v(m),$$
$$y \cdot v(m) \le c_{i+1}(m) - c_{\min}(m) < (y+1) \cdot v(m), 1 \le i < W\} \tag{15}$$

Step 4. Compute the level transition matrix $T_m(X,Y)$ for each order of MFCC by using $G_m(x, y)$

$$T_m(x, y) = \frac{|G_m(x, y)|}{\displaystyle\sum_{x=0}^{Q-1}\sum_{y=0}^{Q-1}|G_m(x, y)|}, \quad 0 \le m < L \tag{16}$$

Step 5. Compute and sort the eigenvalues of $T_m(X,Y)$, $\lambda_m^1 \ge \lambda_m^2 \ge ... \ge \lambda_m^Q$, $0 \le m < L$.

Step 6. Form the feature vector QE by using all the eigenvalues

$$QE = \lambda_0^1,...,\lambda_0^Q, \lambda_1^1,...,\lambda_1^Q,...,\lambda_{L-1}^1,...,\lambda_{L-1}^Q, \; 0 \le m < L \tag{17}$$

2.2.3 Construct the Feature Vector by Using Mean, QI and QE

Combining the three features forms a $15+S \cdot L+Q \cdot L$ dimensional feature vector, of which QI and QE gave the largest number of components. This large dimensional feature vector is unpractical for real application, so before forming the feature vector, the Linear Discriminant Analysis (LDA) was applied to the feature vector form by QI and QE.

The LDA [16] transforms data from the original space to a new space which is better for classification. To find such a transformation matrix W, it requires maximizing the Fisher criterion

$$\max_W J(W) = \max_W \frac{tr(W^T S_b W)}{tr(W^T S_w W)}. \tag{18}$$

The matrices S_w and S_b, called within-class scatter matrix and between-class scatter matrix, are computed by the following equations:

$$S_w = \sum_{j=1}^{C}\sum_{i=1}^{N_j}(\mathbf{x}_i^j - \boldsymbol{\mu}_j)(\mathbf{x}_i^j - \boldsymbol{\mu}_j)^T. \tag{19}$$

$$S_b = \sum_{j=1}^{C} (\mathbf{\mu}_j - \mathbf{\mu})(\mathbf{\mu}_j - \mathbf{\mu})^T \cdot \tag{20}$$

in which $\mathbf{x}_i^j$ denotes the ith vector in class j, $\mathbf{\mu}_j$ is the mean vector of class j, C is the number of classes, N_j is the number of vectors in class j and $\mathbf{\mu}$ is the mean of all data vectors. It was found that the optimal matrix W_{opt} solved by Eq. (18) is composed of the principal eigenvectors of the matrix $S_w^{-1}S_b$. The principal eigenvectors of a matrix are defined by the corresponding eigenvalues. The eigenvectors whose corresponding eigenvalues are the largest d eigenvalues of a matrix form the d principal eigenvectors of the matrix. Determination of d can be accomplished by the following equation

$$d = \min_t \sum_{i=1}^{t} \lambda_i \geq \theta \cdot \sum_{i=1}^{m} \lambda_i \cdot \tag{21}$$

where λ_i is the ith largest eigenvalue, m is the number of eigenvalues and θ is a parameter to be set.

After the LDA of QI and QE, the dimension of the feature vector formed by the three features was reduced. Nevertheless, a birdsong is usually composed of a lot of syllables belonging to several types. To obtain representative feature vectors for a birdsong requires the clustering of the syllable feature vectors. In this study, the clustering process was accomplished by using the fuzzy c-mean (FCM) clustering method. The FCM, proposed by Dunn in 1973 and enhanced by Bezdek in 1981, is an un-supervised clustering algorithm iterative tuning the cluster centers and the cluster memberships of data vectors. The clustering process is described in the following.

Step 1: Select the cluster number c.

Step 2: Set the initial fuzzy pseudopartition at $t = 0$ satisfying

$$\sum_{i=1}^{c} \mu_{ij}^{(t)} = 1, \quad j = 1,2,...,J, \tag{22a}$$

$$0 < \sum_{j=1}^{J} \mu_{ij}^{(t)} < J, \quad i = 1,2,...,c \cdot \tag{22b}$$

In these two equations, $\mu_{ij}^{(t)}$ denotes the membership grade of feature vector $\mathbf{v}_{s_j}$ belonging to cluster i at time t, and J is the number of feature vectors to be clustered.

Step 3: Set the initial performance index $J_m^{(t)}$, $t = 0$, as 0.

Step 4: Calculate the c cluster centers $\mathbf{v}_1^{(t)},...,\mathbf{v}_c^{(t)}$ by

$$\mathbf{v}_i^{(t)} = \frac{\sum_{j=1}^{J} (\mu_{ij}^{(t)})^m \cdot \mathbf{v}_{s_j}}{\sum_{j=1}^{J} (\mu_{ij}^{(t)})^m}, \quad i = 1, ..., c, \ 1 < m < 2. \tag{23}$$

Step 5:   Update the membership grade for each feature vector $\mathbf{v}_{s_j}$,

$$\mu_{ij}^{(t+1)} = \left[\sum_{k=1}^{c} \left(\frac{\left\| \mathbf{v}_{s_j} - \mathbf{v}_i^{(t)} \right\|^2}{\left\| \mathbf{v}_{s_j} - \mathbf{v}_k^{(t)} \right\|^2} \right)^{\frac{1}{m-1}} \right]^{-1}. \tag{24}$$

Step 6:   Compute the performance index

$$J_m^{(t+1)} = \sum_{j=1}^{J} \sum_{i=1}^{c} \left[(\mu_{ij}^{(t+1)})^m \cdot \left\| \mathbf{v}_{s_j} - \mathbf{v}_i \right\|^2 \right]. \tag{25}$$

Step 7:   If $\left| J_m^{(t+1)} - J_m^{(t)} \right| \geq \varepsilon$ (a threshold), then $t = t + 1$, go to step 4.

Step 8:   Stop

Applying the FCM algorithm requires the determination of the optimal cluster number, that is, to treat the cluster validity problem. In this study, the WB index proposed in [17] was applied to solve it. The WB index has the purpose of finding cluster number c that minimizes the intra-group variance $W(\mu, \mathbf{v})$ and maximizes the inter-group variance $B(\mu, \mathbf{v})$. That is, to find c_{opt} such that

$$c_{opt} = \arg \max_c WB = \arg \max_c \frac{B(\mu, \mathbf{v})}{W(\mu, \mathbf{v})}. \tag{26}$$

The two terms $W(\mu, \mathbf{v})$ and $B(\mu, \mathbf{v})$ are defined as

$$W(\mu, \mathbf{v}) = \sum_{i=1}^{c} \sum_{j=1}^{J} (C_i)^{-1} \left\| \mathbf{v}_{s_j} - \mathbf{v}_i \right\|^2. \tag{27}$$

$$B(\mu, \mathbf{v}) = \frac{1}{C_2^c} \sum_{\lambda=1}^{c-1} \sum_{m=\lambda+1}^{c} \left(\frac{\sum_{j \in S_\lambda \cup S_m} (\mu_{\lambda j} \cdot \mu_{mj})}{\left| S_\lambda \right| + \left| S_m \right|} \right)^{-1} \left\| \mathbf{v}_\lambda - \mathbf{v}_m \right\|^2. \tag{28}$$

in which

$$C_i = \frac{\sum_{j=1}^{J} \mu_{ij}^2}{\left| S_i \right|}, \quad i = 1, 2, ..., c. \tag{29}$$

where

$$S_i = \left\{ j \mid I_{ij} = 1 \right\}. \tag{30}$$

and

$$I_{ij} = \begin{cases} 1, & \text{if } \mu_{ij} = \max_{1 \leq k \leq c} \mu_{kj} \\ 0, & \text{otherwise} \end{cases}. \tag{31}$$

and C_2^c is a combination computation.

After the FCM clustering, several mean vectors were obtained as the feature vectors of each bird species. These mean vectors, though applicable for the recognition process, are still too large dimensionally. So before applying them, the LDA was applied again to extract the principle components of the feature vector and improve the recognition rate.

2.3   Recognition

In the recognition process, after the same feature extraction procedure (without the clustering process), as shown in Fig. 1, the feature vector of a testing syllable was matched to those of the template bird species. A template bird species usually has several syllable feature vectors and so do the matching degrees defined by the inverse of the Euclidean distance between the feature vectors of the testing syllable and the template syllables. The recognition of the testing syllable was accomplished by finding the template bird species that had syllable with the largest matching degree.

3   Experimental Results

The bird species vocalization database used in this study was obtained from a commercial CD [18] containing both birdcall and birdsong files of 420 bird species recorded in the field in Japan. Each file contains vocalizations of the same bird species. The database of 420 bird species made it much larger than any other used in previous studies. Meanwhile, recordings in the field were usually in noisy environment, incomplete and interrupted. The sampling rate of these vocalization signals was 44.1 kHz with 16-bit resolution and a monotone type PCM format.

In the experiment, the frame size was set as 512 samples with one-half frame overlapping and the Q value for computing both QI and QE was set as 5. Half the syllables of each birdsong file were randomly selected for training and the remaining for testing. The recognition rate RR was defined as

$$RR(\%) = \frac{\text{number of syllables recognized correctly}}{\text{number of all syllables}} \cdot 100\% \cdot \qquad (32)$$

3.1   RRs of Using the Proposed Structure

The proposed two-stage structure shown in Fig. 1 performed LDA of QI and QE before the FCM clustering. Usually the threshold θ used in the LDA is set as 0.95. In this experiment various values from 0.6 to 0.95 were tested to examine the RRs. The RRs and corresponding feature dimensions using the proposed structure are shown in Table 1. It can be seen that when θ was 0.95, the RR of the feature mean was increased from 79.52% to about 82% if QI, QE or both was added. In addition, a RR of 83.3% was achieved and the feature dimension was reduced to 31 when θ was 0.75.

For objectivity, this structure with θ equaling 0.75 was performed 20 times, and the statistics of the resulting RRs are shown in Table 2. Table 2 shows that a maximum RR of 84.34% can be achieved under a relatively low standard deviation of RRs. Meanwhile, feature vector with dimension of 31 is more practical for real application.

Table 1. *RRs* of using the proposed structure under various values of θ

Dim: dimension of feature vectors

features θ	mean, QI		Mean, QE		mean, QI, QE	
	RRs	Dim	*RRs*	Dim	*RRs*	Dim
0.95	81.85	38	82.18	27	82.09	66
0.90	82.03	32	82.41	22	82.7	53
0.85	82.1	28	82.4	19	83.04	43
0.8	82.07	24	82.09	17	83.17	36
0.75	81.99	22	81.59	16	83.30	31
0.7	81.87	20	81.11	15	83.28	27
0.65	81.58	18	80.70	14	83.13	24
0.6	81.22	16	80.67	14	82.94	20

Table 2. Statistics of *RRs* using the proposed structure under $\theta = 0.75$

RR(%)	Max	Min	Avg	S
mean, QI	82.93	79.51	81.99	0.92
mean, QE	82.68	78.98	81.59	1.08
mean, QI, QE	84.34	81.02	83.30	0.81

Table 3. Comparison of LDA and PCA in the first stage dimension reduction

Threshold of LDA or PCA in the first stage	RR(%) by using LDA	RR(%) by using PCA
0.95	82.8142	68.1191
0.9	83.3573	67.7633
0.85	83.5445	68.3376
0.8	83.8067	68.3001
0.75	83.9878	68.2627
0.7	84.0252	67.9006
0.65	83.7193	68.1129

3.2   A Comparison of LDA and PCA

In the proposed system, LDA was applied to reduce the feature dimension and retain the principal features of the syllable. To reduce the feature dimension another method, called the principle component analysis (PCA), is also frequently used [19], [20], [21]. To check the advantage of using LDA in the proposed system, the first stage LDA was replaced with PCA to extract the principal features of QI and QE. The thresholds of both LDA and PCA used in this stage varied between 0.65 and 0.95, while the threshold of the second stage LDA was fixed as 0.95. The RRs of both systems (LDA and PCA in the first state) under various threshold values are shown in Table 3 exhibiting the superior performance of LDA.

4   Conclusions

The investigation of bird species diversity is the key in monitoring environment and ecosystem recovery, and automatic bird species recognition based on their songs has become an invaluable study method in the long-term investigation of bird species. In the design of a voice recognition system, a well-known feature that has been widely applied is the MFCC. Nevertheless, designing a MFCC-based birdsong recognition system requires advanced feature extraction processes for obtaining a satisfactory recognition rate because birdsongs are usually recorded in a noise environment, are incomplete or interrupted. In this study, two novel features based on the MFCCs were presented. The first is QI, used to capture the time-varying property of the MFCCs, and the second is QE for capturing the amplitude transition properties of the MFCCs between frames. Adding the techniques of LDA and the FCM algorithm, the mean, QI and QE were applied to develop a birdsong recognition system. The proposed system was applied for birdsong recognition with 420 bird species. Experiments with an analysis of the using of LDA and FCM clustering, a discussion of using different threshold values, and a comparison between the using of LDA and PCA were given to examine the efficiency of the proposed recognition system.

Acknowledgments. This work was supported by the National Science Council of Taiwan R.O.C. under the Grant NSC96-2221-E-216-031

References

[1] Lee, S.M., Fang, S.H., Hung, J.W., Lee, L.S.: Improved MFCC feature extraction by PCA-optimized filter-bank for speech recognition. In: IEEE Workshop, Automatic Speech Recognition and Understanding, pp. 49–52 (2001)

[2] Lee, C.H., Hyun, D.H., Choi, E.S., Go, J.W., Lee, C.Y.: Optimizing feature extraction for speech recognition. IEEE Transactions on Speech and Audio Processing 11, 80–87 (2003)

[3] Skowronski, M.D., Harris, J.G.: Increased MFCC filter bandwidth for noise-robust phoneme recognition. In: IEEE International Conference on Acoustics, Speech, and Signal Processing, vol. 1, pp. 801–804 (2002)

[4] Skowronski, M.D., Harris, J.G.: Improving the filter bank of a classic speech feature extraction algorithm. Circuits and Systems 4, 281–284 (2003)

[5] Bou-Ghazale, S.E., Hansen, J.H.L.: A comparative study of traditional and newly proposed features for recognition of speech under stress. IEEE Transactions on Speech and Audio Processing 8, 429–442 (2000)

[6] Ricotti, L.P.: Multitapering and a wavelet variant of MFCC in speech recognition. In: IEE Proceedings - Vision, Image and Signal Processing, pp. 29–35 (February 2005)

[7] Hung, W.W., Wang, H.C.: On the use of weighted filter bank analysis for the derivation of robust MFCCs. IEEE Signal Processing Letters 8, 70–73 (2001)

 [8] Kwan, C., et al.: An automated acoustic system to monitor and classify birds. EURASIP Journal on Applied Signal Processing, Article ID 96706, 1–19 (2006)
 [9] Somervuo, P., Harma, A., Fagerlund, S.: Parametric Representations of Bird Sounds for Automatic Species Recognition. IEEE Transactions on Audio, Speech and Language Processing 14, 2252–2263 (2006)
[10] Rabiner, L.R., Sambur, M.R.: An algorithm for determining the endpoints of isolated utterances. Bell System Technical Journal 54(2), 297–315 (1975)
[11] He, S.N., Yu, J.B.: A novel Chinese continuous speech endpoint detection method based on time domain features of the word structure. In: IEEE International Conference on Communications, Circuits and Systems and West Sino Expositions, vol. 2, pp. 992–996 (2002)
[12] Zhang, W.J., Xie, J.Y.: Endpoint detection based on MDL using subband speech satisfied auditory model. In: IEEE International Conference on Neural Networks and Signal Processing, vol. 2, pp. 892–895 (2003)
[13] Bou-Ghazale, S.E., Assaleh, K.: A robust endpoint detection of speech for noisy environments with application to automatic speech recognition. In: IEEE International Conference on Acoustics, Speech, and Signal Processing, vol. 4, pp. 3808–3811 (2002)
[14] Wu, B.F., Wang, K.C.: Robust Endpoint Detection Algorithm Based on the Adaptive Band-Partitioning Spectral Entropy in Adverse Environments. IEEE Transactions on Speech and Audio Processing 13(5), 762–775 (2005)
[15] McIlraith, A.L., Card, H.C.: Bird song identification using artificial neural networks and statistical analysis. In: Canadian Conference on Electrical and Computer Engineering, vol. 1, pp. 63–66 (1997)
[16] Duda, R., Hart, P., Stork, D.: Pattern Classification. Wiley, New York (2000)
[17] Tan, J.H.: On cluster validity for fuzzy clustering. Master Thesis, Applied Mathematics Department, Chung Yuan Christian University, Taiwan, R.O.C (2000)
[18] Kabaya, T., Matsuda, M.: The Songs & Calls of 420 Birds in Japan. SHOGAKUKAN Inc., Tokyo (2001)
[19] Hung, J.W., Tsai, W.Y.: Constructing Modulation Frequency Domain-Based Features for Robust Speech Recognition. IEEE Transactions on Audio, Speech, and Language Processing 16(3), 563–577 (2008)
[20] Minh, V.D., Lee, S.Y.: PCA-based human auditory filter bank for speech recognition. In: International Conference on Signal Processing and Communications, pp. 393–397 (2004)
[21] Takiguchi, T., Ariki, Y.: Robust Feature Extraction using Kernel PCA. In: IEEE International Conference on Acoustics, Speech and Signal Processing, vol. 1, pp. I509–I512 (2006)

Punishment or Reward: It Is a Problem in Anonymous, Dynamic and Autonomous Networking Environments

Yufeng Wang[1], Athanasios V. Vasilakos[2], and Jianhua Ma[3]

[1] Nanjing University of Posts and Telecommunications, China
wfwang@njupt.edu.cn
[2] University of Western Macedonia, Greece
vasilako@ath.forthnet.gr
[3] Hosei University, Japan
jianhua@hosei.ac.jp

Abstract. Recently, service differentiation based incentive mechanisms are proposed in dynamic networking environments like Peer-to-Peer (P2P), wireless Ad hoc networks, etc.: define small meaningful classes of services and assign participants to these classes according to their overall resource contribution. Basically, there exist two fundamental components: How to define different classes? And who can assign autonomous participants to these classes? We argue that those environments are intrinsically anonymous, dynamic and autonomous, which has the following implications: Users can change their identities with near zero cost (cheap pseudonyms); most interactions in autonomous networks should be one-time (that is, each peer has no idea about other peers' behavior history, except their current behaviors); and all behaviors and actions are all endogenous, voluntarily chosen and determined by independent and rational peers. Specifically, in the simplest case, service differentiation based incentive mechanisms could be provided with two ways: punish defect behavior (punishment-based scheme), or reward cooperative behavior (reward-based scheme). This paper preliminarily investigated the effectiveness of punishment-based and reward-based incentive mechanisms in anonymous, dynamic and autonomous environments. Our contributions are following: first, under the above networking environment, we found that the traditional service differentiation based incentive schemes could not work, irrespective of punishment-based and reward-based schemes; then, if peers can voluntarily join the system, and small entry fee is set for participation, we got that the performance of punishment-based scheme (first providing high-level service plus punishment) is always better than that of reward-based scheme (first providing low-level service plus reward).

1 Introduction

Many networking environments, like P2P, wireless Ad hoc networks, etc. are with the features of self-organizing and distributed resource-sharing. By pooling together the resource of many autonomous machines, they are able to provide an inexpensive and highly scalable platform for distributed computing, storage, or data-sharing, etc. Note that there are two extreme cases in resource management: resource allocation (allocation of the existing resource) and resource provision (provision of resource shared by

C.-H. Hsu et al. (Eds.): UIC 2011, LNCS 6905, pp. 197–208, 2011.
© Springer-Verlag Berlin Heidelberg 2011

all participants). In the first case, the designer should decide whether and what percentage of a good (with given predefined capacity) each peer should consume. In the second case, the designer's task is to entice independent participant to provide resource (with its' right share). In this paper, we focus on the latter case.

In those environments, it is imperative for each peer to voluntarily contribute resources (e.g., storage, bandwidth, and contents, etc.). However, intuitively, each peer would prefer to "free ride" on the contribution of other peers by consuming available resources and services without contributing anything, and thus avoid the corresponding costs. It was reported that nearly 70% of Gnutella users shared nothing with other users (these users simply free-ride on other users who share information), and nearly 50% of all file search responses come from the top 1% of information sharing nodes [1]. In following-up study (five years later), it was found that 85% of users share nothing [2], which implies the free-riding problem had got worse in the intervening years.

Generally, lack of cooperation is one of the key problems that confront today's autonomous systems. Incentive mechanisms play a crucial role to encourage cooperation among autonomous nodes. Specifically, a simple rule-based (differential service based) incentive mechanism is preliminarily advocated by [3], to encourage the resource provision in PlanetLab (http://www.planet-lab.org/), the most popular shared network testbed. However, the above work did not investigate the following two basic problems at all: how to define the different service classes? And who can assign autonomous participants to these classes? In this paper, we thoroughly investigated the above questions.

We argue that those networking environments are dynamic and autonomous. By dynamic it means that most interactions among peers are one-time, which implies that each peer has no idea about other peers' behavior history, except their current behaviors; By autonomous it means that there exist no central management entity to assign peers to different classes. Specifically, each strategy and action are voluntarily chosen and determined by independent, rational and autonomous peers, and all behaviors are all endogenous, that is, no exogenous organization to enforce the punishment and/or reward. Under the above networking environment, basically in the simplest case, we could define two categories of services: high-level and low-level. Naturally, from practical viewpoint, the following two service differentiation based incentive schemes are possible:

- Initially, all peers will be served with high-level class, and then, according to each peer's behaviors, voluntary punishers lower the defectors' service level provided by those punishers, which is called punishment-based scheme in our paper;
- Initially, all peers will be served with lower-level class, and then, according to each peer's behaviors, voluntary rewarders promote the cooperators' service level provided by those rewarders, which is called reward-based scheme. Note that, in reward-based incentive scheme, the reason why low-level service should be initially provided, lies in that, in dynamic and autonomous networks, no exogenous organization to enforce the punishment and/or reward, like reimbursing the cooperative behaviors with some out-of-band extra resource (or money), thus, rewarder has to set aside some resource for its rewarding behaviors in future, which lead to the fact that those peers have to provide relative lower-level class initially.

Then, under the above dynamic and autonomous networking environments, the resulted question is: between the above two service differentiation schemes, which is better to incentivize peers' cooperative (or reciprocation) behavior? This paper attempts to answer the above question based on evolutionary game model.

The paper is organized as follows: Section 2 briefly describes the related work of service differentiation based incentive mechanisms, and their differences from our work. Section 3 briefly analyzes the reason why, in the above environment, traditional service differentiation based incentive mechanisms could not work, and, based on the Public goods game, provides the analytical models of punishment-based and reward-based incentive mechanisms for resource provision. Preliminary simulations in section 4 illustrates, when punishment-based scheme performs always better than reward-based scheme. Finally, we briefly conclude this paper.

2   Related Work

Recently, some price-based market approaches (e.g., free markets, commodity markets and auctions, etc.) have been proposed to maximize certain system-level goal, when facing peers' rational behaviors [4]. However, even though such mechanisms might theoretically lead to optimal allocation in economic terms, they are extremely complex, unpredictable and unattractive: for example, require proper virtual currency, trusted third parties, and detailed accounting; suffer from standard problems of virtual currencies (inflation, deflation, etc.). Thus, instead of trading resource units, a large part of the research (and practice) on incentives mechanisms for P2P systems considers the design and deployment of simple rules based on reciprocity or fixed contributions. Specifically, a simple fixed-contribution scheme was proposed to alleviate the free-riding [5], in which each peer merely pays the same fixed fee toward the total cost, and peers unwilling to do so are excluded. Furthermore, it is found that imposing penalty on all users that join the system is effective under many scenarios, and, in particular, system performance degrades significantly only when the turnover rate among users is high [6]. One of the weakpoints of the above fixed-contribution schemes lies in that, instead of the arbitrary value, the fixed contribution should be set as specific value, which should be calculated based on global information in network. Thus, our previous work proposed a punishment-based resource provision mechanism in P2P networks, based on Public goods game, in which an arbitrarily small entry fee is set for all peers, and peers can voluntarily join P2P resource provision system. Theoretical analysis and experimental results show that the proposed mechanism can incentivize peers to contribute resource, and the whole P2P network will almost converge to the state of punisher [7]. This paper extends our previous work: investigate and compare the effectiveness of punishment-based and reward-based incentive mechanisms.

Similarly as our previous work [7], this paper adopts EGT (Evolutionary Game Theory) inspired approach, in which individuals attempt to optimize their utilities by imitating the behaviors of peers with better payoff. The above stochastic learning is a backward-looking approach, and thus assumes much lighter cognitive capabilities on the part of individuals than does traditional rationality. Note that a general framework is proposed to analyze and design the reciprocation-based incentive protocols in P2P networks [8-9], in which peers distributively learn and adapt their actions. Particularly, the authors preliminarily show the correlation between evaluating the incentive protocols and EGT. In order to solve several weakpoints in the above work, our previous work [10] thoroughly investigated the evolutionary dynamics of soft security mechanism, namely, reciprocity-based incentive mechanism, in P2P systems based on EGT. Instead of the pair-wise interaction model that are often adopted to characterize peers' interactions, this paper uses the more realistic Public goods game to characterize the interaction among peers, and design Markov models to calculate the stationary distribution of various strategies.

3   Assumptions and Models

Basically, in traditional punishment-based incentive mechanism, there exist two types of peers, the punishers and defectors, respectively denoted as P and D. P is cooperative with all other peers through offering benefit α_1 to the system (and bearing the corresponding service provision cost c_s). And meanwhile, P voluntarily punishes the defectors: c_p represents the penalty that each P peer imposes on each D peer; c_u the incurred cost to P peer. D does not provide resource to the system, and only consumes resource provided by whole system. Similarly, in traditional reward-based incentive mechanism, there also exist two types of peers: rewarder and defector, respectively represented as R and D. R is cooperative with all peers through offering benefit α_2 to the system, and bearing the corresponding service provision cost c_s. And meanwhile, R voluntarily offers extra reward b_r, to each peer who provides resource to the whole system, and bears the incurred cost, c_r, for the benevolent behavior. Normally, b_r is larger than c_r. Then, the following corollary can be straightforwardly obtained:

Corollary 1. *Under the dynamic, anonymous and autonomous networking environment, when there exist some 'C' mutants, the traditional service differentiation based incentive mechanisms could not work, irrespective of punishment-based and reward-based schemes.*

The brief proof is given as follows:

Specifically, for punishment based scheme, based on peers' behaviors, the payoff matrix is given as follows:

$$\begin{array}{cc} \quad\quad P \quad\quad\quad\quad D \\ \begin{array}{c} P \\ D \end{array} \begin{pmatrix} \alpha_1 - c_s & -c_s - c_u \\ \alpha_1 - c_p & 0 \end{pmatrix} \end{array} \tag{1}$$

Obviously, P and D are bistable, which means that, choosing between P and D, each strategy is a best response to itself. Specifically, the typical dynamics is given as follows: if the frequency of P peers, x_p, satisfies the inequality $x_p > \dfrac{c_s + c_u}{c_p + c_u}$, then P will dominate, otherwise, D dominates. Usually, $c_p \gg c_s$, thus, P always dominates the system.

Similarly, for reward based scheme, the payoff matrix is given as follows:

$$
\begin{array}{cc}
 R & D \\
\begin{array}{c} R \\ D \end{array}
\left(
\begin{array}{cc}
\alpha_2 - c_s + b_r - c_r & -c_s \\
\alpha_2 & 0
\end{array}
\right)
\end{array}
\tag{2}
$$

Then, R and D are bistable, and if the frequency of R peers, x_R, satisfies the inequality $x_R > \dfrac{c_s}{b_r - c_r}$, then R dominates, otherwise, D dominates.

In brief, if, as wished ideally, there only exist two strategies P and D (or P and R) in punishment-based (or reward-based) service differentiation incentive mechanism, then the scheme always works, that is, P (or R) will dominate in P2P network.

However, as dynamic and autonomous network, each peer could independently determine its behaviors, thus, in the above punishment-based and reward-based incentive mechanisms, with small mutation probability, some peers might conceive the following simpler (and more "stupid") strategy: do not assume other jobs (punishment or reward), only provide resource (or service) for the P2P network, so-called C strategy.

It is important to note that, for punishment-based scheme, due to the dynamic characteristics, P peers can only determine whether to punish peers or not, totally according to other peers' current behaviors (i.e., provide/do not provide service to system), thus it is feasible to assume that P can only punish the D peers. Then, for the 3-strategy punishment-based scheme (C, D and P), the payoff matrix can be given as follows:

$$
\begin{array}{ccc}
 C & D & P \\
\begin{array}{c} C \\ D \\ P \end{array}
\left(
\begin{array}{ccc}
\alpha_1 - c_s & -c_s & \alpha_1 - c_s \\
\alpha_1 & 0 & \alpha_1 - c_p \\
\alpha_1 - c_s & -c_u & \alpha_1 - c_s
\end{array}
\right)
\end{array}
\tag{3}
$$

Briefly, the dynamics based on the payoff matrix (3) will finally converge to D. The reason lies in that: considering C peer obtain the same payoff as P peer, for small mutation, cooperators can invade and replace punishers through neutral drift. Once cooperators have taken over the whole system, defectors are advantageous and take over. Furthermore, as described above, P and D are bistable, which means that each strategy is a best response to itself. That is, a small percentage of P mutants could not successfully invade the population of D. Thus, the final state will be stuck in D. Actually, the same conclusion was also provided in [11]. Note that recently, the costly punishment has been shown to invade when a rare percentage of individuals are allowed to opt out of cooperative ventures [12].

In reward-based scheme, similarly, R peers have to reward both R and C peers (because, in the very time, R and C peers all provide good service to system), thus, in this scenario, the pair-wise payoff matrix can be given as follows:

$$
\begin{array}{cc}
& \begin{array}{ccc} C & D & R \end{array} \\
\begin{array}{c} C \\ D \\ R \end{array} &
\left(
\begin{array}{ccc}
\alpha_2 - c_s & -c_s & \alpha_2 - c_s + b_r \\
\alpha_2 & 0 & \alpha_2 \\
\alpha_2 - c_s - c_r & -c_s & \alpha_2 - c_s + b_r - c_r
\end{array}
\right)
\end{array}
\tag{4}
$$

The above matrix implies the following characteristics: R will always transfer into C (because, in comparison with R peers, C peers get the extra reward, and do not bear any reward cost); C will always transfer into D; R and D are bi-stable, which means that a small percentage of R mutants can not invade the D population. Thus, finally, the whole population will be converged to the D state.

In summary, for service differentiation based incentive schemes (punishment-based or reward-based), if, as initially wished, there only exist two strategies, P and D in punishment-based scheme (or R and D in reward-based scheme), then under appropriate conditions, P (or R) will dominate, that is, the differential service based schemes will work. But, unfortunately, if the C peers appear (due the mutation) that only provide service, and do not conduct punishment (or reward) behavior, then service differentiation based incentive mechanisms could not work at all, irrespective of punishment-based or reward-based schemes.

For the simplicity, in the above derivation, we only use the pairwise interaction payoff matrix to characterize the dynamics of whole system. Basically, there exist positive externalities associated with peer's contribution (i.e., one's contribution benefits equally all other peers since it increases the value of the system as a whole). Thus, naturally, we could use the public goods game to model the punishment-based [7] and reward-based service differentiation incentive mechanisms.

In order to provide an escape hatch out of the state of stalemate (mutual defection) in the above service differentiation based incentive mechanisms, which can operate under full anonymity, we assume that, besides the above three strategies, there also exist an extra strategy, L, denoted as the loners, who just stand by the resource provision scheme. And if those loners want to join the system, small entry fee will be exerted (for all peers who want to join the resource provision scheme), and after joining, they could choose to be one strategy of other three strategies C, D and P in punishment-based scheme (or C, D and R in reward-based scheme).

Fig.1 illustrated punishment-based incentive mechanism scheme. Normally, there exist four types of users in autonomous systems: C, D, P, and L. The L peers, represent individuals who, by default, just stand by (do not join the public enterprise), and thus do not pay the entry fee, and the other users include D peers who participate, but do not contribute, C peers who contribute but do not punish the defectors, and P peers, who not only contribute to the commonwealth but also punish the defectors. As shown in Fig. 1, L peers can voluntarily join the resource provision scheme, and all participants can voluntarily quit the scheme. For simplicity, we assume that each C (and P) peer will provide benefit α_1 to resource pool, and bear service-providing cost c_s. Furthermore, each P peer will impose penalty c_p, on D peer, and similarly incur punishment cost c_u for this behavior.

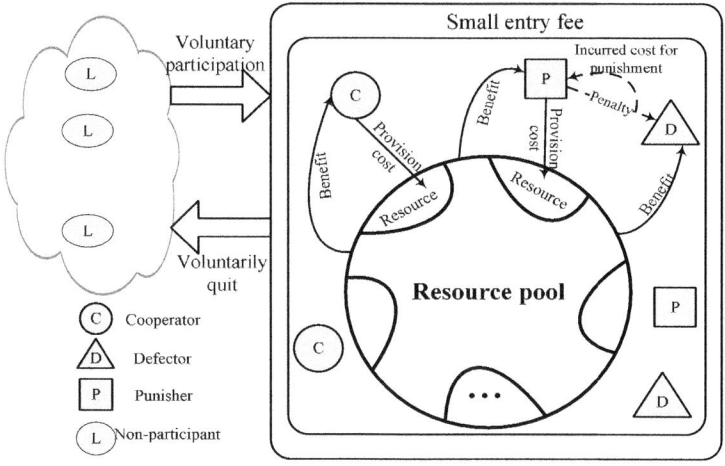

Fig. 1. Schematic illustration of punishment-based incentive mechanism

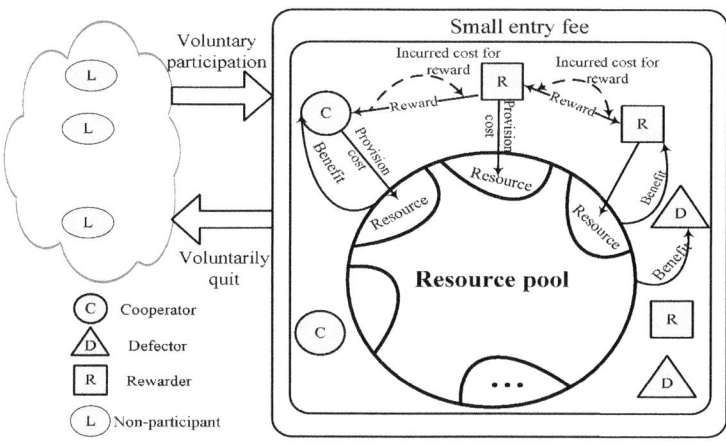

Fig. 2. Schematic illustration of reward-based incentive mechanism

Similarly, Fig.2 shows the reward based incentive mechanism. In reward based incentive mechanism, there exist four types of users: C, D, L and R. The behaviors of C, D and L peers are same as the punishment based scheme. The difference lies in that: the R peers not only cooperate, but voluntarily provide extra reward, b_r for other peers who provide resource to the system, which bring them small cost, c_r. As shown in Fig.2, the rewarder's behavior implies that they not only reward to other R peers, but also reward the C peers.

Considering the inherent dynamics of peer's behavior, we simply assume that each peer imitates the strategy of peer with better utility. Actually, in real-world situations, costs and benefits should be carefully defined and measured empirically. But, even though the model is very simplified, it still illuminates some interesting results. The following tables provide a list of symbols and their definitions used in this paper.

And, in the following description, we let the number 1, 2, 3 and 4 denote the strategies of cooperators, defectors, punishers (or rewarders in reward-based scheme), and loners respectively.

Table 1. Common symbols used in punishment-based and reward-based incentive mechanisms

Symbol	Definition
M	The total number of peers in system
N	The average number of peers in each group
μ	The strategy mutation probability in evolutionary phase
β	The intensity of selection
c_s	The cost that cooperators (or punishers and rewarders) incur by provision of resource. without loss of generality, let $c_s=1$.
c_e	The entry fee set for peers who will join the resource provision scheme

Table 2. The specific symbols used in punishment-based incentive scheme

Symbol	Definition
α_1	The benefit that one peer would voluntarily provide to the system
c_p	The penalty that P peer imposes on D peer
c_u	The incurred cost for P peer for conducting the punishment behaviors

Table 3. The specific symbols used in reward-based incentive scheme

Symbol	Definition
α_2	The benefit that one peer would voluntarily offer to the system
b_r	The extra benefit that R peer offers to peers who provide service to system
c_r	The incurred cost for R peer for conducting the reward behaviors

4   Simulations

In this section, we preliminary investigate and compare the performances of the proposed punishment-based incentive scheme and reward-based scheme. Considering that the performances of punishment-based scheme were already discussed in our previous work [7], this paper mainly focuses on the performances of reward-based scheme and their comparison with punishment-based scheme. Due to the lasting dynamics of imitating and mutating process in the proposed schemes, in our simulations, we define the homogeneous state of each strategy as follows: whenever more than 90% of the peers opt for one strategy, then it is counted as being in the respective homogeneous state. Then, based on the number of homogeneous states, we calculate the ratio of time average for each strategy.

4.1   Illustration of Strategy Frequencies in Punishment-Based Incentive Scheme

Fig. 3 shows the changes of strategy frequencies, as evolutionary rounds go by. The strategy frequency denotes how many percentages of peers with specific strategy are in system. Clearly, after some initial oscillations, P peers usually dominate the whole network. In longer runs, their regime can occasionally break down as a result of C peers invading by neutral drift, but after another series of oscillations among C, D, and L peers (rock-paper-scissors-like succession), the P peers dominate the whole network again.

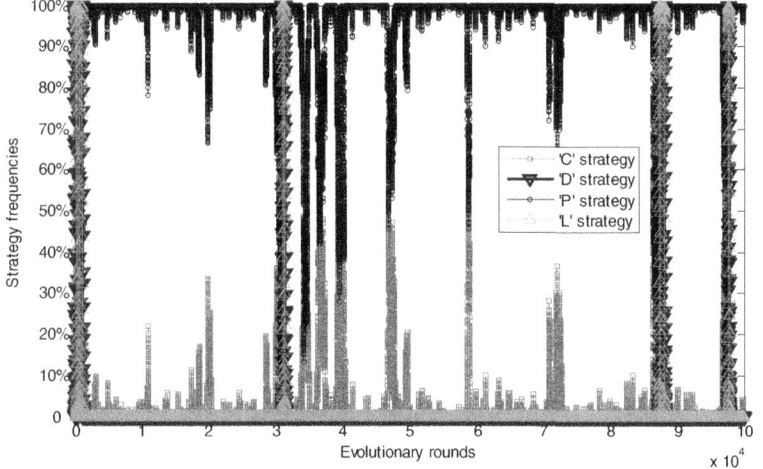

The scenario: $M=500$, $N=50$, $\mu=0.0001$, $\beta=5$, $\alpha_1=10$, $c_s=1$, $c_e=0.1$, $c_p=0.2$, $c_u=0.1$

Fig. 3. Illustration of strategy frequencies in punishment-based scheme (with entry fee)

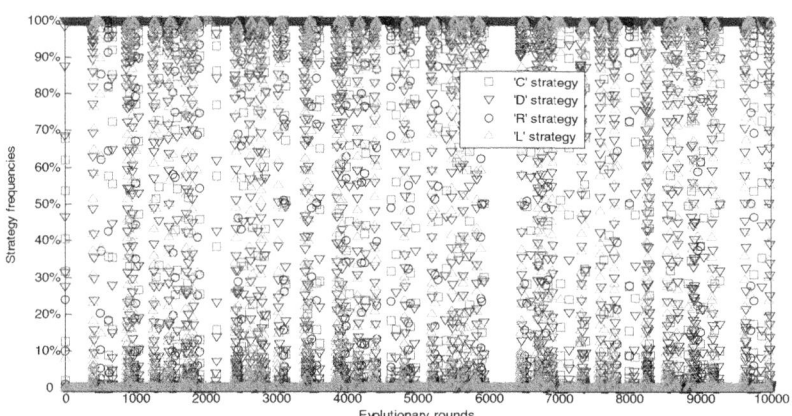

The scenario is: $M=500$, $N=50$, $\mu=0.0001$, $\beta=5$, $\alpha_2=5$, $c_s=1$, $c_e=0.1$, $b_r=0.2$, $c_r=0.1$

Fig. 4. Illustration of strategy frequencies in reward-based scheme

4.2 Illustration of Strategy Frequencies in Reward-Based Incentive Scheme

Fig. 4 illustrates the strategy frequencies, and the stationary probability distributions as well as transition probabilities, when exist entry fee. Unlink the punishment-based incentive mechanism, as shown in Fig. 3, the state of whole system appears unorderly, which implies that reward-based incentive scheme can not make the system "almost stable", that is, the whole system is mostly located at P state. And moreover, intuitively, we can observe that D state occupies the largest ratio of time average.

4.3 Ratio of Time Averages in Reward-Based Incentive Scheme with the Changes of Benefit and Reward

Fig. 5 illustrates, with the increase of the benefit, the experimental time averages of various strategies in reward-based scheme. The time averages of R and C states do not increase correspondingly, and, on the contrary, the time average of D state increases slightly. The above phenomenon is intuitive: with the increase of benefit, D peers would exploit the system more.

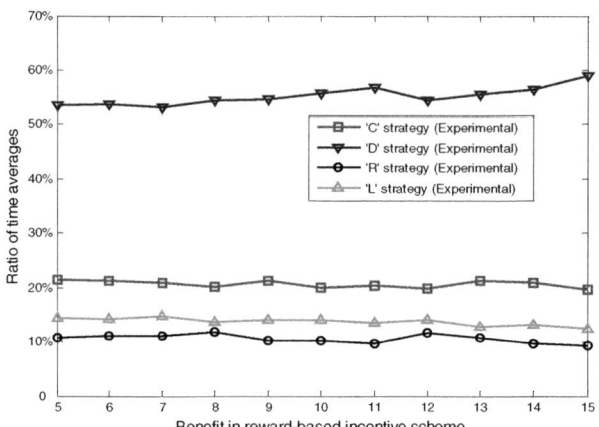

The scenario is: M=500, N=50, μ=0.0001, β=5, c_s=1, c_e=0.1, b_r=0.2, c_r=0.1

Fig. 5. Time average of various strategies with the change of benefit in reward-based scheme

Fig. 6 illustrates the experimental time averages of various strategies in reward-based scheme, with the increase of the extra reward that the R peer provides to C peers and other R peers. Interestingly, only when extra reward is extremely large, the time averages of C and R states can increase slightly.

In brief, as Fig. 5 and Fig. 6 show, even with the increase of the benefit and extra reward, the reward-based incentive mechanism doesn't work well in dynamic and autonomous networks.

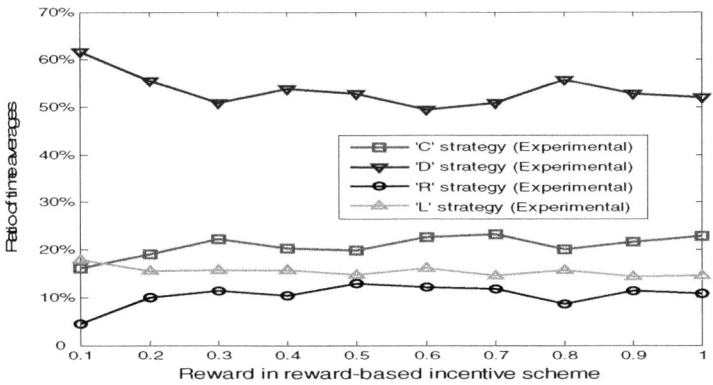

The scenario is: $M=500$, $N=50$, $\mu=0.0001$, $\beta=5$, $\alpha_2=5$, $c_s=1$, $c_e=0.1$, $c_r=0.1$

Fig. 6. Time average of various strategies with the change of reward in reward-based scheme

5   Conclusion and Future Work

Generally, most networking environments are anonymous, dynamic and autonomous, in which most interactions among peers are one-time, each strategy and action are voluntarily chosen and determined by independent, rational and autonomous peers, and all behaviors and actions are all endogenous. Under the above considerations, this paper preliminarily investigated and compared the effectiveness of punishment-base (first providing high-level service plus punishment) and reward-based (first providing low-level service plus reward) incentive schemes. We draw the conclusion that, in anonymous, dynamic and autonomous networking environment, if peers can voluntarily join the system, and small entry fee is set for participation, the performance of punishment-based scheme is always better than reward-based scheme. The philosophy implication in our paper is that: for providing service (or resource) in dynamic, anonymous and autonomous networks, the appropriate way should be: first to be generous, then to be harsh according to peers' current behaviors.

This paper only preliminarily examined, through simulations, the effectiveness of punishment based and reward based incentive mechanisms. The future work includes the following aspects.

- To theoretically analyze and compare both kinds of incentive mechanisms, especially through inferring the fixation probability between pair of pure strategies.
- It is shown that reward is as effective as punishment for maintaining public cooperation and leads to higher total earnings [13]. But the above conclusions rely on truly repeated games, in which player identities persist from round to round. Thus, for anonymous, dynamic and autonomous networking environments, it is interesting to deeply investigate the average earnings of both incentive mechanisms.

Acknowledgments. This work is partially support by the 973 Program 2007CB310607, 863 Projects 2007AA01Z206 and 2006AA01Z235, NSFC Grant 60802022.

References

1. Adar, E., Huberman, B.: Free Riding on Gnutella. First Monday Online Journal (2000)
2. Hughes, D., Coulson, G., Walkerdine, J.: Free Riding on Gnutella Revisited: the Bell Tolls? IEEE Distributed Systems Online 6 (2005)
3. Antoniadis, P., Friedman, T., Cuvellier, X.: Resource Provision and Allocation in Shared Network Testbed Infrastructures. In: The Workshop on Real Overlays and Distributed Systems (2007)
4. Feldman, M., Lai, K., Zhang, L.: A Price-Anticipating Resource Allocation Mechanism for Distributed Shared Clusters. In: ACM Conference on Electronic Commerce (2005)
5. Courcoubetis, C., Weber, R.: Incentives for Large Peer-to-Peer Systems. IEEE Journal on Selected Areas in Communications 24(5) (2006)
6. Feldman, M., Papadimitriou, C., Chuang, J., Stoica, I.: Free-Riding and Whitewashing in Peer-to-Peer Systems. IEEE Journal on Selected Areas in Communications 24(5) (2006)
7. Wang, Y., Nakao, A., Ma, J.H.: A Simple Public-Goods Game Based Incentive Mechanism for Resource Provision in P2P Networks. In: Yu, Z., Liscano, R., Chen, G., Zhang, D., Zhou, X. (eds.) UIC 2010. LNCS, vol. 6406, pp. 352–365. Springer, Heidelberg (2010)
8. Zhao, Q., Lui, C.S., Chiu, D.M.: Mathematical Modeling of Incentive Policies in P2P Systems. In: ACM Workshop on Network Economics (2008)
9. Zhao, Q., Lui, C.S., Chiu, D.M.: Analysis of Adaptive Incentive Protocols for P2P Networks. In: INFOCOM (2009)
10. Wang, Y.F., Nakao, A., Vasilakos, A.V., Ma, J.H.: P2P Soft Security: On Evolutionary Dynamics of P2P Incentive Mechanism. Computer Communications 34(3) (2011)
11. Hauert, C., et al.: Exploration Dynamics in Evolutionary Games. Proceedings of the National Academy of Sciences 106(3) (2009)
12. Hauert, C., et al.: Via Freedom to Coercion: the Emergence of Costly Punishment. Science 316(5833), 905–1907 (2007)
13. Rand, D.G., Dreber, A., Ellingsen, T., Fudenberg, D., Nowak, M.A.: Positive Interactions Promote Public Cooperation. Science (325) (2009)

event.Hub: An Event-Driven Information Hub for Mobile Devices

Adrian Hornsby and Tapani Leppanen

Nokia Research Center, Tampere, Finland
`name.surname@nokia.com`

Abstract. In this paper, we present a novel architecture and implementation of an information hub for mobile devices that we call the event.Hub. The event.Hub allows mobile users to share events, implicit or explicit, happening in their lives following a publish-subscribe model. The event.Hub design follows a decentralized architecture that also takes into account the privacy and data ownership problems of current service offers. The event.Hub is implemented using event-driven programming paradigms and utilize the XMPP protocol for its real-time communication support. As an example application using the event.Hub, we also present an extended address-book application.

1 Introduction

The mobile ecosystem has undergone dramatic changes in the last decade; the mobile device is no longer a simple communication device, extension of a fix line phone, but it has evolved to become a hyper-connected device, transforming the traditional Internet of connected computers to a more global, almost organic and ever changing ecosystem of human relations, information flow and computing resources. Within this new environment, people have fully embraced the possibility to become an architect of this new Internet, publishing information and sharing resources of their daily life to their social networks, without geographic, linguistic or time barriers.

An example of this surge for architecting the web is best seen with social networking services that have become a cultural phenomenon [5] and one of the most popular activities on the web, with sites like Flickr, Facebook or Twitter harboring millions of users. However, despite their very high popularity, social networking services often offer low quality of privacy policies, usability problems, poor security [6] and ownership policies, preventing people from fully using those services [7].

People's expectations have also evolved and today's mobile users expect to have an immediate, almost real-time access to information, where only the relevant, fresh and meaningful data is brought to attention, encouraging user engagement and social interactions.

Along with this transformation from a static to an organic Internet of people and devices, the patterns governing the design and behavior of data flow are evolving to incorporate more social, sensory and personal information.

C.-H. Hsu et al. (Eds.): UIC 2011, LNCS 6905, pp. 209–223, 2011.

To support this revolution, event-driven paradigms have emerged and gained growing interest. Popularized by Graphical User Interface (GUI), the flexibility and asynchronous-friendly behavior of event-driven communication model has gained popularity in every application area, from programming environment to large-scale internet services [11].

Event-driven communication plays an important role in applications, centralized or distributed, that require components to react to a change of state from another component. This communication paradigm is essentially asynchronous, resulting in architectures where the system's components are clearly decoupled from one another, fitting particularly well in mobile environment where entities usually have only a very limited knowledge from each others, and where that knowledge is mainly information about shared interfaces. Decoupled architectures allows for changes to happen in the system without affecting other parts.

The following sections detail an event-driven event.Hub which aims at becoming the key element in our architecture. It uses XMPP [9] as the main communication protocol since it enables real-time event-based interactions through the use of its build-in federation and publish-subscribe features. Section 2 explores the possibilities and opportunities offered by the event.Hub, supporting both software and social real-time interactions. Section 3 presents the architectural details of the event.Hub and in Section 4, the implementation details are presented. Section 5 discusses the consequences of the choices made and Section 6 concludes the article.

1.1   Motivations

Our main motivation for doing this work can be summarized with the following questions:

How do we make it possible for geographically separated people to remain connected with and aware of each other?

How do we emulate the sensation of being "together"?

How do we let people be aware and select certain social bonds to concentrate on to keep in touch?

How to we let people manage there own intimacy, privacy and ownership, in a granular fashion?

How do we let people share information without having to subscribe to a dedicated social website service?

And finally, how do we do that using and open platform?

2   The Power of Events

Whether we refer to a gathering of people (e.g. party, festival), a scientific outcome (e.g. computing, mathematics, physics) or even a philosophical mindset (e.g. thoughts, feelings), events, or any observable phenomenon occurrences, are occupying a primordial importance in our daily lives and each of them is likely to have an impact on our actions. Events also serve our communication needs and social behavior in often very complex and interconnected networks, where individuals are tied together by interdependencies such as family, friendship, appearances, beliefs, customs, practices or knowledge. This extent to which individuals share characteristics that define their identity is known as the social distance [2].

In the light of capturing those life events and nurturing our relationships, we propose a social and event driven middleware that provides a friendly way to share events with our social networks while protecting our privacy.

A typical way in which information is disseminated within a network is using a binary model -on/off-, selecting whether or not the information is transmitted to all other parties. This model is not satisfying since communication between people is not binary, but it evolves with time or through shared activities.

In order to avoid this limited binary classification of communication mode, we arrange events in topics, which are in turn categorized following a three-layer model: superordinate, basic and subordinate [1] . For example, Jazz (subordinate) is a type of music (basic) which is a type of entertainment (superordinate). The level to which events are presented to people is supervised by the social distance (close, somewhat close, not close) separating people within an information network. Let's look at some examples and see how events are shared between people through what we call an *event.Hub*.

2.1 Scenario 1a

Juliet and Romeo share a passion for music and in particular jazz. During a festival, they engage in a conversation about their shared passion and decide to keep in touch. While Juliet adds Romeo's details to her phone's address book, her mobile phone automatically goes on and queries the *event.Hub* that Romeo is sharing. From the list of events suggested by her mobile phone, Juliet decides to subscribe to musical events shared by Romeo. Few days later, while setting up a calendar event for his favorite Jazz band concert, Romeo's mobile phone suggests the publishing of this events to his *event.Hub*. Since Romeo agrees to publish this event, Juliet, who subscribed to musical events from Romeo, receives the notification that Romeo is going to a jazz concert next Saturday. She eventually decides to buy herself a ticket and join Romeo for the concert.

2.2 Scenario 1b

After several concerts and a growing shared affinity, Romeo decides to modify Juliet's contact details in his address book: He subscribes to location events shared by Juliet and modify is perceived social distance to "close". Since Juliet also likes Romeo, she allows him to subscribe to those events and reciprocate the social distance change to "close". After few days without any news, Romeo decides to contact Juliet to see if she wants to join him for tonight's jazz concert. While browsing her contact details, Romeo quickly realize that since Juliet is traveling in southern Spain, Valencia, she cannot be reached easily. Instead, he wishes her a nice trip by sending her a message through her *event.Hub*. Carol, Carlos and Charlie have also subscribed to Juliet's location events but are not close friends; their address book only notifies them that Juliet is away from the country, traveling somewhere in southern Europe.

3   The event.Hub

The event.Hub is an entity by which a mobile user can share (publisher) to her/his contacts, events that she/he encounters. Contacts can subscribe (subscriber) to those events through a publish-subscribe mechanism [3] also known as the observer pattern. As oppose to previously proposed publish-subscribe systems where mobile users are only subscribers and anonymous [4], our proposed architecture defines mobile user as both publishers and subscribers (as shown in Fig.1), the address book contacts defining the extend of the network in which the events can be published and subscribed to. When the publisher's hub updates a particular event collection, an event notification is then sent to all contacts that have subscribed to this particular event collection. Events can for example describe a geographic situation, a mood, an activity (taking a photo), a change of context, an encounter with a friend, a work meeting, a game result, etc. As mentioned previously, events are arranged in topics. A user expresses her/his interest in receiving a certain type of events from her/his address book contacts by subscribing to a particular or a set of topics shared by a particular contact. The list of available subscriptions is directly related to the social distance separating those two contacts. The address book contact list and the social distance separating the owner and her/his contacts is used to control the level of event sharing, enabling controlled privacy through supervised distribution of information. While some events might only be relevant for the mobile users, it is important to note that some might be relevant only for the software platforms or infrastructure (see the Discussion section).

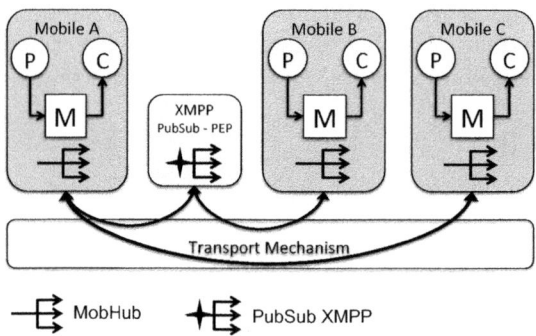

Fig. 1. MobHub model: Distributed PubSub Event System with collocated producer and consumer

3.1   Event-Driven Architecture and the Hub

From the previous example scenarios, one can notice that the flow of Romeo's and Juliet's life is determined by events: Romeo and Juliet meeting, Romeo and Juliet becoming friends, Romeo contacting Juliet to finally Romeo and Juliet going to a concert. Thus, life can be seen as an event-driven process.

To accommodate this event-driven life pattern, we decided the implement the event.Hub using event-driven programming paradigms. In event-driven programming, the flow of the program is also determined by events: e.g. user interaction through the mouse or the keyboard, events from network layer (message received) or event from other threads. Event-driven architectures are usually composed of an event detection mechanism called event dispatcher and one, or several, event handler. When events are generated, the event dispatcher takes care (by checking the event type and producer) to forward the event to the correct event handler.

The event.Hub event handling is using three asynchronous queue mechanisms (for Subscription, Presence and Notification messages) managed by an event-handler, a subscription management and a filter unit and a database to store incoming and outgoing events. All three queues implement the multi-producer, multi-consumer principle especially useful in event based and threaded programming where data needs to be exchanged carefully between multiple threads, producing a fully asynchronous communication service. The network handler is also event driven. When an event occurs on the socket, an event handler is fired and the event is passed to the Queue. The event type defines the routing of the event to the appropriate Queue. This way, no thread awaits on network I/O to complete. The architecture of the hub is shown in Fig.2.

3.2   Requirements

The event.Hub must respect the following principles:

1. Identity: The hub must support identity management and have only one owner. Any given event published on the hub is owned and tied to hub's owner identity and profile. The identity of the hub is also the one of its owner and is identified as a unique resource in the form (owner@domain.org/ event.Hub).
2. Follower-Following model: The hub must support a publish-subscribe model that supports information diffusion granularity through filters.
3. Relationship: The hub must be able to manage relations: discover, add and remove contacts.
4. Privacy and Security: The hub must support and manage the privacy and security of all communication, data exchange and data ownership. This also includes the supervision of the owner on information published by the hub.
5. Formatting: Events must be published in a standardized notification message format (Atom or JSON), and must support interaction on published items.
6. Persistence: The hub must be accessible from any network interface, supporting both local and distant interaction.

In order to fulfill those aforementioned principles, we utilize the XMPP protocol, topic of the following section.

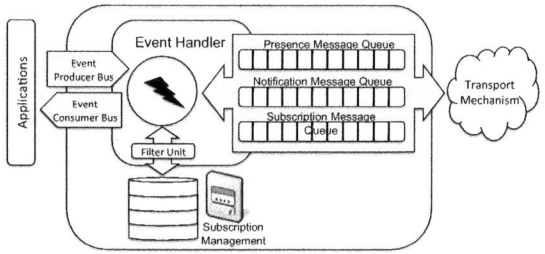

Fig. 2. Overall software architecture of the MobHub

4   Using the XMPP Protocol

Initially developed as an open, presence aware messaging protocol, the XMPP protocol [9] also known as Jabber, has been adapted for a wide range of solutions, from simple instant messaging to complex cloud computing systems [10]. In a nutshell, XMPP is a federated, decentralized and open protocol, built on three core stanzas (elements), presence, message and info/query (iq) that provide the basis for synchronous and asynchronous real-time communication with contact list management (roster). XMPP entities are identified with a unique Jabber ID (JID) in the form of *user@domain*.

XMPP supports logging from multiple clients (or locations), specified as a resource (e.g. home, work, or mobile) each having a priority value. This can be added in the JID in the form of *user@domain/resource*. Messages sent to *user@domain* will be delivered to the client with the highest priority, those sent to *user@domain/resource* will only be delivered to the specified resource.

XMPP uses a push mechanism [8] where entities can register to each other to receive messages using publish-subscribe, preserving bandwidth and giving low latency, thus enabling near real-time event-based interactions (See Fig.3).

In XMPP, nodes (or topics) are things users subscribe to and are handled by a so called publish-subscribe service. This service is, among other things, in charge of keeping an accurate and up-to-date list of subscribers and delivering notifications.

In standard XMPP, publish-subscribe services can either be designed as a dedicated publish-subscribe services with its own domain (e.g. pubsub.example.org) or a publish-subscribe services related to a specific user account. This user centric publish-subscribe, subset of the pubsub specification[1], is known as Personal Eventing Protocol (PEP). PEP-nodes have interesting properties; the ability to directly associate a particular node with a particular person and the possibility to control the user's contact list (roster).

Another important feature of XMPP, is its robust security (via SASL and TLS) that has been built-into the core XMPP specifications. To further secure communications, XMPP enables server identity validation through the use of

---

[1] XMPP Extensions (XEP): `http://xmpp.org/xmpp-protocols/xmpp-extensions/`

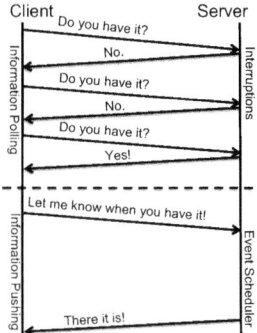

Fig. 3. Polling versus Pushing Model

Certified Authorities, removing the complexity of existing web-based mechanisms that forces securing communication through complex signature exchange.

XMPP as defined in the RFC 3920 does not directly support client-to-client interactions since it requires clients authentication to the XMPP federation through XMPP servers; if the client fails to authenticate to the XMPP server, it won't be able to access the federation and all XMPP communications will fail.

However, the XMPP Serverless extension makes it possible to establish an XMPP-like communication system on a local network using the principles of zero-configuration networking: clients can bypass the core XMPP requirements for server authentication by using zero-configuration networking to establish serverless communication using the DNS SRV service type. Once the discovery is completed, clients can exchange XMPP messages using the message and the iq stanzas.

In our architecture, we utilize both standard and serverless communication, so that the event.Hub can be accessed through local interaction using for example Bluetooth as transport mechanism on top of which XMPP messages will be exchanged (See Fig.1). Moreover, instead of locating the publish-subscribe service on the server side, we build it on the mobile device itself, keeping it accessible through local interaction.

4.1   The Hub's XMPP API

We have implemented the Hub using python since it is extensible and portable and it support object-oriented programming paradigms. As mentioned earlier, the hub (as shown in Fig.2) is implemented using the producer-consumer model using Queue objects, providing an inter-thread communication mechanism.

Three queues are used to pass event message information between the XMPP interface and the message handlers: one queue for managing received subscription messages, one for the received presence information messages and one for sending out notification messages. The queues are used to prioritize the event hub execution, to avoid locks, and to allow the different parts of the hub to run independently from each other.

The event.Hub expose some of its functionality through the Application Programming Interface (API), the following methods representing the main ones (type: method):

. `Request:addMeToContact`

Request the hub to start an exchange contact procedure (I add you, you add me) with supervised authorization (requires user interaction for allowing the procedure to conclude).

. `Get:getContactInfo`

Get information about the owner of the hub.

. `Get:getHubInfo`

Get information about the hub (version, support, api).

. `Get:getSubscriptionInfo`

Get the list of available subscriptions for the requester.

. `Get:getMySubscription`

Get the list of subscriptions active from the requester.

. `Get:getSubscriberList`

Get the list of contacts that have subscribed to a particular topic (if authorized).

. `Subscribe:subscribeToEvent`

Subscribe to a particular type of Events (e.g. musical, calendar, location).

. `Subscribe:unsubscribeToEvent`

Unsubscribe to a particular type of Event.

Those APIs are implemented on top of the XMPP *message* stanza the main reason being the server side support for offline message handling. Indeed, iq stanzas are lost if a connection happens to go offline while message stanza are kept stored on the server until the receiving party comes online again, ensuring better liability. We simply defined a custom message stanza type so that message filtering can be done very easily based on the message type, without requiring the hub to parse for every message body. The subject of the message is specified by the particular API method invoked and is defined in the subject element of the message, ensuring the message to be XMPP standard compliant. This is then followed by the body of the message, containing the method name and the details needed by the hub to understand the invocation.

```
<message
    to = "juliet@capulet.com/eventhub"
    from = "romeo@montague.lit/eventhub"
    type="event"
    xml:lang="en">
    <subject>method_type</subject>
    <body>method_name:details</body>
</message>
```

4.2   Sending and Receiving Events

When a new event occurs on the mobile device, the event.Hub publishes a new entry to the correct event topic collection and an event notification is sent to all the consumers that have successfully subscribed to the particular event topic.

In the following example, Romeo has subscribes to the location events of Juliet. When Juliet gets on the balcony, a event notification message is sent to Romeo. The notification message is sent using the following XMPP/Atom feed format:

```
<message
    to = "juliet@capulet.com/eventhub"
    from = "romeo@montague.lit/eventhub"
    type="event"
    xml:lang="en">
    <subject>Location Event</subject>
    <body>
    <feed xmlns="http://www.w3.org/2005/Atom">
     <title>Example Event Feed</title>
     <link href="capulet.com/eventhub/locations"/>
     <updated>2011-04-26T18:30:02Z</updated>
     <author>
     <name>Juliet</name>
     </author>
     <id>urn:uuid:xxxx</id>
     <entry>
        <title>On my balcony</title>
        <geo:lat>61.4484</geo:lat>
        <geo:long>23.8633</geo:long>
        <link href="/2011/04/atom01"/>
        <id>urn:uuid:xxxx</id>
        <updated>2011-04-26T18:30:02Z</updated>
     </entry>
    </feed>
    </body>
</message>
```

Before composing the message, the filter unit shown in 2 takes care of matching the social distance to the granularity of information shared. In our case, Juliet and Romeo have defines their social distance as close, therefor the information shared is very precise; the very geographic coordinates of the balcony. In our example and to perform the filtering on geographic location, we query a Google location service API for the coordinate[2] and filter back the answer and extract the different levels of geographic location (street, locality and country) serving the different levels of information granularity.

4.3   Integrating with Existing Social Network Services

Since, as mentioned earlier, social networking services have become very popular in mobile devices, it makes great sense to integrate those existing services with our proposed event.Hub, using XMPP to push desired information similarly as to other contacts within the address book. Treating those social services as regular contacts allows users to fine tune the type of information she/he wants to publish on those services. Fortunately, social networking services like Twitter, Facebook, OneSocialWeb, Identica and Superfeedr, just to name a few, already offer some XMPP interface to their services, making the integration relatively easy.

Another solution is to use an XMPP to HTTP gateway. This can also be done relatively easily by mapping XMPP IQ stanza to HTTP request and keeping a uniform query model using the following approach.

```
<iq type="get"
    from="juliet@capulet.com"
    to="gateway.example.com"
    id-"1234">
    <query
      method="GET"
      url="http://shakespeare.lit/romance.html"/>
</iq>
```

The gateway can then easily transform the IQ request into an HTTP request by first opening a socket to the host shakespeare.lit, on the port 80, then, send the following through the socket:

```
GET /romance.html HTTP/1.0
From: gateway.example.com
```

The result of the HTTP GET will then be returned by the gateway as part of the XMPP IQ response message back to the event.Hub.

4.4   Why XMPP for Event-Driven Approach?

It has now been widely recognized that HTTP polling (see Fig.3) doesn't work well in high-data flow and fast changing environments [8]. Of course, there are several ways to emulate push mechanism using HTTP protocol:

(1) Poll for new information very frequently. Unfortunately, this adds a great deal of load to the web server.

---

[2] Example   query: http://maps.google.com/maps/api/geocode/xml?latlng=61. 448,23.863&radius=10&sensor=false

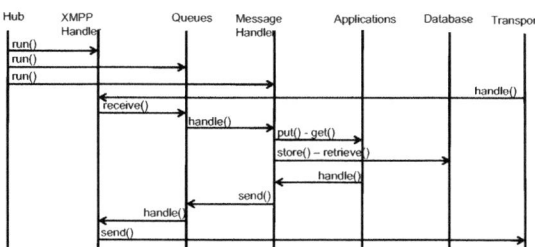

Fig. 4. Event Hub flow diagram

(2) Maintain a persistent, long lasting HTTP connection with the server with a request that only gets answered when new data is available; e.g using long polling or streaming with Comet to simulate server push[3]. Unfortunately, current web servers were not developed nor optimized for maintaining large numbers of open sockets at the same time and for a undefined amount of time, resulting in complex implementation techniques.

(3) Using HTTP callback mechanism where a "reply to" URL is called or pinged when new information is made available. This, however, requires an externally-reachable web server (similarly to Pubsubhubbub[4] and Web hooks[5]).

Those methods require a dedicated TCP three-way handshake and SSL negotiation to operate and also an authentication and/or authorization layer for the communicating parties to identify each other. Using XMPP solves many of those problems since both the sender and the receiver authenticate to an XMPP server, they can express interest in notifications using a publish-subscribe paradigm, they have a build-in presence mechanism and offline message handling, an encryption, authentication and authorization method build-in the XMPP layer and an unique identifier enabling endpoints to easily communicate. All this makes XMPP to fit a lot better for our event-driven approach of real-time information sharing in mobile environment.

4.5 Short Summary on How XMPP Fulfills the Previously Listed Requirements

1. Identity: XMPP support identity management through the JID (user@domain). Moreover, one can use an JID for OpenID authentication using dedicated XMPP OpenID servers[6].
2. Follower-Following model: Since we position the publish-subscribe service on the hub side and not on the server, we break the standard XMPP pubsub conformity. However, defining your own custom message type and payload is

---

[3] http://www.webreference.com/programming/javascript/rg28/
[4] http://code.google.com/p/pubsubhubbub/
[5] http://blog.webhooks.org/about/
[6] OpenID Server for XMPP, http://openid.xmpp.za.net

permitted by the standard, so is the creation of a custom client side pubsub service. This service won't however operate with standard XMPP clients out of the box.

3. Relationship: In XMPP, the contact list is called a roster, and consists of items (contacts) being identified by a unique JID (contact@domain). The roster is stored on the user's server (domain) and is accessible from any resource.
4. Privacy and Security: XMPP uses the Transport Layer Security (TLS) method along with a "STARTTLS" extension for securing the stream from tampering and eavesdropping. Moreover, XMPP also includes a Simple Authentication and Security Layer (SASL) method for authenticating a stream.
5. Formatting: XMPP offers a generalized, extensible framework for exchanging XML data.
6. Persistence: XMPP offers an extension for serverless communication allowing direct client-to-client communications.

5   Example Application Build on the event.Hub

To demonstrate the potential use of our proposed event.Hub, we implemented an enhanced address book application (see screenshot in Fig.5). This application use the event.Hub to exchange contextual information about the contacts, informing in real-time the timezone, the weather, the status information, the location and the current music being listened by each contact. On top of this contextual information, the event.Hub exchange information in forms of hourly digest, shown in the recent activity element. In this screenshot, we can see that Christian took 107 photos in last week and also seemed to have lots of coffee.

The application is build using Qt QML[7] following the message-based MVC architecture and using event-based programming concepts as presented in [12].

6   Discussion

6.1   Privacy

Social networks like Facebook are offering great user value and delight for people's present communication needs and are also offering new means for social interactions. Many services do this is at the expense of privacy and data ownership. Some people are currently not willing to accept these compromises and the awareness of possible conflicts of interest between users and commercial service providers can be expected to arise in the future. In current social networks, people can themselves monitor the possible problems in privacy and data ownership in explicit humans to humans communication; everyone can easily control the amount of private information they want to share with others and with their service provider.

---

[7] Qt application and UI framework: http://qt.nokia.com

Fig. 5. Screenshot of the example address book application

The privacy and ownership problems prevent people, and machines, to openly communicate. Unlike current systems, the proposed event.Hub provides privacy and does not compromise the data ownership. Its architecture does not centrally store the data but only relays it from the publisher to the subscribers and does so in a secured way. The data is distributed and stored locally on the subscribers devices allowing more private communication to happen as well as more open ones.

6.2 Replication of Private Data across Several Devices Own by One User

The current trend of multi-device ownership requires that very personal user data needs to be accessible from all devices. Publishing the changes to data to all user's devices does not only provide better user experience compared to centrally stored data in the cloud, it also provides very high privacy and does not compromise the data ownership.

6.3 Communication with People Having Very Short Social Distance

People are likely to share more personal and intimate information to very close friends if they can trust on privacy and data ownership. Social distance can be used also to control the data abstraction level i.e. subscribers with long social distance may receive more abstract data from publishers context information.

6.4 Machine-to-Machine Communication

In addition to human-to-human communication, machine-to-machine communication of events can provide novel functionalities, use cases and experiences to the users of mobile devices. In addition to user created content, mobile devices can be very aware of user's current and past actions and contexts. This data can be collected in the operating system and middleware SW layers and published according to user's privacy settings. Publishing this type of data is typically implicit, user does not see all the events that the device is publishing. This type of hidden communication can be unacceptable to users if there is a risk of compromised privacy and ownership.

6.5   Information Overflow

Many people are struggling with the vast amount of information from the social networks. The event-driven event.Hub easily creates even more information leading to unmanaged information overflow. We are using the publish-subscribe mechanism for basic management of what data is published by providers and what is subscribed by consumers. To overcome the information overflow problem, following design principles and solutions are applied:

Event Categories. The events are categorized to topics with three layer-model (superordinate, basic and subordinate, see section 2). This enables the publisher to easier control the amount of data to be published and the subscriber to receive only relevant information.

Event Filtering According to Social Distance. Subscribers with longer social distance typically receive information less frequently and the information includes less details. Event filtering according to geographical distance. Some events are relevant only within certain distance of the publisher. This can be useful in human-to-human communication and especially in machine-to-machine communication. Many social interactions and smart space applications are bound to situations where devices are in the same space.

7   Conclusions

This paper describes a novel concept and architecture for an event-driven information hub for mobile devices. The design is inspired by peoples natural forms of communication and comprising producers and consumers. Even though existing popular social networking services provide people with means for communication and information exchange, the presented event.Hub provides a number of benefits over the current solutions. Instead of using a centralized back-end server approach, we are proposing a device-centric information hub that can be used to both subscribe and publish information to/from contacts, using the mobile devices address book as a natural social network. The event.Hub offers privacy and data ownership due to the distributed data model enabling new types of interaction both in human-to-human and machine-to-machine communication. The design is based on events as basic elements of communication as well as a software design pattern, the XMPP protocol being the foundation of which identity management, push mechanism, publish-subscribe mechanism, on-line/off-line use and security are implemented.

Acknowledgment. The authors would like to thank Vladimir Halinen, Joonas Mykkanen, Juha Tapanila and Joni Rissanen for their valuable contribution to the designing and coding of the address book example application.

References

1. Rosch, E., Mervis, C.B., Gray, W.D., David, M., Boyes-braem, P.: Basic objects in natural categories. Cognitive Psychology (1976)
2. Akerlof, G.A.: Social Distance and Social Decisions. Econometrica 65(5), 1005–1028 (1997)
3. Gamma, E., Helm, R., Johnson, R.E., Vlissides, J.: Design Patterns: Elements of Reusable Object-Oriented Software. Addison-Wesley, Amsterdam (1995), ISBN:978-0-201-63361-0
4. Huang, Y., Garcia-Molina, H.: Publish/subscribe in a mobile environment. Journal of Wirel. Netw. 10(6), 643–652 (2004)
5. Boyd, D.M., Ellison, N.B.: Social network sites: Definition, history, and scholarship. Journal of Computer-Mediated Communication 13(11) (2007)
6. Bonneau, J., Preibusch, S.: The privacy jungle: On the market for data protection in social networks. In: Proc. of the Eighth Workshop on the Economics of Information Security (2009)
7. Reese, W., Beckland, J.: Lost in Geolocation White Horse Production, Mobile Marketing Report (2011)
8. Pohja, M.: Server push with instant messaging. In: Proc. of the ACM Symposium on Applied Computing, pp. 653–658 (2009)
9. Saint-Andre, P., Smith, K., TronCon, R.: XMPP: The Definitive Guide: Building Real-Time Applications with Jabber Technologies (2009) ISBN:059652126X
10. Hornsby, A., Walsh, R.: From instant messaging to cloud computing, an XMPP review. In: Proc. of the IEEE 14th International Symposium on Consumer Electronics (2010)
11. Meier, R., Cahill, V.: Taxonomy of Distributed Event-Based Programming Systems. The Computer Journal, 585–588 (2002)
12. Hornsby, A.: XMPP message-based MVC architecture for event-driven real-time interactive applications. In: Proc. of the IEEE International Conference on Consumer Electronics (2011)

A Non-functional Property Based Service Selection and Service Verification Model

Yu Bai[1], Yaoxue Zhang[1], Yuezhi Zhou[1], and Laurence T. Yang[2]

[1] Key Laboratory of Pervasive Computing, Ministry of Education,
Tsinghua National Laboratory for Information Science and Technology,
Department of Computer Science and Technology,
Tsinghua University, Beijing 100084, China
baiyu85@gmail.com, zyx@moe.edu.cn,
zhouyz@mail.tsinghua.edu.cn
[2] Department of Computer Science, St .Francis Xavier University,
Antigonish, Canada
ltyang@gmail.com

Abstract. As the number of web services increases rapidly, there are two problems puzzling the customers. The first is how to get an optimal service from a set of functionally equivalent services, which mainly results from the absence of the description for non-functional properties. In this paper, we propose to add non-functional properties into WSDL, which can narrow down the scope of the service selection results according to individual preferences. The second problem is that, as customers' requirements are more complicated, several atomic services need to be composed together to satisfy their requirements. Due to the complex interactions, the process of service composition is error-prone and it may cause the system to crash. In this paper, we use Process Algebra-based Model Checking method to detect logical errors in order to guide the design of service composition. At last, an example is given to demonstrate the effectiveness of our methods.

Keywords: Model Checking, service description, non-functional property, Process Algebra.

1   Introduction

The rapid development of web technology and the gradual maturity of service science make the amount of web service increasing dramatically. Because of the natural features of web services, such as reusability, programming language independent and cross-platform, more and more companies [1, 2, 3] encapsulate their applications as services and publish the services onto Internet for the end customers to use.

To help customers easily call the services, service description languages are given to formalize the interface of web services. In the meanwhile, as customers' requirements are more personalized and more complex, single service or simple function cannot meet all customers' demands alone. Therefore, service composition modeling languages are used to describe the process of service composition. As service description and service

C.-H. Hsu et al. (Eds.): UIC 2011, LNCS 6905, pp. 224–236, 2011.

composition modeling become two hot topics, a lot of researches have been done in these two research fields. For service description, WSDL (Web Service Description Language) [4] is a W3C's recommendation to describe service syntactic and service interface. Its abstract definitions of *ports* and *messages* are separated from their concrete instance, allowing the reuse of these definitions. However, WSDL does not support the description for composite service or the description for semantic information [8]. OWL (Web Ontology Language) and OWL-S (Web Ontology Language for Services) [12] use ontology to classify the service function and the class of service to provide partial semantic information, but they cannot exactly infer the functions which a service can actually provide. Based on WSDL and OWL, USDL (Universal Service-Semantics Description Language) can provide syntactic information and part of service semantics [8], but it cannot distinguish the functionally equivalent services. For service composition modeling, BPEL (Business Process Execution Language) is well known for its orchestration [5]. It defines an interoperable integration model that can facilitate the expansion of automated process integration both within and between the businesses. But BPEL can only describe the static result of service composition and it cannot guarantee the validity of the service composition result. WS-CDL and COSMO [9] must be specified with the exact and complete sequence of activities to be executed. Although this adds a lot to the control over the service composition process, it comes at the expense of process flexibility and they cannot verify the result of service composition either [10]. Petri Nets and Promela are high-level formal description languages which support service verification. The meaning of their formula is precise and expressive, but they cannot cooperate with currently popular service composition modeling language (such as BPEL) [7]. The existing Model Checking tools, such as SPIN, NuSMN and PRISM are based on CTL or LTL, but they do not support the description and verification for non-functional properties [13].

In the following, we use an example to summarize the weakness of existing service description and service composition modeling languages. In Fig.1, we suppose an author will attend UIC 2011 holding in Banff. On one hand, from the perspective of functionality, existing service description languages cannot help him choose one trip plan between flight, bus and car. Because all of them can provide the same function which is to make the author arrive at Banff. On the other hand, in addition to selecting a vehicle, the author needs to reserve a local hotel. To satisfy these two requirements, Vehicle Selection service and Hotel Agency service need to be composed together. But the process of service composition is always error-prone, it may cause some unexpected logic errors. For example, what if the Vehicle Selection service succeeds while the author cannot get a hotel reservation? That means he has ALREADY paid for Vehicle Selection service but get a FAIL result from Travel Agency service.

To help customer select their optimal service from several functionally equivalent services and verify the result of service composition, we introduce the concept of non-functional property, which corresponds to the semantic description of service information and can be regarded as a complementary to the syntactic description of service information. The relationship between service functionality and non-functional property is that, the former is used to define what the system behavior is, while the latter is used to define to what extent the system implements the behavior. The importance of non-functional property shows in two aspects:

- can narrow down the search scope of the service selection results and can help customers distinguish the services which are functionally equivalent
- can be used as test conditions for service verification at the design-phrase of service composition

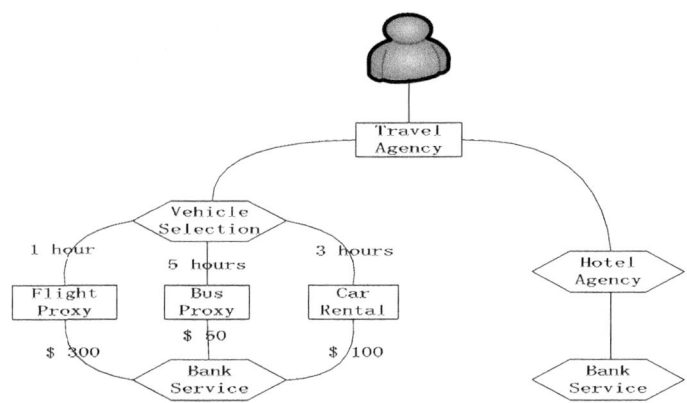

Fig. 1. A simplified Tourism Example

Based on non-functional properties, to compensate the weakness of the existing methods mentioned above, we introduce service 7-tuple [6] and Process Algebra-based Model Checking method. On the basis of WSDL's description for service syntax, service 7-tuple also takes non-functional properties into account, such as Time, Space, Quality and Price etc. In this paper, we propose a method called WSDL2S7Tuple, which is used to translate from WSDL to service 7-tuple. The non-functional properties in service 7-tuple can help customers find their optimal service more quickly. For the second issue, we introduce Process Algebra-based Model Checking method. Process Algebra is one kind of formal logic languages, which can provide a high-level description of interaction, communication and synchronizations between independent processes. It can also provide algebraic laws for formal reasoning. Since BPEL is essentially a process description language, it is compatible with the Model Checking tools of Process Algebra. In the Process Algebra-based Model Checking method, we will rewrite BPEL file in the format of Process Algebra and use Model Checking tools to verify the validity of the composition result.

This paper is organized as following. In next section, we will explain how to translate a WSDL file to a service 7-tuple profile and discuss how to generate non-functional properties. In Section 3, we will make a brief introduction for the basic concepts of Process Algebra and Model Checking. We will use an example to illustrate how to use non-functional properties to distinguish functionally equivalent services and the importance of verifying the composition result in Section 4. Finally, we will address the conclusion and the future work in the last section.

2   From WSDL to Service 7-Tuple

As non-functional property becomes an effective complementary to service description, we propose service 7-tuple in [6]. Service 7-tuple is based on WSDL and it also takes non-functional properties into account, in order to describe web services both from syntactic aspects and semantic aspects. Furthermore, service 7-tuple can be used as the basis for service verification. In the following, we first give an overview for WSDL and service 7-tuple. Then we will describe the mapping relationship between WSDL and service 7-tuple (WSDL2S7Tuple). At last, we will discuss how to generate the non-functional properties.

2.1   Introduction for WSDL and Service 7-Tuple

2.1.1   WSDL

WSDL is a web service description specification which is based on XML grammar. These are 8 major elements in WSDL:

- *definitions* - is the root element of one WSDL documents. It defines service name and declares all namespaces used throughout the remainder of the document
- *message* - is the abstract description of the data being exchanged. It is always used to parameterize the *input message* and *output message*, which are two main parts of the element *operation*
- *types* – is to define all the data types used by the request message (*input message*) and response message (*output message*). It chooses XSD as its default namespace
- *portType* - is a function library which defines all service operations
- *operation* - is composed of *input message* and/or *output message*. There are four basic patterns of operations, which are *one-way*, *request-response*, *solicit-response* and *notification* respectively
- *binding* - connects the abstract description for service *operation* with the concrete implementation code. To improve the reusability, it is feasible to assign several bindings for a single *portType*
- *service* – is an address information for locating or invoking the specified service
- *documentation* - is a textual description to outline service function, service provider, price, response time or other non-functional properties

2.1.2   Service 7-Tuple

Service 7-tuple is designed to describe both service syntax and service semantics. We borrow two main parts (*portType* and *message*) from WSDL to describe service interface. In addition, we add some non-functional properties such as *Space*, *Time* and *Quality* into service 7-tuple to support the automation of service discovery, service substitution and service composition. (The details for service 7-tuple can be found in [6]). Therefore, service 7-tuple can be regarded as a semantic complement to WSDL. It can be also used as the basis to describe customized services and can be regarded as the foundation of service composition. Each element of service 7-tuple can be identified by their first letter and our framework supports dot operation to display service hierarchy. For example, S.F.C means *Service.Function.Constraint*. In the following, we will discuss how to translate WSDL to service 7-tuple.

2.2   WSDL2S7Tuple

The objective of WSDL2S7Tuple (WSDL to Service 7-tuple) is to generate a sketchy profile described by service 7-tuple. The incompleteness is due to the absence of non-functional properties in WSDL. Therefore, the result of the translation lacks non-functional properties related information. Furthermore, WSDL has no description of composite service, let alone the verification for the result of service composition. In the following of this section, we will discuss the details of the translation between WSDL and service 7-tuple.

As mentioned above, we cannot translate from WSDL to Service 7-tuple directly. Therefore, we divide the process of the translation into two main parts (in Fig 2). The first part is to build a rough mapping relationship between the basic elements of WSDL and the basic elements of service 7-tuple. The second part is to fill up the non-functional properties missed in WSDL, such as Time, Space and Quality.

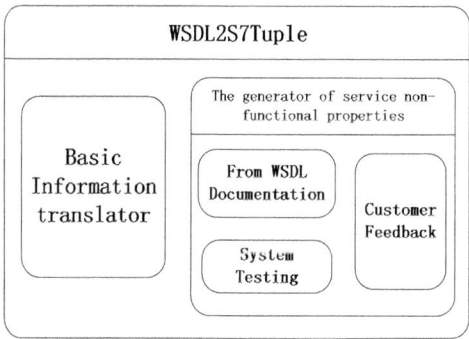

Fig. 2. The structure for WSDL2S7Tuple

In Fig 3 we give the basic mapping relationship between WSDL and Service 7-tuple. The concrete mapping procedure is describing in the next subsection.

2.2.1   Mapping Relationship between Basic Elements
1. *Service* element of service 7-tuple corresponds to the *definition* element in WSDL and it becomes the root element of service 7-tuple. The *name* attribute of WSDL becomes the name of the corresponding *Service* name in service 7-tuple
2. *Service.Function* element of service 7-tuple corresponds to *portType* element in WSDL and it is mainly described by the elements *Service.Input* and *Serivce.Output*
3. *Service.Input* element and *Service.Output* element of service 7-tuple corresponds to *input message* and *output message* in WSDL (also contains the functionality of *fault message*). They mainly describe the message parameters such as message *name* and message *type*
4. *Service.Function.Binding* has the same function with *binding* in WSDL. It describes how to bind the abstract description with the concrete implementation

5. *Service.Quality* element of service 7-tuple can be partly generated from *documentation* of WSDL. We will discuss the details in next subsection

Furthermore, in consideration of WSDL's lack of service composition description and hoping to describe service description and service composition at one step, we add some elements into service 7-tuple.

1. *Service.Function.Subservice* is used to describe the atomic services which are contained in a composite service
2. *Service.Function.Subservice.Context* is used to describe the dependency relationships between the subservices
3. *Service.Function.Message* represents the communication information between the subservices, which is different from *message* in WSDL
4. *Service.Function.Order* represents the assembly orders of a composite service, which can be described in Process Algebra.

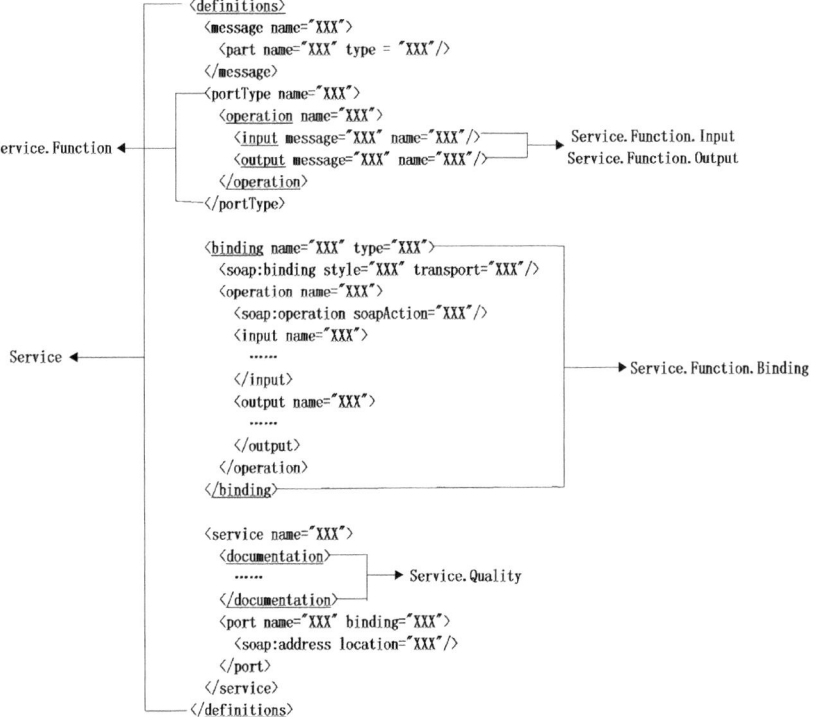

Fig. 3. The mapping relationship between WSDL and service 7-tuple

2.2.2   How to Add Non-functional Properties
Because of the increasing importance of the non-functional properties, we propose to collect non-functional properties from three aspects, which are WSDL *documentation* element, System Testing and User Feedback respectively.

- **WSDL documentation**. WSDL uses the optional *documentation* element as a container for human readable documentation. The content of the element is arbitrary text and elements. *documentation* always includes a simple textual document for describing basic service function, execution time, service quality or other non-functional related properties. Therefore, we can abstract the function-keywords from *documentation* and use WordNet [11] to map the keywords into the existing ontology tree. Then we can analyze the relationship between the keywords in *documentation* and the keywords in the ontology tree. We can also abstract the price information to fill up *Service.Price* element in Service 7-Tuple and the execution time to fill up *Service.Time* element
- **System Testing.** Before publishing the web services to Internet, we should give a system testing for their performance. There are three reasons for the testing. The first is that some service does not contain any description for the service performance. The second is that some service providers may exaggerate the service performance. Furthermore, we should test the performance of the services at regular intervals, in order to update the non-functional properties and filter the services which are no longer available. SPNs (Stochastic Petri nets) can be used to make performance evaluation for web services [13]
- **User Feedback.** The former two methods consider the problem from the general perspectives, but different users may have different user experiences while using the same service (such as response time and network delay). Therefore, we should collect the evaluation and the rating results from the customers to improve the accuracy of the non-functional properties

3   Process Algebra Based Model Checking

Along with customers' increasing demands for the diversity of service functionalities, single service or simple function cannot satisfy all customers' requirements alone any more. We need to compose several atomic services together to form a composite service to meet all of the customers' demands. As a result, the process of service composition becomes more complex and the composite service becomes more complicated.

The generation of composite services is error-prone, because it is difficult to coordinate several distributed web services or monitor all the processes of messages exchanging at the same time. States rely on exchanging messages to get a new state (through state transition). Therefore, it is far from enough that only guarantee the partial correctness (verify the correctness of the output according to the given input) [13]. We need to verify the validity of all the possible states before executing the composite service.

Model Checking is proposed under such a background. The original intention of Model Checking is to solve the following question: given the possible behaviors of the system (system model) and the desirable behaviors (the specification of the properties), and test automatically whether this model meets the given specification. Model Checking checks whether the system exists logical errors or coarse mistakes in design-phrase, such as deadlocks, misspelling, synchronizations missing or other similar issues which may cause the system to crash. To solve such a problem algorithmically, both the model and the properties need to be formulated in some precise mathematical languages. Models are always described by high-level description languages, such as Petri Nets, Promela and Process Algebra [13], and properties are specified in temporal logic such as CTL (Computation Tree Logic) [14] or LTL (Linear Temporal Logic) [15]. Formally, the problem can be stated as follows: given a desired property, expressed as a temporal logic formula p, and a structure M with initial state s, decide if [16]

$$M, s \vDash p$$

Process Algebra is a formal description technique used to describe the dynamic behaviors, compositional modeling and operational semantics between a collection of concurrent and communicating components. The other significant cause for choosing Process Algebra is its ability of formal reasoning. It uses *properties* to check whether the system model satisfies the requirements of the desirable behaviors. Furthermore, Process Algebra is known for its flexibility and precision which is due to its basic elements and operations. These basic elements are sufficiently expressive and can be easily understood. As Process Algebra had been proposed for 30 years, there exist plenty of powerful reasoning tools which can provide algebraic laws that allow process descriptions to be manipulated and analyzed. Some research claims that Process Algebras can provide a very complete and satisfactory assistance to the whole process of web service development [7].

BPEL is one kind of web service orchestration description languages. It is essentially a process description language which is based on primitives for behavior description and message exchange. So it is easy for BPEL to work with Process Algebra. BPEL is useful to describe the process of how to make plenty of independent processes or distributed web services work cooperatively.

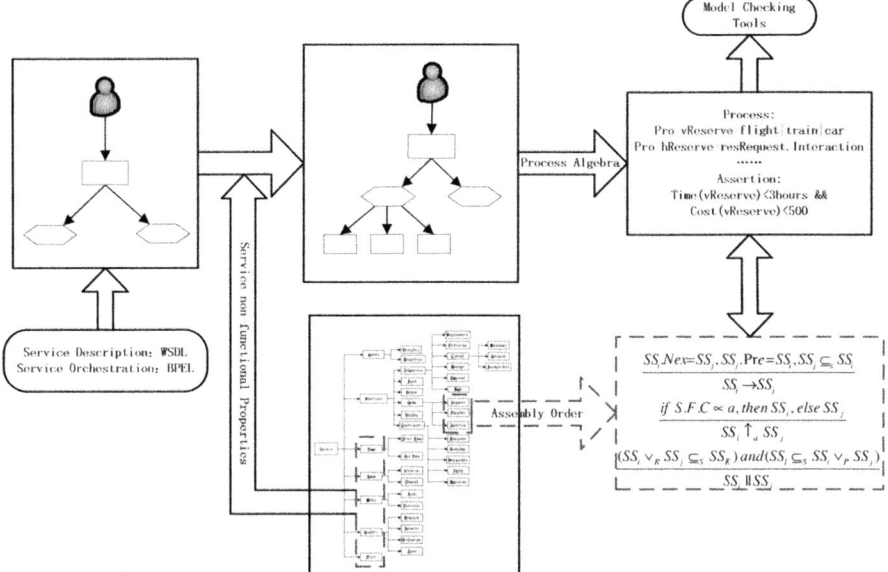

Fig. 4. The system flow chart

The existing Model Checking methods mainly focuses on how to solve the question of service verification or how to evaluate service performance, and some research is trying to combine these two different aspects together [13]. In this paper, with the consideration of the importance of non-functional properties, we translate WSDL file into a service 7-tuple profile in order to represent the services from both the syntactic aspects and the semantic aspects, expecting to help customers select the optimal service more conveniently. Then, we use BPEL to describe the process of service composition. At last, according to the basic guideline to make a mapping between the CCS processes (abstract specifications) and the BPEL code (concrete executable code) [18], we can translate BPEL to Process Algebra and use Model Checking tools (such as CWB-NC [17]) to verify the validity of service composition result. Fig 4 illustrates the structure of how to use service 7-tuple to make service selection and service verification.

4   Case Study

In this section, we will use the simplified tourism example, which is mentioned in the second section, to illustrate how to translate from a WSDL file to a service 7-tuple profile. Then we will represent the structure details of the composite service (containing three subservices) describing by service 7-tuple and discuss how to use non-functional properties to help customers choose their optimal service from several functionally equivalent services.

Before the introduction of service 7-tuple, we need to use four different WSDL files to describe service Vehicle Selection, which are VehicleSelectionService, FlightProxyService, BusProxyService and CarRentService respectively. For space reasons, we can only give a brief description for service VehicleSelectionService (the WSDL structures of the other three services are similar with it). From the following file describing by WSDL, we can find that VehicleSelectionService is a *Request-Response* service (which means VehicleSelectionService needs an *input-message* proposed by the customers and will return them an *output-message*) and we are clear that its basic function is to select one trip plan for the customers (from *documentation* element). Fig 5 is the WSDL file of service VehicleSelectionService.

After the translation from the WSDL file (VehicleSelectionService) to Service 7-tuple and combinating the four atomic files into one composite service (FlightProxyService, BusProxyService and CarRentService are regarded as the subservices of service VehicleSelectionService), we can use only one composite service to represent the four independent services easily. The assembly order of these three subservices is *Selection*, which means these subservices are function-equivalent processes and the author can only select one from them as his trip plan. At last, we abstract some non-functional properties, such as *Service.Quality.Time* and *Service.Quality.Price*, from service *documentation* in WSDL to fill the related elements in the description of service 7-tuple. After the combination, we can set the non-functional properties of service 7-tuple as conditions to filter out the services which cannot satisfy customers' non-functional properties requirements. Furthermore, because the composite services shorten the time of service composition, we can store the composite services in the service data base for customers' using. Besides these, we can also introduce Process Algebra-based Model Checking method to verify the result of service composition. It can be regarded as a complementary for BPEL, which can only be used as a static service composition tool and cannot guarantee the validity of the service composition results. Fig 6 represents the structure of VehicleSelectionService describing by service 7-tuple.

```
<definitions name="VehicleSelectionService">
        ......
        <message name="vehicleSelectionRequest">
                <part name="vehicleType" type="xsd:string"/>
        </message>
        <message name="vehicleSelectionResponse">
                <part name="result" type="xsd:string"/>
        </message>
        <portType name="VehicleSelection_PortType">
                <operation name="vehicleSelection">
                        <input message="tns:vehicleSelectionRequest"/>
                        <output message="tns:vehicleSelectionResponse"/>
                </operation>
        </portType>
        <binding name="VehicleSelection_Binding"
        type="tns:VehicleSelection_PortType">
                ......
                <operation name="vehicleSelection">
                        ......
                </operation>
        </binding>
        <service name="VehicleSelection_Service">
                <documentation>It is for vehicle selection.</documentation>
                <port binding="tns:VehicleSelection_Binding"
                    name="Vehicleselection_Port">
                        ......
                </port>
        </service>
</definitions>

<definitions name="FlightProxyService">......</definitions>

<definitions name="BusProxyService">......</definitions>

<definitions name="CarRentService">......</definitions>
```

Fig. 5. WSDL file for VehicleSelectionService

In the following, we will discuss how to use Model Checking tools to verify the validity of the service composition result. We verify the validity through two main parts, which are *safety property* and *non-functional property*. The importance of verifying the safety property is that, we can write our desirable properties in CTL and use its construct to allow all the states in a formal way. The logic makes all the states respect the desirable properties at every step. The role of non-functional property is helping customers to determine the optimal service according to their personal requirements. Because of the simplicity of this case, we will only emphasize on service duration and service price.

```
<service name="VehicleSelectionService">
        ......
        <function name="vehicleSelection_function">
                <subservice name="FlightProxyService">
                        <requirement name="flightNumber" type = "xsd:string"/>
                        <provision name="price" type="xsd:float"/>
                        <quality>
                                <time>1 hour</time>
                                <price>$300</price>
                        </quality>
                        ......
                </subservice>
                <subservice name="BusProxyService">
                        <requirement name ="busNumber" type="xsd:string"/>
                        <provision name="price" type="xsd:float"/>
                        <quality>
                                <time>5 hours</time>
                                <price>$50</price>
                        </quality>
                        ......
                </subservice>
                <subservice name="CarRentService">
                        <requirement name="carType" type = "xsd:string"/>
                        <provision name="price" type="xsd:float"/>
                        <quality>
                                <time>3 hours</time>
                                <price>$100</price>
                        </quality>
                        ......
                </subservice>
                <order>Selection</order>
                <binding>......</binding>
        </ function>
        ......
</definitions>
```

Fig. 6. Service 7-tuple file for VehicleSelectionService

Safety property is always used to claim that one situation should never happen. In this example we set the following condition as the safety property, which is, the author has paid the VehicleSelectionService but he cannot finish the reservation for the hotel or vice verse. That is, no matter which service returns FAIL, the author need not to pay for any of the two services. As a result, we need to create a communication between the subservice VehicleSelection and the subservice HotelAgency by using *message* element in service 7-tuple. The author will pay for the services after both of the services succeed.

Non-functional property is used to help the author to select optimal service from several functionally equivalent services. In this case, the author has three choices according to the vehicles' different duration and price. System recommends different services to him by distinguishing his different requirements. For example, if the author submits his requirements as (VehicleSelectionService. Price < \$350) ∧ (VehicleSelectionService. Time < 5 hs), both car and flight can meet his demands. But if the author thinks time is more important, his requirements may change to (VehicleSelectionService. Price < \$ 500) ∧ (VehicleSelectionService. Time < 1.5 hs). As a result, he can only choose flight as his trip plan.

5   Conclusion and Future Work

The increasing amount of web services makes the customers difficult to find the optimal service from several functionally equivalent services. In this paper, we propose to use non-functional property to narrow down the scope of the service selection result, in order to help customers quickly find the optimal service according to their personal requirements. On the other hand, because the process of service composition is error-prone, we introduce Model Checking method to verify the result of service composition. It can avoid some coarse mistakes or logic errors at the design-phrase. In the future, we will improve the automation from service selection to service verification, in order to make Process Algebra Model Checking method to leverage the result of WSDL2S7Tuple directly. We hope to provide users with a unified platform including service selection, service composition and service verification.

Acknowledgments. This paper is funded partially by the China Academic Library & Information System (CALIS) project (third level). We would like to thank the anonymous reviewers for their helpful comments on this paper.

References

1. Amazon Web Services, http://aws.amazon.com/products/
2. Mueller, J.P.: Mining Google Web Services: Building Applications with the Google API, 1st edn. Publisher: Sybex (April 23, 2004) ISBN-10: 0782143334
3. Microsoft services, http://www.microsoft.com/microsoftservices/en/us/home.aspx
4. Web Service Description Language, http://www.w3.org/TR/wsdl
5. Michael, C.: What is BPEL and why is it so important to my business. White paper. SoftCare EC, Inc. (c) (2004)
6. Yu, B., Yaoxue, Z., Yuezhi, Z., Yang, L.T.: A novel framework for service description and operations. In: 7th Proceedings of International Conference on Ubiquitous Intelligence and Computing, Xi'an China (2010)
7. Salaun, G., Bordeaux, L., Schaerf, M.: Describing and reasoning on Web services using process algebra. In: 2nd Proceedings of IEEE International Conference on Web Services, San Diego, California, USA, pp. 43–50 (2004)
8. Bansal, A., Kona, S., Simon, L., Hite, T.D.: A Universal Service-Semantics Description Language. In: Proceedings of the Third European Conference on Web Services, pp. 214–225. IEEE Computer Society, Washington, DC (2005)

9. Quartel, D.A.C., Steen, M.W.A., Pokraev, S., van Sinderen, M.: Cosmo: A conceptual framework for service modeling and refinement. Information Systems Frontiers 9(2-3), 225–244 (2007)

10. Ehtesham, Z., Olivier, P., Claude, G..: DISC: A declarative framework for self-healing Web services composition. In: 8th Proceedings of IEEE International Conference on Web Services, Miami, Florida, USA, pp. 25–33 (2010)

11. WordNet, http://wordnet.princeton.edu/

12. Ontology Web Language for Services,
    http://www.ai.sri.com/daml/services/owl-s/1.2/

13. Baier, C., et al.: Performance Evaluation and Model Checking Join Forces. Communications of ACM 53(9) (September 2010)

14. Bianco, A., Alfaro, L.D.: Model checking of probabilistic and non-deterministic system. In: Thiagarajan, P.S. (ed.) FSTTCS 1995. LNCS, vol. 1026, pp. 499–513. Springer, Heidelberg (1995)

15. Vardi, M.Y.: Automatic verification of probabilistic concurrent finite-state programs. In: 26th IEEE Symp. on Foundations of Comp. Science (FOCS), pp. 327–338. IEEE CS Press, Los Alamitos (1985)

16. Clarke, E.M.: Model checking. In: Ramesh, S., Sivakumar, G. (eds.) FST TCS 1997. LNCS, vol. 1346, pp. 54–56. Springer, Heidelberg (1997), doi:10.1007/BFb0058022

17. http://www.cs.sunysb.edu/~cwb/

18. Paolucci, M., Srinivasan, N., Sycara, K., Nishimura, T.: Towards a Semantic Choreography of Web Services: from WSDL to DAML-S. In: 1st Proceedings of IEEE International Conference on Web Service, Las Vegas, Nevada, USA (2003)

Exploring an Adaptive Architecture for Service Discovery over MANETs

Beihong Jin, Fusang Zhang, and Haibin Weng

Institute of Software, Chinese Academy of Sciences, Beijing, 100190, China

Abstract. What a service discovery system (SDS) pursues is to successfully discover the services at low costs if the qualified ones exist. However, dynamics and diversification in MANETs increases the complexity to achieve SDS's goal. This paper develops a SDS over MANETs named SCN4M-H. To enhance system quality, SCN4M-H combines two architecture styles and provides two working modes: basic mode and volunteer mode. In the basic mode, nodes in SCN4M-H work together as peer partners, mapping and discovering the services in a P2P style, and in the volunteer mode, the nodes who declare as volunteers will play the role of servers, they are responsible for dealing with the service discovery requests targeted for the nodes within specified regions. Depending on their own states as well as their neighbors' states, nodes in SCN4M-H can switch automatically from one mode to another. Moreover, two working modes can coexist in SCN4M-H at the same time, which enables a service discovery request to be dealt with in a locally optimal way. Some system properties are revealed and then extensive experiments are conducted. Experimental data indicate that SCN4M-H adapts well to various dynamic scenarios and shows satisfying software quality in terms of discovery success rate and corresponding costs.

Keywords: service discovery, MANET, software quality, pervasive computing.

1 Introduction

MANET (Mobile Ad hoc NETwork) is a kind of wireless ad hoc networks with the feature of dynamics and diversification. Communication quality of a MANET is often unstable and poor, from time to time, it suffers low bandwidth, high latency and frequent disconnection; nodes in a MANET may move around and the nodes may join or leave randomly; the majority of nodes are heterogeneous and differ in resources, some are rich in resources and some not. The latter point was usually simplified into "nodes in a MANET are resource-constrained", but current trend is that nodes begin to widely vary, equipping different hardware configurations.

In order to share resources and integrate services among nodes in a MANET, a service discovery system (SDS), as an infrastructure, is indispensable. For a SDS over MANETs, the quality goal that it pursues is to successfully discover the services at low costs if the qualified ones exist. But the dynamic and diversified situations mentioned above may interfere with the achievement of its goal. A plausible solution to enhance the quality of a SDS is to develop an adaption mechanism, which may be relevant to system architecture, resource management, etc.

C.-H. Hsu et al. (Eds.): UIC 2011, LNCS 6905, pp. 237–251, 2011.
© Springer-Verlag Berlin Heidelberg 2011

So far, there have been many research effects on developing a service discovery system over MANETs. From the point of software architecture, existing SDSs can be categorized into two kinds: one adopts directory-based architecture [2, 3, 4] and the other adopts directory-less architecture [1, 5, 6], where the directory plays the role of a server in charge of service storage and matching. In general, the directory-based solutions are adequate for the scenarios where relatively stable nodes with rich resources in a MANET can be found to act as directories, but they cannot work while no stable node can be found and this situation often occurs in a MANET. The directory-less solutions are more suitable for the scenarios where none of the nodes in a MANET are relatively stable, but they cannot take full advantage of the resources in relatively-stable powerful nodes, in other words, they do not give the corresponding strategies for all potential states of nodes. After all, neither of above solutions can run well in all the scenarios. In response, we implement a SDS with a dynamic architecture, which is named SCN4M-H and characterized by its adaptation mechanism for MANET environments.

SCN4M-H assumes that MANET applications cover a finite geographic region and it is easy for a node in a MANET to know its geographic location. Therefore, SCN4M-H builds a geographic overlay for the nodes in a MANET in terms of their geographic locations and communication transmission range. Based on the overlay, SCN4M-H maps a service and its XML-format description into the overly by applying a consistent hash function, i.e., a service is bound to some geographic locations, and the node at those locations or the nearby nodes are responsible for managing the service. As thus, the service discovery issue is transformed to find the service at certain geographic locations or nearby. SCN4M-H designs two working modes: basic mode and volunteer mode. In the basic mode, the requests related with a certain geographic location are handled by a group of nodes surrounding the geographic location. In the volunteer mode, the same requests are dealt with by the volunteers whose management scopes cover that location. In a detail, once SCN4M-H is started on a node, it automatically runs on the basic mode. Since the service register and discovery are performed in a P2P style, negative effects caused by dynamics in a MANET environment can be alleviated. At any time, a capable node can declare itself as a volunteer node. If a node makes such an announcement, then it turns into the volunteer mode. Afterwards, the nodes within a volunteer's management scope will turn into the volunteer mode. These nodes can also change their modes into the basic modes in a bounded interval while detecting the volunteer leaves or fails. The reason why the volunteer mode is designed is for adapting to node's diversification. The volunteer mode explores the potentials of capable nodes for improving the system quality. In spite of theoretical analyses, extensive simulation experiments are conducted to evaluate whether SCN4M-H can exhibit its good quality even if facing dynamic and diversified MANET environments. For service discovery requests, their success rates and their corresponding costs are collected and analyzed. Experimental data are positive and supportive to our view that SCN4M-H combining two architecture styles is well suited to various scenarios and shows excellent software quality.

The rest of this paper is organized as follows. Section 2 overviews the related work. Section 3 introduces the outline of the system. Section 4 describes the basic mode and the volunteer mode in SCN4M-H. Section 5 shows the evaluation experiments on SCN4M-H. The final section concludes the paper.

2 Related Work

Enhancing adaptation or autonomy in software can help software to achieve the desired quality goals within a reasonable cost, and to reduce the complexity in software management [7, 8, 9]. Usually, adaptive software systems embody a closed-loop mechanism, which consists of monitoring, detecting, deciding, and acting phases. Here, the technologies from different domains can be borrowed and adopted in each phase.

In the existing research work, GSD [1] is a pioneer SDS for MANET environment. It adopts a directory-less architecture, where the services are advertised through periodical n-hop broadcasting. The node which receives advertisements will cache the services embedded in the advertisements. Moreover, GSD classifies the services into several groups based on services' semantic types. The node collects the names of the groups which the sender of advertisement sees along the road of advertising, and then selectively forwards the discovery requests according to service's group information. GSD updates services in time by an advertisement strategy so as to adapt to MANET environment. SPIZ [5] is another directory-less SDS. It extends underlying routing packets to piggyback the information about service advertisement and discovery request. Meanwhile, it provides an adaptive control strategy for advertisement radius. Our early work [6] builds a directory-less SDS on the top of the geographic routing algorithm GOAFR. We present an algorithm to register a service on the nodes in a geographic ring and also the corresponding discovery algorithm. Besides, we provide the means for service cancellation and refreshment to increase the adaptability to MANET environments and dynamic service availability.

Considering that relatively stable nodes can be found in some MANET scenarios, some SDSs are designed to rely on a group of directories for registering and locating available services. For example, Ariadne implements the ideas proposed in [2] where some nodes are elected as directories. While a node cannot receive the directory's presence message, it will initiate the election of a directory so that any node can reach a directory within the specified hops. Ariadne builds service indexes in the form of bloom filters on the directories. Directories advertise their service indexes through 2-hops broadcasting. Ariadne can control the frequency of broadcasting service indexes to guarantee the freshness of information on directories and alleviate the problem of environment changes. However, in DSDM [3], some nodes are chosen as directories by grading their resource capabilities, and then nodes can get up-to-date routing information from the underlying DSDV protocol and find the nearest directories to direct the discovery requests to them. Since DSDM can know the departure information of nodes (including the nodes as directories and/or the nodes as service providers) from the proactive DSDV protocol, it can take following actions. If the offline of a directory is detected, the first available directory candidate (ordered by the score) will take over the role of the offline directory and service providers will register their services again. If the offline of a service provider is detected, the directories will delete the corresponding services. As an alternative solution, [4] organizes the nodes in a MANET into a hierarchical structure, electing different coordinators to act as the directories and take charge of a zone, a region or entire area. [4] provides the coordinator management mechanism which can handle service state changing, and the node's joining and leaving. Specifically, if the nodes do not receive its coordinator's surviving message, they will elect a new coordinator. Moreover, [4] designs a self-adaptive on-demand geographic routing protocol to meet different routing requirements in the service provision scenarios.

This paper differs from the above work in that (1) it presents a new mode for service discovery, i.e. volunteer mode. As we know, volunteer computing in Internet has been proven its viability and practicality. The most famous project is SETI@Home [10], in which volunteers donate their spare computing resources to participate in searching for the intelligent life outside the earth. We claim that a powerful node in a MANET is likely to be willing to be a volunteer so as to undertake much work, just as the rich tends to work for charity. It is expected that the volunteers in MANETs will emerge, what justifies presenting the volunteer mode. (2) it implements the system which supports two working modes: the volunteer mode and the basic mode, the latter adopts the ring-based register and discovery strategy that we first presented in [6]. Moreover, the nodes in the system can switch automatically from one mode to another so as to make the most of the resources in a changing environment. (3) it conducts probabilistic analyses for the basic mode which are lacked in our early work [6]. Compared with [6], it also conducts extensive experiments to evaluate under the basic mode the effects of the movement speeds of nodes and system configurable parameters on system quality.

3   System Overview

3.1   Underlying Geographic Overlay

In SCN4M-H, a geographic overlay is built for the nodes in a MANET. Node N in a MANET chooses the nodes within one hop as the candidates of N's neighbor in the overlay. Specifically, N deems that its neighbors in the Gabriel graph are its neighbors in the overlay, where the Gabriel graph is constructed from the unit disk graph which a MANET is usually modeled as [11]. Moreover, by heartbeat messages, node N can periodically get the latest information of the nodes within one hop and update its neighbors in the overlay. By this way, the overlay can reflect the up-to-date states of node movements and communication connection, meantime, the maintenance cost of the overlay is also less than the maintenance cost of the other logical overlays such as Chord, CAN.

On the other hand, in order to implement the routing to a designated geographic location, SCN4M-H employs the geographic routing algorithm GOAFR [11] as its underlying routing. GOAFR can promise that, when the routing ends, the last node is the nearest one to the destination among all nodes on the perimeter of the destination. Another reason of choosing GOAFR is its worst-case optimal and average-case efficient feature.

3.2   Request Processing Procedures

No matter what kind of working mode the node is in, both service register requests and service discovery requests are converted into the routing messages over the overlay.

When a service is to be registered by a service provider, its XML-based service description is first decomposed into suffixes, each of which is a path from an inner node to a leaf node in an XML file. Then each suffix of the service description and the service itself are packed into a packet p, and sent to the geographic location (x,y), which is calculated by *HashToPos(suffix's first tag)*. GOAFR help the packet p to reach N_{cr}, the closest node to (x,y). The working mode of N_{cr} determines which nodes will store the service itself.

However, since a service discovery request submitted by a service requestor follows XQuery-like format, it is first factored into the several primitive requests which do not contain the logical operator "AND" or "OR", and then for every primitive request, the service requestor's information including its ID *IDreq* and its geographic information T are added into the routing packet p. The destination (x,y) of the routing packet p is decided by hashing the element name in the primitive request. GOAFR help the packet p to reach N_r, the closest node to (x,y). The working mode of N_r decides which nodes the packet p is sent to for executing the discovery request, i.e. matching the request against local services. The part from receiving a discovery request to finding the matched services is referred to as the searching phase of the whole discovery request processing procedure.

After a node finishes executing the discovery request, it will deliver the matched services back to the service requestor. This part is called the return phase. During this phase, GOAFR uses the requestor's location T as the destination location and send the matched services to N_c, the closest node to T. Then the node N_c broadcasts the matched services to all nodes within 1-hop range of N_c.

As long as the node submitted the original discovery request is still within the N_c's communication range, it can get the service; otherwise, it fails to get the discovery response.

3.3 Working Mode Switching

In SCN4M-H, if node N_v can satisfy the following conditions: (1) it is rich in computation capability, bandwidth and power; (2) it seldom moves in its recent history, (3) it is willing to be a volunteer to serve for other nodes, then it is regarded as capable of becoming a volunteer node and allowed to play the role of a directory.

From then on, node N_v will piggyback a volunteer advertisement in its periodically-sent heartbeat messages, so the circular region W with N_v as the center and $Rc/2$ as the radius (Rc denotes the wireless transmission range) will be the region that N_v is in charge of, and the nodes in the circular region W will change their working modes into the volunteer modes after they receive the volunteer advertisement. As a result, in a certain region of a MANET, some nodes work in a client/server style and a capable node volunteers to undertake much work.

If the volunteer node N_v leaves or shuts down, then after a period of time (the value is given in Section 4.2), the nodes in the circular region W will automatically switch their working modes to the basic modes.

4 Two Working Modes

4.1 Basic Mode

The basic mode is a kind of directory-less mode where the nodes involved are peer partners.

In this mode, when a register request with *(x,y)* as its destination location reaches the node N_{cr}, the closest node to *(x,y)*, the service in it will be stored in the nodes which are on the perimeter enclosing the destination *(x,y)* and also in the geographic ring with *(x,y)* as the center, L as the inner radius and $L+rw$ as the outer radius, where L denotes the distance between N_{cr} and destination *(x,y)*, and rw is the predefined value of the width of the ring. Here, the ring is called the register ring, and the node N_{cr} is called the master node of storing the service; the other nodes for storing the service are called mirror nodes.

Similarly, as to the discovery request whose corresponding destination location is *(x,y)*, it is first delivered to N_r, the closest node to *(x,y)*, then sent to the nodes on the discovery ring for further local service matching. Here, the discovery ring is defined as a ring with *(x,y)* as its center, L' as inter radius and $L'+rw$ as the outer radius, where L' denotes the distance between N_r and destination *(x,y)*.

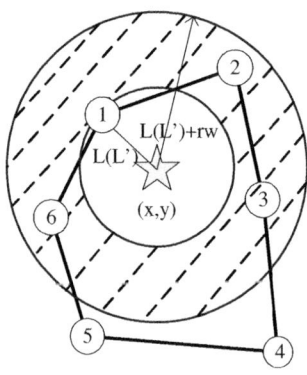

For example, as shown in Fig. 1, the star represents the destination (x,y). N_1 (the circle with ID 1 inside), N_2, N_3, N_4, N_5, N_6 forms perimeter enclosing the star. For a register request, since N_1 is the nearest node to *(x,y)*, it is the master node, N_2, N_3 and N_6 are the mirror nodes. For a discovery request, N_1, N_2, N_3 and N_6 will be the nodes to execute local service matching.

Please note that since the nodes in a MANET can move, join or leave randomly, N_{cr} at the register phase may be different from N_r at the discovery phase. As a result, the register ring may be different from the discovery ring even they have same width. There is a chance that the above ring-based discovery strategy cannot find the registered

Fig. 1. Ring in the basic mode

services. In detail, for a service with *(x,y)* as its destination location, the nodes in the vicinity of *(x,y)* will store the service, but afterwards these nodes may leave the original locations, and the other node which has no desired service may become the closest node to *(x,y)*, what is worse is that when a discovery request arrives the closest node to *(x,y)*, in the current discovery ring, there is not any node storing the desired service. In this case, the above discovery strategy will fail. Therefore, we introduce success rate $P_{success}$ as an important metrics for system quality, which denotes a probability of discovery requests finding existing qualified services.

In order to reduce the decrease of success rates while facing the following situation: (1) the communication between these nodes breaks down, (2) these nodes leave or move, (3) new nodes join, a service renewal policy is employed among the nodes working in the basic mode: for every renewal period ri, every master node will submit the requests to re-register the local services. As thus, the services will be re-registered on the node which is close to the destination location at present. The value of ri is suggested to be set to less than rw/v, where v denotes the average movement speed of a node. The above service renewal policy can mitigate effects caused by the dynamic environment in some degree.

Probability Analyses of Success Rate

Since the total discovery procedure can be divided into two phases: the searching phase and the return phase, we build the probability models for searching and return respectively, and then estimate the effects of parameters on the success rate.

We assume that the n nodes are distributed in a rectangle with length L_{area} and width W_{area} according to the random Poisson distribution, and the destination location of a service is T. At the time point of service registering, the distance between T and its nearest node N_{cr} is L, then N_{ring}, the number of the nodes in the register ring is as follows:

$$N_{ring} = \frac{\pi(L + rw)^2 - \pi L^2}{L_{area} \times W_{area}} \times n = \frac{\pi(2Lrw + rw^2)n}{L_{area} \times W_{area}} \tag{1}$$

where rw denotes the width of the ring.

So, $N_{register}$, the number of nodes which store the service, is in the interval between 1 and N_{ring}.

Assuming that after Δt, the node N_r becomes the node closest to T and the distance between T and N_r is L'. The probability of a node in the register ring not in the current discovery ring is given by:

$$P_{node\_in\_ring} = 1 - \frac{\pi(L' + rw)^2 - \pi L'^2}{L_{area} \times W_{area}} \tag{2}$$

So, $P_{searching}$, the probability of the success rate in the searching phase of a discovery request, is given by:

$$P_{searching} \in \left[\frac{\pi(2L'rw + rw^2)}{L_{area} \times W_{area}}, 1 - (1 - \frac{\pi(2L'rw - rw^2)}{L_{area} \times W_{area}})^{N_{ring}} \right] \tag{3}$$

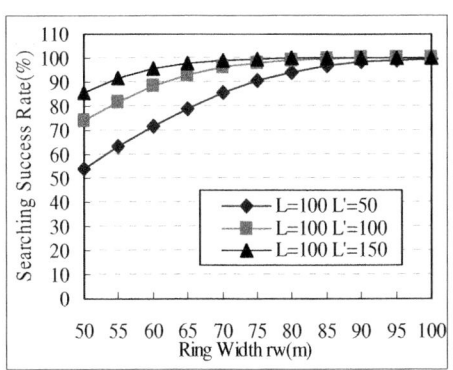

Fig. 2. Estimated $P_{searching}$ versus the ring width

Given that n is 50, both L_{area} and W_{area} are 500m, $N_{register}$ equals to N_{ring}, L is set to 100m, L' is set to 0.5L, 1L, or 1.5L respectively, we can get $P_{searching}$ under different rw, as shown in Fig. 2. From Fig. 2, we find that the success rate at the searching phase is roughly proportional to the width of ring rw. In other words, the large width of the ring will bring the high success rate.

However, the tangible value of above analyses is to give a guideline for users on setting appropriate system parameter rw by (3) and expected success rate.

On the other hand, we note that movement of a service requestor is one of important reasons why the requestor fails to receive the discovery results. Assuming that a node N_{req} at location T sends a discovery request and the discovery results arrival at N_c, the nearest node to T after Δt. If current N_{req} is still the nearest node to T (i.e. $N_c = N_{req}$), then N_{req} can get the discovery results obviously. Otherwise, current N_{req} must be at some position of the ring with T as the center, d as the inner radius, $v \times \Delta t$ as the outer radius, where d denotes the distance between T and N_c. According to our discovery strategy, only the nodes at the positions which are covered by the communication range of N_c can receive the results. As shown in Fig. 3, if and only if N_{req} locates in the shadow part, it can receive the qualified services, where Rc denotes communication radius of a node. Therefore, P_{return}, the probability of successful return to N_{req} is the ratio of the area of shaded part to the area of the ring S_{ring}.

We find that the area of the shaded part, S_{shadow}, is the area of the intersection part TA minus the area of the intersection TB, where TA denotes the intersection part of the circle with T as the center and $v \times \Delta t$ as the radius and the circle with N_c as the center and Rc as the radius, TB denotes the intersection of the circle with T as the center and d as the radius and the circle with N_c as center and Rc as the radius. As thus, S_{shadow} can be given by

$$S_{shadow} = S_{T\text{-}v\Delta t} \cap S_{Nc\text{-}Rc} - S_{T\text{-}d} \cap S_{Nc\text{-}Rc}, \tag{4}$$

where $S_{*\text{-}**}$ stands for the area of the circle with $*$ as the center and $**$ as the radius.

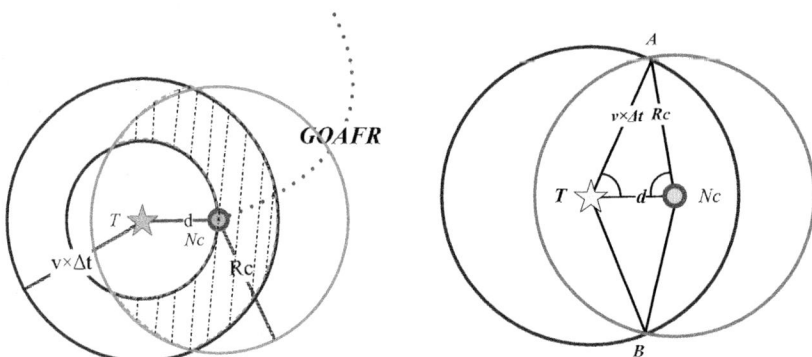

Fig. 3. N_{req} at T and N_c in the return phase　　**Fig. 4.** Two intersecting circles

Now we turn to calculate the area of the intersection part s of two circles.

Fig. 4 shows two intersecting circles, where one circle is with T as the center and $v \times \Delta t$ as the radius, another is with N_c as the center and Rc as the radius. By calculating the angle between line AT and line TN_c and the angle between line AN_c and line TN_c by (5.1) and (5.2) respectively, we can get the area of s by (6).

$$\angle ATN_c = \arccos((d^2 + (v \times \Delta t)^2 - Rc^2)/(2 \times d \times v \times \Delta t)) \tag{5.1}$$

$$\angle AN_cT = \arccos((d^2 + Rc^2 - (v \times \Delta t)^2)/(2 \times d \times Rc)) \tag{5.2}$$

$$s = \frac{2\angle ATN_c}{360} \times \pi \times (v \times \Delta t)^2 + \frac{2\angle AN_cT}{360} \times \pi \times Rc^2$$

$$-2 \times \frac{1}{2} \times v \times \Delta t \times d \times \sin \angle ATN_c \tag{6}$$

$$= \frac{\angle ATN_c}{180} \times \pi \times (v \times \Delta t)^2 + \frac{\angle AN_cT}{180} \times \pi \times Rc^2$$

$$-v \times \Delta t \times d \times \sin \angle ATN_c$$

So, we can get the area of shaded part S_{shadow} by

$$S_{shadow} = S_{T-v\Delta t} \cap S_{Nc-Rc} - S_{T-d} \cap S_{Nc-Rc}$$

$$= [\frac{\angle ATN_C}{180} \times \pi \times (v \times \Delta t)^2 + \frac{\angle AN_CT}{180} \times \pi \times Rc^2$$

$$- v \times \Delta t \times d \times \sin \angle ATN_C] - [\frac{\angle ATN_C}{180} \times \pi \times d^2 + \tag{7}$$

$$\frac{\angle AN_CT}{180} \times \pi \times Rc^2 - d \times d \times \sin \angle ATN_C]$$

Finally, we get P_{return} as follows.

$$P_{return} = S_{shadow} / S_{ring}$$

$$= [\frac{\angle ATN_C}{180} \times \pi \times (v \times \Delta t)^2 + \frac{\angle AN_CT}{180} \times \pi \times Rc^2$$

$$-v \times \Delta t \times d \times \sin \angle ATN_C - \frac{\angle ATN_C}{180} \times \pi \times d^2 - \frac{\angle AN_CT}{180} \times \pi \times Rc^2 \tag{8}$$

$$+ d \times d \times \sin \angle ATN_C] / [\pi \times (v \times \Delta t)^2 - \pi \times d^2]$$

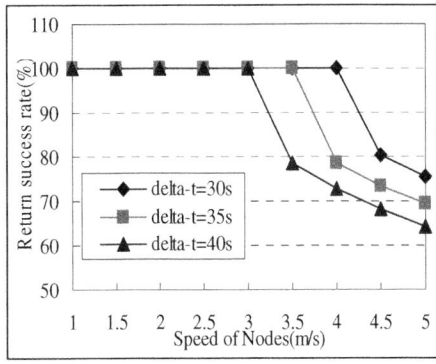

Fig. 5. Estimated P_{return} versus speed of nodes

Given that n is 100, both L_{area} and W_{area} are 1000m, Rc is 250m, and d is 130m, we can get P_{return} under different speed of nodes, as shown in Fig. 5.

From Fig. 5, we find that P_{return} remains 100% while the nodes move at a low speed and then it drops dramatically. As thus, we can use $P_{searching}$ to roughly estimate $P_{success}$ in the case of slow movement of nodes. Meantime, contrasting the data in Fig. 5 with the experimental data in Fig. 7 and Fig. 10 of Section 5, we find that when the nodes move at a high speed, the main reason for the failure of a discovery request may well be that the discovery results cannot be delivered to the requestor, which gives a direction of system optimization.

4.2 Volunteer Mode

When the nearest node Nq to the geographic location T which a register or discovery request binds to is working under the volunteer mode, the request will be sent to the volunteer node Nv which is in charge of Nq. The volunteer node acts as a directory, storing the services which ought to have held in surrounding nodes in the basic mode and searching whether the services matched against a service discovery request exist locally. Particularly, we prove the following theorem is true.

Theorem 1. If a discovery request reaches the node Nq, the nearest node to destination location T by GOAFR, and T is covered by the management scope of a volunteer Nv, then the discovery request is bound to find Nv.

Proof From Fig. 6, we have:

$$| Nv, Nq | \ \le \ | Nv, T | \ + \ | Nq, T | \ < \ 2 \times | Nv, T |$$

Since volunteer Nv is in charge of the circular region W with Nv as the circle and $Rc/2$ as the radius,

$$| Nv, Nq | \ < \ 2 \times | Nv, T | \ < \ Rc$$

where $|a,b|$ denotes the distance between location a and location b. As a result, the discovery request can reach Nv.

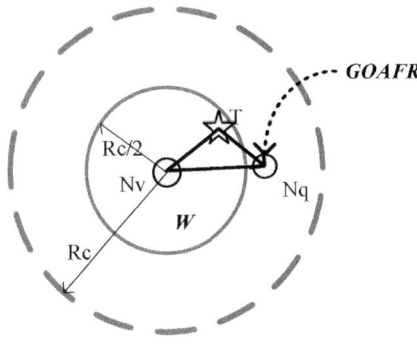

Fig. 6. Estimated P_{return} versus speed of nodes

The above theorem guarantees any discovery request will be executed in the volunteer mode.

Moreover, in order to avoid the services on the volunteer nodes become unavailable while the volunteer nodes leave or shut down, the volunteer nodes periodically execute the backup strategy, i.e., the volunteer nodes copy the local services to multiple backup nodes. The backup strategy is configurable. Users can specify two parameters in the backup strategy: the maximum quantity of backup nodes K and the minimal backup cycle Tb. The value of K is suggested to be set in terms of the density of nodes. Assuming that nodes are deployed according to the random Poisson distribution with density ρ, then K can be given by

$$K = \rho \times \pi \times Rc^2 / 16 , \tag{9}$$

where Rc is communication radius of a node. For example, 100 nodes are distributed in a $400 \times 400\text{m}^2$ square according to the random Poisson distribution, and Rc is 250m, then K is appropriately set to 7 by (9).

As to the value of Tb, the maximum speed of a node is a consideration for specifying Tb. While the nodes have fast movement speed on the average, Tb should be set to a relatively small value.

Further, the backup cycle Tr, i.e. the interval between two successive backup operations, will be decided according to the value of Tb and the node's running states. Tr is calculated in SCN4M-H by

$$Tr = \begin{cases} Tb & \text{if } D_{max} \in ((Rc - (Tb \times V_{max})), Rc) \\ D_{max}/V_{max} & \text{if } D_{max} \in (0, (Rc - (Tb \times V_{max}))) \end{cases} \tag{10}$$

where $Vmax$ denotes the maximum movement speed of a node, and $Dmax$ denotes the farthest distance between the volunteer node and its backup node.

Mode Switching Interval

Mode switching interval Tt is the interval required from when a volunteer node leaves until the surrounding non-volunteer nodes detect the volunteer node's leaving and changes their modes into the basic modes. During this interval, the services registered on the volunteer node will become unavailable, and the discovery requests sent to the volunteer node will be lost. It means the value of Tt has a direct influence on the success rate of discovery requests. By analyzing the system procedure, we find Tt depends on the backup cycle Tr, in other words, it takes one cycle Tr at most to detect whether the volunteer node is leaving. This means that Tt is bounded, it satisfied the following constraint:

$$Tt \in (Tb, Rc/V_{max}) . \tag{11}$$

5   Evaluation

5.1   Experimental Methodology

The motivation behind the following experiments is to observe the behaviors of SCN4M-H in different MANET environments. We adopt as the metrics the service discovery's success rate $P_{success}$ and its corresponding costs including the memory consumption and cumulative network traffic.

For preparing to conduct the experiments under the mobile environments, we modify the implemented SCN4M-H so as to integrate SCN4M-H with J-SIM simulator [12], especially replacing J-SIM's routing algorithm with the geometric routing algorithm implemented in SCN4M-H. After that, we design the following experiment framework.

Initially, 100 nodes are distributed over a 1000×1000 m^2 region. The communication radius of each node is set to 250m. Node's movement is at the speed of pedestrian and conforms to the random waypoint model. Each node can get the MANET field's information (i.e. its length and width).

After the experiment has run for 5 seconds as a warm up, each node begins to register one generated service. The service is registered in the MANET by hashing all its service suffixes to the Euclidean locations, mapping the Euclidean locations onto the locations in the region covered by the MANET, and placing the service on the corresponding locations in the MANET region. As thus, the total number of services generated is 100. At the time point of 40 seconds, the service discovery requests, which follow the similar rules of service generation so as to find the matched services, are generated at a rate of 10 queries per second on the randomly chosen nodes, and the procedure of request generation lasts 100 seconds. Consequently, 1000 queries are generated in total.

We instantiate the above experiment framework by inputting different mobile parameters (e.g. movement speed, the number of volunteers) or system parameters (i.e. refresh interval, ring width), and then conduct the experiments. We record their success rates, memory consumption and network traffic in the experiments and then analyze the impact of varying mobile/system parameters.

5.2 Experimental Results and Analyses

In the first set of simulation experiments, all nodes run in the basic mode. Figs 7-9 plot the success rates, memory consumption and network traffic with the ring width rw of 50 meters and different refresh intervals when the movement speeds of the nodes vary from 1m/s to 5m/s with the step of 0.5m/s. Figs 10-12 show the same measurements with the refresh interval ri of 10s and different ring widths when node movement speeds change. Also Figs 10-12 record the measurements of the perimeter-based register and discovery strategy while executing the same tasks. The perimeter-based strategy is the variant of the ring-based strategy. If the ring is extended to entire plane, then the ring-based strategy becomes the perimeter-based strategy.

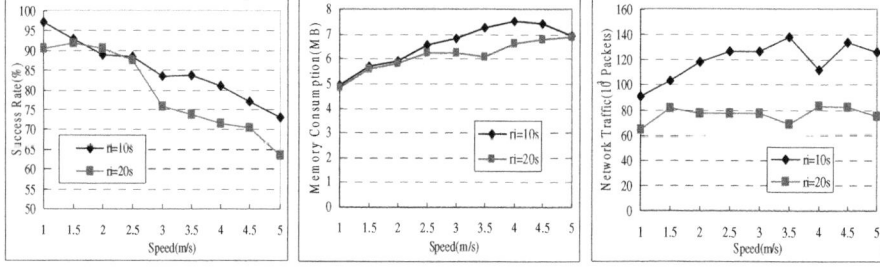

Fig. 7. $P_{success}$ versus movement speed under different refresh intervals

Fig. 8. Memory consumption versus movement speed under different refresh intervals

Fig. 9. Network traffic versus movement speed under different refresh intervals

It is seen from Fig. 7 and Fig. 10 that when the movement speed is less than or equals to 2.5m/s, all the success rates are greater than 85%, no matter which ri or rw is set. This is because the nodes move at such a slow speed that they cannot leave the ring during the refresh interval. While nodes move quickly, reducing ri can help update the services on nodes more frequently and keep services available, which improves the success rates. As shown in Fig. 7 and Fig. 9, while ri is changed from 10s to 20s, the success rate is improved by nearly 10% but larger ri results in more network traffic. In general, the ring width rw is set to less than the communication radius of nodes. Working on the basis of this premise, memory consumption and network traffic have little difference under different rw in our strategy and the success rate stays at a high level (more than 72%), which are illustrated by the data in Figs 10-12.

From the data shown in Figs 10-12, we find that the perimeter-based strategy indeed needs more memory consumption than our basic mode; while their network traffic has no obvious difference, as we expected. Besides, the perimeter-based strategy has lower success rates than our strategy. In sum, it is inferior to our strategy.

Fig. 13 gives the success rates under different number of nodes entering into the network or leaving the network dynamically, which indicates how the dynamic situations affect on request's success rates. Herein, +10% or +20% means that there are 10% or 20% nodes entering the network, while -10% or -20% means leaving. As shown in Fig. 13, node leaving has less influence on success rate than node entering does. The reason behind this result is that the mirror nodes will take the role of a backup node when the master node leaves.

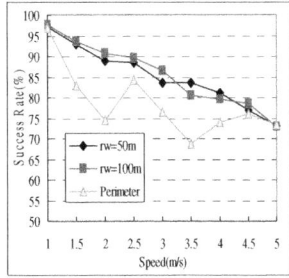 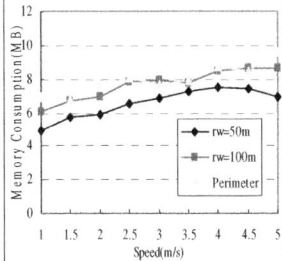 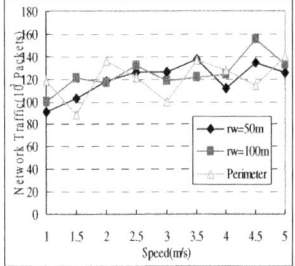

Fig. 10. $P_{success}$ versus movement speed under different ring widths

Fig. 11. Memory usage versus movement speed under different ring widths

Fig. 12. Network traffic versus movement speed under different ring widths

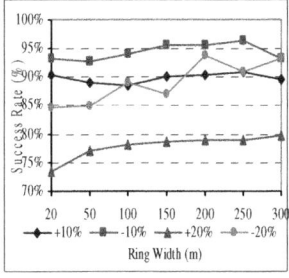

Fig. 13. $P_{success}$ under different dynamic situations

In the second set of simulation experiments, some nodes run in the basic mode, some nodes (i.e. 2-30 nodes) run in the volunteer mode. In these experiments, the following system parameters are also preset: refresh interval ri is set to 20s, ring width rw is set to 100 m, K is set to 3, Tb is set to 20s.

Figs 14-16 show the success rates, memory consumption and network traffic with the 6 volunteer nodes when node movement speeds vary from 1m/s to 5m/s with the step of 0.5m/s.

From the data in Figs 14-16, we note that the occurrence of volunteers can increase the success rate and decrease the resource consumption in contrast to the no-volunteer scenario, no matter what speed the nodes move. For example, while the nodes move with 4m/s, the success rate in the 6-volunteer scenario is about 13% higher than the one in the no-volunteer scenario. On the other hand, while the nodes move at an average speed of 1m/s, there is a negligible difference in success rate regardless of whether volunteers occur. But while the nodes reach a speed of 5m/s, the 6 volunteers will contribute to about 15.2% increasing of success rate. It shows the occurrence of volunteers can bring better effects while the nodes move at a relatively-fast speed. In total, the data in Figs 14-16 shows the occurrence of volunteers can increase the system adaptation to node movements.

Figs 17-19 give the success rate, memory consumption and network traffic when the number of volunteers varies from 2 to 30 and the nodes move at a speed of 4m/s or 2m/s. We find the success rate keeps on rising from 67.3% to 98.9% while the number of volunteer varies from 2 to 30 and the nodes are kept to move randomly at a speed of 4m/s. But success rate remain stable after the number of volunteer reaches 14 or more, at the same time, both the memory consumption and the network traffic show steady declines. The experimental results illustrate the appropriate quantity of volunteer can effectively enhance the system quality.

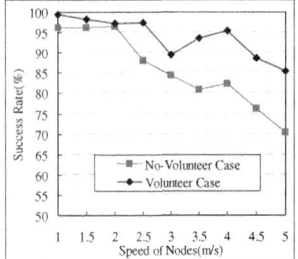 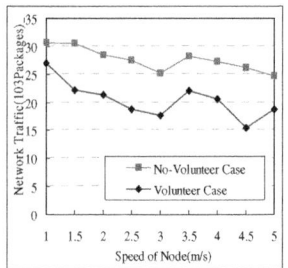 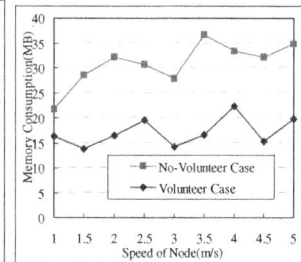

Fig. 14. $P_{success}$ versus different speed of nodes

Fig. 15. Network traffic versus different speed of nodes

Fig. 16. Memory consumption versus different speed of nodes

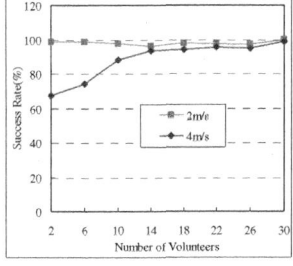 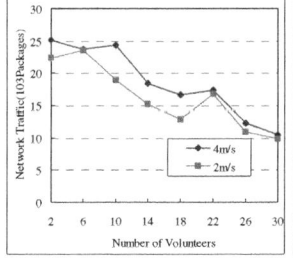 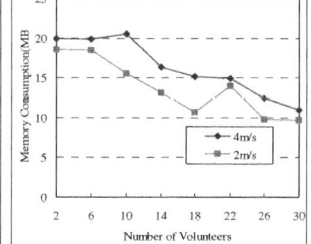

Fig. 17. $P_{success}$ versus different number of volunteers

Fig. 18. Network traffic versus different number of volunteers

Fig. 19. Memory consumption versus different number of volunteers

6   Conclusions

SCN4M-H, as a service discovery system over MANETs, provides its quality assurance from multiple aspects. It constructs the geographic overlay and adopts a geographic routing algorithm GOAFR. On the top of these components, two working modes, i.e. basic mode and volunteer mode, are provided. In the basic mode, nodes work together as peer partners. Services storage and discovery are performed by a P2P style in order to deal with the node mobility and dynamics. However, in the volunteer mode which aims at mining the node's diversity, the nodes who declare as volunteers will play the role of servers; they take advantage of their own abundant resources and relatively static positions to enhance the success rate for discovery requests. SCN4M-H lets a node decide its working mode and switch to the chosen mode smoothly according to its local dynamic states. From system perspective, P2P and C/S architecture styles can coexist simultaneously and switch adaptively in SCN4M-H, therefore, a service discovery request can be dealt with in a locally optimal way.

In addition, the paper gives some guidelines on setting system parameters (including *rw*, *ri*, *K* and *Tb*), and shows some inherent properties in SCN4M-H: (1) the volunteer mode is feasible in terms of motivation and technical design details, (2) the effects of the node movement on success rate in the basic mode are analyzed and $P_{searching}$ can be used to roughly estimate $P_{success}$ in the case of slow movement of nodes, (3) the bound of mode switching interval is given.

Finally, extensive experiments are conducted. Experimental data indicate that SCN4M-H adapts well to various MANET scenarios and shows satisfying software quality.

Acknowledgment. This work was supported by the National Natural Science Foundation of China under Grant No. 60970027.

References

1. Chakraborty, D., Joshi, A., Yesha, Y., Finin, T.: Toward Distributed Service Discovery in Pervasive Computing Environments. IEEE Transactions on Mobile Computing 5(2) (2006)
2. Sailhan, F., Issarny, V.: Scalable Service Discovery for MANET. In: The 3rd IEEE International Conference on Pervasive Computing and Communications, PerCom 2005 (2005)
3. Artail, H., Mershad, K.W., Hamze, H.: DSDM: A Distributed Service Discovery Model for Manets. IEEE Transactions on Parallel and Distributed Systems 19(9) (2008)
4. Xiang, X., Wang, X.: A Scalable Geographic Service Provision Framework for Mobile Ad Hoc Networks. In: The Fifth Annual IEEE International Conference on Pervasive Computing and Communications, PerCom 2007 (2007)
5. Noh, D., Shin, H.: SPIZ: An Effective Service Discovery Protocol for Mobile Ad Hoc Networks. EURASIP Journal on Wireless Communications and Networking (2007)
6. Weng, H., Wen, Y., Jin, B., Zhang, B.: SCN4M-DL: An Adaptive Directory-Less Service Discovery System for MANETs. In: The Fifteenth International Conference on Parallel and Distributed Systems, ICPADS 2009, Shenzhen, China (2009)
7. Baldauf, M., Dustdar, S., Rosenberg, F.: A Survey on Context-aware systems. Journal International Journal of Ad Hoc and Ubiquitous Computing 2(4) (2007)
8. Salehie, M., Tahvildari, L.: Self-Adaptive Software: Landscape and Research Challenges. ACM Transactions on Autonomous and Adaptive Systems 4(2) (2009)
9. Huebscher, M.C., Mccann, J.A.: A survey of autonomic computing — degrees, models, and applications. ACM Computing Surveys 40(3) (2008)
10. Korpela, E., Werthimer, D., Anderson, D., Cobb, J., Lebofsky, M.: SETI@home — Massively Distributed Computing for SETI. Computing in Science and Engineering 3(1) (2001)
11. Kuhn, F., Wattenhofer, R., Zollinger, A.: An Algorithmic Approach to Geographic Routing in Ad Hoc and Sensor Networks. IEEE/ACM Transactions on Networking 16(1) (2008)
12. J-Sim (2009), http://www.j-sim.org

Web Quality Assessment Model: Trust in QA Social Networks

Tomáš Knap and Irena Mlýnková

Department of Software Engineering
Faculty of Mathematics and Physics
Charles University in Prague, Czech Republic
{tomas.knap,irena.mlynkova}@mff.cuni.cz

Abstract. The Web Quality Assessment (WQA) model formalizes the customizable quality assessment (QA) process on the Web – every information consumer can define a set of QA policies, which are then, as part of the QA process, applied to the set of resources requested by the consumer to deduce the quality of the resources. To improve the result of such QA process, we introduced a concept of *QA social networks* – a mechanism to share QA policies among trustworthy entities to reinforce the number of QA policies applied during the QA process in the WQA model. In this paper, we detail the trust model underpinning the QA social network, i.e. what we mean under "trusting another entity" and how trust can be expressed and persisted; we propose a scalable and robust trust algorithm GriTa capable of deriving trust between arbitrary two entities in the QA social network. The goal of the WQA model is to provide a generally usable QA model with the social network dimension in mind – this paper contributes to that goal by presenting computation of trust in QA social networks.

Keywords: Trust, Social Network, Quality Assessment, Linked Data.

1 Introduction

The advent of Linked Data [4] in the recent years accelerates the evolution of the Web into a giant information space where the unprecedented volume of resources will offer to the information consumer a level of information integration and aggregation that has up to now not been possible. Consumers can now 'mashup' and readily integrate information for use in a myriad of alternative end uses. Indiscriminate addition of information can, however, come with inherent problems such as the provision of poor quality, inaccurate, irrelevant or fraudulent information. All will come with an associate cost which will ultimately affect decision making, system usage and uptake.

Therefore, the ability to assess the *information quality (IQ)* presents one of the most important aspects of the information integration on the Web and will play a fundamental role in the continued adoption of Linked Data principles [27]. Nevertheless, Naumann and Rolker [27] argue that assessing IQ is rightly considered difficult, because IQ dimensions are "often of subjective nature and can

C.-H. Hsu et al. (Eds.): UIC 2011, LNCS 6905, pp. 252–266, 2011.

therefore not be accessed automatically". Knight and Burn [1] argue similarly that the perception of IQ is highly dependent on the fitness for use being relative to the specific task that entities have at their hands. Furthermore, the Web is emerging as a global information space where the documents and data can be reused, aggregated and interconnected in new and unexpected ways, thus, we have to cope with the data with the beforehand unknown structure.

To that end, we have proposed in [18] a generic social network-based *Web Quality Assessment model* (*WQA model*), where customizable sets of *QA policies* drive the *QA process* assessing the quality of resources based on a set of IQ dimensions preferred by the information consumer. The use of QA policies in the WQA model is not novel and was successfully used by variety of access control mechanisms [20,26,7]. What is novel is the concept of *QA social network* representing a social network [28,24] an information consumer is part of, where every entity can (1) specify its QA policies and (2) express trust in another entity represented as an edge – *trust relation* – weighted by the amount of trust the entity ascribes to another entity. As a result, the QA policies can be shared among entities trusting each other above the certain threshold to reinforce the number of QA policies applied during the QA process. Since it has been widely documented that social networks have the properties of small world networks, where the average distances between entities in the network are small and connectance of entities is high [28,24], there is a chance of obtaining substantial amount of valuable QA policies from other entities in the QA social network. Furthermore, QA policies sharing can be exploited by environments with hierarchical structures to prescribe certain QA policies for subordinated entities; e.g. a department can prescribe certain QA policies for all its research groups and, in a similar way, research groups can prescribe several more QA policies for its members – thus, apart from their own QA policies, all the group members have to obey QA policies of the department and the particular research group they belong to.

To enable sharing of QA policies, we introduce in this paper the underlying trust model – in particular we define the notion of trust and a trust algorithm deriving trust between arbitrary two entities, not necessarily connected by a trust relation. Since the social networks on the Web (1) can be huge and (2) full of (unintentionally) malicious entities, the proposed trust algorithm must be scalable and robust, with a reasonable computation complexity.

The paper is organized as follows. Section 2 illustrates the QA process in the WQA model on a financial scenario. Section 3 defines the concept of trust in social networks and Section 4 introduces the algorithm GriTa for deriving trust in social trust networks. Section 5 introduces the preliminary evaluation of the trust algorithm's scalability. Section 6 reviews related work. The paper is rounded off with a conclusion and discussion of future work in Section 7.

2   Financial Motivational Scenario

We have chosen a *financial scenario* to motivate the needs for the WQA model incorporating QA social networks. Alice, a financial analyst and the information consumer, is part of the social network depicted in Figure 1(a). The social network consists of trust relations between Alice and (1) her colleague Bob working in the same group, (2) other financial experts, such as Cyril, and (3) the Analysts working group she is part of.

The Alice's goal is to prepare the financial report focusing on the summarized overview of the economic context of the executives of Fortune500 companies in the first quarter 2010. To achieve her goal, she is using a Linked Data [4] *mashup application* consuming and aggregating information included in stock markets time series, financial reports, government data, demographics, previous analysis, and third-party qualitative and quantitative analysis, physically distributed in various resources, such as RDF/XML documents, database tables, and XHTML pages.

The aggregated data Alice is interested in poses many non-trivial questions she has to face, such as: (Q1) Are the raw stock market information published by the operator NYSE[1] considered trustworthy? (Q2) Is the quarterly US GDP projection provided by Bloomberg[2] original or derived from another source? If derived, which source is quoted? (Q3) Is the euro exchange rate up-to-date? (Q4) How many organizations/people support the investment risk analysis score provided for Ireland? (Q5) Which of several contradicting statements for US unemployment rate should be preferred? (Q6) Does the entity have the rights to reuse the US Government data in a report?

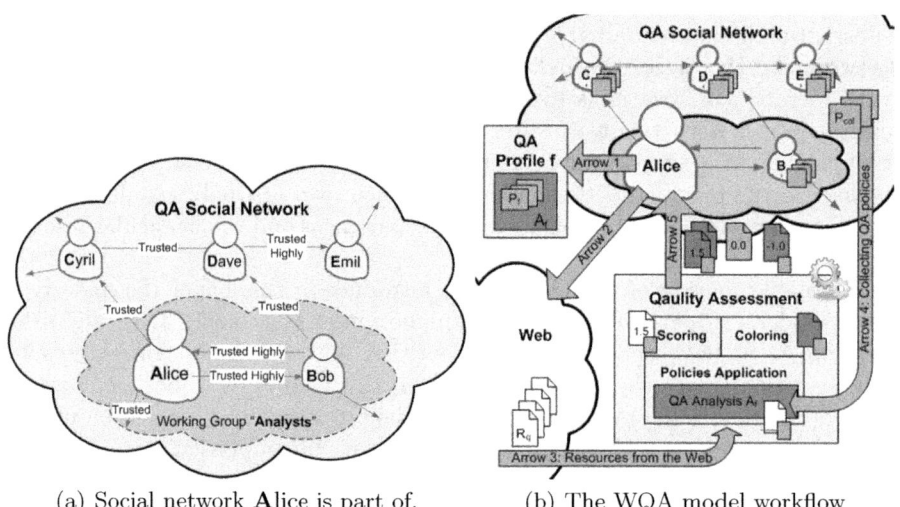

(a) Social network **A**lice is part of.   (b) The WQA model workflow

Fig. 1. Financial motivational scenario

Since provenance or lineage of data (1) provides the necessary contextualization for the information consumer to analyze the quality of the information [25,8,13] and (2) allows the transfer of trust from entities behind the resources to the information in the resources [9], the provenance metadata – the

---

[1] http://www.nyse.com/
[2] http://www.bloomberg.com/

data describing the resources at Alice's hands – helps Alice to answer all the questions Q1 – Q6, as long as the provenance metadata is available.[3] Nevertheless, without any automated solution, Alice has to deliver an enormous effort to filter the possible resources before they can be used by the mashup application.

Therefore, Alice decided to use Grian, the WQA model's implementation. From her perspective, the basic workflow of the QA process in the WQA model is depicted in Figure 1(b). Firstly, Alice defines her QA profile f involving the desired QA analyses A_f and QA policies P_f (Arrow 1). Since Alice understands the importance of the data provenance, she decides to incorporate Provenance QA Analysis as the (only) analysis in her QA process. The QA policies P_f are formed by mapping the questions Q1 – Q6 to the language of QA policies (see Table 3 in [18]).

Afterwards, Alice (or the mashup application on behalf of Alice) queries the Web (Arrow 2); the set of resources R_q relevant to the query q is returned, based on the result of the conventional search engine, such as Google, or semantic search engine, such as Sindice[4] (Arrow 3). At this moment, the QA process is entered – the QA analyses A_f are launched and the collected QA policies P_{col} ($P_f \subseteq P_{col}$) belonging to the analyses A_f (Arrow 4) are tried to be applied to the resources R_q; P_{col} is the set of Alices's QA policies and QA policies of the entities in her QA social network, which is based on the social network depicted in Figure 1(a)[5]. The successfully applied QA policies are reflected in the QA score and the QA color computed for each processed resource $r \in R_q$ (Blue box "Quality Assessment"). Although the QA score is the primary indicator of the resource's quality, the QA color serves as a first signal to Alice whether the resource r is recommended to be included to the report (green color), recommended with warnings (yellow), unknown, in the sense that no QA policy was successfully applied to this resource (grey), or not recommended at all (red). Afterwards, the resources R_q with the corresponding QA scores, colors, and sets of successfully applied QA policies are returned to Alice (Arrow 5).

The WQA model is detailed in [18]. In further sections, we will focus on the underlying trust model.

3   Trust in QA Social Networks

A *social network* [28,24] is typically modeled as a directed graph $sn(\mathcal{V}, \mathcal{E})$, where the vertices represent entities of the network (persons, groups) and the edges, $\mathcal{E} \subseteq \mathcal{V} \times \mathcal{V}$, *friendship relations*[6] between them [11,32]. Such a social network provides a suitable mechanism for sharing QA policies between the entities participating

---

[3] The current activities in the area of data provenance and annotations show that these assumptions are being fulfilled by more and more resources, see [25] and http://twiki.ipaw.info/bin/view/Challenge.

[4] http://sindice.com/

[5] We suppose that all trust relations in Figure 1(a) are w.r.t. the context of financial QA policies.

[6] Persons are friends of each other or persons belong to groups.

in the social network; obviously, the information consumer is more willing to inherit QA policies of entities he *trusts* more.

3.1 Concept of Trust

Manifestations of trust are easy to recognize because we experience and rely on it every day, but at the same time trust is quite challenging to define because it manifests itself in many different forms and it is used with wide variety of meanings [14,2,10,23].

Definition 1, based on the definition proposed by McKnight and Chervany in [23], drives the comprehension of trust in the further text. We selected Definition 1 from lots of other definitions, because it comprehends trust as the subjective opinion of an entity about another entity and it embodies five essential elements of trust: (a) potential negative consequences, (b) dependence, (c) feeling of security, (d) situation specific context, and (e) lack of reliance and control; the necessity of these elements is justified in [23].

Definition 1. *Trust (trusting intention) is the extent to which one entity is willing to depend on the other entity (the other entity's QA policies) in a given situation with a feeling of relative security, even though negative consequences are possible.*

The *extent* in Definition 1 can be quantified either on a discrete [21,11] or continuous scale [22,12,32,30,11]. In general, discrete trust levels are easily seizable by humans when expressing trust between each other, on the other hand, continuous trust values provide more accurate expressions of trust.

In our trust model, trust of an entity u (trustor) in the entity (trustee) v's QA policies w.r.t. the context (domain of expertise) c is internally quantified as continuous *trust value* $\tau_{u,v,c}^t \in [0,1] \cup \bot$, a frequent representation of trust [30,12,32,2,10], computed by the *trust function* $\tau : V \times V \times C \times \mathbb{N} \rightarrow [0,1] \cup \bot$; hence $\tau_{u,v,c}^t = \tau(u,v,c,t)$. As depicted in [19], selecting the proper set of contexts (topics), C, is difficult and is out of the scope of this paper; in [19], several topic hierarchies are compared w.r.t. several criteria. Since trust between entities is evolving in time, t in $\tau_{u,v,c}^t$ represents the time $t \in \mathbb{N}$ in which the given trust value is valid. We discuss the *trust dynamics* in Subsection 3.1.1 in [18]. In the further text, $\tau_{u,v}$ holds the current trust value w.r.t. to the topic (context) "Finance", which is relevant for the motivational scenario.[7]

The trust value $\tau_{u,v}$ is ranging from "absolute distrust" ($\tau_{u,v} = 0$) to "absolute trust" ($\tau_{u,v} = 1$), the value $\tau_{u,v} \geqq 0.3$ expresses that the entity v is comprehended as trusted (to some extend); $\tau_{u,v} = \bot$ if the trust value is unknown. Furthermore, we assume that $\tau_{u,u} = 1$ and $\tau_{u,v} = 1$ ($u \neq v$) only if the entity u is enforced to trust the entity v, e.g. the researcher u trusts the research group v to which it belongs. A trust value $\tau_{u,v} = 0$ can be ascribed through a thoughtful judgement typically based on the bad experience of the entity u with the entity v in the past [22] – the entity u never wants to use any single QA policy of the entity v.

---

[7] Hence $\tau_{u,v} = \tau_{u,v,c}^t$, so that $\neg \exists t' > t \wedge c = $ "*Finance*".

Table 1. Trust Levels

Trust Level Label	Abbreviation	$\tau_{u,v}$
DISTRUSTED	λ_D	0.1
KNOWN	λ_K	0.3
TRUSTED	λ_T	0.7
TRUSTED_HIGHLY	λ_{TH}	0.9

We agree that discrete trust levels are easily seizable by human information consumers. Regrettably, it is hard to imagine that entities will consistently subjectively map their trust to others on a ten point scale (as proposes Golbeck in [11]) – there is no guarantee for the information consumer that someone "really trusted" is always expressed as 9 or 8. Therefore, we externally use only four trust levels depicted in Table 1 together with the corresponding abbreviations for them and $\tau_{u,v} \in [0,1]$. In case of the level *TRUSTED_HIGHLY* the entity u can be almost sure that the entity v provides trustworthy QA policies according to Definition 1. The trust level *TRUSTED* should be assigned to all other entities not classified as TRUSTED_HIGHLY, however, still rather trustworthy – we can expect that they will provide trustworthy QA policies. The trust level *DISTRUSTED* expresses that the entity u rather does not want to use QA policies of v. Finally, the trust level KNOWN expresses the implicit trust of entity u in v, if there is an edge $(u,v) \in \mathcal{E}$ in the underlying social network $sn(\mathcal{V}, \mathcal{E})$.

3.2 Social Trust Networks

We define a *social trust network*[8] as a directed weighted graph $stn(V, E, [\tau]_{stn})$, where $V \subseteq \mathcal{V}$, $E \subseteq \{V \times V\}$, and $[\tau]_{stn} : V \times V \times C \times \mathbb{N} \to [0,1] \cup \perp$ represents the *realization* of the trust function τ in the social trust network stn. Each edge – *trust relation* – $(u,v) \in E$ is weighted by the function $[\tau]_{stn}$ determining how much trust an entity u assigns to another entity v w.r.t. the given context c and in the time t.

Example 1. *In the social network visualized in Figure 1(a), Alice specifies that Bob is "Trusted Highly" in the context of "Finance".*

Persistence of Social Trust Networks. In this Subsection, we propose a persistence of trust relations between entities. We would like to persist data in the (1) application independent and (2) machine understandable way.

In most cases, social networks coexisting in the Web information space[9] are tightly connected with the applications utilizing them (such as MySpace[10]). Contrary, the Friend of a Friend (FOAF) project[11] is an ontology enabling to

---

[8] A concept of social trust networks is similar to the web of trust introduced in PGP system.

[9] See [11, p. 10 – 28] for the list of web-based social networks.

[10] http://www.myspace.com

[11] http://xmlns.com/foaf/spec/

describe, using RDF model, (1) entities as instances of RDF class `foaf:Agent` and (2) relations between entities as instances of the predicates `foaf:knows` (in case of two users) and `foaf:member` (in case of a group involving a user). Since there are no other open, application independent, machine readable, and widely used implementations of social networks, we decided to use FOAF ontology as a cornerstone ontology for representation of entities and trust relations in social trust networks.

Unfortunately, the FOAF ontology does not define the concept of trust, therefore, we developed an extension of the FOAF ontology, WQA Trust Module[12], having the capability to express and persist the trust levels λ_{TH}, λ_T, and λ_D.

4   Deriving Trust in QA Social Networks

Suppose that entities c, v are not connected by a trust relation; then, the information consumer $c \in \mathcal{V}$ can either use only QA policies of trustworthy *neighbors* (entities connected by a trust relation in the social trust network stn_c), or we need to compute a quantitative estimate – *a mediated trust value* – of how much trust an entity c should accord to the entity v in stn_c. Before defining the trust algorithm used in QA social networks to compute the mediated trust value, we need to discuss its desired properties.

Ziegler and Lausen [32] present a categorization of trust algorithms (metrics) – they distinguish global and local trust algorithms. Global trust metrics, such as [16,29], violate our assumption about subjectiveness of the trust (according to Definition 1), because they compute the *reputation* of entities in social trust networks. Therefore, our trust algorithm is a local trust metric comprehending trust as a subjective opinion of the particular entity – the information consumer in the financial motivational scenario.

Another question concerns the transitivity of trust. As stated in [30]: *"[...] from the perspective of network security (where transitivity would, for example, imply accepting a key with no further verification based on trust) or formal logics (where transitivity would, for example, imply updating a belief store with incorrect, impossible, or inconsistent statements) it may make sense to assume that trust is not transitive"*. On the other hand, Golbeck [11] and Guha et al. [12] show experimentally that trust is transitive and may propagate along the trust relations in social networks. In contrary to Golbeck's approach, Guha et al. suggest appropriate trust discounting with the increasing lengths of trust relation paths between two entities, which is a reasonable property of trust – one trusts more his direct friends than friends of friends of his friends. Since the context and the networks in which trust is used by Guha and Golbeck are similar to the social trust networks proposed in Subsection 3.2, we comprehend trust as transitive with appropriate trust discounting.

Let us formally define an already mentioned concept – a *trust relation path*, $\pi_{u,v} \in TP$, between entities u and v in some $stn(V, E, \tau)$ – as a progression of trust relations $(u = v_0, v_1), \ldots, (v_i, v_{i+1}), \ldots, (v_{n-1}, v_n = v)$, $v_i \in V$, $0 \leqq i \leqq n$;

---

[12] `http://www.ksi.mff.cuni.cz/~knap/wqa/tm.owl`

each $e_j = (v_j, v_{j+1}) \in E$ and $\forall e_j, e_k \in \pi_{u,v} : e_j \neq e_k$, where $0 \leqq j, k \leqq n - 1$. The expression $e \in \pi_{u,v}$ ($x \in \pi_{u,v}$) denotes that $e \in E$ ($x \in V$) is part of the path $\pi_{u,v}$. The number of trust relations involved in $\pi_{u,v}$ is denoted as $|\pi_{u,v}|$, whereas $\#\pi_{u,v}$ ($\#\pi^{\chi}_{u,v}$) denotes the number of vertex-disjoint (edge-disjoint) trust relation paths between u and v – two paths $\pi_{u,v}$ and $\pi'_{u,v}$ are vertex-disjoint if $\neg\exists x \in \pi_{u,v}$, $x \neq u, v$, so that $x \in \pi'_{u,v}$, two paths $\pi_{u,v}$ and $\pi'_{u,v}$ are edge disjoint if $\exists e \in \pi_{u,v}$, so that $e \notin \pi'_{u,v}$ or $\exists e \in \pi'_{u,v}$, so that $e \notin \pi_{u,v}$. We define a function $\tau_{path} : TP \rightarrow [0,1]$ computing the trust along the trust relation path according to Formula 1 – it multiplies the trust values along the path; we denote the computed trust value $\tau_{path}(\pi_{u,v})$ as $\tau_{\pi_{u,v}}$.

$$\tau_{\pi_{u,v}} = \tau_{path}(\pi_{u,v}) = \prod_{j=0}^{|\pi_{u,v}|} \{\tau_{x_j, x_{j+1}} \mid x_j \in \pi_{u,v}, x_0 = u, x_{|\pi_{u,v}|} = v\} \qquad (1)$$

Apart from trust transitivity, Golbeck [11] particularizes three other properties of trust: *personalization*, *asymmetry*, and *composability*. The first two properties are already satisfied by the chosen Definition 1 and by assuming only local trust algorithms. Composability means that if there exist more trust relation paths between entities u and v, the mediated trust value is based on more/all these path. Composability is a reasonable property for the algorithm deriving trust in social trust networks in the open environment, such as the Web, where intentionally or unintentionally malicious users occur, because it increases the robustness of the proposed trust algorithm [18].

4.1   Trust Algorithm GriTa

The discussion above lead to a proposal of the local trust algorithm *GriTa* quantified by a function $\tau_{gt} : V \times V \rightarrow [0,1] \cup \perp^{13}$. We will explain the algorithm on the computation of a mediated trust value $\tau_{gt}(c, v)$ between the consumer c and the entity v in the social trust network $stn_c(V, E, [\tau])$.

If there is a trust relation (c, v), then, $\tau_{gt}(c, v) = \tau_{c,v}$. Otherwise, $|\pi_{c,v}| \geqq 2$ for arbitrary $\pi_{c,v} \in TP$. In that case, we distinguish two types of trust: a trust of $x \in \pi_{c,v}$ in v, $x \neq c, v$, $(x, v) \in E$, and a trust of the consumer c in an entity x which has trust relation to v. Both these types of trust satisfy Definition 1, the former – *direct trust* – is about x's trust that the v's QA policies are trustworthy and the latter one – *trust in mediator* – is about how much the consumer c trusts that x's trust estimation in v is correct. Trust in mediator is quantified by the function $\overline{\tau} : V \times V \rightarrow [0,1]$, abbreviated as $\overline{\tau_{c,x}}$ (in case of the consumer c and the mediator x).

The trust algorithm GriTa has two phases. Phase 1 establishes a set of *mediators* V_{med} – the entities in which the consumer has trust value $\overline{\tau_{c,x}} \in [0,1]$, $x \in V_{med}$. Phase 2 uses the trust value $\tau_{x,v}$, $x \in V_{med}$, meliorated by the trust in mediator x, to compute the mediated trust value $\tau_{gt}(c, v)$.

---

[13] We again suppose that the trust algorithm is dealing only with current trust relations w.r.t. context "Finance".

Phase 1 - Establishing Mediators. Since $stn_c(V, E, [\tau])$ can be huge, we suppose that the consumer c defines $\kappa_{med} \in \mathbb{N}$ specifying the desired $|V_{med}|$. Final mediators V_{med} are selected in several steps – V_{med}^{Si} holds the mediators selected in Step i.

Firstly, in Step 1, $V_{med}^{S1} = \{x \in V \mid \overline{\tau_{c,x}} > \lambda_K\}$, where the mediated trust $\overline{\tau_{c,x}}$ is equal to the trust along the most trustworthy path as depicted in Formula 2. The function $\overline{\tau}$ comprehends trust as transitive, with the appropriate trust discount due to the use of multiplication in Formula 1. The time complexity of Formula 2 is $O(|V|log|V| + |E|)$, because it can be computed using Dijkstra algorithm with a heap[14].

$$\overline{\tau_{c,x}} = max_{i=1}^{\#\pi_{c,x}^X}\{\tau_{\pi_{c,x}^i}\} \tag{2}$$

Typically $|V_{med}^{S1}| >> \kappa_{med}$, therefore, in Step 2 we restrict the number of entities involved in Step 3 by setting V_{med}^{S2} to contain at maximum $\overline{\kappa_{med}} = \psi\kappa_{med}$ entities $v \in V_{med}^{S1}$ with the highest $\overline{\tau_{c,v}}$; $\psi \in (1, \infty)$ is a parameter of the algorithm. Since Step 3 is going to throw out some entities $u \in V_{med}^{S2}$, we increased the desired κ_{med} by ψ.

Since the algorithm GriTa must be robust, the algorithm should not rely on one trust relation path with the highest trust computed according to Formula 2. Suppose that a malicious entity m tricks an entity $y \in V_{med}^{S2}$, thus, $\tau_{y,m} = \lambda_{TH}$. As a result, such a malicious entity can easily become part of V_{med}^{S2} during Steps 1 and 2. What is more, the malicious entity m can introduce trust relations to other malicious entities and, thus, polluting the set of mediators V_{med}^{S1} and V_{med}^{S2} with lots of malicious entities.

To avoid that situation, Step 3 further refines the set V_{med}^{S2}: $V_{med}^{S3} = \{x \in V_{med}^{S2} \mid \#\pi_{c,x} \geqq \kappa_{supp}\}$. To compute $\#\pi_{c,x}$ we need to introduce an auxiliary network $g(V', E', cp) \in G'$, where V' is a set of vertices, E' set of edges, and $cp: E' \to 1$ defines a unit capacity for every edge of the network g. Then, according to Theorem 11.4 [5], network flow represented by a function $fl: G' \times V' \times V' \to \mathcal{R}^+$ launched on the network g, a source $a \in V'$, and a sink $b \in V' - fl(g, a, b) -$ holds the maximum number of **edge**-disjoint paths between the vertices a and b in the network g [5]. We use Edmond-Karp's algorithm for the computation of the network flow (the function fl), with a time complexity $O(|V||E|^2)$.

When computing $\#\pi_{c,x}, \forall x \in V_{med}^{S2}$, we cannot simply set $V' = V_{med}^{S1}, E' = E_{|V_{med}^{S1} \times V_{med}^{S1}}$, and call $fl(g, c, x)$, because we are interested in the maximum number of **vertex**-disjoint trust relation paths. To construct V', E', and, thus, convert the task of searching the number of **vertex**-disjoint trust relation paths to searching the number of **edge**-disjoint trust relation paths, we use the approach suggested in the proof of Theorem 11.6 [5] and described by Algorithm 1. Then, calling $fl(g, c^+, x^-)$ computes $\#\pi_{c,x}$ [5].

Finally, V_{med} is set to be equal to V_{med}^{S3} containing at maximum κ_{med} entities v with the highest $\overline{\tau_{c,v}}$. If $V_{med}^{S3} \leqq \kappa_{med}$, we repeat Step 3 with the higher ψ.

---

[14] Since the Dijkstra algorithm is searching "shortest" paths, the weights on the edges must be $1 - \tau_{x,y}, \forall(x, y) \in E$.

Algorithm 1 . Constructing the sets V', E'

Input: V_{med}^{S1}, c
Output: $(V', E') = construct(V_{med}^{S1}, c)$
1: $V' \leftarrow \{c^+\}$
2: $E' \leftarrow \emptyset$
3: **for all** entities $v \in V_{med}^{S1}$ **do**
4:     $V' \leftarrow V' \cup \{v^-, v^+\}$
5:     $E' \leftarrow E' \cup \{(v^-, v^+)\}$
6: **end for**
7: **for all** trust relations $e = (u, v) \in E_{|V_{med}^{S1} \times V_{med}^{S1}}$ **do**
8:     **if** $\tau_{u,v} > \lambda_K \wedge v \neq c$ **then**
9:         $E' \leftarrow E' \cup \{(u^+, v^-)\}$
10:     **end if**
11: **end for**
12: **return** (V', E')

Thanks to Step 3, the computed $\overline{\tau_{c,v}}$, $v \in V_{med}$, is supported by at least κ_{supp} vertex-disjoint trust relation paths $\pi_{c,v}^i$, $1 \leq i \leq \#\pi_{c,x}$.

The time complexity of Phase 1 is $O(|V_{med}^{S2}||V'||E'|^2)$ due to $|V_{med}^{S2}|$ runs of the Edmond-Karp's algorithm using the graph g.

Phase 2 - Computing Mediated Trust Value. Phase 2, which is executed for the given consumer c and the target entity v, selects the set of mediators $V_{med}^{c,v}$, $V_{med}^{c,v} = \{x \in V_{med} \mid (x, v) \in E\}$. If $|V_{med}^{c,v}| \geq \kappa_{minMed}^c$, where $\kappa_{minMed}^c \in \mathbb{N}$ defines the c's desired minimum number of mediators (e.g. $\kappa_{minMed}^c = 3$), the final mediated trust value $\tau_{gt}(c, v)$ of the entity c in v is computed according to Formula 3 as a weighted average over the trust values $\tau_{x,v}$ with the weights $\overline{\tau_{c,x}}$, $x \in V_{med}^{c,v}$. Otherwise the entity's v trustworthiness cannot be judged, i.e. $\tau_{gt}(c, v) = \bot$.

$$\tau_{gt}(c, v) = \frac{\sum_{x \in V_{med}^{c,v}} \overline{\tau_{c,x}} \tau_{x,v}}{\sum_{x \in V_{med}^{c,v}} \overline{\tau_{c,x}}} \tag{3}$$

Formula 3 supports the composability of trust. The time complexity of Phase 2 is $O(|V_{med}^{c,v}|)$.

5   Evaluation

In Section 5 in [17], we have shown the contribution of QA policies inheritance to the QA process in the WQA model. In this section we conduct a preliminary evaluation of the GriTa algorithm's scalability when deriving trust in social trust networks.

To obtain real world social networks as a base for the evaluation, we implemented a crawler, downloading from the Web instances of the RDF class `foaf:Person` and RDF predicate `foaf:knows` to get entities and relations between them. In this way, we obtained two social networks – $sn_a(V_a, E_a)$ and $sn_b(V_b, E_b)$. In case of sn_a, the crawling process started from the FOAF profile of Tim Berners-Lee[15] and extracted $|V_a| = 2887$ entities with the average number of 8.47 relations between them from the social network behind the Advogato web site[16]. In case of sn_b, the crawling process started from the randomly chosen FOAF profile[17] from the FOAF social network behind the web site "http://my.opera.com"[18] and extracted $|V_b| = 289811$ entities with the average number of 10.50 relations between them.

We define social trust networks $stn_a(V_a, E_a, [\tau]_a)$ and $stn_b(V_b, E_b, [\tau]_b)$ with the trust function τ and its realizations $[\tau]_a$ and $[\tau]_b$ randomly assigning trust levels λ_{TH}, λ_T, λ_K, and λ_D as weights of the edges E_a and E_b according to the distribution of the trust levels depicted in Table 2.

Table 2. Determining $[\tau]_{a|b}$ for the arbitrary edge based on the distance of the the randomly generated value $gv \in \mathbb{R}$ from the mean (measured in the multiples of the standard deviation σ)

Ranges	$[\tau]_{a\|b}$
$\|gv\| < 0.5\sigma$	λ_T
$0.5\sigma \leqq gv < \sigma,\ 2\sigma \leqq gv < 3\sigma,\ gv \geqq 3\sigma$	λ_{TH}
$(-1)\sigma < gv \leqq (-0.5)\sigma,\ (-3)\sigma < gv \leqq (-2)\sigma,\ gv \leqq (-3)\sigma$	λ_K
$(-2)\sigma < gv \leqq (-1)\sigma,\ \sigma \leqq gv < 2\sigma$	λ_D

To measure the scalability of the algorithm GriTa, we introduce the *entities reached metric* $\#er^{stn}$ for computing the average number of entities visited per one execution of the algorithm GriTa in the social trust network stn, and *time metrics* $time_{P1}^{stn}$, $time_{P2}^{stn}$, with results in seconds, computing the average time necessary to perform Phase 1, respectively Phase 2, of one execution of the algorithm GriTa in the social trust network stn.

5.1   Simulation and Results

In our simulation, κ_{med} is initially set to 100, κ_{supp} to 5. After performing 100 executions of Phase 1 and 10000 executions of Phase 2 of the GriTa algorithm in both social trust networks, we obtained the results as follows: $Time_{P1}^{stn_a} = 0.872$, $Time_{P2}^{stn_a} = 0.086$, $Time_{P1}^{stn_b} = 1107.76$, $Time_{P2}^{stn_b} = 2.982$, $\#er^{stn_a} = 2359$, and $\#er^{stn_b} = 11542$.

Regarding the scalability w.r.t. to the time needed to finish the computation, Phase 2, which is going to be executed whenever the QA process in the WQA model is executed, is fast in both social trust networks. If we compare $\dfrac{Time_{P2}^{stn_b}}{Time_{P2}^{stn_a}}$

---

[15] http://www.advogato.org/person/timbl/foaf.rdf

[16] Advogato.com, a free software developer's advocate and a research testbed for Advogato trust algorithm [21].

[17] http://my.opera.com/kjetilk/xml/foaf#me

[18] A site where users can blog, share photos, meet their friends.

and $\frac{|V_b|}{|V_a|}$, the growth in time seems to be linear[19] (note that the average number of relations is higher in stn_b). Further, to decrease $Time_{P2}^{stn_b}$, we can lower κ_{med} to decrease $\#er^{stn}$. The execution time of Phase 1 is approximately 18 minutes for $|V_b|$, which has to be decreased in the future work, however, it is still acceptable, because Phase 1 can be executed only once per a certain period of time (e.g. once per day).

Regarding the scalability w.r.t. to the number of processed entities, comparing $\frac{\#er^{stn_b}}{\#er^{stn_a}}$ and $\frac{|V_b|}{|V_a|}$, $\#er^{stn_b}$ is increasing much more slowly than $|V_b|$. Moreover, $\#er^{stn_b}$ is decreasing proportionally with the decreasing κ_{med}; e.g. for $\kappa_{med} = 50$, $\#er^{stn_b} = 6734$. Furthermore, we can introduce a cap for the maximum number of entities reached. As a result, the algorithm is scalable with the reasonably chosen κ_{med};

We try various settings of κ_{supp} with small impact on the time metric and on the entities reached metric as long as $V_{med}^{S3} \geq \kappa_{med}$ is valid after the first run of Phase 1 (hence Step 3 is not repeated with higher ψ). We will conduct more experiments in the future, the important observation is that the trust algorithm GriTa seems to scales well (w.r.t. to the consumed time and number of processed entities) with the increasing size of the social trust network.

6 Related Work

Researchers have developed and investigated various policy languages to describe trust and security requirements on the Web [15,3]; a variety of access control mechanisms generally based on policies and rules have been developed [20,26,7]. Although these approaches support customization of the policies, to the best of our knowledge, they do not utilize the power of social networks to share policies. Paper [6] coins the term Data Quality Social Network. Nevertheless, their social network is not intended to be used for sharing policies – it is used merely for adjusting weights of the quality dimensions in the QA process.

6.1 Trust in Social Networks

Ziegler and Lausen [32] proposed Appleseed trust metric (as an improved version of the Advogato[20] trust metric [21]) calculating trust for a collection of entities at once by energizing the selected entity (a consumer) and spreading the energy to other entities connected by trust relations. The problem of this algorithm is the normalization of the trust values - the more trust relations the entity defines, the less energy (trust) each target entity of these trust relations receives. The algorithm GriTa does not have this problem.

Guha et al. [12] introduced several ways of propagating trust in a social network. Except of *direct propagation* (use of trust transitivity), they propose other

---

[19] We would need more experiments to state that the growth actually is linear.
[20] http://www.advogato.org/

atomic propagations – *co-citation* (if $\tau_{u_1,v_1} > \lambda_K$, $\tau_{u_1,v_2} > \lambda_K$, and $\tau_{u_2,v_2} > \lambda_K$, we can infer $\tau_{u_2,v_1} > \lambda_K$), *transpose trust* (if $\tau_{u,v} > \lambda_K$, then $\tau_{v,u} > \lambda_K$), and *trust coupling* (if $\tau_{u_1,v} > \lambda_K$, $\tau_{u_2,v} > \lambda_K$, then $\tau_{u,u_1} > \lambda_K$ implies $\tau_{u,u_2} > \lambda_K$). The algorithm GriTa uses the transitivity of trust. Other atomic propagations are too vulnerable to malicious entities, which can easily simulate the prerequisites of these propagations and obtain an extra trust.

Furthermore, Guha et al. [12] and Ziegler and Lausen [32] dealt with the propagation of distrust and observed that the semantics of transitivity is not clear: if $\tau_{u,v} \leqq \lambda_K$ and $\tau_{v,w} > \lambda_K$, the mediated trust value of u in w is rather low, although the only way to deduce the trust in the entity w is from the distrusted entity v. In the algorithm GriTa, we simply do not use mediators v with $\tau_{u,v} < \lambda_K$, u is the consumer. To derive trust of u in w in QA social networks, we should employ algorithms for computing reputation of entities [16,29] or algorithms for finding experts among entities [31].

In [30], Walter et al. propose a model of trust based recommender system involving the set of agents (entities) connected with each other by trust relations. When comparing with the WQA model, instead of applying policies collected from the neighbors, they ask the neighbors for their recommendation. Nevertheless, their algorithm for deriving trust between the consumer and the recommending agent is not deterministic – the trust relation paths are probabilistically selected based on their trustworthiness.

7 Conclusions and Future Work

In this paper, we (1) defined a trust model describing the notion of trust and a way of expressing and persisting trust of an entity in another entity in the social trust networks, and (2) proposed a trust algorithm GriTa capable of deriving trust between arbitrary two entities in the social trust network.

We have done a preliminary evaluation of the scalability of the trust algorithm GriTa w.r.t. to the time needed to finish the computation and w.r.t. to the number of processed entities. The results are promising, showing that the algorithm is suitable for the environments with hundreds of thousands of entities.

In future work, we will empirically evaluate the robustness of the algorithm GriTa and measure scalability of the QA process as a whole. Furthermore, we need to extend the trust model to support various domains of human expertise – someone who may be trusted to provide financial QA policies may not be trusted to provide QA polices regarding programming. We are persuaded that QA social networks significantly increase the ability to assess the quality of information on the exponentially growing Web.

Acknowledgments. The work presented in this article has been funded in part by the Czech Science Foundation (GACR, grant number 201/09/H057) and GAUK 3110.

References

1. Ann Knight, S., Burn, J.: Developing a Framework for Assessing Information Quality on the World Wide Web. Informing Science Journal 8, 159–172 (2005)
2. Artz, D., Gil, Y.: A Survey of Trust in Computer Science and the Semantic Web. Web Semant. 5(2), 58–71 (2007)
3. Bizer, C., Cyganiak, R.: Quality-driven Information Filtering Using the WIQA Policy Framework. Web Semant. 7(1), 1–10 (2009)
4. Bizer, C., Heath, T., Berners-Lee, T.: Linked Data - The Story So Far. International Journal on Semantic Web and Information Systems 5(3), 1–22 (2009)
5. Bondy, A., Murty, U.S.R.: Graph Theory, 3rd corrected printing edn. Graduate Texts in Mathematics. Springer, Heidelberg (2007)
6. Caballero, I., Verbo, E., Serrano, M.A., Calero, C., Piattini, M.: Tailoring Data Quality Models Using Social Network Preferences. In: DASFAA Workshops, pp. 152–166 (2009)
7. Cantor, S., Kemp, J., Philpott, R., Maler, E.: Assertions and Protocols for the OASIS Security Assertion Markup LanguagE (SAML) V2.0. Technical report (2005)
8. Freitas, A., Knap, T., O'Riain, S., Curry, E.: W3P: Building an OPM based provenance model for the Web. Future Generation Computer Systems (2010), http://www.sciencedirect.com/ (in press) (accepted manuscript)
9. Gil, Y., Artz, D.: Towards Content Trust of Web Resources. Web Semant. 5(4), 227–239 (2007)
10. Golbeck, J.: Trust on the world wide web: a survey. Found. Trends Web Sci. 1(2), 131–197 (2006)
11. Golbeck, J.A.: Computing and Applying Trust in Web-based Social Networks. PhD thesis, College Park, MD, USA (2005)
12. Guha, R., Kumar, R., Raghavan, P., Tomkins, A.: Propagation of Trust and Distrust. In: International World Wide Web Conference (2004)
13. Hartig, O.: Provenance Information in the Web of Data. In: LDOW 2009, Madrid, Spain (April 2009)
14. Josang, A., Ismail, R., Boyd, C.: A survey of trust and reputation systems for online service provision. Decision Support Systems 43(2), 618–644 (2007)
15. Kagal, L., Finin, T., Joshi, A.: A Policy Based Approach to Security for the Semantic Web. In: Fensel, D., Sycara, K., Mylopoulos, J. (eds.) ISWC 2003. LNCS, vol. 2870, pp. 402–418. Springer, Heidelberg (2003)
16. Kamvar, S.D., Schlosser, M.T., Garcia-Molina, H.: The Eigentrust algorithm for reputation management in P2P networks. In: Proceedings of the 12th International Conference on World Wide Web, WWW 2003, pp. 640–651. ACM, New York (2003)
17. Knap, T.: Trust in QA Social Networks. Technical Report (2011), http://www.ksi.mff.cuni.cz/~knap/wqa/Trust.pdf
18. Knap, T., Freitas, A., Mlynkova, I.: Web Quality Assessment Model. Technical Report (2011), http://www.ksi.mff.cuni.cz/~knap/wqa/tr201102.pdf
19. Knap, T., Mlýynková, I.: Towards Topic-Based Trust in Social Networks. In: Yu, Z., Liscano, R., Chen, G., Zhang, D., Zhou, X. (eds.) UIC 2010. LNCS, vol. 6406, pp. 635–649. Springer, Heidelberg (2010), http://www.ksi.mff.cuni.cz/~knap/wqam/tt10.pdf
20. Lawrence, K., Kaler, C.: WS-Trust Specification. Technical report (2007)
21. Levien, R.: Attack-Resistant Trust Metrics, pp. 121–132 (2009)
22. Marsh, S.: Formalising Trust as a Computational Concept (1994)

23. Harrison Mcknight, D., Chervany, N.L.: The Meanings of Trust. Technical report, University of Minnesota, Carlson School of Management (1996)
24. Milgram, S.: The Small World Problem. Psychology Today 1, 61 (1967)
25. Moreau, L.: The Foundations for Provenance on the Web. Foundations and Trends in Web Science (November 2009)
26. Moses, T.: Extensible Access Control Markup Language Version 2.0. Technical report (2005)
27. Naumann, F., Rolker, C.: Assessment Methods for Information Quality Criteria. In: Proceedings of the International Conference on Information Quality, pp. 148–162 (2000)
28. Newman, M.E.J.: Models of the Small World. J. Stat. Phys., 819–841 (2000)
29. Richardson, M., Agrawal, R., Domingos, P.: Trust Management for the Semantic Web. In: Fensel, D., Sycara, K., Mylopoulos, J. (eds.) ISWC 2003. LNCS, vol. 2870, pp. 351–368. Springer, Heidelberg (2003)
30. Walter, F., Battiston, S., Schweitzer, F.: A model of a trust-based recommendation system on a social network. Autonomous Agents and Multi-Agent Systems 16(1), 57–74 (2008)
31. Zhang, J., Ackerman, M.S., Adamic, L.: Expertise networks in online communities: structure and algorithms. In: WWW 2007: Proceedings of the 16th International Conference on World Wide Web, pp. 221–230. ACM, NewYork (2007)
32. Ziegler, C.-N., Lausen, G.: Propagation Models for Trust and Distrust in Social Networks. Information Systems Frontiers 7(4-5), 337–358 (2005)

Context-Aware Service Composition

Ichiro Satoh

National Institute of Informatics
2-1-2 Hitotsubashi, Chiyoda-ku, Tokyo 101-8430, Japan
ichiro@nii.ac.jp

Abstract. This paper presents a framework for providing context-aware services. It supports the separation of services and location, so that application-specific services can be defined independently of any location information. It also provides a mechanism for loosely and dynamically binding the locations of users and physical entities and services for supporting the users and entities. These are useful in the development of software for context-aware services in ambient computing environments. We describes the design and implementation of the framework and two practical applications.

1 Introduction

In recent years, the vision of ambient computing has produced considerable research efforts in corporated with sensing technologies, including computer vision. Computing and sensing devices are already present in almost every room of a modern building or house and in many of the public facilities of cities. Context-aware services are one of the most typical applications of ambient computing. They are provided for users with services according to their context, e.g., users, locations, and time. For example, location-aware services depend on particular locations, but software for defining such software should be independent of the locations.

Context-aware services depend on particular context, but software for context-aware services tend to depend on such context. The former is reasonable but the latter often makes a serious problem to reuse it in other services. For example, software for location-aware annotation services about such exhibits in a museum need to be changed and modified, when the exhibits are changed or replaced at other locations. Furthermore, such software has another dependency problem. It depends on the underlying systems, e.g., sensing systems, operating systems, and middleware systems. Therefore, software for a context-aware system may not available in other systems. To solve this problem, several researchers introduce the notions of world models (or location models) to abstract away differences between sensing systems.

We need a mechanism for loosely coupling between software for context-aware services and contexts. This paper proposes a framework for maintaining spatial relationships between users and their services to offer a variety of location-aware services. The idea behind this framework is to loosely link between users and software for defining services and to dynamically deploy the software at computers when users move from location to location. Therefore, software for services are independent of any location-dependent aspects.

C.-H. Hsu et al. (Eds.): UIC 2011, LNCS 6905, pp. 267–279, 2011.

2 Design Principles

This section outlines our approach. To enable services that enhance user interaction with his/her current environment, we need to enrich his/her physical surrounding, e.g., shopping malls and trade fares, with dedicated computing resources that enable service to be provided. One example scenario is a shopping mall that offers ambient services to customers, enabling them to navigate through the mall and find certain products quickly. Users moving from shop to shop should have their services deployed and executed at stationary terminals close to them to support them. Annotation services on appliances, e.g., electric lights, may be provided in shops. Such services depend on context. For example, they present digital signage for sales promotions while their target appliances are displayed on shelves. For example, shops frequently replace and relocate their products inside them. The services need to follow the movement of their targets. Annotation services in appliances are needed not only at shops to explain what the appliances are but at users' homes to explain how they are to be used. Furthermore, such annotation services may depend on users. Some may want audio annotations but others may want visual annotations.

Computing devices in ambient computing environments may only have limited resources, such as restricted levels of CPU power and amounts of memory. They cannot support all the services that may be needed. We therefore have to deploy software that can define services at computers only while those services are needed. The deployment of services at computers does not only depend on the requirements of the services. For example, if a user has a portable computer, his/her services should be provided from the portable computer. Otherwise, such services should be provided from stationary computers close to him/her, even when the services may be initially designed to run on portable computers. Our framework enables us to define application-specific services independently of any location information and the deployment policy of services.

We introduce three notions to support the above example scenarios. (Fig. 1)

- The *virtual-counterpart* agent is a digital representation of a user, physical entity, or computing device. When its target moves to another location, it is automatically deployed at a computer close to the current location of the target by using location-sensing systems.
- The *service-provider* agent is a programmable entity for defining application-specific services and it can be deployed at computers, even which they are running.
- The *spatial-connector* is a relationship between the locations of at least one virtual-counterpart and service-providers. When the former moves to another location, the latter is migrated to an appropriate computer according to its policy.

The virtual-counterpart is responsible for abstracting away differences between the underlying location sensing systems. Each service-provider can explicitly specify at most one spatial connector. The current implementation provides two types of spatial-connectors, as shown in Fig. 1. The first enables a service-provider agent to follow at most one virtual-counterpart and the second enables a service-provider agent to migrate to the source location of at most one virtual-counterpart. The third relationship above is our key idea. It enables service-provider agents to specify their placement outside them. Each connector is declared a relocation between its target service-provider agent

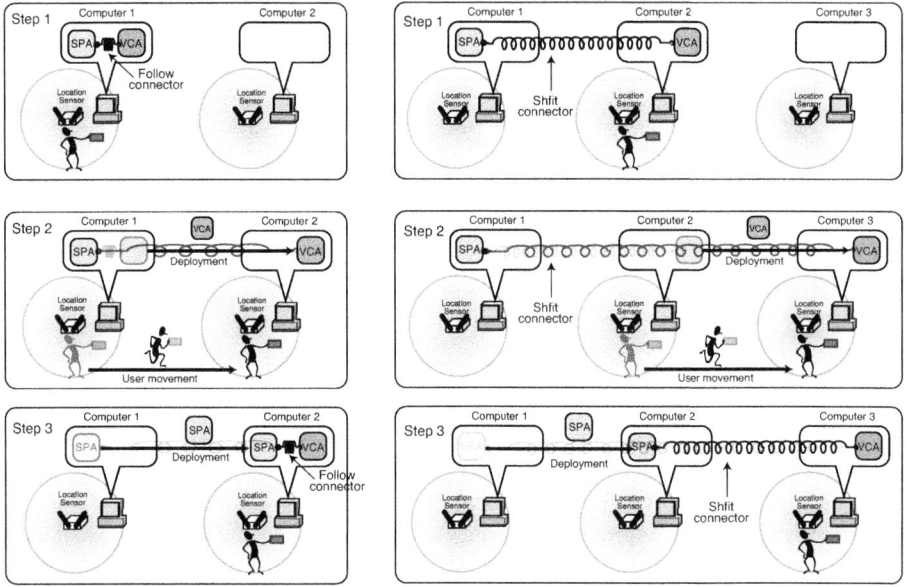

VCA: Virtual-Counterpart Agent   SPA: Service-Provider Agent

Fig. 1. Spatial-coupling between virtual-counterparts and services

and virtual-counterpart agent. The current implementation provides the following built-in connectors.

- If a service-provider agent declares a *follow* connector for at most one virtual-counterpart agent, when the latter migrates to a computer in another location, the former migrates to the same or another computer in the latter's destination location.
- If a service-provider agent declares a *shift* connector for at most one virtual-counterpart agent, when the latter migrates to a computer in another location, the former migrates to the latter's source or another computer in the latter's source location.

These can be dynamically bound between virtual-counterparts and service-providers. By using these relations, service-provider agents are independent of their locations and their deployment policies. When a user is in front of a product, his/her virtual-counterpart agent is deployed at a computer close to his/her current location by using a location-sensing system. Service-provider agents that declare follow policies for the virtual-counterpart agent are deployed at the computer. That is, our service-provider agents should accompany their users and annotate exhibits in front of them in the real-world. Nevertheless, users and service-provider agents are loosely coupled, because the agents are dynamically linked to the virtual-counterpart agents corresponding to the users.

3 Implementation

Our user/location-aware system to assist users is managed in a non-centralized manner. It consists of four subsystems: 1) location-aware directory servers, called LDSs,

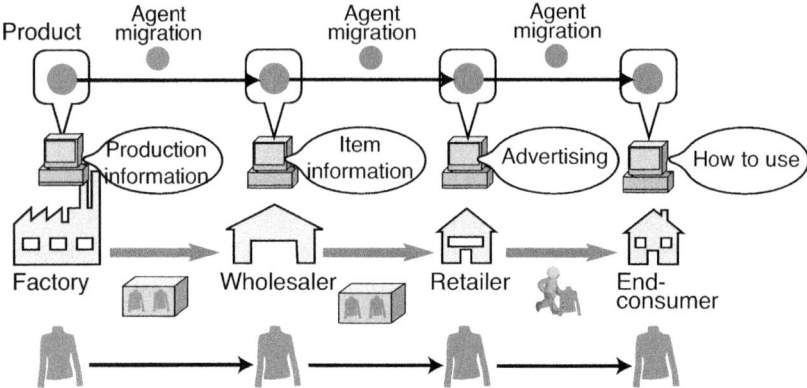

Fig. 2. Forwarding agents to digital signage when user moves

2) agent runtime systems, 3) virtual-counterpart agents, and 4) service-provider agents. The first is responsible for reflecting changes in the real world and the locations of users when services are deployed at appropriate computers. The second runs on stationary computers located at specified spots close to physical entities. It can execute service-provider agents, where we have assumed that the computers are located at specified spots in public spaces and are equipped with user-interface devices, e.g., display screens and loudspeakers. The third and fourth are implemented as mobile agents. Each mobile agent is a self-contained autonomous programming entity. Application-specific services are encapsulated within the fourth, so that the first, second, and third are independent of any application specific services. Figure 2 shows that, when a product is carried by a customer, a virtual-counterpart agent bound to the product is migrated from computer to computer.

Our system can consist of multiple LDSs, which are individually connected to other servers in a peer-to-peer manner. Each LDS only maintains up-to-date information on partial contextual information instead of on tags in the whole space. All LDSs and runtime systems periodically multicast their network addresses to other LDSs and runtime systems through UDP-multicasting. Therefore, when a new LDS or runtime system is dynamically added to or removed from the whole system, other systems are aware of changes in their network domains.

3.1 Location Management System

Each LDS is responsible for monitoring location-sensing systems and spatially binding more than one virtual-counterpart agent to each user or physical entity (Fig. 3). It maintains two databases. The first stores information about all the runtime systems and the second stores all the agents attached to users or physical entities. It can exchange this information with other LDSs in a peer-to-peer manner. When some LDSs and runtime systems are inactive, it automatically removes the inactive LDSs or inactive runtime systems from a set of its neighboring LDSs and runtime systems.

Tracking systems can be classified into two types: proximity and lateration. The first approach detects the presence of objects within known spots or close to known points,

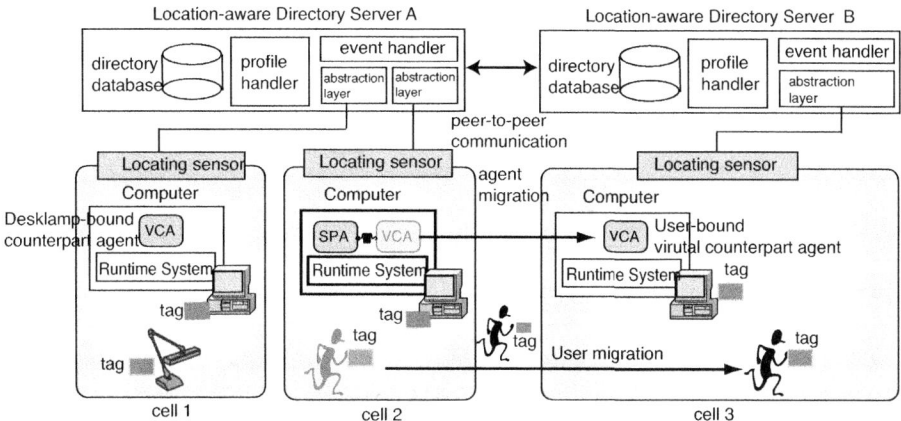

When a user (his/her tag) moves to another cell, location-aware directory serviers deploy his/her
virtual counterpart agents at a computer within the destination cell.

Fig. 3. Location-aware directory server

and the second estimates the positions of objects from multiple measurements of the distance between known points. The current implementation assumes that have provided users or physical entities with tags. These tags are small RF transmitters that periodically broadcast beacons, including the identifiers of the tags, to receivers located in exhibition spaces. The receivers locate the presence or positions of the tags. To abstract away differences between the underlying location-sensing systems, the LDSs map geometric information measured by the sensing systems to specified areas, called *spots*, where the exhibits and the computers that play the annotations are located.

3.2 Agent Runtime System

Each runtime system is responsible for executing and migrating service-provider agents to other runtime systems running on different computers through a TCP channel using mobile-agent technology. It is built on the Java virtual machine (Java VM version 1.5 or later), which conceals differences between the platform architectures of the source and destination computers (Fig. 4). It governs all the agents inside it and maintains the life-cycle state of each agent. When the life-cycle state of an agent changes, e.g., when it is created, terminates, or migrates to another runtime system, its current runtime system issues specific events to the agent. Some navigation or annotation content, e.g., audio-annotation, should be played without any interruptions.

   When an agent is transferred over the network, not only the code of the agent but also its state is transformed into a bitstream by using Java's object serialization package and then the bit stream is transferred to the destination. Since the package does not support the capturing of stack frames of threads, when an agent is deployed at another computer, its runtime system propagates certain events to instruct it to stop its active threads. The runtime system on the receiving side receives and unmarshals the bit stream. Arriving agents may explicitly have to acquire various resources, e.g., video and sound, or release previously acquired resources.

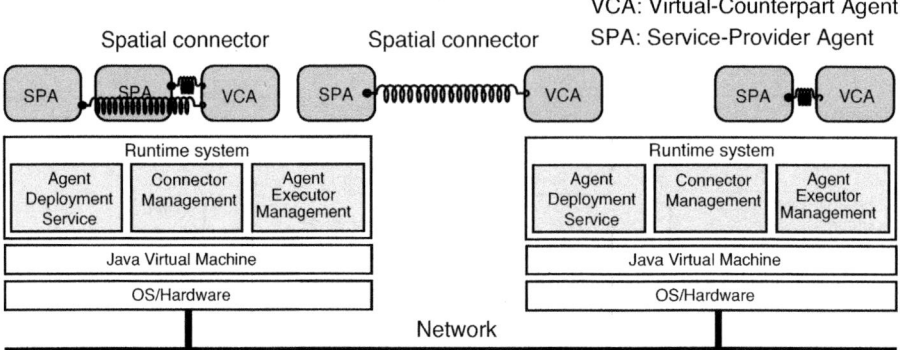

Runtime systems execute SPAs and deploys SPAs at computers according to spatial connections, when VCA moves to other computers by location-aware servers.

Fig. 4. Runtime systems

3.3 Virtual-Counterpart Agent

Each virtual-counterpart agent is attached to at most one user. Each virtual-counterpart agent keeps the identifier of its target or RFID tag attached to the target. It is automatically deployed at a computer in a cell that contains its target by using the underlying location sensing systems.

3.4 Service-Provider Agent

Each service-provider agent in the current implementation is a collection of Java objects in the standard JAR file format and can migrate from computer to computer and duplicate itself by using mobile agent technology.[1] Each agent must be an instance of a subclass of the `MobileAgent` class.

```
class MAgent extends MobileAgent implements Serializable {
  void go(URL url) throws NoSuchHostException { ... }
  void duplicate() throws IllegalAccessException { ... }
  setConnector(CompomnetProfile cref,
    MigrationConnector mconnector) { ... }
  setTTL(int lifespan) { ... }
  void setAgentProfile(AgentProfile cpf) { ... }
  boolean isConformableHost(HostProfile hfs) { ... }
  void send(URL url, AgentID id, Message msg)
    throws NoSuchHostException, NoSuchAgentException, ... { ... }
  Object call(URL url, AgentID id,
    Message msg) throws NoSuchHostException,
      NoSuchAgentException, ... { ... }
  ....
}
```

---

[1] JavaBeans can easily be translated into agents in this platform.

Each agent can execute `go(URL url)` to move to the destination specified as a `url` by its current platform, and `duplicate()` creates a copy of the agent, including its code and instance variables. The `setTTL()` specifies the life span, called the time-to-live (TTL), of the agent. The lifespan decrements TTL over time. When the TTL of an agent reaches zero, the agent automatically removes itself. Each agent can explicitly declare its own spatial connector inside it, although we basically assume a connector is assigned to each service-provider agent. We also provides containers to use JavaBeans or OSGi components as service providers.

Each agent can specify a requirement that its destination host must satisfy by invoking `setAgentProfile()`, with the requirement specified as `cpf`, where it is defined in Composite Capability/Preference Profiles (CC/PP) form [17], which describes the capabilities of the agent host and the agents' requirements. The class has a service method called `isConformableHost()`, which the agent uses to determine whether the capabilities of the agent host specified as an instance of the `HostProfile` class satisfy it requirements. Runtime systems transform the profiles into their corresponding LISP-like expressions and then evaluate them by using a LISP-based interpreter. When an agent migrates to the destination according to its policy, if the destination cannot satisfy the requirements of the agent, the runtime system recommends candidates that are hosts in the same network domain to the agent. If an agent declares repulsive policies in addition to a gravitational policy, the runtime system detects the candidates using the latter's policy and then recommends final candidates to the agent using the former policy, assuming that the agent is in each of the detected candidates.

3.5 Spatial Connector

The framework enables users to explicitly assign a spatial connector to each service-provider agent through its management GUI, even while the agent is running.

Each spatial connector is activated when its target virtual-counter agent migrates to a computer in another cell due to the movement of the agent's target in the physical world. We first explain how to deploy virtual-counterpart agents according to changes in the real world. When the underlying sensing system detects the presence (or absence) of a tag in a spot, the LDS that manages the system attempts to query the locations of the virtual-counterpart agent tied to the tag from its database. If the database does not contain any information about the identifier of the tag, it multicasts a query message that contains the identity of the new tag to other LDSs through UDP multicasting. It then waits for reply messages from the other LDSs. Next, if the LDS knows the location of the agent tied to the newly visiting tag, it deploys the agent at a computer close to the spot that contains the tag.

Next, we will explain how to deploy service-provider agents with spatial connectors according to the deployment of the virtual counterpart agents that are specified in the connectors as their targets. The deployment of each service-provider agent is specified in its connector and is managed by runtime systems without any centralized management system. Each runtime system periodically advertises its address to the others through UDP multicasting, and these runtime systems then return their addresses and capabilities to the runtime system through a TCP channel.[2] The procedure involves four steps. 1) When a virtual-counterpart agent migrates to another runtime system (in a different cell), 2) The destination sends a query message to the source of the visiting virtual-counterpart agent. 3) The source multicasts a query message within current or neighboring sub-networks. If a runtime system has a service-provider agent whose connector specifies the visiting virtual-counterpart agent, it sends the destination information about itself and its neighboring runtime systems. 4) The destination next instructs the service-provider agent to migrate to one of the candidate destinations recommended by the target, because this platform treats every agent as an autonomous entity.

4   Current Status

A prototype implementation of this framework was constructed with Sun's Java Developer Kit, version 1.5 or later version. Although the current implementation was not constructed for performance, we evaluated the migration of a service-provider agent based on spatial connectors. When an agent declares a *follow* or *shift* connector for a virtual-counterpart agent, the cost of migrating the former to the destination or the source of the latter after the latter has begun to migrate is 89 ms or 88 ms, where three computers over a TCP connection is 32 ms.[3] This experiment was done with three computers (Intel Core Duo-1.8 GHz with MacOS X 10.6 and Java Development Kit ver.6) connected through a Fast Ethernet network. Migrating agents included the cost of opening a TCP-transmission, marshalling the agents, migrating them from their source computers to their destination computers, unmarshalling them, and verifying security.

Support for location-sensing systems. The current implementation supports two commercial tracking systems. The first is the Spider active RFID tag system, which is a typical example of proximity-based tracking. It provides active RF-tags to users. Each tag has a unique identifier that periodically emits an RF-beacon (every second) that conveys an identifier within a range of 1-20 meters. The second system is the Aeroscout positioning system, which consists of four or more readers located in a room. These readers can measure differences in the arrival timings of WiFi-based RF-pulses emitted from tags and estimate the positions of the tags from multiple measurements of the distance between the readers and tags; these measurement units correspond to about two meters.

Security. To prevent malicious agents from being passed between computers, each runtime system supports a Kerberos-based authentication mechanism for agent migration. It authenticates users without exposing their passwords on the network and generates secret encryption keys that can be selectively shared between parties that are mutually suspicious. Since it can inherit the security mechanisms provided in the Java language environment, the Java VM explicitly restricts agents so that they can only access specified resources to protect computers from malicious agents.

---

[2] We assumed that the agents comprising an application would initially be deployed at runtime systems within a localized space smaller than the domain of a sub-network.

[3] The size of each virtual-counterpart agent was about 8 KB in size.

Queuing mechanism. As there are many customers in shops, we cannot adequately cope with conflicts caused by multiple users. For example, more than two people may simultaneously view and hear at most one annotation provided from a stationary computer in an exhibition space under the impression that the annotation is for them. To solve this problem, we support two approaches. The first is to use the visual representation of agents, e.g. characters, as a method of assisting customers to identify who the annotation is for. The second is to provide each agent runtime system with a queuing mechanism for exclusively executing agents for multiple simultaneous users. When two users enter the same spot, the LDS sends two notification messages to the runtime system in the spot in the order in which they entered. The runtime system can send events to the agents bound to the two users in that order, or it can explicitly send an event to one of the agents. After the first has handled the event, it sends the same event to the second one. The current implementation supports several queuing policies, e.g., LIFO and synchronization among more than two users.

5   Application: Support to Lifecycle Support of Products

We experimented on and evaluated a context-aware annotation service for appliances, e.g., electric lights. This is unique to other existing active content for digital signage because it does not support advertising of its target appliance but assists users with controlling and disposing of the appliance. We attached an RFID tag to an electric light and provided a virtual-counterpart agent and connected the agent and one of the four service-provider agents for the target by using spatial connectors according the locations of the light, e.g., a warehouse, store, and home. These service-provider agents supported the lifecycle of the light from shipment, showcasing, assembly, usage, and disposal.

In Warehouse. While the light was in the warehouse, its virtual-counterpart agent was automatically deployed at a portable terminal close to the light. Two kinds of service-provider agents were provided for the experiment. The first was attached to the virtual-counterpart agent through the *follow* connector. This notified a server in the warehouse of its specification, e.g., its product number, serial number, and date of manufacture, size, weight, serial number, the date of manufacture. The second was attached to the virtual-counterpart agent through the *shift* connector and ordered more lights.

In Store. While the light was being showcased in a store, we assumed that it had two service-provider agents The first declared the *follow* connector and was deployed at a computer close to its target object so that it displayed advertising content to attract purchases by customers who visited the store. Figures 5 a) and b) have two images maintained in the agent that display the price, product number, and manufacture's name on the current computer. The second declared the *shift* connector. When the light was sold, it notified the warehouse server that the light was out of stock.

In House. When the light was bought and transferred to buyer's house, a service-provider agent, which was attached to the virtual-counterpart agent through the *follow*

Fig. 5. Digital signage for supporting appliance

connector, migrated to a computer in the house and provided instructions on how it should be assembled. Figure 5 c) has the active content for advice on assembly. The agent also advised how it was to be used as shown in Fig. 5 d). When it was disposed of, the agent presented its active content to give advice on disposal. Figure 5 e) illustrates how the appliance was to be disposed of.

These service-provider agents could be defined independently of any locations. This is useful to separate services in developing application-specific services.

We can provide another service-provider agent in buyers' houses that controls appliances, which may not have any network interfaces. The agent allows us to use a PDA to remotely control nearby lights. Place-bound controller agents, which can communicate with X10-base servers to switch lights on or off, are attached to places with room lights in this system. Each user has a tagged PDA, which supports the agent host with WindowsCE and a wireless LAN interface. When a user with a PDA visits a cell that contains a light, the framework moves a controller agent to the agent host of the visiting PDA. The agent, now running on the PDA, displays a graphical user interface to control the light. When the user leaves that location, the agent automatically closes its user interface and returns to its runtime system.

6   Related Work

There have been numerous projects on context-aware services. For example, Cambridge University's Sentient Computing project [6] provided a platform for location-aware applications using infrared-based or ultrasonic-based locating systems in a building. Microsoft's EasyLiving project [3] enabled services running on different computers to be combined dynamically according to contextural changes in the real world. Most of these selected and customized services according to contexts, e.g., locations, users, and time and provided them from mobile or stationary computers. There has been a gap between between low-level sensing systems and higher-level application-specific services. However, unfortunately most of these have been inherently designed for particular location sensing systems or application-specific services. To bridge the gap, several researchers have proposed world models or location models, e.g., NEXUS [1], Cooltown [8], RAUM [2] Sentient Computing [6], EasyLiving [3], and Virtual Counterpart [12].

Although such models could have abstracted away differences between location sensing systems, context-aware services themselves might often be defined to be dependent on their underlying models and target locations. Existing location models can be classified into two types: physical-location and symbolic-location [2,11]. The former represents the position of people and objects as geometric information. A few outdoor-applications like moving-map navigation can easily be constructed on such physical-location models. Most emerging applications, on the other hand, require a more symbolic notion: place. Generically, place is the human-readable labeling of positions. A more rigorous definition is an evolving set of both communal and personal labels for potentially overlapping geometric volumes, e.g., the names of rooms and buildings. An object contained in a volume is reported to be in that place. Most location-aware services explicitly or implicitly assume their underlying models, e.g., absolute geometric information instead of relational and tiled places instead of overlapping places. The definitions of context-aware services may contain information about their target places. Such services cannot be reused for other places.

Our spatial connector may be similar to the dynamic layout of distributed applications in the FarGo system [7]. However, FarGo only supports just a distributed system without any notion of location in the physical world. FarGo's policies aim at allowing an agent to control others, whereas our connectors aim at allowing an agent to describe its own individual migration. FarGo's policies may conflict when two agents can declare different relocation policies for a single agent. However, our platform is free of any conflict because each agent can only declare a policy to relocate itself instead of other agents.

This paper presents two context-aware services for shopping as applications of our framework. Several projects have explored context-aware services for shopping [5]. The *Shopper's Eye* [4] proposed a location-aware service with wirelessly enabled portable terminals, e.g., PDAs and smart phones. As a shopper travels about, his or her personal terminal transmits messages, which include information about his or her location, shopping goals, preferences, and related purchase history. The MyGROCER project [9] provided smart shopping carts, which could automatically scan supermarket products while simultaneously providing valuable information to the customer through a display device, thus creating a fully interactive shopping trip.

We proposed several mobile agent frameworks for building context-aware services [14,15]. However, the previous frameworks could not distinguish between virtual-counterparts and service-providers and had no notion of spatial connectors. We introduced the notion of deployment policy as a relationship between the computers of two agents [13]. The previous work aimed at building test-bed bio-inspired and self-organized approaches on distributed systems and had no notion of locations in the physical world unlike the framework presented in this paper.

7   Conclusion

We designed and implemented a framework for providing context-aware services in private/public spaces, e.g., home and office. It had two novel notions. The first was the separation of services and location, so that we could define application-specific services independently of any location information. The second was a mechanism for loosely and dynamically binding the locations of users and physical entities and services for supporting the users and entities. It enabled us to dynamically modify where and when services should be activated. The two examples presented in this paper were not expressively large-scale spaces and consequently did not have as many users as cities. Nevertheless, our final goal is a city-wide ambient computing environment, which will provide a variety of services to massive numbers of users from numerous heterogenous computers. Therefore, our system itself is designed for a city-wide context-aware system.[4] In fact, Since the framework had no centralized management system, we believe that it was useful in city-wide context-aware services.

Acknowledgments. This research was supported in part by a grant from the Promotion program for Reducing global Environmental loaD through ICT innovation (PREDICT) made by the Ministry of Internal Affairs and Communications in Japan.

References

1. Bauer, M., Becker, C., Rothermel, K.: Location Mmodels from the Perspective of Context-Aware Applications and Mobile Ad Hoc Networks. Personal and Ubiquitous Computing 6(5-6), 322–328 (2002)
2. Beigl, M., Zimmer, T., Decker, C.: A Location Model for Communicating and Processing of Context. Personal and Ubiquitous Computing 6(5-6), 341–357 (2002)
3. Brumitt, B.L., Meyers, B., Krumm, J., Kern, A., Shafer, S.: EasyLiving: Technologies for Intelligent Environments. In: Proceedings of International Symposium on Handheld and Ubiquitous Computing, pp. 12–27 (2000)
4. Fano, A.: Shopper's eye: using location-based filtering for a shopping agent in the physical world. In: Proceedings of International Conference on Autonomous Agents, pp. 416–421. ACM Press, New York (1998)
5. Galanxhe-Janaqi, H., Nah, F.F.-H.: U-commerce: emerging trends and research issues. Industrial Management and Data Systems 104(9), 744–755 (2004)
6. Harter, A., Hopper, A., Steggeles, P., Ward, A., Webster, P.: The Anatomy of a Context-Aware Application. In: Proceedings of Conference on Mobile Computing and Networking (MOBICOM 1999), pp. 59–68. ACM Press, New York (1999)
7. Holder, O., Ben-Shaul, I., Gazit, H.: System Support for Dynamic Layout of Distributed Applications. In: Proceedings of International Conference on Distributed Computing Systems (ICDCS 1999), pp. 403–411. IEEE Computer Society, Los Alamitos (1999)
8. Kindberg, T., et al.: People, Places, Things: Web Presence for the Real World, Technical Report HPL-2000-16, Internet and Mobile Systems Laboratory, HP Laboratories (2000)
9. Kourouthanassis, P., Roussos, G.: Developing Consumer-Friendly Pervasive Retail Systems. IEEE Pervasive Computing 2(2), 32–39 (2003)
10. Kruppa, M., Krüger, A.: Performing Physical Object References with Migrating Virtual Characters. In: Maybury, M., Stock, O., Wahlster, W. (eds.) INTETAIN 2005. LNCS (LNAI), vol. 3814, pp. 64–73. Springer, Heidelberg (2005)

---

[4] It is almost impossible to experiment academic systems in city-wide spaces without any pre-evaluation in small-spaces.

11. Leonhardt, U., Magee, J.: Towards a General Location Service for Mobile Environments. In: Proceedings of IEEE Workshop on Services in Distributed and Networked Environments, pp. 43–50. IEEE Computer Society, Los Alamitos (1996)

12. Romer, K., Schoch, T., Mattern, F., Dubendorfer, T.: Smart Identification Frameworks for Ubiquitous Computing Applications. In: IEEE International Conference on Pervasive Computing and Communications (PerCom 2003), pp. 253–262. IEEE Computer Society, Los Alamitos (2003)

13. Satoh, I.: Test-bed Platform for Bio-inspired Distributed Systems. In: Proceesings of 3rd International Conference on Bio-Inspired Models of Network Information, and Computing Systems (November 2008)

14. Satoh, I.: An Agent-Based Framework for Context-Aware Digital Signage. In: Augusto, J.C., Corchado, J.M., Novais, P., Analide, C. (eds.) ISAmI 2010. AISC, vol. 72, pp. 105–112. Springer, Heidelberg (2010)

15. Satoh, I.: Context-aware Media Agent for Public Spaces. In: Proceedings of European Conference on Artificial Intelligence (ECAI 2010), pp. 407–412. AAAI Press, Menlo Park (2010)

16. Tewari, G., Youll, J., Maes, P.: Personalized location-based brokering using an agent-based intermediary architecture. Decision Support Systems 34(2), 127–137 (2003)

17. World Wide Web Consortium (W3C), Composite Capability/Preference Profiles, CC/PP (1999), http://www.w3.org/TR/NOTE-CCPP

Implementation of a Green Power Management Algorithm for Virtual Machines on Cloud Computing[*]

Chao-Tung Yang[1], Kuan-Chieh Wang[1], Hsiang-Yao Cheng[1],
Cheng-Ta Kuo[1], and Ching-Hsien Hsu[2,**]

[1] High-Performance Computing Laboratory, Department of Computer Science
Tunghai University, Taichung, Taiwan 40704, R.O.C.
ctyang@thu.edu.tw, {acanwang,hsycheng,superada0923}@gmail.com
[2] Department of Computer Science and Information Engineering
Chung Hua University, Hsinchu, Taiwan 300, R.O.C.
chh@chu.edu.tw

Abstract. With the development of electronic of government and business, the implementation of these services are increasing the demand for servers, each year a considerable number of the procurement server and out of the server are too old to provide better service. However, due to the speed of the server out of nowhere near the rate of increase, the continued expansion of the server, on behalf of our need to prepare more space, power, air conditioning, network, human and other infrastructure. Derived from these costs, long years, the often less than the purchase price of the server. And the provision of these services is actually quite energy-intensive, especially when the server is running at low utilization, the making idle resources, waste, which is caused by the energy efficiency of data centers the main reason for the low. Even in a very low load, such as 10% CPU utilization, the total power consumption is more than 50% in the peak. Similarly, if the disk, network, or any such resource is the bottleneck, it will increase the waste of other resources. The "Green" became a hot key word recently. And we aimed the topic and proposed power management approach with virtualization technology.

Keywords: Green Cloud Computing, OpenNebula, Virtualization, Green Power Management (GPM).

1 Introduction

Cloud is actually refers to network, the name came from engineers in the schematic drawing, often represented by a cloud network. Therefore cloud services are the network services. Ones can be presented as a layered architecture that can be viewed as a collection of IT services referred to Software-as-a-Service (SaaS), Platform-as-a-Service (PaaS), and Infrastructure-as-a-Service (IaaS). Among these type SaaS allows users to run applications remotely from the cloud. PaaS includes operating systems with a custom

---

[*] This work is supported in part by the National Science Council, Taiwan R.O.C., under grants no. NSC 100-2218-E-029-004, NSC 99-2218-E-029-001, and NSC 99-3113-S-029-002.

[**] Corresponding author.

C.-H. Hsu et al. (Eds.): UIC 2011, LNCS 6905, pp. 280–294, 2011.

software stack for given application. IaaS refers to computing resources as a service, includes a virtualized computer that is dividing hard ware resources to unit, means virtualization machine that is the key to enable elastic computing delivering an infrastructure service.

Virtual machines are separated into two major categories, based on their use and degree of correspondence to any real machine. A system virtual machine provides a complete system platform which supports the execution of a complete operating system (OS). In contrast, a process virtual machine is designed to run a single program, which means that it supports a single process. An essential characteristic of a virtual machine is that the software running inside is limited to the resources and abstractions provided by the virtual machine—it cannot break out of its virtual world.

Cloud and Virtualization to accelerate not only accelerate the data center building, but also brings the possibility of green energy. When the data center application based on a generic virtual machine, allowing the application workload combined in a smaller number of virtual machines, which can help more efficient use of resources. If workload size could allocated in different resource depend time and space, it could improve the energy efficiency and avoiding waste resource [29].

In this paper, the Green Power Management (GPM) for loading balance approach was proposed by our thesis and in this thesis it including three main phrases: (1) The Virtualization management (2) The Dynamic Resource Allocation mechanism (3) The Green Power Management approach. This paper is organized as follows. In Section 2, we introduce the background and related works, section 3 describes the system design and more detail of entire system, in section 4, we show up the experiment and results, and finally section 5 outlines the main conclusion and the future work.

2 Background and Related Work

2.1 Energy Aware Consolidation

Energy consumption in hosting Internet services is becoming a pressing issue as these services scale up. Dynamic server provisioning techniques are effective in turning off unnecessary servers to save energy. Such techniques, mostly studied for request-response services, face challenges in the context of connection servers that host a large number of long-lived TCP connections. In this paper, we show that our algorithms can save a significant amount of energy without sacrificing user experiences. Consolidation of applications in cloud computing environments presents a significant opportunity for energy optimization. The goal of energy aware consolidation is to keep servers well utilized such that the idle power costs are efficiently amortized but without taking an energy penalty due to internal contentions.

There are several different issues; first of all, the merger must be carefully considered combination of different workload on a common physical suitability of the host. Therefore, understanding the nature of the work to determine which components of critical workloads can be packaged together. Second, there is a performance and energy optimization. This is because it can cause performance degradation, leading to increased execution time, which would eat up the energy derived from the lower idle energy savings. In addition, there are many problems affecting the integration, including the behavior of servers and workloads, the performance from the implementation of change and the optimal combination of different applications that can accept the optimal solution does not interrupt the work load to keep track of changes, which become important the integration of energy efficiency [5].

2.2 Virtualization

Virtualization is simply the logical separation of the request for some service from the physical resources that actually provide that service. In practical terms, virtualization provides the ability to run applications, operating systems, or system services in a logically distinct system environment that is independent of a specific physical computer system. Obviously, all of these have to be running on a certain computer system at any given time, but virtualization provides a level of logical abstraction that liberates applications, system services, and even the operating system that supports them from being tied to a specific piece of hardware. Virtualization, focusing on logical operating environments rather than physical ones, makes applications, services, and instances of an operating system portable across different physical computer systems. Virtualization can execute applications under many operating systems, manage IT more efficiently, and allot resources of computing with other computers.[2]

It's not a new technique, IBM had implemented on 360/67 and 370 on 60, 70 eras. Virtualization gets hardware to imitate much hardware via Virtual Machine Monitor, and each one of virtual machines can be seemed as a complete individual unit. For a virtual machine, there are memories, CPUs, unique complete hardware equipment, etc... It can run any operating systems, called Guest Os, and do not affect other virtual machines.

In general, most virtualization strategies fall into one of two major categories:

Full virtualization (also called *native virtualization*) is similar to emulation. As in emulation, unmodified operating systems and applications run inside a virtual machine. Full virtualization differs from emulation in that operating systems and applications are designed to run on the same architecture as the underlying physical machine. This allows a full virtualization system to run many instructions directly on the raw hardware. The hypervisor in this case monitors access to the underlying hardware and gives each guest operating system the illusion of having its own copy. It no longer must use software to simulate a different basic architecture as shown in Figure 1.

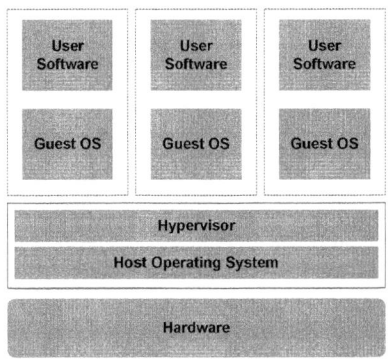

Fig. 1. Full Virtualization

Para-virtualization: In some instances this technique is also referred to as enlightenment. In Para-virtualization, the hypervisor exports a modified version of the underlying physical hardware. The exported virtual machine is of the same architecture, which is not necessarily the case in emulation. Instead, targeted modifications are introduced to make it simpler and faster to support multiple guest operating systems.

For example, the guest operating system might be modified to use a special hyper call application binary interface (ABI) instead of using certain architectural features that would normally be used. This means that only small changes are typically required in the guest operating systems, but any such changes make it difficult to support closed-source operating systems that are distributed in binary form only, such as Microsoft Windows. As in full virtualization, applications are typically still run without modifications.

Para-virtualization, like full virtualization, Para-virtualization also uses a hypervisor, and also uses the term virtual machine to refer to its virtualized operating systems. However, unlike full virtualization, Para-virtualization requires changes to the virtualized operating system. This allows the VM to coordinate with the hypervisor, and reduce the use of the privileged instructions that are typically responsible for the major performance penalties in full virtualization.

The advantage is that Para-virtualized virtual machines typically outperform fully virtualized virtual machines. The disadvantage, however, is the need to modify the Para-virtualized virtual machine or operating system to be hypervisor-aware. The framework of Para-virtualization is shown in Figure 2.

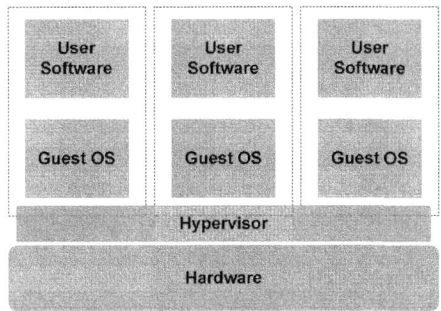

Fig. 2. Para-virtualization

In order to evaluate the viability of the difference between virtualization and non-virtualization, the virtualization software we used in this thesis is Xen. Xen is a virtual machine monitor (hypervisor) that allows you to use one physical computer to run many virtual computers — for example, running a production Web server and a test server on the same physical machine or running Linux and Windows simultaneously. Although not the only virtualization system available, Xen has a combination of features that make it uniquely well suited for many important applications. Xen runs on commodity hardware platforms and is open source. Xen is fast, scalable, and provides server-class features such as live migration.

Xen is chosen to be our system's virtual machine monitor because it provides better efficiency, supports different operating system work simultaneously, and gives each operating system an independent system environment.

This free software is mainly divided into two kinds of simulate types, Para-virtualization and Full virtualization, as mentioned before. Para-virtualization implements virtualization technology, mostly via the modified kernel of Linux.

The characteristic of Para-virtualization is as follows:

- Virtual machine quite like real machine on operating efficacy
- At most supporting more than 32 cores of computer structures
- Supporting x86/32, with PAE technique and x86/64 hardware platform
- Good hardware driver support, almost for any Linux device driver

There are restricts with full virtualization, and it can be only executed when the hardware satisfy these conditions in the following:

- Intel VT technique (Virtualization Technology, Intel-VT)
- AMD SVM technique (Secure Virtual Machine, AMD-SVM or, AMD-V)

Besides, PAE is the Intel Physical Addressing Extensions technique, and this method enables 4 gigabytes physical memory of 32 bits hardware platform to support the platform that is only supported by 64 gigabytes memory. Then Xen could almost execute on all P-II or more high level hardware platform.

As a result of the widespread of virtual machine software in recently years, two best x86 CPU manufacturers Intel/AMD, with efficiency of x86 computers and increasing of compute core of CPU, both have published the new integrated virtualization on CPU, one for Intel Vander pool and another for AMD Pacifica. These technologies also support Xen, and make efficiency step up more than initial stages[3].

VMs can run on a single hardware unit (server consolidation). Therefore, less hardware is needed overall, thus reducing energy wasted for cooling, while the deployed hardware utilization increases. Consolidating hardware and reducing redundancy can achieve energy efficiency. Unused server can be turned off (or hibernated) to save energy. Some hardware gets higher load, which reduces the number of physical servers needed.

2.3 OpenNebula

The OpenNebula is a virtual infrastructure engine that enables the dynamic deployment and re-allocation of virtual machines in a pool of physical resources. The OpenNebula system extends the benefits of virtualization platforms from a single physical resource to a pool of resources, decoupling the server, not only from the physical infrastructure but also from the physical location [4]. The OpenNebula contains one frontend and multiple backend. The front-end provides users with access interfaces and management functions. The back-ends are installed on Xen servers, where Xen hypervisors are started and virtual machines could be backed. Communications between frontend and backend employ SSH. The OpenNebula gives users a single access point to deploy virtual machines on a locally distributed infrastructure.

OpenNebula orchestrates storage, network, virtualization, monitoring, and security technologies to enable the dynamic placement of multi-tier services (groups of interconnected virtual machines) on distributed infrastructures, combining both data center resources and remote cloud resources, according to allocation policies [4]. The architecture of OpenNebula can be described as Figure 3.

Live migration is the movement of a virtual machine from one physical host to another while continuously powered-up. When properly carried out, this process takes place without any noticeable effect from the point of view of the end user. Live migration allows an administrator to take a virtual machine offline for maintenance or upgrading without subjecting the system's users to downtime. When resources are virtualized, additional management of VMs is needed to create, terminate, clone or move VMs from host to host. Migration of VMs can be done off-line (the guest in the VM is powered off) or on-line (live migration of a running VM to another host).

One of the most significant advantages of live migration is the fact that it facilitates proactive maintenance. If an imminent failure is suspected, the potential problem can be resolved before disruption of service occurs. Live migration can also be used for load balancing, in which work is shared among computers in order to optimize the utilization of available CPU resources.

However the OpenNebula lacks a GUI management tool. In previous works, we built virtual machines on OpenNebula and implemented Web-based management tool. Thus, the system administrator can be easy to monitor and manage the entire OpenNebula System on our project. OpenNebula is composed of three main components: (1)the *OpenNebula Core* is a centralized component that manages the life cycle of a VM by performing basic VM operations, and also provides a basic management and monitoring interface for the physical hosts (2) the *Capacity Manager* governs the functionality provided by the OpenNebula core. The capacity manager adjusts the placement of VMs based on a set of pre-defined policies (3) *Virtualizer Access Drivers*. In order to provide an abstraction of the underlying virtualization layer, OpenNebula uses pluggable drivers that expose the basic functionality of the hypervisor [5].

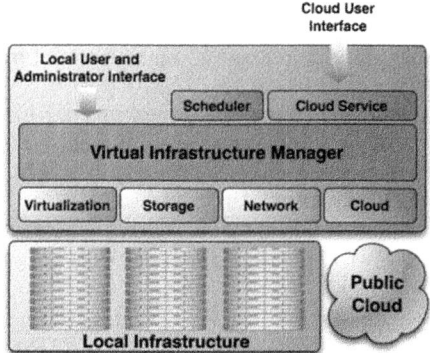

Fig. 3. OpenNebula Architecture

2.4 Dynamic Resource Allocation Algorithm

The Dynamic Resource Allocation (DRA) algorithm [1] focuses on enhancing Hadoop HA architecture problem. However, the purpose of DRA is to reach the best balance between each physical machine. To avoid computing resources centralized on some specify physical machines, how to balance the resources is most important issue. To achieve the maximum efficiency the resource must be evenly distributed.

2.5 Green Power Management

DRA manages the allocation of resources to a set of virtual machines running on a cluster hosts with the goal of fair and effective use of resources. Ones makes virtual machine placement and migration recommendations that serve to enforce resource-based service level agreements, user-specified constraints, and maintain load balance across the cluster even as workloads change.

GPM saves power by dynamically right-sizing cluster capacity according to workload demands. Ones recommend the evacuation and powering of hosts when CPU is lightly utilized. GPM recommends powering hosts back on when either CPU utilization increases appropriately or additional host resources are needed to meet user-specified constraints. GPM executes DRA in a what-if mode to ensure its host power recommendations are consistent with the cluster constraints and objectives being managed by DRA.

Hosts powered of by GPM are marked in standby mode, indicating that they are available to be powered on whenever needed. GPM can be awakened from a powered-of

(ACPI S5) state via either wake-on-LAN (WOL) packets. WOL packets are sent the by front-end host in the cluster, so GPM keeps at least one such host powered on at all times.

2.6 Related Works

Even Internet-based services have been operating for many years; service offerings have recently expanded to include network-based storage and network-based computing. These new services are being offered both to corporate and individual end users. J. Baliga analysis considered both public and private clouds and included energy consumption in switching and transmission as well as data processing and data storage. And after his analysis, he found the number of users per server is the most significant determinant of the energy efficiency of a cloud software service [6].

In power management area, Z. Wu and J. Wang presented a control framework of tree distribution for power management in cloud computing so that power budget can be better managed based on workload or service types [27].

Additionally, R. S. Montero [7] proposes a performance model to characterize these variable capacity (elastic) cluster environments. The model can be used to dynamically dimension the cluster using cloud resources, according to a fixed budget, or to estimate the cost of completing a given workload in a target time.

This paper focuses power management allocation on physical machines with virtual machines. And we will present a green power management mechanism in the following section.

3 System Design

3.1 System Architecture

Besides managing individual VMs' life cycle, we also designed the core to support services deployment; such services typically include a set of interrelated components (for example, a Web server and database back end) requiring several VMs. Thus, we can treat a group of related VMs as a first-class entity in OpenNebula. Besides managing the VMs as a unit, the core also handles the delivery of context information (such as the Web server's IP address, digital certificates, and software licenses) to the VMs. [8]

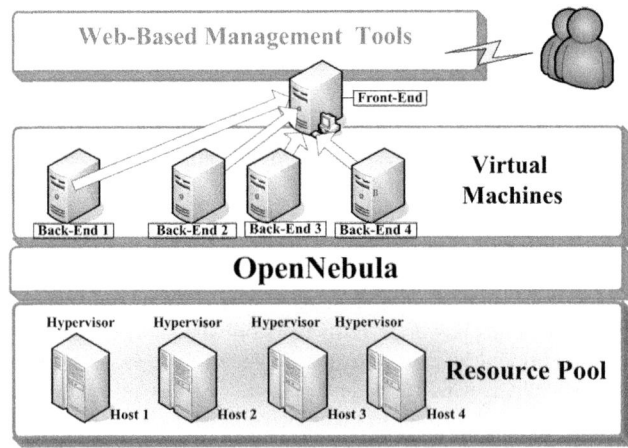

Fig. 4. System Architecture

In Figure 4, it shows the system perspective. According to the previous works we build a cluster system with OpenNebula and also provide a web interface to manage virtual machines and physical machine. Our cluster system was built up with four homogeneous computers; the hardware of these computers is equipped with Intel i7 CPU 2.8 GHz, four gigabytes memory, 500 gigabytes disk, Debian operating system, and the network connected to a gigabit switch.

3.2 Green Power Manager Algorithm

First, DRA defines an ideal ratio. The ones should be equal to the average loading that summary of virtual machine loading divided by the booted hosts. Next, using average loading compare each loading of virtual machine on hosts. Finally, migrate the higher loading of virtual machine to the lower ones. DRA can be regarded as a virtual machine load balance. GPM algorithm archives energy saving which based on the load balance. GPM algorithm is as follow:

$Load_\theta$: Sum of $HOSTi$ loading ratio, there $HOSTi$ is available for allocation, calculation is as follows:

$$Load_\theta = \frac{\sum_{i=1}^{n} HOSTi \; current \; CPU \; usage}{\sum_{i=1}^{n} HOSTi \; total \; CPU \; usage}$$

λ: maximum tolerance ratio of loading.
β: minimum critical ratio of loading.
$HOST_k$: Among of available host for allocation, ones CPU usage is the minimum. calculation is as follows:

$$HOST_k = \min \left(\frac{\sum_{j=0}^{n} HOSTj \; current \; CPU \; usage}{\sum_{j=0}^{n} HOSTj \; total \; CPU \; usage} \right)$$

Suppose there are n virtual machines and $Load_\theta$ is greater than the λ, it shows the loading on physical machine is too much, and then GPM will awake a new a host and apply the DRA to do load balancing. If the $Load_\theta$ is small then β. It expressed resource utilization in most of the time is idle state. So it needs to be turn off the one of the booted hosts. GPM mechanism will decide which one should be shut down. Once target host have determined. The virtual machines on target ones would migrate averagely to the others host, then shut down the target host to attain the purpose of energy saving.

Figure 5 demonstrates GPM process. At the beginning, there are m virtual machines on n hosts (n as booted hosts, N as maximum of n) and resource monitor detects the loading change continuously. There are three circumstances. The first is loading between β (minimum critical ratio of loading) and λ (maximum tolerance ratio of loading), in this state, m VMs do load balance continuously on n hosts. The Second is loading greater then λ and n less than N (if booted hosts equal N, do nothing), then GPM awake a new host to join resource pool, in this state, there are m VMs on $n+1$ host. The third is loading less than β and n greater than 1 (if booted host is only one, do nothing), then the VM on the lowest loading host will be migrated to others, and then turn off the lowest loading host, in this state, there are m virtual machines on n-1 host.

3.3 Management Interface

We design a useful web interface for end users fastest and friendly to Implementation virtualization environment. In Figure 6, it shows the authorization mechanism, through the core of the web-based management tool, it can control and manage physical machine and VM life-cycle.

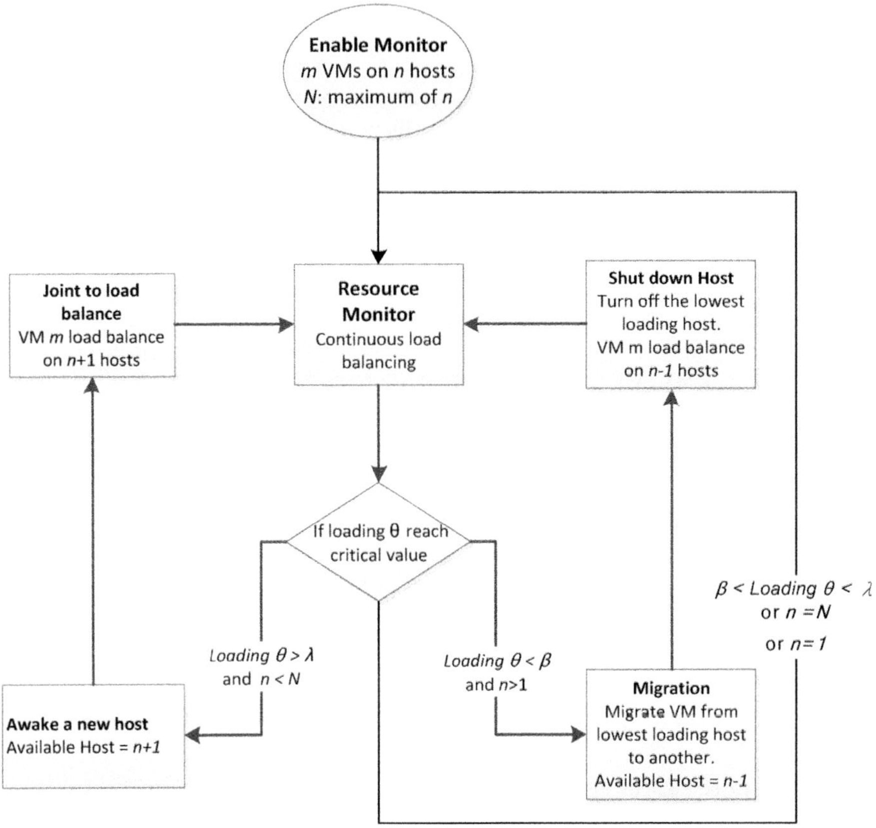

Enable Monitor
m VMs on n hosts
N: maximum of n
Joint to load balance
VM m load balance on n+1 hosts
Resource Monitor
Continuous load balancing
Shut down Host
Turn off the lowest loading host.
VM m load balance on n-1 hosts
If loading θ reach critical value
β < Loading θ < λ
or n = N
or n = 1
Loading θ > λ
and n < N
Loading θ < β
and n>1
Awake a new host
Available Host = n+1
Migration
Migrate VM from lowest loading host to another.
Available Host = n-1

Fig. 5. The Green Power Manager process

Login
User Name
Password
Login
ID NAME CLUSTER RVM TCPU FCPU ACPU TMEM FMEM STAT
0 debian1 default 0 800 790 800 4G 2.9G on
1 debian2 default 0 800 800 800 4G 2.9G on
2 debian3 default 0 800 800 800 4G 2.9G on
3 debian4 default 0 800 800 800 4G 2.9G on
ID USER NAME STAT CPU MEM HOSTNAME TIME IP
vm001 1 1024 140.128.102.192
vm002 1 1024 140.128.102.193
vm003 1 1024 140.128.102.194

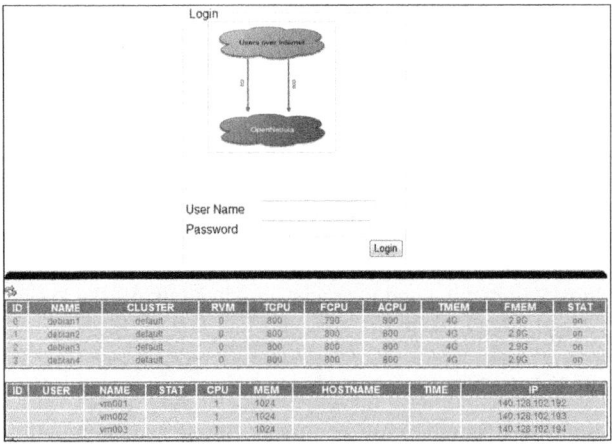

Fig. 6. Web-based Interface

The entire web-based management tool including physical machine management, virtual machine management and performance monitor. In Figure 7 it can set the VM attributes such as memory size, IP address, root password and VM name etc…, it also including the life migrating function. Life migration means VM can move to any working physic machine without suspend in-service programs. Life Migration is one of the advantages of OpenNebula. Therefore we could migrate any VM what we want under any situation, thus, we have a DRA mechanism to make the migration function more meaningful.

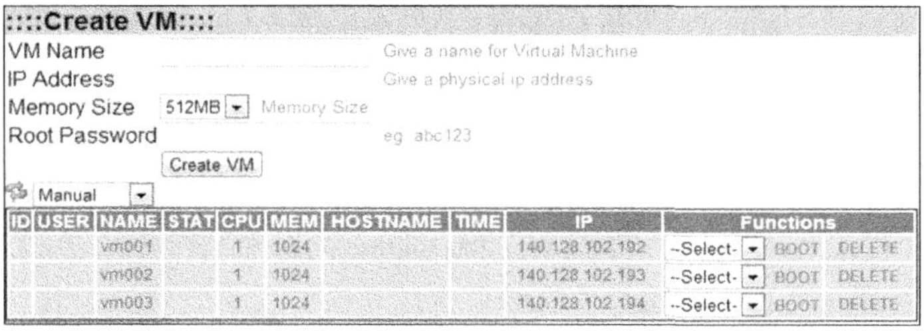

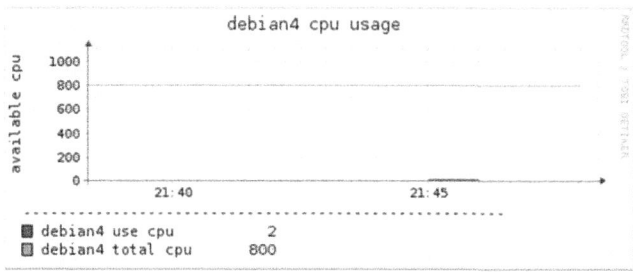

Fig. 7. Virtual Machines Manager

RRDtool is the Open Source industry standard, high performance data logging and graphing system for time series data. Use it to write your custom monitoring shell scripts or create whole applications using its Perl, Python, Ruby, TCL or PHP bindings[10]. In this thesis we use RRDtool to monitor entire system. Figure 8 and 9 show current physical machines CPU and memory usage.

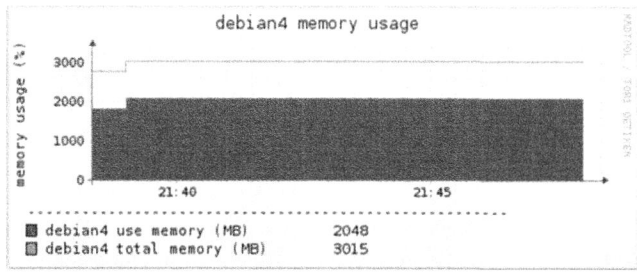

Fig. 8. CPU Performance

Fig. 9. Memory Performance

Figure 10 is a GMP setting page. it show which hosts controled by OPENNEBULA currently, which ones have enabled the GPM mechanism, hosts state of GPM. Moreover once the host enables the GPM, the system will control the VM on the HOST automatically and start loading balance.

Host Name	Description	GPM State	Enable	Host Status of GPM
debian1	OS: Debian 5.0	On	Yes ● No ○	Running
debian2	OS: Debian 5.0	On	Yes ● No ○	Sleep
debian3	OS: Debian 5.0	On	Yes ● No ○	Sleep
debian4	OS: Debian 5.0	Off	Yes ○ No ●	-
debian5	OS: Debian 5.0	Off	Yes ○ No ●	-

Fig. 10. GPM Setting Page

4 Experimental Environments and Results

In this section, we show the results of our efforts. First, we introduce the experimental environment, next is the service was not interrupted. Finally, the results show the mechanism of GPM.

OpenNebula Node-1 and OpenNebula Node-2 are the hosts. They act as backend and sharing storage. DomU VM is living on OpenNebula Node-1 and provides service to external user. The whole lab environment is as shown illustration as Figure 11. We ping service IP on DomU VM continuously. First we migrate DomU VM from OpenNebula Node-1 to OpenNebula Node-2, then power off OpenNebula Node-1. It doesn't cause the service IP stop providing service. You can see the connection status of service IP in Figure 12.

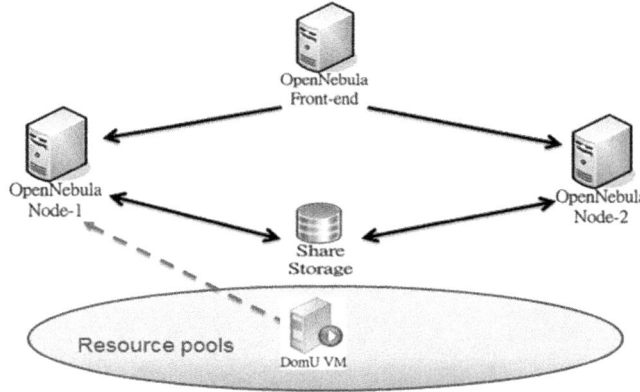

Fig. 11. Experment environment

Furthermore we built up application servers, including the computing service, teaching website, multi-media services contain compression and decompression of media files on virtual environment in HPC lab at Tunghai University. The system architecture has showed in Figure 4. All the services are composed of four physical machines. All of

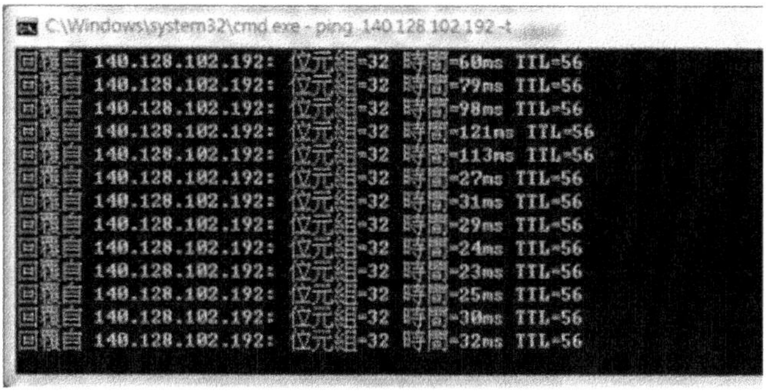

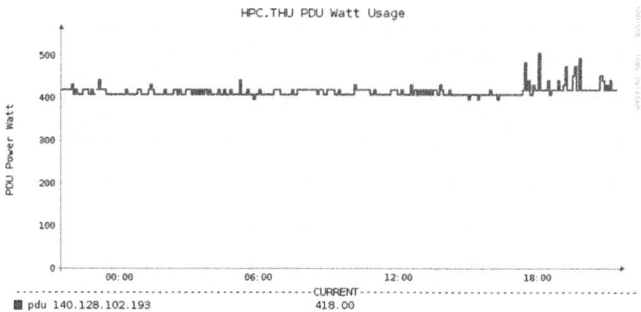

Fig. 12. Shutdown Host and DomU VM

them are on power distribution unit (PDU). A PDU is a device fitted with multiple appliance outlets designed to distribute electric power. It continuously monitors instant wattage consumption for four physical machines (Figure 13). We could observe that changes in wattage over at least 400. The four physical machines as OpenNebula client opened in the above total of four VM. Each VM provide an application service. In Figure 14, within one month, record the four VM CPU averagely total usages per hour. X-axis is time interval (hours), Y-axis is the four VM CPU total usage, here we use the SNMP protocol record the VM CPU usage per hour. We can find between 2 AM to 7 AM, CPU was at lower utilization, 10 AM to 16 PM is relatively high, so VM need more physical resources the interval between 10 AM to 16 PM.

Fig. 13. Power Monitor

Figure 15 has same measuring period as Figure 13, it records averagely total power consumption per hour. X-axis is time (hours), Y-axis as the power consumption total of the four physical machines (watts). The illustration shows that in the case turn off GPM, four machines are in power always, the power consumption has been over the 400W (Diamond marker), but contrast 2 AM to 7 AM of Figure 11, VM CPU demand volume is relatively small, so the decision-making based on GPM, front-end would migrate VM to the same physical machine, and others physical machines shut down to save energy. When the period in 10 AM to 16 PM, GPM was aware of VM CPU demand increasing to exceed a single physical machine can supply, front-end wake up another machine by WOL technology and load balance automatically. System can power or shut down the physical machine according to computing demand, effectively achieve the purpose of saving energy.

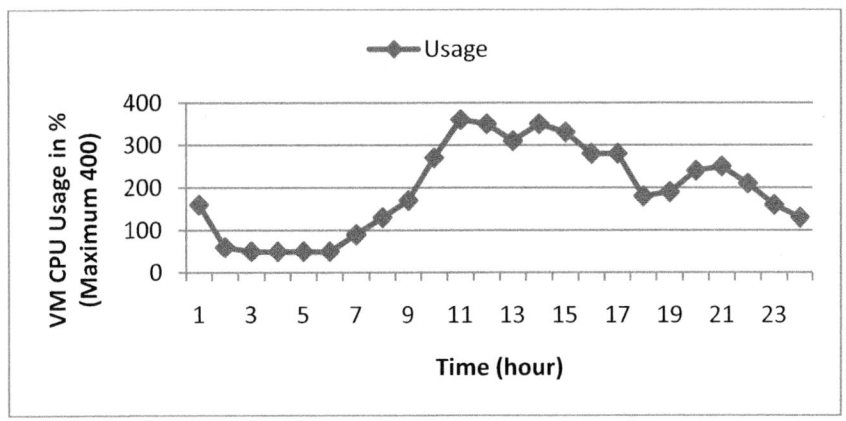

Fig. 14. VM CPU Usage

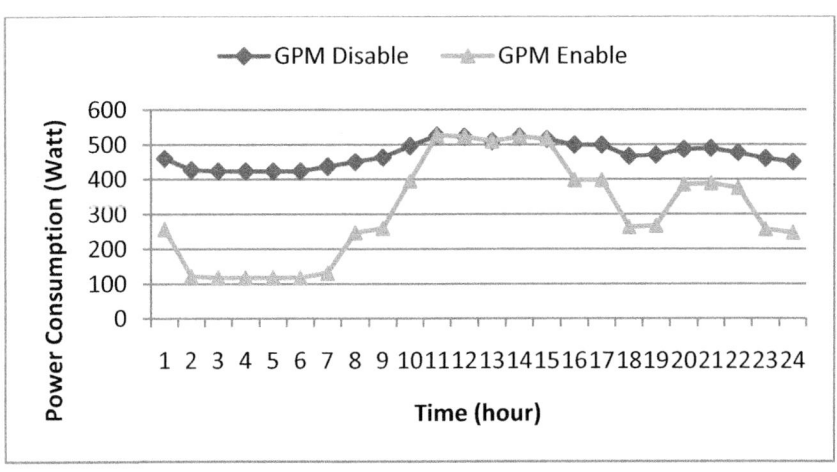

Fig. 15. Power Consumption

5 Conclusion

The "Green" became a hot key word recently. And we aimed the topic and proposed power management approach with virtualization technology. In this paper, the Green Power Management (GPM) is proposed for load balancing for virtual machine management on cloud. It includes supporting green power mechanism and implementing virtual machine resource monitor onto OpenNebula with web-based interface. Moreover, we expect to improve violent CPU highly loading solution. Because in our paper, we assume a prefect smooth virtual machines changes not a dramatic changes. For instance, set sensitivity parameters for entire mechanism and so on. However under our GPM approach, it already got a signification energy saving than traditional approach.

References

[1] Yang, C.-T.: A Dynamic Resource Allocation Model for Virtual Machine Management on Cloud. In: Symposium on Cloud and Service Computing 2011 (2011)

[2] Hagen, W.V.: Professional Xen Virtualization. Wrox Press Ltd., Birmingham (2008)

[3] Chao-Tung Yang, C.-H.T., Chou, K.-Y., Tsaur, S.-C.: Design and Implementation of a Virtualized Cluster Computing Environment on Xen. Presented at the The Second International Conference on High Performance Computing and Applications, HPCA (2009)

[4] OpenNebula, http://www.opennebula.org

[5] Rafael, M.-V., et al.: Elastic management of cluster-based services in the cloud. In: Proceedings of the 1st Workshop on Automated Control for Datacenters and Clouds, pp. 19–24. ACM, Barcelona (2009)

[6] Baliga, J., et al.: Green Cloud Computing: Balancing Energy in Processing, Storage, and Transport. Proceedings of the IEEE 99, 149–167 (2011)

[7] Montero, R.S., et al.: An elasticity model for High Throughput Computing clusters. Journal of Parallel and Distributed Computing (2010)

[8] Borja Sotomayor, R.S.M., Llorente, I.M., Foster, I.: Virtual Infrastructure Management in Private and Hybrid Clouds. IEEE Internet Computing 13 (2009)

[9] Eucalyptus, http://open.eucalyptus.com

[10] Rrdtool, http://www.mrtg.org/rrdtool/

[11] HPCC, http://icl.cs.utk.edu/hpcc/

[12] Soltesz, S., Potzl, H., Fiuczynski, M.E., Bavier, A., Peterson, L.: Container-based Operating System Virtualization: A Scalable, High-performance Alternative to Hypervisors. In: EuroSys 2007 (2007)

[13] Raj, H., Schwan, K.: High Performance and Scalable I/O Virtualization via Self-Virtualized Devices. In: The Proceedings of HPDC 2007 (2007)

[14] Adams, K., Agesen, O.: A Comparison of Software and Hardware Techniques for x86 Virtualization. In: ASPLOS-XII: Proceedings of the 12th International Conference on Architectural Support for Programming Languages and Operating Systems, pp. 2–13. ACM Press, New York (2006)

[15] Emeneker, W., Stanzione, D.: HPC Cluster Readiness of Xen and User Mode Linux. In: 2006 IEEE International Conference on Cluster Computing (2006)

[16] Huang, C., Zheng, G., Kumar, S., Kalé, L.V.: Performance Evaluation of Adaptive MPI. In: Proceedings of ACM SIGPLAN Symposium on Principles and Practice of Parallel Programming 2006 (March 2006)

[17] Wong, F., Martin, R., Arpaci Dusseau, R., Culler, D.: Architectural Requirements and Scalability of the NAS Parallel Benchmarks. In: Supercomputing 1999: Proceedings of the 1999 ACM/IEEE Conference on Supercomputing (CDROM), p. 41. ACM Press, New York (1999)

[18] Dong, Y., Li, S., Mallick, A., Nakajima, J., Tian, K., Xu, X., Yang, F., Yu, W.: Extending Xen with Intel Virtualization Technology. Journal, ISSN, Core Software Division, Intel Corporation, 1–14

[19] Barham, P., Dragovic, B., Fraser, K., Hand, S., Harris, T., Ho, A., Neugebauer, R., Pratt, I., Warfield, A.: Xen and the Art of Virtualization. In: SOSP 2003: Proceedings of the Nineteenth ACM Symposium on Operating Systems Principles, pp. 164–177. ACM Press, New York (2003)

[20] Turner, D., Chen, X.: Protocol-Dependent Message-Passing Performance on Linux Clusters. In: The Cluster 2002 Conference in Chicago (September 25, 2002)

[21] Nagarajan, A.B., Mueller, F., Engelmann, C., Scott, S.L.: Proactive fault tolerance for HPC with Xen virtualization. In: Proceedings of the 21st Annual International Conference on Supercomputing, Seattle, Washington (June 17-21, 2007)

[22] Endo, P.T., Gonçalves, G.E., Kelner, J., Sadok, D.: A Survey on Open-source Cloud Computing Solutions. In: VIII Workshop em Clouds, Grids e Aplicações, pp. 3–16

[23] Zhang, X., Dong, Y.: Optimizing Xen VMM Based on Intel Virtualization Technology. In: 2008 International Conference on Internet Computing in Science and Engineering (ICICSE 2008), pp. 367–374 (2008)

[24] Oi, H., Nakajima, F.: Performance Analysis of Large Receive Offload in a Xen Virtualized System. In: Proceedings of 2009 International Conference on Computer Engineering and Technology (ICCET 2009), Singapore, vol. 1, pp. 475–480 (January 2009)

[25] Hai, Z., et al.: An Approach to Optimized Resource Scheduling Algorithm for Open-Source Cloud Systems. In: 2010 Fifth Annual ChinaGrid Conference (ChinaGrid), pp. 124–129 (2010)

[26] Ruay-Shiung, C., Chia-Ming, W.: Green virtual networks for cloud computing. In: 2010 5th International ICST Conference on Communications and Networking in China (CHINACOM), pp. 1–7 (2010)

[27] Wu, Z., Wang, J.: Power Control by Distribution Tree with Classified Power Capping in Cloud Computing. In: Green Computing and Communications (GreenCom) 2010 IEEE/ACM Int'l Conference on & Int'l Conference on Cyber, Physical and Social Computing (CPSCom), pp. 319–324 (2010)

[28] Figuerola, S., et al.: Converged Optical Network Infrastructures in Support of Future Internet and Grid Services Using IaaS to Reduce GHG Emissions. Journal of Lightwave Technology 27, 1941–1946 (2009)

[29] Srikantaiah, S., et al.: Energy aware consolidation for cloud computing. Presented at the Proceedings of the 2008 Conference on Power Aware Computing and Systems, San Diego, California (2008)

AdPriRec: A Context-Aware Recommender System for User Privacy in MANET Services

Zheng Yan[1] and Peng Zhang[2]

[1] Aalto University, Espoo, Finland; XiDian University, Xi'an China
zheng.yan@aalto.fi
[2] Xi'an University of Post and Telecommunications, Xi'an, China
pengzhangzhang@gmail.com

Abstract. Mobile ad hoc network (MANET) has become a practical platform for pervasive services. Various user data could be requested for accessing such a service. However, it is normally difficult for a user to justify whether it is safe and proper to disclose personal data to others in different contexts. For solving this problem, we propose AdPriRec, a context-aware recommender system for preserving user privacy in MANET services. To support frequent changes of node pseudonyms in MANET, we develop a hybrid recommendation generation solution. We apply a trusted recommendation sever who knows the node's real identity to calculate a recommendation vector based on long term historical experiences. The vector can be also generated at each MANET node according to recent experiences accumulated based on node pseudonyms, while this vector could be further fine-tuned when the recommendation server is accessible. We design a number of algorithms for AdPriRec to generate context-aware recommendations for MANET users. The recommendation vector is calculated based on a number of factors such as data sharing behaviors and behavior correlation, service popularity and context, personal data type, community information of nodes and trust value of each involved party. An example based evaluation illustrates the usage and implication of the factors and shows AdPriRec's effectiveness. A prototype implementation based on Nokia N900 further proves the concept of AdPriRec design.

1 Introduction

A mobile ad hoc network (MANET) is a collection of autonomous nodes that communicate with each other by forming a multi-hop radio network and maintaining connectivity in a decentralized manner. Nowadays, MANET has become a practical platform for pervasive services, i.e., the services that are requested and provided anywhere and anytime in an instant way. For example, a user could access services in vicinity via MANET about restaurant reservation, cost share of on-sale products, and car riding, etc. This kind of service is very valuable for mobile users, especially when fixed networks (e.g. Internet) or mobile networks are temporarily unavailable or costly to access.

For accessing the services, a mobile user may be requested for sharing personal information (e.g. user profile and location information) with other nodes or service

C.-H. Hsu et al. (Eds.): UIC 2011, LNCS 6905, pp. 295–309, 2011.
© Springer-Verlag Berlin Heidelberg 2011

providers. Privacy becomes a crucial issue in pervasive services because it is the ability of an entity to seclude itself or information about itself and thereby reveal itself selectively. However, it is normally difficult for a user to justify whether it is safe and proper to disclose personal data to others in different contexts. This problem becomes even more difficult especially when the user generally uses a pseudonym in MANET communications and the pseudonym could be frequently changed in order to preserve personal privacy and avoid malicious tracking. In addition, privacy is a subjective issue. Different users treat personal privacy differently even in the same situation. To solve all above problems, there is a demand to provide a context-aware recommender system for user privacy that could help the user make a decision on personal data sharing in MANET based pervasive services.

This paper proposes AdPriRec for satisfying this demand. To support frequent changes of node pseudonyms in MANET, we develop a hybrid recommendation generation solution. We apply a trusted recommendation sever who knows the node's real identity to calculate a recommendation vector based on long term historical experiences. The vector can be also generated at each MANET node according to recent experiences accumulated based on node pseudonyms, while this vector could be fine-tuned when the recommendation server is accessible. We further design a couple of algorithms for AdPriRec to generate context-aware recommendations for MANET users. Concretely, the recommendation vector is calculated based on a comprehensive number of factors such as data sharing behaviors and behavior correlation, service popularity and context, personal data type, community information of nodes and trust value of each involved party. It represents recommendation values on different data sharing settings in a given context.

The AdPriRec helps the user make a decision on if it is safe and proper to provide a specific piece of personal information to a third party in a MANET service. The recommendation provided by AdPriRec is personalized based on the correlation of past data sharing behaviors of users in various situations. It represents recommendation values on different user data sharing in a specific context. To the best of our knowledge, few exiting work provides recommendations on user data privacy preservation, especially in pervasive services with context-awareness [5, 10, 17-26]. Although some recommender systems concerns privacy preservation, seldom they support pervasive services [9-16]. The applicability of existing solutions should be further evaluated in order to be applied into our research scenario. Thus, the main contribution of this paper is the AdPriRec system design, presentation and analysis of the AdPriRec algorithms for context-aware personalized recommendations on user data privacy in pervasive services.

The rest of the paper is organized as follows. Section 2 gives a brief overview of related work. Section 3 introduces AdPriRec system. The algorithms used for recommendation generation are described in Section 4. We further evaluate AdPriRec based on a concrete example, followed by system implementation in Section 5. Finally, conclusions and future work are presented in the last section.

2   Related Work

Recommender systems generally apply information filtering technique that attempts to recommend information items (e.g., films, books, web pages, music, etc.) that are likely to be of interest to users [5]. Typically, a recommender system compares a user profile to some reference characteristics, and seeks to predict the 'rating' that a user would give to an item they had not yet experienced [6]. These characteristics may be from an information item (a content-based approach) or the user's social environment (a collaborative filtering approach) [7]. In [8], the authors introduced using trust as both weighting and filtering in recommendations. The recommendation partners should have similar tastes of preferences and they should be trustworthy with a history of making reliable recommendations. This trust information can be incorporated into the recommendation process. But to our knowledge, most characteristics used for recommendations are not based on users' private data sharing behaviors, which however is an important clue to imply users' preferences on privacy. In AdPriRec, we consider both recommender's trust and service provider's trust in the generation of recommendations.

Privacy preservation has been considered in a number of existing recommender systems. A scheme for binary rating-based top-N recommendation on horizontally partitioned data was proposed in [9]. In this scheme, two parties own disjoint sets of users' ratings for the same items to preserve data owners' privacy. In [10], a recommender system applies a privacy-preserving agent that adopts a k-anonymity technique to prevent the data circulated in the system from attackers' access by reasoning, statistic analysis and data mining [10]. Some work improves the collaborative filtering (CF) approach in order to preserve privacy, e.g., a privacy-preserving CF algorithm based on non-negative matrix factorization (NMF) and random perturbation techniques [11], a naive Bayesian classifier-based privacy-preserving recommender system by utilizing pre-processing [12], expert collaborative filtering [13], a CF protocol based on similarity between items, instead of similarity between users [14]. Another classic solution for privacy preservation is applying cryptographic privacy enhancing protocols. However, large overhead in performing cryptographic operations is a practical issue, especially in a mobile domain. A couple of efficient schemes were proposed to reduce the preference matrix of the sets of items and users in order to improve the efficiency of cryptographic operations [15]. Current research focuses on preserving user data provided for generating recommendations without leaking the private information of users to service providers, not on recommendations for the purpose of user data privacy, which is the focus of AdPriRec. Meanwhile, AdPriRec adopts a trusted recommendation server (RS) to support the frequent change of node pseudonyms in order to avoid potential privacy tracking.

We can find a number of solutions for context-aware or personalized recommendations [17-26]. However, none of them provide recommendations on user data privacy preservation. Most of them, e.g. CoMeR [17] and SCAMREF [20], apply client-server architecture, while AdPriRec supports both centralized and distributed recommendation generation at RS and in MANET nodes. Yu et al. proposed a hybrid media recommendation approach CoMeR by integrating content-based approach, Bayesian-classifier approach and rule-based approach together to support context awareness [17]. Yap et al. presented a recommender system based on Bayesian networks (BNs) that minimizes context acquisition. Their context model is trimmed until it contains the minimal set of context parameters that are important to a user [18]. A novel sequential pattern mining algorithm was proposed to mine and group patterns of context [19].

AdPriRec uses a context ID to identify a context that is described with context parameters and their values. It supports context awareness by recommending private data sharing strategy on different types of data in different contexts.

In the literature, distributed trust and reputation evaluations have been studied in MANET [1-3]. Few solutions support node privacy. The existing recommendation based trust/reputation mechanisms aim to support secure node collaboration for the purpose of routing and networking. Seldom, they concern recommendation issues in applications and services using MANET as a communication and computing platform [4].

3 AdPriRec System

3.1 Application Scenario

To facilitate description, we consider a concrete MANET service as a typical scenario for AdPriRec to be applied. In details, there is a big shopping mall with many shops, a number of restaurants/bars and a cinema. During a Christmas season, many shops are on sale, the cinema provides a good offer of 10 ticket package and the restaurants also offer special discounts. The mall estate department provides a pervasive service platform with AdPriRec support to promote all sales. Many users are residents in mall area and come to the mall often. By joining the platform, the users with mobile devices can browse all sales, chat with each other instantly and even share an offer together via MANET in the mall. The pervasive service platform implementing the AdPriRec system also facilitates the trust evaluation of the users and shops. One concrete solution was proposed in [28].

During shopping, a user (i.e., a MANET node) sends a query to its neighbours about today's food quality of restaurants in the shopping mall. Supposed that a number of users respond the query and the user selects one restaurant based on the collected responses and wants to reserve a table. Some personal information is required by the restaurant reservation service (e.g. name, phone number, and credit card number). The user wonders if it is safe and proper to provide these personal data to that restaurant. In order to assist the user's decision, additional query was sent to ask comments on the personal data sharing. The AdPriRec provides the user a recommendation vector based on other users' comments. It helps the user decide if sharing the requested personal data in the underlying context. It is also possible for the user to contact the recommendation server (RS) to get a recommendation. In AdPriRec, each user node can share historical data communication information to RS or with each other (e.g. inside a community).

3.3 AdPriRec Structure

Fig.1 illustrates the structure of AdPriRec. It is a hybrid solution that includes a number of MANET node and a RS server. AdPriRec can work with/without the connection of the RS server. In the case of no RS server, the system works in a fully distributed manner. When the RS server is accessible, the system can use the RS server to provide more accurate and reliable recommendations.

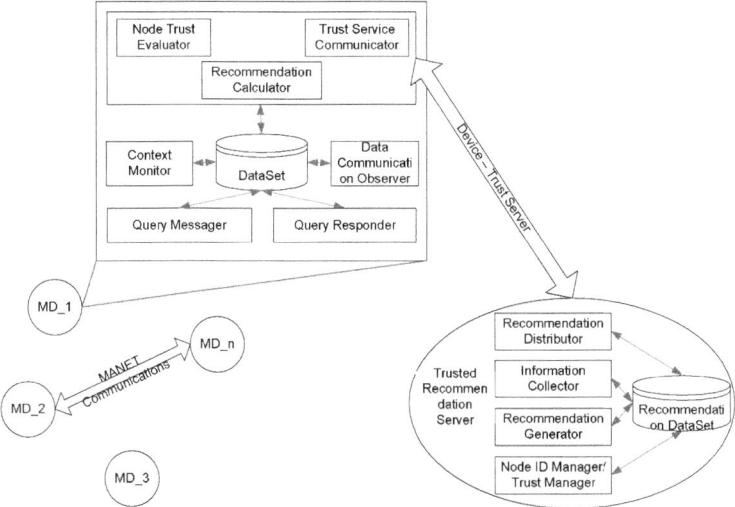

Fig. 1. AdPriRec system structure

At each node device, a query messager sends queries to other MANET nodes and collects responses. A query responder responds the queries received from other nodes. A context monitor extracts context information and classifies contexts based on a context classification model (note that one classification model applied in AdPriRec is based on registered services). A data communication observer observes the user behaviors of personal data sharing in different contexts. A node trust evaluator calculates the trust value of the node based on its recommendation performance and the node trust certificate issued by RS [28]. It is also used to locally calculate the trust value of service providers [28]. A recommendation calculator generates a recommendation vector at the node. The dataset in the device stores the data related to the recommendation vector calculation. A trust service communicator is responsible for communicating RS in a secure measure.

At the RS side, a node ID manager is applied to issue pseudonyms to each node and maintain the node's real ID and its pseudonyms. An information collector collects useful information for user data privacy recommendation. A recommendation generator calculates a recommendation vector according to: service popularity, service context, personal data type, correlation of past user behaviors in personal data sharing, the trust value of recommender nodes, the trust value of the destination party of data sharing, and community information. A trust manager generates the recommendation trust of each node based on recommendation performance, and the reputations of service providers (i.e., the destination party of data sharing). A concrete solution of trust /reputation evaluation is proposed in [28]. Periodically or by request, the RS issues a new trust certificate to each node. The trust certificate contains the node's pseudonym, the node latest recommendation trust value evaluated by the RS and a time

stamp to indicate its valid period. A recommendation distributor sends the recommendation vector to the node. A recommendation dataset stores all data related to
recommendation vector calculation at RS.

Introducing the centralized RS has a number of practical advantages: a) avoid inconsistent recommendation trust problem in MANET [31]; b) support accurate recommendation generation based on registered unique node ID even though the node's
pseudonyms could be frequently changed in MANET communications, thus overcome the Sybil attack [32]; c) provide an economic approach to collect useful data
from pervasive services about user privacy preferences. In AdPriRec, we assume that
the RS is trustworthy enough to preserve user's real ID and private data.

4   Algorithms

Based on the AdPriRec structure, we design a number of algorithms for recommendation generation as described below:

1) When RS is accessible, the recommendation vector is calculated at the RS and
   provided to a requesting node, refer to Algorithm 1 for details.
2) Recommendation vector is fine-tuned/calculated and at the node with/without the
   input from RS server, refer to Algorithm 2 for details.

Note that the algorithms for evaluating node recommendation trust and service provider's trust are proposed and evaluated in our previous publication [28], which are
beyond the scope of this paper. Herein, we assume that these two pieces of trust information are available.

4.1   Recommendation Vector Calculation at RS

When RS is available, it collects historical data communication records and calculates
the recommendation vectors for the node. Suppose a user has a data set
$I = \{i_1, i_2, \ldots, i_L\}$ that contains L types of personal data needed to share in MANET
services. A number M of contexts $C = \{c_1, c_2, \ldots, c_M\}$ could occur in AdPriRec. In
AdPriRec, a specific context is indicated by a context ID and described with context
parameters and their values. For example, a context parameter is *purpose* and its value
is *buy 3 pay 2 offer*. There are K MANET nodes $N = \{n_1, n_2, \ldots, n_K\}$ contributing to
the data privacy recommendation. We use $p_{i,n,c}$ to denote the probability or preference of data i shared by node n in context c, we have

$$p_{i,n,c} = \frac{s_{i,n,c}}{S_{i,n,c} + 1} \tag{1}$$

where $s_{i,n,c}$ is the times of data i shared by node n in context c and $S_{i,n,c}$ is the total
number of sharing requests of data i in context c. The parameter $p_{i,n,c}$ can be easily
calculated based on past data sharing behaviors.

For node n_k, we have the following matrix to present its data sharing behaviors.

$$D(n_k) = \left\{ \begin{bmatrix} p_{i_1, n_k, c_1} \\ p_{i_2, n_k, c_1} \\ \\ p_{i_L, n_k, c_1} \end{bmatrix} \cdots \cdots \begin{bmatrix} p_{i_1, n_k, c_M} \\ p_{i_2, n_k, c_M} \\ \\ p_{i_L, n_k, c_M} \end{bmatrix} \right\} \tag{2}$$

The matrix that represents all nodes' data sharing behaviors is expressed below:

$$D(N) = \left\{ \begin{matrix} \begin{bmatrix} p_{i_1, n_1, c_1} \\ p_{i_2, n_1, c_1} \\ \\ p_{i_L, n_1, c_1} \end{bmatrix} \cdots \cdots \begin{bmatrix} p_{i_1, n_1, c_M} \\ p_{i_2, n_1, c_M} \\ \\ p_{i_L, n_1, c_M} \end{bmatrix} \\ \cdots \\ \cdots \\ \begin{bmatrix} p_{i_1, n_K, c_1} \\ p_{i_2, n_K, c_1} \\ \\ p_{i_L, n_K, c_1} \end{bmatrix} \cdots \cdots \begin{bmatrix} p_{i_1, n_K, c_M} \\ p_{i_2, n_K, c_M} \\ \\ p_{i_L, n_K, c_M} \end{bmatrix} \end{matrix} \right\} \tag{3}$$

According to the similarity of past data sharing behaviors, a personalized recommendation vector $R^p_{n_k, c_m}$ can be pre-calculated for node n_k regarding context c_m at the recommendation server based on Formula (4).

$$R^p_{n_k, c_m} = \frac{\sum_{k'=1}^{K} \left(p_{n_{k'}, c_m} * \mathrm{Re}\, l(n_k, n_{k'}) \right)}{\sum_{k'=1}^{K} \mathrm{Re}\, l(n_k, n_{k'})} \tag{4}$$

where $\quad \mathrm{Re}\, l(n_k, n_{k'}) = \dfrac{1}{M-1} \sum_{\substack{m \neq m', m'=1}}^{M} \left(1 - \sqrt{\dfrac{\sum_{l=1}^{L} \left(p_{i_l, n_k, c_{m'}} - p_{i_l, n_{k'}, c_{m'}} \right)^2}{L}} \right) \tag{5}$

$k' = 1, ..., K$, $p_{n_{k'}, c_m}$ is a vector that denotes the probability of data set I shared by node $n_{k'}$ in context c_m. Herein, $k' \neq k$; $\mathrm{Re}\, l(n_k, n_{k'})$ is applied to calculate the correlations of data sharing behaviors by considering both contexts and data types.

Based on a user study conducted in both Finland and China, we found that users show more trust in an item if more people would like to recommend it [30]. Considering the influence of the number of recommenders (i.e., service popularity), we set

$$N_p = 1 - \exp\left(\frac{-K^2}{2\sigma^2}\right) \tag{6}$$

where $\sigma > 0$, is a parameter that inversely controls how fast the number of recommenders impacts recommendation. It increases as K increases. The parameter σ can be set from 0 to theoretically ∞, to capture the characteristics of different scenarios. We set $\sigma = 1.01$ in our experiment. We use N_p to adjust the recommendation vector $R^p_{n_k, c_m}$, where N_p plays as the credibility of recommendation contributed by the service popularity.

Particularly, the recommendations from trustworthy recommenders should be weighted higher than those from distrusted ones. This could benefit AdPriRec against a number of attacks. Similarly, the trust of destination party should also be considered in data sharing. In addition, the recommendations from the members in the same community with similar interests and/or having interaction experiences should be paid more attention than those from other communities. If $T_{n_k'}$ denotes the trust value of recommender node $n_{k'}$ and T_d denotes the trust value of the destination party d, Ad-PriRec considers a comprehensive number of factors, such as service popularity, community information, and the influence of both $T_{n_{k'}}$ and T_d in the generation of recommendation. Thus, the recommendation vector R_{n_k, c_m} for node n_k in context c_m can be tailored as

$$R_{n_k, c_m} = \frac{\sum_{k'=1}^{K}\left(p_{n_{k'}, c_m} * \mathrm{Re}\, l(n_k, n_{k'}) * \lambda T_{n_{k'}}\right)}{\sum_{k'=1}^{K}\left(\mathrm{Re}\, l(n_k, n_{k'})\right)} * N_p * T_d \tag{7}$$

where λ is a community factor, $\lambda = \omega$ if n_k and $n_{k'}$ are in the same community (e.g., with common shopping interests) and $\lambda = \omega'$ if n_k and $n_{k'}$ are in different communities; and $\omega > \omega'$. The algorithm used for recommendation vector calculation at RS is described in Algorithm 1.

Algorithm 1. Recommendation vector calculation at RS

---
1. Input:
2.   - $D(n_k)$, $D(n_{k'})$, ($k'=1,..., K; k \neq k'$): the matrix of data sharing behaviors;
3.   - $T_{n_{k'}}$, ($k'=1,..., K$): the trust value of node $n_{k'}$;
4.   - T_d: the trust value of destination party with whom to share private data;
5.   - K: the total number of recommenders; λ;

---

6. - n_k : the recommendee node;

7. - c_m : a specific context for recommendation.

8. Generate R_{n_k,c_m} based on (4-7).

9. Output: R_{n_k,c_m} .

4.2   Recommendation Vector Calculation at MANET Nodes

Similarly, a recommendation vector R'_{n_k,c_m} can be generated at the node n_k based on locally collected data $D'(n_{k'})$ according to formula (8),

$$R'_{n_k,c_m} = \frac{\sum_{k'=1}^{K}\left(p_{n_{k'},c_m} * \mathrm{Re}\,l\left(n_k,n_{k'}\right) * \lambda T'_{n_{k'}}\right)}{\sum_{k'=1}^{K}\left(\mathrm{Re}\,l\left(n_k,n_{k'}\right)\right)} * N_p * T'_d \tag{8}$$

where $T'_{n_{k'}}$ and T'_d are trust values of node $n_{k'}$ and destination party d, generated based on the locally accumulated experiences at n_k [28].

Considering the recommendation vector generated at RS, we have the final recommendation vector as described below:

$$R^f_{n_k,c_m} = \alpha R'_{n_k,c_m} + (1-\alpha)R_{n_k,c_m} \tag{9}$$

where $0 \leq \alpha \leq 1$, it is a parameter used to weight considerations on R'_{n_k,c_m} and R_{n_k,c_m} .

The algorithm used to calculate the recommendation vector at a MANET node is described in Algorithm 2.

Algorithm 2. Recommendation vector calculation at node n_k

1. Input:
2.   - $D'(n_k)$, $D'(n_{k'})$, ($k'=1,...,K; k \neq k'$): the matrix of data sharing behaviors collected by node n_k ;

3. - $T'_{n_{k'}}$, ($k'=1,...,K$): the trust value of node $n_{k'}$ at n_k ;

4. - T'_d : the trust value of destination party d evaluated by n_k ;
5. - K : the total number of recommenders; λ ; α ;
6. - R_{n_k,c_m} got from RS if any

7. Generate R'_{n_k,c_m} based on (8);

8. Aggregate R'_{n_k,c_m} and R_{n_k,c_m} based on (9) if R_{n_k,c_m} is input.

9. Output: $R^f_{n_k,c_m}$.

5 Evaluation and Implementation

5.1 An Example Based Evaluation

We illustrate AdPriRec with the example described in Section 3.1 to show its effectiveness. We concern 4 users who have consumed three services: the "buy 3 pay 2" offer in a leather bag shop; the 10 cinema ticket package and the dinner offer. In this case, we have example data as

$N = \{n_1, n_2, n_3, n_4\}, K = 4$, where n_1 is a university girl, n_2 is a university boy, n_3 is a middle-age lady, and n_4 is a middle-age man.

$C = \{c_1, c_2, c_3\}, M = 3$, where $c_1 = purpose$: buy 3 pay 2 offer; $c_2 = purpose$: buy 10 cinema ticket package; $c_3 = purpose$: consume a dinner offer.

$I = \{i_1, i_2, i_3, i_4, i_5\}, L = 5$, where $i_1 =$ name, $i_2 =$ phone number, $i_3 =$ gender, $i_4 =$ credit card number, $i_5 =$ age.

According to personal preferences and historical private data sharing statistics of the users, the data sharing behavior matrix $D(n_k)$ can be generated and stored at the user's device. For example, if n_1 shares i_1 in c_1 3 times in 9 requests, we have $p_{1,1,1} = 0.3$ based on Formula (1). The data sharing behavior can be automatically observed by mobile devices in MANET. For n_1, she is not very interested in c_1 "buy 3 pay 2 offer" but more interested in sharing her personal information in c_2 to buy 10 time cinema ticket. She is also interested in the dinner offer. For a young girl, she always dislikes disclosing her age. Similarly, the university boy n_2 has similar historical behaviors as n_1 except that he is even less interested in c_1 and generally fine to disclose his age. The user n_3 is interested in c_1 and c_3, but less interested in c_2. The user n_4 is more interested in c_2 and c_3 and less interested in c_1 than n_3. Thus, we have example $D(n_k)$ as below:

$$D(n_1) = \left\{ \begin{bmatrix} 0.3 \\ 0.3 \\ 0.3 \\ 0.1 \\ 0.0 \end{bmatrix} \begin{bmatrix} 0.9 \\ 0.9 \\ 0.7 \\ 0.7 \\ 0.0 \end{bmatrix} \begin{bmatrix} 0.8 \\ 0.7 \\ 0.9 \\ 0.6 \\ 0.0 \end{bmatrix} \right\}; \quad D(n_2) = \left\{ \begin{bmatrix} 0.2 \\ 0.2 \\ 0.2 \\ 0.1 \\ 0.5 \end{bmatrix} \begin{bmatrix} 0.7 \\ 0.7 \\ 0.7 \\ 0.6 \\ 0.5 \end{bmatrix} \begin{bmatrix} 0.8 \\ 0.7 \\ 0.9 \\ 0.6 \\ 0.5 \end{bmatrix} \right\};$$

$$D(n_3) = \left\{ \begin{bmatrix} 0.8 \\ 0.8 \\ 0.6 \\ 0.3 \\ 0.0 \end{bmatrix} \begin{bmatrix} 0.3 \\ 0.3 \\ 0.2 \\ 0.2 \\ 0.0 \end{bmatrix} \begin{bmatrix} 0.8 \\ 0.7 \\ 0.6 \\ 0.5 \\ 0.0 \end{bmatrix} \right\}; \quad D(n_4) = \left\{ \begin{bmatrix} 0.3 \\ 0.3 \\ 0.8 \\ 0.3 \\ 0.5 \end{bmatrix} \begin{bmatrix} 0.6 \\ 0.6 \\ 0.7 \\ 0.7 \\ 0.5 \end{bmatrix} \begin{bmatrix} 0.9 \\ 0.8 \\ 0.7 \\ 0.8 \\ 0.5 \end{bmatrix} \right\}.$$

Meanwhile, there are two other users n_5 and n_6. They are interested in c_3 but they do not have any experience on it. Thus, when accessing the service for c_3, they would like to get a recommendation for sharing requested personal data. Their data sharing behavior matrixes are exampled as below.

$$D(n_5) = \left\{ \begin{bmatrix} 0.9 \\ 0.9 \\ 0.8 \\ 0.7 \\ 0.0 \end{bmatrix} \begin{bmatrix} 0.2 \\ 0.2 \\ 0.2 \\ 0.1 \\ 0.0 \end{bmatrix} \{?\} \right\}; \quad D(n_6) = \left\{ \begin{bmatrix} 0.1 \\ 0.1 \\ 0.1 \\ 0.1 \\ 0.9 \end{bmatrix} \begin{bmatrix} 0.9 \\ 0.9 \\ 0.9 \\ 0.9 \\ 0.9 \end{bmatrix} \{?\} \right\}.$$

Herein, we illustrate how AdPriRec assists n_5 and n_6 in c_3 on their personal data sharing through recommendations. We design a number of experiments to test the performance of AdPriRec and discover the implication of the factors considered in AdPriRec. The experimental results are shown in Fig.2, Fig.3, Fig.4 and Fig.5. In our experiments, we assume that the trust values of nodes are the same in different contexts for simplifying the experiments. Note that $D(n_k)$, $D(n_{k'})$, $(k'=1,...,K; k \neq k')$ denote the matrix of data sharing behaviors collected by RS; $D'(n_k)$, $D'(n_{k'})$, $(k'=1,...,K; k \neq k')$ denote the matrix of data sharing behaviors collected by node n_k.

We have the following observation from the experiments.

(1) Since n_5's past data sharing behaviors are close to n_3, the recommendation vector R_{n_5,c_3}^f generated is similar to $p_{3,3} = \{0.8, 0.7, 0.6, 0.5, 0\}$, referring to the case 1 and case 2 in Fig.2.

(2) From Fig.2, we see the influence of the community factor on recommendation generation: AdPriRec weakens the influence of recommendations from different community due to preference or interest diversity, comparing the case 1 and case 2 in Fig.2

(3) Comparing the results R_{n_5,c_3}^f and R_{n_6,c_3}^f in case 1 and case 3 in Fig.2, we can see that the recommendation vectors generated by AdPriRec are personalized and different for different users even though in the same context.

(4) From Fig.3, we see the influence of recommendation trust: AdPriRec considers recommendation contributions based on recommendation trust by comparing case 1, 2, 3, and 4 in Fig.3.

(5) Comparing case 1 with case 2 and case 3 with case 4 in Fig.4, we can observe the influence of $D'(n_{k'})$ influence on the recommendation generation. $D'(n_{k'})$ in case 1 and case 3 is bigger than $D'(n_{k'})$ in case 2 and case 3, thus R_{n_5,c_3}^f is bigger in case 1/3 than case 2/4, respectively.

(6) Comparing case 1 with case 3, case 2 with case 4 in Fig.4, we observe that R_{n_5,c_3}^f becomes smaller in case 1/2 than case 3/4. This is caused by the low trust value of recommender n_2 detected at n_5 ($T_{n_2}' = 0.1$) in case 3 and 4.

(7) Looking at the result of Fig.5, we can see parameter α's influence: locally generated recommendation based on $D'(n_{k'}) = D(n_{k'}) + 0.1$ is concerned more in the
final recommendation vector when α is increasing.

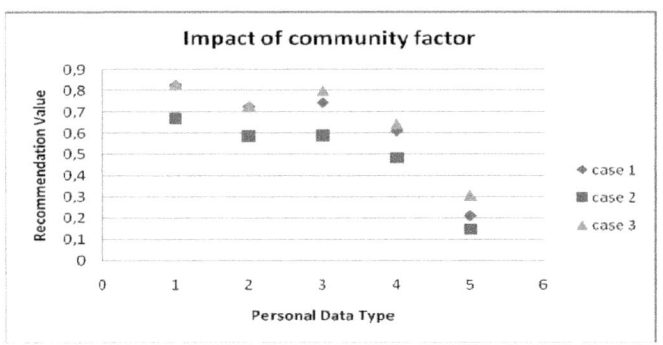

Fig. 2. Impact of community factor λ ($\omega = 1; \omega' = .7$; $\alpha = .5$; $T_{n_k} = \{1,1,1,1\}$; $T'_{n_{k'}} = \{1,1,1,1\}, k' = 1,...,4$; $k = 5$; $D(n_k) = D'(n_k)$; $D(n_{k'}) = D'(n_{k'})$). In case 1, all nodes are in the same community, $k = 5$; in case 2, n_5 are only in the same community with n_3, $k = 5$; in case 3, all nodes are in the same community, $k = 6$.

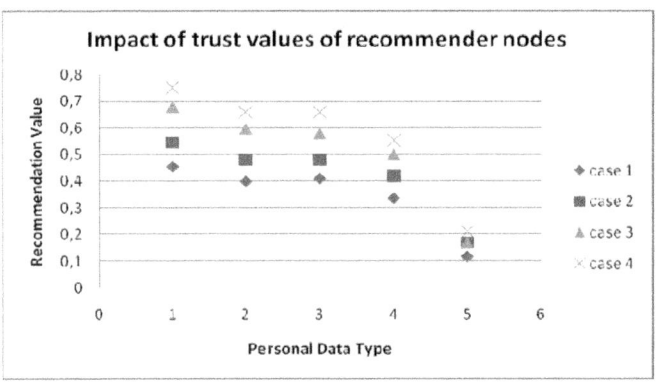

Fig. 3. Impact of trust values of recommender nodes ($\omega = 1; \omega' = .7$; $T'_{n_{k'}} = \{1,1,1,1\}, k' = 1,...,4$; $k = 5$; $D(n_k) = D'(n_k)$; $D(n_{k'}) = D'(n_{k'})$, all nodes are in the same community). In case 1, $T_{n_1} = .1$, $T_{n_2} = .1$, $T_{n_3} = .1$, $T_{n_4} = .1$; in case 2, $T_{n_1} = .1$, $T_{n_2} = .1$, $T_{n_3} = .1$, $T_{n_4} = 1$; in case 3, $T_{n_1} = .1$, $T_{n_2} = .1$, $T_{n_3} = 1$, $T_{n_4} = 1$; in case 4, $T_{n_1} = .1$, $T_{n_2} = 1$, $T_{n_3} = 1$, $T_{n_4} = 1$.

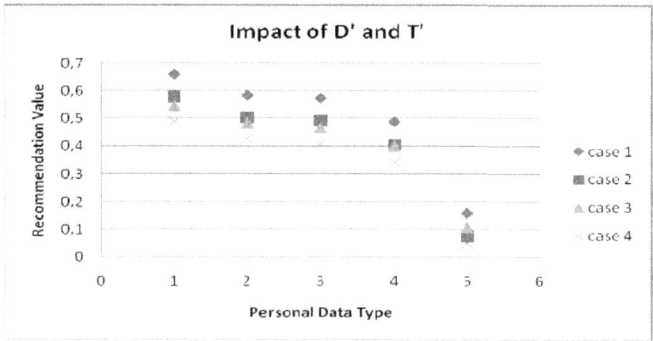

Fig. 4. Impact of D' and T_{n_k}' ($\omega=1; \omega'=.7$; $\alpha=.5$; $T_{n_k'}=\{1,0.1,1,1\}$; $k'=1,...,4$; $k=5$; n_5 are only in the same community with n_3). In case 1, $D'(n_{k'})=D(n_{k'})+0.1$, $T_{n_{k'}}'=\{1,1,1,1\}$; in case 2, $D'(n_{k'})=D(n_{k'})-0.1$, $T_{n_{k'}}'=\{1,1,1,1\}$; in case 3, $D'(n_{k'})=D(n_{k'})+0.1$, $T_{n_{k'}}'=\{1,0.1,1,1\}$; in case 4, $D'(n_{k'})=D(n_{k'})-0.1$, $T_{n_{k'}}'=\{1,0.1,1,1\}$.

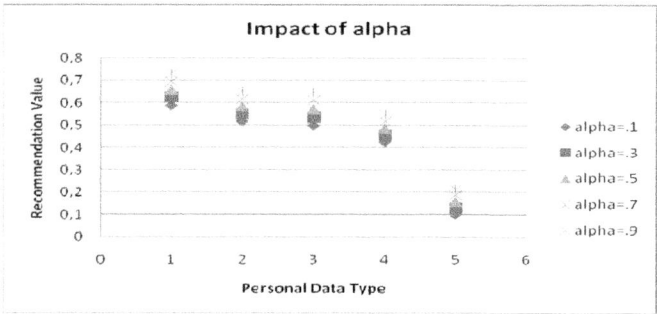

Fig. 5. Impact of α ($\omega=1; \omega'=.7$; $T_{n_{k'}}=\{1,0.1,1,1\}$; $T_{n_{k'}}'=\{1,1,1,1\}$; $k'=1,...,4$; $k=5$; n_5 are only in the same community with n_3 ; $D'(n_{k'})=D(n_{k'})+0.1$).

The above results show the implication of the parameters considered in AdPriRec and prove the effectiveness of AdPriRec.

5.2 Implementation

To prove the feasibility of AdPriRec, we implemented an AdPriRec prototype system based on a pervasive social networking platform [27]. This platform provides an energy-efficient and fully distributed social networking environment via MANET. We develop MANET nodes using Nokia N900 with Python and GTK binding. The MANET communications are based on wireless LAN. The recommendation server is implemented with Apache and PHP in Linux platform (Ubuntu 9.04). The prototype system provides essential security protection on node-server communications with Open SSL and node-node communications by utilizing a community symmetric key. The implementation satisfies the above constraints and proves the feasibility of Ad-PriRec. One future work is to carry out an extensive experiment with the real system.

6   Conclusions and Future Work

In MANET, users lack visibility and trust with each other. Thus, it is difficult for them to make decision when personal data is required for accessing a service. To solve this problem, we presented AdPriRec for user privacy recommendation in MANET services. The system is a hybrid solution that can work in a fully distributed mode or with the support of a recommendation server. Thus, AdPriRec can support frequent changes of node pseudonyms by providing accurate recommendations according to real node ID through the RS. We also designed a number of algorithms for AdPriRec in order to generate context-aware personalized recommendations for MANET users. An example based evaluation shows AdPriRec's effectiveness. A prototype implementation based on Nokia N900 further proves the concept of AdPriRec system design. Regarding the future work, we will conduct a user study based on the prototype system to research AdPriRec's usefulness and further improve the system in such aspects as usability and context sensibility.

References

1. Sun, Y., Yu, W., Han, Z., Liu, K.J.R.: Information Theoretic Tramework of Trust Modeling and Evaluation for Ad Hoc Networks. IEEE Journal on Selected Area in Communications 24(2), 305–317 (2006)
2. Theodorakopoulos, G., Baras, J.S.: On Trust Models and Trust Evaluation Metrics for Ad Hoc Networks. IEEE Journal on Selected Areas in Communications 24(2), 318–328 (2006)
3. Raya, M., Papadimitratos, P., Gligory, V.D., Hubaux, J.-P.: On Data-Centric Trust Establishment in Ephemeral Ad Hoc Networks. In: IEEE INFOCOM, pp. 1912–1920 (2008)
4. Zouridaki, C., Mark, B.L., Hejmo, M., Thomas, K.R.: Robust Cooperative Trust Establishment for MANETs. In: SASN 2006: Proceedings of the Fourth ACM Workshop on Security of Ad Hoc and Sensor Networks, pp. 23–34(2006)
5. Resnick, P., Varian, H.R.: Recommender Systems. Communications of the ACM 40(3), 56–58 (1997)
6. Hancock, J.T., Toma, C., Ellison, N.: The Truth about Lying in Online Dating Profiles. In: Proceedings of the ACM CHI 2007, pp. 449–452. ACM, New York (2007)
7. Su, X., Khoshgoftaar, T.M.: A Survey of Collaborative Filtering Techniques. In: Advances in Artificial Intelligence vol. 19 (2009), doi:10.1155/2009/421425
8. O'Donovan, J., Smyth, B.: Trust in Recommender Systems. In: IUI 2005, pp. 167–174 (2005)
9. Polat, H., Du, W.L.: Privacy-Preserving Top-N Recommendation on Horizontally Partitioned Data. In: The 2005 IEEE/WIC/ACM International Conference on Web Intelligence, 725–731 (2005)
10. Luo, Y., Le, J., Chen, H.: A Privacy-Preserving Book Recommendation Model Based on Multi-agent. In: WCSE 2009, pp. 323–327 (2009)
11. Li, T., Gao, C., Du, J.: A NMF-Based Privacy-Preserving Recommendation Algorithm. In: ICISE 2009, pp. 754–757 (2009)

12. Bilge, A., Polat, H.: Improving Privacy-Preserving NBC-Based Recommendations by Preprocessing. In: WI-IAT 2010, pp. 143–147 (2010)
13. Ahn, J., Amatriain, X: Towards Fully Distributed and Privacy-Preserving Recommendations via Expert Collaborative Filtering and RESTful Linked Data. In: WI-IAT 2010, pp. 66–73 (2010)
14. Tada, M., Kikuchi, H., Puntheeranurak, S.: Privacy-Preserving Collaborative Filtering Protocol Based on Similarity between Items. In: AINA 2010, pp. 573–578 (2010)
15. Kikuchi, H., Kizawa, H., Tada, M.: Privacy-Preserving Collaborative Filtering Schemes. In: ARES 2009, pp. 911–916 (2009)
16. Katzenbeisser, S., Petkovic, M.: Privacy-Preserving Recommendation Systems for Consumer Healthcare Services. In: ARES 2008, pp. 889–895 (2008)
17. Yu, Z., Zhou, X., Zhang, D., Chin, C., Wang, X., Men, J.: Supporting Context-Aware Media Recommendations for Smart Phones. IEEE Pervasive Computing 5(3), 68–75 (2006)
18. Yap, G., Tan, A., Pang, H.: Discovering and Exploiting Causal Dependencies for Robust Mobile Context-Aware Recommenders. IEEE Transactions on Knowledge and Data Engineering 19(7), 977–992 (2007)
19. Wang, J., Kodama, E., Takada, T., Li, J.: Mining context-related sequential patterns for recommendation systems. In: CAMP 2010, pp. 270–275 (2010)
20. Zhang, D., Yu, Z.: Spontaneous and Context-Aware Media Recommendation in Heterogeneous Spaces. In: IEEE VTC 2007, pp. 267–271 (2007)
21. Chuong, C., Torabi, T., Loke, S.W.: Towards Context-aware Task Recommendation. In: JCPC 2009, pp. 289–292 (2009)
22. Liiv, I., Tammet, T., Ruotsalo, T., Kuusik, A.: Personalized Context-Aware Recommendations in SMARTMUSEUM: Combining Semantics with Statistics. In: SEMAPRO 2009, pp. 50–55 (2009)
23. Liu, D., Meng, X., Chen, J.: A Framework for Context-Aware Service Recommendation. In: ICACT 2008, pp. 2131–2134 (2008)
24. Xiao, H., Zou, Y., Ng, J., Nigul, L.: An Approach for Context-Aware Service Discovery and Recommendation. In: IEEE ICWS 2010, pp. 163–170 (2010)
25. Seetharam, A., Ramakrishnan, R.: A context sensitive, yet private experience towards a contextually apt recommendation of service. In: IMSAA 2008, pp. 1–6 (2008)
26. Berkovsky, S., De Luca, E.W., Said, A.: Proceedings of the Workshop on Context-Aware Movie Recommendation (2010)
27. Ahtiainen, A., Kalliojarvi, K., Kasslin, M., Leppanen, K., Richter, A., Ruuska, P., Wijting, C.: Awareness Networking in Wireless Environments: Means of Exchanging Information. IEEE Vehicular Technology Magazine 4(3), 48–54 (2009)
28. Yan, Z., Chen, Y.: AdContRep: A privacy enhanced reputation system for MANET content services. In: Yu, Z., Liscano, R., Chen, G., Zhang, D., Zhou, X. (eds.) UIC 2010. LNCS, vol. 6406, pp. 414–429. Springer, Heidelberg (2010)
29. Wang, J., Wang, F., Yan, Z., Huang, B.: Message Receiver Determination in Multiple Simultaneous IM Conversations. IEEE Intelligent Systems 26(3), 24–31 (2011)
30. Yan, Z., Liu, C., Niemi, V., Yu, G.: Trust information indication: effects of displaying trust information on mobile application usage. Technical Report NRC-TR-2009-004, Nokia Research Center, http://research.nokia.com/files/NRCTR2009004.pdf
31. Hu, J., Burmester, M.: LARS: A locally Aware Reputation System for Mobile Ad Hoc Networks. In: Proc. of the 44th ACM Annual Southeast Regional Conf., pp. 119–123 (2006)
32. Douceur, J.R.: The sybil attack. In: Druschel, P., Kaashoek, M.F., Rowstron, A. (eds.) IPTPS 2002. LNCS, vol. 2429, pp. 251–260. Springer, Heidelberg (2002)

Ensuring Security and Availability through Model-Based Cross-Layer Adaptation

Minyoung Kim, Mark-Oliver Stehr, Ashish Gehani, and Carolyn Talcott

SRI International
{mkim,stehr,gehani,clt}@csl.sri.com

Abstract. Situation- and resource-aware security is essential for the process control systems, composed of networked entities with sensors and actuators, that monitor and control the national critical infrastructure. However, security cannot be addressed at a single layer because of the inherent dependencies and tradeoffs among crosscutting concerns. Techniques applied at one layer to improve security affect security, timing, and power consumption at other layers. This paper argues for an integrated treatment of security across multiple layers of abstraction (application, middleware, operating system including network stack, and hardware). An important step in realizing this integrated treatment of situation- and resource-aware security is first understanding the cross-layer interactions between security policies and then exploiting these interactions to design efficient adaptation strategies (i) to balance security, quality of service, and energy needs, and (ii) to maximize system availability. We propose a novel approach that employs a compositional method within an iterative tuning framework based on lightweight formal methods with dynamic adaptation.

1 Introduction

Physical infrastructure availability relies on the process control systems that can gather, handle, and share real-time data on critical processes from and to networked entities. For example, wireless sensor networks now are being applied in industrial automation to lower system and infrastructure costs, improve process safety, and guarantee regulatory compliance [1]. Harsh environments such as remote areas with potential toxic contamination where mobile ad hoc networks can be the only viable means for communication and information access often necessitate the use of mobile nodes (e.g., surveillance robots with camera and position-changing capability). Optimized control based on continuous observation is an integral part because availability is becoming a fundamental concern in reducing the vulnerability of such systems.

To concretize our approach, we illustrate ideas by using the following motivating scenario. Consider a surveillance system, consisting of a collection of sensors deployed at fixed locations together with mobile nodes, that monitors critical national infrastructure by distributed sensing and actuating. Because of possible jamming attacks and the mobility of nodes, the wireless sensors and mobile

C.-H. Hsu et al. (Eds.): UIC 2011, LNCS 6905, pp. 310–325, 2011.

nodes need to communicate via opportunistic links that enable the sharing and evaluation of data such as video streams in the presence of unstable connectivity. The challenge here is enabling networked entities to respond to dynamic situations in an informed, timely, and collaborative manner so that the physical infrastructure can safely recover after a cyber-disruption.

The operating scenarios are highly networked, and involve interactions among multiple abstraction layers (application, middleware, OS, hardware) in a distributed real-time environment. Typical wireless sensors and mobile units are limited in communication range, processing power, bandwidth, and residual energy. Often, an emergency situation generates a large volume of communication that must be carefully controlled. Clearly, in such a scenario, the dual goals of ensuring security (with respect to data integrity, confidentiality, authentication, and infrastructure protection) and optimizing resource utilization present a significant challenge. In this paper we focus on integrity and confidentiality for group communication, but we believe that a similar cross-layer treatment of authentication and infrastructure protection would be equally important and possible within the same conceptual framework, e.g., by adopting a situation- and resource-aware posture for authentication and against denial-of-service attacks. Research is needed to develop situation- and resource-aware security solutions that investigate the security implications of existing strategies and integrate them across multiple layers.

We propose the idea of automated verification and configuration of situation- and resource-aware cross-layer security. While existing work has shown the effectiveness of cross-layer adaptation [2], many of these efforts try to address the average-case behavior for energy reduction without verifiable guarantees on their solutions. Our recent work, xTune [3], attempts to provide a comprehensive design methodology, based on formal reasoning that can provide an effective basis for tuning mobile embedded systems under a multitude of constraints. These studies successfully addressed system adaptation and explored the tradeoff with performance, energy, quality of service (QoS), and timeliness for mobile multimedia applications. However, security issues across system abstraction layers in a situation- and resource-aware manner with multidimensional objectives have not been considered until now.

Security goals at each layer can be counterproductive and even harmful. Consider, for instance, the need to protect critical sensor nodes from detection and subsequent subversion by avoiding or reducing their transmissions versus the need of authorized parties to remotely access information. A secure group communication system enables the sharing and evaluation of sensor data. The need for beaconing[1] and rekeying[2] in group membership protocols (at the middleware layer) is in direct conflict with the objective of preventing detection (at the hardware layer). Furthermore, the implementation of security goals is constrained

---

[1] In wireless communication, beaconing refers to the continuous transmission of small packets that advertise the sender's presence.

[2] In cryptography, rekeying refers to the process of changing the encryption key of an ongoing communication to limit the amount of data encrypted with the same key.

by the available resources. Various solutions ranging from event-driven or on-demand power cycling to reduce transmission power are possible, but the security effects cannot be understood at a single layer. For example, reduced transmission power influences routing and hence requires more reliance on potentially less trustworthy intermediate nodes. In the extreme case, even acknowledgments may have to be avoided due to more opportunities for sniffing and packet loss may need to be compensated for by higher redundancy from the sender (e.g., forward error correction) at the link/network layer. This is why security should be viewed as a multidimensional cross-layer objective for which reasonable tradeoffs must be found in a situation- and resource-aware manner.

This approach posits that cross-layer security opens a large space of feasible solutions exhibiting a range of power, performance, and cost attributes, enabling system designers to optimize and trade off between security, QoS, and resource utilization in response to the operating conditions (i.e., situation and resources). A unified framework is needed to derive, analyze, and validate cross-layer policies and parameters while proving various properties pertaining to security, energy usage, delays, bandwidth, storage, and processing, as the system evolves over time. xTune [3] has demonstrated the feasibility of applying lightweight formal methods to cross-layer adaptation for mobile multimedia with QoS constraints. In this paper, we extend xTune to cope with security issues across layers.

To focus our efforts, we use an existing simulation environment of self-organizing mobile nodes (with sensors and actuators) in wireless networks [4] with a description of our threat model in Section 2. Section 3 surveys security policies for different layers. In Section 4, we explain the extension of the existing cross-layer system tuning framework, xTune, based on a compositional formal approach to accommodate situation- and resource-aware security. A prototype implementation and experimental results are presented in Section 5 and Section 6, respectively. We present related work in cross-layer security in Section 7. Section 8 concludes our paper with future research directions.

2   Threats

We aim to protect physical infrastructure under the following threat model: Rogue sensors or mobile nodes may pretend to be valid entities and, therefore, fraudulent data can be injected to severely compromise the *availability* of infrastructure.

Given this threat model, consider a sensor reading that will trigger a chain of events in response to an emergency (e.g., gas leakage). A video stream must be obtained from the area where gas leakage has been sensed. The video footage then should be delivered via opportunistic network links to the control center. Data may need to be encoded to reduce its volume or to be transmitted in raw data format to save computation time and energy. First, the fraudulent sensor reading will be propagated. This incurs communication overhead in terms of transmission power and bandwidth for data forwarding, which need to be managed. Second, every hop must include a phase of mutual authentication since the node cannot be trusted. Third, the fraudulent nodes should be detected and declared malicious. Finally, the resources of the wireless sensors and mobile nodes need to be provisioned to ensure a certain level of security while avoiding the depletion of residual energy and avoiding congestion. This requires dynamic configuration of individual (seemingly independent) techniques to compose appropriate protections against attack situations while also making optimal use of resources.

3   Security Policies for Different Layers

Specific adaptation policies have been developed within each abstraction layer to enhance a security measure. *Policies* define the individual security techniques available to the system. *Parameters* determine the behavior of a policy. We identify layers, policies, and parameters of interest to effectively demonstrate our concept using the following examples.

Application Layer — In our sample scenario, surveillance is done by sensor readings including video streaming. There is a need to develop techniques that exploit the structure of the data to maximize the efficiency of encryption algorithms. In particular, selective encryption [5] aims to reduce the computational cost of encryption by partial encryption of multimedia content. An example would be encryption of intra-coded blocks, without which the video stream cannot be decoded, to enhance the security of the encoded bitstream.

Middleware Layer — The video data of our sample scenario must be accessed only by authorized consumers. A secure group communication system can be used to enforce this protection. We use a generalization of Secure Spread [6], whose adaptation parameters enable the system to dynamically tailor data transmission to the application requirements and environmental conditions. In the security dimension, this mechanism enables each group to specify the degree of laziness of the key establishment protocol: (i) eager keying will trigger a rekey after every membership change; (ii) key caching will reuse previously cached keys; and (iii) lazy keying will delay rekeying until a message needs to be sent. In the synchrony[3] dimension, groups with different degrees of synchrony can coexist. Taking into consideration the tradeoffs between security and synchrony, we can explore various solutions (e.g., less stringent synchrony semantics with lazy keying protocol) while preserving required security guarantees.

Operating System (OS) Layer — The video sensor stream is received on nodes using an OS. We consider the network stack as part of the OS layer. At the file system level, OS functionality to transparently audit data provenance was prototyped in our recent work, SPADE [7], for software implementation of provenance certification. Continuing this line of research, ciphertext-policy attribute-based encryption (CP-ABE) [8] can provide the desired flexibility in security policy. Using configurable rules, each provenance element will transparently be encrypted at the time of creation with a policy stating which attributes

---

[3] In a group communication system, the synchrony property ensures that all group members see the same events (group membership changes and incoming messages) and in the same order.

are needed to access it, satisfying the flexible security goal. For example, the provenance record can be verified at runtime to establish mutual authentication to attest the trustworthiness of sensor readings or to be retrospectively checked for forensic purposes.

Hardware Layer — Typical wireless sensors and mobile nodes in our sample scenario are resource constrained. As we explained in Section 1, energy management at the hardware layer has a dramatic impact on the other layers' policies. To save energy or to reduce the risk of an eavesdropping attack, a node can decide to reduce its transmission power [9], which results in residual energy savings at the cost of less coverage (i.e., more hops for end-to-end message delivery). Resource saving on transmission propagates to upper layers (i.e., encryption can consume more energy) and can lead to adaptations there. We analyze this inherent relationship because residual energy is one of the key factors for other layers' decisions regarding whether they can perform computationally intensive tasks (e.g., encryption at the application layer, eager rekeying at the middleware layer) to enhance a corresponding layer's own security level.

4   Cross-Layer Security

4.1   Understanding the Problem of Cross-Layer Security

To enhance security in the context of wireless mobile applications, researchers have proposed several techniques at various system layers, as described in Section 3. Note that one key performance metric for such techniques is how well they manage security under a multitude of constraints in a dynamic situation. Since security comes with cost in terms of performance, energy consumption, storage requirements, and bandwidth used, one needs to optimize security in the context of the operating conditions. However, most security techniques consider only a single system layer remaining unaware of the strategies employed in the other layers. A cross-layer approach that is cognizant of features, limitations, and dynamic changes at each layer enables better optimization than a straightforward composition of individual layers, because solutions for each individual layer can be globally suboptimal.

To coordinate the individual techniques in a cross-layer manner based on the operating condition, one needs to

- Quantify the effect of various security policies at each layer on system properties
- Explore methods of taking the impact of each policy into account and compensating for it at other layers

4.2   Supporting Security Composition within xTune

As explained in Section 1, we extend our earlier research on cross-layer system tuning. In particular, we extend the xTune framework [3] to accommodate the cross-layer security concerns and evaluate various strategies for cross-layer adaptation.

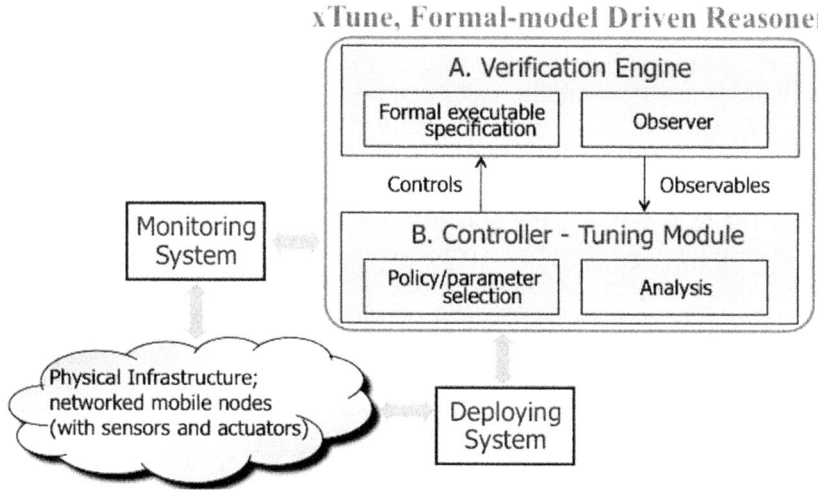

Fig. 1. xTune Cross-layer System Tuning Framework

Figure 1 illustrates how we envision the xTune framework. Here the monitoring system observes the current status of the nodes and environment that compose the physical infrastructure. The tuning module decides which strategy will be deployed for each node. The tuning module may consult the verification engine to ensure the quality of solution. The xTune framework supports a methodology for tuning that attempts cross-layer adaptation, and for verification that performs formal analysis to quantify utility and cost.

Initially, our framework performs property checking and quantitative analysis of candidate policy and parameter settings via formal executable specifications (i.e., formal models of the system that are executable) and statistical techniques. In particular, *Box A* in Figure 1 represents the formal modeling. The core of our formal modeling approach is to develop formal executable models of system components at each layer of interest. Our formal modeling is based on an executable specification language called Maude [10]. Its theoretical foundation is rewriting logic, a logic with operational as well as model-theoretic semantics. This formal prototyping enables us to experiment with an abstract mathematical but executable specification of the system.

Box B in Figure 1 shows the evaluation phase of given specifications that generate statistics for properties and values of interest, to come up with the cross-layer policies and parameters. The policy and parameter selection is achieved by the compositional method by constraining the behavior of the local optimizers working at each abstraction layer. As proposed in [11], we iteratively tune the system parameters by monitoring the current status of a system via the *observables* to generate the appropriate *control* of the corresponding subsystem. Subsequently, each local optimizer uses the other optimizers' refinement results as its *constraints*.

Given an optimization problem with model $\mathcal{M}$ and parameter space $\mathbb{P}$ (e.g., $\mathbb{P} = \mathbb{P}_{App} \times \mathbb{P}_{HW}$ with $\mathbb{P}_{App} = \mathbb{R}$ and $\mathbb{P}_{HW} = \mathbb{N}$), the constraint refinement attempts to quickly find a region $P \in \mathcal{R}(\mathbb{P})^4$ containing a nearly optimal solution. For instance, a resulting region can be represented as $P = P_{App} \times P_{HW} = [Th_{min}, Th_{max}] \times [Tx_{min}, Tx_{max}] = [0.2, 0.3] \times [10, 25]$, where Th and Tx indicate paramaters of selective encryption and transmission range control policies, respectively. In particular, we obtain observables by Monte Carlo sampling over the current region $P_i \in \mathcal{R}(\mathbb{P})$ and subsequently refine P_i to P_{i+1}. The refinement such that the utility is maximized based on the samples available, and $size(P_{i+1}) = size(P_i) \cdot \tau_i$, where τ_i $(0.0 < \tau_i < 1.0)$ represents the i-th refinement ratio. The new region P_{i+1} is then used as the current region and the process is repeated.

The input P_i and output P_{i+1} of each refinement step are sets of feasible policies/parameters, and our approach treats P_i as *constraints* when we restrict the candidate policy/parameter space to find P_{i+1}. For example, if the application layer optimizer refines its parameters (e.g., threshold for intracoding; $P_{App} = [Th_{min}, Th_{max}] = [0.1, 0.8]$), then the hardware layer optimizer refines its parameters (e.g., transmission range; $P_{HW} = [Tx_{min}, Tx_{max}] = [1, 60]$), taking the application layer parameter ranges as constraints. The hardware layer results are transmitted to the application layer optimizer for further refinement. In [11], this process is referred to as *constraint refinement*. In this way, the constraint language can be used as the generic interface among different local optimizers, which enables cross layer coordination of security policies by composition. We explore the above constraint refinement approach to determine the specifics of cross-layer security strategies.

5   Implementation

Figure 2 illustrates our system implementation. Our motivating scenario — distributed surveillance with mobile robots — is described in a declarative manner. The system goal is to collect information in areas where noise or motion is detected. The mobile robots have camera devices that can record short video footage of a target area. The raw video may be directly sent to other nodes if the network supports it, or it can be preprocessed, e.g., by encoding, and then communicated to other nodes. The encoded video can be further encrypted to enhance data confidentiality, which requires a key distribution among mobile robots. The application interacts with a logical engine to perform inferences based on forward and backward reasoning. A detailed explanation on the inference system and a declarative specification of a snapshot-based surveillance scenario can be found in [12].

Our motivating scenario is programmed and executed on top of our cyber-application framework (cyber-framework, for short) via cyber APIs [4]. The

---

^{4} Region $P \in \mathcal{R}(\mathbb{P}) \iff P \subseteq \mathbb{P}$ is a closed convex set (i.e., if $(x, z \in P) \bigwedge (x < y < z)$, then $(y \in P)$) and P is finitely representable (e.g., interval based). For simplicity we use regions defined by the Cartesian product of intervals for each parameter.

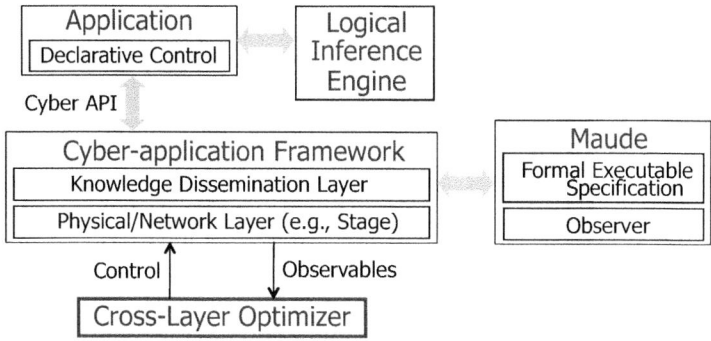

Fig. 2. System Implementation

cyber-framework implements the knowledge dissemination layer that propagates the current progress of the distributed surveillance, in the form of a knowledge unit, on top of an underlying physical/network layer. We use the Stage multi-robot simulator [13] that provides both physical device models and wireless network models to simulate losses and delays associated with packet transmissions. The cyber-framework also interacts with Maude for formal prototyping of a group communication system among mobile robots. The cross-layer optimizer in Section 4.2 iteratively tunes the security policies/parameters (i.e., *control*) by monitoring the current status (i.e., *observables*)

At the application layer, a selective video encryption scheme based on secret key cryptography [5] is used to enhance multimedia data security. For this purpose, we build on our earlier work, PBPAIR (Probability Based Power Aware Intra Refresh) [14], which can effectively control partial intracoding, as a component of a selective encryption scheme. We manipulate the algorithmic parameters of PBPAIR to cope with security demands of the application and with the other layers' operating conditions. For example, PBPAIR can be controlled to insert more intramacro blocks (IMBs), leading to more encryption and less coding efficiency with the benefit of less coding energy, which in turn affects other layers' decisions. In this scheme, the number of IMBs can be an approximate measure of data security, bandwidth requirement, and encoding/encryption energy consumption.

As a middleware layer policy, we use the Maude formal specification presented in [6] for secure group communication with relaxed synchrony — virtual synchrony (VS) and extended virtual synchrony (EVS) — and various rekeying mechanisms explained in Section 3. In this work, we explore six different policies. In the case of VS, we use eager keying with i) blocking and ii) nonblocking data multicast while rekeying proceeds. In the case of EVS, iii) eager keying, iv) key caching, v) lazy keying, and vi) a combination of caching and lazy keying are explored with the nonblocking mode.

At the hardware layer, we consider transmission power control as an effective way to minimize the eavesdropping risk as proposed in [9]. The authors of [9] define the w-th eavesdropping risk as the maximum probability of packets being eavesdropped with w adversarial nodes present in an ad hoc wireless network. Subsequently, they prove that in an arbitrary random network consisting of n nodes, the 1st order eavesdropping risk is bounded below by $\frac{1}{3}r$, where r is the normalized transmission radius. The OS policy is ongoing research. We will discuss its implication in the concluding remarks (Section 8).

6 Experiments

We evaluated the effectiveness of our approach by carrying out a variety of experiments. Our first set of experiments is concerned with understanding the impact of various policies at different layers. In our second set of experiments, we focused on the effect of composition in the context of cross-layer optimization. Currently, cross-layer optimization is performed on the observables from all robots, and the same optimization results (i.e., parameter settings) are applied to all robots. In reality, each robot needs to autonomously tune its parameters at runtime, which is a topic of future research.

Given the inherent complexity due to dependencies among layers, the first goal is to perform quantitative analysis to determine the appropriate design tradeoff between security, QoS, and resource utilization. For this purpose, we perform an exhaustive exploration on two sublayer optimizers: the keying policy in group communication at the middleware layer and the policy for wireless transmission range control at the hardware layer. Figure 3 compares them in terms of security (eavesdropping risk), QoS (travel distance, mission completion time, communication overhead, network dynamicity), and resource (power consumption). Figure 3(a)-(e) show that the larger the communication range the better the QoS since the stable connectivity among mobile robots reduces the necessity of keying and also leads to immediate propagation of current progress toward mission completion. However, Figure 3(f) presents opposite results since the larger communication range requires more transmission power for wireless devices and higher chances of being eavesdropped, which indicates that single-layer policy often cannot accommodate the inherent complexity.

In the next set of experiments we study the effect of composition as a coordination mechanism for cross-layer security management. To capture the effectiveness of given parameter settings, we define a *utility* function based on the observables and user-defined *soft* and *hard* requirements. The situation that the system behavior resides below the soft requirement is most desirable. When the system is observed in between soft and hard requirement, however, the optimizer needs to tune the parameters. Hard requirement indicates an upper limit, above which a user cannot tolerate the quality degradation. We define the cost function of the observables $X = (x_e, x_t, x_m, x_k, x_b, x_r)$ as

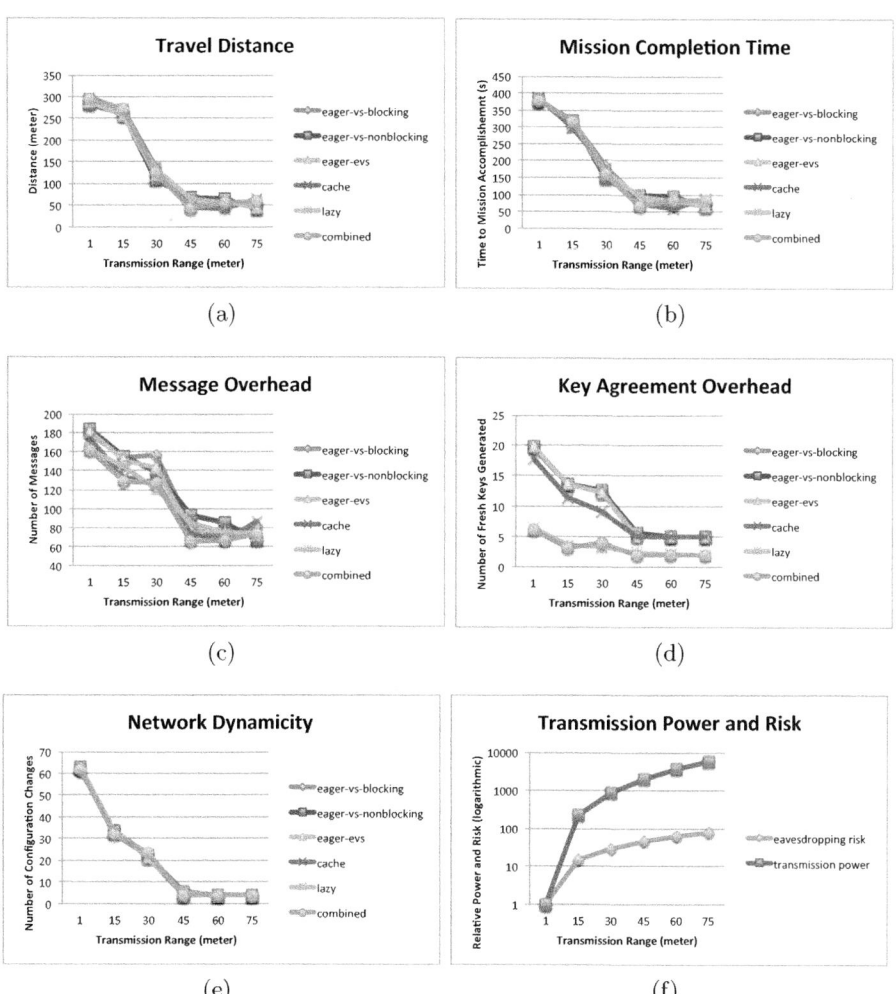

Fig. 3. Effect of Various Group Communication Schemes and Transmission Range Control (a) Total Travel Distance of All Robots, (b) Mission Completion Time, (c) Message Overhead for a Secured Dissemination, (d) Key Agreement Overhead for a Secure Group Communication, (e) Network Dynamicity in Terms of View Changes in a Group Communication, (f) Eavesdropping Risk [9] and Transmission Power Consumptions

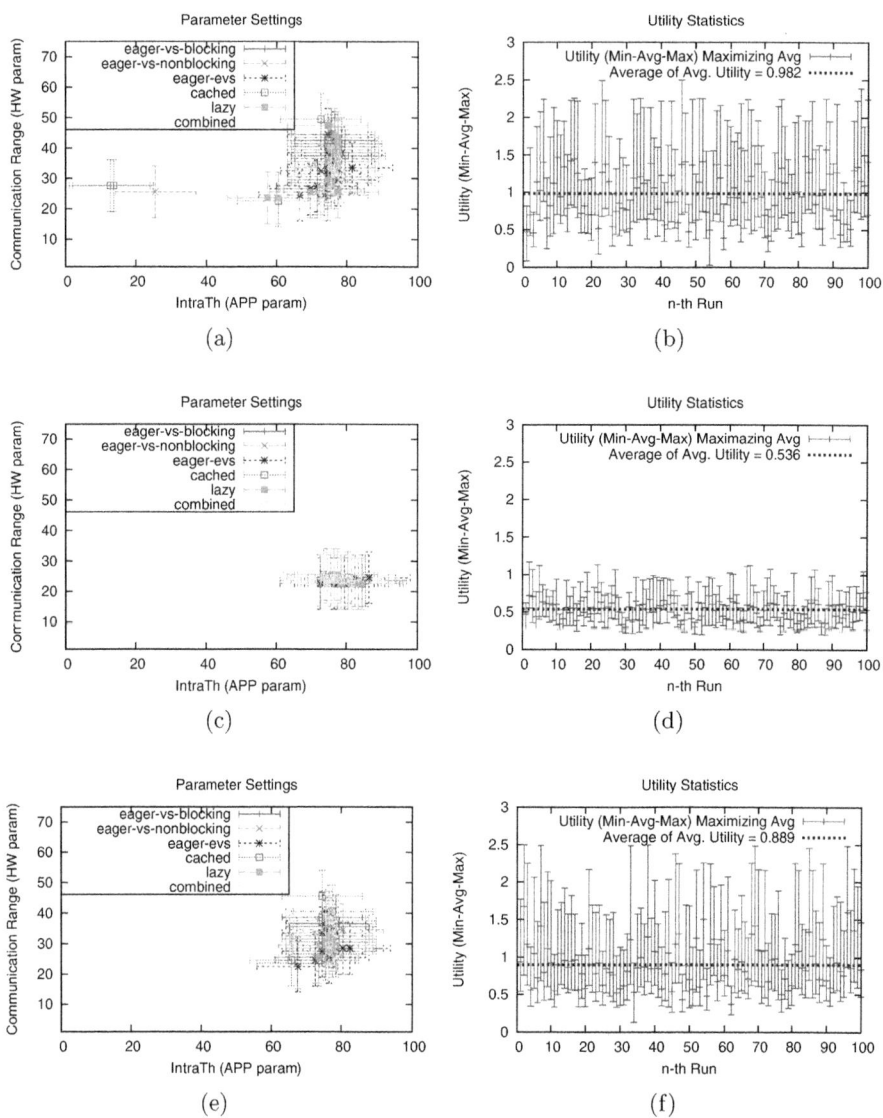

Fig. 4. Effect of Cross-Layer Optimization (Constraint Refinement for Maximizing Average of Utilities) — Parameter Settings and Utility Statistics from 100 Runs (a),(b) Global Cross-Layer Optimization; (c),(d) Without Cross-Layer Optimization; (e),(f) Compositional Cross-Layer Optimization

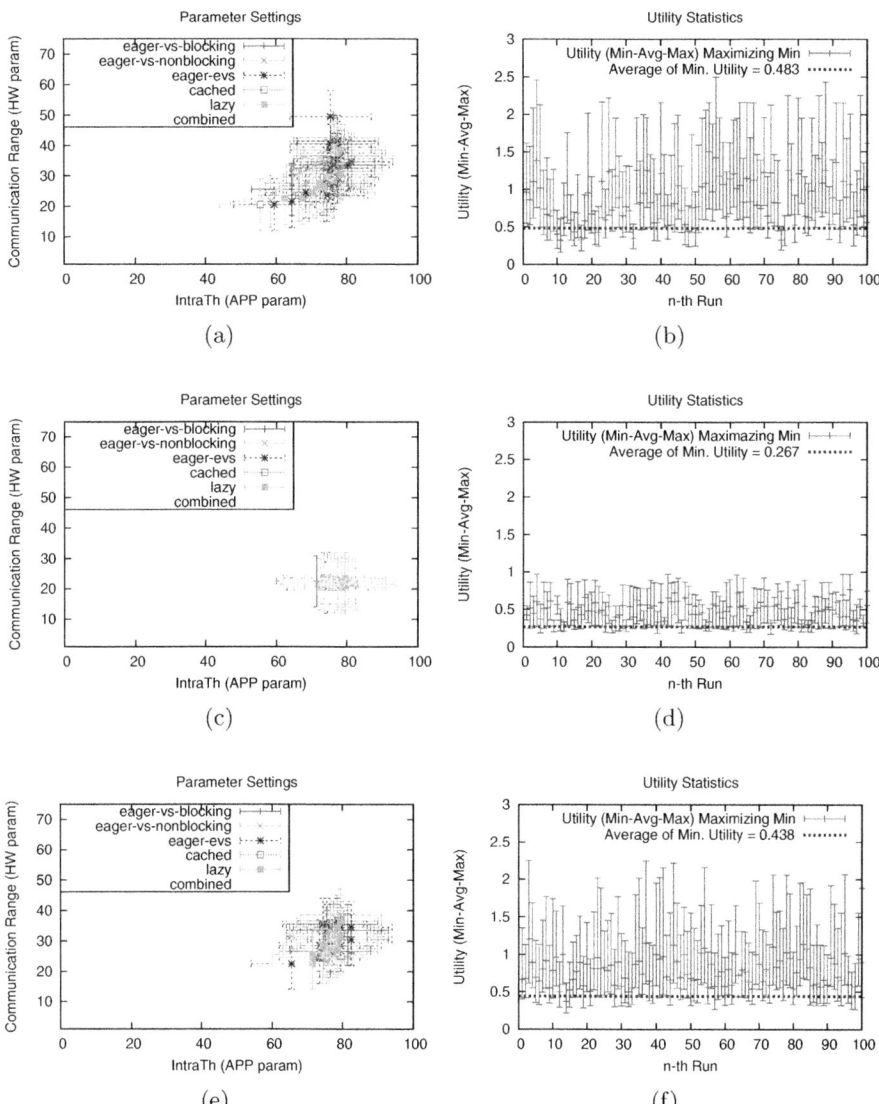

Fig. 5. Effect of Cross-Layer Optimization (Constraint Refinement for Maximizing Minimum of Utilities) — Parameter Settings and Utility Statistics from 100 Runs (a),(b) Global Cross-Layer Optimization; (c),(d) Without Cross-Layer Optimization; (e),(f) Compositional Cross-Layer Optimization

$$cost(x) = \begin{cases} \infty & \text{if } x \geq h \\ \frac{1}{h-x} - \frac{1}{h-s} & \text{if } h > x \geq s \\ 0 & \text{otherwise} \end{cases}$$

where h and s represent user-defined *hard* and *soft* requirement, respectively. The observables x_e, x_t, x_m, x_k, x_b concern energy consumption, mission completion time, messaging overhead, keying overhead, bandwidth, respectively. A risk measure $x_r = \frac{r}{e}$ takes into account of eavesdropping risk r and the amount of encryption e. The utility is defined as follows:

$$utility(X) = \frac{1}{\sum_i cost(x_i)}$$

We use the constraint refinement in sublayer optimizers with two different objectives. First, the sublayer optimizer attempts to guarantee average-case performance. In this case, the average of utilities in a region is maximized. Second, to prevent worst-case performance, the sublayer optimizer maximizes the minimum of utilities in a region. For both cases, failures (i.e., zero utility) are avoided by the sublayer optimizers that refine towards a region with fewer numbers of parameter settings leading to a failure. We compare a compositional approach with two extreme techniques: *global* and *local* optimizations. Global optimization is fully aware of sublayers' decisions, which local optimization lacks. In this work, we use a uniform refinement ratio $\bar{\tau}$ for the recursion (i.e., $\tau_0 \cdots \tau_{t-1} = \tau$ and $\forall i \in [0, \cdots, t-1] : \tau_i = \bar{\tau}$) and a constant number of iterations t. For simplicity, we fix a sequential order for the sublayer optimizers. Arbitrary interleaving and distributed optimization are future research topics.

The results for improving average-case and worst-case performance are presented in Figure 4 and Figure 5, respectively. We evaluated the performance of compositional cross-layer optimization in terms of resulting utilities and parameter selections in solving the scenario in Section 5. We compare our compositional optimization (Figure 4(e)(f) and Figure 5(e)(f)) with the two extremes: without cross-layer optimization (i.e., *local* optimization) in Figure 4(c)(d) and Figure 5(c)(d) vs. *global* optimization in Figure 4(a)(b) and Figure 5(a)(b). In Figure 4(a)(c)(e) and Figure 5(a)(c)(e), the X-axis represents the application layer parameter while the Y-axis represents the hardware layer parameter. The various group communication schemes are pictured in different colors. The parameter settings are depicted as cross bars parallel with the x-y axes to represent a region. In Figure 4(b)(d)(f) and Figure 5(b)(d)(f), x-axis and y-axis represent n-th trial and utility distribution in terms of minimum-average-maximum utilities of a resulting region, respectively.

The *compositional* cross-layer optimization in Figure 4(e)(f) and Figure 5(e)(f) presents solutions reasonably close to the *global* approach since the values of resulting utilities reside between that of local and global optimization. By a blue dashed line in Figure 4(b)(d)(f), the average of the objective (i.e., maximizing the average utilities in a resulting region) from compositional optimization leads to 0.889, which resides between that of local (0.536) and global (0.982) optimization. Similarly in Figure 5(b)(d)(f), the compositional optimization leads to the average value of minimum utilities in a resulting region as 0.438, which resides much closer to that of global (0.483) than local (0.267) optimization. The relative execution time of our compositional approach is 8 times faster than the global approach. It should be noted that the speedup can be further improved because the compositional approach can be naturally parallelized. Finally, the refined solution region is very different from that of the global approach, while our compositional optimization gives similar results.

7 Related Work

The authors of [15] formulated the network resource allocation problem as a cross-layer decision of transmission strategies across the APP, MAC and PHY layers of a traditional network protocol stack to maximize multimedia quality with rate and delay constraints. In [16], the authors modeled the communication network as a generalized utility maximization problem to provide a systematic optimization method by analysis of layered decomposition, where each layer corresponds to a decomposed subproblem and the interfaces among layers are quantified as functions of the optimization variables coordinating the subproblems. Those efforts are, however, mainly focused on the architectural decisions in networking, not tuning the system parameters for energy-quality-security gain.

The author of [17] presented a quality-driven security design and resource allocation framework for wireless sensor networks with multimedia selective encryption and stream authentication schemes proposed at the application layer and network resource allocation schemes at low layers. In particular, an unequal (partial) error protection-based network resource allocation scheme is proposed by jointly designing selective multimedia encryption and multimedia stream authentication with communication resource allocation. Their cross layer resource management framework for secure multimedia streaming solves a global optimization problem requiring full awareness of the system dynamics while our compositional approach leads to acceptable solution quality at low complexity. Also, the composition can be fully distributed and capable of utilizing different even conflicting local objectives through the generic interface of constraint language.

8 Concluding Remarks

We have presented first steps toward situation- and resource-aware cross-layer security by investigating the security implications of existing policies and integrating them across all layers, which aims at automating verification and configuration of security policies to respond to cyber-attacks with minimum availability degradation. The existing xTune cross-layer optimization methodology, on which our approach is based, is general enough to handle simple versions of the cross-layer security problem. A compositional approach to enforcing security policies, while enabling desired activities, has the advantage of being agile and flexible. We build upon substantial preliminary efforts to facilitate the understanding of complex distributed multilayered systems. We believe that our work has broad implications for security analysis of application protocol optimization. In principle, it facilitates security-aware tradeoffs to improve system availability and the utilization of limited resources. We have attempted to illustrate the benefit through a sample scenario that involves cooperative operations of mobile nodes and physical infrastructure.

While this work focuses specifically on the surveillance of physical infrastructure, the approach directly applies to many distributed, dynamically reconfigurable architectures. Furthermore, the techniques described in this paper can apply to broader domains, such as vehicular networks (for both civilian and military usage), instrumented cyber-physical spaces [18], and search/rescue operations by first responders who carry mobile devices. More broadly, the proposed approach gives the basic methodology for future work in understanding runtime assurance techniques because model-based distributed control and optimization methods are especially useful for phenomena with significant uncertainty or failure in input. We are currently extending our models to include provenance at the OS layer, which will enable the detection of malicious nodes based on the examination of provenance data as described in our threat model (Section 2). We also plan to improve our composition methods to handle horizontal compositions and more complex constraint solving needed in many cyber-attack scenarios. Accommodating alternative ways of defining utility (e.g., by enforcing an ordering among the observables and using the induced lexicographic ordering or by adapting the concept of a Pareto front) with composite evaluation metrics for security is another interesting research avenue since our approach does not rely on a specific of the utility function

Acknowledgments. This material is based in part upon work supported by the U.S. Department of Homeland Security under Grant Award Number 2006-CS-001-000001, under the auspices of the Institute for Information Infrastructure Protection (I3P) research program. The I3P is managed by Dartmouth College. The views and conclusions contained in this document are those of the authors and should not be interpreted as necessarily representing the official policies, either expressed or implied, of the U.S. Department of Homeland Security, the I3P, or Dartmouth College.

Additional support from National Science Foundation Grant 0932397 (A Logical Framework for Self-Optimizing Networked Cyber-Physical Systems) is gratefully acknowledged. Any opinions, findings, and conclusions or recommendations expressed in this material are those of the author(s) and do not necessarily reflect the views of NSF.

References

1. Pister, K.: From smart dust to smart plants the evolution of wireless sensor networking. In: ISA EXPO 2008: Keynote Speech (2008), http://www.dustnetworks.com

2. Mohapatra, S., Dutt, N., Nicolau, A., Venkatasubramanian, N.: DYNAMO: A cross-layer framework for end-to-end QoS and energy optimization in mobile handheld devices. IEEE Journal on Selected Areas in Communications 25(4), 722–737 (2007)

3. xTune Framework, http://xtune.ics.uci.edu

4. Kim, M., Stehr, M.-O., Kim, J., Ha, S.: An application framework for loosely coupled networked cyber-physical systems. In: 8th IEEE Intl. Conf. on Embedded and Ubiquitous Computing (EUC 2010), Hong Kong (December 2010), http://ncps.csl.sri.com/papers/cyberframework.pdf

5. Bhargava, B., Shi, C., Wang, S.-Y.: MPEG video encryption algorithms. Multimedia Tools Appl. 24, 57–79 (2004)

6. Gutierrez-Nolasco, S., Venkatasubramanian, N., Stehr, M.-O., Talcott, C.: Exploring adaptability of secure group communication using formal prototyping techniques. In: ARM 2004: Workshop on Adaptive and Reflective Middleware, pp. 232–237 (2004)

7. SPADE Project, http://spade.csl.sri.com.

8. Bethencourt, J., Sahai, A., Waters, B.: Ciphertext-policy attribute-based encryption. In: SP 2007: Proceedings of the IEEE Symposium on Security and Privacy, pp. 321–334 (2007)

9. Kao, J.-C., Marculescu, R.: Minimizing eavesdropping risk by transmission power control in multihop wireless networks. IEEE Trans. Comput. 56(8), 1009–1023 (2007)

10. Maude System, http://maude.csl.sri.com.

11. Kim, M., Stehr, M.-O., Talcott, C., Dutt, N., Venkatasubramanian, N.: Constraint refinement for online verifiable cross-layer system adaptation. In: DATE 2008: Proceedings of the Design, Automation and Test in Europe Conference and Exposition (2008)

12. Stehr, M.-O., Kim, M., Talcott, C.: Toward distributed declarative control of networked cyber-physical systems. In: Yu, Z., Liscano, R., Chen, G., Zhang, D., Zhou, X. (eds.) UIC 2010. LNCS, vol. 6406, pp. 397–413. Springer, Heidelberg (2010)

13. Rusu, R.B., Maldonado, A., Beetz, M., Gerkey, B.: Extending Player/Stage/Gazebo towards cognitive robots acting in ubiquitous sensor-equipped environments. In: IEEE Intl. Conf. on Robotics and Automation Workshop for Network Robot Systems (2007)

14. Kim, M., Oh, H., Dutt, N., Nicolau, A., Venkatasubramanian, N.: PBPAIR: An energy-efficient error-resilient encoding using probability based power aware intra refresh. ACM SIGMOBILE Mob. Comput. Commun. Rev. 10(3), 58–69 (2006)

15. Schaar, M.V.D., Shankar, S.: Cross-layer wireless multimedia transmission: challenges, principles, and new paradigms. IEEE Wireless Communications 12, 50–58 (2005)

16. Chiang, M., Low, S.H., Calderbank, A.R., Doyle, J.C.: Layering as optimization decomposition:a mathematical theory of network architectures. Proceedings of the IEEE 95(1), 255–312 (2007)

17. Wang, W.: Quality-driven cross layer design for multimedia security over resource constrained wireless sensor networks. University of Nebraska, Lincoln, Dept. of Computer and Electronics Engineering, Ph.D. Dissertation (2009)

18. Kim, M., Massaguer, D., Dutt, N., Mehrotra, S., Ren, S., Stehr, M.-O., Talcott, C., Venkatasubramanian, N.: A semantic framework for reconfiguration of instrumented cyber physical spaces. In: Workshop on Event-based Semantics, CPS Week (2008)

Chameleon: A Model of Identification, Authorization and Accountability for Ubicomp

Alireza Pirayesh Sabzevar and João Pedro Sousa

Computer Science Department, George Mason University,
4400 University Drive, Fairfax, Virginia, 22030
{apirayes,jpsousa}@gmu.edu

Abstract. This paper introduces a model for invisible security. Our model provides an unobtrusive multi-factor authentication and context-aware authorization based on a probabilistic approach that takes into account social relationships and natural behaviors of the user, such as sharing objects or borrowing credentials as a form of access delegation. We believe the traditional model with sequential authentication, authorization and accounting modules is not suitable for smart spaces. Instead we propose a "probabilistic-spiral" model that can be as dynamic as the space itself.

Keywords: Identification, Authorization, Bayesian Network, Ubicomp.

1 Introduction

Ubicomp needs to be secure to be of practical use and its security must become just as invisible and non-intrusive as the rest of ubicomp. The large number of computing objects (some with limited I/O capability, confine processing power or small storage), many-to-many relationship between the users and devices, platform differences among devices, and last but not the least, the device and user mobility make the challenge of ubicomp a totally new one.

A frequent approach to identification and authentication in ubicomp is to ask users to carry a device (i.e. a credential of type *something the user has*). For example, one of the earliest ubicomp applications, the Active Badge [1], uses RFID tags to identify users moving around an office space. More recently, the popularity and increasing processing power of cell phones has allowed researchers to use cell phones in ubicomp applications including, but not limited to, authentication and authorization.

Requiring users to carry a particular device is in violation of the ubicomp invisibility. In addition, relying chiefly on personal devices such as badges and phones brings a fair amount of risk and inaccuracy. A primary concern is the protection of the device itself. First, devices may be misplaced or stolen. Smart devices, carrying personal data in addition of being used for authentication, increase the exposure and potential damage resulting from having the device stolen. Second, smart devices are also at risk of viruses, malware, and other cyber attacks. Compared to professionally administered equipment, personal devices are likely to be less protected and they may engage in network exchanges with any of the spaces visited by the user. Since these devices are now used as an entry point for ubicomp security, compromising a device

C.-H. Hsu et al. (Eds.): UIC 2011, LNCS 6905, pp. 326–339, 2011.

opens the gate for compromising the entire system. And third, *anyone* carrying the device will be wrongly identified as the owner of the device, possibly leading to unintended authorizations, and inaccurate auditing information.

In this paper we introduce Chameleon, a novel approach to ubicomp security that incorporates *unobtrusive* authentication mechanisms and accommodates the *uncertainty* that such mechanisms bring to the forefront. Furthermore, Chameleon is aware of the *natural behaviors* and *social relationships* of users: badges or passwords may be borrowed among colleagues and family members as an impromptu form of delegation, similar to borrowing car keys. Rather than designing security mechanisms that try to fit user behaviors to the mechanism's assumptions, we propose to leverage such behaviors to make security less intrusive and more effective overall.

While desktop computing model follows a *deterministic-waterfall* approach to Authentication, Authorization and Auditing, we propose a *probabilistic-spiral* model. Our model focuses on Identification, Authorization and Follow-up, where the security control receives feedback from the environment and adjusts itself based on new facts on the ground.

The rest of the paper is organized as follows: Section 2 explains our vision for Chameleon. In this section we also discuss a hypothetical scenario which helps us to elaborate our vision. In the rest of the paper, this scenario shows how Chameleon solves various aspects of ubicomp security. Section 3 lays down our proposed model, its entities and their relationships. Section 4 describes how the model and entities all work together to achieve a usable security in ubicomp environment. Section 5 looks at the state of the art and compares Chameleon with other studies and previously proposed models. Section 6 concludes our paper and talks about future work to move Chameleon forward.

2 Vision

In order to make user identification and authentication accurate and unobtrusive, the system should leverage multiple identification factors, such as personal devices, biological identifiers (e.g. face recognition) as well as conventional credentials. It should also factor in social relationships among users as well as contextual information, such as user location and time of day. User identification should be flexible and robust in the face of natural behaviors such as users misplacing or borrowing each other's credentials. On the authorization and auditing front, the system should consider dynamism of the environment and enforce *continues control*: an access that is authorized right now might not be valid a minute later or an authorized access may invalidate accesses that were granted in the past. It is also important to factor the size of the display and people who are around it. Based on who are standing in front of a large screen, request for opening a file by a user may get denied despite the fact that user has permission to access the file. Due to this volatility, a richer logging and accounting is required.

Security for ubicomp in general and for smart spaces in particular, should provide:

1. Balance of usability and security: offering mechanisms with low overhead for users, but with adequate levels of deterrence, confidentiality, integrity, and non-repudiation. Rather than supporting a one-size-fits-all solution, it should be easy

for users to tune a range of solutions from "low overhead-low protection" to "high overhead-high protection", depending on the resources to be protected.

2. Accurate and unobtrusive identification of users: The system should leverage probabilistic reasoning about multiple identification factors, such as face recognition and conventional credentials, and factoring in social relationships among users as well as contextual information, such as user location and time of day. User identification should be flexible and robust in the face of natural behaviors such as users misplacing or borrowing each other's credentials.

3. Users' expectations of authorization: The system should consider the presentation of another user's credentials as a proxy for delegation of authority, in addition to the authorization that derive from one's own identity. It should be easy for users to tune the rules for authorization and delegation, e.g. with respect to required credentials, as opposed to requiring complex configuration by a system administrator.

4. Robust and proactive auditing: in addition to logging the (most likely) user identity for each access, auditing should also log the identification factors that led both to the identification and to the authorization decisions. Furthermore, auditing should act proactively in warning a user when others use his or hers credentials to gain access to important resources.

5. Support for simultaneous use of multiple devices and multiple users per device: The system should be able to address the above challenges when multiple users share devices within a space and in particular when a single device, such as a large collaborative surface, is simultaneously used by several users.

To elaborate our vision we employ a hypothetical scenario:

> *Consider a television set in a household. In general, anybody with physical access to the set can Watch TV. The family living in our imaginary household has 3 members: Dad (40 years old), Mom (36 years old) and Son (15 years old). There are TV channels which content might not be suitable for the Son. Furthermore, there are cases when the Son is grounded and he is not allowed to watch TV. When grounded, the Son still may get some TV-time awarded by parents.*

Currently access to channels with age-restricted content can be managed by what so called *parental control*; a 4-digit password. To control the TV usage some TVs offer another password. In absence of such, families may find low-tech alternatives e.g. locking up the TV room or removing the power cord.

In contrast, in an ideal ubicomp environment the TV can recognize who is in front of it and depends on the age of that person, access to restricted channels are either allowed or disallowed. At the same time, when it comes to age restricted content, the identification and authorization are more precise than when a regular channel is watched. If there are two or more users in the room, the most restricted permission prevails. The 4-digit password would still exist to provide backward compatibility, as a last resort to resolve uncertainty around users' identity or overwrite the applied permissions with less restricted ones. Similar argument can be made for turning-on the TV. Everybody in the household should be able to turn on the TV but if the Son is grounded he should not be able to turn-on or watch TV. If the grounded Son gets some TV time, as reward for example, there should be any easy way to grant the Son a temporary access to the TV.

Detecting who is standing in front of TV can be done by evidences such as the car parked in the garage, the cell phones and notebooks inside the house and finally a camera that's installed on top of the TV and a face recognition process that is running in background. Hints such as user behavior can also be used to identify the user. None of these methods is 100% accurate but the synergy among them can add up to certainty about the user's identity. This is similar to idea behind "Multi-Factor Authentication": one method may not be very strong but the combination of multiple methods provides a "Strong Authentication" [2].

Existing security models adopt the classical separation of concerns between authentication and authorization: Once the user's identity is authenticated the authorization proceeds based on that identity. Unfortunately, that may be the wrong identity in the situations where the natural behaviors of users do not match the assumptions of the security model. For example, in a situation that Dad leaves the house and forget to turn off the TV, Son may find a chance to watch TV despite the fact that he is grounded. Similarly, the Dad has to enter the parental control code every time he wants to see what is on a particular channel.

The security model we envision revisits these assumptions. First, given Son's age should automatically restrict access to certain programs or channels. At the same time, when Dad leaves home the system should adjust itself and revisit the issued accesses.

It is important to note that we are not suggesting a replacement for text-based authentication or a new model of authorization. Our model is a smarter security mechanism that can benefit from all the existing methods and technologies.

3 Model

In our model we have a group of users in an environment such as home or office. Each user in the environment has a *Social Network Profile* which provides some information about users such as age or users' social relationships. The system can handle outsiders and label them as a *Guests* or *Strangers*. An environment may be divided into hierarchical *Zones,* corresponding to rooms, and *Sub-zones*. For example, the kitchen is a zone and it has subzones: near the fridge, near the stove, etc. There might be zero or more ubicomp *Objects* in each zone.

Our model has multiple categories for the objects: they are either *Fixed* or *Portable*. TV set or an oven which are usually fixtures of a house are examples of fixed objects. The TV might be in the living room and the oven is usually in kitchen. Both kitchen and living room are sub-zones of the house. House is an *Environment*, i.e. an administrative unit and the *Super-zone*. A car, cell phone and keychain are examples of portable objects. Portable objects move in and out of zones frequently.

The environment is equipped with various *Sensors* which can report the presence of portable objects in a particular zone. For the purpose of this paper, we assume the sensors are all healthy and report accurate readings. Each portable object has an *Owner*. The presence of a portable object contributes to the likelihood of the presence of the owner in a particular zone. All objects are sharable among the users. For example a TV can be watched by all family members or car parked in the garage which is owned by Dad, makes it more likely that somebody who is eligible to drive the car, including but not limited to, the owner, Dad, is at home.

Devices are also categorized based on the level of user interaction they support: A keychain or an RFID tag is a *Non-interactive* object. On the other hand, the TVs or the cell phones are *Interactive* objects. Interactive objects can facilitate the Identification and Authorization process. For example they can display or utter a message challenging the user to clarify his or her identity.

Portable objects can be also categorized as *Authoritative, Non-Authoritative* or *Neutral*. Both authoritative and non-authoritative objects are involved in process of identification and authorization of a user. On the other hand, neutral objects have no role in such. The difference between authoritative and non-Authoritative objects is in the semantics of sharing. Presence of both authoritative and non-authoritative objects contributes to the likelihood of presence of the owner in the environment and a particular zone. Labeling an object as non-authoritative means beside the owner, other users who are eligible to use the object might be in the environment as well. On the other hand, authoritative objects in presence of a non-owner may indicate delegation of some rights. Fig. 1 shows the discussed object categories and their relationship with each other.

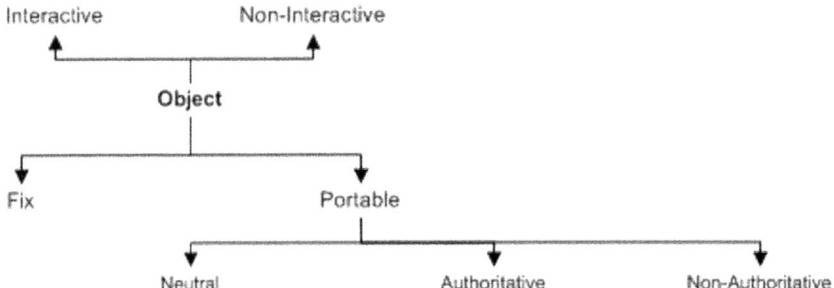

Fig. 1. Object categories

Objects offer *Services*, for example, an oven offers a *Cooking Service* with some *Operations* such as "Turn-on", "Turn-off", and "Set Temperature". Several objects in the environment may offer a similar service. *Watching TV* is an example of such: a user can watch TV on a computer, a TV set, a cell phone or listen to the sound track of the movie on a radio. Such service has some operation such as "Start", "Stop", "Fast Forward" and "Rewind".

Each object, interactive or non-interactive, may be used by one or multiple *object-independent identification services*. For example, a camera can be used by *Face Recognition* service. A smart phone can be used by *Voice Recognition, Face Recognition* and *One-time SMS based pass-code* services.

To put these definitions in context, the mapping of TV watching scenario to our model is as follows:

Users: The family living in our imaginary household has 3 members: Dad, Mom and Son.

Zones: We have only one Zone and that's the "House".

Fixed Object: TV and the camera installed on top of the TV are both fixed objects installed in the "House" zone.

Portable – Authoritative objects: All 3 members of the family have their own cell phones. They don't switch or share phones. They carry their phones with them to work and school but there is always a possibility that some of them forget his or her cell phone at home. Dad also has a USB key fob that can be programmed with well defined access levels to some services.

Portable- Non-Authoritative objects: The family has 2 cars; one owned by dad the other one by mom. Dad and mom switch their cars 5% of the time and 5% of the time they may use only one of the cars and go out together. Son can ride with Mom and/or Dad in either car.

Interactive objects: The TV and cell phone in this scenario are considered interactive objects. As mentioned, interactive devices have the capability of challenging users' identity.

Non-Interactive objects: The car and USB key fob are examples of non-interactive objects.

Sensors: If the cell phone is inside the house, it usually switches to the WiFi network. So it is relatively easy to detect if a phone is inside the house or not. The house has a garage equipped with sensors that can detect if the car is parked in the garage.

Services: "Turn-on", "Turn-off" and "Chang Channel" are the services provided by TV.

In addition to the concepts above, Chameleon's model stores authorization rules. Authorization rules are defined by the owner of an Object or Service for controlling the access to its Operations. A Wizard-based interface guides the users through the steps of defining the access rules. The high level rules for Watching TV looks like:

— *If the user is one of the Parents 'Turn-on' is ALLOWED (Relax)*
— *If the user is SON 'Turn-on' is ALLOWED (Relax)*
— *If the user is UNKNOWN 'Turn-on' is DENIED (Relax)*
— *If Program Content has Nudity or Strong Language, if the User's Age is <=20 'Play' is DENIED (Restrict)*

Each rule is labeled with a conflict resolution instruction. Any time a *Relax* access conflicts with a *Restrict* access, the Restrict access will prevail. The access can be defined using a role-based access control which can handle users and devices relationship similar to what has been proposed in [3]. It has been shown that it is possible to generate discretionary access control from role-based access policies [4]. During the run-time, these rules will be translated to an Extended Access Control List (EACL). In Section 4 we talk about the Extended Access List in more details.

Fig. 2 shows the high level architecture and relationship between different modules in our proposed model. To identify the users, Chameleon employs active and passive identifications. In *Passive Identification* the system tries to identify users based on the values reported by the sensors in the environment. For example a car parked in the garage can indicate the presence of the owner of the car or another person who is eligible to drive at home. Similar inferences can be made based on the presence of a cell phone. In contrast, the *Active Identification* engages user into a series of actions to prove his or her identity, for example, asking user to stand in front of a camera, swipe a card, or enter a pass-code. Chameleon is able to detect all the amenities in the environment and select the best Active Identification method. To choose the best available method, the system should be able to rank the mechanisms based on factors such as ease of use, accuracy, delay and user's preference.

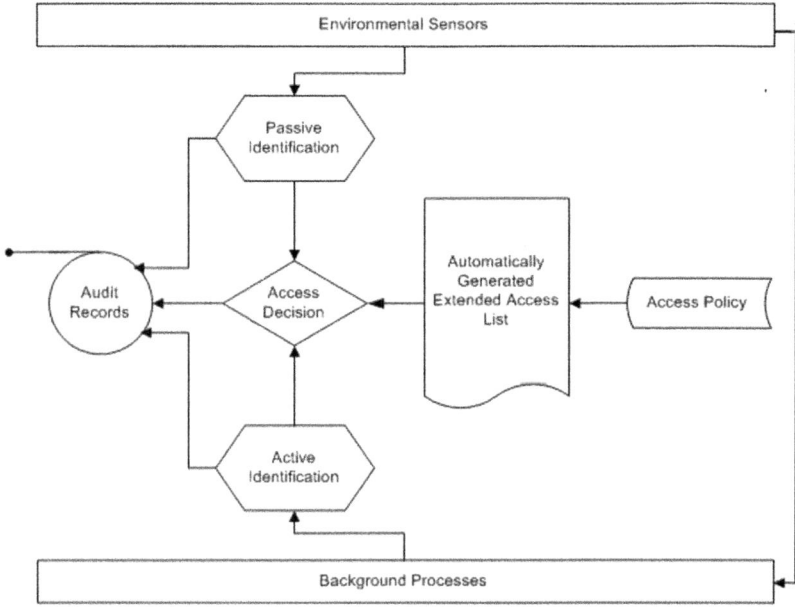

Fig. 2. High level Architecture of the proposed model

Similar to traditional systems when a user wants to access a service, there is a binary decision to be made: access is either allowed or denied. There are 2 reasons for an access denied decision: the user is not identified accurately or the user doesn't have access to the service. In case of insufficient identification or misidentification, the user has a chance to employ one or multiple "active identification" method and pass through. If the user is identified correctly and based on the policy access is denied, the user has a chance to provide a sign of delegation (an Authoritative object) or ask the service owner to delegate him a temporary or permanent access. We will talk more about the Identification and Access Decision in section 4.

The last piece in Chameleon is the *Audit Records* module. This module has two responsibilities. One is to record the events as they are happening. This is very similar to what *syslogd* process does for a UNIX machine. However Chameleon should record a reacher log to capture all the rational beind granting or blocking an access. The second responsibility is to detect the anomalies in the environment and raise the appropriate flag for it.

4 Inference

The purpose of "Inference" is to reason about the world based on observed evidences. Inference can be deterministic: Dad's car is parked in the garage and his cell phone is inside the house, thus Dad is at home. What makes such inference uncertain is the possibility of Dad and Mom leaving together in Mom's car forgetting Dad's cell phone behind.

In general, there are three ways of dealing with uncertainty: non-numerical methods mainly non-monotonic logic, numerical representations such as fuzzy logic or Dempster-Shafer and probabilistic methods such as Bayesian Network [5]. The difference between numerical and probabilistic method is rather superficial [5]. While there are many differences between, for example, Dempster-Shafer and Bayesian Network, there are also many commonalities between the two and they have roughly the same expressiveness power [6].

Probability theory is the most widely applied formalism for reasoning under uncertainty [7] which can represent conditional and independent assumptions [8]. We use Bayesian Network to perform inference for our model.

Fig. 3 shows the decision network that models our TV Watching scenario. This model should be created every time a service is accessed and it should be maintained as long as the service is in use. As shown, the reasoning for presence of user at home depends on the time of the day and presence of certain car or cell phone at home.

The "Extended Access Control" is the translation of access rules defined by the user to a format that can be used for decision making in Bayesian Network. The line in the policy which says "if the user is one of the Parents access is ALLOWED" is translated into "Dad is 100% allowed to watch TV, so are Mom and Dad&Mom". Following the same thought "Dad is 0% denied from watching TV, so are Mom and Dad&Mom". There are several factors that control the size and content of the EACL:

1- The users whose access has been explicitly defined: The rest of the users, if any, can be considered as one user (i.e. named Unknown and denied).
2- The users in the environment: we can cut the branches of the Bayesian tree which are generated for users who are not in the environemnt. This makes the tree smaller and makes the conclusion faster. If the user is not in the tree, we don't need to have the user in the EACL.
3- Size of the screen: If the output is shown on the large screen permission of all the users in the environment should be checked. In contrast smaller (i.e. personal screens) should be only checked for one user.

The "Decision" node is the system response to the request for turning on the TV. We can define a threshold so if "Allow" percentage is equal or greater than the threshold, the function "Turn-on" will be executed on the TV. In case, evidences are not enough to support a definitive decsion, the system should ask for extra evidences or challende the user with a more robust identification method.

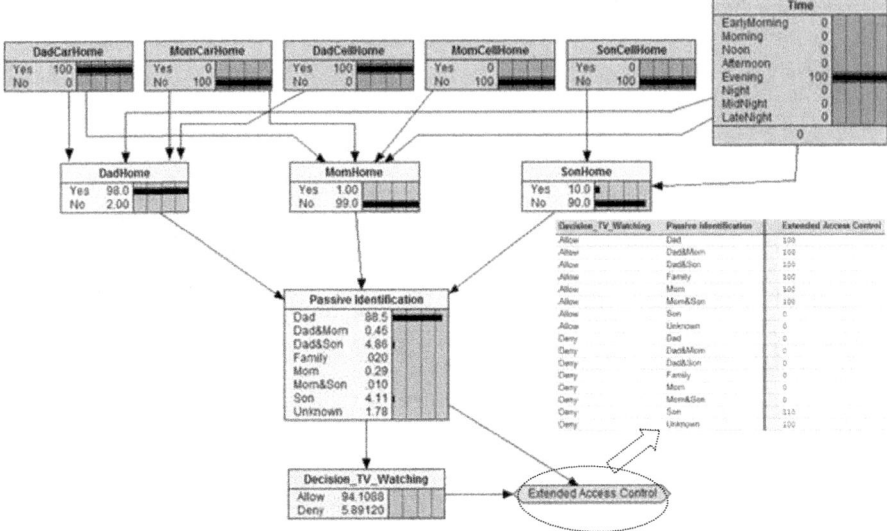

Fig. 3. Bayesian network for TV Watching scenario and the "Access Control" table

User Being At Home-Behavioral			
Time (military format)	Dad	Mom	Son
0001-0800	100%	100%	100%
0801-1000	2%	98%	2%
1001-1200	1%	95%	1%
1201-1400	1%	78%	1%
1401-1600	1%	86%	97%
1601-1800	20%	95%	98%
1801-2000	99%	99%	99%
2001-2200	99%	99%	99%
2201-2400	99.9%	99.9%	99.9%

User Being At Home-Cell Phone at Home		
Dad	Mom	Son
98%	95%	99%

User Being At Home-Car parked in the garage				
Dad Car	Mom Car	Dad	Mom	Son
No	No	1%	1%	N/A
No	Yes	3%	98%	N/A
Yes	No	98%	3%	N/A
Yes	Yes	99.9%	99.9%	N/A

Users Watching TV When at Home		
Dad	Mom	Son
20%	40%	30%

Fig. 4. Example of conditional probability tables

As mentioned before, for the sake of simplicity we have ignored the measurement errors of the sensors meaning that we always assume the reported value of the sensor is accurate. However since we use the Bayesian network, our model is inherently able to handle the probability of inaccuracy. In order to have more accurate results during the run-time, the historical information about users' behavior should be collected and presented to our model. Fig. 4 shows examples of such tables which can be gathered as the system operates.

In Bayesian terminology, these historical values are called conditional probability tables. In case if Passive Identification is not enough, an "Active Identification"

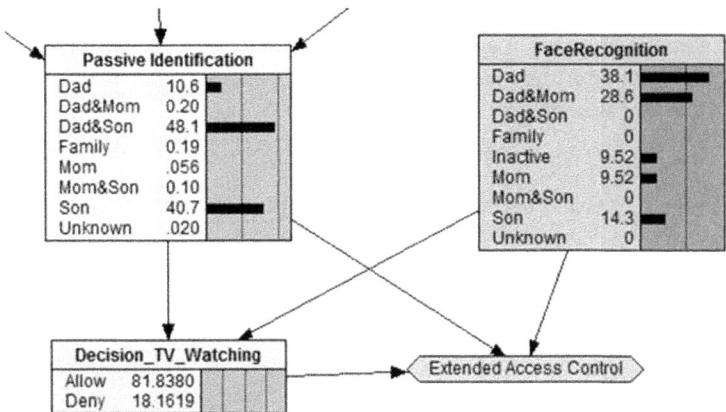

Fig. 5. Partial view of decision network after adding active identification method

method will be invoked. Depends on the type of available Services and Interactive Objects in the environment and their characteristics such as ease of use, accuracy and latency as well as the amount of deficit in user's identity, the system chooses a method of Active Identification.

Choosing the interactive method can be the result of another multi-criteria decision making or a simple predefined priority list. After choosing the method, the system invites the user to participate in series of actions to clarify user's identity. To that end, the system also adds a new node to the decision tree as it can be seen in Fig. 5.

If the user is identified correctly and based on the policy access is denied, the user has a chance to provide a sign of delegation (an Authoritative Object) or ask the service owner to delegate him a temporary or permanent access. Access to Watch TV can be delegated from Dad to Son using Interactive Objects (e.g. a phone call to Dad's cell phone) or Non-Interactive Objects (e.g. a USB key fob that's programmed by Dad and given to Son). Delegation act will simply modify the Extended Access Control to permit the access otherwise banned by the permissions.

We mentioned earlier that we can define a threshold for certainty of "Allow". Therefore, if the calculated value for "Allow" is equal or greater than the threshold, the function "Turn-on" will be executed. In other words, depends on the the treshold level, we are accepting a degree of risk where our decision might not be correct. This leads us to another question that how much risk is acceptable? In the best case scenario we have absolute certainty and zero-risk. A rational person would not accept any risk at all except possibly in return for the benefits that come along with it [9]. The cost of absolute certainty is usually high and for some applications the cost might not be justified. That's why in traditional AAA systems, risk and uncertainty are ignored altogether and the system assumes the person who enters the credential is always the actual user.

Cost-benefit model is be a better alternative where availability is the benefit and protection is the cost. This method can also represent the tradeoff between security and usability in a more meaningful way. In presence of uncertainty, the system permits access (i.e. availability) by risking the protection. In contrast, it sometimes should compromise the availability for the sake of higher protection.

In Chameleon generally we have 2 risks: Allowing unauthorized access and blocking authorized access. Let R be the risk of operation O executed by the users U_i. If there are n users in the environment affecting the decision, then the risk of the operation can be calculated as:

$$R = \sum_{i=1}^{n} Uncert(Ui) \times Dmg\ (Ou) + \sum_{i=1}^{n} Uncert(Ui) \times Dmg\ (Ob) \quad (1)$$

where $Uncert\ (U_i)$ is the uncertainty around identity of users U_i and $Dmg\ (O_u)$ and $Dmg\ (O_b)$ are the damages caused by allowing unautorised access or blocking the authorized access. The Bayesian network can provide us with the uncertainty around identity. We also need a scale quantifying and measuering the damages.

Similarly, benefits in Chameleon's access control are allowing authorized accesses and blocking unauthorized ones. With the similar assumptions, the benefit (B) of operation O can be calculated as:

$$B = \sum_{i=1}^{n} Cert(Ui) \times Bnf\ (Oa) + \sum_{i=1}^{n} Cert(Ui) \times Bnf\ (Ob) \quad (2)$$

$Cert\ (U_i)$ is the certainty around identity of users U_i and $Bnf\ (O_a)$ and $Bnf\ (O_b)$ are the benefits of by allowing autorised access and blocking the unauthorized access. Now, the treshold can be defined based on $B\ /\ R$ outcome.

5   Related Work

Previously we have surveyed existing security mechanisms for various ubicomp environments [10]. The obvious pattern among most of the works we reviewed is that they require the users to carry a specific device with them (See **Table 1**).

We believe such an approach is neither in harmony with the promise of ubiquitous computing, nor necessary for providing effective security. While using a specific device is a transition strategy to move from desktop computing to the ubicomp, we suggest a user identification method that doesn't limit the user to a specific technology or device.

Table 1. Summary of the ubicomp studies and their authentication factor reviewed in [10]

Research Project	Institute/Sponsor	Authentication Factor
Bardram et. al[11]	University of Aarhus, Denmark	RFID tags
ZIA[12]	University of Michigan, US	Cryptography Token
Zero-Stop Auth.[13]	Keio University, Japan	RFID tags, Handhelds
RAUM [14]	University of Karlsruhe, Germany	Handhelds
My Campus[15]	Carnegie Melon University, US	Handhelds
Cerberus[16]	University of Illinois, US	RFID tags
iSecurity[17]	Stanford university, US	Certificate on personal device
Vigil[18]	University of Maryland, US	Bluetooth enabled Handhelds

Among all the proposed solutions, Gaia [19] is the closet to our idea. Gaia is a distributed middleware system from University of Illinois at Urbana-Champaign that enhances the user's activities with ubiquitous computing devices to form an interactive, programmable computing and communication system. Cerberus is the security scheme of Gaia [16]. Similar to our suggested model, Cerberus doesn't require the user to carry a special device and it supports various authentication methods. A user can only access a service if the authentication system identifies her with a confidence value of more than an administratively defines value.

However, the way to reach the necessary confidence is completly different than our approach. In Cerberus, the confidence level of each authentication method is a fix number. The the net confidence value V_{net} to authentication of a user who owns and users n difference authentication methods with confidence values of V_1, V_2, .. V_n is calculated as:

$$V_{net} = 1 - (1-V_1)(1-V_2)\ldots(1-V_n) \tag{3}$$

While the confidence value may work for some situation, it is not flexible enough. For example the confidence in an RFID tag when there is no evidence of presence of the owner in the environment should be significantly lower than when the owner is in the environment. Cerberus doesn't calculate the combined access permission. This is especially important if large screens are employed. It also doesn't consider user's habits to share credential or devices. Cerberus also keeps silence about concepts such as delegation and auditing

Uncertainty is always associated with every aspect of human life. Hence, when the technology gets integrated into life activities, it has to also deal with uncertainty and unpredictability. For the first time Satyanarayanan in [20] talks about accuracy of knowledge around users' intent as one of the implementation problems of pervasive computing. We use Bayesian Network to deal with uncertainty. Bayesian network has been previously used in other ubicomp studies such as Location Stack [21]. Location tracking is a challenging subject in ubicomp in which uncertainty plays an important role. Location Stack is a six-layer sensor fusion library that can provide location information for location-aware application. It introduces a layered approached for ubicomp multi-sensor location systems by performing multi-sensor fusion using a variety of Bayesian filtering and estimation techniques such as adaptive particle filtering.

Our idea of continues authorization is similar to what UCON suggests [22]. Usage Control, UCON, combines ideas from traditional access control, trust management, and digital rights management. UCON's model refines the notion of access rights into access rules, conditions, and obligations. Rules capture the traditional relation between requesters, and the allowed kinds of access to resources. Conditions may be used to capture additional constraints such as access location, time of day, number of allowed accesses per period of time, etc. Obligations capture actions that requester commits to perform during or after the access, e.g. metered payments during access to online media. In UCON users' access right can be checked once before granting the access or continually during the access.

6 Conclusion and Future Work

In this paper, we introduced Chameleon, a security mechanism for ubicomp which provides a secure, usable and flexible identification, authorization and auditing mechanisms. Our goal is to hide the security as much as possible and at the same time cope with users' behavior and their technology usage patterns. To that end, we have to deal with many uncertainties that traditional security mechanisms simply ignore. Chameleon is designed to verify the true identity of the users based on the evidences in the environment, authorize the access according to the defined permissions and adjust the access based on changes in the environment. To make this happen, we employ a probabilistic approach to reason about identity and permissions.

Though we believe Chameleon is a promising model for next generation of ubiquitous security, there are many details that need to be considered. At the current stage, we have finished a high level design of the model and started to design the modules. We are also working on security policy specification and a user friendly way of defining the policy. On the theoretical side, we are defining more details about the cost-benefit model discussed in Section 4 to find a suitable mathematical tradeoff between availability and protection. The work will continue to build an initial prototype which will be evaluated extensively in real environments with real users.

References

1. Want, R., Hopper, A., Falcao, V., Gibbons, J.: The active badge location system. ACM Transactions on Information Systems 10, 102 (1992)
2. Snyder Jr., G.F., Pardoe, T.: Network Security. Delmar Cengage Learning (2004)
3. Barkley, J., Beznosov, K., Uppal, J.: Supporting relationships in access control using role based access control. In: Proceedings of the Fourth ACM Workshop on Role-Based Access Control, pp. 55–65. ACM, New York (1999)
4. Configuring role-based access control to enforce mandatory and discretionary access control policies. ACM Transactions on Information and System Security 3, 85–106 (2000)
5. Pearl, J.: Probabilistic reasoning in intelligent systems: networks of plausible inference. Morgan Kaufmann, San Francisco (1988)
6. Cobb, B.R., Shenoy, P.P.: A comparison of Bayesian and belief function reasoning. Information Systems Frontiers 5, 345–358 (2003)
7. Laskey, K.B.: MEBN: A language for first-order Bayesian knowledge bases. Artificial Intelligence 172, 140–178 (2008)
8. Ginsberg, M.: Essentials of artificial intelligence. Morgan Kaufmann, San Francisco (1994)
9. Kaplan, S., Garrick, B.J.: On The Quantitative Definition of Risk. Risk Analysis 1, 11–27 (1981)
10. Sabzevar, A.P., Sousa, J.P.: Authentication, authorization and auditing for ubiquitous computing: a survey and vision. International Journal of Space-Based and Situated Computing 1, 59–67 (2011)
11. Bardram, J.E., Kjær, R.E., Pedersen, M.Ø.: Context-aware user authentication – supporting proximity-based login in pervasive computing. In: Dey, A.K., Schmidt, A., McCarthy, J.F. (eds.) UbiComp 2003. LNCS, vol. 2864, pp. 107–123. Springer, Heidelberg (2003)
12. Corner, M.D., Noble, B.D.: Zero-interaction authentication. In: Intl. Conf. on Mobile Computing and Networking, pp. 1–11. ACM, Atlanta (2002)

13. Matsumiya, K., Aoki, S., Murase, M., Tokuda, H.: Zero-stop authentication: Sensor-based real-time authentication system. In: Chen, J., Hong, S. (eds.) RTCSA 2003. LNCS, vol. 2968, pp. 296–311. Springer, Heidelberg (2004)
14. Beigl, M.: Using spatial co-location for coordination in ubiquitous computing environments. In: Gellersen, H.-W. (ed.) HUC 1999. LNCS, vol. 1707, pp. 259–273. Springer, Heidelberg (1999)
15. Sadeh, N.M., Gandon, F.L., Kwon, O.B.: Ambient Intelligence: The MyCampus Experience, TR CMU-ISRI-05-123. School of Computer Science, Carnegie Mellon U, Pittsburgh, PA (2005)
16. Al-Muhtadi, J., Ranganathan, A., Campbell, R., Mickunas, M.D.: Cerberus: a context-aware security scheme for smart spaces. In: IEEE Intl. Conf. on Pervasive Computing and Communications, pp. 489–496. IEEE CS, Los Alamitos (2003)
17. Song, Y.J., Tobagus, W., Leong, D.Y., Johanson, B.: iSecurity: A Security Framework for Interactive Workspaces, Technical Report. Stanford University (2003)
18. Kagal, L., Undercoffer, J., Perich, F., Joshi, A., Finin, T., Yesha, Y.: Vigil: Providing trust for enhanced security in pervasive systems. Technical Report, University of Maryland, Baltimore County (2002)
19. Roman, M., Campbell, R.H.: Gaia: Enabling active spaces. In: ACM SIGOPS European Workshop, pp. 229–234. ACM, Kolding (2000)
20. Satyanarayanan, M.: Pervasive computing: Vision and challenges. IEEE Personal Communications 8, 10–17 (2001)
21. The Location Stack, http://portolano.cs.washington.edu/projects/location/
22. Park, J., Sandhu, R.: The UCON ABC usage control model. ACM Trans. on Information and System Security 7, 128–174 (2004)

The Safety Related Legal Issues and Privacy Protection for Intelligent Vehicle Telematics in the United States

Fa-Chang Cheng[1] and Wen-Hsing Lai[2,*]

[1] Graduate Institute of Science and Technology Law, National Kaohsiung First University of Science and Technology, No. 2, Jhuoyue Rd., Nanzih District, Kaohsiung City 811, Taiwan
fachang1@hotmail.com
[2] Dept. of Computer and Communication Engineering, National Kaohsiung First University of Science and Technology, No. 2, Jhuoyue Rd., Nanzih District, Kaohsiung City 811, Taiwan
lwh@nkfust.edu.tw

Abstract. Intelligent Vehicle Telematics has been a promising industry in the world. This new development of telecommunication technology has emerged with some legal concerns, especially in the liability for failure of safety devises and the protection of information privacy within Intelligent Vehicle Telematics. The purpose of this article is to gain experiences from the discussion for these issues in academic papers and related cases within the United States, in order to depict the possible solution for safety related legal issues and the protection of privacy with regard to developing Intelligent Vehicle Telematics.

Keywords: Intelligent Vehicle Telematics, product liability, strict liability, information privacy.

1 Introduction

The Intelligent Vehicle Telematics is highly valued by the government in the world as having a lot of beneficial potential to the transportation infrastructure in such sovereignty. Some aspects of Intelligent Vehicle Telematics are mainly designed for the safety reason. These safety features for Intelligent Vehicle Telematics have some significant meaning to the legal infrastructure. At one hand, those safety devises may increase the safety of transportation; on the other hand, the failure of such safety devises may cause a lot of trouble. Therefore, the liability for system provider and devise manufacture (distributor) is one important safety legal issue with regard to Intelligent Vehicle Telematics. Apart from the safety related legal issues, the protection of privacy in the operation of Intelligent Vehicle Telematics is also another big legal issue for Intelligent Vehicle Telematics. It is planed in this article to introduce the concept of information privacy in the United States and bring up the suggestion of how to comprise the confliction between the protection of information privacy of other legal interests while facing problems. Besides the general technology description of Intelligent Vehicle Telematics and its safety features in the beginning, this

---

* Corresponding author.

C.-H. Hsu et al. (Eds.): UIC 2011, LNCS 6905, pp. 340–349, 2011.

article will center the discussion for these issues to academic papers and related cases within the United States, in order to depict the possible solution for safety related legal issues and the protection of privacy with regard to developing Intelligent Vehicle Telematics.

2 The Technology of Intelligent Vehicle Telematics and Its Safety Features

Vehicle Telematics is the integrated use of telecommunications and informatics within road vehicles. The objectives of Intelligent Vehicle Telematics are to improve safety, reduce traffic congestion, fuel consumption and carbon dioxide emissions, and increase comfort and convenience or even entertainment. Among these, safety normally gets top priority, though there is a trend that entertainment and convenience have rapidly caught up to safety as the impetus for new in-car electronics development [1].

To make the transport intelligent, knowing the accurate position and status of vehicles is the first thing to do. Then, this information should share with other vehicles and the infrastructure by communication. The accuracy of standard Global Positioning System (GPS), which is generally 5 to 10 meters, is not enough. In addition, the accuracy and reliability are degraded in urban environments due to satellite visibility and multipath effects. For example, tunnels or buildings may lead to outages. Therefore, other technologies like Triangulation Method using mobile phones or inertial navigation by the sensors via dead reckoning could be integrated to improve the accuracy. Video cameras can also be fused [2] to help measure traffic flow or the distance between lane lines. The computer vision technology can not only be used to look out of the vehicle to detect and track roads, but simultaneously look inside the vehicle to monitor the attentiveness or intentions of the driver [3]. Besides camera, multiple Sensors including radar and lidar can also be used to help detect various statistic or moving on-road obstacles [4].

A vehicle may communicate with other vehicles (vehicle-to-vehicle, V2V) or the infrastructure (vehicle-to-infrastructure, V2I) by using Dedicated Short Range Communication (DSRC), cellular communication, satellite communication, WiFi, Bluetooth or RFID. Among them, DSRC is short to medium range wireless communication promoted by US Department of Transport and specifically designed for vehicle use. US Federal Communications Commission (FCC) has allocated 75MHz in the 5.9GHz band for DSRC. Longer range communications can be accomplished by GSM, 3G, or WiMAX. It is noted that to prevent accidents, very low latency and short response times are needed for vehicle-to-vehicle communications [5].

IEEE 802.11p, which is the groundwork for DSRC, is an IEEE standard to add wireless access in vehicular environments (WAVE). It defines enhancements to 802.11 to support intelligent transportation system (ITS). That is, it is specially designed for data exchange among moving vehicles and road infrastructure.

Many Applications of Vehicle safety systems employing DSRC including Vehicle-Vehicle and Vehicle-Infrastructure communications are: Cooperative forward collision warning, Emergency braking notification, Lane or road departure warning, Pre-crash sensing, Curve speed warning, Right turn assistance, Give way junction assistance, Traffic signal violation warning, Intersection collision warning, Road / rail collision warning, Road condition warning, Approaching emergency vehicle warning, Emergency vehicle signal pre-emption, Road works warning, and Motorway merge assistance [6].

While full autonomous, unmanned vehicles are still remained as a research topic, nowadays the function of intelligent vehicle system generally focuses on assisting drivers and preventing driver errors. However, these systems may compete for driver attention and the message they provide can be confusing [7]. There is concern that telematics use is a contributing factor for crashes due to multitasking, distraction and longer duration usage time than conventional in-vehicle tasks [8].

Even though there are some solutions have been proposed. For example, a work-load manager is set to help determine if a driver is overloaded or distracted [8]. In addition, a structured procedural approach for the safety assessment of intervening systems which interact directly with the vehicle is proposed [9]. Nevertheless, unless we can totally understand the driving behavior [10] - [12], including driver intentions, how people make decisions, and how people interact with vehicle, and modeling the behavior, there are still risks.

Besides, more and more car innovations are from computer systems and software and such complexity brings with it reliability issues [13]. Ivan Berger [14] questioned three growing challenge for carmakers. First, the more complex a car electronic system, the more failure points it offers. Second, the growing reliance on software raises more risk of fail. Third, the hardware environment becomes more demanding because of heat and electromagnetic interference (EMI).

3   The Liability of System Provider and Devise Manufacture (Distributor) for Safety Legal Issues

At the first sight, there could be three potential possible kinds of liability, negligence, warranty in contract or strict liability, for the system provider and four potential possible kinds of liability for devise manufacture (distributor) with regard to the safety legal issues, adding product liability to the three just mentioned before. The difference between the system provider and the devise manufacture (distributor) for potential liability to the safety legal issues is the product liability because the product liability is only eligible for the harm done by the tangible product, but not the services. In this paragraph, it will briefly introduce the concepts of negligence, warranty, strict liability and product liability, respectively. Since there is no real case handed down related to the safety legal issues for Intelligent Vehicle Telematics in the United States judicial system, based on the understanding and characteristics of those legal infrastructure, it will argue in this article that the strict liability theory is most appropriate to those situations. The following will stick with the thinking process mentioned here and be divided into three parts discussion: the theories among negligence, warranty, product liability and strict liability; the comparison among negligence, warranty, product liability and strict liability for the culpability; the reason for choosing strict liability for the system provider and devise manufacture (distributor) as the liability solution for the related safety legal issues to Intelligent Vehicle Telematics.

3.1 The Theories Among Negligence, Warranty, Product Liability and Strict Liability

The first liability theory for system provider and devise manufacture (distributor) related to the safety devise for Intelligent Vehicle Telematics is negligence. The theory of negligence is really based upon the idea of fault. It means the defendant in the case violates the duty of care imputed by the society. And generally speaking, e xcept for some specific groups, the standard of care is either based upon the reasonable person [15] or professional reaction [16] under the circumstances. Another specific feature for the theory of negligence is the requirement for proximate cause for reason of controlling the amount of damages. Even the cause in fact between the wrongdoer and the consequences invoked by such wrongdoer is required in every tortious cause of action, the proximate cause is not a prerequisite for the cause of action in torts, for example the intentional torts or product liability etc. and the proximate cause is really a means to the policy concern's ends [17]. So, in order to substantiate in a negligence case, there are four elements need to be proved: duty of care, breach duty of care, causation (including the cause in fact and proximate cause) and damages.

The second possible legal theory of the liability for system provider and devise manufacture (distributor) related to the safety devise for Intelligent Vehicle Telematics is warranty. This cause of action is really something between the contract theory and the torts theory. There are two kinds of warrant theory; one is called express warrant, the other is named implied warranty. In the express warranty, it could be the contract liability which needs to prove the contract privity between the parties. The express warrant could also be the torts liability which needs to prove the reliance of the injured party, even though there is no requirement for proving the privity between the parties [18]. And the adoption of implied warrant theory is, to some extent, depending on the willingness of the court and mostly used in the issue of fitness of the object to its common application [19].

The third possible legal theory of the liability for system provider and devise manufacture (distributor) related to the safety devise for Intelligent Vehicle Telematics is strict liability. In the strict liability theory, there is no need to prove the defendant's fault, the contract privity, the reliance of the injured or even pending on the court's interference. The only thing by asserting the strict liability claim is to prove some basic facts and establish that these facts results in the consequences need to be remedies. Traditionally, there are two types of strict liability: the wild or vicious animal strict liability and the extremely dangerous activity strict liability. And it has to be mentioned that, under this stringent liability, there still has some exceptions to the general rule, like the comparative negligence of plaintiff [20] or the Act of God [21].

The last possible legal theory of the liability mentioned in this paragraph for system provider and devise manufacture (distributor) related to the safety devise for Intelligent Vehicle Telematics is product liability.

The main purpose of product liability is to protect the user or consumer injured by the product threw in the stream of commerce. Generally speaking, there have three different types of product liability claims: manufacturing defect, design defect and lack of warning [22]. The legal theory behind product liability has several possible legal interpretations, negligence, warranty and strict liability, as we mentioned in this paragraph. It means, traditionally under the title of product liability, a product liability case can really be a negligence case [23], a warrant case [24] or a strict liability case [25]. Especially, if there is a product liability case based upon the strict liability theory, the distributor between the manufacture and the user would also easily be involved in such case. According to Restatement (Second) of Torts § 402A which is accepted by some of the states in the United States, one who sells any product in a defective condition unreasonably dangerous to the user or consumer or to his property is subject to liability for physical harm thereby caused to the ultimate user or consumer, or to his property, even the seller has exercised all possible care in the preparation and sale of his product or the user (or consumer) has not brought the product from or entered into any contractual relation with the seller. Even the Restatement (Second) and following courts take the position that both the manufacture and the distributor shall bear the strict liability [26], it seems there are still some jurisdictions which follow the Restatement (Second) would like to prove the breach of duty based upon design defect and lack of warning claims in a product liability litigation [27]. And just similar to the strict liability, there are also a couple possible defenses, comparative negligence of plaintiff [28] and statutory immunity (preemption) [29] or unforeseeable misuse of the product [30], could be used as the defense against the product liability. To sum up the statement with regard to product liability, the product liability is the liability to harm caused by the product which liability is one of the three possible choices: negligence, breach of warranty or strict liability.

3.2   The Comparison among Negligence, Warranty, Product Liability and Strict Liability for the Culpability of Wrongdoer

From the explanation in this paragraph, it is possibly said the negligence cause of action is the most difficult liability to prove because, unlike warranty or strict liability, the duty of care need to be substantiated. And the strict liability might be the most easier to satisfy in the burden of prove evidence. As to the warranty cause of action, the liability would either rely on the contract privity or reliance in express warranty or count on the court intervention in implied contract. To estimate the strength of liability or culpability, the warranty cause of action seems to stand in between of the negligence and the strict liability. The last possible liability mentioned in this article-product liability, is really a mixture type of theory of liability among the negligence liability, warranty liability and the strict liability. Observing the history of the policy attitude toward the product liability, the way to deal with product liability is really swinging between the negligence and the strict liability and some commentator believes the current court attitude is more lenient toward the manufacture [31].

3.3   The Reason for Choosing Strict Liability for the System Provider and Devise Manufacture (Distributor) as the Liability Solution for the Related Safety Legal Issues to Intelligent Vehicle Telematics

It is argued in this article that those safety devises to Intelligent Vehicle Telematics are presenting really high social responsible concerns. So, the first thought is the policy thinking should be that the manufacture of these safety devise to Intelligent Vehicle Telematics is going to hold the highest legal responsibility under the current legal theory to the injured person or property based upon the strict product liability. And the system provider for the operation of these safety devises to Intelligent Vehicle Telematics is the same important as the manufacture. If anything goes wrong with the system, it could cause a catastrophe to the transportation. Therefore, the system provider for the operation of these safety devises to Intelligent Vehicle Telematics should take the strict liability. The liability here is nothing like the liability to the cell phone manufacture or the communication services provider for the user talking over the cell phone while he or she was driving because the cell phone is not designed to the protection of transportation safety and it is the user who initiates communication and cause the distraction which results in the traffic incident [32]. As to the distributor between the manufacture and the user or consumer, because the distributor doesn't directly contribute to the safety legal issue with regard to safety devises within Intelligent Vehicle Telematics, it is suggested the distributor doesn't need to be strictly liable to the injury caused upon product liability by the failure of these safety devises. In this article, it will treat the current situation for different options for liability to the distributor as remain the same for further consideration through the case decision in the future.

4 The Protection of Information Privacy in Intelligent Vehicle Telematics

As mentioned in the beginning of this article, in applying Intelligent Vehicle Telematics to the real world, often times, it will acquire, collect or use personal information in the process of operating these devises or systems. This could arouse a lot of concerns to the legal issue of information of privacy. In this section, it intends to introduce the idea of information privacy in the United States, the protection of this legal interest in the United States and also the observation of suggested model to build up such protection in the legal arena for Intelligent Vehicle Telematics.

4.1 The Concept of Information Privacy and the Protection in the United States

The protection of "privacy" is not articulated in the Constitution in the United States, instead it is interpreted by the Supreme Court to say "The forgoing cases suggest that special guarantees in the Bill of Rights have penumbras, formed by emanations from those guarantees that help give them life and substance. Various guarantees create zones of privacy." in order to "create" the protection of privacy [33]. Through the years, the Supreme Court has recognized several kinds of privacy as the fundamental human rights [34], for example the right to marriage, breeding the child etc., but not the information privacy. The significant legal meaning of information privacy as a non-fundamental human rights on the Constitutional level is that the right of privacy will probably be restricted when it directly conflicts with the protection of other fundamental human rights or important social rights, for example the freedom of speech [35]. And it is fairly to say, other than conflicting with the protection of other fundamental human rights or important social rights, the protection of information privacy is really the balance of interests between the protection of privacy and other affected legal interests, except it wouldn't affect any legal interests, for example, to the protection against unauthorized invasion of information privacy. From the experience of the United States in protection of information privacy, there are three auspicious trends worth to draw attention. The first one is to use informed consent mechanism for reducing or eradicating the controversy of reasonable expectation of privacy. The second one is to emphasize the importance of technology prevention of information privacy infringement. And the last one is to enhance the liability of data collector for notification of the security breach to the information provider in case of some special kind of personal information been unauthorized disclosed by the third party.

First of all, the best way to eliminate the issue of whether or how the information privacy shall be protected is to receive the consent of personal information provider in gathering the personal information. The legal thinking behind this is that the information privacy is a personal right and can be reduced or eliminated by way of the consent of the information provider. It can be seen from a flood of statements related to privacy policy within a variety of contract in the United States. Also, this idea of executing informed consent appears in some federal legislation and administrative regulation. For example, in HIPAA (Health Insurance Portability and Accountability Act) [36], the Congress require in this act that the entities for health care will basically get the informed consent for any disclosure of personal medical information. The new drug application for biological product and the human body test for genetic therapy will need the informed consent from the test or research subject before the approval of such application or test [37]. And, the informed consent requirement also happens in The Gramm-Leach-Bliley Act and Privacy of Consumer Financial Information, Regulation P for electronic commerce.

Secondly, beside the informed consent methodology, to put a high value of technology prevention in protecting information privacy is the other current trend of preventive measure for the information privacy infringement. The best example for the emphasis of technology security is the infrastructure for establishing technology standard in American Recovery and Reinvestment Act of 2009 [38]. Generally speaking, from Subtitle C SEC 3001-3003 in American Recovery and Reinvestment Act of 2009, Congress design to establish the Office of the National Coordinator for Health Information Technology for the purpose of setting up the technology standard, including the purpose of protection in information privacy, in order to promote the electronic medical records system.

The last observed tendency for the issue of protecting information privacy is to add the obligation of notification to who preserves the individual information when such information has been unauthorized accessed by the third party. This measurement is a fairly new legal remedy for the harm to the information privacy. For example, the detailed mechanism for how to work the requirement of notification in electronic medical records security breach is regulated in Subtitle D Part I SEC 13400 and 13402 of American Recovery and Reinvestment Act of 2009. There are also other legislations in the United States embracing the similar regulation [39].

4.2 The Observation of Suggested Model Builds Up Such Protection in the Legal Arena for Intelligent Vehicle Telematics

After understanding the general idea of information privacy and the tendency of protecting such legal interest in the United States, how to build the protection infrastructure of information privacy for Intelligent Vehicle Telematics operation brings the discussion to the next level. With regard to the issue of protection of information privacy in Intelligent Vehicle Telematics operation, this article would attempt to divide it into two different aspects: non-legal –binding self regulation and legal measurements for preventive or remedial purpose to the system operator. First, to the part of self regulation within the system operator, the proposed estimation in this article is that the self regulation wouldn't be able to play any significant role in striving to preserve the legal interest of information privacy before the competition in market has reached sufficient status. So, it is argued in this article, in this stage, there is no substantial meaning to emphasize the mechanism of self regulation. As to the preventive or remedial legal measurements for the protection of information privacy related to the system provider for Intelligent Vehicle Telematics, the bottom line is described as the old saying: "One stitch in time safes nine.". That leads to the indication that the preventive measurements of informed consent and technology prevention are much better than the remedial measurements (the obligation of notification, civil liability or even criminal punishment). And in comparing the different interests to confirm the legitimacy of information privacy in the situation of Intelligent Vehicle Teleatics, the safety concern will definitely get its priority to the information privacy concern. To other comparisons between the protection of information privacy and proprietary interests of the system operator, the odds are that the information privacy will have a good chance to fight in the battlefield of balancing interests. To sum up the situation for the protection of information privacy in Intelligent Vehicle Telematics, it is fairly to say in protecting information privacy in operating Intelligent Vehicle Telematics, there is a hierarchy to construct the protection, from the legal to the non-legal in general concept, from the preventive to the remedial measurement in real practice.

5 Conclusion

It often times comes with the legal concern when the advanced technology seems to promise the society a better life. And this is exactly what happens to the Intelligent Vehicle Telematics. These two mainly legal concerns which are the liability both for the safety devise manufacture and the system provider, and also the protection of information privacy, under the discussion in this article, shall move toward the intensive way to go. There should be nothing wrong to be cautious about the new technology after balancing the benefits and the potential harm of such technology to reveal that it could do more harm than good to the society as a whole, especially such harm is imminent. And it is suggested in this article that the potential harm to the safety devise in Intelligent Vehicle Telematics could be a disaster for the reason of estimating human life as high-value. And also the same seriousness to the invasion of information privacy would happen because the unauthorized use or security breach of the extensive gathering of personal information in operating Intelligent Vehicle Telematics could be fatal to the trend of enhanced protection of information privacy. For all the reasons mentioned here, this article will hold the position that the most restrictive legal responsibility under the current legal theory shall apply to these two issues respectively. The development of Intelligent Vehicle Telematics technology is still in its primitive stage. And it is the purpose (intention) of this article to pinpoint the legal issues for Intelligence Vehicle Telematics in front and try to come up the positive solutions in the hope of that the discussion could, at least, have some referential value for the possible future policy making decision.

References

1. Jones, W.D.: Smarter Cars? There's an App. for That (February 2011),
   `http://spectrum.ieee.org/green-tech/advanced-cars/`
   `smarter-cars-theres-an-app-for-that/0`
2. Rae, A., Basir, O.: Reducing Multipath Effects in Vehicle Localization by Fusing GPS with Machine Vision. In: 12th International Conference on Information Fusion, Seattle, WA, USA, July 6-9, pp. 2099–2106 (2009)
3. Trivedi, M.M., Gandhi, T., McCall, J.: Looking-In and Looking-Out of a Vehicle: Computer-Vision-Based Enhanced Vehicle Safety. IEEE Transactions on Intelligent Transportation Systems 8(1), 108–120 (2007)
4. Cheng, H., Zheng, N., Zhang, X., Qin, J., van de Wetering, H.: Interactive Road Situation Analysis for Driver Assistance and Safety Warning Systems: Framework and Algorithms. IEEE Transactions on Intelligent Transportation Systems 8(1), 157–167 (2007)
5. Blau, J.: Car Talk (October 2008),
   `http://spectrum.ieee.org/green-tech/advanced-cars/car-talk`
6. Bell, M.G.H.: Policy issues for the future intelligent road transport infrastructure. IEE Proceedings - Intelligent Transport Systems 153(2), 147–155 (2006)
7. Amditis, A., Bertolazzi, E., Bimpas, M., Biral, F., Bosetti, P., Lio, M.D., Danielsson, L., Gallione, A., Lind, H., Saroldi, A., Sjögren, A.: A Holistic Approach to the Integration of Safety. IEEE Transactions on Intelligent Transportation Systems 11(3), 554–566 (2010)
8. Green, P.: Driver distraction, telematics design, and workload managers: Safety issues and solutions. In: Proceedings of the 2004 International Congress on Transportation Electronics, pp. 165–180 (2004)
9. Carsten, O.M.J., Nilsson, L.: Safety Assessment of Driver Assistance Systems. European Journal of Transport and Infrastructure Research 1(3), 225–243 (2001)
10. Brackstone, M.A., Sultan, B., McDonald, M.: Findings on the Approach Process Between Vehicles - Implications for Collision Warning. Transportation Research Record - Journal of The Transportation Research Board (1724), 21–28 (2000)
11. Misener, J.A., Jacob Tsao, H.-S., Song, B., Steinfeld, A.: Emergence of a Cognitive Car-Following Driver Model - Application to Rear-End Crashes with a Stopped Lead Vehicle. Transportation Research Record - Journal of The Transportation Research Board (1724), 29–38 (2000)
12. Smiley, A.: Behavioral Adaptation, Safety, and Intelligent Transportation Systems. Transportation Research Record - Journal of The Transportation Research Board (1724), 47–51 (2000)
13. Charette, R.N.: This Car Runs on Code (February 2009),
    `http://spectrum.ieee.org/green-tech/advanced-cars/`
    `this-car-runs-on-code/0`

14. Berger, I.: Can You Trust Your Car? (April 01, 2002),
    `http://spectrum.ieee.org/green-tech/advanced-cars/`
    `can-you-trust-your-car/0`
15. Freeman v. Adams, 63 Cal. App. 225 (1923)
16. Heath v. Swift Wings. Inc., 252 S.E.2d. 526 (1979)
17. Synder v. LTG L Lufttechnische, GmbH, 955 S.W.2d 252 (Tenn. 1997)
18. Wade, J.W., et al.: Prosser, Wade and Schwartz's Torts-Cases and Materials, 10th edn., p. 721 (2000)
19. Henningsen v. Bloomfield Motors, Inc., 161 A.2d 69 (1960)
20. Andrade v. Shiers, 564 So.2d 787 (La. App. 1990)
21. Golden v. Amory, 109 N.E.2d 131 (1952)
22. Wikipedia, Product liability,
    `http://en.wikipedia.org/wiki/Product_liability`
    (last visited March 23, 2011)
23. MacPherson v. Buick Motor Co., 217 N.Y. 382 (1916)
24. Henningsen v. Bloomfield Motors, Inc., 161 A.2d 69 (1960)
25. Greenman v. Yuba Power Products, Inc., 377 P.2d. 897 (1963)
26. Wade, J.W., et al.: Prosser, Wade and Schwartz's Torts-Cases and Materials, 9th edn., p. 794 (1994)
27. Alberts, J.R., et al.: Survey of Recent Developments in Indiana Product Liability Law. Ind. L. Rev. 43, 873–887 (2010)
28. Daly v. General Motors Corp., 575 P.2d 1162 (1978)
29. King v. Collagen Corp., 983 F.2d 1130 (1993)
30. Erkson v. Sears, Roebuck & Co., 841 S.W.2d 207 (Mo. App. 1992)
31. MacDougall, V.L.: 8 Oklahoma Practice Product Liability Law § 1, at 1-2 (2010)
32. Amendola, A.F.: Can You Hear Me Now?: The Myths Surrounding Cell Phone Use While Driving and Connecticut's Attempt at a Remedy. Conn. L. Rev. 41, 339 (2008)
33. Griswold v. Connecticut, 381 U.S. 479 (1965)
34. Emanuel, S.L.: Constitutional Law, 16th edn., p. 152 (1998/1999)
35. Hall v. Post, 323 N.C. 259 (N.C. 1988)
36. American College of Emergency Physician, From Hippocrates to HIPAA: Privacy and Confidentiality in Emergency Medicine-PartI: Conceptual, Moral, and legal foundations, http://www.acep.org/NR/rdonlyres/DE534243-E7D5-4A51-9827-1D95828DA45C/0/hippocrateshopaaI.pdf (last visited March 29, 2011)
37. Andrews, L.B., et al.: Genetics: ethics, law and policy, vol. 88, pp. 391–401 (2002)
38. American Recovery and Reinvestment Act of 2009,
    `http://www.gpo.gov/fdsys/pkg/PLAW-111publ5/pdf/`
    `PLAW-111publ5.pdf` (last visited March 30, 2011)
39. Smedinghoff, T.J.: Security Breach Notification Law: Defining a New Corporate Obligation,
    `http://www.wildman.com/resources/articles-pdf/`
    `Security_Breach_Notification_Law.pdf` (last visited March 30, 2011)

PreCon – Expressive Context Prediction Using Stochastic Model Checking*

Stefan Föll, Klaus Herrmann, and Kurt Rothermel

Institute of Parallel and Distributed Systems
Universität Stuttgart
Universitätstrasse 38, 70569 Stuttgart, Germany
{stefan.foell,klaus.herrmann,kurt.rothermel}@ipvs.uni-stuttgart.de

Abstract. Ubiquitous systems need to determine the context of humans to deliver the right services at the right time. As the needs of humans are often coupled to their future context, the ability to predict relevant changes in a user's context is a key factor for providing intelligence and proactivity. Current context prediction systems only allow applications to query for the next user context (e.g. the user's next location). This severely limits the benefit of context prediction since these approaches cannot answer more expressive *time-dependent queries* (e.g. will the user enter location X within the next 10 minutes?). Neither can they handle predictions of multi-dimensional context (e.g. activity *and* location). We propose PreCon, a new approach to predicting multi-dimensional context. PreCon improves query expressiveness, providing clear formal semantics by applying *stochastic model checking* methods. PreCon is composed of three major parts: a *stochastic model* to represent context changes, an *expressive temporal-logic query language*, and *stochastic algorithms for predicting context*. In our evaluations, we apply PreCon to real context traces from the domain of healthcare and analyse the performance using well-known metrics from information retrieval. We show that PreCon reaches an F-score (combined precision and recall) of about 0.9 which indicates a very good performance.

1 Introduction

Ubiquitous systems are expected to provide a new level of computational intelligence, where personalized services are tailored to fit the dynamic needs of humans. One big challenge in this respect is to proactively identify the individual needs of humans in the real world without requiring explicit input. As the user's needs are often connected to the physical context of human behaviour (e.g., where humans are going and what they are doing) ubiquitous systems have to be *context-aware*. However, in order to be proactive, knowledge about the user's *future* context is of major importance. For instance in mobile advertising [1], personalized information such as special offers or cultural events are delivered

---

* This research has been supported by FP7 EU-FET project ALLOW (contract number 213339).

C.-H. Hsu et al. (Eds.): UIC 2011, LNCS 6905, pp. 350–364, 2011.

to mobile users. Incorporating the future context, the relevance of the advertisements can be enhanced, e.g. based on the user's next locations on his shopping tour. Similarly, in domains like home automation or health care, awareness of future context yields more effective services [2]. However, future context is an implicit piece of information as it resides in the routines and habits inherent to our daily lives. Therefore, context prediction approaches have been devised to uncover the patterns of human behaviour and provide the gained knowledge to ubiquitous applications. The level of how intelligently applications can understand and respond to user needs is strongly connected to the expressiveness of queries a context prediction system can answer.

Current approaches to context prediction [3], [4], [5], [6], [7], [8] only allow for very simple queries for the most probable next user context (e.g. the user's next location). Hence, their expressiveness is severely limited since applications are not able to extract any information on the expected time of such a context change. We argue that intelligent ubiquitous applications need therefore the ability to submit *time-dependent queries* (e.g. "Will user A be at location x within the next 10 minutes?"). Likewise, queries for multi-dimensional context (e.g. "Will the user be executing *activity* Y at *location* X within the next 10 minutes?") must be possible. A system that can answer such expressive queries accurately, provides applications with more flexibility and allows them to act in a more goal-oriented way for their user.

We propose PreCon, a new approach to context prediction that allows time-dependent multi-dimensional context prediction queries. PreCon applies well-known methods of *stochastic model checking* [9] (used e.g. for the verification of distributed communication protocols) to the analysis and prediction of human behaviour. While classical model checking relies on fixed hand-crafted models of computer systems, our models (called *stochastic user models* (SUM) in the following) are representations of human behaviour that are learned from traces of past context changes. We represent SUMs as *Semi-Markov Chains* such that the changes in context are regarded as a stochastic process. We use *temporal logics* as a query language, enabling applications to specify expressive temporal properties on future context. For a prediction, our system verifies with which probability these properties hold on a given SUMs. Our evaluations show that PreCon delivers a high *precision* and *recall* for a real-world health-care scenario.

The rest of the paper is organized as follows. First, we give an overview of our approach in Section 2. In Section 3, we present the concepts of SUMs and describe our context prediction query language in Section 4. We then discuss the stochastic algorithms for query evaluation in Section 5. Section 6 presents the related work before we present the evaluation of our approach in Section 7 and conclude the paper in Section 8.

2   Overview of the PreCon Approach

Figure 1 gives a high-level overview of our approach. We assume that a context recognition system monitors the context of the user and records *context*

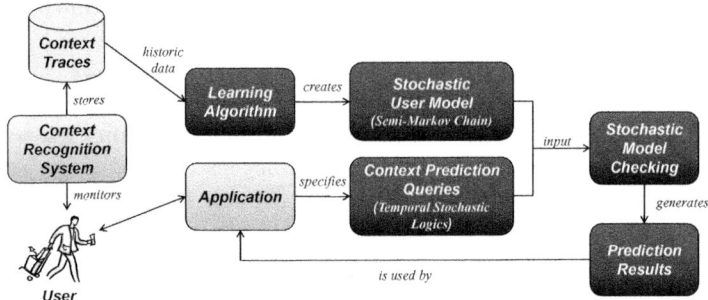

Fig. 1. Overview of the PreCon approach – Concepts specified by PerCon are shown in dark boxes

traces (time-stamped series of consecutive context changes) in user histories. For instance, a context trace may contain information about which activities have been executed at what time and location. The context traces are given as input to our *learning algorithm*, which processes them to obtain an SUM. Our framework allows context traces to be processed either in a *batch-like* fashion or in *real-time*. For the batch-like approach, the learning algorithm processes one or more context trace and creates a new SUM, while for the real-time approach, the algorithm updates the existing SUM each time a relevant context change has been observed. In both cases, the information about sequential changes in user context is used to build a *Semi-Markov Chain* (SMC) – a well-known stochastic process model that we use to represent SUMs. A SMC is a probabilistic state transition system that maintains the discrete states of the user behaviour and the associated state transition probabilities. Furthermore, the temporal characteristics of context changes (the so-called *dwell times*) are modelled by the SMC. This is the key to PreCon's concept of time-dependent queries.

Applications can specify *context prediction queries* using different temporal operators that are part of a temporal stochastic logic. This query language provides well-defined semantics to express *reachability properties* (e.g. will the user arrive at a certain location) and *invariant properties* (e.g. will the user stay at a certain location). A context prediction query is evaluated on an SMC to calculate the probability with which the specified properties hold. A querying application can specify a probability threshold with which the resulting probability is compared, and a *true* or *false* is returned depending on the outcome. Finally, the querying application may use this result to take proactive decisions in terms of, e.g. user interaction and context-aware services, to enhance the user's experience. In the following sections, we will investigate each element of PreCon in turn.

3   Stochastic User Model

People follow varying behavioural patterns in their daily lives, such that real world user behaviour can not be described in a deterministic way. Consequently, we require a user model that is able to deal with this probabilistic nature of human behaviour. In the following, we give a precise formal definition of the SUM. Subsequently, we present our approach for learning such a SUM from observations recorded in real-world context traces.

3.1   Semi-Markov Chain

We represent an SUM as a Semi-Markov Chain (SMC) [10]. In general, Markov Chains are a popular means for describing stochastic processes with discrete state spaces. In addition to that, SMCs specify a so-called *state dwell time* – an arbitrary probability distribution that is associated with every state transition specifying the amount of time spent in a given state. Formally, a SMC M is a 3-tuple defined as:

$$M = (S, p, q)$$

where S is the state space, $p : S \times S \to [0, 1]$ with $\forall s \in S : \sum_{s' \in S} p(s, s') = 1$ is the transition probability function, and $h : (s, s', t) \mapsto [0, 1]$ with $t \in \mathbb{R}^+$ represents the distribution of dwell times associated with a state transition $(s, s') \in S \times S$. For $h : (s, s', t)$, we will also write $h_{s,s'}(t)$ for brevity reasons. The SMC allows us to describe a user's behaviour in the following manner: At each point in time, a user is in a state $s \in S$ that is identified by his current context (cf. Section 3.2). While the user acts in the real world, his context changes and his SMC moves to a new state $s' \in S$ representing the new context. s' is called the *successor state* of s, and s' is visited with a certain probability $p(s, s')$. Before leaving the current state s, s is active for a limited amount of time (the dwell time represented by $h_{s,s'}(t)$). During this time period the user's context does not change.

3.2   Learning a SMC

In contrast to classical model checking, we do not expect a designer of the system to define the SMC underlying the real world behaviour. Instead, we apply a *learning approach* and derive the SMC from the observations of a context recognition system. In the following, we describe the basic elements of an SMC as well as the procedure of how to process context observations in order to learn an SMC.

User States. A user state $s = (c_1, ..., c_n)$ is an n-dimensional vector of context information. Each component c_i of s is of a specific *context type* C_i, and $C_1, ..., C_n$ are the context types known to the system with domains $Dom(C_1), ..., Dom(C_n)$. E.g. c_i may be an integer value from $Dom(C_i) = \mathbb{N}^+$, and C_i may be the *ambient temperature* type. Other types could be *location* and *activity*, and the corresponding domains could be enumerations of possible activities and symbolic location identifiers respectively. For example, the state $s = ($ *"meeting room"*, *"give presentation"* $) \in Dom(Location) \times Dom(Activity)$ describes the fact that the user executes the activity *give presentation* in a location referred to as *meeting room*. Whenever a combination of context information $(c_1, ..., c_n)$ is detected that has not already been encountered for the specific user, a new user state $s = (c_1, ..., c_n)$ is added to the SMC.

Transition Probabilities. A concrete series of consecutive user states is represented as a stochastic process of random variables $X_1, X_2, X_3, ...$, where X_i refers to the state occupied after the i-th state transition. In order to learn the state transition probabilities, we assume the Markov property: The probability $p(s, s')$ for the state s' to be visited next only depends on the current state s, and is independent of all previous state changes. This assumption can be extended such that $p(s, s')$ depends on the k last visited states (k-order Markov models [3]) if needed, and PreCon operates on these more general k-order models. However, for simplicity, we assume $k = 1$ here. The math is essentially the same.

Assuming a stationary probability distribution, the probabilities $p(s, s')$ can be estimated from the history of past state transitions: Let $w_{s,s'}$ be the *transition weight*, which denotes the number of transitions from s to s' as observed in the history. The transition probability $p(s, s')$ is defined as $p(s, s') = P(X_{n+1} = s'|X_n = s) = \frac{w_{s,s'}}{\sum_{s'' \in S} w_{s,s''}}$. Thus, the probability is the ratio of the number of observed state transitions from s to s' to the number of all observed transitions from s.

Dwell Time Distribution. The dwell time in state s is modelled as a random variable D_s. We learn the probability distribution of D_s conditioned on each transition such that $h_{s,s'}(t) = P(D_s = t|X_{n+1} = s', X_n = s)$. For this purpose, we observe the time periods that pass between consecutive changes in user state. In order to limit the storage and computation overhead, we apply a discretization and divide time into intervals of equal size Δt, such that the i-th time interval is defined as $I_i = [i \cdot \Delta t, (i+1) \cdot \Delta t)$. The distribution $h_{s,s'}$ can then be derived as follows: Let $w_{s,s'}^i$ be the number of transitions (s, s') that occurred in the interval I_i such that $w_{s,s'} = \sum_i w_{s,s'}^i$ is the total number of observed transitions (s, s'). Then the probability for spending exactly time t in state s before leaving to successor state s' is calculated as

$$h_{s,s'} : t \mapsto \frac{w_{s,s'}^{\lfloor \frac{t}{\Delta t} \rfloor}}{\Delta t \cdot w_{s,s'}}. \tag{1}$$

In equation 1, we use Δt as a normalization factor to ensure that $\int_0^\infty h_{s,s'}(t)\, dt = 1$ for the cumulative distribution. As we deal with a discrete representation of the dwell time distribution, the cumulative distribution function $\int_a^b h_{s,s'}(t)\, dt$ is computed as a sum of intervals over the probability mass function. More precisely, the cumulative probability is determined by the sum over the intervals which are enclosed by the integral ranges between a and b. As a and b may fall into discretization intervals, we interpolate the probability associated with the fraction of the corresponding intervals based on a linear function. The cumulative distribution is later used in Section 5 to determine the probability resulting from time-bounded queries.

4   Prediction Query Language

PreCon's prediction query language is based on *Continuous Stochastic Logic* (CSL) [11], a probabilistic derivative of branching-time temporal logics (applied in classical model checking). CSL provides operators for verifying *temporal properties* of probabilistic state transition systems. Applications construct queries from these *temporal operators* and submit them to PreCon. The operators are then evaluated on the learnt SMC to verify the specified properties.

The state space S can be traversed by going from one state to the next as the transitions among the states permit. The resulting series of visited states (called a *path*) models one possible temporal behaviour of the user. For a context prediction, PreCom starts at the state $s \in S$ the user currently occupies in the real world and evaluates the given query from there, possibly considering all possible paths starting at s (depending on the temporal operators in the query). The query language is defined as follows:

Let $p \in [0,1]$ be a probability threshold, let $\lhd \in \{\leq, \geq\}$ be a comparison operator, let $t \in \mathbb{R}^+$ be a time bound, and let $(C_i, c \in Dom(C_i))$ be a contextual value c of type C_i. Queries can be composed from CSL using the following grammar:

A query is a temporal-logic formula Φ with

$$\Phi = true \mid (C_i, c) \mid \Phi \wedge \Phi \mid \neg\Phi \mid \mathbb{P}_{\lhd p}(\varphi),$$

where φ is a *path formula* defined as

$$\varphi = X^{\leq t}\Phi \mid F^{\leq t}\Phi \mid G^{\leq t}\Phi \mid \Phi_1 U^{\leq t}\Phi_2$$

Using CSL, we can investigate *reachability properties* (using operators X and F) and *invariant properties* (using operators G and U) of future user behaviour. X is the *Next* operator. It evaluates a condition Φ on all immediate successor states of the current user state s. Φ is expressed as a name-value pair (C_i, c) consisting of the name of a context type C_i (e.g. *location*) and a specific context value c (e.g. *office*). The query "Will the next location be the office?" can be expressed by applying the *Next* operator to $\Phi = (location, office)$, resulting in $X(location, office)$. F is the *Eventually* operator and can be used to verify if a condition Φ holds in any state reachable from s through paths in the SMC. G is the *Globally* operator and can be used to check if the condition Φ holds in every state on all paths starting in s. U is the *Until* operator and expresses that eventually Φ_2 must hold and Φ_1 must hold on all paths starting at the current state until Φ_2 holds.

Time is a first order construct of the prediction query language. All operators are associated with a time constraint t, defining an upper bound on the time, which may pass until the desired property holds. Having such a time bound and using the dwell time distributions to evaluate time-bounded queries enables us to formulate time-dependent queries.

The *raw* predictions are always probabilistic in nature when a query is evaluated. So the answer of the model checking algorithm is of the form "The user enters his office within the next 10 minutes with probability 0.74". A querying application, however, usually expects a *true* or *false* as an answer. Therefore, the calculated probabilities are compared to a probability threshold p, which is expressed in the subscript of a query formula ($\mathbb{P}_{\lhd p}(\varphi)$). The querying application specifies this probability and gets a boolean result depending on whether the outcome of the query evaluation exceeds the threshold or not[1].

In Table 1, we give some examples for behavioural properties which can be expressed as CSL formulas. The examples demonstrate the range of different use cases for context predictions, including queries with different semantics and context types.

Table 1. Examples of context prediction queries

Query	Explanation
$\mathbb{P}_{\geq 0.8}(X^{\leq 10min}(location, office))$	Will the office be the uer's next location within the next 10 minutes with a probability of ≥ 0.8?
$\mathbb{P}_{\geq 1.0} \quad (location, home) \wedge$ $\mathbb{P}_{\geq 0.8}F^{\leq 30min}(\neg(location, home))$	Is the user currently at *home* and will he *eventually* leave with a probability ≥ 0.8 within the next 30 minutes ?
$\mathbb{P}_{\geq 0.6} \; G^{\leq 30min} \; (activity, walking)$	Will the user be *walking* within the next 30 minutes with a probability ≥ 0.6?
$\mathbb{P}_{\geq 0.2} \qquad ((location, stuttgart)$ $U^{\leq 60min} \; (location, home))$	Will the user be in Stuttgart with a probability ≥ 0.2 until he eventually reaches his *home* within the next hour ?
$\mathbb{P}_{\geq 1.0}(activity, biking) \qquad \wedge$ $\mathbb{P}_{\geq 0.8}(F^{\leq 60min} \; (location, home) \wedge$ $(activity, sitting))$	Is the user currently biking (anywhere) and will *eventually* relax (*activity = sitting*) at his home with a probability ≥ 0.2 within the next hour?

The probability threshold p is an application-dependent value to influence the trade-off between *false positives* (queries that evaluate to *true* but prove to be false later on) and *false negatives* (queries that evaluate to false but actually become true in reality): A higher threshold reduces the number of false positives and increases the number of false negatives. A lower threshold has the opposite effect. Consequently, the concrete threshold defines the ratio of false negative and false positives that the application is willing to accept. The choice for the threshold is dependent on the application semantics. For example, in security critical applications it is usually beneficial to prepare for exceptional cases even if they might not occur. Hence, such applications may tolerate a higher number of false positives rather than false negatives. On the contrary, a large number of false positives may negatively impact the satisfaction of a user in an application that delivers advertisements based on his predicted future location. In this case a higher probability threshold is beneficial to prevent the user from being overwhelmed by irrelevant advertisements.

---

[1] Applications can also access the raw prediction result in case they require more complex threshold comparisons.

5   Query Processing

Classical model checking algorithms assume static state transition systems, where the system is analysed at design-time and behavioural properties are only studied at state entry times. In our case, the system that is subject to the verification is dynamic. In particular, the probability resulting from the evaluation of a query is depending on the time Δd, that has passed since the current state s was entered. Therefore, we have to extend the standard model checking approach to account for Δd (referred to as the *running dwell time* in the following) by devising new ways of evaluating the temporal operators X and U. This is sufficient since it can be shown that, F and G can be expressed using the X and U operators [9]. For example, the reachability property $F^{\leq t}\Phi$ can be transformed to the equivalent expression $(true\, U^{\leq t}\Phi)$. We refer to X and U as the *basic operators* in the following. Arbitrarily complex temporal-logic formula can be evaluated in a bottom-up manner based on a tree representation [9] using only the basic operators. Thus, evaluating a query requires two things:

1. We need to be able to determine whether a given state s satisfies a basic context constraint $\Phi = (C_j, c)$. The basic satisfaction relation is defined as $(s = (c_1, ...c_j, ..., c_n) \models \Phi) \Leftrightarrow c_j = c$.
2. We need the ability to calculate the probability of $X^{\leq t}\Phi_1$ and $\Phi_2 U^{\leq t}\Phi_1$ for some basic context constraints Φ_1, Φ_2. Intuitively speaking, this involves calculating the probabilities of reaching a state s with $s \models \Phi_1$ and of traveling a path where $s_i \models \Phi_2$ holds for every state s_i.

Our model checking problem can be solved by evaluating a satisfaction relation $\models$ for the path formula φ enclosed by the probabilistic operator $\mathbb{P}_{\triangleleft p}(\varphi)$ as follows:

$$(s, \Delta d) \models \mathbb{P}_{\triangleleft p}(\varphi) \Leftrightarrow P(s, \Delta d \models \varphi) \triangleleft p$$

In other words, the path formula φ is satisfied after Δd time units have passed in state s iff the probability $P(s, \Delta d \models \varphi)$ for the occurrence of φ satisfies the threshold condition $\triangleleft p$.

In the following, we will present the evaluation approach for the two basic operators in detail. Let i be the index of the last state transition that was observed, such that $X_i = s$ denotes the current state and $D_s = \Delta d$ is the current dwell time that has passed in this state. As a common basis for the computations, we define the probability for moving from the state s to a successor state s' within time t using the information present in the SMC as follows:

$$P(X_{i+1} = s', D_s \leq \Delta d + t | X_i = s, D_s > \Delta d) \tag{2}$$

$$= \frac{P(X_{i+1} = s', \Delta d < D_s \leq \Delta d + t | X_i = s)}{\sum_{s' \in S} P(X_{i+1} = s', D_s > \Delta d | X_i = s)} \tag{3}$$

$$= \frac{p(s, s') \cdot \int_{\Delta d}^{\Delta d + t} h_{s,s'}(x)\, dx}{\sum_{s' \in S} p(s, s') \cdot \int_{\Delta d}^{\infty} h_{s,s'}(x)\, dx} \tag{4}$$

We use Baye's rule to transform formula (2) into (3), which is free of the dwell time distribution in the conditional probability. Thus it can be computed using the state transition probabilities and the dwell time distribution present in the SMC (Equation 4).

5.1 Next Operator X

The next operator limits the search space for the satisfaction of property φ to the immediate successor states of the current state s. Due to the running dwell time, we have to consider the dwell time distribution only from the time Δd onwards and express this using a subscript in $X^{\leq t}_{\Delta d}$. We extend the model checking approach given by Lopez et al. [12] accordingly, as follows:

$$P(X^{\leq t}_{\Delta d}(\varphi)) \tag{5}$$

$$= \sum_{s' \in S \land s' \models \varphi} P(X_{i+1} = s', D_s \leq \Delta d + t | X_i = s, D_s > \Delta d) \tag{6}$$

$$= \frac{\sum_{s' \in S \land s' \models \varphi} p(s, s') \cdot \int_{\Delta d}^{\Delta d + t} h_{s,s'}(x)\, dx}{\sum_{s' \in S} p(s, s') \cdot \int_{\Delta d}^{\infty} h_{s,s'}(x)\, dx} \tag{7}$$

We can calculate $P(X^{\leq t}_{\Delta d}(\varphi))$ directly, using Equation 4. The denominator is the probability of reaching arbitrary next states in greater than Δd time units, whereas the nominator reduces this probability to states where the φ holds. This ratio represents the desired probability considering the running dwell time Δd.

5.2 Until Operator U

For the until operator, the satisfaction of the property φ must be evaluated along all paths which can be reached from the current state within the given time bound. The exploration of the state space is therefore not necessarily bound by the immediate successor states. Again, we extend the approach of Lopez et al. [12] by additionally considering the running dwell time Δd. This is expressed using a subscript in $U^{\leq t}_{\Delta d}$. The probability for the satisfaction of $U^{\leq t}_{\Delta d}$ can then be calculated as follows:

$$P(\Phi_1 U^{\leq t}_{\Delta d} \Phi_2) = F_a(s, s', t, \Delta d) \tag{8}$$

$$F_a(s, s', t, \Delta d) = \begin{cases} 1, \text{ if } s \models \Phi_2 \\ \frac{1}{\sum_{s' \in S} p(s,s') \cdot \int_{\Delta d}^{\infty} h_{s,s'}(t)dt} \cdot \sum_{s' \in S} \int_{\Delta d}^{\Delta d + t} p(s, s') \\ \quad \cdot h_{s,s'}(x) \cdot F_b(s, s', t - x)dx, \text{ if } s \models \Phi_1 \land \neg \Phi_2 \\ 0, \text{ otherwise} \end{cases} \tag{9}$$

$$F_b(s, s', t) = \begin{cases} 1, \text{ if } s \models \Phi_2 \\ \sum_{s' \in S} \int_0^t p(s, s') \cdot h_{s,s'}(x) \cdot F_b(s, s', t - x) dx \\ \qquad , \text{ if } s \models \Phi_1 \wedge \neg \Phi_2 \\ 0, \text{ otherwise} \end{cases} \qquad (10)$$

The extension of the standard algorithm results in two functions F_a (9) and F_b (10). Function F_a is used in the first step of the verification, starting from the current user state s taking the running dwell time in s into account. Function F_a uses F_b for calculating the probability over all the possible paths starting at s. F_b calculates the probabilities recursively using convolution of dwell time distributions, taking into account that a state may be left at each point in time within the remaining time horizon.

6   Related Work

Context prediction in pervasive computing has attracted much attention in recent years. Maryhofer proposed a general architecture for context prediction [2] and used methods from time series analysis (e.g. ARMA) for prediction. Other approaches have used Markov Models [5], [3], [8], compression algorithms [3], [7], n-gram tries [6], or machine learning techniques [4] to predict context. However, the predictions supported by these approaches only compute the most probable next context in a single-dimensional context space. They do not allow queries for temporal relations in a multi-dimensional context space. Semi-Markov Chains as we use them have also been employed by Lee and Hou for an analysis of transient and stationary features of user mobility on the Dartmouth campus network [13]. However, they also did not consider a sophisticated query language that supports temporal relations. PreCon is the first system to investigate the application of temporal logics as a powerful and expressive query language for context predictions.

For the calculation of the predictions, we adopt the techniques from the field of stochastic model checking [14], which has been thoroughly studied by Baier et al. for Continuous Time Markov Chains [11]. Lopez et. al have worked on the extension of the model checking algorithms for Semi Markov Chains [12]. In our approach, we leverage on their results. However, we extend their original model checking algorithms by including the running dwell time of the states, allowing for accurate real-time predictions. In contrast to classical model checking approaches, PreCon does not rely on a design-time specification of a state transition system. Instead, we apply a learning algorithm for building an SMC in an online fashion. This allows us to incorporate newly available data at any time, making the predictions more accurate.

The combination of SMCs, a query language based on temporal logic, and the online learning approach represents an important new step in the area of context prediction.

7   Evaluation

We have evaluated PreCon using real-world context traces from a case study in a German geriatric nursing home. The nursing home is an intensive care station for elderly people suffering from dementia and other old-age diseases. The patients are accommodated in rooms on a nursing ward, where they receive care from nurses throughout the day. Each nurse visits patients in different rooms and performs treatment activities (e.g., the patient morning hygiene). PreCon predicts the future context of the nurses, in order to optimize the tasks scheduled by an intelligent workflow management system. The integration of context prediction into the scheduling decisions is part of the European research project ALLOW [15]. In order to obtain context traces, the nurses were accompanied over the course of 25 days during 3-5 hours in the morning shift. The traces consist of time-stamped entries of (1) the activities performed by nurses (2) the locations of their visits and (3) the ids of the patients they took care of. Thus, the records define a time series of multi-dimensional context, where each entry denotes a discrete change of context associated with a nurse. Given the context traces, PreCon learns a SMC to represent the behaviour of each nurse. In order to evaluate the impact of different context types on the prediction outcome, we varied the types of context used to learn the SMCs. We investigated three different state spaces, i.e., $s \in Dom(Location)$, $s \in Dom(Location) \times Dom(Activity)$ and $s \in Dom(Location) \times Dom(Activity) \times Dom(Patient)$.

It is important to note that comparisons with existing context prediction systems are not possible at this time as they cannot produce the type of temporal predictions generated by PreCon. Since PreCon is the first system to venture into this area, we use metrics from the area of information retrieval (as explained in the following) to asses the general performance of PreCon.

Metrics. We performed the evaluations using the metrics *precision*, *recall* and *F-score* known from the area of information retrieval. If a query result exceeds the probability threshold, we count it as either *true positive* (TP) or *false positive* (FP), depending on whether the prediction matches the real-world context. Otherwise, in case the prediction remains below the probability threshold, we distinguish between *true negatives* (TN) or *false negatives* (FN). We count the occurrences of (TP), (FP), (TN), and (FN) in order to calculate the metrics. This way, we can evaluate the influence of a varying probability threshold p on the *precision* defined as $\frac{TPs}{TPs+FPs}$ as well as on *recall* defined as $\frac{TPs}{TPs+FNs}$. While precision is a measure of the exactness of the predictions, recall is used to quantify the completeness of the predictions. Additionally, we evaluate the *F-score* which gives a combined measure of both and is defined as $2 \cdot \frac{precision \cdot recall}{recision+recall}$. The performance of these metrics gives important insight in how proactive applications are affected by a choice of the probability threshold as will be discussed in the next subsection for different queries.

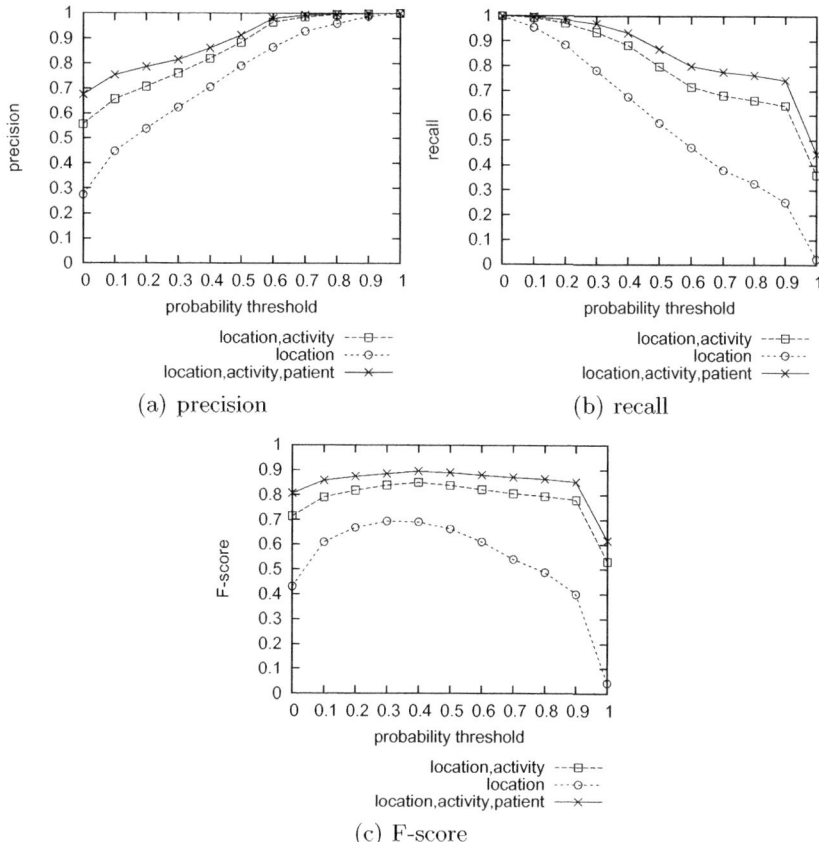

(a) precision

(b) recall

(c) F-score

Fig. 2. Evaluation results for the Next operator

Basic Queries. We evaluated our approach for two exemplary queries $\mathbb{P}_{\lhd p}(X_{\bar{f}}^{\leq t}(\varphi))$ and $\mathbb{P}_{\lhd p}(\ F^{\leq t}\varPhi_2) = \mathbb{P}_{\lhd p}(\ true\ U^{\leq t}\varPhi_2)$. We generated queries for the future location of a user. The time constraint associated with these queries is set to $t = 10$ minutes. We evaluated the queries repeatedly, i.e, predictions were computed upon a state change and periodically after $\Delta E = 10$ seconds have passed in a state. The results discussed in the following show the average of 2000 query evaluations.

Figures 2(a)-(c) illustrate the results for the *Next* operator $X_{\bar{f}}^{\leq t}(\varphi)$. Figure 2(a) shows the impact of a varying probability threshold on the precision metrics. As expected, the precision gains from an increase of the probability threshold. The reason is that the number of FP decreases because an increasing portion of the predictions with a low probability is discarded. At the same time, we can observe the highest precision if states are composed of the multi-dimensional context "concrete activities", "location" and "patient". In contrast, the precision remains lowest when states only contain location information (single-dimensional).

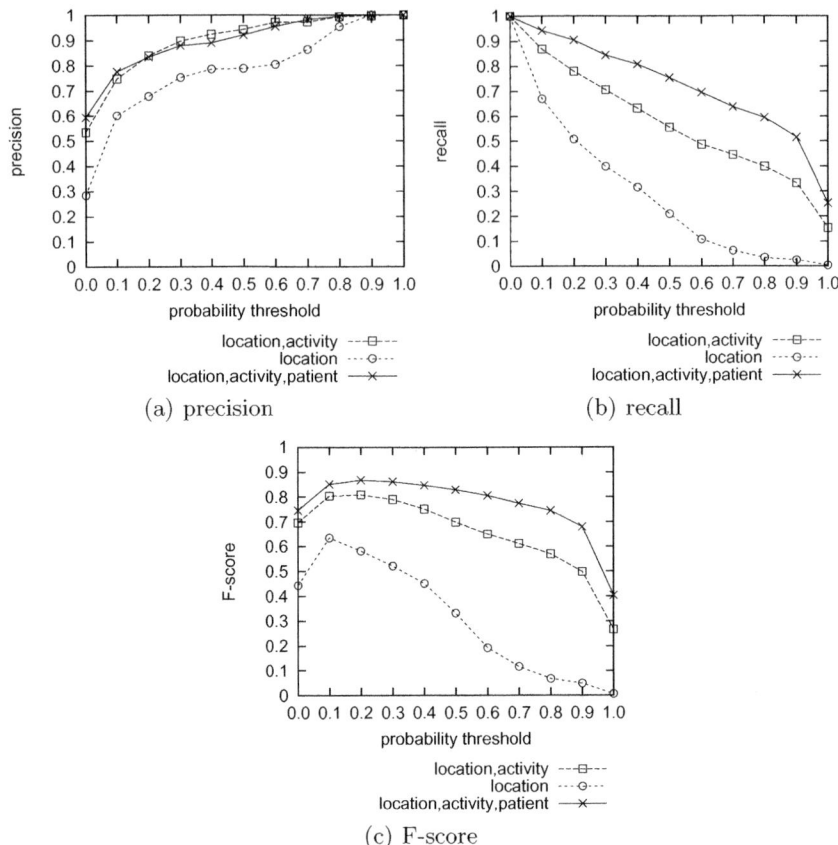

(a) precision

(b) recall

(c) F-score

Fig. 3. Evaluation results for the Until operator

Hence, the evaluation results show that additional context is relevant to discriminate user states such that more accurate predictions can be expected. Figure 2(b) shows the recall as a function of the probability threshold. The results are reciprocal to the precision results: For an increasing probability threshold the number of FN increases, as more and more predictions are discarded that actually match the future behaviour. This result illustrates the trade-off between precision and recall for different values of the probability threshold: If the threshold is increased to guarantee more reliable predictions, the risk of discarding correct predictions with a low probability rises. Figure 2(c) shows the F-score and reveals the characteristics of this trade-off: The F-score rises as the threshold increases from 0 to 0.4. Up to this threshold, the gain from a higher precision outweighs the loss in recall. However, for a threshold higher than 0.4, the loss due to the loss in recall becomes more significant, so that the score is negatively affected. For applications that are interested in a good trade-off, we therefore recommend $p = 0.4$ as a probability threshold. In this case, we achieve a F-score of 0.86, which indicates a very good performance.

Figures 3(a)-(c) depict the evaluation results for the until operator. Figure 3(a) shows that the precision significantly gains already for lower thresholds $p > 0$. The reason is that Φ_2 can be fulfilled in all states reachable within the time constraint. Thus, the chance to encounter the expected context is increased. In contrast, the same chance is limited to the state successors in case of the next operator. At the same time, the recall is highly reduced by an increasing threshold as shown in Figure 3(b). Since the evaluated queries also address future context, which appears in states reachable over multiple transitions that are uncertain to occur, a significant amount of predictions has only a minor probability. This large number causes a lot of FNs in total, so that a significant amount of correct predictions is discarded. This observation is also reflected in Figure 3(c), which shows the F-score. For a threshold $p > 0.2$ the high loss in recall dominates the gain in precision. Compared to the next operator, the until operator is more sensitive to the choice of the probability threshold. We therefore recommend $p = 0.2$ as a threshold for applications to deal with the inherent trade-off for the until operator. In this case, a good result with an F-score of 0.87 can be achieved.

8   Conclusion

We presented PreCon, a novel approach to context prediction that enables intelligence in ubiquitous system by allowing for much more expressive queries than existing systems. In PreCon, user behaviour is represented by Semi-Markov Chains (SMC), and temporal-logics is used as a query language. We extended well-known model-checking techniques to deal with the online character of context predictions and to allow for continuous learning of SMCs. PreCon's query language provides a powerful means for applications to pose temporal queries for reachability and invariant properties of future context. Thus, PreCon goes far beyond existing approaches and represents a new class of context prediction systems that enable intelligent ubiquitous applications to take much more educated decisions.

We evaluated PreCon based on a real-world case study in the area of healthcare using metrics from information retrieval and showed that it exhibits a good performance. Moreover, our evaluations yielded indications for choosing sensible parameters for different classes of applications.

In our future work, we will extend our approach to probabilistic LTL as another variant of temporal logics. This will enable us to define further types of queries, which can not be expressed in CSL. Furthermore, we are working on a distributed context prediction system where prediction models are cached on mobile devices such that a user always has access to the future context that is relevant for him.

References

1. Krumm, J.: Ubiquitous advertising: The killer application for the 21st century. Pervasive Computing 10(1), 66–73 (2011)
2. Mayrhofer, R.M.: An Architecture for Context Prediction. PhD thesis, Johannes Kepler University of Linz (2004)

3. Song, L., Kotz, D., Jain, R., He, X.: Evaluating next-cell predictors with extensive wi-fi mobility data. IEEE Transactions on Mobile Computing 5, 1633–1649 (2004)
4. Anagnostopoulos, T., Anagnostopoulos, C., Hadjiefthymiades, S., Kyriakakos, M., Kalousis, A.: Predicting the location of mobile users: a machine learning approach. In: Proc. of the 6th Intl. Conf. on Pervasive Services (2009)
5. Katsaros, D., Manolopoulos, Y.: Prediction in wireless networks by markov chains. IEEE Wireless Communications 16, 56–63 (2009)
6. Hartmann, M., Schreiber, D.: Prediction algorithms for user actions. In: Proc. of Intl. Conf. on Adaptive Business Information Systems (2007)
7. Gopalratnam, K., Cook, D.J.: Online sequential prediction via incremental parsing: The active lezi algorithm. IEEE Intelligent Systems 22, 52–58 (2007)
8. Davison, B.D., Hirsh, H.: Predicting sequences of user actions. In: Workshop on Predicting the Future: AI Approaches to Time Series Analysis (1998)
9. Baier, C., Katoen, J.P.: Principles of Model Checking. MIT Press, Cambridge (2008)
10. Howard, R.A.: Dynamic Probabilistic Systems: Semi-Markov and Decision Processes. John Wiley & Sons, Chichester (1971)
11. Baier, C., Haverkort, B., Hermanns, H., Katoen, J.P.: Model-checking algorithms for continuous-time markov chains. IEEE Transactions on Software Engineering 29, 524–541 (2003)
12. López, G.G.I., Hermanns, H., Katoen, J.-P.: Beyond memoryless distributions: Model checking semi-markov chains. In: de Luca, L., Gilmore, S. (eds.) PROBMIV 2001, PAPM-PROBMIV 2001, and PAPM 2001. LNCS, vol. 2165, pp. 57–70. Springer, Heidelberg (2001)
13. Lee, J.K., Hou, J.C.: Modeling steady-state and transient behaviours of user mobility: Formulation, analysis, and application. In: Proc. of the 7th ACM International Symposium on Mobile Ad Hoc Networking and Computing (2006)
14. Kwiatkowska, M., Norman, G., Parker, D.: Stochastic model checking. In: Bernardo, M., Hillston, J. (eds.) SFM 2007. LNCS, vol. 4486, pp. 220–270. Springer, Heidelberg (2007)
15. Herrmann, K., Rothermel, K., Kortuem, G., Dulay, N.: Adaptable pervasive flows - an emerging technology for pervasive adaptation. In: Proc. of the Workshop on Pervasive Adaptation at the 2nd Intl. Conf. on Self-Adaptive and Self-Organizing Systems (2008)

A Virtual Channel Technique for Supporting P2P Streaming[*]

Jau-Wu Huang, Nien-Chen Lin, Kai-Chao Yang,
Chen-Lung Chan, and Jia-Shung Wang

Department of Computer Science
National Tsing Hua University
Hsinchu, Taiwan
jwhuang@vc.cs.nthu.edu.tw

Abstract. Nowadays, some powerful client devices, e.g., smart phone, set top boxes and digital video recorders, are commonly used to enhance digital TV broadcasting services. This paper proposes a virtual channel platform by organizing these client devices to virtually support each user a dedicated channel according to her/his demand. In the proposed platform, each video is partitioned into many small segments before it is shared in a peer-to-peer network. A virtual channel is constructed by composing these video segments into a long video playout sequence. However, retrieving these small segments from a large scale peer-to-peer network could cause relatively large query overhead. To reduce the number of queries, we propose a virtual stream mechanism by aggregating popular adjacent video segments to logically form a long video object. The simulation results demonstrate that the proposed virtual channel platform can improve the service performance.

1 Introduction

The Digital TV (DTV), which is a new type of TV broadcasting technology, has become the most popular home entertainment nowadays. In addition, some powerful client devices, for example, smart phone, Set Top Box (STB) and Digital Video Recorder (DVR), are now widely integrated to the TV broadcasting service. Since these client devices usually have some computation powers, some storage spaces, and a network interface for Internet access, we then attempt to organize these client devices to provide a more flexible TV broadcasting service that delivers a sequence of demanded programs to each user via a "virtual channel", which is a personalized channel composed by her/his favorite programs.

In this paper, we propose a virtual channel platform to support an efficient virtual channel service. The idea of this platform is to organize the client devices to share their resource efficiently; therefore the availability of the videos in the system can be improved. We assume that all video programs are encoded into a common media format for compatibility, for exzample, MPEG-4 or H.264, before sharing them to all clients.

---

[*] The research is supported by the NSC99-2221-E-007-077-MY3, National Science Council, R.O.C.

C.-H. Hsu et al. (Eds.): UIC 2011, LNCS 6905, pp. 365–378, 2011.

We also propose a cache-and-share mechanism to improve the availability of the videos. Once a client obtains a video, this video will be stored and shared to others by means of a peer-to-peer file sharing technique, e.g., structured P2P (Pastry[2], Chord[3], CAN[4], CoopNet[5]), unstructured P2P (Gnutella[6], Napster[7], KaZaA[8]), or P2P streaming (CoolStreaming[9], PPLive[12], UUSee[13], SopCast[14]). These works are good for file sharing or video streaming; however, directly implementing them to support virtual channel service is not appropriate. The reasons will be stated later.

To support each user a dedicated virtual channel, we summarize the general viewing behaviors of users to four modes as follows:

A. Live mode

In this mode, users always watch the live program (for instance, live basketball game). In Fig. 1, we let the four users all watch a live video program A. When a user is coming, she/he always watches the latest frame of the live program.

B. Review mode

The review mode is based on the live mode. When a user is watching a live program, she/he could want to review some scenes, for example, splendid scenes or the scenes she/he just missed. Consider the example in Fig. 2. Let the live program A have a splendid scene at time 3. Therefore, some users, such as the user 1 and user 2 in this example, are probably to watch the scene A3 again.

C. Serial-play mode

In this mode, a user always watches an entire TV program from the head to the tail sequentially. Consider the example in Fig. 3. When a user requests the program A, she/he always stays in this channel until the entire program has end.

D. Interest-based mode

In this mode, a user can randomly access the TV programs according to her/his interest. Consider the example in Fig. 4. As the figure illustrates, the request sequences are irregular and are difficult to model.

Based on the above, we can summarize these general modes to two types: 1) sequential access; 2) random access. Undoubtedly, a perfect TV broadcasting platform should consider two goals as below:

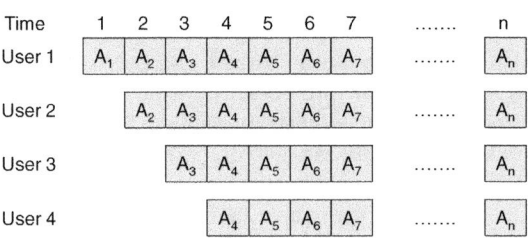

Fig. 1. The behavior of live viewing

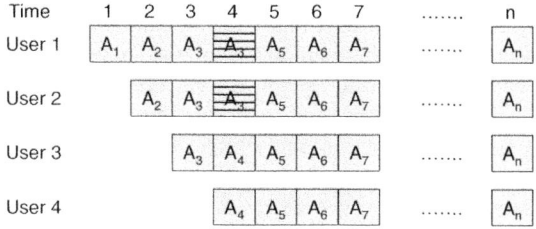

Fig. 2. The behavior of review viewing

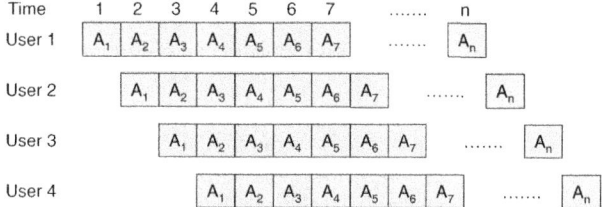

Fig. 3. The behavior of serial-play viewing

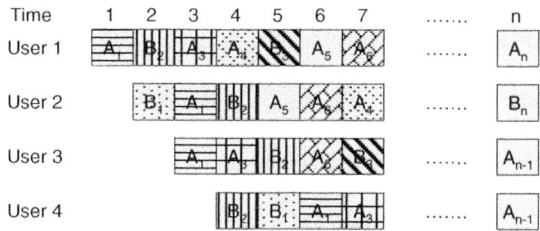

Fig. 4. The behavior of interest-based viewing

(1) supporting all the user viewing behaviors

Sequential access is a special case of random access. To support the above viewing behaviors, we assume that the platform must provide a random access interface to users.

(2) optimizing the system performance

A random access request pattern is not appropriate for performance optimization due to its irregularity. Therefore, we should try to aggregate some segments into a long video stream thus the system can deliver them sequentially.

Because 1) the system must provide a random access interface and 2) different parts of a video could have different popularities, we make an important assumption that the proposed platform partitions each video program into many small segments, such as [10][11][15][16] do. Then, a virtual channel can be constructed by retrieving these video segments and composing them into a long video playout sequence.

The rest of this paper is organized as follows. Section 2 introduces the concept of the proposed virtual channel platform and formulates its problem on query overhead. Section 3 then presents a virtual stream mechanism for reducing the query overhead. Section 4 presents some simulation results to evaluate the performance of the platform. Finally, the conclusion and future works are given in Section 5.

2   A Framework of Virtual Channel

2.1   Overview of the Proposed Platform

The primary components of the proposed platform can be summarized as follows:

A. The video source provider

With the rapid advances on network communication technologies, a client which can access the Internet and has some videos to share can also operate as a video source provider. Unfortunately, the storage and the reliability would be limited. To eliminate these restrictions in our platform, a backup service, which contains a large storage and has high reliability, to store the videos supported from the video source providers is essential. The details of the backup service will be introduced later.

B. The client

In the proposed virtual channel platform, each client could generate a request sequence including a series of video segments according to her/his demanded. To satisfy the demands of each client at anytime, we must increase the availability of each video program. Therefore, we not only introduce a backup service to store these videos but also adopt a cache-and-share mechanism to each client.

C. The backup service/the lookup service

In this paper, we introduce a backup service and a lookup service to increase the availabilities of the videos which are summarized as follows:

The backup service

In this paper, we adopt a backup service to store the video programs from the video source providers. The main functionalities of the backup service are 1) partitioning each video program into many small video segments; 2) storing these video segments in the buffers; 3) sharing these video segments to the clients. However, the storage of the backup service could still be exhausted. Therefore, we also adopt a LRU algorithm to replace the video segments which are not accessed for a long time.

The lookup service

In the current peer-to-peer file/video sharing platforms, each file/video is usually identified by a unique hash key. Thus, we introduce a lookup service to keep the mapping of the hash keys to the corresponding video segments.

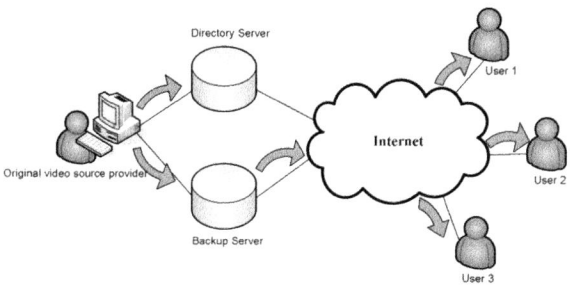

Fig. 5. An illustrative example of the proposed virtual channel platform

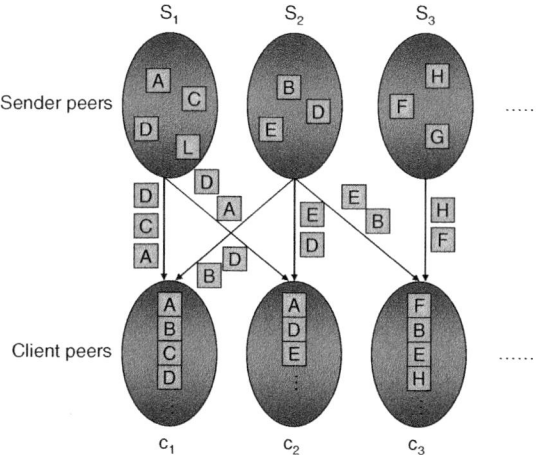

Fig. 6. An illustrative example of the delivery architecture

2.2   The Proposed Virtual Channel Platform

In this subsection, we introduce an illustrative example of the proposed virtual channel platform, as depicted in Fig. 5. The backup service and the lookup service can be implemented as a centralized or a distributed architecture. To simplify the following illustrations, we assume that the backup and lookup services are both implemented in a centralized way. Then, we will describe the details of the platform from three parts: 1) publishing a video program; 2) locating the sender peers; 3) retrieving the video segments.

A. Publishing a video program

When a video source provider publishes a video program, it will simultaneously forward the video stream to the backup server and the directory server. The backup server will partition the video into many small video segments and store them in its local buffer. On the other hand, the directory server will associate a unique hash key to each generated video segment and maintain the mapping in a hash table.

B. Locating the sender peers

When a client gets the hash key of a video segment, it still has to retrieve the video segment from one or more sender peers. The process to locate the sender peers can be implemented in either a centralized model or a peer-to-peer model.

(1) Centralized model

In the centralized model, the strategy is for each segment to publish the information of its contributed sender peers. However, this model would result in a performance bottleneck on the server of a large scale service.

(2) Peer-to-peer model

In a structured P2P system, a video source provider usually publishes the essential information to specific peers where requesters can easily discovered by means of a DHT (Distributed Hash Table) mechanism. However, maintaining such a DHT over a large scale P2P network will require considerable management overhead, and any update on peer status and system information will also cause an update on the content of the DHT. In the proposed virtual channel platform, a client can dynamically join or leave the system, and the cached video segments in its buffer could also update frequently. Thus, the structured P2P is not appropriate for our platform. Based on the above, we develop the delivery architecture of the proposed virtual channel platform based on the concept of unstructured P2P, just as CoolStreaming [9] does.

C. Retrieving the video segments

After locating the possible sender peers, the client then must retrieve the desired video segments from these sender peers. Fig. 6 shows an illustrative example of the delivery architecture in the proposed virtual channel platform. (It is important to remember that a sender peer could be the local buffer, another client, or the backup server.) As Fig. 6 illustrates, the client c_1 has gathered the hash keys $\{A, B, C, D\}$ of its desired video segments. c_1 also understands that it can get the segments corresponding to $\{A, C, D\}$ from S_1 and the segments corresponding to $\{B, D\}$ from S_2.

2.3   The Details of the Proposed Delivery Architecture

In this subsection, we will discuss the details of a client to retrieve the desired video segments as follows:

(1) hash key conversion

After receiving the request sequence from a client, the directory server transforms the request sequence into a series of hash keys for P2P sharing.

(2) query and delivery

After receiving the responded hash keys, the user attempts to obtain the corresponding video segments according to these hash keys. First, the client checks if the video segments are already cached in its local buffer. If the segments are not cached in the local buffer, the client floods a query message to find at most w sender peers among all other peers and wait for responses. Let the number of available sender peers be x. Then, the delivery process would be either of the following cases:

Case I. x $\geq$ w: The available number of sender peers is larger than the requirement. In this case, this client will choose w peers as the video sources.

Case II. x < w and x > 0: The available number of sender peers is smaller than the requirement, so the client will simultaneously get the video segment from all of these x sender peers.

Case III. x = 0: The video segment is not cached in any peer in the P2P network. Therefore, the client must get the video segment from the backup server.

(3) local caching

After obtaining the desired video segments, the client will cache these video segments into its local buffer simultaneously with a LRU algorithm.

3   Overview of the Virtual Stream Mechanism

3.1   Definition of a Virtual Stream

A virtual stream is a set of video segments which are generated by the directory server and adopted to reduce the query overhead. In the proposed virtual channel platform, the virtual streams can be divided into two types: 1) beneficial virtual stream, and 2) elemental virtual stream. A beneficial virtual stream is a series of video segments which are frequently accessed by user requests, whereas an elemental virtual stream is formed with only one video segment. In other words, each individual video segment is called an elemental virtual stream. Then the directory server will associate an unique hash key with each virtual stream and record these hash keys into a hash table. To simplify the discussions, we assume that the size of each video segment is equal and is normalized to minutes of video data. Then, the directory server will 1) check all useable beneficial virtual streams and try to use them to replace the matched request subsequence of each user; 2) use the elemental virtual streams to replace the user request segments which are not matched by the beneficial virtual streams; 3) convert the request sequence to a series of hash keys associated to the virtual streams.

3.2   Definition of Popular Subsequences

Let the proposed virtual channel platform have n clients, and let each client C_i ($1 \leq i \leq n$) send out a request sequence q_i ($1 \leq i \leq n$), which is composed by d_i ($1 \leq d_i \leq y$) video segments, to the directory server. (Note that y is the maximum number of video segments that a request sequence can contain.) Then, we have, $q_i = \{R_1, R_2, ..., R_{di}\}$. Consider a request subsequence v' with y' video segments ($2 \leq y' \leq L$), i.e., $v' = \{U_1',$ $U_2', ...U_y'\}$. (Note that L is the maximum length of a virtual stream.) Then we define the term "match measure" MM as

$$MM(q_i, v') = \begin{cases} 1, & \text{if } v' \text{ is occurred in } q_i. \\ 0, & \text{if } v' \text{ is not occurred in } q_i. \end{cases} \tag{1}$$

We use this match measure MM to check if the request subsequence v' is matched in the request sequence q_i. If v' is found in q_i, then we have $MM(q_i, v') = 1$. Otherwise, we have $MM(q_i, v') = 0$. The match ratio of the request subsequence v' is then defined as follows:

$$MR(v') = \frac{\sum_{i=1}^{n} MM(q_i, v')}{n} \tag{2}$$

The above match ratio MR function for v' is equivalent to the probability that a request sequence contains v'. Then, if the match ratio of v' is larger than or equal to a threshold δ, i.e., $MR(v') \geq \delta$, the request subsequence v' is referred to as a popular subsequence and is treated as a beneficial virtual stream in this paper.

3.3   A Naïve Approach

A. Virtual stream generation

A naïve approach is to list all possible subsequences, check their match ratio MR, and select the highest ones as the beneficial virtual streams. However, this naïve approach requires too much memory space and computation overhead.

For example, we assume that the system have 10,000 video segments, whose lengths are all five minutes long. Let the system have 10,000 clients, and let each client request 60 video segments (i.e., 5 hours). Therefore, the number of possible request subsequences in worse case will be $10,000^{60} = 10^{240}$, because a video segment could be requested many times by a client. To find the most popular subsequences, we must derive all the possible subsequences in advance, and then check the match ratio MR of each one. Since a beneficial virtual stream will be at least two segments long, the amount of possible subsequences will be

$$\sum_{i=2}^{60} 10000^i,$$

which is an incredible large number. Based on the above, we can make two essential assumptions for virtual stream generation: 1) the number of subsequences to be checked must also be restricted, and 2) the length of each subsequence must be restricted.

B. Virtual stream scheduling

To reduce the query overhead, the directory server should reschedule the request sequences and try to replace with the beneficial virtual streams. The scheduling approach can be further divided into two steps: 1) sequentially scan all request sequences to check if any beneficial virtual stream is matched; 2) replace the matched subsequences with the corresponding beneficial virtual streams. However, this naïve scheduling approach has some problems: 1) too large memory space and computation overhead. 2) the match probability is low.

3.4 The Proposed Approach

In Section 1, we have summarized that the request sequences of the sequential access behaviors are more regular than those of the random access behaviors, so these request sequences are easily to find beneficial virtual streams with high match rates. Although this problem is caused by the request sequences themselves and looks impossible be solved by the directory server, it is not so serious because a user issues a random access based request sequence may not extremely care the playout order of demanded segments.

Based on the above, we let the directory server rearrange the "interest-based" user request sequences to increase the match probability of the beneficial virtual streams.

A. Virtual stream generation

To restrict the number of subsequences to be checked, we apply an interval batching mechanism to the directory server. Consider the example in subsection A again. The directory server will only deal with the request sequences which contain at most 12 segments. Therefore, the amount of possible subsequences will be

$$\sum_{i=2}^{12} 10000^i,$$

which is much smaller than the original one. However the result is still too large to be stored in memory. To reduce the number of possible subsequences to be checked, define a cost function to accurately evaluate the impact of a virtual stream.

In this paper, we define a cost function, which is called "estimated performance gain", to estimate the performance gain of each subsequence. The subsequences with the largest performance gains will be selected as beneficial virtual streams. The estimated performance gain ($E(G)$) is defined as below:

After the virtual stream is applied, assume that the amount of query messages becomes n_Q', the total number of requests becomes r', and the number of requests served by the local buffers becomes r_L'. Then the amount of query messages n_Q' can be represented as

$$n_Q' = ((r' - r_L') \cdot n_P) \tag{3}$$

Let r_B' be the number of segments delivered by the backup server after the virtual stream is applied. Therefore, the estimated performance gain ($E(G)$) will be

$$E(G) = (n_Q - n_Q') \cdot o_Q - (r_B' - r_B) \cdot o_S \tag{4}$$

The algorithm of virtual stream generation, which is designed based on the equation (4), is illustrated as follow:

In this paper, we only focus on the popular video segments and the directory server applies a heuristic to generate the beneficial virtual streams in every interval time as follows:

First, the directory server finds the most M frequently accessed video segments in this interval. Then, it generates all possible subsequences by spanning the frequently accessed video segments. Since a request sequence can be rearranged, we only generate the subsequences by composing the segments as a nondecreasing order on the segment generating time. For example, let the popular segments be A, B, and C. So the possible subsequences will be {A, B}, {A, B, C}, {B, C}, and {A, C}. Finally, the directory server evaluated the estimated performance gains $E(G)$ based on the equation (4) and selects the subsequences with the largest F gains as the beneficial virtual streams, and then it will associate each of them an unique hash key.

B. Virtual stream scheduling

In this subsection, we will introduce the proposed approach for virtual stream scheduling with a rearranging strategy. Note that while rearranging a request sequence, each demanded video segment R_i can not be scheduled to a time slot before its generating time $t(R_i)$, i.e., can not cause a "time violation". However, this procedure could take a lot of computation overhead. To reduce the computation complexity, we let the directory server sort the interest-based request sequences to a nondecreasing order on the segment generating time $t(R_i)$.

4   Simulation Results

In this section, we propose two platforms based on the Gnutella P2P overlay network to compare their system performance over various physical network topologies, as illustrated in Table 1.

We let each client have 10 neighbors, and let the TTL of each query message be 5 hops for limiting the query range of a request. Besides, we assume that all video programs are originally from several TV broadcasting channels. Let the lengths of all videos be one hour, and let each video be divided into 12 five-minute video segments (M = 12). The execution time of each simulation is 24 hours. In each scheduling interval which is one hour long, the directory server will generate at most 10 beneficial virtual streams, and each virtual stream could have at most five segments. We use the term "normalized load" to evaluate the system performance of both platforms:

$$\text{normalized load} = \frac{\text{system cost in the enhanced platform}}{\text{system cost in the baseline platform}}$$

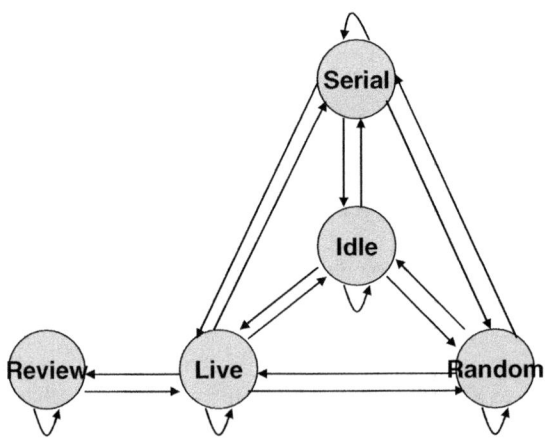

Fig. 7. The finite state machine to model the user viewing behavior

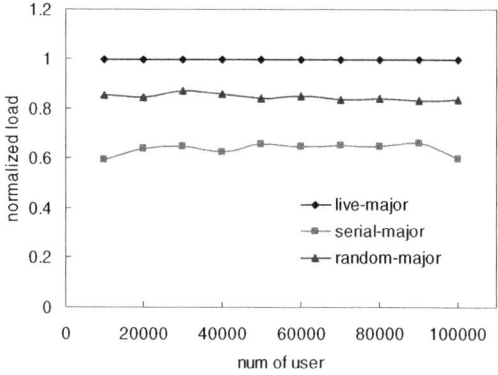

Fig. 8. The impacts of request patterns

Table 1. The two platforms for comparison

Baseline platform	Without beneficial virtual streams
Enhanced platform (our scheme)	Schedule the user request sequences with beneficial virtual streams.

4.1 The Model to Formulate the User Requests Determining the State of Viewing Behavior

In this subsection, we use a finite state machine to model the behavior of each user, as illustrated in Fig. 7. Under this finite state machine, the user can start from one of these four states (i.e., live, serial, random, idle), and then she/he can select to stay at the same state or go to another state in the next time slot.

Choosing the Channel

As mentioned above, we have assumed that the simulated system have three channels and define a channel table to specify the weight on each state for accessing each channel in the simulation. Table 2 shows an illustrative example of a channel table. In this example, if a user is in the Live state, she/he has a 50% to choose channel 1, a 30% to choose channel 2, and a 20% to choose channel 3.

Table 2. An example of channel table

	Channel 1	Channel 2	Channel 3
Live state	50%	30%	20%
VoD state	20%	70%	10%
Random state	10%	30%	60%

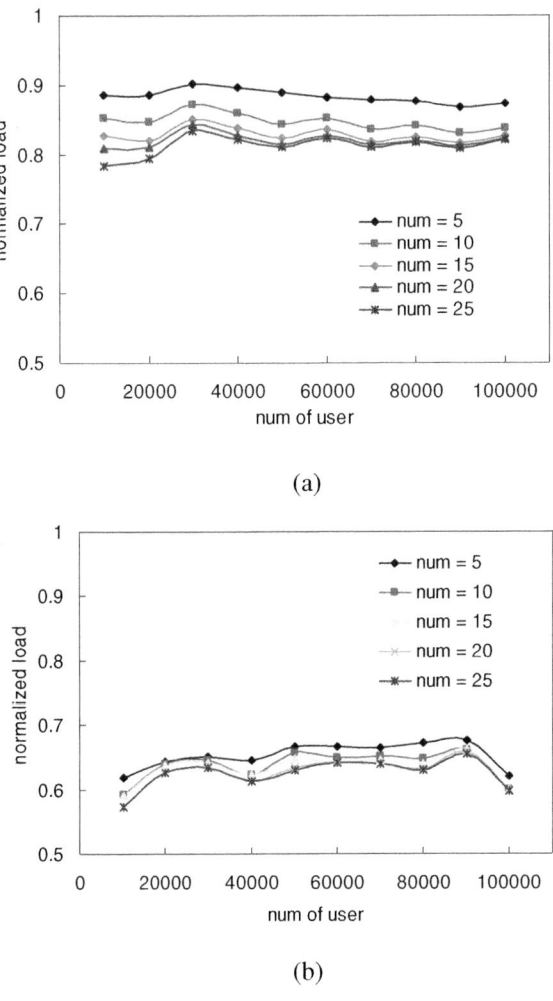

(a)

(b)

Fig. 9. The impact of the number of generated beneficial virtual streams F: (a) for random-major, (b) for serial-major

Requesting a video segment

After the viewing state and the demanded channel have been determined, we have to combine the finite state machine with the channel table to model the user viewing behaviors.

4.2   Performance Evaluation

A. Impact of the request patterns

Now we evaluate the system performance of the baseline platform and the enhanced platform under different request patterns: 1) live-major: with high ratio of live viewing; 2) serial-major: with high ratio of serial-play viewing; 3) random-major: with high ratio of interest-based viewing. In this simulation, each client averagely issues 0.97 requests every five minutes, and the request distribution is determined by the model as mentioned above. We then vary the number of clients from 10,000 to 100,000 to investigate the normalized load under these settings.

In Fig. 8, the result agrees that the serial-play mode is much easier to generate both long and frequently accessed beneficial virtual streams. Therefore, in the following simulations, we only focus on the viewing behaviors based on random-major and serial-major mode, and modify the number of the beneficial virtual streams in a scheduling interval, the maximum length of a virtual stream, to investigate the corresponding service performance.

B. Impact of the number of beneficial virtual streams

We adjust the maximum number F, of beneficial virtual streams generated in each scheduling interval time. Fig. 9(a) and Fig. 9(b) illustrate the simulation results of a random-major and a serial-major request pattern, demonstrating that a larger F implies a lower normalized system load, and the request pattern in a serial-major mode has a larger improvement than in a random-major mode.

5   Conclusions

We have proposed a virtual channel platform, which organizes DTV client devices to virtually support each user a dedicated channel according to her/his favor. We have introduced a peer-to-peer overlay network for sharing their resources, such as their buffers and network bandwidth, to each other, thus improving overall video availability. In addition, each video program is partitioned into many small segments before it is shared in this peer-to-peer network. However, such a peer-to-peer delivery architecture would cause considerable query overhead, so we also have proposed a virtual stream mechanism which aggregates the popular connected video segments into a large video stream to reduce the amount of query messages. The simulation results demonstrate that our virtual stream mechanism can significantly reduce the query overhead by increasing tiny backup server load, thus the system performance can be improved. Our future work is to develop a more efficient algorithm for generating beneficial virtual streams to further improve service performance.

References

1. Digital Video Broadcasting Project (DVB), http://www.dvb.org
2. Rowstron, A., Druschel, P.: Pastry: Scalable, distributed object location and routing for large-scale peer-to-peer systems. In: Liu, H. (ed.) Middleware 2001. LNCS, vol. 2218, pp. 329–350. Springer, Heidelberg (2001)
3. Stoica, I., Morris, R., Kaashoek, M., Balakrishnan, H.: Chord: A scalable peer-to-peer lookup service for Internet applications. In: Proc. ACM SIGCOMM 2001 (August 2001)
4. Ratnasamy, S., Francis, P., Handley, M., Karp, R., Shenker, S.: A scalable content-addressable network. In: Proc. ACM SIGCOMM 2001 (August 2001)

5. Padmanabhan, V.N., Wang, H.J., Chou, P.A., Sripanidkulchai, K.: Distributing streaming media content using cooperative networking. In: Proc. ACM NOSSDAV (May 2002)
6. Gnutella, http://www.gnutella.com/
7. Napster, http://www.napster.com
8. KaZaA, http://www.kazaa.com
9. Zhang, X., Liu, J.C., Li, B., Peter Yum, T.-S.: CoolStreaming/DONet: A data-driven overlay network for efficient live media streaming. In: Proc. IEEE INFOCOM (March 2005)
10. Viswanathan, S., Imielinski, T.: Metropolitan area video-on-demand service using pyramid broadcasting. Multimedia Systems 3, 197–208 (1996)
11. Hua, K.A., Sheu, S.: Skyscraper broadcasting: a new broadcasting scheme for metropolitan video-on-demand systems. In: Proc. ACM SIGCOMM 1997 (1997)
12. PPLive, http://www.pplive.com/
13. UUSee, http://www.uusee.com/
14. SopCast, http://www.sopcast.com/
15. Chi, H., Zhang, Q., Jia, J., (Sherman) Shen, X.: Efficient Search and Scheduling in P2P-based Media-on-Demand Streaming Service. IEEE Journal on Selected Areas in Communications 25(1) (January 2007)
16. Cheng, X., Liu, J.: NetTube: Exploring Social Networks for Peer-to-Peer Short Video Sharing. In: Proc. IEEE INFOCOM 2009, Rio de Janeiro, Brazil (April 19-25, 2009)

System-Level Power-Accuracy Trade-Off in Bluetooth Low Energy Networks

Jürgen Sommer, Simon Lüders,
Stephen Schmitt, and Wolfgang Rosenstiel

Wilhelm-Schickard-Institut für Informatik
Department of Computer Engineering
University of Tübingen
Sand 13, 72076 Tübingen
Germany
jsommer@informatik.uni-tuebingen.de

Abstract. Location awareness is a key service in mobile devices. For indoor localization, radio frequency (RF) based distance estimation methods are the most viable. An economically favorable method using RF is received signal strength indication (RSSI) as there is no additional hardware required in the mobile devices. Localization is performed relative to fixed landmark nodes. Bluetooth (BTH) is a widely available standard that can be employed for such purpose. This work explores the potential of BTH and Bluetooth Low Energy (BLE) protocols in terms of power consumption and position accuracy. At time of writing there are no known simulators with support for BLE. The major contribution of this work is the design of a simulation infrastructure that supports BLE.

1 Introduction

Location-sensitive services have become popular especially on mobile devices like smartphones and handsets as well as in logistics and robotics. Unlike the GNSS standard for outdoor localization a de facto standard for indoor positioning systems is still missing. Instead, a variety of physical sensor infrastructures and location positioning methods are competing. Radio frequency based distance estimation methods require, in case of received signal strength analysis, no additional hardware and effort. Bluetooth is the most available short and medium range communications standard available in portable devices like mobile phones or smartphones and therefore presents an excellent solution for use in an indoor positioning system. For a location infrastructure consisting of battery supplied Bluetooth landmarks the energy consumption should be as low as possible in order to reduce maintenance costs. On the other hand it should adhere to a defined precision-accuracy ratio. For the consideration of Bluetooth Low Energy devices that will soon be on the market a virtual prototyping environment is being proposed.

C.-H. Hsu et al. (Eds.): UIC 2011, LNCS 6905, pp. 379–392, 2011.

1.1   State-of-the-Art

Indoor Localization of Mobile Consumer Devices. Several methods exist for position estimation. Each method consists of a sensor type, the observed phenomena and the fusion algorithms.

Sensors. Determining a mobile terminal's position requires sensor information to capture location sensitive data. These sensors can either be placed on mobile devices or can be distributed on a number of (fixed) nodes with known positions, denoted as landmarks. Sensor nodes relying on signals from sending devices, e.g. landmarks, normally find a harsh environment for precise indoor positioning due to signal degradation from obstacles and walls inside buildings. This circumstance could explain the magnitude of current indoor position sensing systems [5]. Inertial measuring units (IMU) do not require signal emission and are typically mounted on the mobile part in order to aid iteratively refining or updating a previous absolute position estimation by means of dead reckoning. If the focus is laid on mobile consumer devices such as mobile phones, smartphones, PDA or tablet PCs, only a few sensors remain available for absolute position information: Built-in communication standards such as UMTS/GSM, WiFi, Bluetooth and RFID, and proprietary sensors such as cameras and microphones. Since the latter need at least a time consuming offline phase for scene analysis preparation radio frequency based methods are favorable.

Phenomena. In general, localization methods in wireless communication networks rely on time-of-flight (ToA, TDoA, RTT), angle-of-arrival (AoA), received signal strength indication (RSSI) or connectivity properties of the transmitted signals. For an overview the reader is referred to [4]. RSSI-based approaches are the only economically sound method for use in mobile devices. Many cheap mobile devices using Bluetooth are already capable of measuring signal strength without the need for extra hardware which makes Bluetooth an excellent candidate for use in localization. On the other hand, scattering, occlusion and damping can degrade the signal strength quite severely which can lead to inaccurate results making it necessary to intelligently fuse the RSSI data.

Fusion Algorithms. Given the results of time-of-flight, angle-of-arrival or received signal strength sense data actual positioning algorithms can be divided in non-iterative and iterative position determination algorithms. The non-iterative algorithms instantly fuse multiple sensor data inputs into a position calculation. Prominent algorithms are linearization based and quasi least-quare (QLS) as well as spherical interpolation (SI) methods. Iterative positioning algorithms fuse the date over space (multi-sensor) and time. In this case, an initial position estimation is successively updated and refined. Important representatives of iterative filtering are Kalman and Particle Filtering, which are based on the recursive Bayesian Filter [3].

Power Saving Strategies in Bluetooth Networks. Mobile communication has to rely on power supplied by batteries. Therefore, all components should consume as little power as possible to achieve a long runtime of the device. Especially radio transceivers contribute a large part to the power consumption of landmark nodes and mobile devices.

From the beginning, Bluetooth has been conceived for low power consumption offering three power saving modes: Hold, Sniff and Park. In Hold mode, the communication between the master and slave in a Bluetooth connection can temporarily be put on hold for a limited amount of time (12.5 ms to 20.48 s) to allow the devices to enter a low-power sleep mode. In Sniff mode, the time slots that a slave is listening to are reduced and the master only transmits to that slave in specified time slots, called anchor points, which are separated by the sniff interval (3.75 ms to 840 ms). In Park mode, the slave exchanges its piconet address for a parked member address and goes to sleep, only to wake up at specified intervals (8.75 ms to 2.56 s) to listen for unpark messages from the master. [6] and [7] describe an FSM based methodology for selecting the best Bluetooth low-power mode (and interval settings) in point-to-point and scatternet scenarios given a set of traffic requirements. For a power consumption analysis of Bluetooth's power saving modes the reader is referred to [2].

The low complexity Bluetooth Low Energy (BLE) Specification [1] was designed for very low power from the ground up. In order to achieve long battery life BLE devices have lower peak power and are able to connect to other devices much faster. The Inquiry and Paging states of Bluetooth have been replaced by the Advertising state in BLE, which is also connectible. When in the Advertising state, the BLE Link Layer periodically sends out up to 3 Advertising packets on the 3 Advertising channels spaced less than 10 ms apart. A BLE device in the Scanning or Initiating state can directly respond to an Advertising packet in the following slot to initiate a connection. In the Connection state communication between the Master (Initiator) and Slave (Advertiser) is controlled by connection events set by the Master. The connection event interval is in the range of 7.5 ms to 4.0 s. Connection events remain open while either device has data to send. For each new connection event the channel index is determined by the frequency hopping selection scheme.

Measurements and analysis of the power consumption of consumer-ready BLE hardware were unfortunately not available at the time of writing.

A comparison between Bluetooth and Bluetooth Low Energy properties is shown in table 1.

There are several Bluetooth simulators available that ease Bluetooth energy analysis, i.e. [6] and [7]. To the best of our knowledge none of these simulators supports the specified Bluetooth Low Energy standard yet.

1.2   Contribution and Organization

The major contributions of this work are the design of virtual Bluetooth Low Energy (BLE) prototypes out of the actual specification, the injection of communication and measurement errors on physical level (RSSI), the annotation

Table 1. Comparison of Bluetooth and Bluetooth Low Energy

	BTH	BLE
Protocol Complexity	High	Low
Network topology	Scatternet	Star
Data channels	79	37
Advertising channels	32	3
Connectible advertising	No	Yes
Radio activity (Advertising)	11.25 ms	1.2 ms
Connection setup	∼ 100 ms	< 3 ms
Packet size (bytes)	9 to 358	10 to 47
Connection type	Polling	Events

of technology typical power consumption values to the relevant states of the communication controller, and finally, the integration of the devices into the location sensing and testing platform.

The following chapters are organized like this: In chapter 2 the methodology, namely the simulation modelling, the model and dataset generation is explained. In chapter 3 an analysis of power and performance records is shown and the discussion of the results is given. Finally, we conclude the paper in chapter 4.

2   Methodology

2.1   Simulation Environment

The experiments build upon the OSCI SystemC TLM-2.0 [8] based SySifoS Simulator [10]. In the simulator, devices can be modeled on hardware and software level. On the hardware level we have implemented core system packages of the Bluetooth and Bluetooth Low Energy protocol. On the software level of the application a particle filtering algorithm for position determination is running. An overview of the simulator's architecture is given in figure 1.

The *Input and Output* of the simulator take place in the form of XML-files. An input file contains configuration parameters for the simulator and descriptions of the networked devices and their environment as well as parameters for the radio transmission model (Fault Model). At the end of a simulation run, results gathered during the simulation are written to a XML results file which can be post-processed easily for analysis.

After reading the configuration file, the *Simulation Controller* prepares the simulation environment and required objects before starting the simulation. It then updates the simulator's *World Model* continuously which controls all objects until the end of the simulation.

The *World Model* describes a virtual environment for the network devices so that, for example, effects like radio signal degradation due to occlusion can be computed. At the beginning of a simulation run the description of the World Model is directly loaded from the simulator configuration file. Shapes in this virtual environment are represented by triangles which allows for easy ray intersection tests.

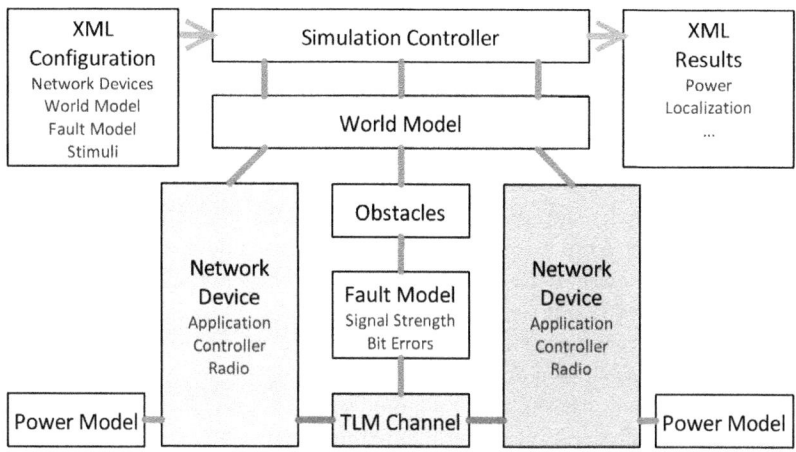

Fig. 1. Simulation Environment

The abstract *Network Device* module in the simulator models the properties and functionality of a real network device. This module can internally be designed according to any number of layers from the OSI Reference Model. In the SySifoS Simulator these layers correspond to parts of the Bluetooth and Bluetooth Low Energy protocol stack. On the application layer any user code can be run using SystemC threads. The application layer communicates directly to the device's hardware via a host controller interface layer. The management and scheduling of connections is handled by a Link Layer or Link Manager layer. The Link Layer or Link Controller is responsible for the Bluetooth states, protocol timing and link control. The lowest layer in the Bluetooth network devices is a Radio layer which provides access to the physical medium for sending and receiving packets. Abstract TLM Channels are used to model the physical medium.

Very often the power consumption of mobile wireless devices is of great interest. With their limited power capacity it is important to optimize their efficiency early in the development process. To be able to conduct power related analyses we have annotated the radios of the network devices with power consumption information contained in a *Power Model*. The Power Model is time-based and keeps track of how long a certain power consumption state is active. We decided to use 3 different states, namely Sleep, RX and TX, which mirror the states of the device's radio. The annotated power consumption values have been extracted from data sheets of actual BTH and BLE devices. In the Sleep state we assume that the device is idle (not connected, or waiting for the next connection event) and that the radio is off, only requiring little power (0.015 mA). For the RX and TX states we assume a low base power consumption for the device and a large consumption for the radio of 20 mA and 24 mA respectively. At simulation time the total power consumption is computed automatically and is written to the XML results file for further analysis.

The communication between networked devices is realized by an abstract transaction level model of a *Communications Channel* based on the OSCI TLM-2.0 library. All devices are connected to each other in a star topology network where all network devices communicate over a central interconnect hub. In this approach the interconnect hub acts as an abstract communications channel. For communication to take place in the network, a sending device wraps its network packets into TLM transactions before they get sent over the channel. Indifferent of the used approach, the abstract communications channel is responsible for passing transactions from a source to a target network device. Inside the channel the transaction is evaluated by a *Fault Model*, which may indicate that the transaction does not reach its target.

The *Fault Model* is responsible for applying environmental effects and faults to transactions sent over the communications channel in the network. It computes the signal strength between any two devices and considers effects like signal degradation and bit errors in the transmitted data.

2.2   Datasets

The Datasets provide the empirical stimuli for the simulator. We denote empirical stimuli the part of the *World Model* which is related to physical environmental effects that are relevant for our simulation results. In the simulation setup the RSSI values influence the results (cf. box *XML Results*) in two aspects: Firstly, the RSSI dataset quality directly influences the distance estimation accuracy. Secondly, connection losses force transitions in the finite-state-machine of the connection controller which lead to changes in the energy consumption.

To conclude, we have identified the physical path loss and degradation of the signal through walls, obstacles, etc. as the key physical measure which is highly environmentally sensitive and difficult to model. As a consequence, we can stimulate the simulator with two types of datasets, real data, that is recorded along a reference trajectory and synthetic data, that aim to model the signal strength propagation on basis of specified walls and obstacles.

For signal strength based distance estimation the attenuation factor model presented in [9] was used.

3   Simulations

3.1   Experiments

We employ the simulator to study the precision and power performance of a Bluetooth-based location service. Our experiments use different strategies based on either the Bluetooth or Bluetooth Low Energy standard. Strategies:

- BTH Connection + Hold: The mobile device searches for and connects itself to found landmarks. To achieve longer update intervals and to save power, the connection must be put into the low power Hold state periodically.

- BTH Inquiry: The idea here is to retrieve signal strength information from the landmarks solely from their inquiry responses. For this purpose the mobile device spends as much time as possible in the Inquiry mode and the landmarks in the Inquiry Scan mode. However, the mobile device must establish and disconnect a one time connection to any yet unknown landmarks to retrieve their world space positions required for location computation.
- BLE Advertising: Mobile device remains in the Scanning state while landmarks run the Advertising state which can also include the landmark's position in the payload.
- BLE Connection: The mobile device is in the Scanning state and connects to advertising landmarks. Landmarks use the advertising state until a connection can be established and then turn advertising off.
- BLE Connection + Advertising: Landmarks keep running the advertising state and can also be connected to. The mobile device receives signal strength information from both arriving advertising packets as well as from the connection to the landmarks.

As an example, we plot in figure 2 the paths of position estimation in relation to the ground truth position.

The black structure depicts a virtual representation of the laboratory while small circles indicate Bluetooth landmarks with their device address next to them. The ground truth path of a mobile device is drawn in blue color, the Bluetooth-based path of position estimation in light purple color. The path for a BLE-based approach is shown in darker purple color.

3.2   Analysis of Power and Performance Records

Power Savings Potential. Average power consumption information of the landmarks was the second point of interest in the localization scenario. The relation between the used intervals and the consumed power is shown in figure 3.

The overall highest power consumption is caused by *BTH Connection + Hold*, which stays fairly constant up to 1 s intervals, then drops more quickly with increasing intervals. *BTH Inquiry* requires significantly less power than maintaining a Bluetooth connection. Increasing the Inquiry Scan interval further reduces power consumption and brings it close to that of Bluetooth Low Energy. The lowest power curve is that of *BLE Connection* which always stays below all other curves. With *BLE Advertising* the power consumption is a bit higher than a pure BLE connection but progresses analogous to it within the possible advertising intervals. *BLE Connection + Advertising* is the combination of maintaining a connection to the master and also running the advertising state. The power consumption almost directly mirrors the combination of both of these states.

Analysis of Power States. From the power model we get information about how long each power state has been active. In figure 4 we present this information from experiments using a 100 ms interval. We observe that *BTH Connection + Hold* is spending a lot of time in the RX state compared to its own TX activity as

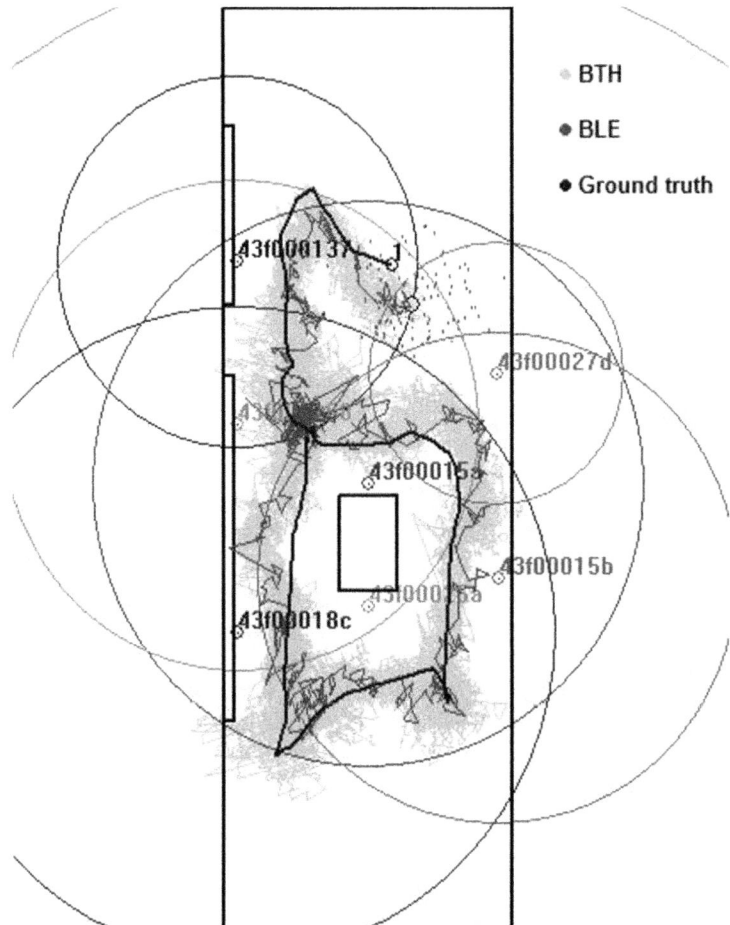

Fig. 2. Position estimation paths of BTH and BLE in the virtual environment

well as compared to the other technologies. This is likely the result of excessive polling by the master while no data is being transfered. For *BTH Inquiry* the landmarks are listening for inquiry requests from mobile devices and only then spend time in TX for the response. In the *BLE Connection* experiment only a small amount of time is spent in both RX and TX states. During this connection both master and slave exchange packets of same size which leads to about the same RX/TX time spent in these states. *BLE Advertising* transmits 3 times more than a *BLE Connection* with the same interval but with larger packets and does not receive anything which leads to more time spent in the power expensive TX state. With *BLE Connection + Advertising* we can again see that this is pretty much the combination of both Advertising and Connection states.

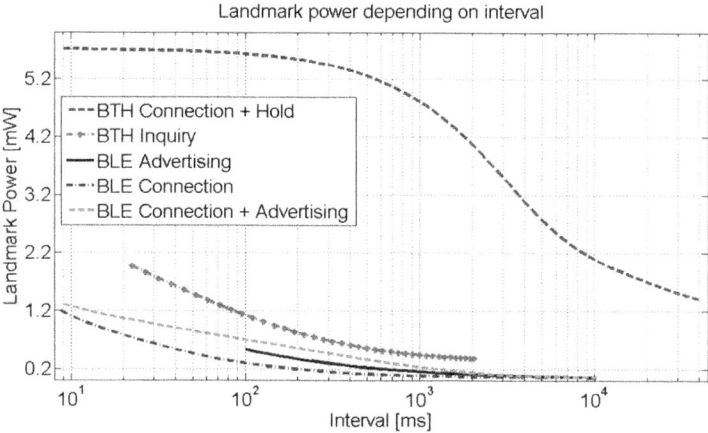

Fig. 3. Power savings with increasing sampling interval

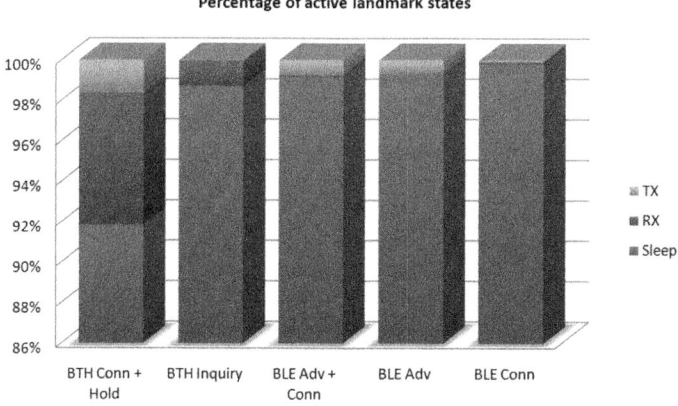

Fig. 4. Percentaged comparison of the active landmark states

Statistical Accuracy. In our simulations we have investigated the accuracy of several different communication methods in the localization scenario using BTH and BLE. The position error in relation to the used communication intervals is shown in figure 5.

Both *BTH Connection + Hold* and *BLE Connection* curves start out at about the same position error at the lowest possible connection intervals. Then, however, the error of *BTH Connection + Hold* increases more rapidly than the one of *BLE Connection* which hardly increases until short of the 1 second interval. The curve of *BTH Inquiry*, starting at 22.5 ms has a significantly higher RMSE than all other curves and deteriorates rapidly at intervals higher than about 700 ms ending up at a position error close to 2 m at the highest interval. *BLE*

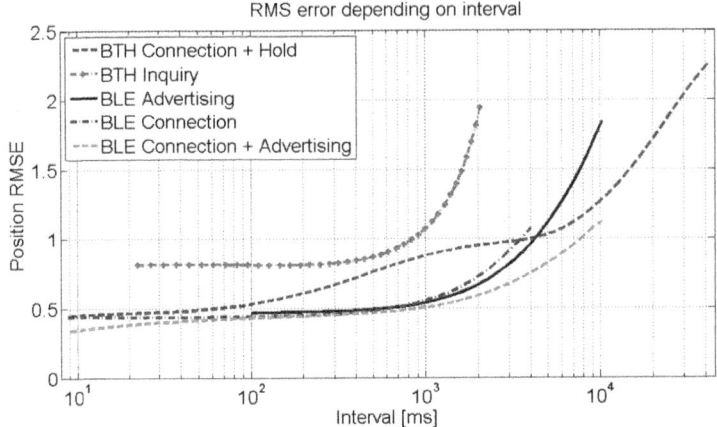

Fig. 5. RMS error with increasing sampling interval

Advertising starts off with an interval of 100 ms and yields very similar results to *BLE Connection* until the highest interval giving slightly worse results towards the end compared to *BLE Connection*. The combination of advertising with a connection shows a small improvement in position accuracy in the intervals less than 100 ms compared to a pure connection. *BLE Connection + Advertising* then starts performing a fair deal better than the pure advertising or connection modes until the top end of the interval range.

3.3   Synthetic Dataset Validation

In order to validate the adequacy of the synthetic RSSI propagation model we repeated the accuracy experiments for *BTH Connection + Hold* and *BLE Connection + Advertising* with the real RSSI stimuli datasets. For this purpose we captured approximately 28000 RSSI measures from 7 landmarks along the predefined trajectory. Figure 6 shows the RMSE differences of both approaches for the *BTH Connection + Hold* experiment.

The curves are quite similarly shaped and close enough together for the simulated RSSI model to be used as a fair estimation. The same holds true for the *BLE Connection + Advertising* experiment seen in figure 7. Here the match between model and real dataset is even closer.

3.4   Discussion of Results

Power Savings Potential. The most power efficient method is *BLE Connection* even though it can not use intervals longer than 4 s. *BLE Advertising* can work up to a 10 s interval but does not gain a power advantage over *BLE Connection*. This is because the advertising state sends out 3 packets per interval, while the connection state only sends and receives a single packet (which is enough for positioning). Combining both of these states (*BLE Connection +*

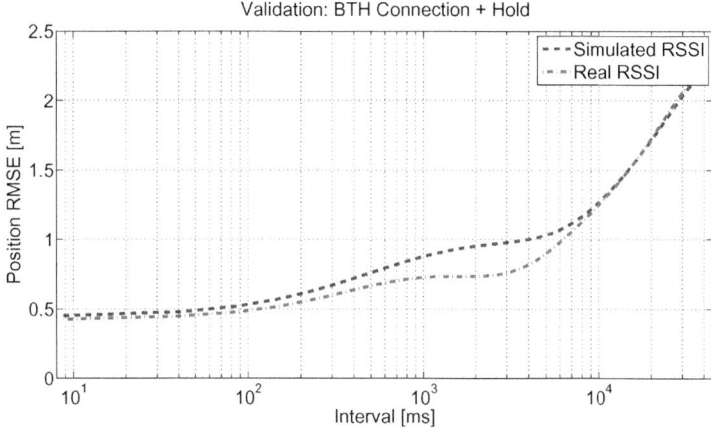

Fig. 6. Validating BTH Connection + Hold experiment

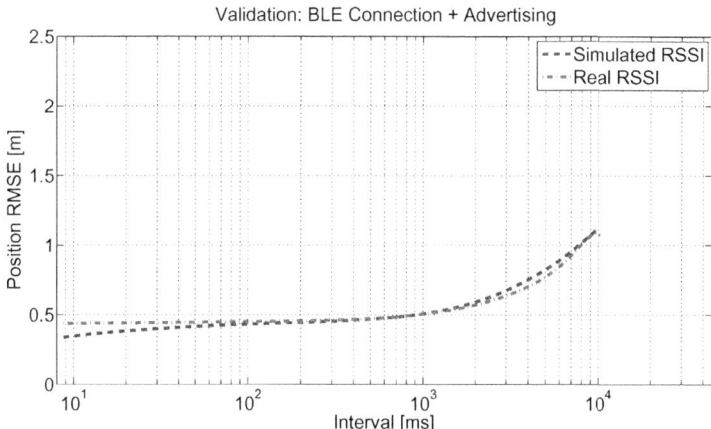

Fig. 7. Validating BLE Connection + Advertising experiment

Advertising) means that besides maintaining a connection, a beacon will also keep advertising regularly, which increases the power consumption, of course. A visual representation of these methods is shown in figure 8.

BTH Connection + Hold consumes significantly more power than all other methods across all intervals. Excessive polling and larger packet sizes are partly responsible for this. The delay from when the hold mode is negotiated until the connection actually enters hold mode also plays a part.

Shorter packets are used for the *BTH Inquiry* method where the positive effects on power consumption is clearly visible. However, a lot of time is spent listening for inquiry requests on 32 inquiry channels. BLE has a clear advantage in this regard because it only has 3 advertising channels.

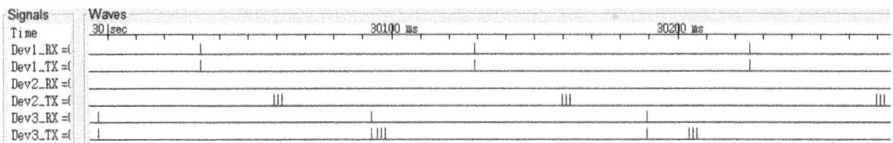

Fig. 8. BLE Connection (Dev1) vs. Advertising (Dev2) vs. Connection + Advertising (Dev3)

As we have seen in figure 3, the power usage difference between BTH and BLE is quite high. As an example: With an interval of 100 ms *BTH Connection + Hold* draws 10 times more power than *BLE Advertising*.

Statistical Accuracy. If we compare the positioning accuracy of both BTH and BLE, we notice that they both give about the same accuracy at low intervals. Position accuracy for BTH degrades more quickly than BLE though which we attribute to the fact that the BLE protocol can cope more efficiently with packet loss and retransmission for landmarks that move near the edge of detectability. *BLE Advertising* gives very similar accuracy to *BLE Connection* from 100 ms until 4 s intervals. *BLE Advertising* then degrades to worse than *BTH Connection + Hold* for longer intervals. The reason for this is probably because the BTH Connection leaves us with several RSSI values per interval whereas we only get a single one from *BLE Advertising* per interval. *BTH Inquiry* starts out with worse position accuracy than all other methods and degrades more quickly as well. This method yields the worst accuracy at small intervals. The best performer in terms of accuracy is the *BLE Connection + Advertising* mode. Across all intervals this mode delivers the highest accuracy due to the arrival of more RSS values.

3.5   Trade-Offs

Let us start looking for good power/precision trade-offs. Bluetooth Low Energy is clearly superior to standard Bluetooth both in regards to power consumption and positioning error in the scenario with one exception. The accuracy of the *BLE Advertising* method decreases below that of *BTH Connection + Hold* intervals greater than about 4 seconds. In a real time location scenario, however, such long intervals do not make much sense.

For practical purposes, maintaining a BLE connection to landmarks does not gain a huge precision benefit but drains power more rapidly. Furthermore the Bluetooth Low Energy protocol only allows the landmarks to maintain a single connection at any time. A landmark should always be discoverable which makes the use of the advertising mode a necessity. The advertising mode in itself gives good enough location accuracy which makes the use of additional connections unnecessary.

A very good accuracy is achieved by all BLE methods around the 500 ms to 1000 ms interval. The power consumption here is also very favorable for all BLE methods which makes this interval a very good power/precision trade-off.

4   Conclusion

An ad-hoc network of virtual Bluetooth and Bluetooth Low Energy devices has been setup and analyzed for beacon energy consumption and location accuracy. The goal is to help system and protocol designers obtain a satisfactory compromise relevant for their specific scenario. In order to provide meaningful data, environmental conditions were generated synthetically and validated with measured reference data. Realistic energy consumption values have been annotated to the different transceiver activities.

The simulation shows that BLE is roughly 4 times more power efficient over standard Bluetooth given the same intervals and transceiver hardware. This is due to a shorter duty cycle, shorter packets and lower overhead for connection establishment. From the simulated ambient localization scenario it can be concluded that BLE is clearly the better choice in ad-hoc networks with rare and small traffic as well as in fixed or adaptive interval communication. BLE offers system designer maximum flexibility, since no complicated design decisions are necessary to select the best power savings mode for a given scenario. Standard Bluetooth on the other hand offers higher bandwidths than BLE (3 Mb/sec compared to 1 Mb/sec, 54 Mb/sec with Bluetooth v3.0). With the anticipated fusion of Bluetooth and Low Energy standards into a single chip solution we expect to see hybrid solutions in the future that can easily adapt to current bandwidth demands. For the growing ad-hoc and sensor networking market Bluetooth is a very capable candidate in the scope of 802.15 communication whose wide adoption may very well replace proprietary solutions in the end.

Acknowledgment. This work was funded by the Baden-Württemberg Stiftung in the scope of the BW-FIT project AmbiSense.

References

1. Bluetooth SIG, Inc.: Bluetooth core specification v4.0 (June 2010), http://www.bluetooth.com
2. Cano, J.C., Cano, J.M., González, E., Calafate, C., Manzoni, P.: Evaluation of the energetic impact of bluetooth low-power modes for ubiquitous computing applications. In: Proceedings of the 3rd ACM International Workshop on Performance Evaluation of Wireless Ad Hoc, Sensor and Ubiquitous Networks, PE-WASUN 2006. ACM, New York (2006), http://doi.acm.org/10.1145/1163610.1163612
3. Fox, D., Hightower, J., Liao, L., Schulz, D., Borriello, G.: Bayesian filtering for location estimation. IEEE Pervasive Computing 2, 24–33 (2003)
4. Liu, H., Darabi, H., Banerjee, P., Liu, J.: Survey of wireless indoor positioning techniques and systems. IEEE Transactions on Systems, Man, and Cybernetics, Part C 37(6), 1067–1080 (2007)
5. Mautz, R.: Overview of current indoor positioning systems. Geodesy and Cartography 35(1), 18–22 (2009), http://dx.doi.org/10.3846/1392-1541.2009.35.18-22

6. Negri, L., Sami, M., Macii, D., Terranegra, A.: Fsm–based power modeling of wireless protocols: the case of bluetooth. In: Proceedings of the 2004 International Symposium on Low Power Electronics and Design, ISLPED 2004, pp. 369–374. ACM, New York (2004), http://doi.acm.org/10.1145/1013235.1013323
7. Negri, L., Zanetti, D.: Power/performance tradeoffs in bluetooth sensor networks. In: Hawaii International Conference on System Sciences, vol. 9, p. 236b (2006)
8. Open SystemC Initiative: SystemC Version 2.0, User's Guide (2001), www.systemc.org
9. Seidel, S.Y., Rappaport, T.S.: 914 MHz path loss prediction for indoor wireless communications in multifloored buildings. IEEE Transactions on Antennas and Propagation 40, 207–217 (1992)
10. Sommer, J., Lüders, S., Subramanian, S., Schmitt, S., Rosenstiel, W.: SySifoS: SystemC simulator for sensor and communication systems. In: Proceedings of the 6th International Conference on Mobile Technology, Applications and Systems, Mobility 2009. ACM, New York (2009), http://doi.acm.org/10.1145/1710035.1710054

Hidden Node and Interference Aware Channel Assignment for Multi-radio Multi-channel Wireless Mesh Networks

Fei Hao[1], Jin Ma[1], and Chunsheng Zhu[2]

[1] Department of Computer Science,
Korea Advanced Institute of Science and Technology,
305-701, Daejeon, South Korea
{fhao,jinma}@kaist.ac.kr
[2] Department of Computer Science,
St. Francis Xavier University,
B2G 2W5, Antigonish, Canada
chunsheng.tom.zhu@gmail.com

Abstract. Carrier sense interference and hidden terminal problem are two critical factors, which limit the performance of wireless mesh networks. In order to increase the throughput of the network, multi-radio and multi-channel technology has been put forward to address this problem, since more channels can be used simultaneously to avoid collisions. In this paper, we propose a new scheme for hidden node and interference aware channel assignment, in which both hidden terminal problem and carrier sense interference are taken into consideration. This scheme is put forward in the link layer instead of network layer, which is a pre-determined approach. Our simulation results show that this optimum channel assignment scheme which has the least carrier sense interference and hidden terminal problem will be proposed before the establishment of network infrastructure.

1 Introduction

Wireless Mesh Networks (WMNs) have attracted a lot of attention due to the wide coverage, convenient access, and robustness. They are multi-hop wireless networks composed of wireless mesh routers (MRs) and mesh end devices. Since the capacity of single-radio mesh networks is seriously affected by the nature of half-duplex of the wireless medium [1], multi-radio and multi-channel wireless mesh networks play a key role in the development of WMNs. In multi-radio multi-channel WMNs, how to assign the appropriate channels to appropriate radios to maximize the throughput of network is a key problem. A simple way to realize multi-radio and multi-channel is to make use of static channel assignment. However, with the increased number of wireless APs, the adjacent AP might use the same channel as well, which will cause conflictions [2]. Generally, there are three kinds of classifications of optimal model for channel assignment

C.-H. Hsu et al. (Eds.): UIC 2011, LNCS 6905, pp. 393–404, 2011.

in multi-radio multi-channel WMNs, *i.e.*, 1) Minimize the interference of network; 2) Increase the Bandwidth of link; 3) Increase the bandwidth of dataflow from point to point. However, 2) and 3) are optimal plans in the network layer and meet the bandwidth of networks. The first one is an optimal plan which works in the link layer. Furthermore, most previous work mainly focus on the carrier sense interference when proposing a channel assignment model. However, the past recent years' researches [3,4] show that carrier sense interference has been over estimated. In fact, the degradation resulting from carrier sense interference is not as serious as previous understanding. The literature [5] shows the hidden terminal problem, actually, has much more effects on the performance degradation than the carrier sense interference.

To the best of our knowledge, the existing literatures usually ignore that the hidden terminal problem is an important factor which needs to be considered when designing the channel assignment. Besides, fewer researches care about establishing networks before potential collisions. In this paper, we explore our model in the link layer and try to find all of the collisions' relations between links according to carrier sense interference (CS) and hidden terminal problems (HD) and investigate an optimal channel assignment which has the fewest collisions. In our opinion, predetermined network is quite important because of better design of network with consideration of potential collisions. To the best of our knowledge, our work is the first to incorporate the hidden terminal problems in channel assignment for multi-radio multi-channel WMNs and to predetermine the network to avoid carrier sense interference and hidden terminal problem as much as possible. Intuitively, when we reduce the effects of carrier sense interference and hidden node interference together, the throughput will increase a lot.

In this paper, our contributions are mainly twofold. First, we consider the collisions resulting from both carrier sense interference and hidden terminal perspective and introduce a tunable parameter to balance the collisions to get the best channel assignment scheme. Second, we come up with an approach to predetermine the establishment of the networks which have the least collisions caused by carrier sense interference and hidden terminal problems.

This paper is organized as follows: Section 2 introduces the related work. Section 3 presents the problem definition. Our proposed approach is explored in Section 4. We evaluate the proposed approach with simulations in Section 5. Section 6 concludes the work.

2   Related Work

An integer linear programming (ILP) model was proposed by Arindam K. Das *et al.* [6]. In their paper the authors maximized the number of links being active simultaneously based on assumption that each node had the same number of radios. They ignored the serious effects caused by hidden terminal problem. Kyasanuretal. *et al.* [7] studied multi-radio mesh networks, assuming that the network can switch interface from one channel to another dynamically without considering the traffic characteristics. Draveset *et al.* [8] investigated multi-hop multi-radio mesh networks and introduced WCETT which was implemented in Multi-Radio Link-Quality Source Routing (MR-LQSR), where all nodes were assumed to be stationary. The channel assignment can be predetermined as well. Their results show that classical shortest path routing was not appropriate when multiple radios were deployed. Dasetal. *et al.* [9] proposed a Multiple Access Control (MAC) protocol for multiple radios, using an extra busy tone interface. However, the paper did not show the number of radios which should be used. Das *et al.* [10] minimized total network interference to solve the problem of assigning channels to communication links in the network. But they did not consider the interference brought in by carrier sense interference and hidden terminal problem together. Deema *et al.* [6] took both carrier sense interference and hidden terminal problem into account and proposed a HIAM-Based routing protocol, with which routing stability and throughput can be higher and control packet overhead can be lower than existing approaches. However, they did not consider avoiding collisions before establishment of the network firstly.

3   Problem Statement

In multi-radio multi-channel WMNs, there are two limitations on channel assignment.

1. Number of channels. Each link is assigned for a channel.
2. Number of radios on each node should be more than the number of channels.

$$N(Channel) \leq N(Radio)$$

If a channel meets the above two limitations, then it is a "feasible" channel. Since we may have many assignment plans, optimization of channel assignment is to select the best channel assignment from the "feasible" channels. With better and more efficient channel assignment, we can minimize the collisions and maximize the throughput of the network in terms of carrier sense interference and hidden nodes problem. With multi-radio and multi-channel, transmission simultaneously can be realized and collisions can be avoided as much as possible. The target of this paper is to maximize the total throughput of the network by having optimal channel assignment to reduce collisions, in which both hidden node problem and carrier sense interference are considered.

4   Proposed Approach

With our model, different kinds of schemes of channel assignment will be proposed. Each scheme will have different characteristics, e.g., throughput, interference caused by hidden terminal problem and carrier sense interference, packet loss. Throughput is important to evaluate the performance of the network. We make the assumption that the throughput only depends on the collisions from carrier sense interference and hidden terminal problem without the effects like packet loss rate, jitter, and delay and so forth.

The example of carrier sense interference in our model is described in Figure 1.(a). Specially, if the used channel by link $\overline{AB}$ is the same as that by link $\overline{BC}$, which means they use the same channels, carrier sense interference will happen. If the channel utilized by link $\overline{AB}$ is the same as the channel utilized by link $\overline{AD}$, carrier sense interference will also happen.

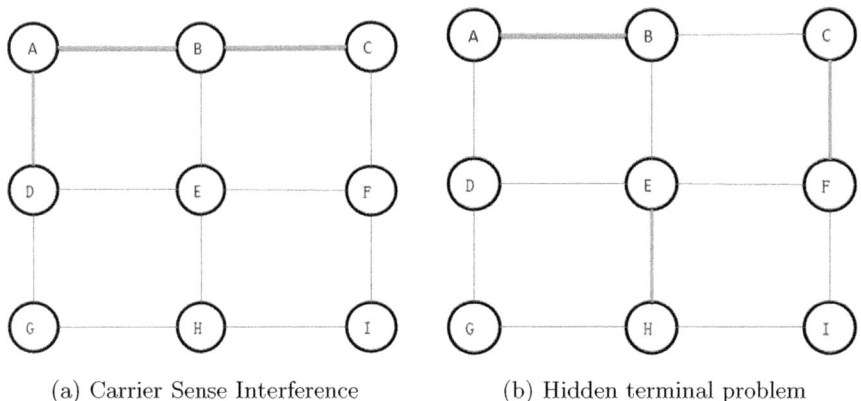

(a) Carrier Sense Interference   (b) Hidden terminal problem

Fig. 1. (a)Example of Carrier Sense Interference. If link $\overline{AD}$ and link $\overline{AB}$ use the same channel, they cannot transmit data at the same time. (b) Example of hidden terminal problem. If link $\overline{AB}$ and link $\overline{EH}$ use the same channel, they cannot transmit data at the same time.

Figure 1.(b) shows the situation of hidden terminal. If the channel on link $\overline{AB}$ is the same as the channel on link $\overline{CF}$ and $\overline{EH}$, hidden terminal will occur. When node A tries to send data to node B, if node C is transmitting data to F, then the channel on link $\overline{CF}$ is used, which means the channel on link $\overline{AB}$ cannot be used at that time.

According to the experiment in [6], the result shows that hidden terminal problem makes more contributions to the degraded throughput of the network compared with carrier sense interference. Moreover, it is difficult to avoid hidden terminal problem and carrier sense interference completely. What can be done is to minimize the total collisions to maximize the throughput of the network. Our approach is to keep the number of hidden terminal nodes smaller so that hidden terminal problem has fewer effects. And we also try to eliminate the carrier sense interference so that a trade-off between the CS nodes and HD nodes is made.

Hence, we introduce a tunable parameter, $\beta \in [0, 1]$, to balance the effects caused by CS interference and hidden terminal problem. We assume an intuition that more CS nodes and less HD nodes will lead to higher capacity compared with that of more HD nodes and less CS nodes, even though we hope both the number of CS nodes and HD nodes can be decreased. If more CS nodes and less HD nodes result in the interference, the total capacity will be increased.

Our proposed model consists of two parts. The first part is CS interference and the latter part shows the effect of HD problem. We use β to adjust the total interference. When β changes to a certain value, the total collisions should be the fewest.

Definition 1. *Interference*

$$\Omega = \frac{1}{L}\sum_{i=1}^{L}\beta\phi_i^{(CS)} + \frac{1}{L}\sum_{i=1}^{L}(1-\beta)\phi_i^{(HD)}$$

$$= \frac{1}{L}(\beta\sum_{i=1}^{L}\sum_{j=1}^{L}I_{ij}^{'(CS)} + (1-\beta)\sum_{i=1}^{L}\sum_{j=1}^{L}I_{ij}^{'(HD)}) \tag{1}$$

where β is a tunable parameter, L is the total number of links, $\phi_i^{(CS)}$ is the carrier sense interference, $\phi_i^{(HD)}$ is the hidden node interference. $I_{ij}^{'(CS)}$ is the CS nodes-based link collision matrix, $I_{ij}^{'(HD)}$ is the HD nodes-based link collision matrix.

Definition 2. *Node-Link Matrix*

$$S_{ij} = \begin{cases} 1, & v_i \quad \text{is the vertex of} \quad e_j, \\ 0, & \text{otherwise.} \end{cases} \tag{2}$$

Definition 3. *CS Node-Based Potential Link Collision Matrix*

$$I_{ij}^{(CS)} = \begin{cases} 1, & e_i \quad \text{is the neighboring link of} \quad e_j, \\ 0, & \text{otherwise.} \end{cases} \tag{3}$$

Definition 4. *HD Node-Based Potential Link Collision Matrix*

$$I_{ij}^{(HD)} = \begin{cases} 1, & e_i \quad \text{is the 2-hop neighboring link of} \quad e_j, \\ 0, & \text{otherwise.} \end{cases} \tag{4}$$

Definition 5. *Link-Channel Assignment Matrix*

$$A_{jk} = \begin{cases} 1, & \text{Channel } k \quad \text{is assigned to} \quad e_j, \\ 0, & \text{otherwise.} \end{cases} \tag{5}$$

Definition 6. *Node-Channel Assignment Matrix*

$$A_{jk}' = \begin{cases} 1, & \text{Channel } k \quad \text{is assigned to} \quad v_j, \\ 0, & \text{otherwise.} \end{cases} \tag{6}$$

Definition 7. *CS nodes-based Link Collision Matrix*

$$I_{ij}^{'(CS)} = \begin{cases} 1, & e_i \quad \text{is conllided with} \quad e_j, \\ 0, & \text{otherwise.} \end{cases} \tag{7}$$

Minimize

$$\Omega = \frac{1}{L}\sum_{i=1}^{L}\beta\phi_i^{(CS)} + \frac{1}{L}\sum_{i=1}^{L}(1-\beta)\phi_i^{(HD)}$$

$$= \frac{1}{L}(\beta\sum_{i=1}^{L}\sum_{j=1}^{L}I_{ij}^{'(CS)} + (1-\beta)\sum_{i=1}^{L}\sum_{j=1}^{L}I_{ij}^{'(HD)})$$

Subject to:

$$0 \le 2A'_{ik} - \frac{1}{P}\left(\sum_{j=1}^{L}S_{ij}A_{jk}\right) < 2$$

$$\forall P > L, 1 \le i \le N, 1 \le k \le K$$

$$I_{ij}^{'(CS)} = (\sum_{k=1}^{K}A_{ik}\bullet A_{jk})\bullet I_{ij}^{(CS)} \qquad I_{ij}^{'(HD)} = (\sum_{k=1}^{K}A_{ik}\bullet A_{jk})\bullet I_{ij}^{(HD)}$$

$$\sum_{k=1}^{K}A_{jk}^i = 1, \forall 1 \le j \le L \qquad \sum_{k=1}^{K}A'_{jk} \le R_i, \forall 1 \le j \le N$$

$$A_{jk} = 0 \ or \ 1, \forall 1 \le j \le L, 1 \le k \le K$$
$$A'_{ik} = 0 \ or \ 1, \forall 1 \le i \le L, 1 \le k \le K$$

Fig. 2. Proposed model

Definition 8. *HD nodes-based Link Collision Matrix*

$$I_{ij}^{'(HD)} = \begin{cases} 1, & e_i \ \ is \ conllided \ with \ \ e_j, \\ 0, & otherwise. \end{cases} \tag{8}$$

Figure 2 shows our proposed model in this paper. Obviously, the proposed model is a heuristic-based integer quadratic programming (HIQP) model. HIQP model is composed of objective function and some constraints of optimal channel assignment.

- **Objective function**: The optimal object Ω is to optimal an optimal parameter β in order to minimize the CS-node based interference and HD-node based interference
- **Constraints**: Basically, the constraints satisfy the requirements of feasible channel.
  1. $0 \le 2A_{ik}^i - \frac{1}{P}(\sum_{j=1}^{L}S_{ij}A_{jk}) < 2$ indicates a relationship among the S_{ij}, A_{jk} and A'_{jk}. If $\sum_{j=1}^{L}S_{ij}A_{jk} \ge 1$, due to $\sum_{j=1}^{L}S_{ij}A_{jk} \le L$, then $A'_{ik}=1$.
  2. $I_{ij}^{'(CS)} = (\sum_{k=1}^{K}A_{ik}\bullet A_{jk})\bullet I_{ij}^{(CS)}$ and $I_{ij}^{'(HD)} = (\sum_{k=1}^{K}A_{ik}\bullet A_{jk})\bullet I_{ij}^{(HD)}$ represent the correlations between the CS-based potential link collision matrix and CS-based link collision matrix, and HD-based potential link collision matrix and HD-based link collision matrix, respectively.
  3. $\sum_{k=1}^{K}A_{jk} = 1, \sum_{k=1}^{K}A'_{jk} \le R$ are two basic limitations for channel assignment. In another word, each link is assigned for a channel. The number of radios on each node should be more than the number of channels.

Based on above specific description of HIQP model, the working mechanism of HIQP model is to search the best channel assignment which satisfies the constraints and optimize the objective function with various given tunable parameter β. Henece, to obtain the optimal solutions of this model, Lingo 9.0[1] is utilized.

5 Experiment

In this section, we investigate the correlation among number of radios on each node, number of channels and interference. It is assumed that the carrier sense interference range is equal to hidden terminal range. Then we adjust the value of β to analyze different schemes of channel assignment related to different β to find out the best scheme.

5.1 Evaluation Framework

Our evaluation framework is composed of three modules and two implementation steps:

- Topological information of the network including the number of channels and the number of radios. This module is our input module.
- We obtain the channel assignment candidates using proposed model. This module is our middle module.
- Optimal channel assignment module. This is our output module.

As we can see from Figure 3, we utilize the Lingo 9.0 to obtain the channel assignment candidates based on our proposed model. Furthermore, to extract our optimal channel assignment, we simulate them using Qualnet 5.0[2] and compare the throughput of each channel assignment scheme.

5.2 Experiment Setup

With the HIQP model, we get different channel assignment schemes according to the changes of β. We classify different situations regarding different number of radios and channels. Since grid network is easy to analyze, we first simulate and analyze the grid network. After getting the correlation between the number of channels and collisions, we use Qualnet to simulate each channel assignment scheme and select the scheme which has the highest throughput as the final candidate. This final candidate is regarded as the pre-determined scheme. With this scheme we can make plans before the establishment of the network so that

---

[1] http://www.lindo.com/. Lingo is a comprehensive tool designed to make building and solving Linear, Nonlinear, Quadratic, Quadratically Constrained, Second Order Cone, Stochastic, and Integer optimization models faster, easier and more efficient is used.

[2] http://www.scalable-networks.com/products/qualnet/.

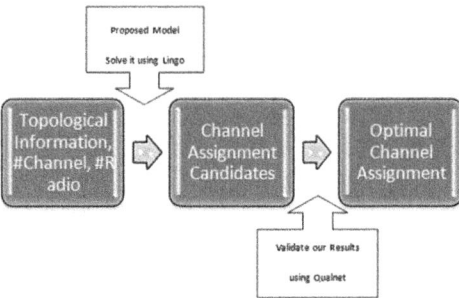

Fig. 3. Evaluation Framework. Make use of mathematics to get the channel assignment schemes, then simulate these schemes to select the scheme which has the highest throughput.

we do not need to modify the infrastructure of the network to address future potential problems like collisions. In addition, if efficient routing algorithm is used based on the final candidate, the performance of the network would be much better. Figure 4 describes the parameters we use for simulation in Qualnet.

Simulation Parameters			
β	0, 0.1, 0.2, ...0.9, 1.0		
Network Type	4 times 4 grid	3 times 3 grid	
Number of channels and radios	3 channels 3 radios	3 channels 3 radios	2 channels 3 radios
Number of Nodes	16	9	
Distance between nodes	350 m		
Radio Protocol	802.11b		
Routing Protocol	AODV		
Transmission range	375 m		
Flow Type	FTP		
Number of flows	4		
Starting time interval of flows	10s		
Simulation time	50s		
Average throughput	$(\sum_{i=1}^{4} Throughput\ of\ flow\ i)/4$		

Fig. 4. Simulation parameters used in QualNet

5.3   Experimental Results

The correlation between the number of channels and interference. In this part we changed the number of channels and radios of 3×3 grid network and 4×4 grid network to get the relation between number of channels and interference as well as radios. Since we just want to know how the interference changes when the number of channels is changed without considering the effect brought in by β, we set the value of β is 0.5.

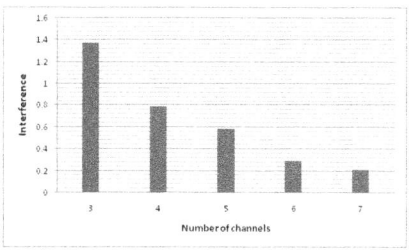

Fig. 5. 4 × 4 grid network, R=3. When the number of channels is larger, the value of interference is smaller. However after the number of channels increases to more than 6, the changes of interference become smaller.

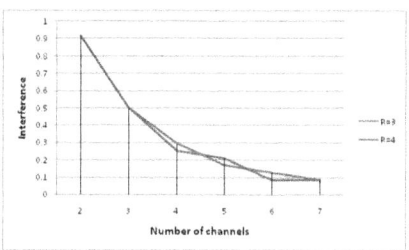

Fig. 6. 3 × 3 grid network, R=3 and R=4. Interference will decrease when number of channels increases.

Table 1. Average Throughput for 4 × 4 grid network When C=3 and R=3. When β is 0.5, the scheme has the highest throughput, thus this is the optimum channel assignment scheme.

β	0.0	0.1	0.2	0.3	0.4	0.5
Average Throughput(bit/s)	74082	51419.75	51419.75	59393.25	53990.75	95676.75
β	0.6	0.7	0.8	0.9	1.0	-
Average Throughput(bit/s)	62034	38949.75	38949.75	38949.75	53752.25	-

Figure 5 and Figure 6 show that when the number of radios is three, with the number of channels being increased, the interference of the 4 × 4 grid network will decrease dramatically. The multi-line chart describes the same phenomenon for 3 × 3 gird network. The changes of the number of radios only have relatively small effects on the interference.

As what have been expected, more channels decrease the interference. However this method has limited effects on the interference. As what can be observed from above charts, when the number of channels increase to more than 5, the decreased interference become smaller and smaller, which means multi-channel and multi-radio has limitations to address channel assignment problem though it has obvious effects on this problem.

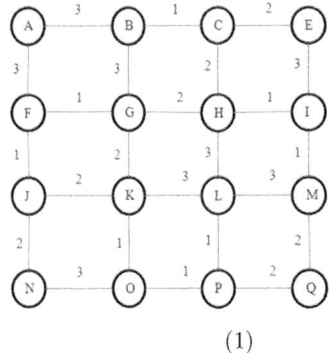
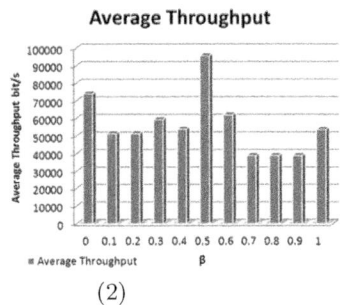

Fig. 7. (1)Best Channel Assignment when β is 0.5. Compared with other schemes, this one has the highest throughput; (2)Average Throughput Comparison Under Various β When C=3 and R=3. When β equals to 0.5, the throughput is the highest.

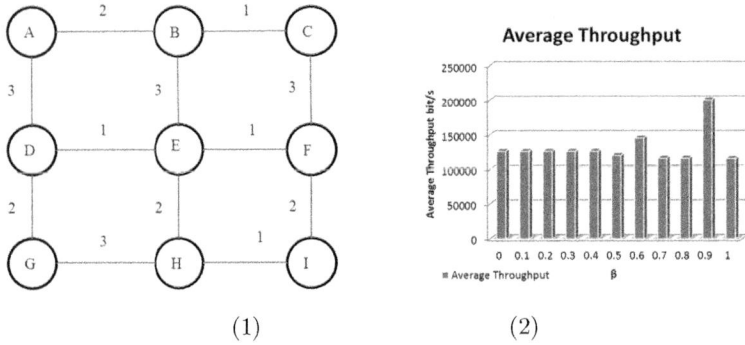

Fig. 8. (1)Best channel assignment for 3×3 grid network when β is 0.9, number of channels and radios are both 3. Compared with other schemes, this one has the highest throughput; (2)Average throughput comparison under various β when C=3 and R=3. When β equals to 0.9, the throughput is the highest.

Comparison experiments on throughput. In this part, we simulate 4×4 grid network when $C = R = 3$ and 3×3 grid network when $C = R = 3$ as well as $C = 2, R = 3$ to make a comparison on how throughput changes when the number of channel changes.

Figure 7.(2) shows that average throughput comparison under various β when C=3 and R=3. It is easily to know that when β=0.5, the average throughput is the highest, which means in this case the scheme of the channel assignment is the best. Figure 7.(1) shows the best channel assignment for 4×4 grid network when $C = R = 3$ and Figure 8 shows 3×3 grid network when $C = R = 3$. To make a comparison for different number of channels, we simulate the 3×3 grid network which has two channels and three radios. The simulation results are shown in Figure 8.(1) and Figure 8.(2). According to Figure 8.(2), when β

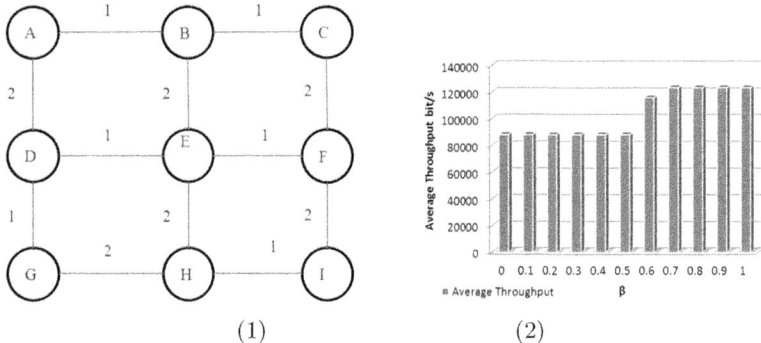

(1)   (2)

Fig. 9. (1)Best channel assignment for 3×3 grid network when β is 0.7~1.0, number of channels is decreased to two. Number of radios is three. Compared with other schemes, this one has the highest throughput. (2)Average throughput comparison under various β when C=2 and R=3. When β is 0.7~1.0, the throughput is the highest.

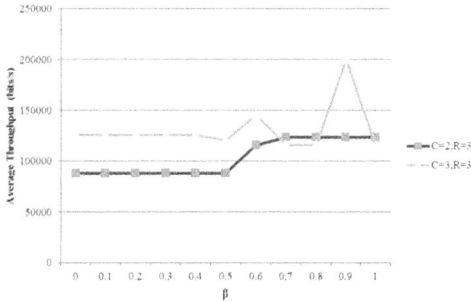

Fig. 10. Throughput comparison between three-channel assignment and two-channel assignment schemes. Both of these two schemes have three radios, and the figure shows three-channel assignment has larger throughput.

is 0.9, the throughput will be the highest and therefore, under this β, Figure 8.(1) shows the related optimum scheme. The results for 3×3 grid network is shown in Figure 9.(2) and Figure 9.(1). Figure 9.(2) shows when β is equal to 0.7~1.0, the throughput can be the the the highest. Actually under these values of β, the model gives the same channel assignment schemes, which is shown in Figure 9.(1). According to Figure 10, we can find that, generally, more number of channels means higher throughput, because more than one channel can be used at the same time to avoid some collisions.

6   Conclusions

In this paper, we address the optimal channel assignment problem in multi-radio multi-channel wireless mesh networks. We present a novel model to minimize the network interference by considering both hidden nodes problem and carrier sense interference. Simulation results indicate that optimal channel assignment should take account of average throughput so as to reduce the network interference further more. We investigate the correlation between the impact of radio and channel constraints. We also study the comparison analysis of various channel assignment schemes on grid networks. The optimum channel assignment scheme which has the fewest collisions can be pre-determined before the establishment of the network infrastructure.

References

1. Gupta, P., Kumar, P.R.: The capacity of wireless networks. IEEE Transactions on Information Theory, 388–404 (2000)
2. Ramachandran, K.N., Belding-Royer, E.M., Almeroth, K.C., Buddhikot, M.M.: Interference-Aware Channel Assignment in Multi-Radio Wireless Mesh Networks. In: INFOCOM (2006)
3. Jamieson, K., Hull, B., Miu, A., Balakrishnan, H.: Understanding the Real-World Performance of Carrier Sense. In: ACM Sigcomm Workshop on Experimental Approaches to Wireless Network Design and Analysis, pp. 52–57 (2005)
4. Vasan, A., Ramjee, R., Woo, T.Y.C.: ECHOS - enhanced capacity 802.11 hotspots. In: INFOCOM, pp. 1562–1572 (2005)
5. Hammash, D., Kim, M., Kang, S., Lee, S., Lee, B.: HIAM: Hidden Node and Interference Aware Routing Metric for Multi-channel Multi-radio Mesh Networks. Submitted for publication in IEEE/ACM Transactions on Networking (2010)
6. Das, A., Alazemi, H.M.K., Vijayakumar, R., Roy, S.: Optimization Models for Fixed Channel Assignment in Wireless Mesh Networks with Multiple Radios. In: IEEE SECON, pp. 463–474 (2005)
7. Kyasanur, P., Vaidya, N.: Routing and interface assignment in multi-channel multi-interface wireless networks. University of Illinois at Urbana-Champaign Technical Report (2004)
8. Draves, R., Padhye, J., Zill, B.: Routing in multi-radio, multi-hop wireless mesh networks. In: MOBICOM, pp. 114–128 (2004)
9. Maheshwari, R., Gupta, H., Das, S.: Multichannel mac protocols for wireless networks. In: IEEE SECON, pp. 25–28 (2006)
10. Subramanian, A., Krishnan, R., Das, S.R., Gupta, H.: Minimum interference channel assignment in multi-radiowireless mesh networks. In: IEEE SECON, pp. 18–21 (2007)

uFlow: Dynamic Software Updating in Wireless Sensor Networks

Ting-Yun Chi, Wei-Cheng Wang, and Sy-Yen Kuo

Electrical Engineering, National Taiwan University, Taiepi 10617 Taiwan(R.O.C)
{Louk.chi,cole945}@gmail.com, sykuo@cc.ee.ntu.edu.tw

Abstract. A wireless sensor network (WSN) consists of spatially distributed autonomous sensors to monitor physical or environmental conditions, such as temperature, sound, vibration, pressure. Due to the maintenance reason, we may update the software to fix bugs. Because there are more and more sensor nodes using in the vehicle, smart environment, Software updating for wireless sensor networks has become an important issue. In previous related works, Update the node usually is required to reboot. However, reboot the nodes is costly since the previous runtime status may be lost. To recover the runtime status for routing, it will take time and bandwidth to synchronize with other nodes. We present uFlow: a programming paradigm and a prototype implementation for wireless sensor networks. uFlow allows application to update the nodes without rebooting. So we can avoid to lost precious runtime status.

Keywords: Software updating, wireless sensor networks, runtime status.

1 Introduction

A wireless sensor network (WSN) consists of spatially distributed autonomous sensors to monitor physical or environmental conditions, such as temperature, sound, vibration, pressure. Because there are more and more sensor nodes using in the vehicle, smart environment, Software updating for wireless sensor networks has become an important issue. By updating the software, we can fix bugs to maintain the senor network. However it is a challenge to update the software with limited hardware resources and environment. Previous works try to save the problems by only distributing the changed parts, but this is not adequate. First, even we change a small part of the code; the binary code will be many differences with the old one. It causes from address relocations of functions and variables. Second, direct function calls makes it hard to safely and dynamically replace the functionalities of the program at runtime. And the worse is that rebooting the entire node after updating is costly – it loses precious status data and waste energy to rebuild the status. A node may take minutes or hours to fully restore the running status.

Our work presents a programming model. The basic functionalities are implemented as tasks and the control flow which is managed by a lightweight engine. By this way, we make dynamic replacement become possible. We not only keep the runtime status data during updating but also avoid unnecessary changes to

C.-H. Hsu et al. (Eds.): UIC 2011, LNCS 6905, pp. 405–419, 2011.
© Springer-Verlag Berlin Heidelberg 2011

the binary image. We only transmit the limited data over the network. In section 1, we explain why the software updating is important to sensor network. The rest of the paper is organized as follows. Section 2 presents the related works around software updating in wireless sensor network field. Section 3 proposes the idea of uFlow and explains system architecture. Section 4 shows the result of prototype implementation engine, example program. We make the conclusion in section 5.

2   Related Works

The Researches for software updating in wireless sensor networks can be divided by three perspectives – dissemination, patch generating, and execution environment. The big picture of related works is illustrated in Figure 1. These perspectives are not fully mutual exclusive but sometimes cooperative to provide a better and integrative approach for software updating.

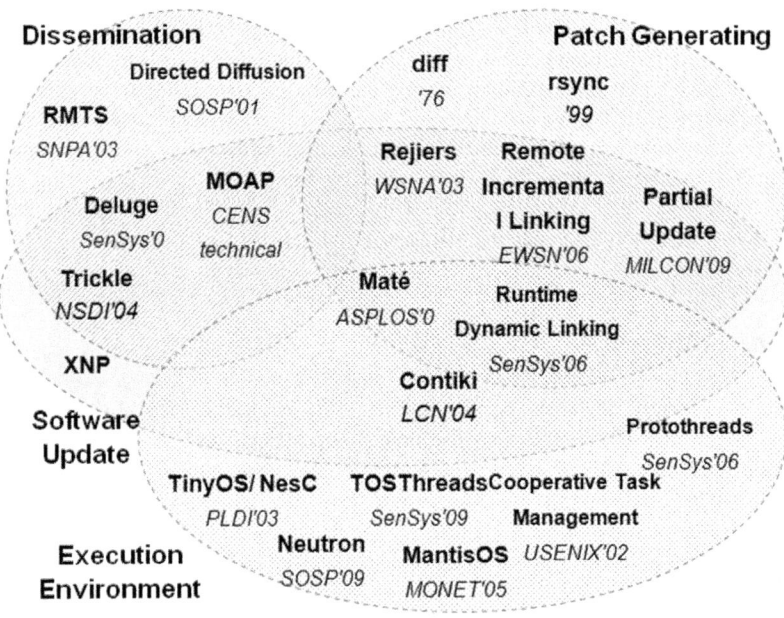

Fig. 1. The big picture - Software Updating for Wireless Sensor Network

2.1   Dissemination

Dissemination concerns about how to spread the message across the network. In wireless sensor network, sensor nodes often cooperate in a distributed manner lacking pre-established infrastructure for routing and forwarding information. In order to exchange information, these nodes have to autonomously build an ad-hoc network to communicate with nodes multiple hops away. Moreover, conventional dissemination approaches for data collection are not adequate when applying to software update. Software program images are usually much larger than sensed data, and hence they will be fragmented into several small chunks before transmitting and assembled, correctly, when receiving. Directed Diffusion [4] is one of the most fundamental approach widely used, and MOAP [6] discussed and analyzed the design goals, constraints, and choices between difference dissemination strategies for software update in wireless sensor network.

2.2   Traffic Reduction

During software update, transmitting the entire program image is not economical, because, in most case, only partial of the program need to be modified. Transmitting unnecessary parts wastes bandwidth, reduces battery life, increase update latency, and more likely to fail.

diff

The rule of thumb is that, only distributing the changed parts. One of the most representative and widely used works is diff [2], a UNIX utility, which was developed in the early 1970s on the UNIX operating system. It is typically used to compare two difference versions of the same text file, and display the changes made per line. The output is called a patch, or an edit script, which is usually very small compared to the original files. Later, one can use the patch file to update the previous version to the newer version. Similarly, one can use the patch file to downgrade the newer version to the previous version. Therefore only the small patch file, instead of the entire newer version file, is needed to update a file.

Revised Diff

Based on the UNIX diff system, Rejiers [7] introduces a revised approach diff-like approach which uses a different operation.

Slop Space

Beyond traffic reduction, another issue [7] emerged from rebuilding a program image. When the size of subroutine is changed to shrink or grow, the addresses of unrelated subroutines may shift backward or forward. Address relocations cause every instruction which referring to the relocated address needs to be patched. Unnecessary patches waste network bandwidth and power. Worse, even a single byte in a flash memory page need to be altered, the entire flash memory page is erased and rewritten with new data. These erase and rewrite operations are slow and power consumed.

2.3   Execution Environment

Instead of writing an application from scratch, reinventing wheel and directly access underlying hardware platform, applications are usually running on top of a hardware abstraction layer [12, 13, 14, 15, 16, and 17]. A hardware abstraction layer is usually provided by an operating system, a middle-ware, or other execution environment. The purpose of hardware abstraction is hide the difference in hardware, hence the application be ported to other hardware more easily. The execution environment may also provide off-the-shelf and try-and-true facilities to programmers that reduce the level of expertise and effort requirement by the programmers.

Task Management

Task management [18-20] is one of the most important functionalities provided by underlying execution environment to coordinate tasks. When multiple tasks are running concurrently, race condition or dead lock may occur if the programmer did not properly use the synchronization tools. To ease the pain of concurrency issue, the execution environment often provides the well-designed concurrency model and programming model to simplify the concurrency issues [18].

Virtual Machine

Maté [13] is a virtual machine designed for sensor network. Compared to native machine code, the bytecode, executed by the interpreter, is very concise. At first glance, running virtual machine on sensor nodes seem impractical due to the cost of interpreting bytecode is quite high. However Maté is based on the assumption that the energy cost of interpreting bytecode is outweighed by the energy saved by transmitting bytecode instead native machine. Although Maté is impressive in terms of code size and the ability of reprogramming, but the results show the interpreting overhead is rather big. According to the conclusion of Maté, in the gdi-comm case, the energy can be saved only when running five days of less.

Table 1. Cost of Maté operations [13]

Operations	Maté Clock Cycles	Native Clock Cycles	Cost
Simple: and	469	14	33.5:1
Downcall: rand	435	45	9.5:1
Quick Splite: sense	1342	396	3.4:1
Long Split: sendr	685+≈20,000	≈20,000	1.03:1

Table 2. Maté application costs [13]

Application	Binary Size	Install Time	Maté Capsules	Instructions
sens_to_rfm	5394B	79s	1	6
gdi-comm	7130B	104s	1	19
bless_test	7381B	108s	7	108

Cost of Reboots

Neutron [17] is a specialized version TinyOS that efficiently recovers from memory safety bugs by only rebooting the faulting units instead of the entire node. The work is based on the assumption – rebooting is costly. When a node is rebooting, the precious runtime state is lost. For example, lost data of weather condition cannot be collected again. Besides a rebooting node takes time to re-synchronize with other nodes, and control packets for routing protocol waste precious network bandwidth and energy.

To preserve these status by rebooting only the faulting units, Neutron can reduce 94% of the cost for time-synchronization for Flooding Time Synchronization Protocol and 99.5% of the cost for a routing protocol for Collection Tree Protocol.

Data-driven, or Dynamic, Programming
In computer programming language [21], static means things are determined during and before the compile-time, whereas dynamic means things are determined when the programming is being executed. Data-driven programming [24], sometimes called dynamic programming, is one of the most classic approaches to dynamically modify a program at run-time. Instead of hardcoding the logic of a program, the logic of the program is separating from the code. Therefore, the logic of a programming can be modified by editing the data structures, even at runtime, instead of the code.

3   System Design

A program is decomposed into tasks and transitions. A task is an application-independent reusable functionality, and a transition describes how execution flow transits from tasks to tasks. A task can be constructed from tasks and transitions to represent a more complex task. For example, three tasks have to be done and the second task invoking 3 steps. They can be illustrated as the following structure.

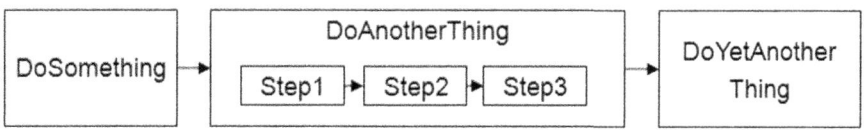

Fig. 2. Structuring of tasks and transitions

Transitions provide the mechanism of conventional control flow statements. As Figure 3 5 shows, the transitions, represented as solid arrow lines, describe the order in which the individual task are executed. That is, DoSomething, Step1 of DoAnotherThing, Step2 of DoAnotherThing, Step3 of DoAnotherThing, and finally DoYetAntoherThing.

Tasks in uFlow
A task is a fundamental building block of a program. It defines what to do, or how to transit the execution flow to next task. There are two types of tasks, simple and composite. A simple task represents a single basic task to be done. It is associated with a subroutine, called execution handler, which is invoked when the task is executed. For example, tasks for blinking LED or transmitting a packet. A composite task contains other child tasks. It plays the role of control flow to coordinate a collection of child tasks to accomplish a more sophisticated task. For example, instead of building a monolithic task for U-turns from scratch, it can be built from reusing two turn-right tasks, and a forward task, off the shelf. Therefore, a composite task is

composed of a collection of child tasks, and a rule of how to execute the child tasks. A rule can be sequence execution, conditional branch, while-loop, or even a programmer defined one. For example, the pseudo code of conditional branch in would be:

```
If condition is true then

    Execute the first child

Else If

    Execute the second child

End If
```

Fig. 3. Pseudo code of conditional branch

The rule of a composite task is implemented by the execution handler and a continuation handler. Similar to simple task, the execution handler is invoked when the task is executed, and the composite task can be notified when a child task complete its execution thought the continuation handler. To elaborate, see EXECUTE UFLOW PROGRAMS. In order to simplify the program structure, localize a modification to prevent from affecting the rest of the program and provide reusability, the composite pattern is adopted [22]. Hereby, a composite task is treated in the same way as a simple task. That is, a task can be composed of tasks, and eventually the hierarchy of task forms a tree which representing the entire program itself. The program starts its execution from the root, then the child tasks, and so forth. The UML diagram of tasks is illustrated in Figure 3 7. Both a simple task and a composite task inherit from the task which provides execution handler to perform a specific work. While a composite task has a list of potential transitions and a continuation handler used to determine which transition to take.

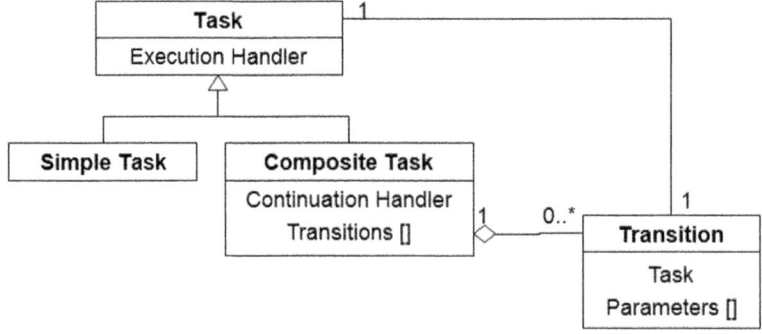

Fig. 4. Task composition

Control Flow in uFlow

As stated previously, a program is a collection of tasks to be done, and transitions are used to define their execution orders. This section describes how uFlow organizes tasks and transitions to into a running program. A task contains other tasks is call a composite task. A composite task manages the execution of is child tasks, and it completes its execution depends on its transition rule. uFlow doesn't use explicit transitions to describe the control flow. Instead, composite tasks are used to structure the control flow. Examples of composite tasks used for control flow are depicted in the following section.

Sequence Execution

Sequence Task is used to run a list of tasks in an ordered manner. The children are executed one by one at a time. When the last child completes, the sequence task per se completes.

Conditional Branch

Conditional branch task is used to execute its child task only if a specified condition is met. It acts like the if-else statement in programming language. A conditional branch task can have one or two children, and a conditional function. If the conditional function is evaluated to true, then the first child is chosen to be run, otherwise the second child, if exists.

While Loop

Loops structure is used to repeatedly execute a task based on a specified condition. For example, while loop, do-while loop, and for-loop.

Hierarchized Structure

These control flow tasks can be combined to form a more sophisticated task. Hereby, although only one or few tasks can be put in a task, but it doesn't mean only a few tasks can be performed.

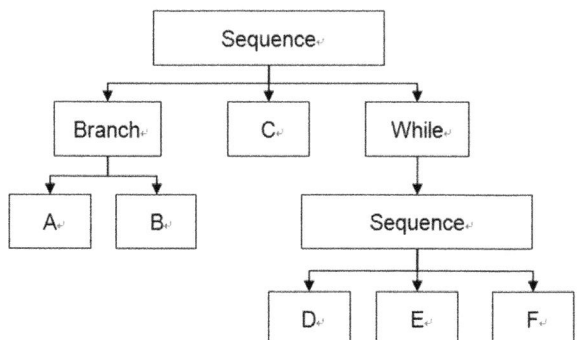

Fig. 5. Hierarchized structure example

Before explaining the example in Figure 5, the tree-style diagrams may look confusing and not straightforward about what it intends to do, because it is used to illustrate the parent-child relationship of a composite task, not the execution flow. A flowchart-style equivalent counterpart of the diagram can be used to represent the execution flow of the tasks.

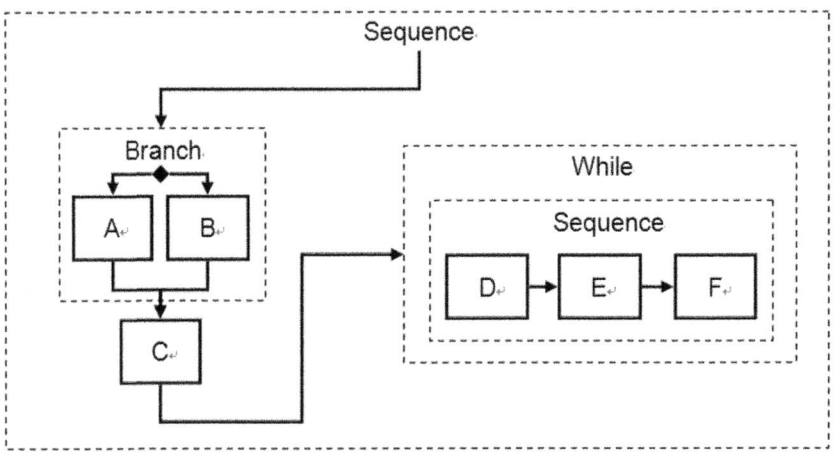

Fig. 6. Flowchart-style representation

The diagram in Figure 6 is the equivalent counterpart of the diagram in Figure 5 in different style and emphasizing on the execution flow the tasks. The solid block represents a task to be done, while the solid arrow denotes the execution order.

It is now straightforward that either A or B will be executed, then C, while D, E, and F as a whole will be executed repeatedly based on a given condition.

Context Stack
A task acts like a blueprint to describe the functionality and the behavior, and it may be used again to repeat a same operation or to cooperate with other task to form a new functionality. However, this leads to two issues. First, each executed task may stay in a different execution state. How to keep track their execution status? Second, no matter how the execution flow traverses down the task tree, it eventually needs to backtrack to the parent task to start next child task. The solution in uFlow is the context along with the context stack. There are two cases of task execution, simple or composite, when the execution flow traverses down the tree. Simple tasks are always leaf nodes of the tree; hence no more than one simple task is executed at the same time. However, execution of tasks may be nested, since a child task of a composite task can also be a composite task and so forth. Furthermore, a child composite task can be the same type of task as its parent, that is, recursion.

Parameter Passing in uFlow
Task acts like a subroutine, which can accept input parameters and return multiple values in the form of output parameters.

Execute uFlow Programs

uFlow engine executes the application in a manner similar to tree traversal. Instead of in a strict order (e.g., preorder, inorder or preoder), it traverses in task-defined order.

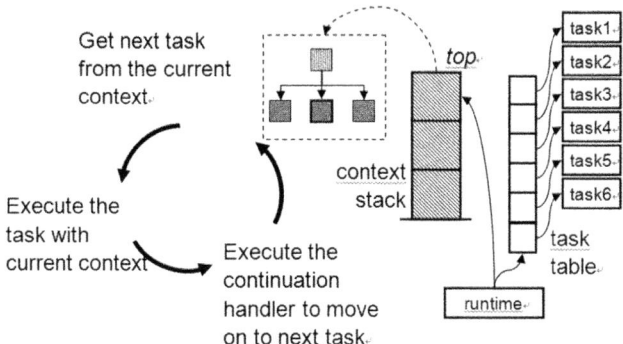

Fig. 7. uFlow Task Loop

The uFlow task loop, as illustrated above, manages to execute the entire program, i tasks. Without loss of generality, the task loop involves three major parts:

1. Looks up the current context to get the next task.
2. Executes the task by invoking the execution handler.
3. Move on the next task by invoking the continuation handler.

Dynamic Replacement

uFlow provides the ability to dynamically update the application behavior by changing the task structures. Structural changing includes adding new tasks, removing unwanted tasks, and even altering the task implantation on the fly without neither stopping the execution before updating nor restarting the program after update to preserve the precious runtime status. The update scenarios are classified into three cases depending on what task structures are modified. In either case, since all the uFlow programs and engine are executed in a single thread, one can easily define inter-task invariants to guarantee the modification will not break the uFlow execution. The following sections discuss the updating procedure in terms of each case.

4   Prototype Implementation and Result

4.1 Engine Task Loop

The engine task loop is illustrated, in Figure 4 1, to explain its implementation code.

4. The context records the execution status of the current executed composite task. If the context is valid, there is a task waiting for execution. Otherwise, the program is terminated.
5. The engine looks up the context to get the next task and executes it by invoking its execution handler.

6. After execution, the execution result shows whether the newly executed task is a composite task. If not, the continuation handler is called to designate the next task.
7. If the newly executed task is a composite task. It is responsible for pushing a new context of it and designating the first child for execution. By this means, the first child of the newly composite task will be executed at the next iteration.
8. If a composite task is finished, the engine will pop out its context, and invokes the continuation handler of its parent to schedule next task.

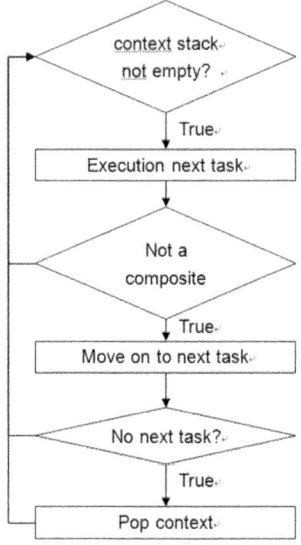

Fig. 8. Change the transition rule

4.2   Engine Task Loop

The example is illustrated below. It repeatedly read to input from user, and sum them up. If the summation is an odd number, it prints "Number %d is Odd" ; otherwise, it prints "Number %d Even" where "%d" will be replaced by the summation. The example demonstrates how to write an application using uFlow and parameter binding in uFlow.

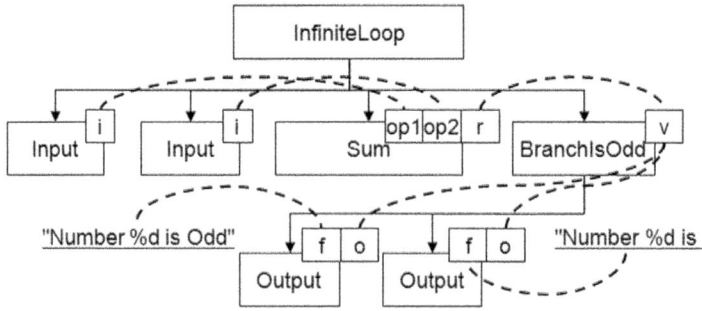

Fig. 9. uFlow example application

4.3 Results

In the following evaluation, the code is compiled with IAR [23] C/C++ Compiler for MSP430 4.21.2 with Debug configuration without optimization. MSP430 is a microcontroller from Texas Instruments. It is designed for low power consumption embedded applications, and widely used in various wireless sensor network environments. For example, the famous Telos from UC and its compatible motes, Tmote Sky from Sentilla and TelosB from Crossbow, are all equipped with MSP430F1611 microcontroller. The compiler is developed by IAR system, a Swedish company, one of the leadership companies providing compilers, debuggers and other tools for various microcontrollers. The compiler is chosen because it is officially suggested by Texas Instruments.

Engine Code Size
The code sizes for required and optional functions are 420 bytes and 146 bytes respectively. The size of each function in detail is listed in the tables below.

Table 3. Code size for required functions

Function	Size (in bytes)
Engine task loop	108
uFlowCompositeTaskExec	24
uFlowGetParameters	38
uFlowGetValue	96
uFlowSetValue	50
uFlowPushContext	68
Total	420

Table 4. Code size for optional helper api

Function	Size (in bytes)
uFlowSetTransition	28
uFlowAllocSimpleTask	20
uFlowAllocCompositeTask	66
uFlowAllocTransitions	32
Total	146

uFlow Program Size
Program size is contributed from the code for execution and related data structures for uFlow. The code may be a simple task which implements a specific work, or a composite task implementation for control flow. No matter using uFlow or not, the code for simple task is usually required, because it is used to actually complete specific task. For example, reading sensor, transmitting packet. However, the code for composite task is often an overhead, because it is used for control flow. In Table5 show in order to organize the task, a collection of data structures are needed to describe to task and their transitions. Hence they are all overhead to the application.

Table 5. The code size of the example application

Function	Task Type	Size (in bytes)
OutputTask	Simple	34
SumTask	Simple	52
InputTask	Simple	52
BranchIsOddExec	Composite	94
BranchIsOddCont	Composite	12
MainLoopCont	Composite	34
Total		278

Table 6. Required data structure size for the application

	Entry	Task	Transition	Parameter	Total
Output	2	2	0	4	8
Sum	2	2	0	6	10
While	2	10	24	0	36
Branch	2	10	26	2	40
Total	10	26	50	14	100

The Table 6 shows the size for a specific type of task is fixed no matter how many times it is used. Instead, a transition structure is needed to refer the task.

Execution Overheads

When executing uFlow program, the engine task loop traverses the tree to find next task for execution. The task loop *per se* does not help to accomplish the work, therefore is an overhead which slows down the execution and wastes extra energy. We compare the overhead with TinyOS and Maté, because TinyOS is one of the most widely used execution environment in sensor networks while Maté show the impressive ability of software update. The overhead of TinyOS comes from the task scheduler. Instead of directly invoke a subroutine, a subroutine is wrapped as a task, and posted in the task queue. At later time, the scheduler pops the tasks for execution one by one. The overheads of Maté are caused by wrapping each instruction to a TinyOS task.The clock cycles for the uFlow task loop is measured and compared to the scheduler in TinyOS-1.1.15.

Table 7. Execution overhead of uFlow, TinyOS and Maté

System	Task Loop	Clock Cycles
uFlow	uFlow engine task loop	58
	Continuation Function	≈ 30
TinyOS	TOS_post	26
	TOSH_run_next_task	30
Maté	TOS_post	$N \times 26$
	TOSH_run_next_task	$N \times 30$

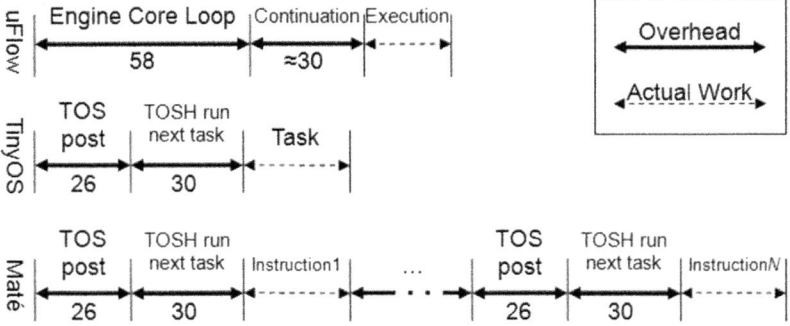

Fig. 10. Execution overhead of uFlow, TinyOS and Maté

5   Conclusion

We present uFlow, a programming paradigm and a prototype implementation for wireless sensor networks. By uFlow, we allow the sensor network nodes to update without rebooting. Therefore the precious runtime status can be keep .we achieve the goal by decomposing the application into reusable task that organized as a tree structure. The engine executes the uFlow tree by traversing the task node and executing the task handlers. All the handlers are run-to-complete and never interrupted by other handlers. It is safe to replace or update tasks but does not interrupt microcontroller execution. Besides, all of the tasks are indirectly accessed via the task table. The Tasks are organized as a tree structure; these two properties keep update away from affecting the entire program and address relocation problems.

The prototype implementation result shows our idea works. The execution overhead in terms of clock cycle which costs around 58 for the engine task loop and around 30 for the extended handler. That is around 1.6 times for TinyOS task scheduler, i.e., around 88 clock cycles. Although the overhead is larger than TinyOS, but the overhead is only introduced at transition between tasks. The engine task loop only costs 420 bytes, helper API for dynamically creating uFlow application costs 146 bytes, the code size for the sample application costs 318 bytes, and the data structure used to describe the application costs 100 bytes. By our proposed idea, we can provide a software updating for sensor network and avoid the reboot.

Acknowledgments
NSC 99-2221-E-002-106-MY3
MOTC-DPT-100-03

References

1. Han, C.-C., Kumar, R., Shea, R., Srivastava, M.: Sensor Network Software Update Management. Intl. Journal of Network Management (15) (2005)
2. Hunt, J.W., Douglas McIlroy, M.: An Algorithm for Differential File Comparison. Computing Science Technical Report, Bell Laboratories 41 (1976)

3. Tridgell, A., Mackerras, P.: The rsync algorithm. Tech. Rep. TR-CS-96-05, Canberra 0200 ACT, Australia (1996), http://samba.anu.edu.au/rsync/
4. Intanagonwiwat, C., Govindan, R., Estrin, D.: Directed Diffusion: A Scalable and Robust Communication Paradigm for Sensor Networks. In: Proc. of the Sixth Annual International Conference on Mobile Computing and Networking (MobiCOM 2000), Boston, Massachussetts (2000)
5. Crossbow Technology Inc. (XNP) Mote In-Network Programming User Reference (2003), http://www.xbow.com
6. Stathopoulos, T., Heidemann, J., Estrin, D.: (MOAP) A remote code update mechanism for wireless sensor networks. Technical report, UCLA, Los Angeles, CA, USA (2003)
7. Reijers, N., Langendoen, K.: Efficient Code Distribution in Wireless Sensor Networks. In: Proc. 2nd ACM International Conference on Wireless Sensor Networks and Applications (WSNA 2003), pp. 60–67 (2003)
8. Jeong, J., Culler, D.: Incremental Network Programming for Wireless Sensors. In: Proc. of Sensor and Ad-Hoc Communications and Networks, SECON 2004 (2004)
9. Koshy, J., Pandey, R.: Remote Incremental Linking for Energy-Efficient Reprogramming of Sensor Networks. In: Proc. of the Second European Workshop on Wireless Sensor Networks, pp. 354–365 (2005)
10. Dunkels, A., Finne, N., Eriksson, J., Voigt, T.: Run-time dynamic linking for reprogramming wireless sensor networks. In: Proc. of the 4th International Conference on Embedded Networked Sensor Systems, SenSys 2006 (2006)
11. Mukhtar, M., Kim, B.W., Kim, B.S., Joo, S.S.: An Efficient Remote Code Update Mechanism for Wireless Sensor. In: Proc. of Military Communications Conference, MILCON 2009 (2009)
12. Gay, D., Levis, P., Behren, R.V., Welsh, M., Brewer, E., Culler, D.: The nesC Language: A Holistic Approach to Networked Embedded Systems. In: Proc. of Programming Language Design and Implementation, PLDI 2003 (2003)
13. Levis, P., Culler, D.: Maté a tiny virtual machine for sensor networks. In: Proc. of the 10th International Conference on Architectural Support for Programming Languages and Operating Systems, ASPLOS X (2002)
14. Abrach, H., Bhatti, S., Carlson, J., Dai, H., Rose, J., Sheth, A., Shucker, B., Deng, J., Han, R.: MANTIS: system support for MultimodAl NeTworks of In-Situ sensors. In: Proc. Mobile Networks and Applications, WSNA 2003 (2003)
15. Dunkels, A., Gronvall, B., Voigt, T.: Contiki - a Lightweight and Flexible Operating System for Tiny Networked. In: Proc. of the 29th Annual IEEE International Conference on Local Computer Networks (LCN 2004), pp. 455–462 (2004)
16. Gnawali, O., Jang, K.Y., Paek, J., Vieira, M., Govindan, R., Greenstein, B., Joki, A., Estrin, D., Kohler, E.: The Tenet architecture for tiered sensor networks. In: Proc. of the 4th International Conference on Embedded Networked Sensor Systems, SenSys 2006 (2006)
17. Chen, Y., Gnawali, O., Kazandjieva, M., Levis, P., Regehr, J. (Neutron): Surviving sensor network software faults. In: Proc. of the ACM SIGOPS 22nd Symposium on Operating Systems Principles, SOSP 2009 (2009)
18. Adya, A., Howell, J., Theimer, M., Bolosky, W.J., Douceur, J.R.: Cooperative Task Management Without Manual Stack Management. In: Proc. of the General Track of the Annual Conference on USENIX Annual Technical Conference, USENIX 2002 (2002)
19. Dunkels , Schmidt, O., Voigt, T., Ali, M.: Protothreads: simplifying event-driven programming of memory-constrained embedded systems. In: Proc. of the 4th International Conference on Embedded Networked Sensor Systems, October 31-November 03 (2006)

20. Klues, K., Liang, C.J.M., Paek, J., Musaloiu-E, Levis, P., Terzis, A., Govindan, R.: TOSThreads: Thread-Safe and Non-Invasive Preemption in TinyOS. In: Proc. of the 7th International Conference on Embedded Networked Sensor Systems, SenSys 2009 (2009)
21. Sebesta, R.W.: Concepts of Programming Languages, 6th edn. Addison Wesley, Reading (2003)
22. Gamma, E., Helm, R., Johnson, R., Vlissides, J.M.: Design Patterns: Elements of Reusable Object-Oriented Software, p. 395. Addison-Wesley, Reading (1995) ISBN 0-201-63361-2
23. IAR Systems, http://www.iar.com/
24. Raymond, E.S.: Art of UNIX Programming, p. 560. The Addison-Welsey, London (1999) ISBN 0131429019

Energy-Balancing and Lifetime Enhancement of Wireless Sensor Network with Archimedes Spiral

Subir Halder[1], Amrita Ghosal[1], Aadirupa Saha[2], and Sipra DasBit[2]

[1] Dept. of Comp. Sc. & Engg, Dr. B. C. Roy Engineering College, Durgapur, India
[2] Dept. of Comp. Sc. & Tech., Bengal Engineering and Science University, Shibpur, India
subir_ece@rediffmail.com, ghosal_amrita@yahoo.com,
siprad@hotmail.com

Abstract. Energy is one of the scarcest resources in wireless sensor network (WSN). Therefore, the need to conserve energy is of utmost importance in WSN. There are many ways to conserve energy in such a network. One fundamental way of conserving energy is judicious deployment of sensor nodes within the network area so that the energy flow remains balanced throughout the network. This avoids the problem of occurrence of 'energy holes' and ensures prolonged network lifetime. In this paper, we have identified intrinsic features of Archimedes' Spiral and shown its suitability to model the layered WSN area. Next we have transformed the same Spiral in its discrete form and proposed this as a deployment function. A node deployment algorithm is developed based on this deployment function. Further, we have identified necessary constraints involving different network parameters to ensure coverage, connectivity and energy balance of the entire network. Performance of the deployment scheme is evaluated in terms of energy balance and network lifetime. Both qualitative and quantitative analyses are done based on these two performance metrics. Finally the scheme is compared with an existing Gaussian distribution-based deployment scheme and the results confirm the superiority of our scheme in respect to both the metrics over the existing one.

Keywords: Wireless sensor network, Archimedes' spiral, Node deployment, Coverage, Connectivity, Energy balance.

1 Introduction

A wireless sensor network (WSN) [1] consists of several hundreds of sensor nodes which collect data from their surroundings and send the data to the sink either directly or via their one hop neighbouring nodes. The sink processes and transmits the received data to the outside world. Sensor nodes are equipped with battery whose charge cannot be replaced easily after deployment and so the need to conserve energy is a major concern of WSN. The rate of energy depletion in the network primarily depends on the deployment nature of the nodes that further depends on the application environment.

Deployment can be random or pre-determined. In random deployment, nodes are randomly deployed generally in an inaccessible terrain. For example, in the application

C.-H. Hsu et al. (Eds.): UIC 2011, LNCS 6905, pp. 420–434, 2011.
© Springer-Verlag Berlin Heidelberg 2011

domain of disaster recovery or in forest fire detection, sensors are generally dropped by helicopter in random manner [2]. In pre-determined deployment, number of nodes in a unit area is known apriori and is used in applications where sensors are expensive or their operation is significantly affected by their positions. These applications include placing imaging and video sensors, populating an area with highly precise seismic nodes etc [2].

One important way of conserving energy is through uniform energy or load distribution all over the network. Non-uniform energy dissipation in any part of the network may result in non-functioning of that part leading to the phenomenon of energy hole problem [3] that affects network lifetime. This arises due to uneven data transmissions by certain nodes resulting in extra energy dissipation of those nodes that causes a substantial amount of energy to remain in the nodes even after network lifetime ends leading to significant wastage of energy [4]. To avoid this, nodes should be deployed in such a manner that the energy dissipation of all nodes takes place uniformly ensuring load balancing throughout the network. A good sensor deployment strategy is one that achieves both energy balance and energy efficiency [5].

Many works reported so far have proposed strategies for ensuring energy balance thereby enhancing network lifetime. In one such work, S. Olariu and I. Stojmenovic [6] have given a network design guideline for maximizing lifetime and avoiding energy hole with uniform node distribution. They show that uneven energy depletion due to energy hole is unavoidable for free-space model, but can be prevented for multipath model. However, they have not explored the potential of non-uniform node deployment.

X. Wu et al. [7] have explored the theoretical aspects of energy hole problem in sensor networks with layered architecture by proposing a non-uniform node distribution strategy. The number of nodes distributed in a layer is determined based on the minimum number of nodes required in the upper adjacent layer. However, the authors are silent about the minimum number of nodes required to be placed in the farthest layer from the sink to maintain connectivity and coverage.

Y. Liu et al. [8] have studied a number of node deployment strategies suffering from energy hole problem and have proposed a non-uniform, power-aware distribution scheme. The authors have shown that their scheme is capable of increasing network lifetime and also improves network service quality. However, the problem of creation of energy hole is not addressed.

C. Efthymiou et al. [9] have proposed an algorithm where a node decides whether to propagate data in multi hop towards the sink or directly forward data to the sink. The choice between the two forwarding methods is based on a proposed probability value. One major drawback of the algorithm is that it does not support network scalability.

J. Luo and J. P. Hubaux [10] have investigated the problem of more data pressure on nodes located closer to the sink than the nodes located farther away from the sink. They have proposed to solve the uneven energy consumption by considering mobile sink. If mobile sink is used, then the nodes lying nearer to the sink keep on changing resulting in even distribution of load among the nodes.

H. M. Ammari and S. K. Das [11] have also provided three different solutions to eliminate energy hole problem. One solution is by adjusting communication range of the sensor nodes while the second is a deployment strategy based on energy heterogeneity in terms of initial energy of nodes. The final one proposes a localized energy aware Voronoi diagram based data forwarding protocol considering homogeneous nodes and mobile sink. The deployment strategy considers the sink as mobile which is a major drawback as sink mobility incurs additional overhead in nodes in terms of energy consumption due to updation of location information.

D. Wang *et al.* [12] have proposed an analytical model for coverage and network lifetime of sensor networks using two dimensional Gaussian distribution. They have proposed two deployment algorithms- one for circular and another for elliptical network area using which larger coverage and longer network lifetime are achieved. But the deployment scheme does not ensure energy balancing in the network.

Most of the distribution-function/scheme based deployment strategies have not addressed all the issues of coverage, connectivity, energy balance and network lifetime simultaneously. In this background, we have proposed a location-wise predetermined node deployment strategy based on Archimedes' spiral [13] to achieve both energy balance and enhancement of network lifetime.

The rest of the paper is organized as follows. Section 2 presents network model considered for the proposed node deployment scheme. The proposed energy balanced node deployment scheme is presented in section 3. In section 4, the performance of the scheme is evaluated based on qualitative analysis and simulation results. Finally the paper is concluded with some mention about the future scope of the work in section 5.

2 Network Model

In this section, we describe the network architecture along with the assumptions. We then present the definitions of coverage, connectivity, energy balance and network lifetime that are considered for this work. Energy model considered for the work is presented at the end of this section.

2.1 Architecture

We consider a square shaped network area a×a which is covered by a set of annuli shown in Figure 1. Each such annuli is designated with width r as layer. The sink is considered to be located at the centre of the network area. Nodes are placed in different layers surrounding a single sink. A layer is identified as L_i where i =1,2,...,N. Here i=1 indicates the layer nearest to the sink and i=N indicates the layer farthest from the sink. We define boundary between layers i & (i+1) as the boundary of layer i (BL_i). So the nodes of layers i & (i+1) share a common boundary BL_i (shown in Figure 1).

We assume all the sensor nodes are static, homogeneous with respect to their initial energy and distributed within the network with a given node density. The node density is defined [3], [7] as the ratio of the number of nodes in a layer and area of the layer. Further we consider that all the sensor nodes generate and send data to the sink at fixed time-interval q(t). We assume that data is transmitted from layers towards the sink following the maximum remaining energy policy [7], where a node in a layer chooses a neighbour as next-hop when the neighbour has the maximum residual energy compared to the other neighbours. Random selection is done if there is more than one node with the same maximum remaining energy.

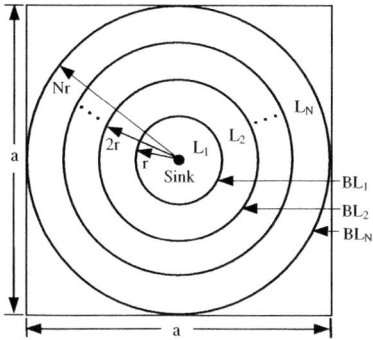

Fig. 1. Layered Network Area

For ease of exposition, we consider the following terms as defined below:

Definition 1 (Coverage). A unit area is said to be covered, if every point in the area is within the sensing range of at least one active node [14]. We assume nodes can perform observation at an angle of $360°$. The maximal circular area centered around a node v that can be covered by it is defined as its sensing area $S(v)$. The radius of $S(v)$ is called the v's sensing range R_s.

Definition 2 (Connectivity). The network is considered to be connected, if any active node can communicate with any other active node either in single hop or in multiple hops [14]. We assume two nodes u and v can directly communicate with each other if their Euclidean distance is less than or equal to the communication range R_c, i.e. $|uv| \leq R_c$.

Definition 3 (Energy Balance). The N-layered network is considered to be energy balanced when the sensor nodes located in layer-i and layer-(i+1) have the same energy consumption rate [6] [7] where i=1,2,...,(N-1).

Definition 4 (Network Lifetime). The network lifetime is defined [3] in terms of coverage of the network. It is the time till the proportion of dead nodes exceeds a certain threshold, which may result in loss of coverage of a certain region, and/or network partitioning.

2.2 Energy Model

We have considered the first order radio model [12] as our energy model where the energy consumption of a node is dominated by its wireless transmissions and receptions; so we have neglected the other energy consumption factors such as for sensing and processing. According to this radio model, energy consumed by a node for transmitting n-bit data over a distance R_c

$$e_{tx}(n, R_c) = e_{elec} \, n + e_{amp} \, n \, R_c^2 = e_t n \text{ where } e_t = e_{elec} + e_{amp} \, R_c^2. \tag{1a}$$

Energy consumption for receiving (e_r) n-bit data from a distance R_c

$$e_{rx}(n, R_c) = e_{elec} \, n = e_r n \text{ where } e_r = e_{elec}. \tag{1b}$$

3 Energy-Balanced Node Deployment

In this section the entire node deployment strategy based on Archimedes' Spiral along with the implementing algorithm is presented.

3.1 Archimedes' Spiral

A spiral is defined as a curve, which emanates from a central point, getting progressively farther away as it revolves around the point. An Archimedes' spiral is a continuous spiral [13] with polar equation $r_d = B\theta$ where r_d is the radial distance, θ is the polar angle and B is a real number which controls the distance between two successive turnings. One of the features of the Archimedes' spiral is that its successive turns have a constant separation distance equal to $2\pi B$ (Refer Figure 2).

3.2 Proposed Deployment with Discrete Archimedes' Spiral

The Archimedes' spiral which is continuous has been discussed in previous subsection. Our objective is to map the layered network architecture with the Archimedes' spiral so that the area covered by two successive turns corresponds to one layer. As the spiral is a continuous curve, to use it for deployment, it should be transformed into discrete form so that nodes may be deployed at those discrete locations on the boundary of the layers. In the context of deployment, for convenience we refer the boundary BL_i as layer-i. We propose the spiral as in equation (2) for modeling the layered network architecture and the discrete form of it as the deployment function.

$$f(\theta) = B\theta \qquad \text{where } \theta \in \left[2(i-1)\pi, 2i\pi\right]. \tag{2a}$$

Further, to transform it into discrete form we propose to choose $\theta(i)$ as follows:

$$\theta(k) = \left(2\pi i - kG(i)\right) \tag{2b}$$

$$\text{and } G(i) = C \times i \tag{2c}$$

for i=1,2,...,N and k=0,1,2,..., $\frac{2\pi}{G(i)}$.

In equation (2c), C is a positive real number. Here $G(i)$ represents the gap between two consecutive nodes in layer-i and it is clear from the relation that for i=N the value of $G(i)$ is maximum and for i=1 it is minimum. In order to map the layered network with the Archimedes' spiral, the radius of layer-i for deployment is considered as $\frac{1}{2}\left[B2\pi i + B2\pi(i+1)\right] = B\pi(2i+1)$.

A typical discrete distribution is shown in Figure 2 where B= 25.46 and C= 0.04. Using equation (2a) the exact locations where the nodes are to be placed can be determined. Figure 2 shows two such locations having polar coordinates $(480, 6\pi)$ and $\left(520, \frac{13\pi}{2}\right)$ for (i, k)=(3, 0) & (4, 30) respectively.

The deployment parameter B decides the width of the layers and its value is constant. The width of layer-i i.e. r is equal to $\left[B\pi(2i+1) - B\pi(2(i-1)+1)\right] = 2\pi B$ for i=1,2,...,N. As B decides the width of a layer so it has an impact on the connectivity of the network. On the other hand, the value of C controls the number of nodes to be deployed in a layer and its value is constant for given network size. C has an impact on the coverage in the network. Now for a N-layered network area, for layer i, the range of θ is to be computed first. Next on layer i, i.e. within the range of θ values, discrete locations $(f(\theta), \theta)$ are to be computed. In this way, discrete locations are to be computed for all the N layers. Nodes are to be deployed at these computed locations.

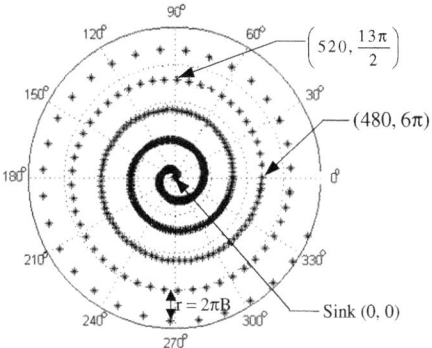

Fig. 2. Archimedes' Spiral

3.3   Analysis on Coverage and Connectivity

This sub-section formulates necessary constraints to be satisfied related to the proposed deployment function for maintaining coverage and connectivity.

Theorem 1: For a given N-layered network area and a set of nodes that at least 1-cover the network area, the communication graph is connected if $R_c \leq 2R_s$.

Proof: We first prove that any two nodes lying in adjacent layers can communicate with each other. As illustrated in Figure 3, the point p lies between layer-i and layer-(i+1). We consider u, v and w are equi-distant from p and these are the closest to p among all other nodes in the respective layers. Hence, p must be covered by u, v and w, otherwise it will not be covered by any nodes. According to the triangle inequality for Δuvp , we have:

$$|uv| \leq |pu| + |pv| . \tag{3a}$$

We now prove the network is connected by showing that there is a communication path between any two nodes in the network belonging to two adjacent layers. In Figure 3, the Euclidean distance between two nodes u of layer-i and v of layer-(i+1) is

$$dl_{i+1} = f(\theta(i+1)) - f(\theta(i))$$

where $\theta(i+1) = 2\pi(i+1) + \phi$, $\theta(i) = 2\pi i + \phi$, where $2\pi \geq \phi \geq 0$.
So, $f(\theta(i+1)) = B \times (2\pi(i+1) + \phi)$ and $f(\theta(i)) = B \times (2\pi i + \phi)$ for i=1,2,...,(N-1).
The Euclidean distance between nodes u and v is

$$dl_{i+1} = |uv| = R_c = [B \times 2\pi(i+1)] - [B \times 2\pi i] . \tag{3b}$$

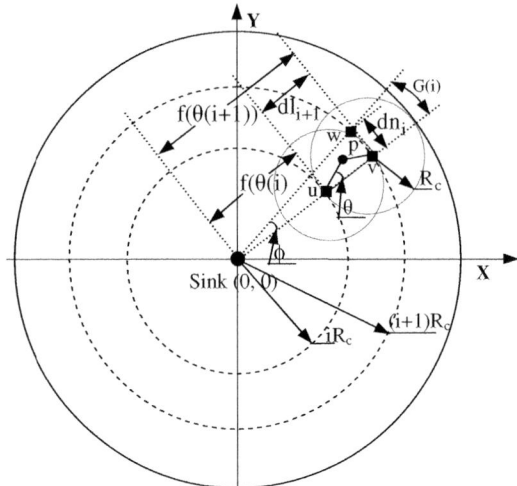

Fig. 3. Coverage and Connectivity with Deployment Function

The Euclidean distance between nodes u and w is

$$dl_{i+1} = |uw| = R_c = \left[B \times (2\pi(i+1)+\phi)\right] - \left[B \times (2\pi i + \phi)\right].$$

It is also noted that the Euclidean distance between two nodes u of layer-i and v or w of layer-(i+1) is equal to the width of a layer i.e. r. So for connectivity, the relationship between r and R_c is

$$r \le R_c.$$

The network is connected when the distance between two adjacent layers is same as given in equation (3b).

We now prove the network is covered by showing that every point in the network is covered by at least one node. Based on the position of the point p there are two possibilities which are given below:

Case I): When p lies between the two adjacent layers shown in Figure 3 it forms Δuvp. According to the triangle inequality, we have-

$$|pu| = |pv| = R_s = \frac{1}{2\cos\theta}\left[f(\theta(i+1)) - f(\theta(i))\right] \text{ where } 0 < \theta < \frac{\pi}{3}. \tag{3c}$$

So the condition for p to be at least 1-cover and communication graph to be connected is formulated from equation (3a). By putting the values of equations (3b) and (3c) in (3a) we have-

$$\left[B \times (2\pi(i+1)+\phi)\right] - \left[B \times (2\pi i + \phi)\right] \le \frac{1}{\cos\theta}\left[f(\theta(i+1)) - f(\theta(i))\right]$$

$$R_c \le 2R_s.$$

Case II): When p lies between two consecutive nodes of a layer. As we consider for node deployment that the inter node gap i.e. G(i) is maximum when i=N, which implies that the network coverage is ensured if coverage is guaranteed at layer-N. The inter distance between two consecutive nodes of layer-i is given by

$$dn_i = f(\theta(i)) \times G(i) \quad \text{for } i=1,2,\ldots,N.$$

Let p lies between v and w on BL_N. Now p is at least 1-cover when the distance between p and w or p and v is-

$$|pw| = |pv| = R_s = \frac{1}{2} \Big[f(\theta(N)) \times G(N) \Big].$$ (3d)

Nodes v and w are connected when the Euclidean distance between nodes v and w is

$$dn_N = |vw| = R_c = f(\theta(N)) \times G(N).$$ (3e)

So the condition for p to be at least 1-cover, connectivity is formulated using equations (3d) and (3e) as-

$$|vw| \leq |pw| + |pv|$$

$$\Big[f(\theta(N)) \times G(N) \Big] \leq 2 \Big[\frac{1}{2} \Big[f(\theta(N)) \times G(N) \Big] \Big]$$

$$R_c \leq 2R_s.$$

Theorem 1 establishes a sufficient condition for a 1-covered network to guarantee 1-connectivity. Under the condition that $R_c \leq 2R_s$, a sensor network only needs to be configured to guarantee coverage in order to satisfy both coverage and connectivity.

Lemma 1: Ensuring connectivity requires the deployment parameter B should stand in relation with R_c as $B = \frac{R_c}{2\pi}$.

Proof: B can be derived from the connectivity relationship given in equation (3b) as shown below.

$$\Big[B \times (2\pi(i+1) + \phi) \Big] - \Big[B \times (2\pi i + \phi) \Big] \leq R_c.$$ (3f)

The above equation is modified for satisfying the minimum distance between the inter-layers and is given as-

$$R_c = \Big[B \times (2\pi(i+1) + \phi) \Big] - \Big[B \times (2\pi i + \phi) \Big].$$

Now this inter-layer distance should be equal to the communication range of a node. We have-

$$R_c = \Big[B \times (2\pi(i+1) + \phi) \Big] - \Big[B \times (2\pi i + \phi) \Big]$$

$$B \times 2\pi = R_c \; or, \; B = \frac{R_c}{2\pi}.$$ (3f)

As we know that communication range of a node is fixed so from equation (3f), we say that B is fixed. Lemma 1 justifies the features of the Archimedes' spiral that is, its successive turns (or width of a layer) have a constant separation distance and in our deployment strategy it is equal to $2\pi B$.

Lemma 2: For a given network area a×a, ensuring coverage and connectivity requires the number of layers (N) should stand in relation with a as $N = \frac{1}{2\pi} \Big(\frac{a}{\sqrt{2}B} - \frac{\pi}{4} \Big)$, where

$B = \frac{R_c}{2\pi}$.

Proof: If the area of the network is a×a, then the distance between the centre, where the sink lies and the farthest corner of the network is given by $\frac{a}{\sqrt{2}}$.

Now for i=N (farthest layer) the distance from the sink to the farthest point can be obtained from equation (2)-

$$f(\theta(i)) = B\theta \text{ and } \theta(i) = 2\pi i + \frac{\pi}{4} \quad \text{for i=1,2,...,N}$$

replacing i by N in the above equations we get

$$f(\theta(N)) = \frac{a}{\sqrt{2}}$$

$$B \times \left(2\pi N + \frac{\pi}{4}\right) = \frac{a}{\sqrt{2}}$$

$$N = \frac{1}{2\pi}\left(\frac{a}{\sqrt{2}\,B} - \frac{\pi}{4}\right). \tag{3g}$$

For a given network area, maximum number of layers can be calculated from equation (3g) while maintaining coverage and connectivity. As B is fixed, maximum number of layers for a given network area depends on the area parameter.

Lemma 3: For a N-layered network area, ensuring coverage requires the deployment parameter C should stand in relation with R_s as $C = \dfrac{R_s}{B\pi N^2}$.

Due to page limitation, the proof of lemma 3 could not be incorporated.

3.4 Analysis on Energy Balance

In this section we formulate the necessary constraints to achieve energy balance.

Lemma 4: Number of nodes T_i in layer-i holds the relationship $T_i = \dfrac{2\pi}{G(i)}$ for achieving energy balance where i=1,2,...,N.

Proof: As mentioned in section 3.2, G(i) denotes the gap between two consecutive nodes in layer-i. The value of G(i) is directly proportional to the layer number.

$$G(i) = C \times i$$

where C is a constant for a given network size. So $G(i) \propto i$ or with the increase in layer number, the gap between the two consecutive nodes increases and vice-versa.
As we know that the angle in possession of a layer is 2π, the number of nodes in layer-i is- $T_i = \dfrac{2\pi}{G(i)} = \dfrac{2\pi}{C \times i}$.

We observe from lemma 4 that as T_i is inversely proportional to G(i), it ensures more number of nodes are deployed in layers nearer to the sink and less number of nodes in layers farther away from the sink. Such type of deployment is necessary for our network architecture for balancing the energy consumption.

Corollary 1: Node density (D(i)) in layer-i holds the relationship $D(i) = \dfrac{2\pi}{G(i) \times A_i}$ for achieving energy balance, where A_i is the area of layer i.

Corollary 2: Node density of a layer is inversely proportional to layer number.

Due to page limitation, the proofs of corollary 1 and 2 could not be incorporated.

4 Performance Analysis

Performance of the present node deployment strategy is measured based on two parameters- energy balance and network lifetime. Both qualitative and quantitative analyses are presented here.

4.1 Qualitative Analysis

In this sub-section, we have identified the parameters involved in achieving energy balance and prolonging lifetime. We have also shown the present scheme's achievement in terms of the identified parameters borrowing the techniques used in [6] [7].

4.1.1   Energy Balance

Our objective is to maximize network lifetime while balancing energy consumption among all the network layers. A WSN with layered architecture is said to be energy balanced when all nodes of the network use up their energy at the same time [6] [7]. Nodes of all layers except those belonging to the farthest layer from the sink, spend their energy for transmitting their own data, receiving data from nodes of adjacent layers farther from the sink and forwarding the received data. Nodes of the farthest layer from the sink spend their energy only for transmitting their own data.

Let ECR_i denotes energy consumption in layer-i per unit time-interval q(t) (section 2.1). As the last layer consumes energy only for transmitting its own sensed data

$$ECR_N = T_N \, n \, e_t, \text{ for i=N.} \tag{4a}$$

As the rest of the layers consume energy both for transmitting their data and for receiving & forwarding the other adjacent layers' (farther from sink) data

$$ECR_i = T_i \, n \, e_t + n \, (e_t + e_r) \sum_{h=i+1}^{N} T_h \, , \text{ for i=1, 2, ..., (N-1)} \tag{4b}$$

where $T_i \, n \, e_t$ is for transmitting its own data and $n \, (e_t + e_r) \sum_{h=i+1}^{N} T_h$ is for receiving and forwarding the adjacent layers' (farther from sink) data.

All the nodes of the network use up their energy at the same time, means that the ratio of total initial energy content of a layer and ECR of that layer is same for all layers in the network. So for energy balancing, the following condition must be satisfied-

$$\frac{T_1 \times E_{Initial}}{ECR_1} = \frac{T_2 \times E_{Initial}}{ECR_2} = \cdots = \frac{T_i \times E_{Initial}}{ECR_i} \tag{4c}$$

where T_i is the number of nodes in layer-i and $E_{Initial}$ is the initial energy in each node.

From equation (4c), the condition required for balancing energy throughout the network is:

$$\frac{ECR_i}{T_i} = \frac{ECR_{i+1}}{T_{i+1}}$$

$$\frac{T_i}{T_{i+1}} = \frac{T_i \, n \, e_t + n \sum_{h=i+1}^{N} T_h \, (e_t + e_r)}{T_{i+1} \, n \, e_t + n \sum_{h=i+2}^{N} T_h \, (e_t + e_r)} . \qquad \text{[using equation (4b)]}$$

Simplifying the above relation by dropping n, $T_{i+1} T_i e_t$ and $(e_t + e_r)$ in sequence, we have

$$T_i \sum_{h=i+2}^{N} T_h \, (e_t + e_r) = T_{i+1} \sum_{h=i+1}^{N} T_h \, (e_t + e_r)$$

$$\frac{T_i}{T_{i+1}} = \frac{\sum_{h=i+1}^{N} T_h}{\sum_{h=i+2}^{N} T_h} \ . \tag{4d}$$

The LHS of equation (4d) is evaluated as-

$$\frac{T_i}{T_{i+1}} = \frac{\frac{2\pi}{C \times i}}{\frac{2\pi}{C \times (i+1)}} = \frac{i+1}{i} = 1 + \frac{1}{i} \ , \qquad \text{for } i=1,2,\ldots,(N-1). \qquad \text{[using lemma 4]}$$

The RHS of equation (4d), we have-

$$\frac{\sum_{h=i+1}^{N} T_h}{\sum_{h=i+2}^{N} T_h} = \frac{T_{i+1} + \sum_{h=i+2}^{N} T_h}{\sum_{h=i+2}^{N} T_h} = 1 + \frac{T_{i+1}}{\sum_{h=i+2}^{N} T_h} \ , \qquad \text{for } i=1,2,\ldots,(N-1).$$

Both the LHS and RHS are ratios where LHS is $\left(1+\frac{1}{i}\right)$ and RHS is $\left(1+\frac{T_{i+1}}{\sum_{h=i+2}^{N} T_h}\right)$.

Therefore these two terms are approximately equal (LHS≈RHS) when the number of layers in the network is more or network size is large. It implies that with the increase in network size, the performance of the network in terms of energy balancing would be more accurate.

4.1.2   Network Lifetime
As defined in section 2.1, network lifetime is the time till the proportion of dead nodes exceeds a certain threshold, which may result in loss of coverage of a certain region, and/or network partitioning. Further, energy consumption rate per node in layer-i (ER_i) is-

$$ER_i = \frac{ECR_i}{T_i} \qquad \text{for } i=1,2,\ldots,N. \qquad \text{[from equation (4c)]}$$

To achieve energy balancing, the lifetime of a node is same as lifetime of a layer or network lifetime. The lifetime of a node of layer-i is

$$LT_i = \frac{E_{Initial}}{ER_i} q(t) \ .$$

Putting the value of ER_i in the above relation, we have

$$LT_i = \frac{E_{Initial} \times T_i}{ECR_i} q(t) = \frac{E_{Initial} \times T_i}{T_i \, n \, e_t + n \, (e_t + e_r) \sum_{h=i+1}^{N} T_h} q(t) \ . \tag{5}$$

Therefore, the parameters $E_{Initial}$, T_i, $q(t)$, e_t, e_r, n affect the lifetime of a node or layer.

4.2   Quantitative Analysis

The effectiveness of the proposed node deployment scheme, reported in section 3.2 is evaluated through simulation. Moreover all the theoretical claims made through qualitative analysis presented in section 4.1 are justified by simulation results.

4.2.1   Simulation Environment
The simulation is performed using MATLAB (version 7.1). Simulation results of our scheme of node deployment with Archimedes' Spiral (NDAS) are compared with one

of the existing schemes, node distribution with Gaussian distribution (NDGD) [12]. In NDGD, the authors have considered the node density function at point $f(x_i, y_i)$ as-

$$f(x,y) = \frac{1}{2\pi\sigma_x\sigma_y} e^{-\left(\frac{(x-x_i)^2}{2\sigma_x^2} + \frac{(y-y_i)^2}{2\sigma_y^2}\right)},$$

where σ_x and σ_y are the standard deviations for x and y dimensions.

We assume perfect MAC layer issues while considering this work. Extensive simulation has been performed and average results of 2000 independent runs have been taken while plotting the simulation graphs.

4.2.2   Simulation Metric

To evaluate the performance of the scheme NDAS, network lifetime and energy balance as defined in section 2.1 have been considered as performance metrics. We have chosen network coverage as the yard-stick for measuring network lifetime. We define two more parameters namely average energy consumption rate per node and average residual energy of each layer for evaluating the extent of energy balance in the network:

Energy consumption rate per node (ER): It is defined as the energy consumption by a node per unit time. It is evaluated as-

$$ER = \frac{\text{Energy consumption of a layer}}{\text{Number of nodes in the layer}}.$$

Average residual energy per layer (Avg RE per layer): It is defined as the residual energy of a layer after network lifetime ends. It is evaluated as-

$$\text{Avg RE per layer} = \frac{\text{Sum of residual energy of nodes in a layer}}{\text{Number of nodes in the layer}}$$

where residual energy of a node is the energy which remains in the node once the network lifetime terminates.

Table 1. Simulation Parameters

Parameters	Value
Initial Energy (E_{Initial})	10 J
e_{elec}	50 nJ/bit
e_{amp}	10 pJ/bit/m^2
B	3.18
C	0.0016~0.0025
Gaussian standard deviation	$\sigma_x = 57$ and $\sigma_y = 37$
Packet size (n)	100 bits
Network area	550m×550m~750m×750m

The energy balance is achieved in full when the average energy consumption rate per sensor node is the same [6] for all layers in the whole network. We conduct two sets of experiments for the scheme NDAS. While one set of experiment measures energy balancing in the network, the other verifies the enhancement of network lifetime. Further, in the second set of experiment, the NDAS is compared with NDGD. The number of deployed nodes is varied from 1500 to 3000 for both NDAS and NDGD. We have considered communication and sensing ranges of each of node as 20m and 10m respectively. We have considered the time-interval between two successive generation & sending data to the sink as 1 min. We have listed all the other parameters and their corresponding values used in simulation in Table I.

4.2.3   Energy Balancing
In this section energy balancing of the scheme is evaluated in terms of the following two parameters.

4.2.3.1 ER
Figure 4 shows ER for different network sizes.

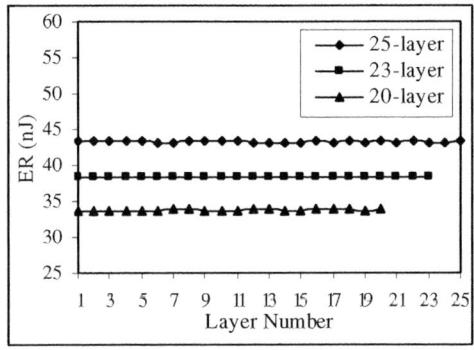

Fig. 4. Energy Consumption Rate per Node for various network sizes

We observe that for NDAS, the ER for a particular network size is constant for all the layers and this rate varies with network sizes. For example, for the 20, 23 and 25-layered network, the ER is 33.7 nJ, 38.3 nJ and 43.2 nJ respectively. These results imply that the ER for NDAS increases with increase in network area. This justifies our claim that NDAS is energy balanced specifically for the networks with 20 or more layers.

4.2.3.2 Avg RE per layer
Figure 5 shows the avg RE per layer when the network lifetime ends. The results are plotted for three different network sizes. For a given network size, average RE for all the layers is nearly equal and it decreases with increase in size of the network. For example, for the 20, 23 and 25-layered network, the avg RE per layer is 31.6 nJ, 27.2 nJ and 22.1 nJ respectively. This is in accordance with our analysis.

4.2.4   Network Lifetime
Network lifetime is evaluated for various network sizes and plotted in Figure 6. The graphs illustrated in Figures 6(a) and 6(b) represent the network lifetime for two different sizes of networks. It is observed that in our scheme the network lifetime is 91.55% (20-layer network) and 79.74% (25-layer network) more than that of NDGD

scheme. Moreover, in NDAS the flat nature of plot ensures that the lifetime terminates in all layers at same time compared to NDGD. This ensures that in NDAS energy is balanced to a greater extent than NDGD.

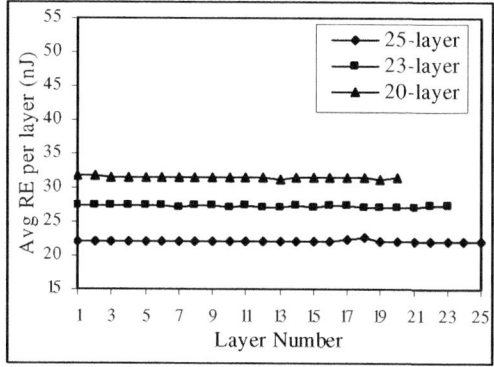

Fig. 5. Average Residual Energy for various network sizes

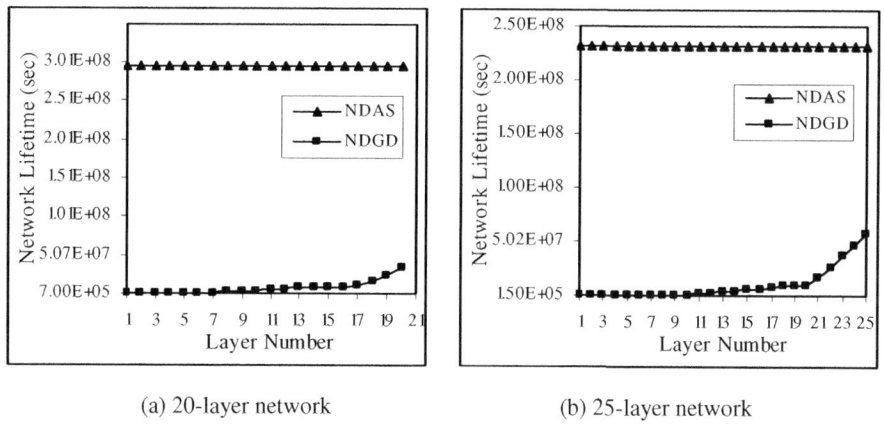

(a) 20-layer network   (b) 25-layer network

Fig. 6. Network Lifetime for various network sizes

5   Conclusion and Future Work

In this paper we have proposed a node deployment strategy in wireless sensor network
using the discrete form of Archimedes' spiral. The deployment strategy is location-
wise pre-determined in nature which is typically used in some application domains
where accurate positioning of nodes is very much essential. We provide theoretical
formulations of coverage, connectivity, energy balancing and network lifetime. Based
on this analytical model we have captured certain constraints to be satisfied involving
various network parameters to achieve the target of energy balancing and increase of
network lifetime. Accordingly we have developed an algorithm to implement such a
node deployment. We claim that the present deployment scheme ensures energy
balancing and thereby increases network lifetime while maintaining coverage and

connectivity. The claim is substantiated by performing qualitative and quantitative analyses. Finally the results of quantitative analysis are compared with a recently published work which establishes the supremacy of our scheme over the existing work.

As a future extension of our work, the deployment strategy may be made more realistic by considering 3-D environment. Moreover, the scheme may be analyzed for further improvement considering various QoS parameters.

References

1. Akyildiz, I.F., Su, W., Sankarasubramaniam, Y., Cyirci, E.: Wireless Sensor Networks: A Survey. IEEE Computer Networks 38(4), 393–422 (2002)
2. Younis, M., Akkaya, K.: Strategies and Techniques for Node Placement in Wireless Sensor Networks: A Survey. Ad Hoc Network 6(4), 621–655 (2008)
3. Li, J., Mohapatra, P.: Analytical Modeling and Mitigation Techniques for the Energy Hole Problem in Sensor Networks. Pervasive and Mobile Computing 3(3), 233–254 (2007)
4. Lian, J., Naik, K., Agnew, G.: Data Capacity Improvement of Wireless Sensor Networks using Non-uniform Sensor Distribution. International Journal of Distributed Sensor Networks 2(2), 121–145 (2006)
5. Cheng, Z., Perillo, M., Heinzelman, W.B.: General Network Lifetime and Cost Models for Evaluating Sensor Network Deployment Strategies. IEEE Transactions on Mobile Computing 7(4), 484–497 (2008)
6. Olariu, S., Stojmenovic, I.: Design Guidelines for Maximizing Lifetime and Avoiding Energy Holes in Sensor Networks with Uniform Distribution and Uniform Reporting. In: Proceeding of IEEE INFOCOM, pp. 1–12 (2006)
7. Wu, X., Chen, G., Das, S.K.: Avoiding Energy Holes in Wireless Sensor Networks with Nonuniform Node Distribution. IEEE Transaction on Parallel and Ditributed Systems 19(5), 710–720 (2008)
8. Liu, Y., Ngan, H., Ni, L.M.: Power-aware Node Deployment in Wireless Sensor Networks. In: Proceedings of IEEE International Conference on Sensor Networks, Ubiquitous, and Trustworthy Computing, vol. 1, pp. 128–135 (2006)
9. Efthymiou, C., Nikoletseas, S., Rolim, J.: Energy Balanced Data Propagation in Wireless Sensor Networks. Wireless Networks 12(6), 691–707 (2006)
10. Luo, J., Hubaux, J.P.: Joint Mobility and Routing for Lifetime Elongation in Wireless Sensor Networks. In: Proceedings of IEEE INFOCOM, pp. 1735–1746 (2005)
11. Ammari, H.M., Das, S.K.: Promoting Heterogeneity, Mobility, and Energy-Aware Voronoi Diagram in Wireless Sensor Networks. IEEE Transactions on Parallel and Distributed Systems 19(7), 995–1008 (2008)
12. Wang, D., Xie, B., Agrawal, D.P.: Coverage and Lifetime Optimization of Wireless Sensor Networks with Gaussian Distribution. IEEE Transactions on Mobile Computing 7(12), 1444–1458 (2008)
13. Liu, M., Myers, T.: Special Plane Curves Archimedes Spiral (May 18, 2005), http://online.redwoods.cc.ca.us/instruct/darnold/CalcProj/sp05/miketim/Archimedes.doc (accessed on May 15, 2010)
14. Halder, S., Ghosal, A., Sur, S., Dan, A., DasBit, S.: A Lifetime Enhancing Node Deployment Strategy in WSN. In: Lee, Y.-h., Kim, T.-h., Fang, W.-c., Ślęzak, D. (eds.) FGIT 2009. LNCS, vol. 5899, pp. 295–307. Springer, Heidelberg (2009)

Bullet-Proof Verification (BPV) Method to Detect Black Hole Attack in Mobile Ad Hoc Networks[*]

Firoz Ahmed, Seokhoon Yoon, and Hoon Oh[**]

School of Electrical Engineering, University of Ulsan,
P.O. Box 18, Ulsan 680-749, South Korea
jewelraaz@yahoo.com, {seokhoonyoon,hoonoh}@ulsan.ac.kr

Abstract. Mobile ad hoc networks are vulnerable to various security attacks due to the fact that a mobile node not only has a freedom of joining or leaving the network but also acts as a router. In this paper, we propose a bullet-proof verification (BPV) method to detect the black hole attack, either single or cooperative, in mobile ad hoc networks. The BPV method consists of two steps: every node first examines suspicious nodes using local neighborhood information and secondly, if a node receives RREP from a suspicious node, it sends an encrypted (bullet-proof) test message to the destination to confirm whether the suspicious node is black hole or not. The two-step approach not only pins down the black hole nodes, but also contributes to reducing control overhead. We prove by resorting to simulation that the BPV can be applied to the AODV without degrading performance notably and also is highly dependable against the black hole attack.

Keywords: Black hole attack, security, mobile ad hoc networks, encryption, AODV.

1 Introduction

Mobile ad hoc networks (hereafter referred to as MANETs) are formed autonomously by a number of mobile nodes without the help of a centralized management entity [1]. Such networks are useful in the battlefields that perform the military operations and the disaster areas that perform the emergency rescue operations [2]. In MANETs, every mobile node (MN) acts as a router that receives data packets or messages from an MN and then forwards them to another MN along a pre-established multi-hop path [3]. Since an MN takes a freedom to join or leave the network, the network topology changes frequently. Such characteristics make it hard to have a centralized security management entity. As a result, MANETs are vulnerable to various kinds of attacks such as

---

[*] This work was supported by the development program of local science park funded by the ULSAN Metropolitan City and the MEST(Ministry of Education, Science and Technology)
[**] Corresponding author.

C.-H. Hsu et al. (Eds.): UIC 2011, LNCS 6905, pp. 435–449, 2011.
© Springer-Verlag Berlin Heidelberg 2011

black hole attack [4], worm hole attack [5], rushing attack [6], gray hole attack [7], flooding attack [8], sinkhole attack [10], byzantine attack [11] and so on. This paper addresses how to efficiently handle the black hole attack.

In ad hoc networks, a node tries to explore a path by flooding the network with an RREQ (route request). While the RREQ is exploring a path, a malicious node responds with an RREP (route reply) including a fake path which is attractive to the source in terms of path selection criteria. Then, the source node sends data packets along the fake path which eventually leads to the malicious node, and the malicious node absorbs data packets. This type of attack is known as a black hole attack. The black hole attacks can be categorized into two types: a single black hole attack and a colluding black hole attack. In the single black hole attack, a malicious node acts alone where the colluding black hole attack involves two or more malicious nodes that collaborate with each other.

The single black hole attack problem has been tackled in a lot of works [4], [12], [13], [14], [15]. In [4], an RREP initiator is required to send next hop information with RREP message to the source node. Upon receiving RREP, the source node floods (the network) with *Further Request* message in search for the next hop of the RREP initiator and checks whether or not it has a route to the destination node as well as the RREP initiator. The source node trusts the RREP and establishes a route if the check result is positive from *Further Reply* message. In [12], an intermediate node that responds with RREP to the source is required to send CREQ (confirmation request) to next hop on the path that the RREP carries. Upon receiving CREP (confirmation reply), the source node compares the path in RREP and the one in CREP to avoid black hole attack. However, these schemes generate a high control overhead due to extra control messages for every RREP. Moreover, they are not appropriate for the colluding attack.

Meanwhile, only a few methods have been proposed to tackle the colluding black hole attack [16], [19]. In [16], every RREP initiator has to issue SREQ (sequence number request) message to destination that has to respond with SREP. Every node monitors the sender and the receiver of SREP to check the fabrication of the SREP. However, this may not always succeed in detecting colluding black hole nodes since the protocol assumes the existence of the third watchdog node that connects in common to the colluding nodes.

In order to address those issues of requiring high control overhead or a watchdog node and also to detect a single and colluding black hole attack effectively, we propose a bullet-proof verification (BPV) method in which it first checks whether the RREP initiator is suspicious or not then it initiates verification process using an encrypted (bullet-proof) test request message only if the RREP initiator is judged to be suspicious. The malicious nodes are not able to spoof the test request message. The BPV can be applied to on-demand routing protocols such as AODV [9] and DSR [18]. In designing the scheme, we take two design principles into account in order to preserve the performance of the original AODV routing protocol. One is that the scheme should not incur a high control overhead. Another is that the scheme should be able to correctly identify the malicious nodes. In BPV, every node collects data routing information from one-hop neighbors by

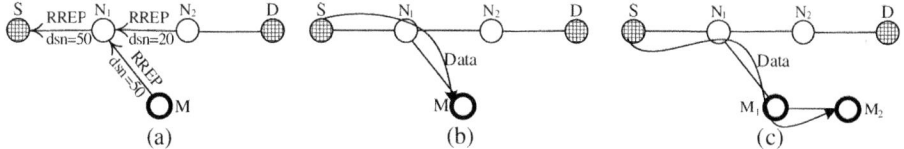

Fig. 1. Examples of single and colluding black hole attacks

overhearing packets and keeps the information in data collection table. Based on the information, a node that receives RREP checks whether the RREP initiator is suspicious or not. Secondly, if the RREP initiator is suspicious, verification process is initiated to detect whether the suspicious node is a black hole or not. The detection node[1] sends an encrypted test message towards destination to prove that the sequence number in the previously received RREP was not faked by any suspicious node. Upon receiving the test reply message from destination, the detection node can identify whether the suspicious node is black hole or not by comparing the destination sequence number in RREP and that in test reply message.

The BPV method produces less overhead since, instead of relying on flooding, it unicasts test message to the destination and it does only when the suspicious node responds with RREP. Furthermore, this proposed method judges the black hole attack correctly since it is impossible for the suspicious node to spoof the test message. Using NS-2 network simulator [20], we conducted performance evaluation when the BPV is applied to AODV. The devastating impact of the black hole attack lies in a drastic reduction in delivery ratio as the number of malicious nodes increases. According to simulation, delivery ratio went down to 0.03 in the presence of five malicious nodes; when BPV is employed, it was around 0.46 in the presence of same number of malicious nodes.

The rest of the paper is organized as follows. In Section 2, we identify the problems of existing methods and outline our method. We present our method formally in Section 3. The evaluation on the effect of BPV is given in Section 4 and is followed by concluding remarks in Section 5.

2   Problem Identification and Overview of Our Approach

The on-demand routing protocols are exposed to the black hole attack of a malicious node: A malicious node consumes the packets destined for some other nodes by having the source establish a fake route. This not only prevents a normal communication, but also may cause the eavesdropping of critical information. For example, in AODV [9][2], a source initiates route discovery by broadcasting

---

[1] If a node receives RREP from a suspicious node, the receiving node is called the detection node.

[2] In this paper, although we only focus on exploits of the destination sequence number to detect black hole node, the BPV can also be applied to DSR by comparing the claimed path in RREP and the actual path taken by TREQ.

RREQ. Upon receiving RREQ, a node rebroadcasts the RREQ if it is neither the destination nor has a fresh route to the destination. A malicious node pretends that it has a fresh and short route to the destination, and then immediately responds with RREP with a large destination sequence number to the source. When the source receives the RREP, it starts sending data packets along the fake route that are consumed by the malicious node. On the other hand, multiple nodes may collude with each other to attack the network. In this case, the black hole problem becomes worse because multiple nodes cooperate to deceive their malicious behaviors.

Let us take some examples. As depicted in Fig.1(a), upon receiving RREQ, the malicious node M replies RREP to N_1 that includes a large destination sequence number ($dsn = 50$). Since M's RREP contains larger dsn than other RREPs, N_1 sets next hop to M in its routing table. Upon receiving data packets, N_1 will forward them to the malicious node M as shown in Fig.1(b). The malicious node M_1 colludes with another malicious node M_2 in Fig.1(c) where M_1 forwards the received packets to M_2 to pretend that it is a normal node.

It is relatively easy to resolve a single black hole attack. However, it is quite challenging to detect colluding black hole attack. The single black hole attack can be resolved by either verifying a data forwarding behavior of a node using watchdog mechanism [13] or by verifying the correctness of the obtained path through the downstream node of the RREP initiator [12]. In the watchdog mechanism [13], every node maintains a buffer to keep the packets after transmitting them, and then it watches out whether the receiving node forwards the packets by overhearing. It deletes the packets if the receiving node behaves correctly according to its role. In the path verification method [12], every RREP initiator is required to send CREQ (confirmation request) to its downstream node that triggers CREP (confirmation reply) to the source node. Upon receiving CREP, the source node compares the path in RREP and the one in CREP to check path validity. However, those schemes do not address colluding attack.

The two-step (judgment and verification) schemes were proposed to detect black hole attack in [17], [19]. In [17], they employ a CTS/RTS value besides the watch dog mechanism in order to increase judgment credibility for a suspicious node. If a certain node has a high CTS/RTS ration (i.e., the number of its receiving packets is much more than that of its transmitting packets), it is more likely to be suspicious. However, this often does not make sense in case that the node is destination and two colluding nodes transmit data packets to each other. In the verification process, they employ a checking method that exploits the reliable neighbors of any suspicious node and uses a limited flooding, causing a lot of overhead. In [16], every RREP initiator is required to issue SREQ (sequence number request) to destination. Upon receiving SREQ, the destination sends SREP (sequence number reply) to the source. In order to detect colluding black hole attack, it requires a third watchdog node that connects simultaneously to a pair of black hole nodes. Note that while the first SREP is moving backward, the change of the sequence number by the black hole node is detected by the node that forwarded the SREP, and the change by the second black hole node is detected by the third watchdog node. However, the third node may not be always available.

In order to tackle the above problems, we propose a bullet-proof verification (BPV) method using a cryptographic mechanism. It consists of two steps: Judgment phase and verification phase. Every node collects the communication behavior of its neighbors and based on the collected information, it judges whether any RREP initiator is suspicious or not. If any node judges that an RREP initiator is suspicious, it initiates verification process by sending an encrypted test request message to destination. Upon receiving the test request message, destination replies with the encrypted test reply message. Then, the node that initiated the verification process can confirm the black hole node by comparing two sequence numbers contained in the RREP and that in the test reply message.

3   Bullet-Proof Verification (BPV) Method

3.1   Identification of Suspicious Nodes

Basically, even though any malicious nodes get into a network, if a node forwards data packets to a reliable node, the network will work safely. The way that a node determines a node's reliability depends on the watchdog method traditionally. Every node observes the communication behaviors of its neighbors by overhearing data packets transmitted by its neighbors. One simple way that decides the reliability of a node is to know whether or not the node has ever sent data packet to any reliable node.

It starts with the fact "I am reliable." A node is said to be *reliable* if it has forwarded data packet(s) to some reliable node. Therefore, if a node has received data packet *from* its neighbor before, the neighbor is *reliable*. A node is said to be *suspicious* if it has never forwarded data packet to any node. So, initially nodes are suspicious to each other. Even though a node has neither received data packet *from* one of its neighbors ever, it cannot say that the neighbor is suspicious, since the neighbor may have forwarded data packet to other reliable node. However, suppose that a node knows that its neighbor has forwarded data packet to some third node, but the node does not know whether the third node is reliable or not. Whenever this situation occurs, if the node initiates any costly inspection algorithm, it may cause too high overhead since those situations occur frequently. The neighbor is said to be *indecisive* for whether it is suspicious or not. In this situation, a node collects further data by inspecting the receiver IDs of the packets transmitted by the indecisive node and judges whether or not the indecisive node can turn to a reliable node based on the data. If the indecisive node received data packets from different nodes (that is, two different sessions are more likely to have the different forwarding paths that share the same indecisive node) and forwarded those packets to different nodes, it may be reliable. This suspicious node needs to be inspected further by some mechanism other than the watchdog mechanism.

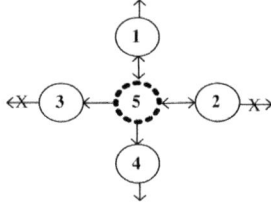

Fig. 2. An example topology to define DCT

Table 1. An example of DCT_5

j	$From_j$	$Through_j$	$Suspicious_j$
1	1	1	0
2	1	0	0
3	0	0	1
4	0	1	indecisive

Each node collects such data by overhearing the packets that its neighbors transmit and maintains a data collection table (DCT) with those data as follows.

$$DCT_i = (j, From_j, Through_j, Suspicious_j), \ j \in i.N,$$

where

- $i.N$ is a set of node i's neighbors;
- $From_j$ indicates whether or not node i has received a packet from node j ever;
- $Through_j$ indicates whether or not node i has routed a packet via node j ever; and
- $Suspicious_j$ indicates whether or not node j is suspicious based on the combination of $From_j$ and $Through_j$ fields.

The values of $From_j$, $Through_j$ and $Suspicious_j$ are given true (1) or false (0).

For an example to show data collection table, we give a small network topology as shown in Fig. 2. Node 5 observes its neighbors 1, 2, 3, and 4 and stores the observed behaviors in its data collection table, DCT_5 as shown in Table 5. For example, node 5 has received data packet from node 1 and node 2 ($From_1 = 1$, $From_2 = 1$), as indicated by the solid arrows. Node 5 can determine that node 1 and node 2 are reliable ($Suspicious_1 = 0$, $Suspicious_2 = 0$). On the other hand, node 5 did not receive any data from node 3 and node 4 and node 3 did not forward my data packet to anyone. Thus node 3 is

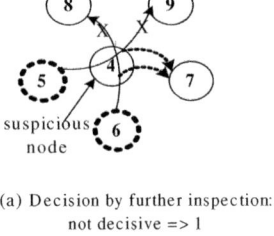

(a) Decision by further inspection: not decisive => 1

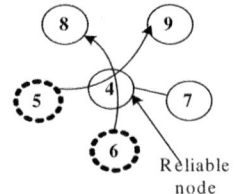

(b) Decision by further inspection: not decisive => 0

Fig. 3. Further inspection

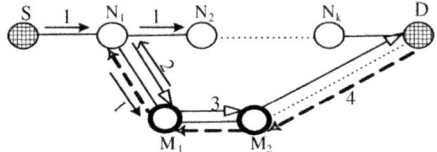

Fig. 4. Bullet-Proof Verification (BPV) process 1. N_1 broadcasts RREQ 2. M_1 responds with the fake RREP 3. N_1 thinks that M_1 is suspicious and sends the encrypted TREQ along the path specified in RREP 4. D receives the TREQ and responds with the encrypted TREP. N_1 judges the reliability of M_1.

determined to be suspicious ($Suspicious_3 = 1$). Although node 5 has routed data packet through node 4, whether node 4 is suspicious or not is indecisive because node 4 may have forwarded to another colluding malicious node. In consequence, further inspection has to be carried out.

Fig. 3 illustrates further inspection and decision mechanism for the indecisive node. According to Fig. 2, node 5 determines that node 4 is an indecisive node. In Fig. 3(a), node 4 received data packets from two different nodes and forwarded to the identical node 7. Thus, the node 4 is determined to be suspicious.[3] On the other hand, Fig. 3(b) shows the opposite case where node 4 is determined to be reliable.

3.2   Bullet-Proof Verification (BPV) Process

Upon receiving RREP from a reliable node, a source starts sending data packets and an intermediate node forwards RREP toward the source as in AODV [9]. If a node receives RREP from a suspicious node, it initiates bullet-proof verification (BPV) process to verify the suspicious node.

Upon receiving an RREP from a suspicious node, it (as detection node) extracts destination sequence number from the RREP and stores it in its cache, and then it generates a test request message, TREQ = (*detection node address, destination node address, timestamp*)where the *timestamp* indicates a current time. The detection node encrypts TREQ using public key cryptosystem, being a bullet-proof message and sends it along the path specified in the RREP towards destination. A node that receives the TREQ relays it to next node. If the destination receives the TREQ, it decrypts the message and creates a test reply message, TREP = (*detection node address, destination node address, timestamp, dsn*) where the *dsn* indicates a destination sequence number. The destination encrypts the TREP and sends it along the reverse path to the detection node. Upon receiving the TREP, the detection node decrypts it. If the detection node finds that the *dsn* in TREP is smaller than that in RREP, it judges the suspicious node as a black hole node and drops the RREP. If the suspicious node is determined to be a reliable node, the detection node forwards the RREP toward the source node.

---

[3] If node 4 is determined to be black hole node in BPV process, node 4 and node 7 must be colluding black hole node.

Fig.4. illustrates a bullet proof verification process. When a suspicious node M_1 responds with RREP, detection node N_1 sends the encrypted TREQ to destination D along the path specified in RREP. When D receives the TREQ, it responds with the encrypted TREP towards N_1. M_1 and M_2 cannot alter the key contents of the encrypted TREP.

3.3   Dropping TREQ or TREP

If the TREQ message is not delivered to destination, the BPV algorithm fails to detect the malicious node(s). Thus, we employ the well known watchdog mechanism to watch the behavior of the suspicious node. When detection node sends TREQ to the suspicious node, it watches whether or not the suspicious node forwards the TREQ to its downstream node. In our approach, if any node that receives TREQ finds its downstream link broken, it is required to send TERR (Test Error) to the detection node. Thus, if the detection node neither watches the suspicious node forward TREQ nor receives TERR from the suspicious node, the detection node determines the suspicious node to be a black hole node.

Meanwhile, the above approach cannot detect a black hole node in case of a colluding black hole attack since the suspicious node will always send TREQ to its downstream node which may cooperate with it. In this case, we rely on a timer to detect a black hole node. The detection node sets a timer as soon as it watches the suspicious node forward the TREQ to its downstream node. The detection node determines that the suspicious node is a black hole node if it does not receive the TREP until its timer expires. Similarly, the timer can handle the dropping of TREP.

Referring to Fig. 5-(a), node 1 determines the node 2 is a black hole node since node 2 does not forward TREQ to node 3. In Fig. 5-(b), node 1 determines node 2 is a black hole node by the expired timer. However, in Fig. 5-(c) node 1 does not determine node 2 is a black hole node since node 3 issues TERR to node 1.

3.4   Encryption and Decryption

We assume that every node has a pair of public and private keys that are used in the RSA public key cryptosystem [21]. The public key of each node can be

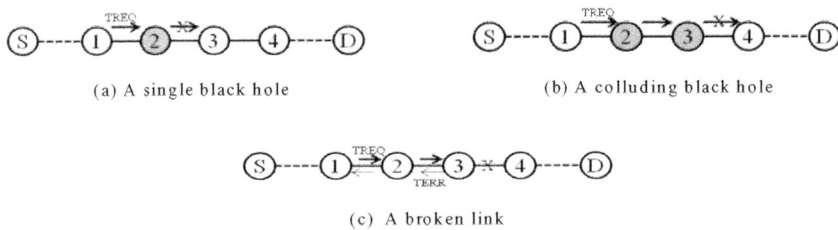

(a) A single black hole   (b) A colluding black hole

(c) A broken link

Fig. 5. Detection of black hole nodes

Table 2. Notations

Notations	Meaning
K_s+	Public key of node s
K_s-	Private key of node s
IP_s	IP address of node s
$[d]K_s+$	Message d encrypted with node s's public key, K_s+
$[d]K_s-$	Message d digitally signed with node s's private key, K_s-
$s \longrightarrow M[d]$	Node s sends a message d to node M

distributed once when it joins a considered network. The newly joined node can get the public keys of the other nodes in the network from one of its neighbors. The notations used in the cryptosystem are summarized in Table 2.

3.5 Control Flow of TREQ and TREP Message

In this section, we describe how TREQ and TREP message flow during the bullet-proof verification (BPV) process.

If a node receives an RREP from a suspicious node, it (or detection node) extracts destination sequence number and stores it in its cache. The detection node creates TREQ and it signs the whole TREQ with its own private key. Now, the detection node forwards the TREQ along the forward path towards destination. The receiving node validates and removes of previous node's signature in the TREQ and checks whether it is the destination or not by checking the destination IP address. If it is not the destination, it takes the same process again. The process continues until the TREQ reaches the intended destination.

Given a forward path $= (N_1, N_2, ..., N_{l-1}, N_l)$ where N_1 and N_l represent *detection node* and *destination node*, respectively, the behavior of each node on the path can be described formally as follows.

$$N_i \longrightarrow N_{i+1}:[IP_{N_1}, IP_{N_l}, timestamp]K_{N_i}-, (1 \leq i \leq l-1)$$

Upon receiving TREQ, the destination node creates TREP packet in which the current *dsn* are encrypted with the public key of detection node. Now, the destination node forwards the TREP along the reverse path after it signs the whole TREP with its own private key. The receiving node validates and removes of previous node's signature in the TREP and checks whether it is detection node or not by checking the IP address of detection node. If it is not the detection node, it takes the same process again. The process continues until the TREP reaches the initiator of TREQ (or the detection node). The behavior of each node can be described formally as follows.

$$N_{l-i} \longrightarrow N_{l-i-1}:[[dsn]K_{N_1}+, IP_{N_l}, IP_{N_1}, timestamp]K_{N_{l-i}}-, (0 \leq i \leq l-1)$$

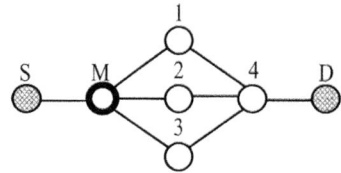

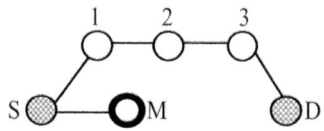

Fig. 7. An example network that blocks the forwarding of a normal packet

Fig. 6. An example network that hinders the flooding of RREQ

4   Performance Evaluation

4.1   Control Overhead Analysis

In this section, we analyze BPV and AODV comparatively in the viewpoint of control overhead. We consider the four cases.

- *AODV w/ BH* when the AODV is used in the network with a black hole node.
- *AODV w/o BH* when the AODV is used in the network without a black hole node.
- *BPV w/ BH* when the BPV is used in the network with a black hole node.
- *BPV w/o BH* when the BPV is used in the network without a black hole node.

We use a notation *OH(A)* to denote control overhead in the scenario A. For example, *OH(AODV w/ BH)* indicates overhead when AODV is used in the network with a black hole node.

OH(AODV w/ BH) < OH(AODV w/o BH) and *OH(BPV w/ BH) < OH(BPV w/o BH)*. Since the presence of a black hole node often hinders the normal operation of the protocol, the protocol in the network with a black hole node generates less overhead than that in the network without a black hole node. Consider the example network in Fig.6 the RREQ issued by the source *S* will never go beyond the malicious node. Similarly the node *M* in Fig.7 will not forward the RREQ.

OH(AODV w/ BH) < OH(BPV w/ BH). Furthermore, BPV will generate much more overhead than AODV in the presence of a black hole node due to the same reason above. Take an example in Fig.6; RREQ will not go beyond the *M* with both AODV and BPV. However, TREQ and TREP with BPV will go through the *M*. In Fig.7, the source *S* will get the fake path with AODV without further initiating a path discovery. However, BPV will detect the malicious node *M* and will choose the other path $(S, 1, 2, 3, D)$. This normal path can trigger a new path discovery at the failure of any link on the path, thereby increasing control overhead.

OH(BPV w/ BH) < OH(AODV w/o BH). In this case, even though BPV uses some additional control messages such as TREQ, TREP and TERR, the

Table 3. Simulation parameters

Parameter	Values
Simulator	NS-2.34
Mobility model	Random waypoint
Traffic	CBR
Transmission range	250m
Number of nodes	50
Terrain range	$1000 * 1000 \ m^2$
Maximum speeds	1, 5, 10, 15, 20 m/s
Pause times	0, 30, 60, 120, 300s
Number of sessions	20
Simulation time	300s
Packet size	512 bytes
Packet rate	4 packets/s
Number of malicious nodes	1, 2, 3, 4, 5

BPV in the network with a black hole node will generate less overhead than the AODV in the network without a black hole node. The reason can be explained as follows. The BPV uses TREQ, TREP and TERR to detect a black hole node, increasing overhead; however since both control messages are unicast, the increase in overhead is not that serious. While the black hole node may limit the flooding of the RREQ partially, with the AODV in the network without a black hole node, the source will flood the network with the RREQ without any hindrance. Note that the increase of overhead by flooding is dominant over that of overhead by the unicast of both TREQ, TREP and TERR.

According to the analysis so far, it generally holds that $OH(AODV \ w/ \ BH)$ $< OH(BPV \ w/ \ BH) < OH(AODV \ w/o \ BH) < OH(BPV \ w/o \ BH.)$ In consequence, we can say that the presence of a black hole node not only degrades delivery ratio, but also it lowers control overhead.

4.2   Simulation Environment

The NS-2 [20] simulator with CMU extension was used to evaluate BPV against standard AODV and AODV with malicious nodes. In order to compare the performance all protocols were run under various mobilities and traffic scenarios. The terrain size was $1000 * 1000 \ m^2$ where 50 nodes were deployed randomly. The simulation was run for 300 seconds.

The IEEE 802.11 with a physical layer data rate of 2Mbps was used for the medium access control. Pairs of source and destination were randomly chosen and mobile nodes use random waypoint model. Each simulation was performed five times and then the average value for each metric was presented. The used simulation parameters are given in Table 3.

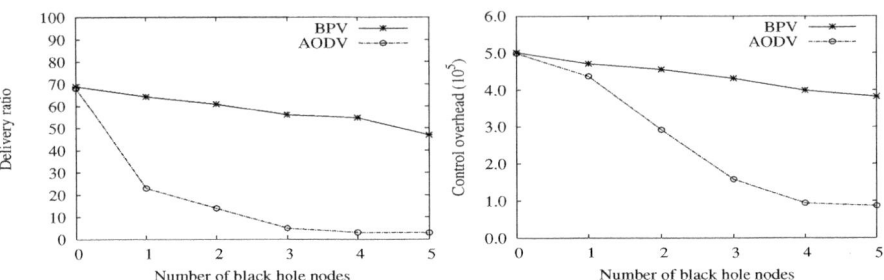

Fig. 8. Delivery ratio versus Number of black hole nodes

Fig. 9. Control overhead versus Number of black hole nodes

4.3 Simulation and Discussion

To evaluate the performance of BPV, we used the following two metrics, packet delivery ratio and control overhead.

$$\text{Delivery Ratio} = \frac{nPacketReceived(i.d)}{nPacketSent(i.s)}, \tag{1}$$

where $nPacketReceived$ $(i.d)$ and $nPacketSent$ $(i.s)$ are the number of packets received at destination d and sent at source s for session i, respectively.

$$\text{Control Overhead} = \sum_{m \in M} \# \text{ of } m\text{'s transmitted} * \text{size of } m, \tag{2}$$

where $M = \{$RREQ, RREP, RERR, TREQ, TREP, TERR$\}$ and # of m's transmitted includes the messages initiated or relayed by the nodes in the network.

Fig.8 shows the delivery ratio of packets by varying the number of malicious nodes from 0 to 5 and setting the pause time to 30s. The delivery ratio of both methods performs well in case of no black hole nodes. The delivery ratio of AODV dramatically drops in the presence of one black hole node and it becomes worse as the number of black hole nodes increases while BPV shows a very stable outcome. On the contrary to our expectation, Fig.9 shows that the control overhead of AODV sharply decreases as the number of malicious nodes increases while that of BPV is not sensitive to the number of black hole nodes. The reason was given in section 4.1.

Fig.10 shows the data delivery ratio of packets by varying maximum speeds as 1, 5, 10, 15 and 20 m/s. We analyze and compare BPV and AODV with and without black hole node. As shown in Fig.10, the delivery ratio of BPV and AODV perform well with no malicious node and slightly decreases as the node mobility increases. With one black hole node and max speed of 20 m/s, the packet delivery ratio of BPV is more than 54 percent while AODV is about 25 percent. This result supports that BPV works efficiently. Fig.11 shows that $OH(AODV\ w/\ BH) < OH(BPV\ w/\ BH)$ and also shows $OH(BPV\ w/\ BH) < OH(AODV\ w/o\ BH)$ as explained in section 4.1.

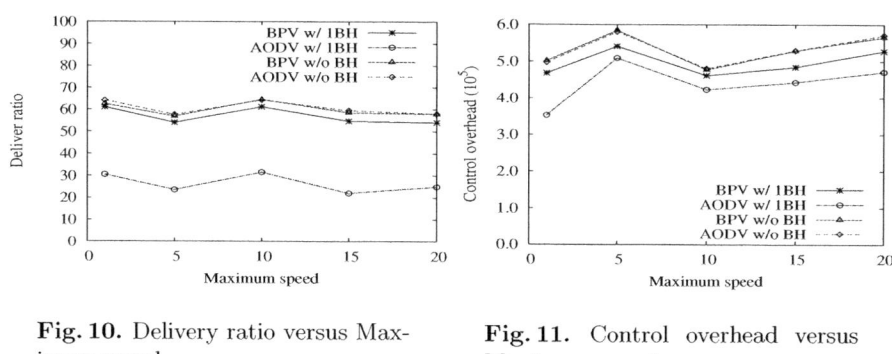

Fig. 10. Delivery ratio versus Maximum speed

Fig. 11. Control overhead versus Maximum speed

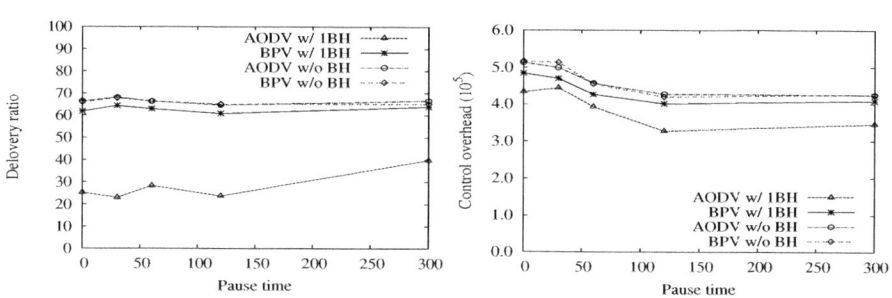

Fig. 12. Delivery ratio versus Pause time

Fig. 13. Control overhead versus Pause time

Fig.12 shows the data delivery ratio of packets by varying the pause times as 0, 30, 60, 120 and 300s. With one black hole node, the delivery ratio of BPV is better than AODV due to the black hole detection mechanism. In the presence of one malicious node, the delivery ratio of AODV becomes worse because malicious node consumes data continuously. On the other hand, the delivery ratio of BPV is well sustained high to almost the same level as that of AODV without a black hole node. Fig.13 shows that $OH(AODV\ w/\ BH) < OH(BPV\ w/\ BH)$, $OH(AODV\ w/o\ BH) < OH(BPV\ w/o\ BH.$, however, it also shows $OH(BPV\ w/\ BH) < OH(AODV\ w/o\ BH)$ as discussed in section 4.1.

5 Concluding Remarks

In this paper, we have proposed an efficient bullet proof verification (BPV) method that resolves a single or cooperative black hole attack in mobile ad hoc networks. The BPV effectively pins down a black hole node by taking two-step black hole detection method using a cryptographic mechanism. It initiates verification process only if it identifies a suspicious node. It does not use flooding to detect black hole node; it unicasts an encrypted (bullet-proof) test message directly to the destination along the established path. In future, we will extend our algorithm to isolate the black hole node from the network and also solve a selective forwarding attack such as gray hole attack.

References

1. Ilyas, M.: The Handbook of Ad Hoc Networks. CRC PRESS, Boca Raton (2002)
2. Leiner, B.M., Ruth, R.J., Sastry, A.R.: Goals and challenges of the DARPA GloMo program. IEEE Personal Communications 3, 34–43 (1996)
3. Siva Ram Murthy, C., Manoj, B.S.: Ad hoc Wireless Networks-Architectures and Protocols. Pearson Education, London (2007)
4. Deng, H., Li, W., Agarwal, D.P.: Routing security in ad hoc networks. IEEE Communications Magazine 40, 70–75 (2002)
5. Hu, Y., Perrig, A., Johnson, D.: Packet Leashes: A Defense against Wormhole Attacks in Wireless Ad Hoc Networks. In: Proc. of IEEE INFOCOM (2002)
6. Hu, Y.-C., Perrig, A., Johnson, D.B.: Rushing Attacks and Defense in Wireless Ad Hoc Network Routing Protocols. In: Proc. of ACM WiSe (2003)
7. Yu, W., Sun, Y., Liu, K.R.: HADOF: Defense Against Routing Disruptions in Mobile Ad Hoc Networks. In: Proc. of the 24th IEEE INFOCOM, Miami, USA (2005)
8. Desilva, S., Boppana, R.V.: Mitigating Malicious Control Packet Floods in Ad Hoc Networks. In: Proc. of IEEE WCNC 2005, pp. 2112–2117 (2005)
9. Perkins, C.E., Royer, E.M., Das, S.: Ad-hoc On demand Distance Vector (AODV) Routing. In: RFC, p. 3561 (2003)
10. Kim, G., Han, Y., Kim, S.: A cooperative-sinkhole detection method for mobile ad hoc networks. AEU-International Journal of Electronics and Communications 64, 390–397 (2010)
11. Awerbuch, B., Holmer, D., Nita-Rotaru, C., Rubens, H.: An on-demand secure routing protocol resilient to byzantine failures. In: ACM Workshop on Wireless Security, WiSe (2002)
12. Lee, S., Han, B., Shin, M.: Robust Routing in Wireless Ad Hoc Networks. In: International Conference on Parallel Processing Workshops, pp. 73–78 (2002)
13. Marti, S., Giuli, T., Lai, K., Baker, M.: Mitigating routing misbehavior in mobile ad hoc networks. In: Proc. of the Sixth Annual Intl. Conference on Mobile Computing and Networking (MOBICOM), pp. 255–265 (2000)
14. Kurosawa, S., Nakayama, H., Kato, N., Jamalipour, A., Nemoto, Y.: Detecting blackhole attack on AODV-based mobile ad hoc networks by Dynamic Learning Method. International Journal of Network Security 5, 338–346 (2007)
15. Al-Shurman, M., Yoo, S.-M., Park, S.: Black hole attack in mobile ad-hoc networks. In: Proceedings of the 42nd Annual Southeast Regional Conference, ACM-SE, pp. 96–97 (2004)
16. Zhang, X., Sekiya, Y., Wakahara, Y.: Proposal of a method to detect black hole attack in MANET. In: International Symposium on Autonomous Decentralized Systems, pp. 1–6 (2009)

17. Yu, C.W., Wu, T.-K., Cheng, R.-H., Yu, K.-M., Chang, S.C.: A Distributed and Cooperative Algorithm for the Detection and Elimination of Multiple Black Hole Nodes in Ad Hoc Networks. IEICE Transactions on Communications E92.B, 483–490 (2009)
18. Johnson David, B., Maltz David, A.: Dynamic source routing in ad hoc wireless networks. Mobile Computing 353, 153–181 (1996)
19. Sanjay, R., Huirong, F., Sreekantaradhya, et al.: Prevention of cooperative black hole attack in wireless ad hoc networks. In: ICWN, pp. 570–575 (2003)
20. ns-2, http://www.isi.edu/nsnam/ns/
21. Stallings, W.: Cryptography and Network Security Principles and Practices, 4th edn. Prentice Hall, Englewood Cliffs (2005)

The Coverage Problem in Directional Sensor Networks with Rotatable Sensors

Yin-Chung Hsu, Yen-Ting Chen, and Chiu-Kuo Liang

Department of Computer Science and Information Engineering
Chung Hua University, Hsinchu, Taiwan 30012, Republic of China
ckliang@chu.edu.tw

Abstract. Directional sensor network is composed of many directional sensor nodes. Unlike conventional omni-directional sensors that always have an omni-angle of sensing range, directional sensors may have a limited angle of sensing range due to technical constraints or cost considerations. Therefore, it is possible that when directional sensor nodes are randomly scattered in the environment, some interested targets cannot be covered due to the limited angle of sensing direction even if the targets are located in the sensing range of sensors. We propose a Maximum Coverage with Rotatable Sensors (MCRS) problem in which coverage in terms of the number of targets to be covered is maximized whereas the angle's degrees to be rotated are minimized. We present two centralized greedy algorithm solutions for the MCRS problem. Simulation results are presented to apply angle adjustment algorithm to enhance the coverage of the directional sensor network.

Keywords: Directional Sensor Networks, Coverage, Rotatable Sensors, Centralized Greedy Algorithm.

1 Introduction

In recent years, wireless sensor networks have received a lot of attention due to their wide applications in military and civilian operations, such as environmental monitoring [1], [2], battlefield surveillance [3], health care [4], [5] and volcanoes monitoring. In wireless sensor networks, target coverage is a fundamental problem and has been studied by many researchers. Most of the past work is always based on the assumption of omni-directional sensors that has an omni-angle of sensing range. However, there are many kinds of directional sensors, such as video sensors [6], ultrasonic sensors [7] and infrared sensors [5]. The omni-directional sensor node has a circular disk of sensing range. The directional sensor node has smaller sensing area (sector-like area) and sensing angle than the omni-directional one.

There are several ways to extend the sensing capabilities of sensor nodes. One way is to put several directional sensors of the same kind on one sensor node, each of which faces to a different direction. One example using this way is in [7], where four pairs of ultrasonic sensors are equipped on a single node to detect ultrasonic signals from any directions. Another way is to place the sensor node onto a mobile device so that the node can move around. The third way is to equip the sensor node with a

C.-H. Hsu et al. (Eds.): UIC 2011, LNCS 6905, pp. 450–462, 2011.

device that enables the sensor node to rotate to different directions. In this study, we adopt the third way to make our sensor nodes to face in different directions.

For simplicity, we consider the following assumptions and notations in this paper. In the directional sensor model, the sensing region of a directional sensor is a sector-like area of the sensing disk centered at the sensor with a sensing radius. When the sensors are randomly deployed, each sensor initially faces to a randomly selected direction. Each sensor node equips with exactly one sensor. Thus, we do not distinguish the terms sensor and node in the rest of the paper. Furthermore, some interested targets with known locations are deployed in the region. When a target is both located in the direction and the sensing region of a sensor, we say that the sensor covers the target.

In directional sensor networks, how to monitor or cover the interested targets is a challenging problem. This is because that a directional sensor has a smaller angle of sensor range than an omni-directional sensor or may not even cover any target when it is deployed. Therefore, we are interested in improving the coverage of targets for a randomly deployed directional sensor network. Such problem is called the coverage problem in directional sensor network. In general, the goal of the coverage problem is to achieve the best coverage for interested targets.

In order to improve the coverage of targets for a randomly deployed directional sensor network, we assume that each sensor is equipped with a device that enables the sensor to rotate with some degrees to face on different sensing directions. Therefore, we are interested in finding a way for each sensor to rotate with some degrees to cover more targets than it is initially deployed. Since sensor nodes are randomly scattered in the environment replacing or charging battery is very difficult. Therefore, power saving is an important issue in sensor network. In this paper, we are asked to develop a method that can maximize the coverage in term of the number of targets to be covered whereas the total rotated degrees are minimized. The problem is called the Maximum Coverage with Rotatable Sensors (MCRS) problem. We present two centralized angle adjustment algorithms, namely the Maximal Rotatable Angles (MRA) scheme and the Maximum Coverage First (MCF) scheme, for the MCRS problem. Simulation results are also presented to show the performance of our proposed angle adjustment algorithms.

The rest of the paper is organized as follows: Section 2 introduces some related literatures dealing with directional sensor networks. In Section 3, the MCRS problem is formally defined and some notations and assumptions are also introduced. In Section 4, our proposed angle adjustment algorithms are presented. In Section 5, some simulation results are presented for showing the performance of our proposed algorithms. Finally, some concluding remarks are given in Section 6.

2 Related Works

The coverage rate of sensor network represents the quality of monitoring. According to monitoring objectives, there are many different coverage models that have been discussed both in omni-directional sensor networks and directional sensor networks. Some researchers study that the area coverage depends on whether the region is covered by sensor nodes, and some studies take into account the strength of regional coverage and network connectivity in omni-directional sensor networks.

The target coverage problem in omni-directional sensor networks is one of the most important issues that have been widely discussed. When a set of target nodes are scattered in an environment, the authors in [8] assumed that each sensor can only cover one target at a time, and built a coverage time table to maximize the network lifetime. The authors in [9], [10] present methods to organize all sensors into subsets that are activated successively to extend the network lifetime.

In recent years, the coverage problem in directional sensor networks has attracted considerable attention. The authors in [11] presented a directional sensor model in which each sensor is fixed to one direction, and analyzed the coverage rate and connectivity problem for the directional sensor networks. Besides that, the directional sensor model that allows each sensor to work in several directions is provided in [12], [13]. Cai et al. proved the problem of finding a cover set named Directional Cover Set problem (DCS) is NP-Complete [14]. In [15] and [16], the authors proposed the centralized and the distributed algorithms independently to use the method of considering the weight of targets so that each sensor can decide a better orientation for reaching the higher coverage rate.

The aforementioned directional sensor network is focused on deciding the sensing orientation from the available orientations of each sensor. However, some directional sensors, like the video sensors [17], [18], [19] and multimedia sensors [20], [21], the rotatable sensing capability is needed. In [17], the authors first introduced the rotatable directional sensing model in which the Sensing Connected Sub-Graph (SCSG) is used to divide a directional sensor network into several sub-graph in distributed way, and model each sensing connected sub-graph as a multi-layered convex hull to enhancing coverage by adjusting the sensing direction of directional sensor to minimize the overlapping sensing area of directional sensors. In [18], the authors presented a potential field based coverage-enhancing algorithm (PFCEA) to eliminate the overlapping regions and coverage holes between sensors.

Zhao et al. proposed a Virtual Potential Field based Coverage Algorithm For Directional Networks (VPFCAFDN) which utilized the virtual repulsive forces by neighboring sensors and virtual attractive forces by uncovered regions of the probable sense regions, so that coverage holes can be eliminated quickly [19]. They also presented Electrostatic Field-based Coverage-Enhancing Algorithm (EFCEA) to build virtual field and grid in the sensing region of sensor. They used the repulsive force between any two neighboring sensors, and calculated the resultant force by the repulsive force with each neighbor sensor, so that sensors can rotated its direction to enhanced the coverage of networks and shut off redundant sensors [20]. They are also presented the third research Virtual Centripetal Force-based Coverage-Enhancing Algorithm (VCFCEA), which used centripetal force replace repulsive force in EFCEA, and more enhance the coverage of networks in [21].

In this paper, we utilize the rotatable directional sensing model of sensor to enhance the target coverage and minimize the rotation angles.

3   Rotatable Sensors for Coverage Problem

In this section, we are going to present some notations, assumptions and definitions for the MCRA problem.

3.1 Rotatable Directional Sensing Model

The sensing model of a directional sensor s can be described as follows and shown as in Fig. 1: (x, y) is the location of the sensor node s, r is the sensing radius, D is a unit vector which cuts the sensing sector into half, and α is the offset angle of the field of view on both side of D. Note that we use the unit vector D to indicate the direction of sensor s. Furthermore, a target t is said to be covered by a sensor s if and only if the following conditions are satisfied:

$$\left\| \overrightarrow{st} \right\| \leq r \tag{1}$$

$$\overrightarrow{st} \cdot \overrightarrow{D} \geq \left\| \overrightarrow{st} \right\| \cos \alpha \tag{2}$$

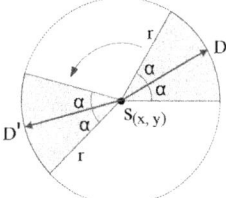

Fig. 1. The directional sensing model

3.2 Problem Definition

As we know that, in a directional sensor network, sensor nodes cannot monitor the target node even if it is within its sensing radius. Fig. 2 presents an example to demonstrate the situation. In Fig. 2(a), there are three targets, say t_1, t_2 and t_3, located within the sensing radius of sensor s. Suppose that, after sensor s is deployed with the original direction D, the sensor s can cover only targets t_1 and t_2. As shown in Fig. 2(b), sensor s can rotate its direction clockwise with some degrees to D' in which target t_3 can be covered.

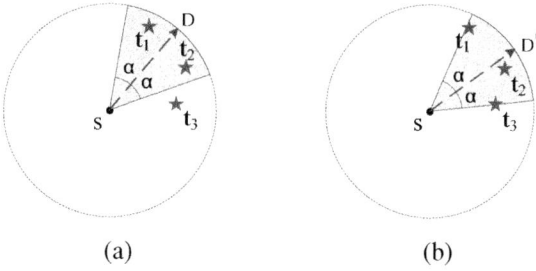

(a)   (b)

Fig. 2. An example for a directional sensor to cover more targets by rotating its direction

Therefore, in this paper, we aim to rotate the angle of the sensing direction of the sensor node to cover as many targets as possible. By doing so, the overall target coverage rate will be increased. In addition, in order to save energy, our goal is to maximize the target coverage rate while minimizing the total rotating angle degrees.

4   Solutions to MCRS Problem

In this section, we propose two different greedy algorithms to solve the MCRS (Maximum Coverage with Rotatable Sensors) problem, that allow directional sensor to rotate its angle in order to cover as many targets as possible which results in higher target coverage rate. In Section 5, we compare the experimental result in term of coverage rate of our algorithms where the directions are rotatable, against those methods in [16] where the directions are not rotatable.

Section 4.1 describes the detailed solutions for Maximal Rotatable Angle (MRA) scheme. The Maximum Coverage First (MCF) scheme is shown in Section 4.2.

4.1   Maximal Rotatable Angle algorithm

In this section, we propose a greedy algorithm, called the Maximal Rotatable Angle (MRA) algorithm, which is based on the maximal rotatable angle policy. The idea of maximal rotatable angle policy is that once a sensor was deployed, the sensor could rotate its direction in order to cover more targets. However, we do not hope the situation that one target (not within the original direction) can be covered by rotating the direction with some degrees and the other target within the original direction will be no longer covered due to the rotation has been done. Therefore, our strategy is to keep the targets in the original direction still in the final direction after the rotation. Fig. 3 shows the situation. In Fig. 3(a), the original direction of sensor s can cover two targets t_1 and t_3. As we can see in Fig. 3(b), since we need to keep targets t_1 and t_3 in the final coverage, the rotation angle will be β_1 and β_2, where β_1 and β_2 are the maximal angles of sensor s to rotate clockwise and counterclockwise, respectively.

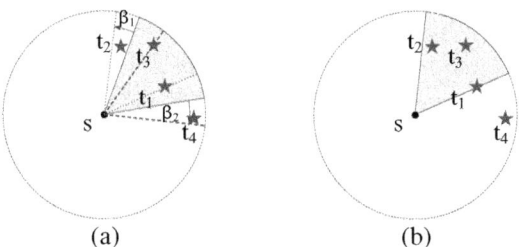

(a)   (b)

Fig. 3. The rotations of MRA policy

The process of our MRA scheme is to apply the MRA policy on every sensor to rotate effectively to cover more targets. Therefore, the order of the chosen sensors to apply the MRA policy may result in different performance in term of the target coverage rate.

Generally speaking, our proposed MRA scheme consists of three major steps: compute the priority of each sensor, choose the sensor with highest priority, and apply the MRA policy on the chosen sensor to rotate. After a sensor has been rotated, the priorities of remaining sensors will be re-calculated and the whole process will be repeated again for the remaining sensors until there is no remaining sensor. In order to calculate the priority of each sensor, some notations are introduced as in the following section.

In order to cover as many targets as possible, we need to identify, for a target t, the number of un-rotated sensors that can cover target t by rotating their directions with some degrees. This number is called the MCN (Maximally be Covered Number) value of a target t [16], which is denoted as MCN(t). We can use the MCN value as the weight of a target to lead us to get a better way for covering more targets. Fig. 4 shows an example. In Fig. 4, there are three sensor nodes, namely s_1, s_2 and s_3, and four targets, namely t_1, t_2, t_3 and t_4, respectively. As shown in Fig. 4(a), the MCN value for t_1 is 3, which means that t_1 can be covered by three sensors. Therefore, the MCN values for t_2, t_3 and t_4 are 2, 1, and 1, respectively. Note that in our greedy algorithm, once a sensor node has rotated its direction, the MCN values will be updated to indicate the latest status of targets. For example, when the sensor node s_3 rotated its direction with some degrees to cover target t_4, it cannot cover the targets t_1 and t_2 at the same time, as shown in Fig. 4(b). Therefore, the MCN values of t_1 and t_2 will be updated as 2 and 1, respectively. With the MCN value for each target, we can then define the target weight as follows to indicate the priority of a target. It can be seen that when a target has a lower MCN value, it implies that the target node can be covered by fewer sensor nodes. Therefore, the target would have higher priority to be covered by a sensor. We use the idea to define the priorities of sensors to be chosen for rotating angles.

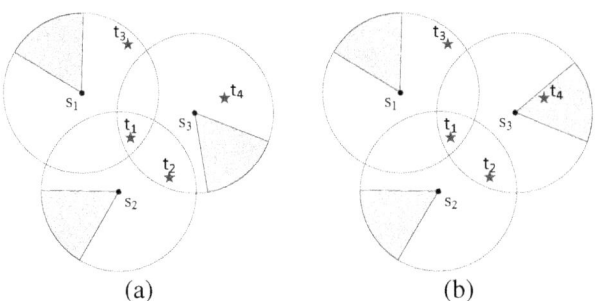

Fig. 4. An example for MCN

Definition 1. Let t be a target and $w(t)$ be the target weight of t. Then, $w(t) = \text{MCN}(t)$.

Definition 2. Let D be a unit vector of a sensor s and $W(D)$ be the direction weight of D. Then, $W(D) = \Sigma\ w(t)$, for all target t located inside the direction D of sensor s. If there is no target located inside direction D, then $W(D) = 0$.

Definition 3. Let D be a unit vector of a sensor s and $P(s)$ be the priority value of s. Then, $P(s) = W(D) / k$, where $W(D)$ is the direction weight of D and k is the number of targets located inside the direction D of sensor s. If there is no target located inside direction D of sensor s, then $P(s) = 0$.

In the following, we briefly present our MRA scheme to increase the target coverage rate.

Algorithm: Maximal Rotatable Angle scheme

Step 0: Let $S = \{s_1, s_2, ..., s_n\}$ denote a set of n sensors that are deployed for covering a set of m targets, denoted as $T = \{t_1, t_2, ..., t_m\}$. Initially, mark all sensors as un-rotated and all targets as un-covered.
Step 1: For each un-rotated sensor $s \in S$, compute the priority value $P(s)$ based on the un-covered targets.
Step 2: Choose the sensor, say s, with the lowest value of $P(s_i)$, where $i = 1, 2, ..., n$.
Step 3: Apply the MRA (Maximal Rotatable Angle) policy on sensor s for rotation.
Step 4: After sensor s is rotated, mark sensor s as rotated and the targets covered by s as covered.
Step 5: If there are un-rotated sensors in S, go to Step 1; Otherwise, algorithm stops.

Here, we demonstrate an example for our proposed MRA algorithm. In Fig. 5, there are three sensors, namely s_1, s_2 and s_3. Initially, s_1 covers no targets, s_2 covers targets t_2 and t_3, and s_3 covers targets t_1, t_4 and t_{10}. Thus, the priority values of s_1, s_2 and s_3 are 0, 5/2, and 4/3, respectively. We can find that s_1 has the highest priority since it has the smallest priority value. Therefore, we first rotate sensor s_1 to cover more targets. It should be noticed that, in this case, sensor s_1 covers no targets in the very beginning, it will rotate its direction until reach the first target, for example is this case t_5. After it covers the first target, the maximal rotatable angle will be the angle of its direction and the sensor will rotate its maximal rotatable angle to cover more targets. In this case, sensor s_1 will cover targets t_4, t_5 and t_8. After sensor s_1 is rotated, the priority values of sensors s_2 and s_3 are updated to 2 and 1, respectively. In this case, sensor s_2 cannot cover more targets than its original cover due to the limitation of MRA policy and sensor s_3 can cover one more target, say t_7. The final coverage is shown as in Fig. 5(b) which enhances the coverage rate from 50% to 80%.

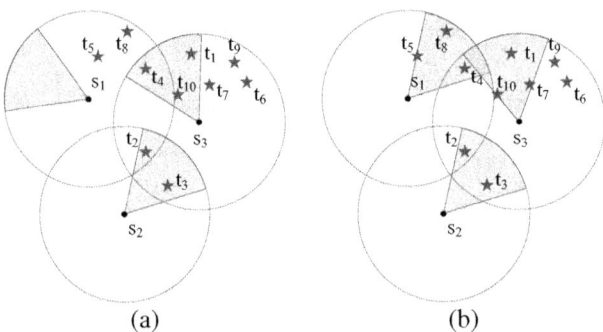

(a)   (b)

Fig. 5. An example of MRA algorithm

4.2 Maximal Coverage First Algorithm

In this section, we propose another greedy algorithm for MCRS problem. Although we can get a better coverage by applying the previous MRA algorithm, there is a limitation on MRA policy. As we can see in the previous section, the original covered targets should be kept in the final coverage regardless the rotation has been applied or not. Therefore, we intended to release the limitation in order to cover more targets. This means that we are looking for the direction that can cover more targets than the original one regardless the rotation angles. Therefore, it is possible that a better coverage can be obtained by uncovering some original targets and covering new targets. Fig. 6 shows the situation. In Fig. 6(a), sensor s covers two targets t_1 and t_3 within its original direction. However, we can find a better coverage which covers t_1, t_4, t_5 and t_6 by rotating some degrees clockwise as shown in Fig. 6(b). Note that target t_3 was uncovered in order to cover more targets. The idea is called the Maximal Coverage First (MCF) algorithm.

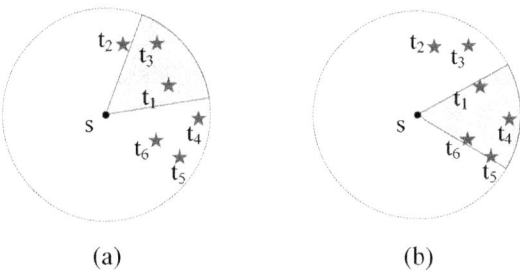

(a)   (b)

Fig. 6. The rotation scheme of MCF algorithm

Basically, the procedure of MCF algorithm is much the same as in the previous MRA algorithm. The main difference between them is in the rotation scheme. In the MCF algorithm, we do not limit the rotation angles while in MRA algorithm the rotation angles are limited by MRA policy. Therefore, we will only demonstrate an example to show how the MCF algorithm works and skip the detailed procedures.

Here we show an example in Fig. 7. In this example, there are three sensors, namely s_1, s_2 and s_3. Initially, s_1 covers no targets, s_2 covers targets t_2 and t_3, and s_3 covers targets t_1, t_4 and t_{10}. According to their priority values, we will first choose sensor s_1 to rotate. At this time, sensor s_1 will rotate its direction to the situation of covering maximal number of targets, say t_4, t_5 and t_8. After sensor s_1 is rotated, the priority values of sensors s_2 and s_3 are updated to 2 and 1, respectively. In this case, the coverage of sensor s_2 remains but sensor s_3 can find the maximal coverage of covering targets t_1, t_6, t_7 and t_9. Note that sensor s_3 uncovers target t_{10} to get a better coverage. The final coverage is shown as in Fig. 7(b) which enhances the coverage rate from 50% to 90%. It can be seen that the coverage rate of MCF algorithm is better than that of MRA algorithm.

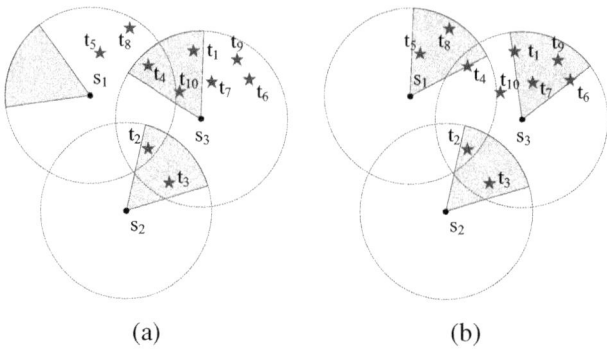

Fig. 7. An example of MCF algorithm

5   Simulation Results

In this section, we will present some simulation results to show the performance of our proposed algorithms. The experimental environment of our simulation is a two-dimensional plane with the size $R \times R$, where $R = 100$ meters. The positions of sensor nodes and target nodes are randomly distributed, but any two sensor nodes cannot be located in the same position. Each sensor has the same sensing radius which is $R/10 = 10$ meters. All sensor nodes are identical and each sensor node is aware of its own location and can detect target nodes within the sensing range. Any two of the sensor nodes can communicate with each other and no communication errors and collisions occur. After all sensor nodes and target nodes are spread in the area, all nodes are unable to move. Furthermore, in our experiments, we have done two different scenarios, which have 400 and 800 targets randomly deployed in the area, respectively. For both cases, the number of sensor nodes is varying from 50 to 225.

Our simulation is designed for the following purposes: evaluating the coverage rate for different approaches, the coverage rate after rotating sensors, and the active sensor rate. In the following, we show the simulation results for the above purposes.

First, we present the simulation result of evaluating the coverage rate for different rotating approaches. The Coverage Rate (CR) is used to measure the ratio of target nodes that can be covered in the network. The coverage rate can be calculated by using equation (3), in which m, m_c, and m_{out} represent the total number of targets, the number of covered targets by using the proposed scheme and the number of targets which no sensor can cover with any rotated angles, respectively.

$$CR = \frac{m_c}{m - m_{out}} \times 100\% \tag{3}$$

It should be noticed that the higher coverage rate is obtained, the better performance of coverage is achieved. Therefore, our purpose is to achieve the higher coverage rate. We evaluate our proposed approaches and compare their performance. The experimental result is shown in Fig. 8. As mentioned above, each sensor of using MCF approach will rotate its sensing direction and try to cover more target regardless the rotated angles.

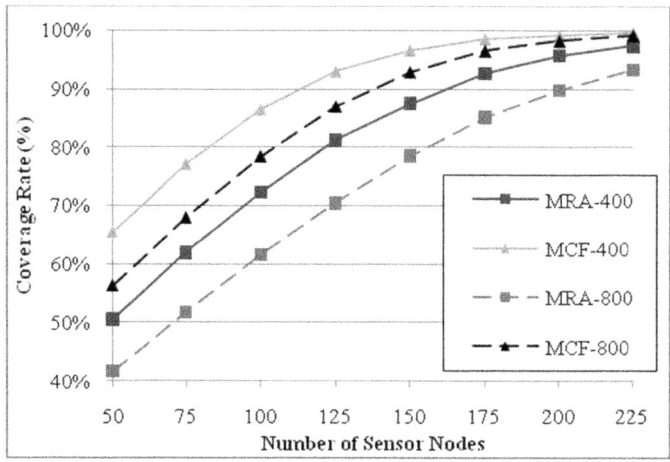

Fig. 8. The Coverage Rate

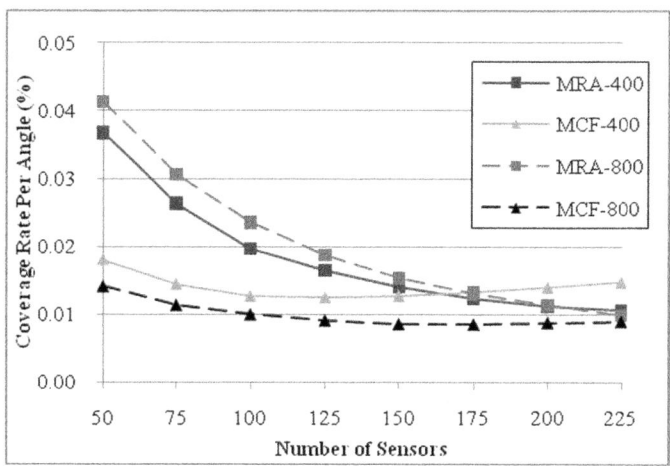

Fig. 9. The Coverage Rate per Angle

As shown in Fig. 8, we can see that the MCF scheme can achieve the higher coverage rate than the MRA scheme. It justifies that we can rotate the sensing direction to get a better coverage rate. This is because that if we allow the sensor to rotate its sensing direction with a large angle, then it can cover more targets.

However, we are also interested in finding the benefit of coverage with regard to the rotated angles. Therefore, we compare the coverage rate after rotating sensors by unit angle with MRA and MCF schemes. In the second experiment, we focused on the performance of the coverage rate for each sensor after rotating a unit of angle. The coverage rate per angle can be calculated by using equation (4). Fig. 9 shows the experimental results. We can see that the coverage rate of MRA approach have better benefit than that of MCF approach. This means that the rotating scheme in MRA approach can achieve more efficient result than MCF approach in term of the coverage rate. But the MCF approach can achieve better coverage rate than MRA approach.

$$Coverage\ Rate\ Per\ Angle = \frac{CR}{total\ rotated\ angles} \qquad (4)$$

The final experiment is focused on the result of active sensor rate. The active sensor rate is the ratio of the number of sensor nodes used for covering the targets to the total number of sensor nodes in the sensor network. The active sensor rate can be used to estimate the power consumption since more sensor nodes being used will consume more energy. The experimental result is shown in Fig. 10. We can see that both of our proposed approaches, MCF approach achieve better performance than MRA approach in term of active sensor rate. This means that MCF approaches can cover targets by using fewer sensors than MRA approach. Therefore, the MCF approach can achieve better performance than MRA approach in term of energy efficiency.

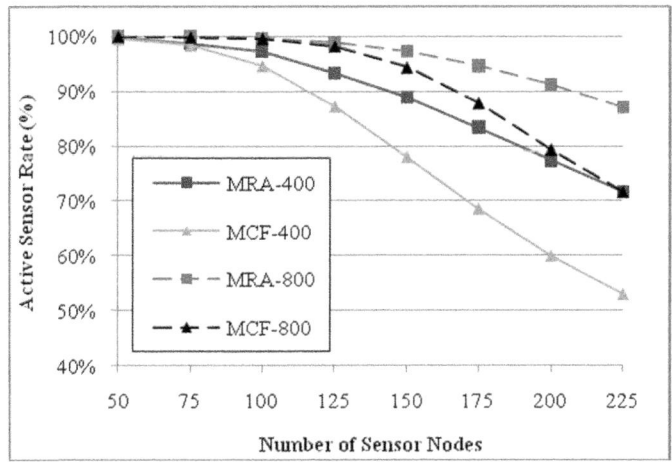

Fig. 10. The Active Sensor Rate

6   Conclusion

In this paper, we propose two centralized greedy algorithms, namely the Maximal Rotatable Angle (MRA) scheme and the Maximum Coverage First (MCF) scheme, to increase the coverage rate after the directional sensors are randomly deployed into the area. Our approaches are using different rotating schemes to increase the coverage rate. Simulation results show that, by rotating the sensing direction of sensors, the active sensor rate of the MCF scheme can be decreased effectively compared with the MRA scheme. Meanwhile, it can also be found that the MCF scheme can achieve better coverage rate than the MRA scheme. However, the rotating cost of MCF scheme is higher than MRA scheme.

References

1. Hefeeda, M., Bagheri, M.: Randomized k-coverage algorithms for dense sensor networks. In: 26th IEEE International Conference on Computer Communications (INFOCOM 2007), pp. 2376–2380. IEEE Press, Anchorage (2007)
2. Chakrabarty, K., Iyengar, S., Qi, H., Cho, E.: Grid coverage for surveillance and target location in distributed sensor networks. IEEE Transactions on Computers 51(12), 1448–1453 (2002)
3. Kininmonth, S., Atkinson, I., Bainbridge, S., Woods, G., Gigan, G., Freitas, D.: The Great Barrier Reef Sensor Network. In: PACEM IN MARIBUS XXXI Proceedings, Townsville, pp. 361–369 (2005)
4. Akyildiz, I.F., Su, W., Sankarasubramaniam, Y., Cayirci, E.: A survey on sensor networks, ACM Trans. on Multimedia Computing. Communications and Applications, 102–114 (August 2002)
5. Szewczyk, R., Mainwaring, A., Polastre, J., Anderson, J., Culler, D.: An analysis of a large scale habitat monitoring application. In: ACM Conference on Embedded Networked Sensor Systems (SenSys), pp. 214–226 (2004)
6. Rahimi, M., Baer, R., Iroezi, O.I., Garcia, J.C., Warrior, J., Estrin, D., Srivastava, M.: Cyclops: In situ image sensing and interpretation in wireless sensor networks. In: ACM Conference on Embedded Networked Sensor Systems(SenSys) (2005)
7. Djugash, J., Singh, S., Kantor, G., Zhang, W.: Range-only slam for robots operating cooperatively with sensor networks. In: IEEE International Conference on Robotics and Automation (2006)
8. Liu, H., Wan, P., Yi, C., Jia, X., Makki, S., Niki, P.: Maximal lifetimescheduling in sensor surveillance networks. In: IEEE INFOCOM (2005)
9. Cardei, M., Thai, M.T., Li, Y., Wu, W.: Energy-efficient targetcoverage in wireless sensor networks. In: IEEE INFOCOM (2005)
10. Cheng, M.X., Ruan, L., Wu, W.: Achieving minimum coveragebreach under bandwidth constraints in wireless sensor networks. In: IEEE INFOCOM (2005)
11. Ma, H.-D., Liu, Y.: On Coverage Problems of Directional Sensor Networks. In: Jia, X., Wu, J., He, Y. (eds.) MSN 2005. LNCS, vol. 3794, pp. 721–731. Springer, Heidelberg (2005)
12. Ai, J., Abouzeid, A.A.: Coverage by directional sensors in randomly deployed wireless sensor networks. Journal of Combinatorial Optimization 11(1), 21–41 (2006)
13. Cai, Y., Lou, W., Li, M., Li, X.-Y.: Target-oriented scheduling in directional sensor networks, pp. 1550–1558 (2007)
14. Cai, Y., Lou, W., Li, M., Li, X.-Y.: Energy Efficient Target-Oriented Scheduling in Directional Sensor Networks. IEEE Transactions on Computers (TC 2009) 58, 1259–1274 (2009)
15. Cai, Y., Lou, W., Li, M.: Cover set problem in directionalsensor networks. In: Future Generation Communicationand Networking (FGCN 2007), vol. 1, pp. 274–278 (2007)
16. Chen, U., Chiou, B.-S., Chen, J.-M., Lin, W.: An Adjustable Target Coverage Method in Directional Sensor Networks. In: IEEE Asia-Pacific Services Computing Conference (APSCC 2008), pp. 174–180 (2008)
17. Tao, D., Ma, H.-D., Liu, L.: Coverage-Enhancing Algorithm for Directional Sensor Networks. In: Cao, J., Stojmenovic, I., Jia, X., Das, S.K. (eds.) MSN 2006. LNCS, vol. 4325, pp. 256–267. Springer, Heidelberg (2006)

18. Tao, D., Ma, H.-D., Liu, L.: A Virtual Potential Field Based Coverage-Enhancing Algorithm for Directional Sensor Networks. Journal of Software 18(5), 1152–1163 (2007)
19. Zhao, J., Zeng, J.-C.: A Virtual Potential Field Based Coverage Algorithm for Directional Networks. In: IEEE Chinese Control and Decision Conference, CCDC (2009)
20. Zhao, J., Zeng, J.-C.: An electrostatic field-based coverage-enhancing algorithm for wireless multimedia sensor networks. In: 5th International Conference on Wireless Communications, Networking and Mobile Computing, WiCom (2009)
21. Zhao, J., Zeng, J.: A Virtual Centripetal Force-Based Coverage-Enhancing Algorithm for Wireless Multimedia Sensor Networks. IEEE Sensors Journal 10(8), 1328–1334 (2010)

A Bayesian Approach to Blind Separation of Mixed Discrete Sources by Gibbs Sampling

Hang Zhang[1], Fanglin Gu[1], and Yi Xiao[2]

[1] Institute of Communication Engineering, PLA University
of Science and Technology, 210007 Nanjing, China
hangzh_2002@163.com, gufanglin@gmail.com
[2] School of Engineering & Information Technology,
the University of New South Wales, Australian
Defence Force Academy, 2006 Canberra, Australia
yix@tpg.com.au

Abstract. Blind source separation (BSS) is the process of separating the original signals from their mixtures without the knowledge of neither the signals nor the mixing process. In this paper, a Bayesian modeling approach for the separation of instantaneous mixture of linear modulation signals with memory in communication systems is developed, in which the finite alphabet (FA) property of the source signals, together with the correlation contained in the source signals are used for the purpose of accurate signal separation. And the Gibbs sampling algorithm is employed to estimate discrete source signals and mixing coefficients. Moreover, the approach takes into account noise levels in the model in order to provide precise estimations of the signals. The simulation results under determined mixture condition show that this new algorithm gives precise estimation of sources and coefficients of mixture. Furthermore, the efficiency of this proposed approach under underdetermined mixture condition is attested by a numerical simulation experiment.

Keywords: Blind source separation, Bayesian Inference, linear modulation with memory, Gibbs sampling.

1 Introduction

A ubiquitous network relies on highly reliable communication and signal processing technology for context extraction, modeling and description. This paper is concerned with BSS techniques which can improve the performance of communication systems amid interference surroundings.

Based on the crucial assumption of mutual statistical independence of source signals, various techniques have been proposed for BSS. A well-known method to solve BSS problem is to employ the contrast functions. A contrast function is any a non-linear function about mixing matrix or separating matrix. It is invariant to permutation and scaling matrices, and attains its minimum value in correspondence of the mutual independence among the output components. A famous contrast function based on Kullback-Leibler divergence [1] is used to

C.-H. Hsu et al. (Eds.): UIC 2011, LNCS 6905, pp. 463–475, 2011.

describe statistical independence between outputs by measuring the distance between separated outputs and source signals. The equivariant adaptive separation via independence (EASI) algorithm [2] is deduced from this criterion. However, the EASI algorithm can't used in the cases of under-determined mixture, i.e., the number of sensors is smaller than the number of sources, because it involves inversed operation on matrix which may not be executed under under-determined mixture condition. Another method to deal with BSS problem is a Bayesian approach which provides a framework to incorporate any prior information of the source to improve the performance of blind separation. The Bayesian approach can be implemented with the Expectation-Maximization (EM) methods [3-5] or Monte-Carlo Markov Chains (MCMC) methods, e.g., Gibbs samplers [6]. The Gibbs sampler can be taken as a stochastic analog to the EM approach to obtain likelihood functions when missing data are presented. The EM method used to compute the maximization can only guarantees theoretical convergence to a local maximum of the posterior density. There is no problem if this density is unimodal. The density, however, might be with a lot of local maxima that makes the direct calculation of the full posterior density impossible. This difficulty can be overcome by performing a global maximization of posterior densities, with a Gibbs sampler described in [7].

The FA properties of communication signals have been shown to be very useful for BSS [8]. In general, the recovered signals in BSS problems can be recorded by a permutation matrix and a scaled diagonal matrix. By exploiting the FA property, the signal's norm is restricted to discrete amplitudes and phase values which take from the considered finite set so that there is no scale ambiguity. On the other hand, Bayesian separation of discrete sources via Gibbs sampling is studied in [9], where the source signals are restricted to the case of binary phase shift keying (BPSK) signals with distribution of $1/2\delta_{+1} + 1/2\delta_{-1}$. This hypothesis is very implicative as it reduces general fields of incertitude of sources separation. In [10], temporally correlated discrete signals, which are modeled by stationary Markov chain with known state spaces but unknown initial and transition probabilities, have been blind restored by Gibbs sampling. In this paper, we consider the BSS problems in communication systems. Especially, we focus on the source signals that are modulation signals with memory in communication systems [11], such as NRZ, miller Code, et al. The Gibbs sampler, a Monte Carlo method, is employed to calculate the full posterior density and determine the minimum square error (MSE) estimation of sources and unknown parameters.

The rest of this paper is organized as followed. In section 2, the BSS problem in communication systems, having linear modulation with memory signals, is described. Section 3 gives the Bayesian framework used for the blind separation. The prior information, including FA property and memory contained in source signals modeled by Markov chain, is incorporated to estimate the most probable solution. The Gibbs sampling algorithm is introduced in Section 4 for the calculation of posterior density and the estimation of source signals, noise levels and mixing matrix. At the same time, the estimating possibility of more sources than sensors is discussed. In section 5, some simulation examples are presented. Finally, conclusions are given in section 6.

2   Problem Formation

In this study, we assume n sources emit n discrete sequences $(s_j(t))_{t=1,\cdots,T,j=1,\cdots,n}$, which are instantaneous linearly mixed and corrupted by additive noise. We denote observed sequences impinging on m sensors by $(x_i(t))_{t=1,\cdots,T,j=1,\cdots,m}$. Then the observed signal is modeled as

$$x_i(t) = \sum_{j=1}^{n} a_{ij} s_j(t) + w_i(t) \tag{1}$$

where a_{ij} is an element in mixing matrix $\boldsymbol{A}$, denoting the mixing filter from source j to sensor i; and denotes $w_i(t)$ noise component i, which is Gaussian white noises with zero-mean and unknown variances σ_i^2 and is independent of $s_j(t)$.

In previous literatures, it is often assumed that the source signals are temporally independent. Here we can relax the limitation. Specifically, we focus on linear modulation signals with memory in communication systems. As [11] points out, we characterize the memory of the modulation signals in terms of Markov chains. And we assume all sources share the same statistical properties. Definitely, this condition can be easily relaxed. We assume that $(s_j(t))_{j=1,\cdots,n}$ are independent Markov processes which take values in $\Omega = \{e_1, \cdots, e_k\}$. $\boldsymbol{p}_{jo} = [p_{j01}, \cdots, p_{j0k}]^T$ denote the initial probabilities of the Markov chain $s_j(t)$, for $k = 1, \cdots, K$, $p_{j0k} \doteq Pr\{s_j(t=1) = e_k\}$. The transition probabilities matrix of the Markov chain is denoted by $\boldsymbol{P}_j \doteq [p_{jkl}], k, l \in \{1, \cdots, K\}$. The kth column of $\boldsymbol{P}_j$ is $\boldsymbol{p}_{jk}(k = 1, \cdots, K)$. It is obvious that the probabilities should satisfy the constraints $\sum_{k=1}^{K} p_{j0k} = 1$ and $\sum_{l=1}^{K} p_{jkl} = 1$ for $k = 1, \cdots, K$. We denote $\boldsymbol{\theta}_j \doteq (\boldsymbol{p}_{j0}, \boldsymbol{P}_j)$ and for $\boldsymbol{\Phi} = [\boldsymbol{\theta}_1, \boldsymbol{\theta}_2, \cdots, \boldsymbol{\theta}_n]$ notation simplification.

Under these assumptions, the main objective of this paper is to simultaneously reconstruct the source signals $(s_j(t))_{t=1,\cdots,T,j=1,\cdots,n}$ and estimate the mixing matrix coefficients $a_{ij}(i = 1, \cdots, m, j = 1, \cdots, n)$ along with the statistical parameters σ_i^2 and $\boldsymbol{\Phi}$ on the basis of the observed signals $(x_i(t))_{t=1,\cdots,T,j=1,\cdots,m}$.

3   The Bayesian Model

For the BSS problem in communication systems, we can make use of some prior information, including the knowledge that the mixing is linear and amplitude densities of source signals can be described by some classes of probability densities. A Bayesian framework is employed with these prior information for achieving more precise separation of the source signals. The general Bayesian algorithm forms a model comprised of a set of parameters, which describes all the relevant features for the source separation problem. One can calculate probabilities of parameters with particular values which provide an accurate description of the physical situation based on acquired data and prior information.

3.1   Prior Distributions

To make the Gibbs sampler computationally efficient, the priors are chosen such that the conditional posterior distributions are easy to simulate. And conjugate priors are used to obtain simple analytical forms for the resulting posterior distributions [10].

The coefficients $a_{ij}(i = 1, \cdots, m, j = 1, \cdots, n)$ of the mixing matrix are unknown. The choice of a prior to these parameters is a difficult problem. To simplify, it is assumed that $a_{ij}(i = 1, \cdots, m, j = 1, \cdots, n)$ are independent to each other and each has a Gaussian distribution as follow

$$a_{ij} \sim N(0, \sigma_a^2) \tag{2}$$

Further, we impose an inverted Gamma distribution [9] $p(\sigma_i^2) \propto IG(\lambda_i, v_i)$ and $p(\sigma_a^2) \propto IG(\lambda_a, v_a)$ for the noise variance and the hyperparameter σ_a^2. The density of inverted Gamma distribution is defined as follow

$$p(\sigma^2|\lambda, v) = \frac{v^\lambda}{\Gamma(\lambda)}(\sigma^2)^{-(\lambda+1)}exp(-\frac{v}{\sigma^2}) \tag{3}$$

where $\Gamma(.)$ denotes Gamma function. Note that small values of the coefficients λ and v correspond to the case of a lack of information on the noise levels σ_i^2 and the hyperparameter σ_a^2. In the end, Independent Dirichlet distributions [10] are used for the prior densities of $\boldsymbol{p}_{jo}$ and $\boldsymbol{p}_{jk}$. More precisely, let $D(\boldsymbol{\alpha})$ denote the Dirichlet distribution with parameters $\boldsymbol{\alpha} = \{\alpha_1, \cdots, \alpha_K\}$. The probability density function (pdf) of $D(\boldsymbol{\alpha})$ is defined as

$$p(\boldsymbol{p}|\boldsymbol{\alpha}) = \frac{\prod_k \Gamma(\alpha_k)}{\Gamma(\Sigma_k \alpha_k)} \prod_k p_k^{\alpha_k - 1} \tag{4}$$

for $\boldsymbol{p} = \{p_1, \cdots, p_K\}$ with $0 < p_k < 1$ and $\sum_{k=1}^K p_k = 1$. Note that $\alpha_k = 1$ for $k = 1, \cdots, K$ correspond to the less informative prior. We assume that $\boldsymbol{p}_{j0} = [p_{j01}, \cdots, p_{j0K}]^T$ and $\boldsymbol{p}_{jk} = [p_{jk1}, \cdots, p_{jkK}]^T$ are independent with $\boldsymbol{p}_{j0} \sim D(\boldsymbol{\alpha}_{j0})$ and $\boldsymbol{p}_{jk} \sim D(\boldsymbol{\alpha}_{jk})$, where $\boldsymbol{\alpha}_{jk} = \{\alpha_{jk1}, \cdots, \alpha_{jkK}\}$. Under these assumptions, the following priors can be obtained for $\boldsymbol{\theta}_j \doteq (\boldsymbol{p}_{j0}, \boldsymbol{P}_j)$ in Markov case, namely $p(\boldsymbol{\theta}_j) = p(\boldsymbol{p}_{j0}, \boldsymbol{\alpha}_{j0}) \prod_{k=1}^K p(\boldsymbol{p}_{jk}, \boldsymbol{\alpha}_{jk})$. When $s_j = (s_j(t))_{t=1, \cdots, T}$ is an independent identically distribution (i.i.d) sequence, the parameters set for $\boldsymbol{\theta}_j$ can be reduced to $\boldsymbol{p}_{j0}$ and the prior distribution of $\boldsymbol{\theta}_j$ becomes $p(\boldsymbol{\theta}_j) = p(\boldsymbol{p}_{j0}, \boldsymbol{\alpha}_{j0})$.

3.2   Bayesian Inference

Since the source signals can be modeled as Markov chains, the distribution of given can be written as

$$p(s_j|\boldsymbol{\theta}_j) = \prod_{k=1}^K p_{jk}^{\delta_{jk}} \prod_{k,l=1}^K p_{jkl}^{n_{jkl}} \tag{5}$$

where n_{jkl} is the number of pairs $\{s_j(t), s_j(t+1)\} = \{e_k, e_l\}$ in s_j, and δ_{jk} is the indictor such that $\delta_{jk} = 1$ if $s_j(t = 1) = e_k$, and $\delta_{jk} = 0$ if $s_j(t = 1) \neq e_k$. In the i.i.d case, the distribution of s_j which is given by $\boldsymbol{\theta}_j = \{p_{j1}, \cdots, p_{jK}\}$, reduces to

$$p(s_j|\boldsymbol{\theta}_j) = \prod_{k=1}^{K} p_{jk}^{n_{jk}} \tag{6}$$

where n_{jk} is the number of $s_j(t)$ in s_j which equals to e_k.

Since $\omega_i(t)$ is white and Gaussian, we can derive the joint posterior distribution of the unknown quantities as

$$
\begin{aligned}
&p(\boldsymbol{A}, s, \boldsymbol{\sigma}^2, \sigma_a^2, \boldsymbol{\Phi}|\boldsymbol{x}) \\
&\propto \prod_{i=1}^{m} (\tfrac{1}{\sigma_i^2})^{\frac{T}{2}} \times exp\{-\tfrac{1}{2\sigma_i^2} \sum_{t=1}^{T} (x_i(t) - \sum_{j=1}^{n} a_{ij}s_j(t))^2\} \\
&\times \tfrac{1}{\sigma_a^2}^{\frac{m \times n}{2}} exp(- \sum_{i=1}^{m} \sum_{j=1}^{n} \tfrac{1}{2\sigma_a^2} a_{ij}^2) p(\boldsymbol{\sigma}^2) p(\sigma_a^2) p(s|\boldsymbol{\Phi}) p(\boldsymbol{\Phi})
\end{aligned}
\tag{7}
$$

where $p(s|\boldsymbol{\Phi}) = \prod_{j=1}^{n} p(s_j|\boldsymbol{\theta}_j)$, since the source signals are independent mutually. Although the joint distribution in Eq. (7) is given explicitly (up to a normalizing constant), the direct calculation of the MAP estimates of the unknowns is computationally forbidding.

4   Gibbs Sampling

The direct calculation of the Bayesian estimation requires multiple integrations. To avoid this complexity, we resort to a Monte Carlo method. The main idea of Monte Carlo method is to generate an ergodic random sample according to the distribution in Eq. (7) and then perform the average. The Gibbs sampler provides a recursive way for generating such a sample. The key of a Gibbs sampler is that one only considers univariate conditional distributions - the distribution where all of the random variables except one are assigned fixed values. Such conditional distributions usually have simple forms and are far easier to simulate than the complex joint distributions. Thus, simulating n-dimensional variables sequentially from univariate conditionals is preferred rather than generating a single n-dimensional vector in a single pass using full joint distributions. Further information and full theoretical details about the Gibbs sampler can be found in [7].

4.1   Conditional Posterior Distributions

In our problem, the implementation of Gibbs sampler requires the following conditional posterior distributions.

A.1. It can be shown that

$$
\begin{aligned}
&p(a_{ij}|\boldsymbol{x}, s, a_{r \neq i, q \neq j}, \boldsymbol{\sigma}^2, \sigma_a^2, \boldsymbol{\Phi}) \\
&\propto p(\boldsymbol{x}_i|s, a_{i,q<j}, a_{ij}, a_{i,q>j}, \sigma_i^2) \times p(a_{ij}|\sigma_a^2)
\end{aligned}
\tag{8}
$$

Since the $x_i(t)$ is independent conditionally to $\boldsymbol{s}, \boldsymbol{A}, \sigma_i^2$ and $\omega_i(t)$ is white and Gaussian noise, we get

$$
\begin{aligned}
&p(\boldsymbol{x}_i | \boldsymbol{s}, a_{i,q<j}, a_{ij}, a_{i,q>j}, \sigma_i^2) \\
&\propto \prod_{t=1}^{T} p(x_i(t) | \boldsymbol{s}(t), a_{i,q<j}, a_{ij}, a_{i,q>j}, \sigma_i^2) \\
&\propto \prod_{t=1}^{T} exp\{-\frac{1}{2\sigma_i^2} \times (x_i(t) - \sum_{q \neq j} a_{iq} s_q(t) - a_{ij} s_j(t))^2\}
\end{aligned} \tag{9}
$$

Thus we obtain a Gaussian likelihood density distribution for $p(a_{ij} | \boldsymbol{x}, \boldsymbol{s}, a_{r \neq i, q \neq j}, \sigma^2, \sigma_a^2) \propto N(\mu_{a_{ij}}, \sigma_{a_{ij}}^2)$ with $\mu_{a_{ij}} = \mu_{ij}/(1 + \sigma_{ij}^2/\sigma_a^2)$ and $\sigma_{a_{ij}}^2 = 1/(1/\sigma_{ij}^2 + 1/\sigma_a^2)$ where

$$
\mu_{ij} = 1/\sum_{t=1}^{T}(s_j(t))^2 \times (\sum_{t=1}^{T} s_j(t)(x_i(t) - \sum_{q \neq j} a_{iq} s_q(t))) \tag{10}
$$

$$
\sigma_{ij}^2 = \sigma_i^2 / \sum_{t=1}^{T}(s_j(t))^2 \tag{11}
$$

A.2. It can be shown that

$$
\begin{aligned}
&p(\sigma_i^2 | \boldsymbol{x}_i, \boldsymbol{s}, \boldsymbol{A}, \sigma_{r \neq i}^2, \sigma_a^2, \boldsymbol{\Phi}) \propto p(\sigma_i^2 | \boldsymbol{x}_i, \boldsymbol{s}, a_{i,1:n}) \\
&\propto \prod_{t=1}^{T} p(\sigma_i^2 | x_i(t), \boldsymbol{s}(t), a_{i,1:n}) \\
&\propto \prod_{t=1}^{T} \frac{1}{\sqrt{2\pi}\sigma_i} exp\{-\frac{1}{2\sigma_i^2}(x_i(t) - \sum_{j=1}^{n}(x_i(t) - a_{ij} s_j(t))^2)\} \\
&\propto (\frac{1}{\sigma_i^2})^{\frac{T}{2}} exp(-\frac{1}{2\sigma_i^2}(x_i(t) - \sum_{j=1}^{n}(x_i(t) - a_{ij} s_j(t))^2))
\end{aligned} \tag{12}
$$

Thus, we can obtain $p(\sigma_i^2 | \boldsymbol{x}_i, \boldsymbol{s}, \boldsymbol{A}, \sigma_{l \neq i}^2, \sigma_a^2, \boldsymbol{\Phi}) \propto IG(\lambda_i^*, v_i^*)$ where

$$
\lambda_i^* = T/2 + \lambda_i \tag{13}
$$

$$
v_i^* = \frac{1}{2} \sum_{t=1}^{T} (x_i(t) - \sum_{j=1}^{n} a_{ij} s_j(t))^2 + v_i \tag{14}
$$

A.3. It is shown that

$$
p(\sigma_a^2 | \boldsymbol{x}, \boldsymbol{s}, \boldsymbol{A}, \sigma^2, \boldsymbol{\Phi}) \propto p(\boldsymbol{A} | \sigma_a^2) \times p(\sigma_a^2) \tag{15}
$$

Since the mixing matrix coefficients $(a_{ij})_{i=1,\cdots,m, j=1,\cdots,n}$ are independent to each other, we can get

$$
p(\boldsymbol{A} | \sigma_a^2) \propto N(0, \sigma_a^2)^{m \times n} \propto (1/\sigma_a^2)^{\frac{m \times n}{2}} exp(-\frac{1}{2\sigma_a^2} \sum_{i=1}^{m} \sum_{j=1}^{n} a_{ij}^2) \tag{16}
$$

Hence

$$
p(\sigma_a^2 | \boldsymbol{x}, \boldsymbol{s}, \boldsymbol{A}, \sigma^2, \boldsymbol{\Phi}) \propto IG(\frac{m \times n}{2} + \lambda_a, \frac{1}{2} \sum_{i=1}^{m} \sum_{j=1}^{n} a_{ij}^2 + v_a) \tag{17}
$$

A.4. Let $\boldsymbol{\theta}_{j[-k]} = [\boldsymbol{p}_{j0}, \boldsymbol{p}_{j1}, \cdots, \boldsymbol{p}_{j,k-1}, \boldsymbol{p}_{j,k+1}, \cdots, \boldsymbol{p}_{jK}]$ for $k = 0, 1, \cdots, K$. Then in the markovian case

$$p(\boldsymbol{p}_{jk}|\boldsymbol{x}, \boldsymbol{s}, \boldsymbol{A}, \sigma^2, \sigma_a^2, \boldsymbol{\Phi}) \propto p(\boldsymbol{p}_{jk}|\boldsymbol{s}_j, \boldsymbol{\theta}_{j[-k]}) \propto D(\boldsymbol{a}_{jk}^*) \tag{18}$$

where $\boldsymbol{\alpha}_{jk}^* = [\alpha_{jk1}^*, \cdots, \alpha_{jkK}^*]$, $\alpha_{jkl}^* = \alpha_{jkl} + n_{jkl}$, and n_{jkl} is the number of pairs of $\{s_j(t), s_j(t+1)\} = \{e_k, e_l\}$ in $\boldsymbol{s}_j$. A.5. For any fixed $t^* \in \{1, \cdots, T\}$, let $\boldsymbol{s}_{j[-t^*]} = \boldsymbol{s}_j/s_j(t^*)$. Since $\omega_i(t)$ is white and Gaussian and the mixing process is instantaneous, this implies

$$p(s_j(t^*) = e_k|\boldsymbol{x}, \boldsymbol{s}_{j[-t^*]}, \boldsymbol{s}_{q<j}, \boldsymbol{s}_{q>j}, \boldsymbol{A}, \sigma^2, \sigma_a^2, \boldsymbol{\Phi})$$
$$\propto \prod_{i=1}^{m} p(x_i(t^*)|s_j(t^*) = e_k, \boldsymbol{s}_{q\neq j}(t^*), \boldsymbol{A}, \sigma^2, \sigma_a^2)p(\boldsymbol{s}_j^*|\boldsymbol{\theta}_j) \tag{19}$$

for $k = 1, \cdots, K$, where $\boldsymbol{s}_j^*$ is obtained by substituting $s_j(t^*)$ with e_k in $\boldsymbol{s}_j$. It is clear that

$$p(x_i(t^*)|s_j(t^*) = e_k, \boldsymbol{s}_{q\neq j}(t^*), \boldsymbol{A}, \sigma^2, \sigma_a^2)$$
$$\propto \exp\{-\frac{1}{2\sigma_a^2} \times (x_i(t^*) - \sum_{q\neq j} a_{iq}s_q(t^*) - a_{ij}e_k)^2\} \tag{20}$$

4.2   Algorithm for Gibbs Sampler

First, initialize the indispensable hyper-parameters involved in the proposed algorithm according to certain law. Then, using the conditional posterior distributions, the Gibbs sampler can be implemented iteratively as follow:

Step.1. Draw $a_{ij}(d)$ from $p(a_{ij}|\boldsymbol{x}, \boldsymbol{s}^{(d-1)}, a_{r<i,q<j}(d), a_{r>i,q>j}(d-1), \sigma^2(d-1), \sigma_a^2(d-1), \boldsymbol{\Phi}(d-1))$ by (8), for $i = 1, \cdots, m$, $j = 1, \cdots, n$.

Step.2. Draw $\sigma_i^2(d)$ from $p(\sigma_i^2|\boldsymbol{x}, \boldsymbol{s}^{(d-1)}, \boldsymbol{A}(d), \sigma_{r<i}^2(d), \sigma_{r>i}^2(d-1), \sigma_a^2(d-1), \boldsymbol{\Phi}(d-1))$ by (13-14) for $i = 1, \cdots, m$, and $\sigma_a^2(d)$ from $p(\sigma_a^2|\boldsymbol{x}, \boldsymbol{s}^{(d-1)}, \boldsymbol{A}(d), \sigma^2(d), \boldsymbol{\Phi}(d-1))$ by (17).

Step.3. For $j = 1, \cdots, n$, $k = 1, \cdots, K$, draw $\boldsymbol{p}_{jk}(d)$ from $p(\boldsymbol{p}_{jk}|\boldsymbol{s}_j^{(d-1)}, \boldsymbol{\theta}_{j[-k]}^{(d-1)})$ by (18), where $\boldsymbol{\theta}_{j[-k]}^{(d-1)} = \{\boldsymbol{p}_{j0}(d), \cdots, \boldsymbol{p}_{j,k-1}(d), \boldsymbol{p}_{j,k+1}, \cdots, \boldsymbol{p}_{jK}(d-1)\}$.

Step.4. For $j = 1, \cdots, n$, $t^* = 1, \cdots, T$, draw $s_j^{(d)}(t^*)$ from $p(s_j(t^*) = e_k|\boldsymbol{x}, \boldsymbol{s}_{j[-t^*]}^{(d)}, \boldsymbol{s}_{q<j}^{(d-1)}, \boldsymbol{s}_{q>j}^{(d-1)}, \boldsymbol{A}(d), \sigma^2(d), \sigma_a^2(d), \boldsymbol{\Phi}(d))$ by (19), where $\boldsymbol{s}_{j[-t^*]}^{(d-1)} = \{s_j^{(d)}(1), \cdots, s_j^{(d)}(t^*-1), s_j^{(d)}(t^*+1), \cdots, s_j^{(d)}(T)\}$, $\boldsymbol{s}_{q<j}^{(d)} = \{\boldsymbol{s}_{q<j}^{(d)}(1), \cdots, \boldsymbol{s}_{q<j}^{(d)}(t^*), \boldsymbol{s}_{q<j}^{(d-1)}(t^*+1), \cdots, \boldsymbol{s}_{q<j}^{(d-1)}(T)\}$, $\boldsymbol{s}_{q>j}^{(d-1)} = \{\boldsymbol{s}_{q>j}^{(d)}(1), \cdots, \boldsymbol{s}_{q>j}^{(d)}(t^*-1), \boldsymbol{s}_{q>j}^{(d-1)}(t^*), \cdots, \boldsymbol{s}_{q>j}^{(d-1)}(T)\}$.

Step.5. Set $d = d+1$ and if $d < iter\_max$ go to step1, else break out, where denote the iterative time.

Finally, if the algorithm has converged, export the recovered source signals and relevant parameters.

4.3   Remarks

In step2, the random variable subject to inverted-Gamma distribution $IG(\lambda, v)$ can be generated by $1/G(\lambda, 1/v)$, where $G(\lambda, 1/v)$ denotes the Gamma distribution with coefficients λ and $1/v$. In step3, $\boldsymbol{p}_{jk} \sim D(\boldsymbol{\alpha}_{jk}^*)$ can be obtained from

Beta random variables by first generate p_l from $Beta(\alpha_{jk,l}^*, \alpha_{jk,l+1}^* + \cdots + \alpha_{jk,K}^*)$ for $l = 1, \cdots, K - 1$ and then set $p_{jk1} = p_1$, $p_{jk,l} = (1 - \sum_{q=1}^{l-1} p_{jk,q}) p_l$ for $l = 2, \cdots, K - 1$ and $p_{jk,K} = (1 - \sum_{q=1}^{K-1} p_{jk,q})$.

A key issue in the successful implementation of Gibbs sampler is burn-in, which means number of runs until the chain approaches stationary. A sufficient burn-in is required to remove effects of initial sampling values. To ensure convergence, a Gibbs sampler is usually carried $N + M$ out times and samples from the last M iterations are used to calculate the Bayesian estimates. The sample means of $\{s^{(d)}\}$, $\{\Phi(d)\}$, $\{\sigma^2(d)\}$ and $\{\sigma_a^2(d)\}$ can be used to approximate the corresponding minimum square error (MSE) estimates. Further more, the sample variances of $\{s^{(d)}\}$, $\{\Phi(d)\}$, $\{\sigma^2(d)\}$ and $\{\sigma_a^2(d)\}$ are approximations to the posterior variances $V(s|x)$, $V(\Phi|x)$, $V(\sigma^2|x)$ and $V(\sigma_a^2|x)$ respectively, which reflect the uncertainty in estimating these unknowns on the basis of x.

Since no computation about the inverse matrix of a mixing matrix is involved in the proposed algorithm, we can infer that the algorithm can be extended to solve the under-determined mixtures. In section 5, blind separation of 2×3 under-determined mixture with BPSK signals is employed to test the validity and efficiency of the algorithm.

5   Simulations

In this section, the following numerical simulation examples are carried out.

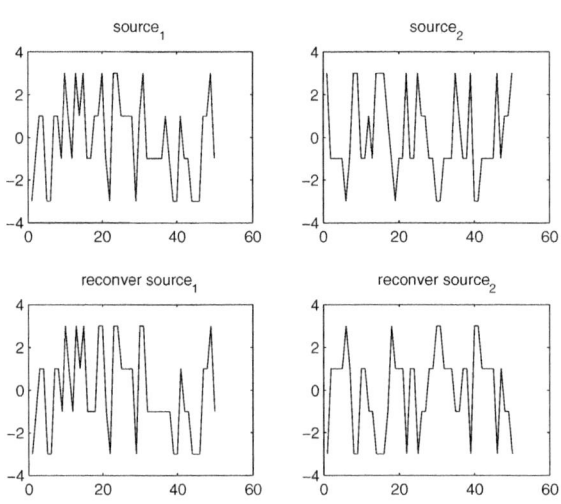

Fig. 1. The original and corresponding recovered source signal by the proposed algorithm

5.1   Determined Mixture

The observed signals are generated according to the following model:

$$\begin{cases} x_1(t) = 4s_1(t) - 3s_2(t) + w_1(t) \\ x_2(t) = s_1(t) + 5s_2(t) + w_2(t) \end{cases}$$

where $\{s_1(t)\}$ both $\{s_2(t)\}$ and are first-order, four-state Markov chains with $\Omega = \{-3, -1, 1, 3\}$ and a transition probabilities matrix of

$$P = \begin{bmatrix} 0.4 \ 0.2 \ 0.2 \ 0.2 \\ 0.2 \ 0.4 \ 0.2 \ 0.2 \\ 0.1 \ 0.3 \ 0.4 \ 0.2 \\ 0.1 \ 0.2 \ 0.3 \ 0.4 \end{bmatrix}$$

The sample variances of $\{w_1(t)\}$, $\{w_2(t)\}$ are adjusted so that the signal-to-noise ratio (SNR) of the observed signals $\{x_1(t)\}$, $\{x_2(t)\}$ are equal to $10dB$ and $3dB$, respectively.

Due to noise levels with their σ_i^2 and hyperparameter σ_a^2 are assumed to be unknown, we choose non-informative priors of the form $IG(\lambda, v)$ for them with coefficients $\lambda_1 = \lambda_2 = 0.1$, $v_1 = v_2 = 0.1$ and $\lambda_a = 0.1$, $v_a = 0.1$. Meanwhile, the non-informative priors forming $D(\alpha)$ with $\alpha = 1$ for the Markov chain coefficients are chosen. Then, 1000 iterations of the Gibbs sampling are executed to compute the estimates of relevant parameters and source signals. The recovered source signals $\hat{s}_1(t), \hat{s}_2(t)$ are equivalent to the original source signals $-s_1(t), s_2(t)$ with error rate (BER) 5.2% and 5.8% respectively. A sample of the original and corresponding recovered source signals are shown in Figure 1.

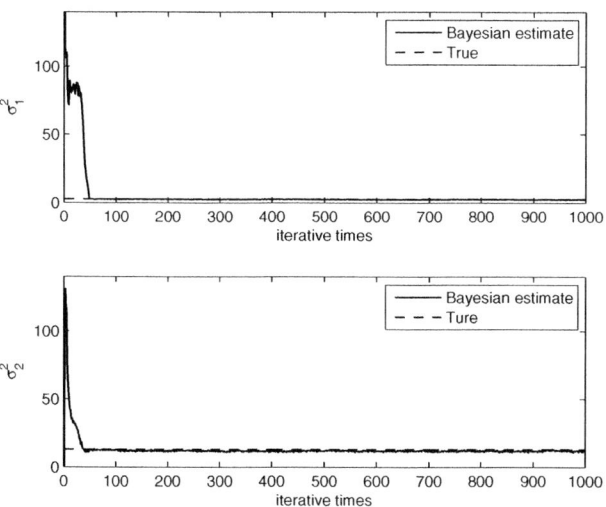

Fig. 2. Estimates of noise levels and respectively

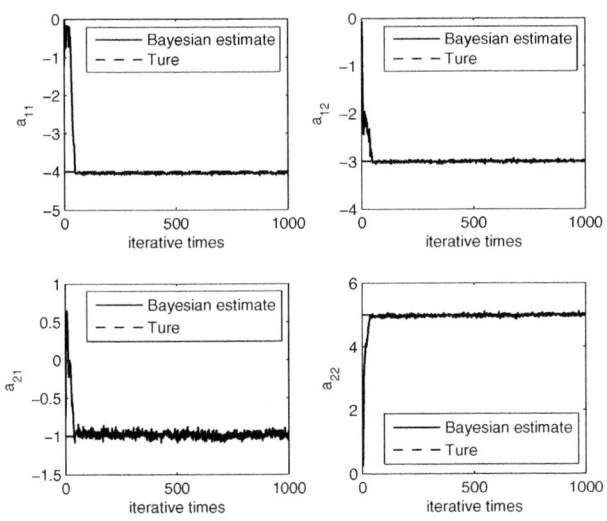

Fig. 3. Estimates of the mixing coefficients

The Gibbs sampling algorithm also gives good estimates about noise levels σ_1^2 and σ_2^2. The convergences of them are shown in Figure 2. It indicates that estimated noise levels are close to true noise levels. Mixing coefficients are also well estimated, and the convergence is shown in Figure 3.

The mean of the estimated mixing matrix computed from the 500th iteration to the 1000th iteration is equal to

$$\widehat{A} = \begin{bmatrix} -4.0419 & -3.0009 \\ -0.9855 & -4.9855 \end{bmatrix}$$

It is shown that the estimate of the mixing matrix approximates the true mixing matrix up to permutation matrix.

The mean and variance of the estimated transition probabilities matrix , are computed from the 500th iteration to 1000th iteration and given in the form of $E(.|x) \pm \sqrt{V(.|x)}$ by

$$\widehat{P}_1 = \begin{bmatrix} 0.4004 & 0.2076 & 0.1977 & 0.1943 \\ 0.1862 & 0.3810 & 0.2103 & 0.2225 \\ 0.1168 & 0.2785 & 0.4128 & 0.1919 \\ 0.1059 & 0.1958 & 0.3239 & 0.3745 \end{bmatrix} \pm \begin{bmatrix} 0.0253 & 0.0210 & 0.0207 & 0.0201 \\ 0.0170 & 0.0211 & 0.0170 & 0.0178 \\ 0.0124 & 0.0188 & 0.0203 & 0.0161 \\ 0.0135 & 0.0180 & 0.0208 & 0.0220 \end{bmatrix}$$

$$\widehat{P}_2 = \begin{bmatrix} 0.3383 & 0.2113 & 0.2280 & 0.2225 \\ 0.1575 & 0.4215 & 0.2192 & 0.2019 \\ 0.1085 & 0.3109 & 0.3790 & 0.2017 \\ 0.0711 & 0.2019 & 0.3380 & 0.3890 \end{bmatrix} \pm \begin{bmatrix} 0.0264 & 0.0235 & 0.0242 & 0.0232 \\ 0.0149 & 0.0208 & 0.0175 & 0.0158 \\ 0.0126 & 0.0192 & 0.0200 & 0.0164 \\ 0.0114 & 0.0170 & 0.0200 & 0.0205 \end{bmatrix}$$

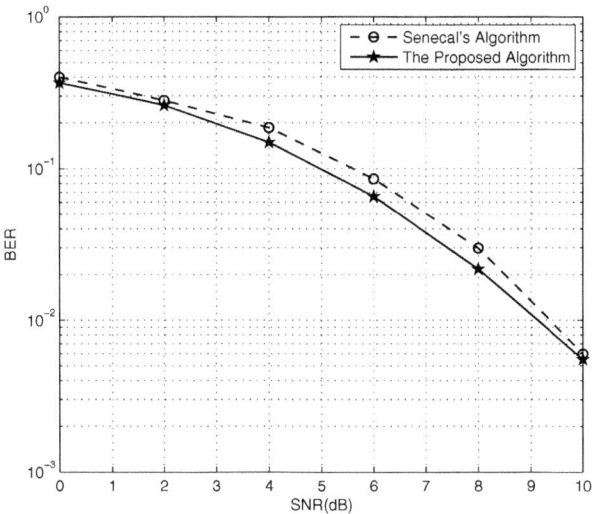

Fig. 4. Contrast the BER performance of the proposed algorithm and the Sénécal's algorithm in [9]

We compare the performance of the proposed algorithm that both the FA property of the source signals and memory contained in source signals modeled by Markov chain are used, with the algorithm in [9] only using the FA property of source signals. We simulate the proposed algorithm under the condition that noise components contaminated observed signals ranging from $0dB$ to $10dB$. The precision is scored by BER and results are shown in Figure 4.

The simulation results show that algorithm proposed in this paper can provide more precise separation by adding the correlation contained in source signals.

5.2 Underdetermined Mixture

We simulate performance of proposed algorithm under underdetermined mixture. Underdetermined mixture of $n = 3$ BPSK source signals and $m = 2$ observations are considered. The mixing matrix is given as follow

$$A = \begin{bmatrix} 4 & -3 & 1 \\ 4 & 5 & 2 \end{bmatrix}$$

We set $\sigma_1 = 3.60$ and $\sigma_2 = 1.732$ respectively, which corresponds to SNR on observations of $3dB$ and $10dB$.

We run 1000 iterations for the Gibbs sampler, and estimate the mixing matrix and source signal which are computed from final 900 samples. After the burn-in process, take mean of samples as the estimate of mixing matrix

$$\widehat{A} = \begin{bmatrix} -2.9832 & 4.0005 & 0.6809 \\ 4.9827 & 1.1383 & 2.0134 \end{bmatrix}$$

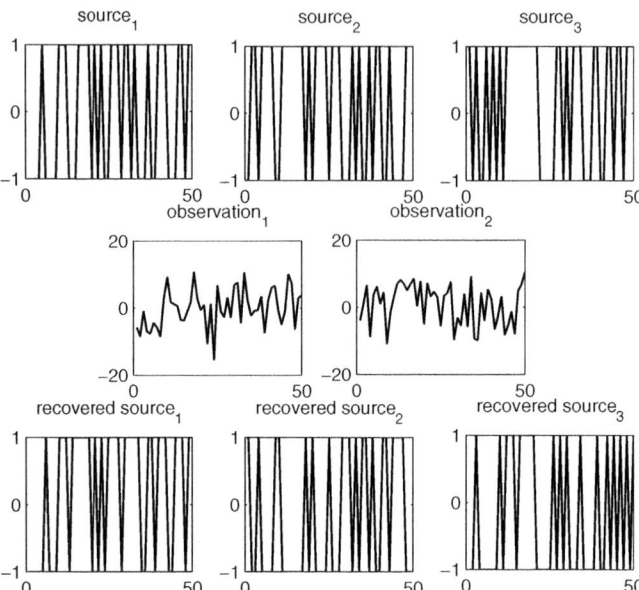

Fig. 5. The original sources, observations, and recovered sources in underdetermined mixture by the proposed algorithm

It shows that the estimation of the mixing matrix is very close to exact mixing matrix up to permutation matrix. Meanwhile, original source signals, observed signals and recovered signals are all shown in Figure 5.

We can see that the algorithm separates the blind source in the underdetermined mixture case successfully.

6   Conclusions

In this paper, a new approach to solve the instantaneous BSS problem under linear modulation signals with memory in communication systems is proposed. Not only the FA property of the source signals, but also the correlation contained in source signals, are used in order to achieve more precise blind signal separation. For this purpose, we develop a framework of Bayesian approach to separation the discrete source signals. Due to the difficulty to direct calculate the posterior density, the Gibbs sampling algorithm is proposed to separate the discrete source signals and estimate the mixing coefficients with accuracy by simulating the univariate posterior densities. Moreover, this approach takes into account noise levels in the model, and provides precise estimates. In contrast to the algorithm proposed by Sncal and Amblard in [9], which considers only the FA property of source signals, the algorithm proposed in this paper is able to give more precise separation.

What's more, the proposed algorithm can be extended to solve under-determined mixture problem. A 2×3 underdetermined case is used to demonstrate the validity and efficiency of the proposed algorithm. Simulation results show that mixing matrix and source signals are well estimated even in an underdetermined case.

Acknowledgments. This work is supported in part by Natural Science Foundation of China under Grant 61001106 and National Program on Key Basic Research Project of China under Grant 2009CB320400.

References

1. Cavalcante, C.C., Romano, J.M.T.: Multi-user pdf estimation based criteria for adaptive blind separation of discrete sources. Signal Processing 85, 1059–1072 (2005)
2. Cardoso, J.F., Laheld, B.H.: Equivariant adaptive source separation. IEEE Trans. Signal Process. 40(12), 3017–3030 (1996)
3. Belouchrani, A., Cardoso, J.F.: Maximum likelihood source separation for discrete sources. In: EUSIPCO 1994, Edinburgh, Scotland, pp. 768–771. Elsevier, Amsterdam (1994)
4. Routtenberg, T., Tabrikian, J.: Blind MIMO-AR System Identification and Source Separation with Finite-Alphabet. IEEE Trans. Signal Process. 58(3) (2010)
5. Bilmes, J.A.: A Gentle Tutorial of the EM Algorithm and its Application to Parameter Estimation for Gaussian Mixture and Hidden Markov Models. International Computer Science Institute, Berkeley, CA, Tech. Rep. TR-97-021 (1998)
6. Rowe, D.B.: A Bayesian Approach to Blind Source Separation. J. Interdis. Math. 5(1), 49–76 (2002)
7. Casella, G., George, E.I.: Explaining the Gibbs Sampler. The American Statistician 46(3), 167–174 (2003)
8. Grellier, O., Comon, P.: Blind separation of discrete sources. IEEE Signal Process. Lett. 5(8), 212–214 (1998)
9. Sénécal, S., Amblard, P.-O.: Bayesian separation of discrete sources via Gibbs sampling. In: International Workshop on Independent Component Analysis and Blind Source Separation, Helsinki, Finland, pp. 566–572 (2000)
10. Chen, R., Li, T.-H.: Blind Restoration of Linearly Degraded Discrete Signals by Gibbs Sampling. IEEE Trans. on Signal Process. 43(10), 2410–2413 (1995)
11. Proakis, J.G.: Digital Communications, 4th edn. House of Electronics Industry, Beijing (2006)

Image Data Hiding Schemes Based on Graph Coloring

Shuai Yue[1], Zhi-Hui Wang[1], Ching-Yun Chang[2],
Chin-Chen Chang[3], and Ming-Chu Li[1]

[1] Department of Software,
Dalian University of Technology, Dalian, China
{peaceful1207,wangzhihui1017}@gmail.com,
Li_mingchu@yahoo.com
[2] Computer laboratory,University of Cambridge,
Cambridge, UK
Ching-Yun.Chang@cl.cam.ac.uk
[3] Department of Information Engineering and Computer Science,
Feng Chia University,Taichung City 40724, Taiwan
alan3c@gmail.com

Abstract. Graph coloring has been applied in a variety of applications, but not for data hiding. Therefore, in this paper, we are proposing two graph coloring-based data hiding schemes that embed secret data in spatial domain of gray scale images. The main idea of our schemes is to use a graph, in which every vertex corresponds to a pixel pair, to hide data by replacing a pair of pixels of one color with a pair of pixels of a different color, with every color corresponding to some bits of the secret message. The performance of the proposed schemes has been evaluated by a joint evaluation of the imperceptibility of the images they produce and their embedding capacity. Also, the validity of the proposed schemes has been proven by comparing them with some other schemes.

Keywords: Data hiding, Graph coloring, Particle swarm optimization.

1 Introduction

Millions of data are exchanged on the Internet every second. It is a challenging job to protect those data from illegal access. So, many techniques have been developed for this purpose, and they can be divided mainly into cryptographic and steganographic techniques. In steganography, data hiding in images is an important and effective method[1]. The schemes proposed in this paper are irreversible data hiding schemes that embed secret data in spatial domain of gray scale images.

In the past few years, many researchers have published irreversible data hiding schemes in the literature [2]. One of the most common and well-known approaches is the Least-Significant-Bit (LSB) scheme that hides data in images by modifying the last few bits of every pixel of a gray image [3]. The LSB scheme

C.-H. Hsu et al. (Eds.): UIC 2011, LNCS 6905, pp. 476–489, 2011.

has good embedding capacity, but it is still far from perfect due to the drawback that the modifications made to the smooth areas of a cover image are obvious [4,5,6]. In 2001, Wang et al. [7] proposed a scheme in which a genetic algorithm was used to try to find an optimal LSB substitution to lower the distortion of the image. However, the results provided by this scheme were not always optimal, and, in 2003, Chang et al. [8] improved the scheme by using a dynamic programming strategy.

Although the papers mentioned above improved the quality of the stego-image, none of the authors considered improving image quality by manipulating the edge areas of images, which can tolerate more changes [9] without undue image distortion. In 2003, Wu and Tsai presented a scheme using pixel differencing to detect the edge areas and hide more data in those areas [10]. In the last few years, many papers on this topic have been published, including Wu et al.'s method in 2005 [11] and Yang et al.'s method in 2007 [12]. In 2008, Wang et al. proposed a method using a combination of pixel-value differencing and modulus function [13] to improve the distortion caused by changing the difference value of two pixels in Wu and Tsai's scheme. However, Wang et al.'s method has limitation in embedding capacity. In 2010, Hsiao et al. proposed an adaptive steganographic method based on just noticeable distortion profile measurement [14] which performs well on both embedding capacity and image quality.

The schemes proposed in this paper hide data in the cover image in a similar way to Wang et al.'s [13] method by modifying the value of two adjacent pixels. However, our schemes manipulate a series of substitution rules, built by graph coloring, instead of the confined rules used in Wang et al.'s scheme and Hsiao et al.'s scheme. Although our proposed schemes do not take into consideration that the edge areas can tolerate more changes, the quality of the stego-images produced by the schemes is better than the quality of the stego-images produced by Wang et al.'s scheme and Hsiao et al.'s scheme due to the use of particle swarm optimization to resolve graph coloring problem. In addition, our proposed scheme uses a key to embed data, which can provide better security.

The format of the remainder of this paper is as follows. In Section 2, we discuss related works. In Section 3 and Section 4, we provide the details of the data hiding and extracting procedures of two proposed scheme respectively. In Section 5, the analysis of our experimental results is given, and our proposed schemes are compared with other schemes. In Section 6, Conclusions are provided.

2   Related Works

In the proposed scheme, the graph-coloring problem and particle swarm optimization are used, and both are described in this section.

2.1   Graph-Coloring Problem

In graph coloring [15], colors are assigned to the elements of a graph subject to certain constraints. The simplest form of graph coloring is vertex coloring, in

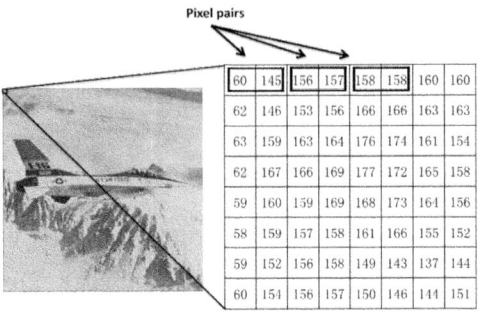

Fig. 1. Pixel pairs

which different colors are assigned to the vertices of a graph such that no two adjacent vertices have the same color. Similarly, edge coloring assigns colors to edges such that no two adjacent edges have same color, and face coloring assigns colors to the faces of a graph so that no two faces that share a common boundary have the same color.

Graph coloring is computationally difficult. So, in our proposed scheme, particle swarm optimization was selected to compute an approximate coloring solution for a graph in which there may be adjacent vertices that have the same color [17].

2.2   Particle Swarm Optimization

Particle swarm optimization (PSO) is a computational method used to optimize a problem [18]. PSO maintains a lot of particles, and every particle has both a position, which is a candidate solution to the problem, and a velocity that indicates the direction of the particle's movement. The PSO algorithm tries to improve every candidate solution in every loop. It updates the position of every particle until the best solution is found or the maximum allowable run time has been reached.

PSO outputs are different for each different run due to the use of a pseudo-random number generator. However, the proposed scheme requires the same color solution for the same graph. So, a fixed integer is selected to initiate the pseudo-random number generator.

3   Proposed Scheme 1

The details of our first proposed scheme are described as follows. Let I represent the cover image and I' represent the stego-image. The terms $I(x, y)$ and $I'(x, y)$ denote the pixel value at the position of the xth row and the yth column of the image, respectively.

The term $G(V, E)$ represents a graph in which every vertex corresponds to a kind of pixel pair in the original image I . The pixel pair indicates two adjacent pixels that are on the same row and in adjacent columns in image I as shown in Figure 1. The term $I(0,0)$ equals 60, and $I(0,1)$ equals 145, so the vertex that the pixel pair corresponds to is noted as $v(60, 145)$. In an image, all the same pixel pairs correspond to the same vertex. For example, the pixel pair $(156, 157)$ in Figure 1, which corresponds to the vertex $v(156, 157)$, appears both at the 0th row, 2nd column and 7th row, 2nd column. The distance between two vertices, $D(v_1, v_2)$, is defined as equation 1.

$$D(v_1, v_2) = |v_1.f - v_2.f| + |v_1.s - v_2.s| . \qquad (1)$$

In Equation 1, $v.f$ indicates the value of the first pixel in the pixel pair, and $v.s$ indicates the second pixel in the pair. When the distance between two vertices is no more than a constant value, noted as adj_thresh, an edge is added between the two vertices.

Let $LastPosition(v)$ denote the last position of the vertex v that appears in image I . For example, the vertex $v(156, 157)$ appears both at the 0th row, 2nd column and at the 7th row, 2nd column, so the $LastPosition(v)$ will be $(7, 2)$, which is the position where $v(156, 157)$ appears last.

When the scheme uses 2^k different colors to color graph G, every color can be noted as an integer, so the set of 2^k different colors can be represented as $C = \{0, 1, ..., 2^k - 1\}$. Let $SM = \{s_b|s_b = \{0, 1\}, for \ b = 0, 1, ..., k \times l\}$ denote the secret message, with $k \times l$ indicating that there are $k \times l$ bits in the secret message. To hide data in an image, first the secret message will be transformed from a sequence of binary numbers to a sequence of colors, $SM = \{s_d|s_d \in C, for \ d = 0, 1, ..., l\}$ by transforming every k bits binary secret message to an decimal integer in C.

The proposed scheme begins with the construction of graph G by scanning the whole image, adding every kind of pixel pairs to the graph as a vertex, then connecting any two vertices when the distance, $D(v_1, v_2)$, between them is less than adj_thresh . Next, graph G is colored using a PSO algorithm that tries to ensure that every two adjacent vertices have the different colors. A secret key KEY is used to initiate the PSO pseudo-random number generator. After that, every vertex is assigned a color that is noted as $Color(v)$.

To ensure that the secret message hidden in the cover image can be extracted with no changes, graph G must be refined before and during the hiding procedure. To refine graph G, every vertex, v, in graph G is checked by iteratively testing whether a color can be found around v through a breadth-first search so that every color can be found in the adjacent vertices that are in a certain distance, noted as bfs_thresh, from v.

3.1   Embedding Phase

The detailed hiding procedure is illustrated in pseudo-code as algorithm 1 shown.

Algorithm 1. Embedding Phase of Scheme 1

Input: a cover image I, a secret message S_d and secret key KEY
Output: a stego-image I'
  Step 1. Construct a graph G with the following steps:
    for every pixel pair (a, b) in every row of the original image **do**
      add a vertex $v(a, b)$ to graph G if $v(a, b)$ is not in graph G
    end for
    for any two vertices, v_1 and v_2, in graph G **do**
      add an edge between them if $D(v_1, v_2) \leq adj\_thresh$
    end for

  Step 2. Coloring graph G with the PSO algorithm using a secret key KEY with k colors
  Step 3. Refine graph G
    for every vertex v in the graph G : **do**
      Use a breadth-first search to determine whether, within a certain distance from the vertex v, there are vertices colored with all the colors in C . If not, delete v from graph G
    end for
  Repeat this step until no vertex must be deleted.

  Step 4. Hide data in a zig-zag scanning manner to process the cover image I
    for a pixel pair in cover image I, find its corresponding vertex, v **do**
      if $LastPosition(v)$ equals the current position **then**
        skip the pixel pair in I, and delete vertex v in graph G .
        Repeat Step 3
      else if $Color(v)$ equals S_d **then**
        go to process S_{d+1} with the next pixel pair
      else
        Use a breadth-first search in graph G to find a vertex that meets the following requirements: $Color(v') = S_d$, $D(v, v') \leq bfs\_thresh$
        Replace the pixel pair in cover image I with another adjacent pixel pair that corresponds to vertex v' in graph G
        Go to process S_{d+1} with the next pixel pair
      end if
      If all the vertices in graph G have been deleted or all the pixel pairs have been processed, the algorithm is terminated
    end for

  Step 5. Output the stego-image I'

3.2 Extracting Phase

The extracting phase is the inverse procedure of the hiding phase.

First, the scheme builds graph G by scanning the stego-image. Because all kinds of pixel pairs are still in the stego-image, graph G that is built based on to the stego-image will be exactly the same as the graph that was built based on the cover image. Then, the scheme uses the PSO algorithm to color the graph using the same KEY to initiate the pseudo-random integer generator, which leads to the same colored graph, G, as the one in the embedding procedure.

Next, the scheme scans the stego-image in a zig-zag manner. When it finds a pixel pair contained in G, the scheme determines whether the pixel pair is the last appearance of that kind of pixel pair. If it is the last position of vertex v, the scheme deletes the vertex from graph G and repeats step 3 to refine graph G. If it is not the last position of vertex v, indicating that there is information hidden in this pixel pair, the scheme checks $Color(v)$, which is just the information hidden in the pixel pair.

Taking the former example as an example, when the scheme finds $(157, 158)$, it determines that the $LastPoint(v(157, 158))$ equals $(5, 2)$, which is not the current place. So the scheme recognizes that information is hidden here. Then, it checks the color of the vertex, i.e. $Color(v(157, 158))$, which equals 1, meaning that the information hidden here is '10'. Now, the scheme goes to the next pixel pair, $(158, 158)$, and finds that it is the last appearance of $(158, 158)$, so the scheme deletes $(158, 158)$ from the graph and repeats Step 3, which leads to the deletion of all the vertices in graph G. Then, the scheme stops when the secret message has been extracted successfully.

4   Proposed Scheme 2

In the first proposed scheme, the way to construct graph G in the proposed scheme 1 helps to achieve better visual quality, however, it also decreases the number of vertices in graph G which leads to a limited embedding capacity. So we proposed the second scheme to fix it. In this section, the details of the second proposed scheme are described as follows.

The second scheme starts with constructing graph G in which every vertex also corresponds to a pixel pair but in a different way by adding every vertex ranging from $(0, 0)$ to $(255, 255)$ into G, and connecting any two vertices, v_1, v_2, that $D(v_1, v_2) \leq 1$. Thus, the constructed graph G is a grid with the size of 256×256.

Next, graph G is colored and refined in the exactly same way with the former scheme while the embedding phase is different. In proposed scheme 1, the last appearing position of a pixel pair in the cover image I has to be saved from embedding secret data, because that if every appearing position of a pixel pair is replaced with other pixel pairs, the constructed graph G in the extracting phase would not contain a vertex that corresponds to this pixel pair. So scheme 1 deletes vertex v when the last appearing position of its corresponding pixel pair is met. Also, because of that the deletion of a vertex also means the deletion of a color for the vertices around v, so the refine step must be repeated after each deletion. However, in proposed scheme 2, due to that the way to construct G does not rely on image I, there is no need to delete vertex in graph G any more. So the scheme does not refine graph G in the embedding phase. Details of the second proposed scheme are illustrated in the following subsection.

4.1 Embedding Phase

The detailed hiding procedure is also illustrated in pseudo-code in algorithm 2.

Algorithm 2. Embedding Phase of Scheme 2

Input: a cover image I, a secret message S_d and secret key KEY
Output: a stego-image I'
  Step 1. Construct a graph G with the following steps:
    for a from 0 to 255 **do**
      for b from 0 to 255 **do**
        add a vertex $v(a, b)$ to graph G
      end for
    end for
    for any two vertices, v_1 and v_2, in graph G **do**
      add an edge between them if $D(v_1, v_2) \leq 1$
    end for

  Step 2. Coloring graph G with the PSO algorithm using a secret key KEY with k colors
  Step 3. Refine graph G
    for every vertex v in the graph G : **do**
      Use a breadth-first search to determine whether, within a certain distance from the vertex v, there are vertices colored with all the colors in C . If not, delete v from graph G
    end for
    Repeat this step until no vertex must be deleted.

  Step 4. Hide data in the cover image in a zig-zag scanning manner to process the cover image I
    for a pixel pair in cover image I, find its corresponding vertex, v **do**
      if $Color(v)$ equals S_d **then**
        go to process S_{d+1} with the next pixel pair
      else
        Use a breadth-first search in graph G to find a vertex that meets the following requirements: $Color(v') = S_d, D(v, v') \leq bfs\_thresh$
        Replace the pixel pair in cover image I with another adjacent pixel pair that corresponds to vertex v' in graph G
        Go to process S_{d+1} with the next pixel pair
      end if
      If all the vertices in graph G have been deleted or all the pixel pairs have been processed, the algorithm is terminated
    end for

  Step 5. Output the stego-image I'

4.2 Extracting Phase

The extracting phase in scheme 2 is similar to the extracting phase in scheme 1. First, the scheme starts the reconstruction of graph G by adding every vertex ranging from $(0,0)$ to $(255,255)$ into graph G. Then the scheme uses the PSO algorithm to color graph G using the same KEY to initiate the pseudo-random integer generator. Next, the scheme scans the stego-image in a zig-zag manner. When it finds a pixel pair corresponding to vertex v in graph, it checks $Color(v)$, which is just the data hidden in stego-image. After every pixel pair is processed, the secret messages are extracted successfully.

5   Experimental Results

To show the hiding capacity and stego-image quality, some experimental results are presented in this section. The experiment was conducted on an Intel Core2 Duo P7450 computer. The proposed scheme conducted experiments on six typical images with sizes 512×512 pixels, as shown in Figure 2.

(a) Airplane   (b) Baboon   (c) Boat

(d) Pepper   (e) Tiffany   (f) Lena

Fig. 2. Images used to test the proposed schemes

5.1   Embedding Rate and Distortion Performance

In image steganography, embedding capacity, which indicates the number of secret bits that can be hidden in a cover image, is preferred to evaluate a data hiding scheme. Peak signal-to-noise ratio (PSNR), which is the most common measurement in image steganography, is used to evaluate the quality of the stego-images. The definition of PSNR is as equation 2:

$$PSNR = 10\log_{10}(255^2/MSE)$$
$$MSE = \frac{1}{W \times H} \sum_{x=0}^{H-1} \sum_{y=0}^{W-1} (I(x,y) - I'(x,y))^2, \tag{2}$$

where $I(x,y)$ and $I'(x,y)$ are the xth row, y^{th} column pixel values of the cover image I and the stego-image I', respectively; The terms W and H denote the width and the height of the image, respectively. A larger PSNR value indicates a better quality stego-image.

5.2 On Parameters of Scheme 1

In the first proposed scheme, there are three parameters that must be set, i.e., k, the number of colors used to color graph G ; adj_thresh, which decides whether two vertices are adjacent; and bfs_thresh, which limits the area of the proposed scheme's breadth-first search. In this subsection, the parameters of the first proposed scheme are described.

Figure 3 shows the influence of adj_thresh on the results of the first proposed scheme. We can observe that, while adj_thresh increases, the embedding capacity does not always increase, but the PSNR decreases significantly. This is due to the fact that, when adj_thresh increases, more edges are added to graph G, leading to a more complicated graph for which PSO has significant difficulty in finding a good coloring solution. Thus, the breadth-first search has difficulty finding a vertex with the required color near the origin vertex, leading to a decrease in the value of the PSNR. Hence, in the following experiment, adj_thresh was set as 1.

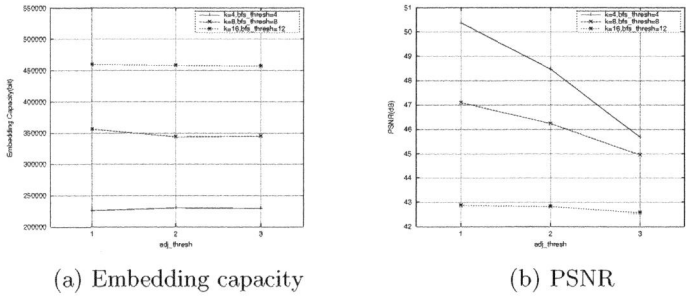

(a) Embedding capacity   (b) PSNR

Fig. 3. Influence of adj_thresh in scheme 1 for image "baboon"

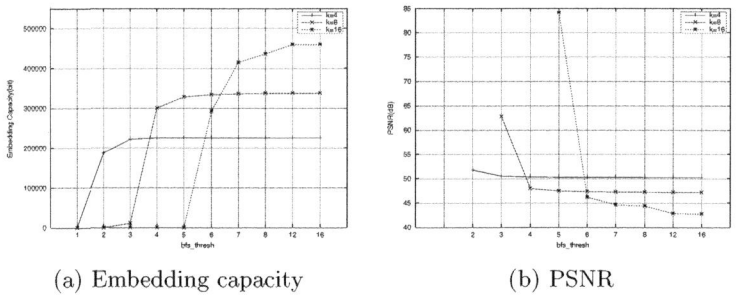

(a) Embedding capacity   (b) PSNR

Fig. 4. Effect of variations of bfs_thresh on embedding capacity and PSNR in Scheme 1 (The test image is baboon.)

Figure 4 shows the influence of bfs_thresh on the result of the first proposed scheme when adj_thresh is set as 1 and k is set as 4, 8, and 16, respectively. We note that the embedding capacity increases as bfs_thresh increases, especially when bfs_thresh is around half of k. However, when bfs_thresh is more than k, both the embedding capacity and PSNR do not vary much. This is because, when bfs_thresh that represents the radius of the breadth-first search area around a vertex, v, is too small, there are not enough vertices around to be colored with all k different colors, which leads to the deletion of the v. Finally, after the step of refining graph G, there are fewer vertices that can be used to hide data. Also, it can be found that when k increases, the embedding capacity also increases, which is illustrated in Figure 5 with the experimental results of more images.

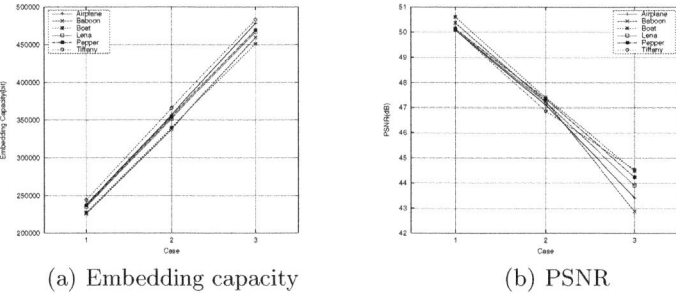

(a) Embedding capacity   (b) PSNR

Fig. 5. Variation of embedding capacity and PSNR as k increases in Scheme 1

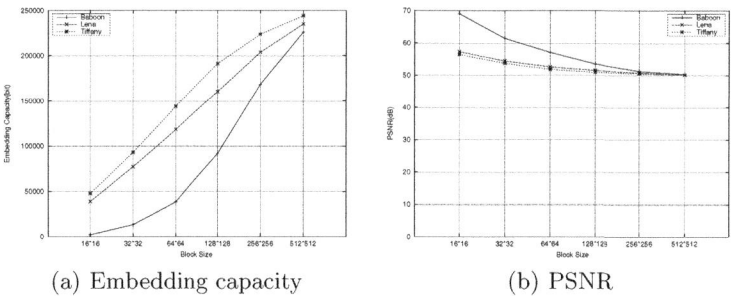

(a) Embedding capacity   (b) PSNR

Fig. 6. Influence of segmenting the cover image into blocks in Scheme 1 when the block size is 16×16, 32×32, 64×64, 128×128, 256×256, and 512×512. The test image is baboon ($k = 4$; $bfs\_thresh = 4$).

In addition to the three constant parameters mentioned above, we segmented the cover images into blocks and performed the scheme on every block, one at a time. As figure 6 shows, it can be observed that the embedding capacity and the PSNR can be controlled manually over a wide range to meet a variety of different needs.

5.3   On Parameters of Scheme 2

In the second proposed scheme, there are 2 parameters that must be set, i.e., k, the number of colors used to color graph G ; and bfs_thresh, which limits

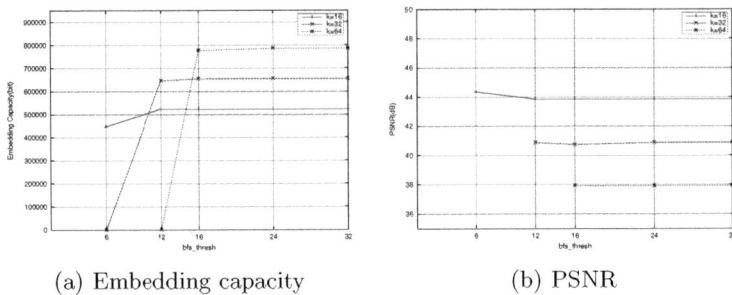

(a) Embedding capacity   (b) PSNR

Fig. 7. Variation of embedding capacity and PSNR in Scheme 2 for image "baboon" as bfs_thresh varies

the area of the proposed scheme's breadth-first search. In this subsection, the parameters of the second proposed scheme are described.

Figure 7 shows the performance of the second proposed scheme when bfs_thresh varies. It is similar to the influence of in Scheme 1 due to the same reason.

Figure 8 shows the result of the second proposed scheme under different k and bfs_thresh. In case 1 to 5, k and bfs_thresh are set as 16/6, 16/10, 32/16, 64/24, 128/32, respectively. It is note that as k and bfs_thresh increase, the embedding capacity increases a lot while PSNR decreases. Different from Figure 5, the embedding capacity of six images shown in Figure 8 is same in Cases 2 to 5. It is because the bfs_thresh is set relatively too large for k leading to every pixel in the stego-image has data embedded in.

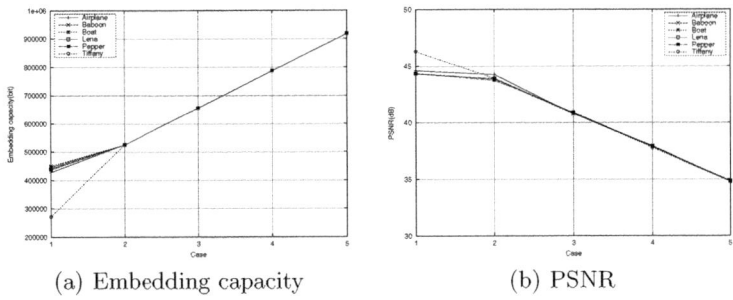

(a) Embedding capacity   (b) PSNR

Fig. 8. Variation of embedding capacity and PSNR in Scheme 2

5.4   Results and Comparisons

Figure 9 shows the stego-images of Scheme 2 with 786432 bits secret data embedded. It can be observed that the modification of the image is still imperceptible.

Table 1 shows the performance of Wang et al.'s scheme [13], Hsiao et al.'s scheme [14] and the proposed schemes. In the experiment of Scheme 1, the adj_thresh is set as 1 for a better speed, while the number of colors used to color

(a) Airplane
PSNR=37.81

(b) Baboon
PSNR=37.92

(c) Boat
PSNR=37.82

(d) Pepper
PSNR=37.85

(e) Tiffany
PSNR=37.74

(f) Lena
PSNR=37.88

Fig. 9. Stego-images of scheme 2($k = 64; bfs\_thresh = 24$;)

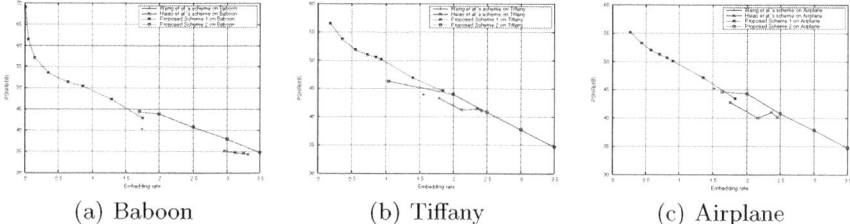

(a) Baboon   (b) Tiffany   (c) Airplane

Fig. 10. Comparisons with Wang et al.'s scheme and Hsiao et al.'s scheme

graph G and the bfs_thresh were set as $4/4$, $8/8$, and $16/12$, respectively. In the experiment of Scheme 2, k and bfs_thresh are set as $16/6$, $16/10$, $32/16$, $64/24$, $128/32$, respectively.

It can be observed that our schemes achieve better quality than both Wang et al.'s scheme and Hsiao et al.'s scheme when embedding capacity is close. Also, our proposed schemes can achieve both stego-images of high quality, limited embedding capacity and stego-images of acceptable quality and high embedding capacity. The range of our proposed schemes is wider than the range of the combination of Wang et al.'s scheme and Hsiao et al.'s scheme. By segmenting the cover image into blocks, the range can be much wider to meet different needs. Besides, our schemes perform much more stable on different images than Wang et al.'s scheme and Hsiao et al.'s scheme. It also can be noted that our scheme 2 has better embedding capacity than that of scheme 1. It is due to that the constructed graph G in scheme 2 contains more vertices than graph G in scheme 1 and the refine step is executed leading to that more pixel pairs are replaced with more secret bits embedded.

Figure 10 shows those points in a more perceptible way. We adopted three images, of which baboon is a complicated image; tiffany is a smooth image; and airplane is a normal image.

Table 1. Performance of Wang et al.'s scheme, Hsiao et al.'s scheme and our proposed schemes

Methods			Ariplane	Baboon	Boat	Pepper	Tiffany	Lena
Wang		bits	397912	457168	421080	407256	407360	409752
et al.'s		PSNR	45.2	40.3	42.1	43.3	43.9	44.1
	JND_2	bits	566074	818413	657468	695244	555779	608746
	Capacity	PSNR	40.0061	34.7143	37.0227	35.5616	41.2102	37.956
	JND_4	bits	643731	870651	723209	753178	634838	680684
Hsiao	Capacity	PSNR	40.1314	34.3178	37.1268	35.7733	41.0367	38.2711
et al.'s	JND_2	bits	459532	775055	540986	540572	468705	476270
	Quality	PSNR	42.7525	35.2057	41.0037	41.6441	43.2631	43.3275
	JND_4	bits	619919	852663	671660	664964	618315	625409
	Quality	PSNR	41.0125	34.5879	39.7253	40.3018	41.3944	41.5383
	k=4; bfs_	bits	238286	225990	227480	236594	244208	235306
	thresh=4	PSNR	50.0810	50.3683	50.6042	50.1421	50.0974	50.0930
Our	k=8; bfs_	bits	356340	337410	339732	354159	365517	351642
Scheme 1	thresh=8	PSNR	47.0994	47.2445	47.3931	47.3388	46.8587	47.2064
	k=16; bfs_	bits	478264	459456	451208	469192	483252	466812
	thresh=12	PSNR	43.4167	42.8732	44.4789	44.2345	44.5323	43.9064
	k=16; bfs_	bits	428012	445980	450220	437576	272184	440976
	thresh=6	PSNR	44.6323	44.3637	44.3159	44.3549	46.2778	44.3331
	k=16;bfs_	bits	524288	524288	524288	524288	524288	524288
	thresh=10	PSNR	44.2764	43.8675	43.8941	43.7599	43.9504	43.9082
Our	k=32; bfs_	bits	655100	654655	655205	655140	655340	655000
Scheme 2	thresh=16	PSNR	40.7552	40.7372	40.8097	40.8828	40.7940	40.8498
	k=64; bfs_	bits	786432	786432	786432	786432	786432	786432
	thresh=24	PSNR	37.8147	37.9264	37.8251	37.8555	37.7406	37.8817
	k=128; bfs_	bits	917504	917504	917504	917504	917504	917504
	thresh=32	PSNR	34.7595	34.8105	34.7466	34.7905	34.7418	34.8369

6   Conclusions

In this paper, we proposed two new, novel, data hiding schemes based on graph coloring to embed secret data in images. The proposed schemes offer several improvements over other schemes, i.e., (1) it performs better in both capacity and imperceptivity of stego-images; (2) it is more flexible than the others because, through segmenting images into different size blocks, it can achieve stego-images with good embedding capacity and good PSNR as well as stego-images with limited embedding capacity and much better PSNR, if needed; (3) the use of the PSO algorithm makes it more secure; and (4) graph coloring was used to solve the data hiding problem, which has never been done before. As stated above, our proposed scheme provides increased embedding capacity, increased quality of the stego-images, security, and innovation.

References

1. Duric, Z., Jacobs, M., Jajodia, S.: Information hiding: steganography and steganalysis, vol. 24, pp. 171–187. Elsevier, Amsterdam (2005)
2. Chang, C.-C., Lin, C.-Y., Wang, Y.-Z.: New image steganographic methods using run-length approach. Information Sciences 176(22), 3393–3408 (2006)
3. Chan, C.-K., Cheng, L.-M.: Hiding data in images by simple LSB substitution. Pattern Recognition 37(3), 469–474 (2004)
4. Thien, C.-C., Lin, J.-C.: A simple and high-hiding capacity method for hiding digit-by-digit data in images based on modulus function. Pattern Recognition 36(12), 2875–2881 (2003)
5. Yang, C.-H.: Inverted pattern approach to improve image quality of information hiding by LSB substitution. Pattern Recognition 41(8), 2674–2683 (2008)
6. Luo, X.-Y., Wang, D.-S., Wang, P., Liu, F.-L.: A review on blind detection for image steganography. Signal Processing 88(9), 2138–2157 (2008)
7. Wang, R.-Z., Lin, C.-F., Lin, J.-C.: Image hiding by optimal LSB substitution and genetic algorithm. Pattern Recognition 34(3), 671–683 (2001)
8. Chang, C.-C., Hsiao, J.-Y., Chan, C.-S.: Finding optimal least-significant-bit substitution in image hiding by dynamic programming strategy. Pattern Recognition 36(7), 1583–1595 (2003)
9. Yang, C.-H., Weng, C.-Y., Wang, S.-J., Sun, H.-M.: Adaptive data hiding in edge areas of images with spatial LSB domain systems. IEEE Transactions on Information Forensics and Security 3(3), 488–497 (2008)
10. Wu, D.-C., Tsai, W.-H.: A steganographic method for images by pixel-value differencing. Pattern Recognition Letters 24(9-10), 1613–1626 (2003)
11. Wu, H.-C., Wu, N.-I., Tsai, C.-S., Hwang, M.-S.: Image steganographic scheme based on pixel-value differencing and LSB replacement methods, Vision, Image and Signal Processing. IEE Proceedings 152(5), 611–615 (2005)
12. Yang, C.-H., Wang, S.-J., Weng, C.-Y.: Analyses of pixel-value-differencing schemes with LSB replacement in stegonagraphy. Intelligent Information Hiding and Multimedia Signal Processing 1, 445–448 (2007)
13. Wang, C.-M., Wu, N.-I., Tsai, C.-S., Hwang, M.-S.: A high quality steganographic method with pixel-value differencing and modulus function. Journal of Systems and Software 81(1), 150–158 (2008)
14. Hsiao, J.-Y., Chang, C.-T.: An adaptive steganographic method based on the measurement of just noticeable distortion profile. Image and Vision Computing (in press, corrected proof)
15. Yanez, J., Ramirez, J.: The robust coloring problem. European Journal of Operational Research 148(3), 546–558 (2003)
16. Guruswami, V., Khanna, S.: On the hardness of 4-coloring a 3-collorable graph. In: IEEE Conference on Computational Complexity Proceedings, pp. 188–197 (2000)
17. Cui, G., Qin, L., Liu, S., Wang, Y., Zhang, X., Cao, X.: Modified pso algorithm for solving planar graph coloring problem. Progress in Natural Science 18(3), 353–357 (2008)
18. Kennedy, J., Eberhart, R.: Particle swarm optimization. In: IEEE International Conference on Neural Networks Proceedings, vol. 4, pp. 1942–1948 (1995)

A Variable Weight Based Fuzzy Data Fusion Algorithm for WSN

Qianping Wang, Hongmei Liao, Ke Wang, and Yuan Sang

School of Computer Science and Technology,
China University of Mining and Technology, Xuzhou, P.R. China
qpwang@cumt.edu.cn

Abstract. Due to the limited energy, storage space and computing ability, data fusion is very necessary in Wireless Sensor Networks (WSN). In this paper, a new variable weight based fuzzy data fusion algorithm for WSN is proposed to improve the accuracy and reliability of the global data fusion. In this algorithm, the weight of each cluster head node in global fusion is not fixed. Time delay, data amount and trustworthiness of each cluster head will all affect the final fusion weight. We get the fusion weights by variable weight based fuzzy comprehensive evaluation or fuzzy reasoning. In the variable weight based fuzzy comprehensive evaluation, by increasing the weight of the factor with too low value, we can give prominence to deficiency and the clusters with too long time delay or too small amount or too low trustworthiness will get smaller weights in data fusion. And therefore, the cluster head node with deficiency will have a small influence in global fusion. Simulation shows that this algorithm can obtain a more accurate and reliable fusion results especially when there are data undetected or compromised nodes compared with traditional algorithms.

1   Introduction

Commercial and military applications have motivated the expeditious development of ubiquitous and pervasive computing environments. Wireless sensor network is a good representation of ubiquitous computing. A wireless sensor network is suitable for special scenarios in which the installment of an infrastructure is impossible due to hostile environments, high costs, or a transient period of use [1].In a typical wireless sensor network, a large number of sensor nodes collect application specific information from the environment and this information is transferred to a central base station where it is processed, analyzed, and used by the application. Wireless sensor network often consists of a large number of low-cost sensor nodes that have strictly limited sensing, computation, and communication capabilities. So, it is important to minimize the amount of data transmission and improve the average sensor life time and the overall bandwidth utilization. Data fusion is the process of summarizing and combining sensor data to reduce the amount of data transmission in the network. Some protocols allow routing and fusing of data packets simultaneously. These protocols can be categorized into two parts: tree-based data fusion protocols [2] and

C.-H. Hsu et al. (Eds.): UIC 2011, LNCS 6905, pp. 490–502, 2011.
© Springer-Verlag Berlin Heidelberg 2011

cluster-based data fusion protocols. To reduce the latency due to tree-based data fusion, recent work on data fusion tends to group sensor nodes into clusters and route fused data over cluster heads. In Cluster-based data fusion protocols, nodes are subdivided into clusters. In each cluster, a cluster head is elected in order to fuse data locally and transmit the fused result to the base station. At the base station, data from different clusters are fused again. We called this process as global fusion. The fusion in cluster is called local fusion.

As wireless sensor networks are usually deployed in remote and hostile environments, sensor nodes are prone to node compromise attacks. A compromised sensor node or data aggregators can inject false data during data forwarding and fusing to forge the integrity of fused data. Security issues in data fusion in WSN are of utmost importance. The trustworthiness of the node sending the fusion data should be taken into consideration also. Some secure data fusion protocols in wireless sensor networks have been proposed. In [3], topological constraints are introduced to build a secure aggregation tree (SAT) that facilitates the monitoring of data aggregators. In [4], the authors improved the main idea of SELDA by introducing functional reputation concept where each functional reputation value is computed over sensor node actions with respect to that function. Hence, security of data fusion process is ensured by selecting trusted data aggregators using fusion functional reputation and by weighting sensor data using sensing functional reputation. In [5] [6], an Extended Kalman Filter (EKF) based mechanism to detect false injected data is proposed. Along with the employment of EKF, the proposed mechanism monitors sensor nodes to predict their future real in-network fused values. In [10], to support data fusion along with false data detection, the monitoring nodes of every data aggregator also conduct data fusion and compute the corresponding small-size message authentication codes for data verification at their pair-mates.

However, in the fusion process of cluster head nodes, besides nodes trustworthiness, different time delay and different amount of data of each cluster head may cause a low accuracy and reliability of fusion. To meet this problem, we propose a *variable weight based fuzzy data fusion algorithm for WSN* in this paper. In this algorithm, data from each cluster head in WSN will be fused in the station with a weight. It is important that this weight is not fixed; it is gotten by a variable weight based fuzzy comprehensive evaluation. With this variable weight based fuzzy comprehensive evaluation, every factor such as trustworthiness, time delay and amount of data will be taken in consideration and any defect factor will be given a larger weight in the comprehensive evaluation algorithm so that the defect is amplified. By this variable weight based fuzzy comprehensive evaluation, the weight of a cluster head with some defect in global fusion will be much smaller and its impact will decrease.

The remainder of the paper is organized as follows: In Section 2, we give introductory information about Cluster fusion model and set the context of the present paper. In Section 3, we explain the fuzzy comprehensive evaluation of fusion weights and Variable Weight based Fuzzy Fusion algorithm in detail.

Simulations and analysis are provided in Section 4. We use Fuzzy Reasoning to get Fusion weights in Section 5.Concluding remarks are presented in Section 6.

2   Problem Definitions

In this paper, we discuss the data fusion in Cluster based WSN.

2.1   Cluster Fusion Model

In Clustering fusion model, the network is divided into several clusters, and each cluster is managed by a cluster head (CH). In the in-network data fusion of a cluster, Mobile Agent Architecture is applied [7]. When the base station sends a query, a mobile agent moves around a cluster for acquiring data sensed by nodes in this cluster at first; After data analysis and fusion, the mobile agent transmits the fused data to cluster head. As described above, mobile agent completes the local fusion in a progressive way. Further, the base station gathers local results from all cluster heads and then the global fusion is accomplished by fusing these local fusion results from cluster heads.

2.2   Different Time Delay, Data Amount and Existence of Compromised Nodes

Commonly used *Weighted Averaging Fusion Algorithm* [8] uses fixed weights for cluster heads in global fusion.

However, in wireless sensor networks, compromised sensor nodes aim to distort the integrity of data by sending false data reports, injecting false data during data fusion, and disrupting the transmission of fused data. Because fused data calculated by a cluster head node represents the data of a large number of normal sensor nodes and the cluster heads can inject false data during data fusion, a compromised cluster head node will have a larger impact on the final result computed by the base station. For the above reasons, our works focus on the global fusion of data from cluster heads in WSN. Besides, due to the heterogeneous character of wireless sensor network, the density of nodes, the time delay that data from cluster head nodes arrive at the base station and the amount of data that each cluster head node collected in a certain period of time are different, which may cause a low accuracy and efficiency of fusion. And therefore WAF is not accurate enough and it may lead to worse accuracy or slower convergence when there is information undetected.

In this paper, we proposed a *fuzzy logic based global fusion algorithm* in which weights of fusion cluster head nodes are obtained by variable weight based fuzzy comprehensive evaluation. Suppose there are trust systems to detect node misbehavior and give the trustworthiness of nodes, mechanisms giving time delay value and data amount. Trust system based on node monitoring mechanisms in WSN has been researched in [4] [9] [10].

3   Fuzzy Comprehensive Evaluation of Fusion Weights

Considering the constraints of limited energy, storage space, and computing ability of sensor nodes, Distributed Kalman Filtering is applied to source nodes in wireless sensor networks [11]. In global Fusion Model, the proposed fuzzy comprehensive algorithm is used to fuse the processed data from cluster heads in WSN.

Weighted Averaging Fusion (WAF) is a fusion method to obtain the average detection value of multi-sensor nodes [12]. In a traditional global weighted averaging data fusion algorithm, each cluster has a different but fixed weight.

As a heterogeneous network, time delay is unavoidable in wireless sensor networks. Here, time delay is defined as the interval between the time data packet is taken out from a cluster head and the time the data packet is received by the base station [12]. Moreover, the amount of transmitted data of cluster heads is not fixed. Therefore, Weighted Average Fusion and other fusion algorithm without consideration of time delay and data amount is not accurate enough in WSN. Especially, the method may lead to worse accuracy or slower convergence when data undetected conditions happened [13]. Besides, compromised sensor nodes sending false data in WSN will distort the integrity of data. In order to improve the performance of the fusion algorithms, a new weighted fusion algorithm is proposed. In this algorithm, the weights of clusters is determined by a Variable Weight based Fuzzy Comprehensive Evaluation and fuzzy reasoning. The fusion weights will be changed with the time delay, data amount and trustworthiness of cluster head nodes. Nodes with less time delay, more amount data and larger trustworthiness will get a bigger weight in the fusion algorithm instead of a fixed weight.

In our new weighted fusion algorithm, every factor play role in deciding the membership degrees of fusion weights to fuzzy sets $U_i(i = 1, 2, \cdots, 6)$. U_1 denotes the *zero* fuzzy set; U_2 denotes the *very small* fuzzy set; U_3 denotes the *small* fuzzy set; U_4 denotes the *middle* fuzzy set; U_5 denotes the *big* fuzzy set; U_6 denotes the *one* fuzzy set.

As we often cannot give precise weights of every cluster in practical fusion computing, fuzzy Comprehensive Evaluation can be used to compute the fusion weights decided by these three factors.

3.1   Ordered Weighted Averaging Operations

Suppose the following is the factors (attributes) aggregation in computing fusion weights of clusters:

$E = \{E_1, E_2, E_3\}$.

E_1 represents time delay, E_2 represents data amount and E_3 represents trustworthiness of the sending node. There may be several subgroup factors in each factor. In this paper, for simplification, we will not discuss the subgroup factors.

Suppose the fuzzy evaluation aggregation of time delay and data amount weights is:

$U = (U_1, U_2, U_3, U_4, U_5, U_6)$.

The relationship R denotes the mapping of E to U. That is, the element r_{ij} in R is the membership degree of E_i to U_j.

Matrix $R = (r_{ij})_{3 \times 6}$ is the fuzzy comprehensive judgment Matrix of clusters' fusion weights.

The final value of fusion weights of clusters in WSN will be combined closely with the value of each evaluation factor in E. The nature of evaluation weight is shown in the different influence from the above three aspects on the fusion weights of clusters in WSN.

Suppose w_i is the weight of the factor E_i. Let $w = (w_1, w_2, w_3)$ be a *weighting vector* such that w_i is in $[0, 1]$ for all i and $w_1 + w_2 + w_3 = 1$. So, the fuzzy fusion weight vector $V = \{v_1, v_2, v_3, v_4, v_5, v_6\}$ of some node can be gotten by the following fuzzy mapping:

$\{v_1, v_2, v_3, v_4, v_5, v_6\} = (w_1, w_2, w_3) \circ (r_{ij})_{3 \times 6}$ And

$v_i = w_1 * r_{1j} + w_2 * r_{2j} + w_3 * r_{3j}, (j = 1, 2, \cdots, 6)$.

This aggregation operation is often called *ordered weighted averaging operations*.

Suppose there are two sets of performance evaluation of factors $\{E_1, E_2, E_3\}$ whose define area is $[0, 1]$. Suppose the values of these two sets of evaluation of some cluster are respectively $[0.2, 0.9, 0.75]$ and $[0.8, 0.3, 0.85]$.

To get the fuzzy comprehensive evaluations of these two groups, we should first change the evaluation on $[0,1]$ into membership degrees in six fuzzy sets mentioned in 3.2. These fuzzy sets are the evaluation reviews of factors E_1, E_2 and E_3. We use the *Trapezoidal Curve Membership Function* to fuzzify the input values such as time delay and data amount. The width and shape of trapezoid curve is decided by four parameters [a, b, c, d]which can be obtained by expert experience. If the fuzzy sets of fusion weights $U_1, U_2, U_3, U_4, U_5, U_6$ adopt trapezoidal membership functions, and parameters [a, b, c, d] are set separately as [-0.18 -0.02 0.02 0.18], [0.02 0.18 0.22 0.38], [0.22 0.38 0.42 0.58], [0.42 0.58 0.62 0.78], [0.62 0.78 0.82 0.98], [0.82 0.98 1.02 1.18]. Then the first set of evaluation $[0.2, 0.9, 0.75]$ can be fuzzyfied and changed into a fuzzy comprehensive evaluation matrix R_1:

$$R_1 = \begin{pmatrix} 0 & 1 & 0 & 0 & 0 & 0 \\ 0 & 0 & 0 & 0 & 0.5 & 0.5 \\ 0 & 0 & 0.4 & 0.6 & 0 & 0 \end{pmatrix}.$$

The second set of evaluation $[0.8, 0.7, 0.85]$ is changed into a fuzzy comprehensive evaluation matrix R_2:

$$R_2 = \begin{pmatrix} 0 & 0 & 0 & 0 & 1 & 0 \\ 0 & 0 & 0 & 0.5 & 0.5 & 0 \\ 0 & 0 & 0 & 0 & 0.7 & 0.3 \end{pmatrix}.$$

Suppose the comprehensive evaluation weights w_{mi} (w_{m1}, w_{m2}, w_{m3}) are set as 0.3, 0.3 and 0.4. Two sets of fusion evaluation $[0.2, 0.9, 0.75]$ and $[0.8, 0.7, 0.85]$ is given. If the delay time is too long, that means the performance evaluation of factor E_1 is poor, the evaluation value of E_1 will be small. If the data amount is too small, that means the performance evaluation of factor E_2 is poor, the evaluation value of E_2 will be small. If the trustworthiness of a node is too small, that means the performance evaluation of factor E_3 is poor, the evaluation value of E_3 will be small.

The comprehensive values of the two sets of fusion evaluation$[0.2,0.9,0.75]$ and $[0.8,0.7,0.85]$ can be separately computed with fixed weight $w_{mi}(w_{m1}, w_{m2}, w_{m3})$: $V_1 = [0 \quad 0.8 \quad 0.2 \quad 0 \quad 0 \quad 0]$; $V_2 = [0 \quad 0 \quad 0.05 \quad 0.35 \quad 0.6 \quad 0]$.

Defuzzification is the reverse process of fuzzification. The value we have gotten above is a *fuzzy* result, that is, the result is described in terms of membership in fuzzy sets. Defuzzification would transform this result into a single number indicating the fusion weights of clusters in WSN. It is necessary to output a real number as the fusion weight. An average of maxima method or a centroid method can be used to do this work. With centroid-based defuzzification, we can get the outcomes V_1=0.38 ; $V_2 = 0.62$.

3.2   Variable Weight Based Fuzzy Comprehensive Evaluation of Fusion Weights

In ordered weighted averaging operations, evaluation weight vector $w = (w_1, w_2, w_3)$ is fixed. That is, once the weight of each factor of these three is set, it will not be changed whatever the actual situation is.

However, if the value of one attribute such as time delay is too long or the value of data amount is too small or the trustworthiness is too low, even if the other attribute is very good, the cluster head should not be given a big fusion weight. In ordered weighted averaging operations, the high value of the other attribute will counteract the low value of the bad attribute.

By increasing the weight of the attribute when its value is too low, we can give prominence to deficiency. That is variable weight based fuzzy comprehensive evaluation of fusion weight which can be described as follows:

1) Suppose the value of evaluation factors (attributes) $E = \{E_1, E_2, E_3\}$ is u_1, u_2, u_3. $u_i \in [0, u_m]$, $i = 1, 2, 3$. When attribute E_i is in the best situation, $u_i = u_m$. When attribute E_i is in the worst situation, $u_i = 0$.

2) The weight of factor E_i in comprehensive evaluation is denoted as w_i, it is function of (u_1, u_2, u_3). That is, $w_i = w_i(u_1, u_2, u_3)$. The weight of factor E_i, depends on the separate values of all factors. $w_i \in [0, 1]$ and $w_1 + w_2 + w_3 = 1$.

Especially, $w_{mi} = w_i(u_m, u_m, u_m)$, $i = 1, 2, 3$, $w_{mi} \in (0, 1)$ and $w_{m1} + w_{m2} + w_{m3} = 1$. w_{mi} is called base weight , and it can be gotten by ierarchical analytic approach. Here

$w_{01} = w_1(0, u_m, u_m)$, $w_{02} = w_2(u_m, 0, u_m)$,
$w_{03} = w_3(u_m, u_m, 0)$, $w_{0i} \in (0, 1)$, $i = 1, 2, 3$.

w_{0i} denotes the weight of factor E_i when E_i has its min value and the other factor have its max values. w_{0i} can be set by the specialist as the max value of weight of factor E_i. So the influence of factor E_i can be amplified.

3) In order to find appropriate variable weight $w(u_1, u_2, u_3)$, which is non-increasing function of u_i and which is non-decreasing function of u_i, we introduce function $\lambda_i(u)(i = 1, 2)$which matches the following criteria

(1)$\lambda_i(u)$ is defined in $[0, u_m]$it is not negative and bounded

(2)u_i is a nonincreasing differentiable function in $[0, u_m]$;

(3)Let $\lambda_i(0) = \lambda_{0i}$, $\lambda_i(u_m) = \lambda_{mi}$. λ_{0i} denotes the maximum of $\lambda_i(u)$ and λ_{mi} denotes the minimum value of $\lambda_i(u)$.

To a given set of single-factor assessment of (u_1, u_2, u_3) a function λ_{u_i} ($i = 1, 2, 3$) can be obtained by the means in literature [14]. Set:

$$w_i(u_1, u_2) = \frac{\lambda_i(u_i)}{\sum_{j=1}^{3} \lambda_j(u_j)}, i = 1, 2, 3.$$

It have been proved that $w_i(u_1, u_2, \cdots, u_n)$, $i = 1, 2, \cdots, n$ in this formula can be the variable weight [14].

Parameters in the variable weight based fuzzy comprehensive evaluation algorithm are shown in Table1.

If the time delay of a cluster head in WSN fusion algorithms is too long or the data amount is little or the trustworthiness is too small, although the other factors are all well, the cluster head node should be given a smaller weight then that computed with fixed Fuzzy Comprehensive Evaluation method to outstand the deficient factor and decrease its impact on the final fusion weights.

Table 1. Variables in Varialble Weight based Fuzzy Comprehensive Evaluation

Parameters	E_1	E_2	E_3
w_{mi}	0.3	0.3	0.4
λ_{0i}	1.63	1.05	2.67
λ^*	3.72	4.3	8.03
λ_{*i}	0.7	0.7	1.6
k_i	0.289	0.09233	0.6737

It can be seen that the value of factors E_1 in factors evaluation [0.2,0.9,0.75] is outstandingly low, that means the delay time is too long. Long delay time means old fashioned data. To decrease the impact of the cluster with too long delay time, we can increase the weight of the deficient factor E_1 in the fuzzy comprehensive evaluation. The final fusion weight which is obtained by fuzzy comprehensive evaluation will be decreased. Variable weight based fuzzy comprehensive evaluation instead of fixed fuzzy comprehensive evaluation is applied in this fuzzy comprehensive evaluation model.

According to variable weight based fuzzy comprehensive evaluation algorithm, we can get the weights of comprehensive evaluation factors and the final fusion weight on these two sets of evaluations [0.2, 0.9, 0.75] and [0.8, 0.7, 0.85].

Variable weights of every factor on evaluations [0.2, 0.9, 0.75] and [0.8, 0.7, 0.85] are as Table2.These values can be computed with the method in literature [14]:

With variable weight based fuzzy comprehensive evaluation algorithm, the comprehensive fusion weight vectors of valuations [0.2, 0.9, 0.75] and [0.8, 0.7, 0.85] can be gotten.

Table 2. Values of Variable Weights when Evaluations are Given

Evaluation	Weight	E_1	E_2	E_3
$[0.2, 0.9, 0.75]$ w_i		0.54	0.22	0.24
$[0.8, 0.7, 0.85]$ w_i		0.3	0.28	0.42

Defuzzify the vectors computed by the above variable weight based fuzzy comprehensive evaluation algorithm by centroid method, we can get the following results:

V_1=0.36, V_2=0.53.

Compare this results computed by variable weight based fuzzy comprehensive evaluation and the results computed by fixed weighted fuzzy comprehensive evaluation, we can find that former is always smaller than the latter except that every single factor in the assessment factors have taken the maximum.

The affection of the ill clusters have low fusion weights by give it a larger weight in variable weight based fuzzy comprehensive evaluation which have three factors, time delay, data amount and trustworthiness. The comprehensive fusion weights of cluster in WSN will then be decreased even if its other factors have high evaluations. By variable weight based fuzzy comprehensive evaluation, the clusters have too much time delay or have too little data amount and too small trustworthiness will get a smaller fusion weights than by fixed weight based fuzzy comprehensive evaluation and then the fusion algorithm is more reliable.

4   Simulations and Analysis

We use 8 random variables respectively subject to normal distribution to simulate the signals of 8 cluster heads for global fusion in WSN. The mean of these variables are all 0, and their standard derivations are separately 1.5, 2.0, 1.0, 1.0, 2.5, 0.3, 0.8, and 3.0.

Weighted Averaging Fusion (WAF) and Variable Weight based Fuzzy Data Fusion Algorithm (VWFFA) are used to fuse the data from these 8 cluster heads respectively. Variable weight based fuzzy comprehensive evaluation is used in VWFFA to compute the weight of every factors of a cluster fusion weight at the base station.

Suppose the collected data by each cluster heads will be sent to base station every 2 seconds. Simulation results in Matlab are shown in Fig1 and Fig2.

Fig1 shows the comparison of the accuracy result between the two algorithms when there is a comprised node. When there is compromised node with low trustworthiness which has reported 6 false data in the past time, the Variable Weight based Fuzzy Data Fusion Algorithm will give low weight 0.33 to the node by giving larger weight 0.76 to the trustworthiness factor with small value. The node with false data will then have minor influence.

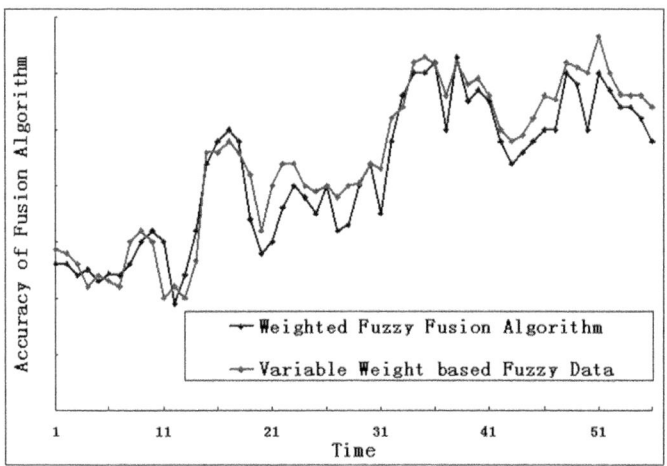

Fig. 1. Comparison of 2 fusion algorithm with a compromised node

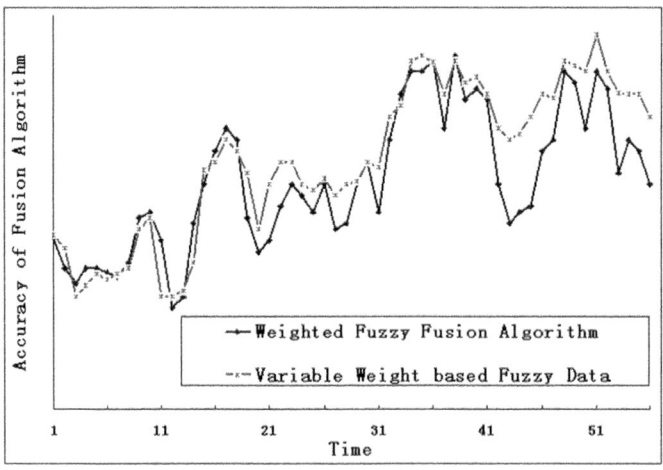

Fig. 2. Comparison of 2 fusion algorithm where there is misdetection after 40s

Suppose one of the cluster heads damaged at 40s. The membership degree to fuzzy set D6 of delay time factor will be 1, and that is the extreme case. Fig2 shows that the accuracy of Weighted Average Fusion is much worse than that of Variable Weight based Fuzzy Data Fusion Algorithm.

Performance analysis and simulation results indicate that the proposed algorithm has a higher accuracy and reliability especially under undetected condition or with compromised nodes.

5 Fusion Weights Obtained by Fuzzy Reasoning and Simulations

In data fusion of WSN, time delay vector, data amount vector and trustworthiness are input and the fusion weights of these clusters are output. By variable weight based fuzzy comprehensive evaluation, we can get the variable fusion weights of clusters in WSN. If the amount of evaluation factors n is small, for example in this paper $n = 3$, this fusion weights can also be obtained by fuzzy reasoning theory.

Set $T_i(i = 1, 2, \cdots, 6), D_i(i = 1, 2, \cdots, 6)$ and $HD_i(i = 1, 2, \cdots, 6)$ as input which denote time delay fuzzy sets, data amount fuzzy sets and trustworthiness fuzzy sets seperately. Output $U_i(i = 1, 2, \cdots, 6)$ denote fusion weights fuzzy sets of clusters. In practice, the fuzzy rules in this algorithm should be more. For simplification, we set eight rules in this paper.

These fuzzy reasoning rules are as follows:

```
1. If (TimeDelay is D1) and (DataAmount is mf1) and (HonestDegree is HD1) then (FusionWeight is U1) (1)
2. If (TimeDelay is D2) and (DataAmount is mf2) and (HonestDegree is HD2) then (FusionWeight is U2) (1)
3. If (TimeDelay is D3) and (DataAmount is mf3) and (HonestDegree is HD3) then (FusionWeight is U3) (1)
4. If (TimeDelay is D4) and (DataAmount is mf4) and (HonestDegree is HD4) then (FusionWeight is U4) (1)
5. If (TimeDelay is D5) and (DataAmount is mf5) and (HonestDegree is HD5) then (FusionWeight is U5) (1)
6. If (TimeDelay is D6) and (DataAmount is mf6) and (HonestDegree is HD6) then (FusionWeight is U6) (1)
7. If (TimeDelay is D1) or (DataAmount is mf1) or (HonestDegree is HD1) then (FusionWeight is U1) (1)
8. If (TimeDelay is D2) or (DataAmount is mf2) or (HonestDegree is HD2) then (FusionWeight is U2) (1)
```

Fig. 3. Fuzzy Reasoning Rules

Fig4 and Fig5 shows the application of these fuzzy rules.

As shown in Fig4, if the value of input T, D and HD are 0.669 , 0.52 and 0.452 separately, we can get the fuzzy vectors by the above fuzzy rules . The defuzzified fusion weight of cluster in fusion algorithm iscan be cacualted as 0.6.

As shown in Fig5, the value of input T, D and HD are 0.91, 0.886 and 0.127 separately, we can get the fuzzy vectors by the above fuzzy rules. Defuzzify these fuzzy vectors, the fusion weight of cluster with time delay, data amount and trustworthiness is: fusion weight=0.183.

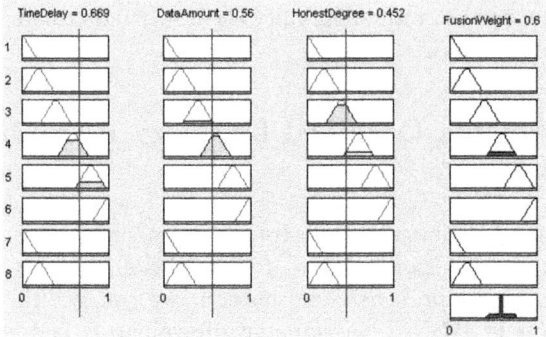

Fig. 4. Results of Fuzzy Reasoning Rules

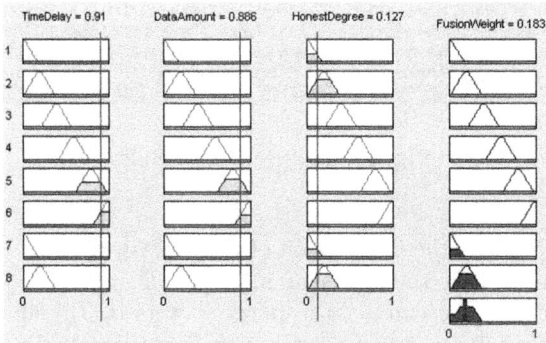

Fig. 5. Results of Fuzzy Reasoning Rules

6   Conclusions

In WSN, different time delay and different amount of sending data, and different trustworthiness of each cluster head node may cause a low accuracy and reliability of fusion. A compromising node may provide false data and disrupting the fusion process. A damage node with too long delay time will affect the fusion result. And therefore, a new *Variable Weight based Fuzzy Data Fusion Algorithm for WSN* is proposed. In this algorithm, the global fusion weights of each cluster head can be obtained by variable weight based fuzzy comprehensive evaluation of or fuzzy reasoning. In the variable weight based fuzzy comprehensive evaluation, any factor of the above mentioned three factors is deficient, that is the time delay it too long or data amount is too little or trustworthiness of node is too small, the weight of this deficient factor will be amplified, and then the final weight of the cluster head node in global fusion algorithm will be decreased.

By increasing the weight of the factor with too low value, we can give prominence to deficiency and the clusters with too long time delay or too small amount or too low trustworthiness will get smaller weights in global data fusion. Simulation shows that this algorithm can obtain a more accurate and reliability fusion estimate especially when there are data undetected or compromised nodes compared with rational algorithms.

References

1. Yiwei, Z., Hong, N.: Research on the Wireless Sensor Network Database. Computer Engineering and Science 28, 73–74 (2000)
2. Xu, Y., Heidemann, J., Estrin, D.: Geography-informed energy conservation for ad hoc routing. In: Proceedings of the CM/SIGMOBILE MobiCom, pp. 70–84 (2001)
3. Wu, K., Dreef, D., Sun, B., Xiao, Y.: Secure data aggregation without persistent cryptographic operations in wireless sensor networks. Ad Hoc Networks 5(1), 100–111 (2007)
4. Ozdemir, S.: Functional reputation based reliable data aggregation and transmission for wireless sensor networks. Elsevier Comput. Commun. 31(17), 3941–3953 (2005)
5. Sun, B., Jin, X., Wu, K., Xiao, Y.: Integration of secure in-network aggregation and system monitoring for wireless sensor networks. In: Proceedings of IEEE International Conference on Communications, pp. 1466–1471 (2007)
6. Sun, B., Chand, N., Wu, K., Xiao, Y.: Change-point monitoring for secure in-network aggregation in wireless sensor networks. In: Proceedings of IEEE Global Telecommunications Conference, IEEE GLOBECOM, pp. 936–940 (2007)
7. Lotfinezhad, M., Liang, B.: Energy efficient clustering in sensor networks with mobile agents. In: Proc of IEEE Conf. on Wireless Communications and Networking, pp. 187–192. IEEE Computer Society, New York (2005)
8. Ganeriwal, S., Srivastava, M.B.: Reputation-based framework for high integrity sensor networks. In: Proceedings of the Second ACM Workshop on Security of Ad Hoc and Sensor Networks, Washington DC, pp. 66–77 (2004)

9. Boukerch, A., Xu, L., Khatib, E.L.: Trust-based security for wireless ad hoc and sensor networks. Computer Communications 30, 2413–2427 (2007)
10. Liu, K., Nael, G., Kyoung, A.: Location verification and trust management for resilient geographic routing. J. Parallel Distrib. Comput. 67, 215–228 (2007)
11. Cam, H., Ozdemir, S., Nair, P., Muthuavinashiappan, D., Sanli, H.O.: Energy-efficient and secure pattern based data aggregation for wireless sensor networks. Comput. Commun. 29(4), 446–455 (2006)
12. Wang, X., Wang, S.: Jiang.A.: Optimized deployment strategy of mobile agent s in wireless sensor networks. In: The 6th Int. Conf. on Intelligent System Design and Applications, pp. 893–898. IEEE Computer Society, Los Alamitos (2006)
13. Gracanin, D.: A service- centric model for wireless sensor networks. IEEE Journal on Selected Areas in Communications 23, 159–166 (2005)
14. Zuzeng, P., Wenyu, S.: Fuzzy Mathematics and its application, pp. 200–210. Wuhan University Press, China (2007)

Threshold Selection for Ultra-Wideband TOA Estimation Based on Skewness Analysis

Hao Zhang[1,3], Xue-rong Cui[1,2], and T. Aaron Gulliver[3]

[1] Department of Information Science and Engineering, Ocean University of China,
Qing Dao, China
zhanghao@ouc.edu.cn, cuixuerong@163.com
[2] Department of Computer and Communication Engineering, China University of Petroleum
(East China), Qing Dao, China
[3] Department of Electrical Computer Engineering, University of Victoria, Victoria, Canada
agullive@ece.uvic.ca

Abstract. Because of the high sampling rate, coherent Time of Arrival (TOA) estimation algorithms are not practical for low cost, low complexity Ultra-Wideband (UWB) systems. In this paper, an Energy Detection (ED) based non-coherent TOA estimation algorithm is presented. The expected values of skewness and kurtosis with respect to the Signal to Noise Ratio (SNR) are investigated. It is shown that the skewness is more suitable for TOA estimation. To improve the precision of TOA estimation, a new threshold selection algorithm is proposed which is based on skewness analysis. The best threshold values for different SNRs are investigated and the effects of integration period and channel modes are examined. Comparisons with other ED based algorithms show that in CM1 and CM2 channels, the proposed algorithm provides higher precision and robustness in both high and low SNR environments.

1   Introduction

Among the potential applications, precision indoor ranging, positioning and tracking have been the most obvious for Impulse Radio Ultra-Wideband (UWB) technology [1-3]. UWB technology is increasingly considered as an ideal radio system to enable accurate indoor positioning for tasks such as asset and people tracking or ambient intelligent sensing, even in dense multipath, Non-Line of Sight (NLOS) fading environments. This is because of the high time resolution (sub-nanosecond to nanosecond) available due to the transmission of very short pulses. In addition, the wide signal bandwidth results in a very low power spectral density, which reduces interference to other RF systems, and the short pulse duration reduces or eliminates pulse distortion (fading) and spurious signal detections due to multipath propagation [4]. In addition, some frequency components may be able to penetrate obstacles to provide a line-of-sight (LOS) signal. Thus, these high resolution, wide bandwidth UWB signals are very suitable for positioning applications [5].

Positioning technologies can be classified into range based [2, 3, 6, 7] and non-range based [8]. For example, Time of Arrival (TOA) [7, 9] and Time Difference of Arrival (TDOA) [10] are range based techniques, while Received Signal Strength (RSS) and Angle-of-Arrival (AOA) [8] are non-range based. Range based positioning

C.-H. Hsu et al. (Eds.): UIC 2011, LNCS 6905, pp. 503–513, 2011.
© Springer-Verlag Berlin Heidelberg 2011

is the most suitable for use with UWB technology [11], as it can take full advantage of the high time resolution available with very short UWB pulses. Accurate TOA estimation is the key to precise ranging, but this is very challenging due to the potentially hundreds of multipath components in UWB channels.

TOA estimation has been extensively studied [9, 12-15]. There are two approaches applicable to UWB TOA estimation, a Matched Filter (MF) [13] (such as a RAKE or correlation receiver) with a high sampling rate and high-precision correlation, or an Energy Detector (ED) [15] with a lower sampling rate and low complex. A MF is the optimal technique for TOA estimation, where a correlator template is matched exactly to the received signal. However, a UWB receiver operating at the Nyquist sampling rate makes it very difficult to align with the multipath components of the received signal [12]. In addition, a MF requires a priori estimation of the channel, including the timing, fading coefficient, and pulse shape for each component of the impulse response [12]. Because of the high sampling rates and channel estimation, a MF may not be practical in many applications. As opposed to a more complex MF, an ED is a non-coherent approach to TOA estimation. It consists of a square-law device, followed by an integrator, sampler and a decision mechanism. The TOA estimate is made by comparing the integrator output with a threshold and choosing the first sample to exceed the threshold. This is a convenient technique that directly yields an estimate of the start of the received signal. Thus, a low complexity, low sampling rate receiver can be employed without the need for *a priori* channel estimation.

The major challenge with ED is the selection of an appropriate threshold based on the received signal samples. In [14], a normalized threshold selection technique for TOA estimation of UWB signals was proposed which exploits the kurtosis of the received samples. In [15], an approach based on the minimum and maximum sample energy was introduced. Threshold selection for different SNR values was investigated via simulation. These approaches have limited TOA precision, as the strongest path is not necessarily the first arriving path.

In this paper, we consider the relationship between the SNR and the statistics of the integrator output including skewness, and kurtosis. A metric based on skewness analysis is then developed for threshold selection. The threshold for different SNR values is investigated and the effects of the integration period and channel are examined. Performance results are presented which show that in both the CM1 and CM2 channels, this proposed algorithm provides high precision and robustness for both high and low SNRs.

The remainder of this paper is organized as follows. In Section 2 the system model is outlined. Section 3 discusses various TOA estimation algorithms based on energy detection. Section 4 considers the statistical characteristics of the energy values. In Section 5 the algorithm based on skewness analysis is proposed, and a novel TOA estimation algorithm is introduced. Section 6 presents some performance results, and Section 7 concludes the paper.

2   System Model

IEEE 802.15.4a [16] is the first international standard that specifies a wireless physical layer to enable precision ranging [6]. It includes channel models for indoor residential, indoor office, industrial, outdoor, and open outdoor environments, usually with a distinction between LOS and NLOS properties. In this paper, a Pulse Position Modulation Time Hopping UWB (PPM-TH-UWB) signal is employed for transmission. It is employed to estimate the propagation delay between the transmitter and receiver for use in positioning and tracking systems.

As shown in Figure 1, after the amplifier, the received signals are squared, and then input to an integrator with integration period T_b. Because of the inter-frame leakage due to multipath signals, the integration duration is $3T_f/2$ [14], so the number of signal values for energy detection is $N_b=(3T_f)/(2T_b)$. The integrator outputs can then be expressed as

$$z[n] = \sum_{j=1}^{N_s} \int_{(j-1)T_f+(c_j+n-1)T_b}^{(j-1)T_f+(c_j+n)T_b} r^2(t)dt \tag{1}$$

where $n \in \{1, 2, ..., N_b\}$ denotes the sample index with respect to the starting point of the integration period and N_s is the number of pulses per symbol. Here, N_s is set to 1, so the integrator outputs are

$$z[n] = \int_{(c+n-1)T_b}^{(c+n)T_b} r^2(t)dt . \tag{2}$$

If z[n] is the integration of noise only, it has a centralized Chi-square distribution, while it has a non-centralized Chi-square distribution if a signal is present. The mean and variance of the noise and signal values are given by [14]

$$\mu_0=F\sigma^2, \ \sigma_0^2=2F\sigma^4, \tag{3}$$

$$\mu_e=F\sigma^2+E_n, \ \sigma_e^2=2F\sigma^4+4\sigma^2E_n \tag{4}$$

respectively, where E_n is the signal energy within the nth integration period and F is the number of degrees of freedom given by $F=2BT_b+1$. Here B is the signal bandwidth.

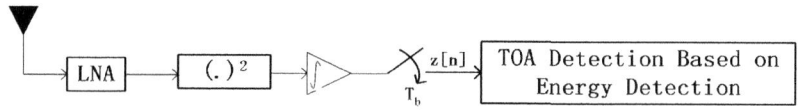

Fig. 1. Block diagram of the energy detection receiver

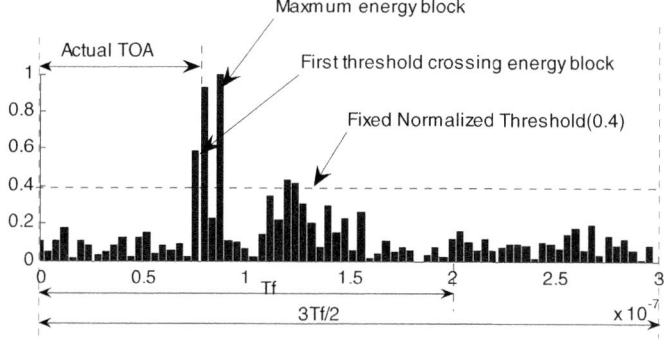

Fig. 2. TOA estimation techniques based on received energy

2.1   TOA Estimation Algorithms

There are many TOA estimation algorithms based on energy detection for determining the start of a received signal, as show in Figure 2. The simplest is Maximum Energy Selection (MES), which chooses the maximum energy value to be the start of the signal value. The TOA is estimated as the center of the corresponding integration period:

$$\tau_{MES} = [\arg \max_{1 \le n \le N_b}\{z[n]\} - 0.5]T_b. \tag{5}$$

However, as show in Figure 2, the maximum energy value may not be the first [13], especially in NLOS environments. On average, the first energy value $z[\hat{n}]$ is located before the maximum $z[n_{max}]$, i.e., $\hat{n} \le n_{max}$. Thus, Threshold-Crossing (TC) TOA estimation has been proposed where the received energy values are compared to an appropriate threshold ξ. In this case, the TOA estimation is given by

$$\tau_{TC} = [\arg \min_{1 \le n \le n_{max}}\{n \mid z[n] >= \xi\} - 0.5]T_b. \tag{6}$$

It is difficult to determine an appropriate threshold ξ directly, so usually a normalized threshold ξ_{norm} is calculated. For example, using kurtosis analysis as in (10) and (11), or the joint metric as in (13) and (14). Using ξ_{norm}, ξ is given by

$$\xi = \xi_{norm}(\max(z(n)) - \min(z(n))) + \min(z(n)). \tag{7}$$

The TOA (τ_{TC}) is then obtained using (6).

A simpler TC algorithm is the Fixed-Threshold (FT) algorithm where the threshold is set to a fixed value, for example $\xi_{norm} = 0.4$.

In [14], a normalized threshold selection technique for TOA estimation of UWB signals was proposed which exploits the kurtosis of the received signal samples. In [15], a normalized threshold selection approach based on (7) was introduced. The problem in this case becomes one of how to set the threshold. It should be based on the statistics of the received signal energy, particularly for multipath, NLOS indoor environments.

2.2   Error Analysis of the TOA Estimation Algorithm

In [15], the Mean Absolute Error (MAE) of TC-based TOA estimation was analyzed, and closed form error expressions derived. The MAE can be used to evaluate the quality of an algorithm, and is defined as

$$MAE = \frac{1}{N} \sum_{n=1}^{N} \left| t_n - \hat{t}_n \right|, \tag{8}$$

where t_n is the nth actual propagation time, $\hat{t}_n$ is the nth TOA estimate, and N is the number of TOA estimates.

3   Statistical Characteristics of the Energy Blocks

In this section, the skewness and kurtosis of the received energy signals are analyzed.

3.1   Kurtosis

The kurtosis is calculated using the second and fourth order moments and is given by

$$k = \frac{1}{(N_b - 1)\delta^4} \sum_{i=1}^{N_b} (x_i - \bar{x})^4 , \tag{9}$$

where $\bar{x}$ is the mean, and δ is the standard deviation. The kurtosis for a standard normal distribution is three. For this reason, k is often redefined as $K=k$-3 (often referred to as "excess kurtosis"), so that the standard normal distribution has a kurtosis of zero, positive kurtosis indicates a "peaked" distribution and negative kurtosis indicates a "flat" distribution.

For noise only (or for a low SNR) and sufficiently large F (degrees of freedom of the Chi-square distribution), z[n] has a Gaussian distribution and $K=0$. On the other hand, as the SNR increases, K will tend to increase.

In [14], the best normalized threshold with respect to the logarithm of the kurtosis and the corresponding MAE were investigated. To model the relationship, a double exponential function was used for $T_b = 4$ns, and a linear function fit was used for $T_b = 1$ns. The resulting functions are

$$\xi_{best}^{(4ns)} = 0.673e^{-0.75\log_2 K} + 0.154e^{-0.001\log_2 K} , \tag{10}$$

and

$$\xi_{best}^{(1ns)} = -0.082\log_2 K + 0.77 . \tag{11}$$

The model coefficients were obtained using data from both the CM1 and CM2 channels. In Section 6, these expressions are used to obtain the performance results.

3.2   Skewness

The skewness is given by

$$S = \frac{1}{(N_b - 1)\delta^3} \sum_{i=1}^{N_b} (x_i - \bar{x})^3 , \tag{12}$$

where $\bar{x}$ is the mean, and δ is the standard deviation of the energy values. The skewness for a normal distribution is zero, in fact any symmetric data will have a skewness of zero. Negative values of skewness indicate that the data is skewed left, while positive values indicate data that is skewed right. Skewed left indicates that the left tail is long relative to the right tail, while skewed right indicates the opposite. For noise only (or very low SNR), and sufficiently large F, $S \approx 0$. As the SNR increases, S will tend to increase.

3.3   Characteristics of the Two Statistical Parameters

In order to examine the characteristics of the two statistical parameters (skewness and kurtosis), the CM1 (residential LOS) and CM2 (residential NLOS) channel models from the IEEE802.15.4a standard are employed. For each SNR value, 1000 channel realizations are generated and sampled at F_c= 8GHz. The other system parameters are T_f = 200ns, T_c = 1ns, T_b= 4ns and N_s = 1. Each realization has a TOA uniformly distributed within $(0, T_f)$.

The two statistical parameters were calculated, and the results obtained are shown in Figure 3. This shows that the characteristics of the parameters with respect to the Signal to Noise Ratio (SNR) are similar for the two channels. Further, Figure 3 shows that the kurtosis and skewness increase as the SNR increases, but the skewness changes more rapidly. Since the skewness changes more rapidly than the kurtosis, it better reflects changes in SNR, and so is more suitable for TOA estimation.

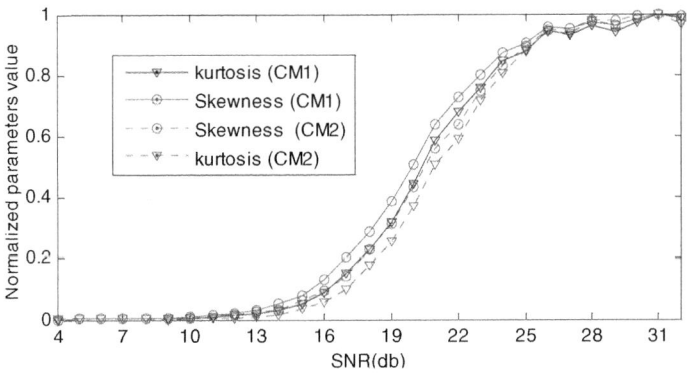

Fig. 3. Two normalized statistical parameters change with SNRs in CM1 and CM2

4   Threshold Selection Based on Skewness

4.1   MAE with Respect to the Normalized Threshold

In order to determine the best threshold (ξ_{best}) based on S, the relationship between MAE and normalized threshold (ξ_{norm}) was investigated. 1000 CM1 and CM2 channel realizations with SNR={4, 5,..., 32} dB were simulated. ξ is the threshold which is compared to the energy values to find the first threshold crossing, and is defined in (7). When ξ is bigger than the maximum energy value (z_{max}), no τ is found, so in this case ξ is set to z_{max}.

To illustrate the results, Figures 4 and 5 show the MAE for S={1,2,3,4,5,6,7,8} with T_b=1ns and T_b=4ns. The relationship is always that the MAE decreases as S increases. Another conclusion is that the minimum MAE is lower as S increases. The normalized threshold ξ_{norm} with respect to the minimum MAE is just the best threshold ξ_{best}. The relationship between ξ_{best} and S is examined in Section 5.2.

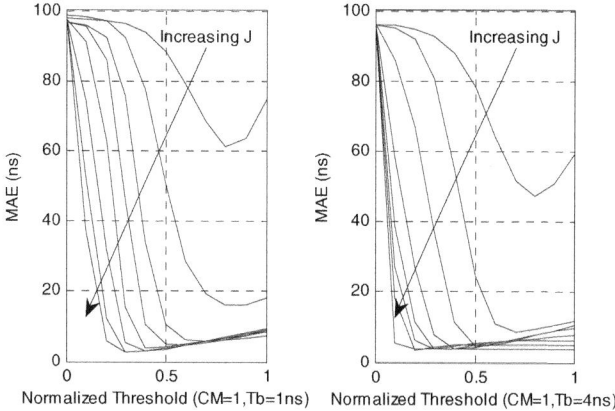

Fig. 4. MAE for normalized threshold values $S=\{1, 2, 3, 4, 5, 6, 7, 8\}$ and $T_b = 4$ns

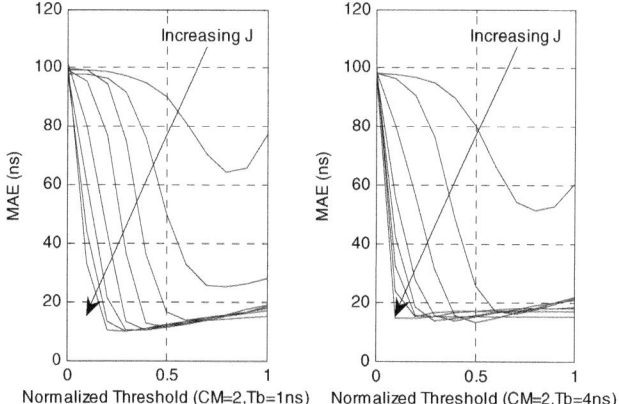

Fig. 5. MAE for normalized threshold values $S=\{1, 2, 3, 4, 5, 6, 7, 8\}$ and $T_b = 1$ns

4.2 Best Normalized Threshold with Respect to S

From the results in the previous section, the best threshold ξ_{best} for each value of S is presented in Figure 6. This shows that the relationship between the two parameters is not affected significantly by the channel model, but is more dependent on the integration period. Therefore, two functions were fitted to these results for $T_b = 4$ns and 1ns, with S as the x-coordinate and ξ_{best} as the y-coordinate. An exponential function was used, giving

$$\xi_{best}^{(1ns)} = 0.9028e^{-0.1347S} , \tag{13}$$

$$\xi_{best}^{(4ns)} = 0.9265e^{-0.2025J} \tag{14}$$

for T_b=1ns and 4ns, respectively.

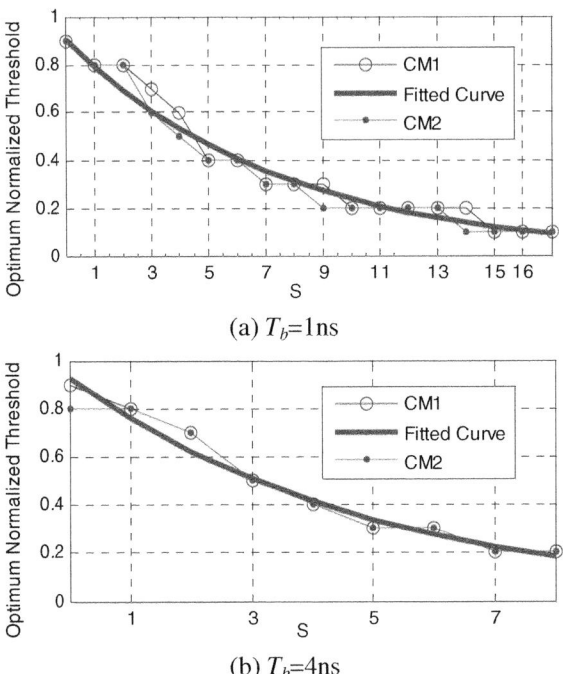

Fig. 6. Best normalized thresholds with respect to S

5   Performance Results and Discussion

In this section, the MAE is examined for different ED-based TOA estimation algorithms in the IEEE 802.15.4a CM1 and CM2 channels. As before, 1000 channel realizations are generated for each case. A second derivative Gaussian pulse with a 1 ns pulse width is employed, and the received signal is sampled at F_c= 8Ghz. The other system parameters are T_f = 200ns, T_b= 4ns and N_s = 1. Each realization has a TOA uniformly distributed within (0, T_f).

Figure 7 presents the TOA estimation MAE for SNR values from 4dB to 32dB in LOS (CM1) and NLOS (CM2) channels with T_b=1ns and 4ns. This shows that the proposed algorithm performs well at high SNRs. The performance in CM1 is better then in CM2 by 3ns to 7ns. When SNR>22dB, the MAE for CM1 is ≈3ns and for CM2 ≈10ns.

Figures 8 and 9 present the MAE performance with four TOA algorithms in channels CM1 and CM2, respectively. Here "MES" is the Maximum Energy Selection algorithm, and the normalized threshold for the Fixed Threshold algorithm is set to 0.4. As expected based on the results in Section 5, the MAE with the proposed algorithm is lower than with other algorithms, particularly at low to moderate SNR values. The proposed algorithm is better except when the SNR is greater than 24dB. In this case, the Kurtosis algorithm is slightly better. For example, when SNR=4dB to 12dB the MAE of the proposed algorithm is better by 20ns~30ns, when SNR=13dB to 20dB the MAE is about 50~80ns better than the Kurtosis algorithm. For SNR>24dB, The MAE of the proposed algorithm is only 0.5ns greater than that of the Kurtosis algorithm.

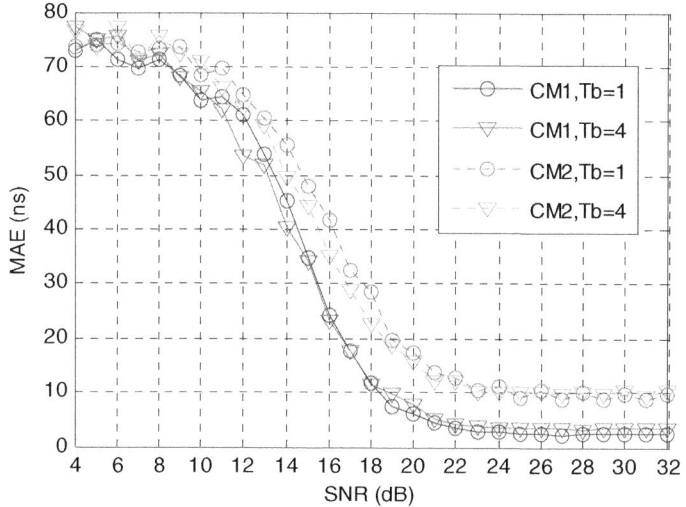

Fig. 7. MAE for channels CM1 and CM2 with T_b=1ns and 4ns

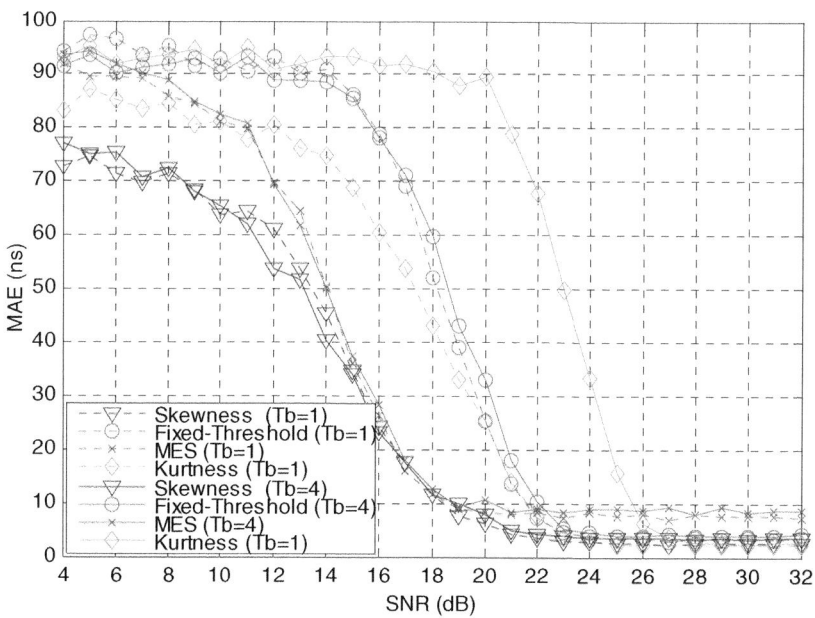

Fig. 8. MAE for different algorithms with channel CM1

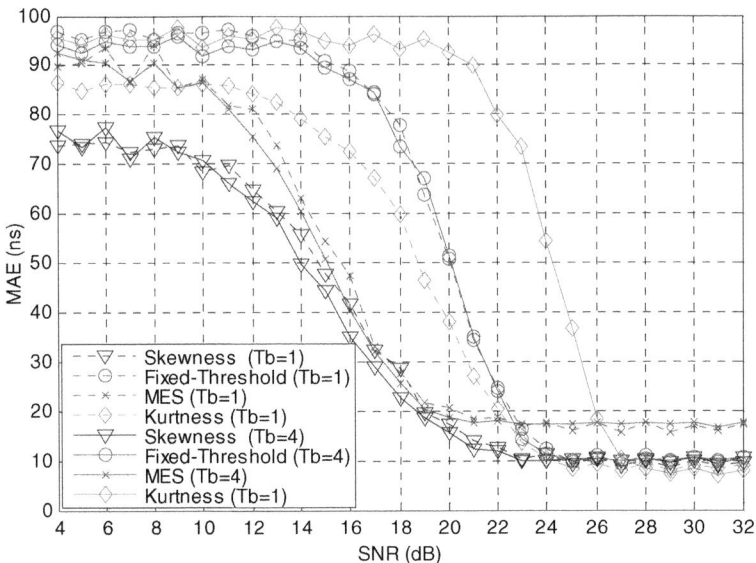

Fig. 9. MAE for different algorithms with channel CM2

The performance of the proposed algorithm is more robust than the other algorithms, as the performance difference between T_b=1ns and 4ns is very small compared to the difference with the Kurtosis algorithm. For almost all SNR values the proposed algorithm is the best. Conversely, the performance of the Kurtosis algorithm varies greatly with respect to the other algorithms, and is very bad for low to moderate SNR values.

6   Conclusions

Low complexity, energy-based TOA estimation algorithms have been examined for UWB ranging, positioning, and tracking applications. Two statistical parameters were investigated, and based on the results obtained, a new algorithm based on skewness was developed for Threshold-Crossing TOA estimation. The best normalized threshold was determined using simulation with the CM1 and CM2 channels and curve fitting. The effects of the integration period and channel model were investigated. It was determined that the proposed threshold selection technique is largely independent of the channel model. The performance of the proposed algorithm was shown to be better than several known algorithms. In addition, the proposed algorithm is more robust to changes in the SNR and integration period.

Acknowledgment. This work was supported by the Nature Science Foundation of China under grant No.60902005, the Outstanding Youth Foundation of Shandong Province under grant no. JQ200821, and the Program for New Century Excellent Talents of the Ministry of Education under grant no. NCET-08-0504.

References

1. Tiuraniemi, S., Stoica, L., Rabbachin, A., Oppermann, I., Tiuraniemi, S.: A VLSI Implementation of Low Power, Low Data Rate UWB Transceiver for Location and Tracking Applications. Journal of VLSI Signal Processing Systems, 43–58 (2006)
2. Jie, D., Cui, X., Zhang, H., Wang, G.: A Ultra-Wideband Location Algorithm Based on Neural Network. In: 6th International Conference on Wireless Communications Networking and Mobile Computing. IEEE Press, New York (2010)
3. Tu, X., Zhang, H., Cui, X., Gulliver, T.A.: 3-D TDOA/AOA location based on Extended Kalman Filter. In: 9th International Symposium on Antennas Propagation and EM Theory. IEEE Press, New York (2010)
4. Rao, D., Barton, R.J.: Performance Capabilities of UWB Location and Tracking Systems. In: Fortieth Asilomar Conference on Signals, Systems and Computers. IEEE Press, New York (2006)
5. Gezici, S., Poor, H.V.: Position Estimation via Ultra-Wide-Band Signals. Proceedings of the IEEE 97(2), 386–403 (2009)
6. Sahinoglu, Z., Gezici, S.: Ranging in the IEEE 802.15.4a Standard. In: IEEE Annual Wireless and Microwave Technology Conference. IEEE Press, New York (2006)
7. Dardari, D., Conti, A., Ferner, U., Giorgetti, A., Win, M.Z.: Ranging With Ultrawide Bandwidth Signals in Multipath Environments. Proceedings of the IEEE 97(2), 404–426 (2009)
8. Zhang, Y., Brown, A.K., Malik, W.Q., Edwards, D.J.: High Resolution 3-D Angle of Arrival Determination for Indoor UWB Multipath Propagation. IEEE Transactions on Wireless Communications 7(8), 3047–3055 (2008)
9. Dardari, D., Giorgetti, A., Win, M.Z.: Time-of-Arrival Estimation of UWB Signals in the Presence of Narrowband and Wideband Interference. In: IEEE International Conference on Ultra-Wideband. IEEE Press, New York (2007)
10. Bocquet, M., Loyez, C., Benlarbi-Delai, A.: Using enhanced-TDOA measurement for indoor positioning. IEEE Microwave and Wireless Components Letters 15(10), 612–614 (2005)
11. Abbasi, A., Kahaei, M.H.: Improving source localization in LOS and NLOS multipath environments for UWB signals. In: 14th International CSI Computer Conference. IEEE Press, New York (2009)
12. Guvenc, I., Sahinoglu, Z.: Multiscale energy products for TOA estimation in IR-UWB systems. In: IEEE Global Telecommunications Conference. IEEE Press, New York (2005)
13. Xu, A.Y.-Z., Au, E.K.S., Wong, A.K.-S., Wang, Q.: A Novel Threshold-Based Coherent TOA Estimation for IR-UWB Systems. J. IEEE Transactions on Vehicular Technology 58(8), 4675–4681 (2009)
14. Guvenc, I., Sahinoglu, Z.: Threshold selection for UWB TOA estimation based on kurtosis analysis. J. IEEE Communications Letters 9(12), 1025–1027 (2005)
15. Guvenc, I., Sahinoglu, Z.: Threshold-based TOA estimation for impulse radio UWB systems. In: IEEE International Conference on Ultra-Wideband, IEEE Press, New York (2005)
16. Molisch, A.F., Balakrishnan, K., Cassioli, D., Chong, C.-C., Emanmi, S., Fort, A., Karedal, F., Kunisch, J., Schantz, H., Schuster, U., Siwiak, K.: IEEE 802.15.4a Channel Model—Final Report, IEEE P802.15-04-0662-00-004a (2006)

Modeling Human Activity Semantics for Improved Recognition Performance

Eunju Kim and Sumi Helal

Mobile and Pervasive Computing Laboratory
The Department of Computer and Information Science and Engineering
University of Florida, Gainesville, FL 32611, USA
{ejkim,helal}@cise.ufl.edu

Abstract. Activity recognition performance is significantly dependent on the accuracy of the underlying activity model. Therefore, it is essential to examine and develop an activity model that can capture and represent the complex nature of human activities precisely. To address this issue, we introduce a new activity modeling technique, which utilizes simple yet often ignored activity semantics. Activity semantics are highly evidential knowledge that can identify an activity more accurately in ambiguous situations. We classify semantics into three types and apply them to generic activity framework, which is a refined hierarchical composition structure of the traditional activity theory. We compare the introduced activity model with the traditional model and the hierarchical models in terms of attainable recognition certainty. The comparison study shows superior performance of our semantic model using activities of daily living scenario.

Keywords: Activity Recognition, Activity Modeling, Activity Semantic Knowledge, Generic Activity Framework, Accuracy and Certainty.

1 Introduction

Human activity recognition (AR) is an essential technology of pervasive computing science because it can be applied to many practical applications including health care, eldercare or smart spaces [1][2]. In spite of the obvious importance of this technology, current AR technology has limited accuracy and further development is required for real world applications. It is because many human activities are so complex that their accurate recognition is a big challenge. To illustrate, when people perform an activity, it is performed in a variety of ways. Also it is often concurrent and interleaved with other activities.

To solve this problem, many activity models and activity recognition algorithms including probability-based or machine-learning based approaches have been developed to improve the recognition performance [11][12][13][14][15]. However, these approaches are not sufficient for practical applications because they do not adequately address complex, ambiguous or diverse human activities. Therefore, a new approach, which can capture and represent such unique characteristics of human activities more precisely, is necessary. Comprehensive understanding of human activities and careful

C.-H. Hsu et al. (Eds.): UIC 2011, LNCS 6905, pp. 514–528, 2011.
© Springer-Verlag Berlin Heidelberg 2011

activity modeling is especially important because other techniques including AR algorithm and AR system are based on the activity model and their accuracy is influenced from the activity model.

In this paper, we propose activity semantic knowledge and a knowledge-assisted activity modeling technique that utilizes the semantic knowledge for accurate modeling of human activities.

1.1 Motivation

Our motivation is developing a new activity modeling approach that can model real world human activities accurately. To achieve this goal, several challenges need to be addressed. In particular, the new approach should address the following characteristics of human activities.

Concurrent activities. People may be involved in actions corresponding to several activities at the same time. For example, people watch TV while talking to friends. These behaviors are not sequential, and therefore, an activity model needs to represent these characteristics of activities [3].

Interleaved activities. In a real world scenario, some activities may be interrupted by other activities before completion whereas some are not. For instance, if a friend calls while cooking, the resident may pause cooking and talk to the friend for a while. After talking, he/she continues to cook [3].

Ambiguity. Even though sensor detects user activities well, the exact interpretation may be difficult. For example, we cannot guarantee that a person really takes a medicine even though a sensor detects opening the medicine bottle because the sensor could be reporting on other related activities such as *checking whether bottle is empty* or *cleaning bottle* but not taking the medicine.

Variety. Humans can perform activities in a variety of ways. For example, there are multiple ways to eating such as *having a meal* or *having a snack*. Typical scenario based activity recognition is not enough to handle this variety.

Multiple subjects. More than one person could occupy the same space and perform activities together sometimes. An activity model needs to be capable of associating the detected activities with the resident who actually executed them [3].

1.2 Proposed Approach

As a solution to the aforementioned problems, we propose a new approach that utilizes activity semantic knowledge for modelling human activities. Activity semantics are the knowledge about the characteristics of activities and it can provide a variety of important information to express activities. For example, no other activity can be performed along with sleeping activity and the person will be in better condition after sleeping, the person will be lying down on the bed, and the next possible location of the person will be near the bedroom. This information constitutes the semantic knowledge of an activity. We named this kind of knowledge as activity semantic knowledge and utilized it for modelling activities. The major advantage of this modelling approach is that it can reduce uncertainty in an activity model and other AR technologies based on the activity model.

First, without prior semantic knowledge, activity models treat all activity components equally because it is difficult to know the differences. But a close look at human activities reveals that activity components have different roles. Some components are essential for an activity whereas some are trivial. Therefore, semantic activity knowledge is helpful for modelling activities more precisely.

Second, activity model can capture activity relationship more accurately. Without prior semantic knowledge, activity models may impose detection conditions that are too strict or too loose. For example, Hidden Markov Model (HMM) model is too strict, as it requires enumerating all possible orders of activities. Conditional Random Field (CRF) model is too loose in that it does not account for the order among activities [3][7][8]. However, if we have semantic knowledge of activities, we can account for the order in which actions are performed only if it is meaningful.

The rest of this paper is organized as follows. In section 2, we discuss the traditional activity models such as activity theory based model and probabilistic graphical models and their limitations. The proposed approach is explained in section 3. A comparison and analysis are represented in section 4. Finally, section 5 concludes the paper.

2 Background

In this section, we describe traditional activity models. There are two popular approaches for modeling activities. One is activity theory based modeling; the other is probabilistic modeling such as Hidden Markov Model (HMM) or Conditional Random Field (CRF) model.

2.1 Activity Theory - Origin of Activity Modeling

Historically speaking, L. S. Vygotsk who was a psychologist during 1920s and 1930s founded the activity theory. Later, the activity theory was further developed by A. N. Leontjev and A. R. Lurija and coined the term "activity" [5][6]. Activity theory was first applied to human-computer interaction (HCI) in the early 1980s [5]. These days, it is applied implicitly or explicitly in a lot of activity recognition research.

The activity theory contains four components (subject, tool, objective, and outcome) [5][6]. A subject is a participant of an activity. An objective is a plan or common idea that can be shared for manipulation and transformation by the participants of the activity. Tool is an artifact a subject uses to fulfill an objective. Outcome is another artifact or activity that are result of the activity. Transforming the objective into an outcome motivates the performing of an activity. For example, having one's own house is an objective and the purchased house is the outcome. Transforming an object into an outcome requires various tools.

As shown in Table 1, activity theory has a three-layered hierarchical structure and activity is composed of actions and an action is composed of operations [5].

Table 1. Hierarchical layers of an activity and an example of activity, action, and operation

Levels	Related Purpose	Example of purpose
Activity	Motive	Completing a software project
Action	Goal	Programming a module
Operation	Conditions	Using an operating system

Activities are composed of cooperative actions or chains of actions. These actions are all related to the motive of an activity. Each action has a goal and consists of operations to reach the goal. Operation is a unit component and it depends on the faced condition where the operation performs. The detailed description of each level can be found in [4][5].

Even though activity theory is well known and is often used in activity recognition research, it has some limitations. First, the border between hierarchical layers is blurred. As described in [5], an activity can lose its motive and become an action, and an action can become an operation when the goal changes [5]. This unclear border makes automated activity recognition difficult because the change of motive of activity and goal of action are not easy to detect. Hence, it is necessary to find clearer ways to determine each layer.

Second, activity theory does not distinguish between tool and object. But, they are needed to be distinguished because the same item may be used as tool or object in several activities. In this case, the item has different meaning for each activity. For example, when a pan is used as a tool for cooking, it implies it contains food. On the other hand, if it is an object for washing dish activity, it means that it is an empty dish.

Last, some activities are too complicated to be represented by a single activity name. For instance, eating has several similar activities such as having a meal or having breakfast, lunch or dinner. Because the top layer is activity in activity theory, the layer includes everything. This makes AR system design cumbersome and difficult to conceptualize. This difference in granularity is not conducive to sharing or modularizing AR systems.

2.2 Probabilistic Activity Models

In probabilistic approach, human activities are continuously performed and each activity is a sequential composition of activity components such as motions, operations or actions according to a temporal sequence. According to this idea, several probabilistic models including Hidden Markov Model and the Conditional Random Field Model have been used to build an activity model because they are suitable for handling temporal data.

Hidden Markov Model (HMM). HMM is a probabilistic function of Markov chains based on the first order Markov assumption of transition [7]. The basic idea of Markov chain of order m is that the future state depends on the past m numbers of states. Therefore, for HMM based on the first order Markov assumption, the future state depends only on the current state, not on past states [7]. Also HMM is a model that is used for generating hidden states from observable data. HMM determines the hidden state sequence $(y_1, y_2, ..., y_t)$ that corresponds to the observed sequence $(x_1, x_2, ..., x_t)$ [3]. In activity recognition, hidden state is human activities and HMM recognizes activities from both sensor observation and previous activity according to the first order Markov chain. However, HMM is also a generative, directed graph model [3]. Generative model means that observation data is randomly generated. In other words, it should enumerate all possible random cases in the model. Directed graph is used capture order between states. Therefore, a generative and directed graph model in activity recognition implies it should find all possible sequences of observations.

However, many activities may have non-deterministic natures in practice, where some steps of the activities may be performed in any order. In practice, although many activities are concurrent or interleaved with other activities, HMM has difficulty in representing multiple interacting activities (concurrent or interleaved) [3]. Also HMM is incapable of capturing long-range or transitive dependencies of the observations due to its very strict independence assumptions on the observations. Therefore, enumerating all possible observation cases and orders is difficult for a practical system. Furthermore, missing an observation or an order will cause the HMM to produce errors in the model.

Conditional Random Field (CRF). CRF is a more flexible alternative to the HMM, which relaxes the strict assumption of HMM [8]. In other words, CRF solves the problems of HMM by neglecting the order constraint. Like HMM, CRF is also used to determine a hidden state transition from randomly generated observation sequences. However, CRF is a discriminative model, which does not generate possible cases from the joint distribution of x and y. Therefore, CRF does not include arbitrarily complicated features of the observed variables into the model. Also, CRF is an undirected acyclic graph, flexibly capturing any relation between an observation variable and a hidden state [8]. Because CRF does not consider order, it considers only relationships such as state feature function (relationship between observations over a period of time and activities) and transition feature function (relationship between past activities and future activities). Even though CRF removes order constraint from an activity model, CRF could outperform HMM [15].

3 Semantic Activity Model

In order to recognize activities accurately, modeling activities precisely is essential because recognition performance will be limited unless activities are analyzed and represented accurately. To illustrate, the knowledge of components of activities, relationships between an activity and components, characteristics of activities, etc. are important for identifying activities. Therefore, this activity knowledge should not be overlooked when modeling activities.

However, as we mentioned in the previous section, both activity theory and probabilistic activity model have limitations and do not represent human activity precisely because they do not consider important activity semantic knowledge. For example, activity theory does not distinguish activity components clearly enough. HMM and CRF apply an order assumption that is too strict or too loose respectively. However, these modeling assumptions should be more adaptive in reality because there are some activities like an instruction, which consider order critical whereas some activities do not.

To solve this issue, the proposed activity semantics based model (Semantic activity model) incorporates substantial semantic activity information in the model. To exploit semantics, we first adopt a generic activity framework that extends the activity theory in section 2.1 because it provides a refined framework of activity model. We use daily living activities as demonstrative examples.

3.1 Generic Activity Framework

Generic activity framework has a hierarchical structure in which each layer of the structure consists of activity components. In total, there are eight primitive components in the framework as shown in Fig. 1. It is not necessary for every activity to contain all eight components as long as the activity is recognized clearly. For example, the walking activity does not require any object. Descriptions of the eight primitive components are summarized below and described in details in [4]:

Subject. A subject is an actor of the activity. Subject has an important role as an activity classifier especially when there are multiple people.

Time. This is the time when an activity is performed. It consists of start time and end time. We can also calculate the duration of an activity using time.

Location. Location is the place where an activity is performed. If an activity is performed in several places, location will have multiple values.

Motive. Motive is the reason or objective why a subject performs a specific activity.

Tool. Tool is an artifact that a subject uses to perform an activity. Tool provides essential information to classify activities. For example, a spoon or a fork is a tool for eating or cooking.

Motion. Motion is defined as the movement performed by a subject for handling tools. Motion explains what a subject does with a tool. For example, cutting and chopping are both performed using the same tool i.e. knife. The different motions associated with cutting and chopping can be used to differentiate between them.

Object. An object can also be any artifact like tool. But, object is the target of an activity whereas a subject uses a tool. Distinction between tool and object is important for accurate activity recognition because some artifacts are tool for an activity and object of another activity.

Context. Context provides information about the "vicinity" in which an activity is performed. Installed sensors directly find some contexts such as temperature or humidity. Other primitive components such as time or location contribute to finding more other contexts such as time to sleep, place to cooking, etc. On the other hand, some contexts like motive of an activity need some artificial intelligence techniques such as reasoning or inference to elicit them.

Fig. 1 shows a composition diagram of the generic activity framework. Rectangles are layers and ellipses are primitive components. According to the composition of components, the activity framework has a hierarchical structure. And the components of each layer are clearly defined. Brief description for each layer is given below (more details in [4]):

Sensors. Sensors are installed in the pervasive space (e.g. a smart home) to collect event information of the space. Based on the installed places of sensors, sensors are classified into four types: motion, tool, object, and context sensor.

Operation. Operation is a composition of tool and motion. The user operates tools with specific motion. For example, if computer is a tool, some hand or arm motion will be performed for typing a keyboard or using a mouse.

Action. Action is determined by combination of operation and object. For instance, if a user clicks a mouse to open a file, using a mouse is an operation and the file is an object and this combination is open file action.

Activity. Activity is a collection of actions. Activity may involve multiple actions and an action belongs to a subject. If a subject is different, we classify the activity separately. If multiple people collaborate for a same activity, the activity belongs to the multiple people.

Meta activity. A meta activity is a collection of activities. It is useful to use when an activity is complicated, in which case it can be composed of several simple activities. For instance, a meta activity *hygiene* is composed of *washing hands, brushing teeth* or *taking a bath*.

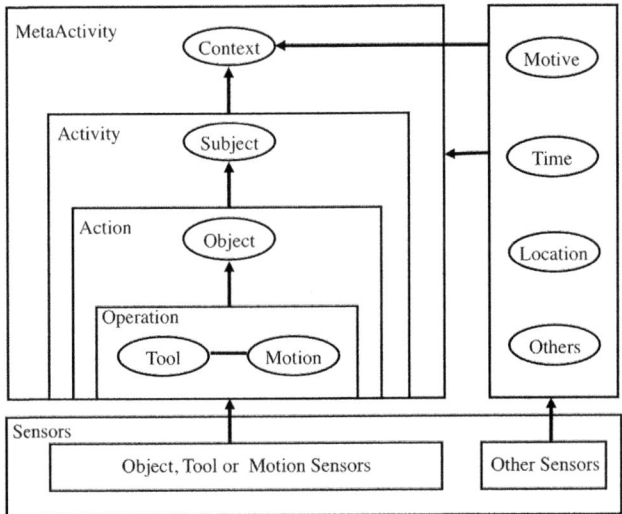

Fig. 1. Composition diagram of a generic activity framework. It is composed of several hierarchies and each hierarchical layer contains classifier components.

The hierarchical structure has several advantages. Firstly, it provides clear distinguish between layers so that user will not confuse operation, action and activity any more. Secondly, it makes the activity recognition system more tolerant to sensor environment change [4]. For instance, even if more sensors are inserted in the AR system, the upper layers in the hierarchy will not be seriously influenced from the change of sensor environment. Lastly, activity recognition using hierarchical structure is analogous to the way people recognize, so it is easier to design more natural and intuitive AR algorithm [4].

3.2 Semantic Activity Model

Even though a generic activity framework in section 3.1 describes the composition hierarchy of activity components, it is a general framework, which does not contain detailed activity semantic knowledge such as role of an activity component, constraint or relationship with other components. The activity semantics should be represented in an activity model because they are important for classifying an activity. For example, *eating* is composed of three actions such as *picking food, chewing food* and *swallowing food*. In this case, if only *picking food* and *chewing food* are detected, then it is not clear whether we consider *eating* is really performed or not because we are not sure the person completes the activity through chews and swallows the food or not. Activity semantics reduce these kinds of ambiguity. There are three activity semantics: dominance semantics, mutuality semantics and order semantics.

Dominance semantics is semantic information of vertical relationship between components in upper layer and lower layer in Fig. 1 (e.g. meta activity and activity, activity and action, or action and operation). In other words, components in upper layer (e.g. activity) are composed of the components in lower layer (e.g. action). In this hierarchical composition structure, the contribution of each action is different. Even though some actions are components of the same activity, some actions are dominantly essential component of the activity whereas some are not. According to the dominance, we classify them as key, unique, optional and conditioned components.

Key component. Key component is a mandatory component for identifying an activity. If an activity has multiple key components, all of them are required to agree with the activity. Otherwise, the activity is not considered performed. To illustrate, *swallowing* is a key action for *eating* because if people don't swallow food, it is not regarded *eating* is completely performed even though there are many other actions such as *picking food*, *scooping food* or *chewing food*.

Unique component. Unique component is a highly evidential component although it is not a key component. For instance, *chewing* is a unique action for *eating* because most *eating* requires chewing. However, *chewing* is not a key component because *chewing* can be omitted if food is soup.

Optional component. If a component is neither a key nor unique component, it is an optional component. It is possible to omit an optional component because it does not always affect activity classification. For example, *cutting food* is an action of *eating* but it may be omitted depending on the food. However, if optional component is detected, it increases the certainty of the recognition of an activity.

Conditioned component. If components should satisfy a specific condition for an activity, it is a conditioned component. For instance, *duration* is an example of condition for *sleeping* because it is highly unlikely that sleeping is performed if the duration is too short (e.g., a few minutes).

Mutuality semantics is semantic information of horizontal relationship between components at the same layer (e.g. meta activity and meta activity, activity and activity, action and action or etc). This semantic knowledge is used to determine whether multiple activities can be concurrently performed or not.

Concurrent component. If two or more components are performed together, they are in concurrent relationship. For example, *laundry* or *watching TV* is concurrent because while the washer is running, the user can watch TV at the same time.

Exclusive component. If an activity cannot be performed simultaneously with another activity, it is an exclusive activity. For example, *sleeping* is an exclusive activity because people cannot perform anything when they sleep.

Ordinary component. Ordinary components are partially exclusive and concurrent. If an activity is performed with a part of the body (e.g. human limb), the activity is both concurrent and exclusive. For example, when people eat food, they cannot sing a song at the same time. In this case, they are exclusive. But if the people take a walk, they can sing a song concurrently. Therefore, *sing a song* is both partially exclusive and concurrent.

Order semantics. Some activities like an instruction should follow a procedural sequence. However, many activities have flexible order or do not have any order. Therefore, the role of order among activity components should be considered depending on the activity.

No order. There is no specific order required between activity components. For example, actions for *eating* such as *cutting, picking* and *scooping food* does not have any order restriction.

Strong order. Some activity requires that activity components (e.g. actions) should be performed in a specific order always. For instance, in case of *sleeping* and *waking-up, waking-up* comes immediately after *sleeping* because people perform another activity before waking up.

Weak order. For many activities, their action components are performed according to a flexible order, which is not mandatory or strict. For example, usually *eating* is performed after *cooking*, but there are exceptions to this order depending on several situations.

Skip chain order. When an activity is interleaved, other activity components may be performed between two ordered activity components. To illustrate, *eating* is usually performed immediately after *cooking*, but sometimes we can do other activities between them.

The Fig. 2 shows the modeling notations of each semantic. A component can have multiple semantics. For example, if a component is unique and exclusive, it is represented with both bold dotted line and filled circle. Also we can find that there are multiple elements like "x,y,z" in some circles whereas there is only "x" in other circles in Fig. 3. The circle that contains multiple elements is a compound component and the circle with an element is an elementary component.

Elementary component. An elementary component such as optional component or ordinary component can have only one element.

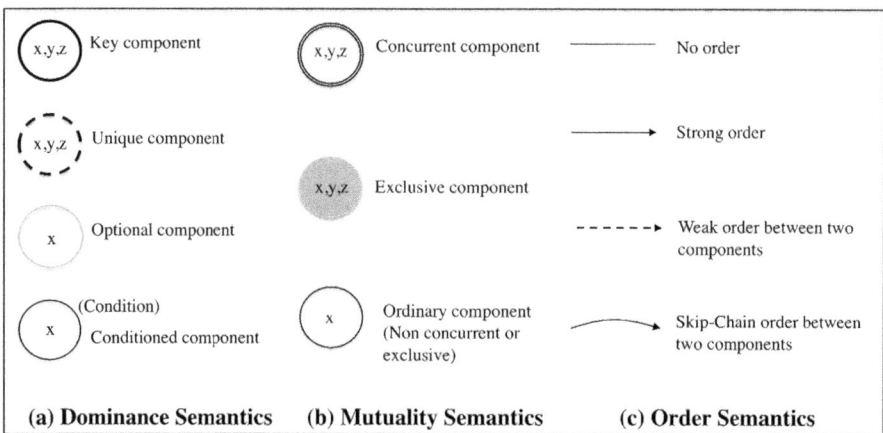

(a) Dominance Semantics   (b) Mutuality Semantics   (c) Order Semantics

Fig. 2. Notations of semantic components. Dominance semantics and mutuality semantics are represented as nodes whereas order semantics are represented as edges.

Compound component. A compound component contains either single or multiple elements. Even though each individual sub-component of a compound component is optional or ordinary component, there are some cases their combination have stronger semantics. For example, *picking food* or *scooping food* is an optional and an ordinary component because we can have food without picking if we can have the food by scooping and vice versa. However, we need to do one of them while eating food. Even though *picking* and *scooping* is less evidential compare to *chewing* and *swallowing*, missing both *picking* and *scooping* will reduce the probability of the activity. In this case, we create a compound component with multiple optional or ordinary components.

Fig. 3 is an example of semantic activity modeling of daily living activities. In this example, *sleeping* is a unique activity and it also exclusive activity where as *watching TV* is a concurrent activity. *Scooping* and *picking* are compound key components of *eating*. There is a skip chain relationship between *preparing meal* and *having a meal* because it can be interleaved by other activities.

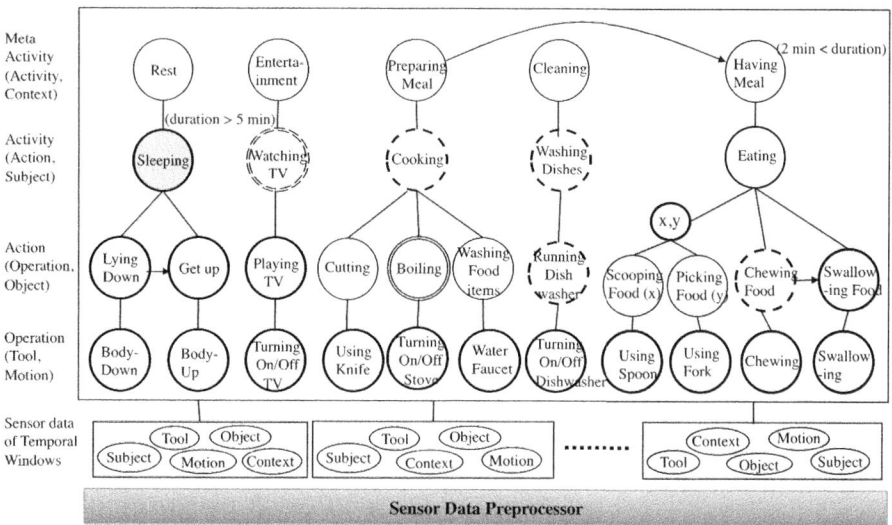

Fig. 3. An example of semantic activity modeling of daily living activities. Semantic components are represented on a hierarchical composition structure, which is based on the generic activity framework.

4   Comparison and Analysis

In this section, we compare the proposed Semantics and Generic Activity Framework based Model (S-GAM) with a Traditional Activity Model based on activity theory (TAM) and the Generic Activity Framework based Activity Model without semantics (GAM). We used a daily living activity scenario. To establish an activity scenario for the comparison, we used the eldercare scenarios of daily living described in [2] instantiated with a real activity dataset provided by University of Amsterdam [15].

The eldercare scenarios in [2] describe 33 different daily living activities of the elderly. The activity data set in [15] is records of activities of daily living performed by a man living in a three-bedroom apartment for 28 days. We named this dataset the Amsterdam dataset. We chose seven activities, which are common in both [2] and [15]. In terms of sensors, we assume the same sensor environment with the Amsterdam dataset are used to see how S-GAM performs in real situations. We add a Bed sensor according to the scenario in [2]. Table 2 lists the seven activities and their components.

Table 2. Activity list collected from the Amsterdam dataset. It shows meta activities, activities, actions, operation tools, objects and related semantics for each activity.

Meta Activity	Activities (Location)	Action			Semantics
		Operation	Tool	Object	
Rest	Sleeping (Bedroom)	-Going to the bedroom -Lying down	 Bed	Bedroom door	Mutuality: Exclusive activity
Hygiene	Taking a bath (Bathroom)	-Taking a shower -Washing face		Bathroom door Restroom door	Mutuality: Exclusive activity
	Using the toilet (Restroom)	-Opening a restroom door -Pressing a toilet flush		-Restroom door -Toilet flush	Dominance: -Key: Toilet flush -Unique: Restroom door
Preparing a meal -Breakfast -Lunch -Dinner	Cooking (Kitchen)	-Preparing food items -Heating food	 -Microwave -Pan	-Groceries -Refrigerator -Freezer	Weak order: -Taking food items -> Heating food
Drinking	Drinking	Taking drink	Cup	Refrigerator	Dominance: Key: Cup
Cleaning	Washing dishes		Dishwasher	-Pans -Cup -Dishes	Mutuality: Concurrent activity
Going out	Leaving the house	Opening front door		Front door	Dominance: -Key: Front door Mutuality: -Exclusive activity

Our activity scenario consists of six meta activities, seven activities, eleven actions, five tools and eleven objects. It also shows the activity semantics of each activity. In Table 2, we can see that many artifacts are used as tools or object in activities. Especially when an artifact is used in several activities, TAM is difficult to recognize activities accurately because it regards artifacts as tools only. For example, in Table 2, an artifact pan is a tool for cooking and it is also an object for washing dishes. Since TAM does not distinguish tool and object, sensing pan is not sufficient to determine which activity is performed. In contrast, GAM and S-GAM consider the usage of artifacts as both tool and object. Especially, S-GAM can recognize activities more accurately because it classifies activities using activity semantics. For example, sensing tools such as pan or microwave and objects like groceries usually mean that *cooking* is performed in GAM model. However, food items should be prepared before turning the microwave on if it is a cooking. Otherwise, it is unlikely the microwave is for cooking. GAM does not check this order semantic that is necessary for accurate activity recognition.

To compare the accuracy of the three activity models, we measured the uncertainty incurred by each model under the same activity scenario. Certainty factor is very effective evaluative analysis used in several areas such as diagnostics and medicine [9]. We briefly define Certainty Factor below.

CF(H, E): CF is a certainty factor from hypothesis H influenced by evidence E [9]. The value of certainty factor ranges from -1(very uncertain) to +1(very certain) through zero (neutral).

$$CF(H, E) = MB(H, E) - MD(H, E) \tag{1}$$

MB(H, E): MB is the measure of increased belief in hypothesis H influenced by evidence E [9]. p(H) and 1-p(H) are the probabilities of that hypothesis being true or false respectively. p(H|E) is a probability of hypothesis given E. If the evidence, E, is very strong, p(H|E) will equal to 1 and p(H|E) - p(H) will be also close to 1 - p(H) and MB will be close to 1 and certainty factor will increase. On the other hand, if the evidence is very weak, then p(H|E) - p(H) is almost zero, and the uncertainty remains about the same with MD (H, E). The function max is used to normalize the MB value positive (between 0 and 1).

$$MB(H, E) = \begin{cases} 1 & \text{if } p(H) = 1 \\ \dfrac{\max(p(H \mid E),\, p(H)) - p(H)}{1 - p(H)} & \text{otherwise} \end{cases} \tag{2}$$

MD(H, E): measure of increased disbelief on hypothesis H influenced by evidence E [9]. If the evidence, E, is very strong, p(H) – min(p(H|E), p(H)) will equal 0 and MD will be 0. On the other hand, if the evidence is very weak, then p(H) – p(H|E) is almost p(H), and the uncertainty will be close to 1. The purpose of function min is to make the MD value positive.

$$MD(H, E) = \begin{cases} 1 & \text{if } p(H) = 0 \\ \dfrac{p(H) - \min(p(H \mid E),\, p(H))}{p(H)} & \text{otherwise} \end{cases} \tag{3}$$

To find MB(H, E) and MD(H, E), the probabilities of hypothesis p(H) and the conditional probability p(H|E) need to be determined. For calculating the probabilities, we enumerate 77 possible cases based on Table 2. For example, to find the probabilities for *sleeping*, we found 6 possible cases with 2 components (bedroom door and bed) and one semantic (if the activity is exclusively performed or not). Then the number of all possible cases is three (detecting bedroom door, bed and both bedroom door and bed) for each semantic case. In TAM, *bedroom door* and *bed* are equally treated as artifacts. In GAM, *bedroom* is an object and *bed* is a tool for lying down. S-GAM adds semantic information in the GAM model. We counted activities for each of the evidences. Table 3 shows an example of *Sleeping*. Sum of probability is calculated using the addition law of probability that is the probability of A or B is the sum of the probabilities of A and B, minus the probability of both A and B. The probabilities of other activities are calculated similarly.

Table 3. The probabilities of *sleeping* activity according to the models

	Evidence (E)	p(H and E)	p(E)	p(H|E)	Sum of p(H|E)
TAM	Artifacts	2	6	0.33	0.33
GAM	Tool	1	4	0.25	0.25
	Object	1	4	0.25	0.44
S-GAM	Tool	1	4	0.25	0.25
	Object	1	4	0.25	0.44
	Semantics	2	7	0.29	0.63

Table 4 represents the conditional probability of hypothesis H given E for every activity. We can observe some semantics are highly evidential whereas some are not according to how much the semantic contribute for identifying activities. However, S-GAF has higher probability overall because it is based on GAF.

Table 4. The probabilities of hypothesis H given evidence E for each model, p(H|E)

Activity	TAM	GAF (Tool)	GAF (Object)	GAF (Tool and Object)	Semantics	S-GAF (GAF and Semantics)
Sleeping	0.33	0.25	0.25	0.44	0.29	0.60
Taking a bath	0.38	0.00	0.38	0.38	0.43	0.64
Using the toilet	0.29	0.00	0.40	0.40	1.00	1.00
Cooking	0.35	0.40	0.40	0.64	0.72	0.90
Drinking	0.06	0.25	0.04	0.28	0.33	0.52
Washing dishes	0.16	0.88	0.19	0.90	0.21	0.92
Leaving the house	0.5	0.00	0.50	0.50	0.14	0.57

Using the estimated probabilities, we computed the certainty factor. Fig. 4 shows the certainty factor for each activity.

Fig. 4 shows that S-GAF has higher certainty for all activities and GAF model has higher or comparable certainty to that of TAM. This is an obvious result because S-GAF and GAF models provide more evidence than TAM and GAF models respectively. If no tool is used for an activity like *using the toilet* or *leaving the house*, GAF and TAM show comparable certainty. We also can see that *cooking, drinking,* and *washing dishes* in TAM have low certainty compared to other activities because their tools or objects have low evidential certainty. The low evidential certainty may be attributed to artifacts such as a pan or a cup being used in multiple activities. Also, we can observe that the certainty of S-GAF for *using the toilet* and *cooking* have

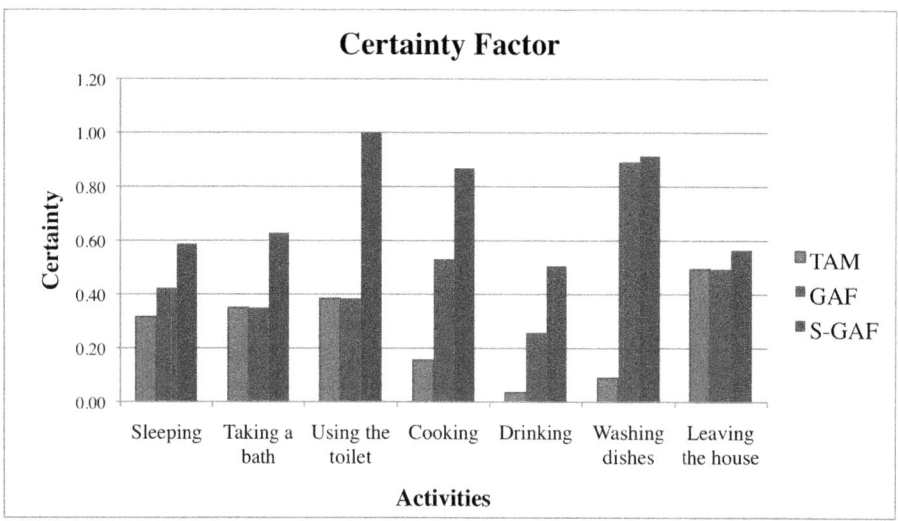

Fig. 4. Uncertainty according to activities. It compares uncertainties of TAM, GAF and S-GAF for each activity.

significant difference with other models. It is because the semantic information for *using the toilet* and *cooking* are more activity centric compared to other activities. For example, mutuality semantic is applied for several activities such as sleeping, *taking a bath* or *leaving the house*. On the other hand, the order semantic for *cooking* is only for the *cooking* activity and it is not applied for another activity of the scenario in Table 2. Therefore, the semantic is highly evidential.

5   Conclusion

Accurate activity modeling is important for increasing activity recognition (AR) performance because AR model affects other AR techniques, which are based on the AR model. However, the characteristics of human activities such as complexity, ambiguity or diversity make accurate activity modeling very challenging. In order to address the challenges, we propose a new activity modeling technique, which is based on both generic activity framework and activity semantic knowledge. The generic activity framework is a refinement of the classical activity theory. And the proposed approach adds meaningful semantic knowledge to the generic activity framework for representing activities more precisely. A major advantage of the proposed approach is that it can represent real world activities accurately by using the eight components of our generic activity framework along with the activity semantics introduced in this paper. This advantage implies reducing a great deal of uncertainty that may inherently exist in the activity model. Therefore, our modeling technique does increase the performance of activity recognition.

References

1. Helal, A., King, J., Zabadani, H., Kaddourah, Y.: The Gator Tech Smart House: An Assistive Environment for Successful Aging. In: Hagrass, H. (ed.) Advanced Intelligent Environments. Springer, Heidelberg (2008)
2. Mann, W., Helal, S.: Smart Technology: A Bright Future for Independent Living. The Society for Certified Senior Advisors Journal 21, 15–20 (2003)
3. Kim, E.J., Helal, S., Cook, D.: Human Activity Recognition and Pattern Discovery. IEEE Pervasive Computing 9(1), 48–52 (2010)
4. Kim, E.J., Helal, S.: Revisiting Human Activity Frameworks. In: 2nd International ICST Conference on Wireless Sensor Network Systems and Software - S-Cube (2010)
5. Kuutti, K.: Activity theory as a potential framework for human-computer interaction research. In: Nardi, B.A. (ed.) Context and Consciousness: Activity Theory and Human-Computer Interaction. MIT Press, Cambridge (1996)
6. Davydov, V. V., Zinchenko, V. P., Talyzina, N. F.: The Problem of Activity. In: The Works of A. N. Leontjev, Soviet Psychology, vol. 21(4), pp. 31–42 (1983)
7. Rabiner, L.R.: A tutorial on hidden markov models and selected applications in speech recognition. Proceedings of the IEEE 77(2), 257–286 (1989)
8. Sutton, C., McCallum, A.: An introduction to conditional random fields for relational learning. In: Getoor, L., Taskar, B. (eds.) Introduction to Statistical Relational Learning, MIT Press, Cambridge (2006)
9. David Irwin, J.: The industrial electronics handbook, p. 829. IEEE Press, Los Alamitos (1997)
10. Kusrin, K.: Question Quantification to Obtain User Certainty Factor in Expert System Application for Disease Diagnosis. In: Proceedings of the International Conference on Electrical Engineering and Informatics, pp. 765–768 (2007)
11. Pentney, W., et al.: Sensor-Based Understanding of Daily Life via Large-Scale Use of Common Sense. In: Proceedings of AAAI 2006, Boston, MA, USA (2006)
12. Surie, D., Pederson, T., Lagriffoul, F., Janlert, L.-E., Sjolie, D.: Activity Recognition using an Egocentric Perspective of Everyday Objects. In: Indulska, J., Ma, J., Yang, L.T., Ungerer, T., Cao, J. (eds.) UIC 2007. LNCS, vol. 4611, pp. 246–257. Springer, Heidelberg (2007)
13. Lefre, P.: Activity-based scenarios for and approaches to ubiquitous e-Learning. In: Personal and Ubiquitous Computing, vol. 13(3), pp. 219–227 (2009)
14. Pentney, W., et al.: Sensor-Based Understanding of Daily Life via Large-Scale Use of Common Sense. In: Proceedings of AAAI 2006, Boston, MA, USA (2006)
15. Kasteren, T., Noulas, A., Englebienne, G., Krose, B.: Accurate Activity Recognition in a Home Setting. In: Proceedings of the Tenth International Conference on Ubiquitous Computing (Ubicomp), Korea, pp. 1–9 (2008)

A Two-Layer Steganography Scheme Using Sudoku for Digital Images[*]

Yi-Hui Chen[1], Ci-Wei Lan[2], and Zhi-Hui Wang[3]

[1] Department of Applied Informatics and Multimedia, Asia University,
Taichung 431, Taiwan
chenyh@asia.edu.tw
[2] IBM Research Collaboratory, IBM Company,
Taipei 110, Taiwan
ciweilan@tw.ibm.com
[3] Department of Software, Dalian University of Technology,
DaLian, China
wangzhihui1017@gmail.com

Abstract. Steganography is a skill to convey the secret data in the digital images without getting any unexpected notices to attackers. LSB replacement, the simplest method, directly replaces the secret bits with LSB bit plane. Unfortunately, it is insecure because it cannot resist against the visual attacks and statistic detection. In 2009, Lin et al. proposed a novel data embedding scheme by using the concept of Sudoku. Lin et al.'s scheme not only improved the performances of traditional LSB-based steganography schemes, but also resist against steganalysis. In this paper, a steganography scheme based on Lin et al.'s scheme is explored. Experimental results show that the proposed scheme can improve the visual quality of stego-images. In addition, the average of hiding capacity is 1.29 bpp (bits per pixel). Therefore, it confirms that our proposed scheme provides higher hiding capacity than that of LSB replacement 0.29 bpp. Furthermore, our method shows the positive results to resist against the visual attacks.

1 Introduction

Steganography [1-4, 8-11] is a skill widely used to conceal secret data in cover digital media, such as images, videos, electronic documents, etc. The secret data embedded in the digital media is usually undetectable and non-statistical so that the hidden data can be securely transferred to the receivers without being noticed by the potential attackers. Three criteria used to evaluate the performances of steganographic schemes are hiding capacity, visual quality of stego-images and security analysis. High performances imply high embedding capacity and good visual quality. However, hiding capacity and visual quality are tradeoff because high hiding capacity often results in low visual quality.

---

[*] I gratefully acknowledge financial support for this research provided by the National Science Council with No. 100-2218-E-468-002-MY2.

C.-H. Hsu et al. (Eds.): UIC 2011, LNCS 6905, pp. 529–535, 2011.

LSB-based (Least Significant Bit Plane) data embedding schemes are roughly divided into two types, namely LSB replacement and LSB matching. The former one is the simplest strategy to directly replace the LSB of a cover image with the secret data. The latter one is to remain, add or subtract the pixel value according to the condition of least significant bit of the pixel equal to the secret data. The distortion of LSB-based data embedding schemes is very low so it can achieve high visual quality; however, some of the LSB-based data embedding schemes are insecure because the hidden data can be detected by the steganalysis [6, 7]. For example, the LSB replacement can be easily detected by visual attack and chi-square analysis [6], which will be described in our experimental results.

In 2006, Mielikainen [10] proposed an improved LSB matching scheme to provide better because only one of the two pixels would be modified during the embedding procedure in the worst case. That is, scheme [10] keeps the same hiding capacity 1 bpp, but provide better visual quality than traditional LSB matching scheme. To enlarge the hiding capacity, Lin et al. [8] proposed a novel data embedding scheme by using the concept of Sudoku. In scheme [8], they adopted 3^n-based notational system to design their hiding strategy. This paper extends the design of Lin et al.'s scheme to propose a two-layered data embedding scheme. The first layer is hiding the secret data through the ordinary design of Lin et al.'s scheme. The second layer embedding strategy modifies the pixel values according to the outcome of the first layered embedding strategy. The experimental results provide positive data to confirm that the proposed scheme has better visual quality than that of Lin et al.'s scheme. In addition, the hiding capacity is larger than scheme [10] 0.29 bpp. Furthermore, the proposed scheme can resist against the security analysis.

The rest of this paper is organized as follows. In Section 2, we shall briefly review the scheme [8]. In Section 3, we shall present the two-layered embedding schemes for digital images. In Section 4, the experimental results will be presented and discussed to show the performances of the proposed scheme with respect to the hiding capacity, visual quality of stego-images and security analysis. Finally, conclusions will be summarized and the future works will be drawn in the last section.

2   Related Works

In Lin et al.'s scheme [8], they first divide pixels into several groups and each group consists of n pixels, denoted as $g = (p_1, p_2, ..., p_n)$. Next, they transform the secret bitstream s into a 3^n-base digit sequence s'. Next, each pixel group can calculate a digit with Equation (1), where function $f()$ is also defined as an extracting function for later extraction.

$$f(p_1, p_2, ..., p_n) = \sum_{i=1}^{n} 3^{i-1} p_i \mod 3^n \cdot \tag{1}$$

For clarity, let the result of $f(p_1, p_2, ..., p_n)$ depict as r. If the r is not equal to s, the pixel values must be changed by using equations (2)-(3), where ℓ is a temporary value generated for each digit in the original pixel group $f(p_1, p_2, ..., p_n)$.

$$\ell = (r - f(p_1, p_2, ..., p_n) + \left\lfloor \frac{3^n - 1}{2} \right\rfloor) \bmod 3^n .$$ (2)

Next, they transform ℓ into a 3-base digital sequence depicted as ℓ^t, where $\ell^t = d_1 d_2 ... d_n$, d_i $d_i \in [0, 1, ..., n-1]$ and $1 \le i \le n$. Later on, each digit of ℓ^t is minus by 1 and the sequence is denoted as $\widetilde{\ell}^t = m_n m_{n-1} ... m_1$, $m_j \in [-1, 0, ..., n-2]$, where $m_j = d_i - 1$ and $j = n-i+1$. Finally, the pixels are modified with Equation (3), where each pixel in group g adds the corresponding digit of $\widetilde{\ell}^t$.

$$p_i' = p_i + m_i, \text{ where } i = 1 \text{ to } n.$$ (3)

Note that some special cases such as underflow or overflow are happened if the embedded pixel p_i' is less than 0 or greater than 255, respectively. When the pixel p_i' is less than 0, its corresponding original pixel pi is added with 1. If p_i' is larger than 255, its corresponding original pixel p_i is subtracted by 1. The modified pixels are formed a new group and repeats the embedding procedure until all pixels in group g do not have the problem of underflow or overflow at all. In the extracting procedure, the receivers divide the image into several groups and each group is composed of n pixels. Later, the receivers can extract the hidden s' by using Equation (1). Finally, the secret data s can be retrieved by transforming s' into bitstream s.

3   Proposed Scheme

This paper proposed a double layers data embedding scheme. The second layer embedding procedure must be adjusted by the results of the first layer embedding procedure. The details of the embedding procedure are described by the following steps.

Step 1: The image is divided into several groups. Each group consists of four pixels denoted as x_1, x_2, x_3 and x_4.

Step 2: Let two pixels be a group, such as two groups $\{x_1, x_2\}$ and $\{x_3, x_4\}$.

Step 3: Compute two differences $d_1 = |x_1 - x_2|$ and $d_2 = |x_3 - x_4|$.

Step 4: Let $p_1 = d_1$, $p_2 = d_2$, and $n=2$. Put into the Lin et al.'s scheme, which is described in Section 2, to get new differences d_1' and d_2' for embedding the secret data s.

Step 5: According to the results d_1' and d_2' generated by Step 4 to modify the pixels x_1, x_2, x_3, and x_4. The pixels x_1 and x_2 in the first one set $\{x_1, x_2\}$ are modified with Equations (4) and (5), respectively, where $i=1$, $j=2$ and $k=1$. Also, the pixels x_3 and x_4 in the second set $\{x_3, x_4\}$ are changed with Equations (4) and (5), respectively, where $i=3$, $j=4$, $k=2$ and LSB() is used to return the value 0 (or 1) when the pixel value is even (or odd).

$$x'_i = \begin{cases} x_i, & if \ s_k = LSB(x_i), \\ x_i+1, & if \ s_k \neq LSB(x_i), \ x_i > x_j \ and \ d'_k \geq d_k \\ x_i+1, & if \ s_k \neq LSB(x_i), \ x_i \leq x_j \ and \ d'_k < d_k \\ x_i-1, & if \ s_k \neq LSB(x_i), \ x_i \leq x_j \ and \ d'_k \geq d_k \\ x_i-1, & if \ s_k \neq LSB(x_i), \ x_i > x_j \ and \ d'_k < d_k \end{cases} \qquad (4)$$

$$x'_j = \begin{cases} x_j, & if \ s_k \neq LSB(x_i), \ d'_k \neq d_k, \\ x_j, & if \ s_k = LSB(x_i), \ d'_k = d_k, \\ x_j+1, & \begin{array}{l} if \ s_k = LSB(x_i), \ d'_k > d_k, \ and \ x_i \leq x_j, \\ if \ s_k \neq LSB(x_i), \ d'_k = d_k, \ and \ x_i > x_j, \\ if \ s_k = LSB(x_i), \ d'_k < d_k, \ and \ x_i > x_j, \end{array} \\ x_j-1, & \begin{array}{l} if \ s_k = LSB(x_i), \ d'_k > d_k, \ and \ x_i > x_j, \\ if \ s_k = LSB(x_i), \ d'_k < d_k, \ and \ x_i \leq x_j, \\ if \ s_k \neq LSB(x_i), \ d'_k = d_k, \ and \ x_i \leq x_j, \end{array} \end{cases} \qquad (5)$$

Step 6: The special cases are happened when the hidden pixel x'_i (or x'_j) is larger than 255 or less than 0, which problem is called overflow (or under-flow) problem. If pixel x'_i (or x'_j) has the overflow problem, the pixel x'_i (or x'_j) must trace back to their original pixel x_i (or x_j) and change the original value as $x_i = x_i-1$ (or $x_j = x_j-1$). As for the underflow problem, the original pixel x_i (or x_j) must be changed as $x_i = x_i+1$ (or $x_j = x_j+1$). After the pixel is changed, pixels go into the Step 2 to Step 5 until pixels are embedded.

The extracting procedure retrieves the secret data by using two layers. The details of extracting procedure are described as follows.

Step 1: The received stego-image is divided into several groups. Each group consists of four pixels, which are denoted as $\overline{x}_1$, $\overline{x}_2$, $\overline{x}_3$ and $\overline{x}_4$.

Step 2: Let two pixels be a group, such as two groups { $\overline{x}_1$, $\overline{x}_2$ } and { $\overline{x}_3$, $\overline{x}_4$ }.

Step 3: Compute two differences $d_1 = |\overline{x}_1 - \overline{x}_2|$ and $d_2 = |\overline{x}_3 - \overline{x}_4|$.

Step 4: Let $p_1 = d_1$, $p_2 = d_2$, and $n=2$. Then, we can calculate the secret data s with Equation (1).

Step 5: Get the secret data s_1 and s_2 by computing LSB($\overline{x}_1$) and LSB($\overline{x}_2$), respectively.

4   Experimental Results

Two criteria for evaluating the performances of data embedding schemes: Hiding capacity and visual quality of stego-image. On average, the hiding capacity in the proposed scheme is 1.29 bpp. In addition, except for exceptional situation, only one of two pixels is incremented or decremented by 1 in worst case. The visual quality of stego-images in our proposed scheme is computed with Equation (6) as PSNR = 51.14 dB. Therefore, there is no change between cover images and stego-images by using naked eyes.

$$PSNR = 10 \times \log_{10}(\frac{255^2}{MSE})dB. \tag{6}$$

Here, 255 is the maximum value of each pixel and the *MSE* for an image is defined in Equation (7).

$$MSE = (\frac{1}{hd \times wd})\sum_{i}^{hd} \sum_{j}^{wd}(\beta_{ij} - \beta'_{ij})^2. \tag{7}$$

Here, *hd* and *wd* denote the height and width of an image, β_{ij} is the pixel value of the location *(i, j)* in an original image, and β'_{ij} is the pixel value after the data embedding procedure.

To prove that our proposed scheme can hide large payload as well as good visual quality, the comparisons among Chang and Tseng's [1], Lin et al.'s [8], and Mielikainen's [10] schemes and our scheme in image quality and hiding capacity are shown in Table 1.

Table 1. Performance of various schemes with different cover images

Images	Lena		Baboon	
Schemes	Capacity (bytes)	PSNR (dB)	Capacity (bytes)	PSNR (dB)
Scheme [1]	48,626	41.20	57,146	34.10
Scheme [8]	51,941	49.88	51,941	49.88
Scheme [10]	32,768	52.38	32,768	52.38
Proposed Scheme	42,270	51.14	42,270	51.14

In Table 1, the hiding capacity of the proposed scheme is higher than that of the LSB replacement strategy about 0.29 bpp on average. The visual quality of the proposed scheme is similar to that of Mielikainen's scheme [10], but the hiding capacity of our scheme is highly significant improvement. The visual quality of our scheme is over 51 dB, which is relatively higher than that of schemes [1, 8].

The security analysis is proved as shown in Table 2. The detected results show that our proposed scheme can resist against the traditional LSB attacks, such as using statistical analysis or visual attack [6]. The traditional LSB replacement replaces the lowest bit plane of pixels with secret data so that it can easily detected by using the statistical analysis. The statistical tools are difficult to analyze the hidden data in stego-images because they do not directly correspond to the lowest bit plan. Table 2 shows the results for original images without embedding any secret, the secret hidden into an image with LSB replacement and our proposed scheme listed as "Embedding no secret data", "LSB replacement" and "Our proposed scheme", respectively. The results of LSB replacement are easily to show some regular patterns appear so it is insecure. Conversely, no clues can be found in our proposed scheme which are similar to the results of without embedding any secret data so the proposed scheme can withstand a visual attack.

Table 2. Comparison of visual attack results with LSB replacement and our proposed scheme

Images	Embedding no secret data	LSB replacement	Our proposed scheme

5   Conclusions

The hiding capacity and visual quality of our proposed scheme are 1.29 bpp and 51.11 dB on average. Moreover, the results show the positive data to confirm its security. In the future, we will extend this version to achieve higher hiding capacity as well as better visual quality.

References

1. Chang, C.C., Tseng, H.W.: A Steganographic Method for Digital Images Using Side Match. Pattern Recognition Letters 25(10), 1431–1437 (2004)
2. Chang, C.C., Lu, T.C., Chang, Y.F., Lee, R.C.T.: Reversible Data Hiding Schemes for Deoxyribonucleic Acid (DNA) Medium. International Journal of In-novative Computing, Information and Control (IJICIC) 3(5), 1145–1160 (2007)

3. Chang, C.C., Wu, W.C., Chen, Y.H.: Joint Coding and Embedding Tech-niques for Mul-timedia Images. Information Sciences 178(18), 3543–3556 (2008)
4. Chen, Y.H., Chang, C.C., Lin, C.C.: Adaptive Data Embedding Using VQ and Clustering. International Journal of Innovative Computing and Information Control (IJICIC) 3(6(A)), 1471–1485 (2007)
5. Fridrich, J., Goljan, M., Du, R.: Detecting LSB Steganography in Color and Gray-Scale Images. Magazine of IEEE Multimedia, Special Issue on Security 8(4), 22–28 (2001)
6. Guillermito, S.: Chi-square Steganography Test Program, http://www.guillermito2.net/stegano/tools/index.html
7. Ker, A.D.: Steganalysis of LSB Matching in Grayscale Images. IEEE Signal Processing Letters 12(6), 441–444 (2005)
8. Lin, C.C., Chen, Y.H., Chang, C.C.: LSB-based High-Capacity Data Em-bedding Scheme for Images. International Journal of Innovative Computing and Information Control (IJICIC) 5(11(B)), 4283–4289 (2009)
9. Lin, S.D., Kuo, Y., Yao, M.: An Image Watermarking Scheme with Tamper Detection and Recovery. International Journal of Innovative Computing, Information and Control (IJICIC) 3(6(A)), 1379–1387 (2007)
10. Mielikainen, J.: LSB Matching Revisited. IEEE Signal Processing Letters 13(5), 285–287 (2006)
11. Weng, S., Zhao, Y., Pan, J.S.: A Novel Reversible Data Hiding Scheme. International Journal of Innovative Computing, Information and Control (IJICIC) 4(2), 351–358 (2008)

Algorithms and Hardware Architectures for Variable Block Size Motion Estimation

Sheng-De Wang and Chih-Hung Weng

Department of Electrical Engineering
National Taiwan University
Taipei 106, Taiwan
sdwang@ntu.edu.tw

Abstract. Multimedia has become more and more important in embedded systems. It is well-known that motion estimation plays an essential role in video coding. It is also one of the key elements that achieve video compression by exploiting temporal redundancy of video data. The latest coding standard H.264 has adopted lots of new features. For instance, in order to adaptively choose the proper block size for frame macroblock, H.264 has used variable block size motion estimation which can significantly improve the coding performance compared to previous techniques. However, the computational complexity of H.264 has also increased drastically. Among all the techniques in the encoder, motion estimation is exactly the most time-consuming function especially when it is implemented in a software approach. In this paper, we combine software and hardware optimizations for variable block size motion estimation. At the software level, we propose a new algorithm that can efficiently select a suitable block size by grouping the motion vectors. At the hardware level, we propose a pipelined and parallel architecture to enhance the performance. Our architecture is implemented on an FPGA platform. It operates at a maximum clock frequency of 311 MHz with gate count 65k. The results show that under a frequency of 248MHz, our architecture allows the processing of 1920x1080 at 30fps with full search motion estimation in a 16x16 search range. This proposed architecture provides a better hardware efficiency in terms of throughput and gate count than previous works.

Keywords: Motion Estimation, Variable Block Size Motion Estimation, Hardware Accelerator.

1 Introduction

Recently, with the growing popularity of multimedia, the demand of high quality video has been stronger than ever. In order to support high quality video, we must put more effort on data compression, which means that computational complexity will also increase. Therefore, how to reduce encoding time without significant loss of subjeplays an important role in video coding. Itctive picture quality is indispensable.

C.-H. Hsu et al. (Eds.): UIC 2011, LNCS 6905, pp. 536–549, 2011.
© Springer-Verlag Berlin Heidelberg 2011

Generally speaking, data compression usually involves a trade-off between speed and quality. It takes advantage of data redundancy of video data to achieve higher compression ratio, since successive frames are usually similar. Data redundancy usually results from temporal, spatial, and statistical correlation. Motion estimation can reduce temporal redundancy between frames and transform coding can reduce spatial redundancy within a frame, while binary coding is used to eliminate statistical dependency.

As we all know, pure software solutions of video coding usually result in large computation. To solve these issues, hardware implementations is often employed. Compared to pure software solution, adopting hardware to enhance video coding seems to have more possibilities. One of an important reason is that the clock speed of central processing unit (CPU) has reached its physical limit, which means it will not be able to run any faster. Under this circumstance, hardware can use parallelism to achieve higher performance. This architecture again attracts the attention of computer scientists. Designing specific hardware, to serve as the auxiliary processor, and to further enhance the system performance seems to be the trend.

Among all the components in a video encoder, motion estimation is the most time consuming part [2]. It is also the critical component that affects video quality and compression ratio. As a result, lots of software and hardware solutions have been proposed to solve this problem. Hence, video coding systems are usually implemented in application-specific integrated circuit (ASIC) or field programmable gate array (FPGA) [3].

Although many algorithms have been proposed, the performance still may not meet the application requirements. The reason is that the complexity of motion estimation has tremendously increased compared to previous coding standards since the introduction of variable block size motion estimation in H.264 [11]. In this paper, we focus on the software and hardware co-design of variable block size motion estimation. Moreover, we will implement our proposed approach in an FPGA evaluation board and analyze the results.

2   Variable Block Size Motion Estimation

The motion estimation unit serves to eliminate the temporal dependency as we mentioned above. The current frame and the reference frame are passed to the unit. Since this two frames are really similar, especially for high frame rates, thus temporal redundancy occurs. By adopting motion estimation, the predicted frame will nearly be the same as the original one. As a result, the difference between adjacent frames can be made smaller, which means data size can be reduced. Typically, since it is well-known that the motion between consecutive frames is really small, the 16x16 search range will almost suffice. Afterward, a motion vector, which represents the relative displacement between current block and reference block in horizontal and vertical direction is generated. And what the best motion vector means is that the difference between reference block in the search area and the current block in the current frame is the least.

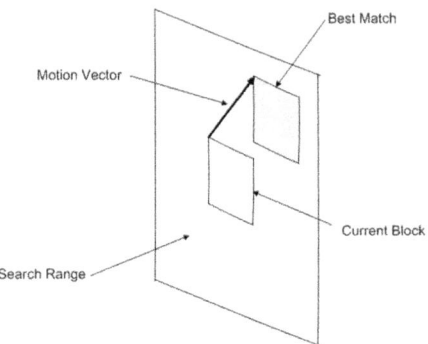

Fig. 1. Motion estimation and motion vector

When the best match is found, as we described earlier, the residue data and the corresponding vectors are passed to the transformation unit and entropy unit and then transmitted to the decoder. As for the motion compensation unit, it serves to reconstruct a compensated frame, from the original frame and motion vectors. At decoder side, it performs the inverse procedures the encoder does to reconstruct the original picture. It should be noticed that the reconstructed image will not be the same as the original one because of the lossy operations in the quantization unit. Figure 1 shows an illustration of the above procedure. In contemporary video coding standards, the number of reference frames referred can vary. The more frames referred, the higher quality it achieves.

2.1   Searching Strategy

There are many matching methods in video coding. The ideal situation is that we partition video into moving objects and describe object motion. Nevertheless, as a consequence of the difficulties in implementation, it is impractical. As for block-based matching proposed by Jain [5], it is the most widely used method since its simplicity and ease of implementation. The frames are partitioned into non-overlapped blocks, usually 16x16 or 8x8 depending on the accuracy needed. In the latest coding standards such as H.264, variable block sizes are supported. Generally speaking, the smaller the block size is, the more accurate the prediction is. Apparently, we can notice that the small blocks favor detailed region while the large blocks favor uniform region such as background. Likewise, searching strategy also has great impact on the results. Among all strategies proposed, only full search guarantees optimal results within the search area. Others only achieves suboptimal results by reducing the search candidates. These suboptimal methods can save time considerably at the risk of being trapped in the local minimum.

In some coding standards, the block size for estimation is fixed, such as 8x8 or 16x16. Thus one motion vector is produced for each block in the frame. Nonetheless, since the demand of high quality video has been stronger than ever, the traditional methods seem not to be suitable. Accordingly, the latest coding standard

Table 1. The profiling result of each function

Function	Proportion
Motion Estimation	82.87%
Transformation	5.11%
Inverse Transformation	6.03%
Quantization	0.3%
Others	5.69%

has employed variable block size motion estimation. Since the introduction of this mechanism, we can adaptively choose the proper block size for macroblock. Compared to fixed block size motion estimation, this method supports 7 block patterns: 16x16, 16x8, 8x16, 8x8, 8x4, 4x8, 4x4 and thus can produce more than one vector for each block[8]. Though it can achieve better estimation for detailed area, the computational complexity increases drastically in a software approach since all the block sizes are performed and the one that results in the least cost is chosen. Even for hardware implementation, the comparators required also increase from 1 to 41.

Table 1 shows the profiling result of each function in our program on a Core 2 Duo 2.66GHz platform. Obviously, motion estimation particularly contributes the most computational complexity to the system. In a software approach, it takes more than 80 percent of the total computation time.

3   Mode Decision

In H.264 coding standard, for every macroblock, various block sizes such as 16x16, 8x16, 16x8, 8x8, 4x8, 8x4 and 4x4 are tried and one that results in the least cost is selected. Notwithstanding the optimal selection of the block size for final encoding, this method requires extreme complexity since the cost is achieved after various operations such as motion estimation, motion compensation, transformation, quantization, inverse quantization, inverse transformation and entropy coding. Accordingly, reduce the complexity of motion estimation without compromising the coding efficiency is necessary .

There have been lots of fast mode decision algorithms proposed for H.264 video coding recently. In [12], D.Wu et al. exploited the spatial homogeneity and the temporal stationarity characteristics of video objects. Simply put, spatial homogeneity is decided by the edge intensity of the macroblock, while temporal stationarity is decided by the difference of the current macroblock and its collocated counterpart in the reference frame. In [7], Feng Pan et al. proposed a fast mode decision algorithm by adopting local edge information. An edge map is created and a local edge direction histogram is then established for each block.

In [9], Sarwer et al. reduced the complexity of the motion estimation with an early termination scheme depending on the statistical characteristics of rate distortion cost regarding current block and previous blocks. In this way, a large number of searches can be terminated. In [14], Zhenyu *et al.* observed that the compensated prediction errors are mainly depending on the textures in the image. The image block containing detailed textures makes variable block size motion estimation necessary. For the homogeneous block, the unnecessary inter-mode motion estimation can be eliminated efficiently.

Although there have been many software optimizations for motion estimation lately, most of those work just focus on how to reduce search points at the expense of video quality. Considering full search motion estimation, its large computational complexity still limits the capability of real time processing. In modern general purpose processors such as Intel Pentium-4, its performance is a few giga operations per second (GOPS) but a full search motion estimation requires at least 15 GOPS for CIF resolutions, so it's totally impractical to perform motion estimation in a software approach. Hence, hardware implementation for motion estimation is the only solution. We will discuss some motion estimation architecture in the following paragraph.

In [1], A. Ben Atitallah *et al.* present a HW/SW implementation of the motion estimation on a FPGA platform using the Nios II softcore processor. Their implemented more than one motion estimation algorithm. The main component of the SAD architecture is the processing element. It is composed by registers, adders, subtractors and a unit of the absolute value. The calculation of the SAD values of a macroblock line is done by applying in parallel of the 4 PEs modules. In this way, the SAD value of the macroblock line is obtained in one clock cycle. Likewise, the calculation of the SAD16x16 is achieved by using the SAD16 module. In fact, A. Ben Atitallah *et al.* discuss on two methods to implement the SAD16x16 operation. When optimizing for speed, they replicate the SAD16 module 16 times in parallel. In this way, the SAD value is obtained in one clock cycle. When optimizing for area, they call the SAD16 module 16 times consecutively. In this case, the SAD computation of the macroblock is obtained in 16 clock cycles. Obviously, the parallel architecture is 16 times faster than the letter regardless of the considerable area.

In [10], An-Chao Tsai *et al.* propose a early termination mechanism for motion estimation at the software level. They observed that if the SAD value of the 4x4 block is small, the SAD of the large block merged by 4x4 block will also have a small SAD and can become the possible candidate. Therefore, in their scheme, the SADs of the large block are generated by combining the SADs of 4x4 blocks. Based on the above observation, they calculated the SAD value of 4x4 block first. And the candidate will be stored into a heap if its SAD value is smaller than the minimum matching error. The heap capacity is defined by the user, so the smaller the capacity is, the faster the motion estimation will be performed. However, the cost is the degeneration of video quality. In their implementation, they set 200 for the capacity of the heap. As for the other 4x4 blocks, the same policy is applied. If the heap is full, the search will be stopped. When calculating the large block size, the heap also defines which is merged by the combination of the 16 4x4 blocks. Therefore, it only needs to search the candidate recorded in the heap for the large block type. As for the hardware implementation, 2D systolic array for variable block size motion estimation architecture are employed.

4   Proposed Algorithms and Architectures

As we described earlier, for mode decision algorithms, most work just focus on the reduction of search points and the pre-processing algorithm is usually too complex. Therefore, we proposed a mode decision algorithm that can efficiently select a suitable block size by analyzing and grouping the motion vectors. As to hardware architecture, although 2D systolic architecture offers better through-put rate, it usually suffers from some problems such as complex data scheduling, huge power consumption and large silicon area. Consequently, it is not suit-able for portable devices. Based on the reasons described above, we proposed a modified 1D architecture that can significantly reduce gate counts with slightly throughput decrease. Hence, the efficiency of our proposed method increases significantly.

Vectors Grouping

In the latest coding standard, intermode motion estimation is performed for different sizes such as 16x16, 16x8, 8x16, 8x8, 8x4, 4x8, and 4x4. For each mac-roblock, all the sizes are tried and the one that leads to the least cost is chosen. Although the selection of block size is optimal, this new features has led to extreme complexity since the cost is achieved after various operations such as motion estimation, motion compensation, transformation, quantization, inverse quantization, inverse transformation and entropy coding. Accordingly, reduce the complexity of motion estimation without compromising the coding efficiency is necessary . As a result, in order to solve this problem, a fast mode decision algorithm is employed. We will describe our method in the following paragraph.

Taking Figure 2 for example, if the objects in a macroblock are inseparable, then the motion vectors of larger blocks will nearly be the same as those of the smaller ones, as Figure 3 shows. Moreover, the bits associated with vectors of larger block are less than the smaller one. Thus, we can choose the larger block for motion estimation. This means that we partition it into four 8x8 subblocks assuming the macroblock size is 16x16. If all the four vectors are almost the same, then we can use 16x16 instead. Otherwise, let's see another example. Figure 4 shows that the motion vectors of larger blocks will not be the same as the smaller one as Figure 5 shows. This distribution means that the macroblock may contain objects moving toward opposite directions. Thus we can use 8x16 instead. If all the four vectors are irrelevant, indicating the movements in this macroblock are not in a single direction, so we should select 8x8 instead.

Motivated by the observations above, we proposed an efficient algorithm by performing vectors grouping. First, we perform motion estimation with 8x8 block size for each 16x16 macroblock. After that, we can obtain four vectors

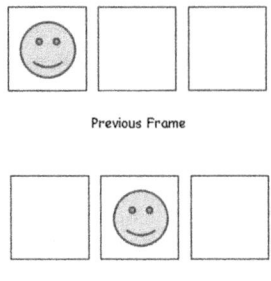

Fig. 2. An example of inseparable objects

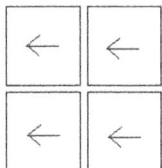

Fig. 3. An example of 16x16 vectors distribution

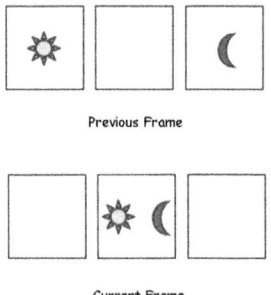

Fig. 4. An example of separable objects

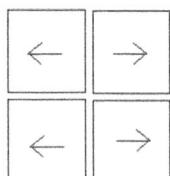

Fig. 5. An example of 8x16 vectors distribution

V_0, V_1, V_2, V_3. Next, we calculate the variance of these vectors. If the variance of both x and y components are less than predefined threshold, this indicates the objects in this macroblock have great probability to be inseparable. In this case, we can choose 16x16 block as the best mode. Otherwise, we calculate the variance of V_0, V_3 and V_0, V_1 and check the variance using the same criteria to decide whether we should choose 16x8 or 8x16 block. Thus, the search procedure of the six remaining modes can be eliminated. If none of the above cases happened, it means that this macroblock is likely to contain many objects which move toward different directions. In such a case, we recursively adopt the same policy described above to perform 4x4 block size motion estimation for each 8x8 subblock. Likewise, after analyzing and grouping these vectors, we can know whether we should select 8x8, 4x8, 8x4, or 4x4 block as the best mode. In the proposed algorithm, we only need to perform 8x8 block size motion estimation for one macroblock in the best-case scenario and the remaining search procedure can be terminated. Even though the worst-case scenario happens, the extra penalty is merely the 4x4 block size motion estimation. In other words, the number of times needed to perform motion estimation is at best 2, which is quite less than the original 7.

Hardware Architecture

As we analyzed earlier, the computational complexity of full search motion estimation is at least 15 giga operations per second, not to mention variable block size motion estimation. Therefore, the contemporary processor cannot achieve this performance. As we all know, one of an important reason is that the clock speed of central processing unit (CPU) has reached its physical limit, which means it will not be able to run any faster. Under this circumstance, hardware accelerator will be the only solution. Considering both speed and area, the 1D architecture is chosen as the basic unit for computing the SAD of 4x4 block. The architecture of our SAD unit is shown in Figure 6.

Our proposed architecture is composed of memories, multiplexers, registers, processing element array, and a comparator for selecting the minimum SAD and

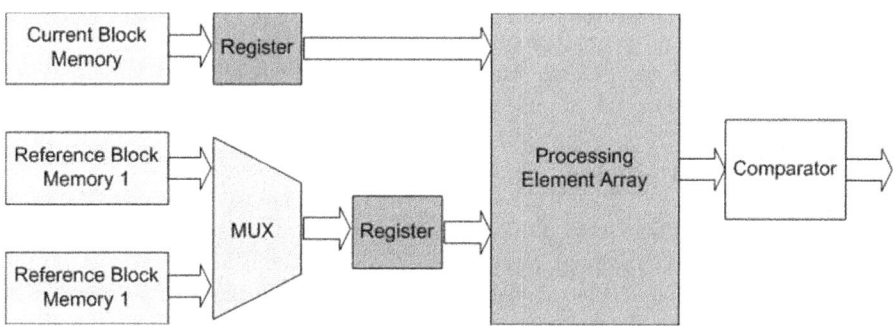

Fig. 6. The SAD4x4 unit

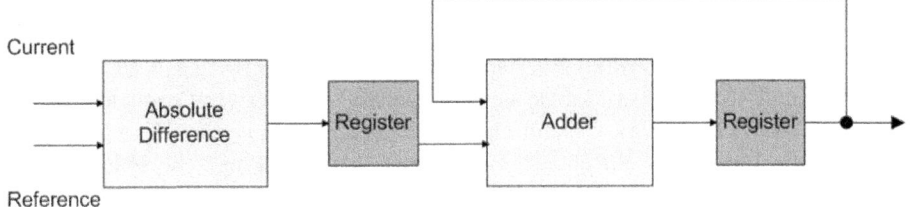

Fig. 7. The processing element

the corresponding motion vector. In this architecture, we have three single port memories. One is for current block data, and others are for reference block data. It should be noticed that the reference data are divided into two parts since we must read two reference pixels at the same time. Each PE array is responsible for the specific block motion estimation. As for the detailed architecture of the processing element array in Figure 6, it is formed by five PEs. Each PE calculates the absolute difference between reference block data and current block data and accumulates the value as shown in Figure 7. Accordingly, we can get five candidate SADs in a row after 20 clock cycles. After achieving the vertical movement in the search window, the same policy is applied to other SAD computations. Thus, after 84 clock cycles, we will get the entire candidate SADs. The detailed data flow schedule is shown in Table 2.

Furthermore, we need additional 1 clock cycle to compare all SADs and generate the corresponding motion vector. The architecture described above is for 4x4 block size. As for larger block size motion estimator, we adopt bottom-up technique and thus we combine these small block size estimators to achieve the larger block size one. Hence, for 8x8 block size motion estimation, we replicate our processing element array 4 times in parallel. Likewise, we can get five candidate SADs in a row after 20 clock cycles, but it should be noticed that in this architecture, an additional adder is used to sum up these four temporary results. Similarly, an extra 1 clock cycle is required to perform comparison between the results. To sum up, in order to support variable block size motion estimation, we need 80 PEs to compute variable block size motion vectors in parallel. It means that we can replicate our processing array 16 times. From the data flow described above, we can get the final results after 84 clock cycles for any block size motion estimation.

Implementation Platform

We use the Evaluation Board DE2 from Altera to test if our motion estimator works and to see its preformance. We have developed the driver and ported uClinux on DE2 to complete hardware and software integration design. The testing process takes the advantage of the NIOS II processor. First, it stores image data into the onchip memory, and then we let the motion estimator to perform motion estimation. After estimation is finished, the reconstructed image

Table 2. The data flow schedule

Clk	Cur	Ref1	Ref2	PE1	PE2	PE3	PE4	PE5
1	(0,0)	(0,0)		(0,0)-(0,0)				
2	(1,0)	(1,0)		(1,0)-(1,0)	(0,0)-(1,0)			
3	(2,0)	(2,0)		(2,0)-(2,0)	(1,0)-(2,0)	(0,0)-(2,0)		
4	(3,0)	(3,0)		(3,0)-(3,0)	(2,0)-(3,0)	(1,0)-(3,0)	(0,0)-(3,0)	
5	(0,1)	(0,1)	(4,0)	(0,1)-(0,1)	(3,0)-(4,0)	(2,0)-(4,0)	(1,0)-(4,0)	(0,0)-(4,0)
6	(1,1)	(1,1)	(5,0)	(1,1)-(1,1)	(0,1)-(1,1)	(3,0)-(5,0)	(2,0)-(5,0)	(1,0)-(5,0)
7	(2,1)	(2,1)	(6,0)	(2,1)-(2,1)	(1,1)-(2,1)	(0,1)-(2,1)	(3,0)-(6,0)	(2,0)-(6,0)
8	(3,1)	(3,1)	(7,0)	(3,1)-(3,1)	(2,1)-(3,1)	(1,1)-(3,1)	(0,1)-(3,1)	(3,0)-(7,0)
9	(0,2)	(0,2)	(4,1)	(0,2)-(0,2)	(3,1)-(4,1)	(2,1)-(4,1)	(1,1)-(4,1)	(0,1)-(4,1)
10	(1,2)	(1,2)	(5,1)	(1,2)-(1,2)	(0,2)-(1,2)	(3,1)-(5,1)	(2,1)-(5,1)	(1,1)-(5,1)
11	(2,2)	(2,2)	(6,1)	(2,2)-(2,2)	(1,2)-(2,2)	(0,2)-(2,2)	(3,1)-(6,1)	(2,1)-(6,1)
12	(3,2)	(3,2)	(7,1)	(3,2)-(3,2)	(2,2)-(3,2)	(1,2)-(3,2)	(0,2)-(3,2)	(3,1)-(7,1)
13	(0,3)	(0,3)	(4,2)	(0,3)-(0,3)	(3,2)-(4,2)	(2,2)-(4,2)	(1,2)-(4,2)	(0,2)-(4,2)
14	(1,3)	(1,3)	(5,2)	(1,3)-(1,3)	(0,3)-(1,3)	(3,2)-(5,2)	(2,2)-(5,2)	(1,2)-(5,2)
15	(2,3)	(2,3)	(6,2)	(2,3)-(2,3)	(1,3)-(2,3)	(0,3)-(2,3)	(3,2)-(6,2)	(2,2)-(6,2)
16	(3,3)	(3,3)	(7,2)	(3,3)-(3,3)	(2,3)-(3,3)	(1,3)-(3,3)	(0,3)-(3,3)	(3,2)-(7,2)
17			(4,3)		(3,3)-(4,3)	(2,3)-(4,3)	(1,3)-(4,3)	(0,3)-(4,3)
18			(5,3)			(3,3)-(5,3)	(2,3)-(5,3)	(1,3)-(5,3)
19			(6,3)				(3,3)-(6,3)	(2,3)-(6,3)
20			(7,3)					(3,3)-(7,3)

will be stored in the file, and we can download the file via network to make sure
if the motion estimator works as exactly as it previously runs on the simulator.

5 Experimental Results

The performance results of our proposed algorithm and architecture will be discussed respectively. We will also compare the required number of processing elements, maximum working frequency, gate count, throughput rate, and efficiency with previous work. Our target device is Altera DE2 and we use Altera Quartus II 6.0 as our synthesizer. The results show that our architecture can operate at 311MHz with about 5k logic elements. The register and memory usage are 2201 and 10240, respectively.

Performance of Proposed Algorithm

To show the simulation results of our fast motion estimation algorithm, several video sequences with CIF resolution are tested to verify the coding efficiency. The vectors analysis results are listed below. From this table, it is notable that for images that show strong stillness, lots of blocks choose 16x16 as best mode and only a few blocks select 8x8. On the contrary, for sequences containing fast movements, we can observe that most blocks select 8x8 as best mode. By adopting this mechanism, for each macroblock at most two block sizes are needed

Table 3. The vectors analysis results

Sequences	16x16	16x8 or 8x16	8x8
Akiyo	81%	4%	15%
Bridge	80%	4%	16%
Bus	19%	14%	67%
Coastguard	65%	7%	28%
Container	67%	4%	29%
Flower	57%	5%	38%
Foreman	44%	10%	46%
Hall	33%	10%	57%
Highway	25%	12%	63%
Mobile	67%	6%	27%
Mother-daughter	48%	7%	45%
News	72%	5%	23%
Paris	73%	6%	21%
Silent	71%	5%	24%
Stefan	39%	10%	51%
Tempete	70%	6%	24%
Waterfall	96%	1%	3%
Weather	74%	7%	19%
Average	59%	7%	34%

to be performed and the search time depends on the probability of 8x8 block size. In other words, the lower the probability of 8x8 block size is, the less time the estimation procedure takes. Thus, we can conclude that for stationary sequences, the time and the bits required for encoding procedure are less. The simulation results show that about 60% of the blocks select 16x16 as best mode, which means we can save much time and lots of storage.

Table 4 shows the simulation results of our proposed algorithm. We can observe that our proposed algorithm can save about 75% motion estimation time on average and the most important of all, the video quality has no significant drop. Also, the pre-processing procedures of many works are based on complex operations such as edge detection. Thus, comparing to the previous works, it should be noted that our procedure is merely a variance calculation, which is very simple.

Performance of Proposed Architecture. As we mentioned in the previous section, 1282 operations are needed for one macroblock SAD computation. In consequence, the total number of operations required is about 4 GOPS for CIF resolution and 80 GOPS for 1920x1080 resolution assuming the frame rate is 30 and the search range is 16x16. Therefore, this huge computational complexity limits the feasibility of real-time processing for modern processor. As to our proposed architecture, it needs only 756 clock cycles to complete a macroblock SAD computation. Hence, it requires about 12M and 248M clock cycles for

Table 4. The simulation results for our proposed algorithm

	D. Wu[12]		A. C. Tsai[10]		Proposed	
Sequences	PSNR(db)	Time(%)	PSNR(db)	Time(%)	PSNR(db)	Time(%)
Akiyo	–	–	-0.01	-75.81	-0.02	-74.17
Bridge	–	–	–	–	-0.01	-74.25
Bus	–	–	-0.02	-70.21	-0.04	-77.21
Coastguard	–	–	-0.01	-71.00	-0.02	-75.18
Container	-0.01	-36.25	-0.02	-74.17	-0.02	-75.23
Flower	–	–	-0.01	-73.53	-0.03	-74.73
Foreman	-0.06	-25.18	-0.03	-71.28	-0.03	-76.92
Hall	–	–	-0.03	-75.57	-0.02	-74.75
Highway	–	–	-0.07	-73.67	-0.05	-74.73
Mobile	-0.01	-9.97	-0.02	-71.98	-0.02	-75.11
Mother-daughter	–	–	-0.03	-74.52	-0.04	-75.62
News	-0.07	-42.62	-0.03	-75.07	-0.02	-74.13
Paris	-0.04	-31.90	-0.03	-75.73	-0.04	-74.96
Silent	-0.02	-45.16	–	–	-0.03	-74.47
Stefan	-0.02	-17.37	-0.03	-71.46	-0.02	-76.24
Tempete	–	–	-0.02	-71.26	-0.02	-75.09
Waterfall	–	–	-0.05	-72.02	-0.05	-73.81
Weather	–	–	–	–	-0.03	-74.74
Average	-0.03	-29.77	-0.03	-72.91	-0.03	-75.09

CIF and Full-HD, respectively. The synthesis reports show that our proposed architecture can be operated at a maximum clock frequency of 311MHz, which means that the real time processing for Full-HD is feasible.

Comparison

We will compare our proposed architecture with previous work. The gate level circuits are based on Synopsys Design Compiler with TSMC 0.13um CMOS standard cell technology. The results show that our architecture only needs 65k gates. By the way, the circuit can work at 311MHz with a search range of 16x16. Moreover, our circuit requires at most 756 clock cycles to process one macroblock and can achieve 93M search points per second. Finally, it is noteworthy that the proposed architecture has the best efficiency, which means that the performance-price ratio is the best. Table 5 shows the comparison between our work and previous work. From this table, we can observe that simple architecture always results in poor throughput like [13], whereas complex structure always results in higher cost but better throughput rate. Notice that in [4] and [10], although their throughput rate are relatively high, the resources needed for the architecture are also huge. Therefore, our proposed work is the trade-off between cost and performance and the experimental results show that the resources required reduce remarkably with only negligible performance degradation.

Table 5. The comparison between our work and previous work

Methods	Deng[4]	Yap[13]	Tsai[10]	Levi[1]	Kthiri[6]	Proposed
Number of PE	256	16	256	64	128	80
Search Range	65x65	16x16	48x32	16x16	16x16(DS)	16x16
Process	0.18um	0.13um	0.13um	–	–	0.13um
Block Size	4x4–16x16	4x4–16x16	4x4–16x16	16x16	4x4–16x16	4x4–16x16
Gate Count	210k	61k	191k	5318(LE)	13068(LE)	5114(LE)65k(gates)
Frequency	260MHz	294MHz	200MHz	120MHz	100MHz	311MHz
Cycles Per MB	5216	4181	1614	961	–	756
Throughput	205M	17M	186M	–	–	93M
Efficiency	1002.8	299.1	998.8	–	–	1598.6

6   Conclusion

In this paper, we have introduced several algorithms and architectures for variable block size motion estimation. Although there are some mode decision and search algorithms that can reduce the complexity of motion estimation, their pre-processing procedures are based on complex operations such as edge detection. In addition, most of them just focus on the reduction of search points. Hence, at the software level, we proposed a new software algorithm for variable block size motion estimation. It can efficiently select a suitable block size by analyzing and grouping the motion vectors. Our proposed methods not only reduce the encoding time notably but also retain both objective and subjective quality performance. The simulation results show our method can save about 75% motion estimation search time on average. As for the hardware architecture, even though two-dimension systolic architecture offers better throughput rate, it usually suffers from some problems such as complex data scheduling, huge power consumption and large silicon area. Thus it is not suitable for portable and embedded devices. Based on these reasons, we focus on a solution that can achieve a better throughput-area ratio. Consequently, we adopt bottom-up technique and thus we combine these small block size estimators to achieve the larger block size one. Our architecture is implemented on an FPGA platform. It can be operated at a maximum clock frequency of 311Mhz with throughput rate 93M search points per second. Based on Synopsys Design Compiler with TSMC 0.13um standard library, it is noteworthy that our work only costs 65k gates, which means that the area is smaller. The results show that under a frequency of 248Mhz, our architecture allows the processing of 1920x1080 at 30fps with full search motion estimation in a 16x16 search range. Comparing to the previous works, our proposed architecture provides a better hardware efficiency in terms of throughput and area.

Although the current implementation of the proposed architecture can satisfy the demand for high-definition television resolutions, there are still several different directions to further extend this architecture. First, the video resolutions will be increasing in the future, so our work can be modified into a two-dimension architecture to allow more pixels to be processed simultaneously. Second, our testing procedure takes the advantage of the Nios II processor, and thus we can integrate a CMOS sensor and a LCD module into our design to achieve real-time processing. Lastly, we can combine the fast mode decision and search algorithms together to further enhance the performance.

References

1. Ben AtItallah, A., KadIonik, P., Masmoudi, N., Levi, H.: HW/SW FPGA architecture for a flexible motion estimation. In: IEEE International Conference on Electronics, Circuits and Systems, pp. 30–33 (December 2007)
2. Chung, W.C.: Implementing the H.264/AVC video coding standard on FPGAs (September 2005)
3. Compton, K., Hauck, S.: Reconfigurable computing: a survey of systems and software. ACM Comput. Surv. 34(2), 171–210 (2002)
4. Deng, L., Gao, W., Hu, M.Z., Ji, Z.Z.: An efficient hardware implementation for motion estimation of AVC standard. IEEE Transactions on Consumer Electronics 51(4), 1360–1366 (2005)
5. Jain, J., Jain, A.: Displacement Measurement and Its Application in Interframe Image Coding. IEEE Transactions on Communications 29(12), 1799–1808 (1981)
6. Kthiri, M., Loukil, H., Werda, I., Ben Atitallah, A., Samet, A., Masmoudi, N.: Hardware implementation of fast block matching algorithm in FPGA for H.264/AVC. In: International Multi-Conference on Systems, Signals and Devices, pp. 1–4 (March 2009)
7. Pan, F., Lin, X., Rahardja, S., Lim, K., Li, Z., Wu, D., Wu, S.: Fast mode decision algorithm for intraprediction in H.264/AVC video coding. IEEE Transactions on Circuits and Systems for Video Technology 15(7), 813–822 (2005)
8. Richardson, I.E.G.: H.264 and MPEG-4 video compression. John Wiley Publisher, Chichester (2003)
9. Sarwer, M.G., Wu, Q.J.: Adaptive variable block-size early motion estimation termination algorithm for H.264/AVC video coding standard. IEEE Transactions on Circuits and Systems for Video Technology (2009)
10. Tsai, A.-C., Lee, K.-I., Wang, J.-F., Yang, J.-F.: VLSI architecture designs for effective H.264/AVC variable block-size motion estimation. In: International Conference on Audio, Language and Image Processing, pp. 413–417 (July 2008)
11. Wieg, T., Pattaya, E.: Draft ITU-T recommendation H.264 and draft ISO/IEC 14496-10 AVC (March 2003)
12. Wu, D., Pan, F., Lim, K., Wu, S., Li, Z., Lin, X., Rahardja, S., Ko, C.: Fast intermode decision in H.264/AVC video coding. IEEE Transactions on Circuits and Systems for Video Technology 15(7), 953–958 (2005)
13. Yap, S.Y., McCanny, J.: A VLSI architecture for variable block size video motion estimation. IEEE Transactions on Circuits and Systems II: Express Briefs 51(7), 384–389 (2004)
14. Zhenyu Liu, S.G., Zhou, J., Ikenaga, T.: Motion estimation optimization for H.264/AVC using source image edge features. IEEE Transactions on Circuits and Systems for Video Technology (2009)

Reliability Comparison of Schedulability Test in Ubiquitous Computing

Fei Teng[1], Lei Yu[2,*], and Frédéric Magoulès[1]

[1] Ecole Centrale Paris, Chatenay-Malabry, France
{fei.teng,frederic.magoules}@ecp.fr
[2] Ecole Centrale de Pekin, Beihang University, Beijing, China
yulei@buaa.edu.cn

Abstract. The development of ubiquitous intelligent has increased the real-time requirements for computing system. If one real-time computation does not complete before its deadline, it is as worse as that the computation is never executed at all. Ineffective computation not only wastes computational resources, but also might bring system overload and collapse. Hence, a schedulability test is necessary to ensure the stability of ubiquitous system. The schedulability test is concerned with determining whether a set of tasks is schedulable on a cluster. Although a number of schedulability tests have been developed, they can not be compared due to distinct test principles. In this paper, we propose a reliability indicator, through which the probability that a random task set succeeds in schedulability test can be evaluated. The larger the probability is, the better the test is. The reliability of two sufficient deadline monotonic tests are compared, and the comparison result is further validated by detailed experiments. Both analysis and experimental results show that the performance discrepancy of schedulability test is determined by a prerequisite pattern. Since this pattern can be deduce by reliability indicator, it may help system designers choose a good schedulability test in advance.

1 Introduction

Ubiquitous computing targets offering everyday assistance when we navigate through our work and personal lives. In such intelligent environments, an application demand may arrive at any time, and should be get response in real time. For instance, to give an assistive transportation consultation, traffic control center needs to collect the state of road by different sensor devices periodically, and make a real-time decision to help drivers choose appropriate control actions. If the consultation can not be finished before a deadline, it will be meaningless for the drivers. Therefore, the future development of ubiquitous intelligent should head for real-time computing category [1].

Real-time computing is subject to real-time constraints that must be met, regardless of system load. If one real-time computation does not complete before its deadline, it is treated as a failed case, as worse as that the computation is never executed at all [2]. Ineffective computation not only wastes computational resources, but also might bring

---

* This work was done in part while the author was visiting Ecole Centrale Paris under the Top Academic Network for Developing Exchange and Mobility program.

C.-H. Hsu et al. (Eds.): UIC 2011, LNCS 6905, pp. 550–562, 2011.

system overload and collapse. Hence, a schedulability test is necessary to ensure the stability of ubiquitous system. Such a test will judge the schedulability of an arriving task together with the tasks already running in a system [3]. Considering the strict time requirements of ubiquitous computing, schedulability test here should be taken online, in predictable running time.

A number of schedulability tests have been developed to provide online control commitments [3, 4, 5, 6, 7], but these tests are incomparable due to different determination conditions. This deficiency arises the difficulty to choose the best test among all available alternatives, which provides the primary motivation of our study. In this paper, we introduce a reliability indicator to evaluate the accuracy of schedulability test. The large the value of indicator is, the more reliable the test is. Different schedulability tests could be compared through examining their reliability indicators. Another key contribution of this work is that the performance discrepancy can be predicated by a prerequisite pattern. This exact pattern helps system designers make a right choice in advance.

This paper is organized as follows. Section 2 introduces the related research of schedulability tests. Next section 3 presents task model and notions. In section 4, reliability is compared between different deadline monotonic tests. Section 5 further validates this comparison result by SimMapReduce simulation. Finally, section 6 concludes the paper.

2   Related Work

In the context of real-time systems, the scheduling algorithm is normally priority driven. The tasks are assigned priorities according to their time constraints. The method for priority assignment is important, generally, the highest priority is given to the most urgent task. Rate monotonic (RM) [4] and deadline monotonic (DM) [8] are commonly used assignment algorithms, and the former can be considered as a special case of the latter where period equals deadline.

Schedulability test is used to predict temporal behaviour of a given task set. It can decide whether the deadlines will be meet in advance, that is, the given task set can be scheduled [9]. Exact schedulability test yields to sufficient and necessary condition, but it requires high computational complexity [10], even in the simple case where task relative deadlines are equal to periods. Audsley [11] proposed an exact schedulability test by searching worst-case response time in an iterative manner. Lehoczky [12] then proposed a more general feasibility test for arbitrary deadlines. Later on, methods for speeding up the analysis of task sets were proposed [13, 14, 15, 16, 17], but the complexity of these approaches always remains pseudo-polynomial in the worst case.

Sufficient test can ensure all passing tasks meet their deadlines. For the tasks that do not pass the test, they still have the possibility to be scheduled. Sufficient tests might somewhat underutilize cluster, but can be finished quickly, with constant-time complexity. Constant complexity tests usually apply the lowest upper bound, such as classic RM bound [4] and DM bound [5]. As long as the utilization of a given task set is under this bound, all tasks can be scheduled for sure. Recently, another load test with $O(1)$ complexity is developed by Masrur [3]. This test is different from all mentioned bound tests that are based system utilization. It calculates the worst response time of accepted tasks. If this worst response time does not exceed the respective deadlines, all tasks can be scheduled. However, the comparison with other bound-based tests is unfinished by the authors.

3 System Model

We first clarify system model and relative terms that will be used in the following sections.

3.1 Task Model

A task set $\Gamma = (\tau_1, \tau_2, \cdots, \tau_n)$ is formulated including n independent periodic tasks. Task τ_i consists of a periodic sequence of requests. A new instance is created when a request arrives. The interval between two successive instances is period T_i. The time taken to execute τ_i is C_i. In the duration of any instance, computation must be completed before a deadline D_i. Herein, we assume $C_i \leq D_i \leq T_i$. Utilization u_i is the ratio of computation time to its period $u_i = C_i/T_i$.

A task τ_i is schedulable with respect to an algorithm if no instance misses its deadline, and a task set Γ is feasible with respect to an algorithm that can schedule all tasks in the set before their deadlines. Each task is assigned to a priority before execution. DM priority assignment refers to that the priority of task is inversely proportional to its period, that is to say, the task with the shortest deadline has the highest priority. DM scheduling is an optimum static algorithm for the cases where task deadline is no longer than its period [8]. If DM can not make a task set schedulable on a cluster, no other rules succeed in scheduling. When a running task with lower priority encounters a new request from a task with high priority, it hands over cluster to the new instance. This behavior is called preemptive, and the overhead of preemption is negligible.

3.2 Probability Distribution

Schedulability tests are used to predict schedulability of a given task set. The effectiveness of an sufficient test can be measured by the accepted ratio of task sets. The larger the ratio is, the reliable the test is. Note that this accepted ratio is different from the similar concept in previous researches [16]. The denominator of this ratio is the total number of participated tests, rather than the feasible ones. Such an adjustment makes our analysis much easier, because finding out all feasibly schedulable task set in an exact test is extremely time consuming. Another advantage is that simple UUniform algorithm turns to be practical in our simulation, which does not work for original test of accepted ratio, owing to a huge number of iterations[6].

Without loss of generality, we suppose that task utilization u_i is uniformly distributed with mean value $1/2$ and variance $1/12$. Two probability distributions will be calculated in the following context.

(1) $X = \sum_{i=1}^{n} u_i$

X is the sum of n independent u_i, and the PDF (probability density function) of X is

$$\mathcal{F}_{PDF}(X) = \frac{1}{(n-1)!} \sum_{k=0}^{\lfloor U \rfloor} (-1)^k \tbinom{n}{k} (U-k)^{n-1} \quad U \in [0, n] \tag{1}$$

Therefore, U has mean value $n/2$ and variance $n/12$. Its CDF (cumulative distribution function) is

$$\mathcal{F}_{CDF}(X) = \frac{1}{n!} \sum_{k=0}^{\lfloor U \rfloor} (-1)^k \binom{n}{k} (U-k)^n \quad U \in [0, n] \tag{2}$$

More generally, for a sequence of independent and identically distributed random variables u_i with expected values μ and variances σ^2, the central limit theorem asserts that for large n, the distribution of the sum X is approximately normal with mean $n\mu$ and variance $n\sigma^2$.

$$X \to \mathcal{N}(\frac{n}{2}, \frac{n}{12}) \tag{3}$$

(2) $Y = \sum_{i=1}^{n} 2u_i/(1+u_i)$ An intermediate variable $y_i = 1/(1+u_i)$ is introduced, and its PDF is expressed as

$$\mathcal{G}_{PDF}(y_i) = \frac{1}{y_i^2} \quad y_i \in [\frac{1}{2}, 1] \tag{4}$$

Mean and variance of y_i are

$$E(y_i) = \int_{\frac{1}{2}}^{1} y_i g(y_i) \mathrm{d}y_i = \ln 2 \tag{5}$$

$$D(y_i) = E(y_i^2) - [E(y_i)]^2 = \frac{1}{2} - (\ln 2)^2 \tag{6}$$

With y_i, we obtain

$$Y = \sum_{i=1}^{n} \frac{2u_i}{1+u_i} = \sum_{i=1}^{n} 2(1 - y_i) \tag{7}$$

Y is approximated by a normal distribution as

$$Y \to \mathcal{N}[2n(1 - \ln 2), 4n(\frac{1}{2} - (\ln 2)^2)] \tag{8}$$

3.3   Reliability Indicator w

We define reliability indicator w as

$$w = \frac{x - \mu}{\sigma} \tag{9}$$

For a generic normal random variable with mean μ and variance σ^2, its CDF can be expressed as $F(x) = \Phi(\frac{x-\mu}{\sigma})$, in which $\Phi(x)$ is the standard normal distribution. Because CDF of $\Phi(w)$ is monotone increasing function with respect to w, w can be used to compare the values of different $F(x)$.

4   Reliability Comparison of Schedulability Tests

In DM scheduling, we analyze two kinds of schedulability test, proposed by Peng and Masrur, respectively.

4.1   Bound Test

Bound test is firstly proposed for RM algorithm. Liu [4] introduced a concept of utilization factor to evaluate the CPU consumption of a single processor, and deduced the least upper bound that is the minimum of the utilization factors over all sets of tasks that fully utilize the processor. Since this bound is minimum value, any task set with a utilization factor under this bound is certainly schedulable on the processor. The bound U of RM algorithm is $n(2^{1/n} - 1)$. In DM scheduling, Peng [5] modified the utilization bound U_p by introducing system hazard $\theta = D_i/T_i, 1 \leq i \leq n$.

Theorem 1. *For a set of n tasks with fixed utilization $u_1, u_2, \cdots, u_n$, there exists a feasible algorithm ensuring all tasks can be scheduled on a cluster if*

$$U_p = \sum_{i=1}^{n} u_i \leq \begin{cases} \theta & \theta \in [0, 0.5) \\ n[(2\theta)^{1/n} - 1] + 1 - \theta & \theta \in [0.5, 1] \end{cases} \quad (10)$$

From the distribution of U_p in (3), we obtain $\mu = n/2$, $\sigma = \sqrt{n/12}$. The reliability indicator w_p of Peng's bound test is

$$w_p = \begin{cases} \dfrac{\theta - \frac{n}{2}}{\sqrt{\frac{n}{12}}} & \theta \in [0, 0.5) \\ \dfrac{n[(2\theta)^{1/n} - 1] + 1 - \theta - \frac{n}{2}}{\sqrt{\frac{n}{12}}} & \theta \in [0.5, 1] \end{cases} \quad (11)$$

4.2   Load Test

Masrur [3] studied a set of tasks with deadline no longer than period. Through comparing the deadline and the least upper bound U_m of the worst case response time of task set, Masrur proposed a load condition to test whether a task set is schedulable on a cluster.

Theorem 2. *For a set of n tasks with fixed utilization $u_1, u_2, \cdots, u_n$, there exists a feasible algorithm ensuring all tasks can be scheduled on a cluster if*

$$\sum_{i=1}^{n} \max(\frac{u_i}{\theta}, \frac{2u_i}{1 + u_i}) \leq 1 \quad (12)$$

Masrur's test contains a maximum operator. For sake of simplicity, we replace the max by introducing two parameters $u_l = (1 + \min u_i)/2$ and $u_h = (1 + \max u_i)/2$. There are m tasks ($m \leq n$) satisfy that u_i/θ is larger than $2u_i/(1 + u_i)$. Then the above inequality is decomposed to

$$U_m = \begin{cases} \frac{1}{\theta} \sum_{i=1}^{n} u_i \leq 1 & \theta \in [0, u_l) \\ \frac{1}{\theta} \sum_{i=i}^{m} u_i + \sum_{j=1}^{n-m} \frac{2u_j}{1+u_j} \leq 1 & \theta \in [u_l, u_h) \\ \sum_{i=1}^{n} \frac{2u_i}{1+u_i} \leq 1 & \theta \in [u_h, 1] \end{cases} \tag{13}$$

A factor α is introduced to represents the ratio $\alpha = m/n$, and the distribution of U_m can be developed as

$$U_m \rightarrow \begin{cases} \mathcal{N}(\mu_1, \sigma_1^2) & \theta \in [0, u_l) \\ \mathcal{N}(\mu_2, \sigma_2^2) & \theta \in [u_l, u_h) \\ \mathcal{N}(\mu_3, \sigma_3^2) & \theta \in [u_h, 1] \end{cases}$$

where:
$$\mu_1 = \frac{1}{\theta} \frac{n}{2}$$
$$\sigma_1 = \frac{1}{\theta} \sqrt{\frac{n}{12}} \tag{14}$$
$$\mu_2 = \frac{\alpha}{\theta} \frac{n}{2} + 2(1-\alpha)n(1 - \ln 2)$$
$$\sigma_2 = \sqrt{\frac{\alpha}{\theta^2} \frac{n}{12} + 4(1-\alpha)n(\frac{1}{2} - (\ln 2)^2)}$$
$$\mu_3 = 2n(1 - \ln 2)$$
$$\sigma_3 = \sqrt{4n(\frac{1}{2} - (\ln 2)^2)}$$

The reliability indicator w_i of Masrur's load test are

$$w_i = \frac{1 - \mu_i}{\sigma_i} \qquad i = 1, 2, 3 \tag{15}$$

4.3   Reliability Comparison

Reliability indicator of the two tests are both piecewise functions. In order to clearly compare them, a factor is defined as

$$\Delta = w_p - w_i \tag{16}$$

The positive value of Δ indicates that a task set is more likely to pass bound test than load test. In other words, the Peng's test is better the Masrur's. Comparison can be detailed in the following four steps.
(1) $\theta \in [0, 0.5)$

$$\Delta_1 = w_p - w_1 = 0 \tag{17}$$

In this part, the value of Δ is always zero, so two tests have the same reliability.
(2) $\theta \in [0.5, u_l)$

$$\Delta_2 = w_p - w_1 = \frac{n[(2\theta)^{1/n} - 1] - 2\theta + 1}{\sqrt{\frac{n}{12}}} < 0 \tag{18}$$

In this part, the value of Δ is always negative, so load test is more reliable than bound test.

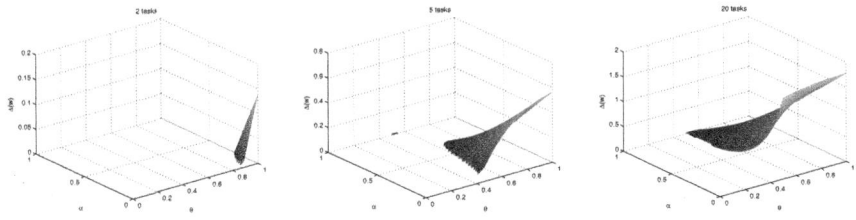

Fig. 1. Better performance of bound test ($\theta \in [u_l, u_h]$)

(3) $\theta \in [u_l, u_h)$

$$\Delta_3 = w_p - w_2 \tag{19}$$

Fig. 1 shows the performance comparison if θ locates in the field $[u_l, u_h)$. The points on each sub-figure stand for the cases where Peng's test exceeds the Masrur's. Especially, Masrur's test is more reliable for most of cases when there are only two tasks in set. Bursting number of tasks results in the degradation of Masrur's advantage, in terms of the enlarging coverage of Peng's test.

Reliability indicator is not only useful for performance comparison, but also capable of specifying exact pattern where the winner can be applied. For example, in Fig. 1, system designer can choose dominated condition based on foreseeable n, α and β. If the point appears on the figure, bound test wins, otherwise, load test is preferred.

(4) $\theta \in [u_h, 1]$

$$\Delta_4 = w_p - w_3 \tag{20}$$

In Fig. 2, bound test wins the competition by expanding almost all the surface. Masrur's test seldom works as the dominated condition for schedulability test, only under strict constraint that the number of tasks is no more than three.

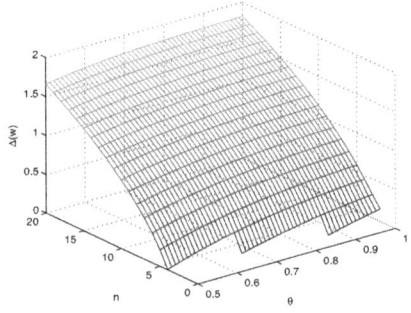

Fig. 2. Better performance of bound test ($\theta \in [u_h, 1]$)

Table 1. Node Characteristics

Characteristics	Parameters
PE rating	100MIPS
PE number	4
node number	50
memory	2G
storage	200G
bandwidth	100Mbps
network	star-shaped

5 Simulation Evaluation

In order to further validate the comparison result deduced by reliability indicator, we compare the two accepted ratio by a MapReduce simulator, SimMapReduce [18]. SimMapReduce models a vivid MapReduce environment with a detailed analysis on task processing. It supports multi-layer scheduling algorithms, such as heuristics. In this work, priority-driven scheduling algorithm is applied to evaluate the scheduling performance for real-time tasks in MapReduce cluster.

5.1 Experiment Setup

A MapReduce cluster with 50 homogeneous nodes is configured. The parameters of node are shown in Table 1.

A certain number of users enter into the cluster simultaneously. Every user τ_i has an unique type of task, which arrives periodically. These periodic tasks construct a sequence, belonging to one specific user. $\tau_{i,k}$ is the kth task in sequence. In this simulation, the size of task sequence is fifty. Users are given priorities before simulation starts, and these priorities are fixed throughout the execution of simulation.

Two concepts concerning utilization should be clarified. Set utilization U_Γ is the sum of all task utilization u_i. Obviously, U_Γ is no more than one if there exists a feasible scheduling algorithm. For every U_Γ, we generate a set of task utilization u_i with UUniFast [19]. The user characteristics are shown in Table 2.

5.2 Experiment Results

Given a fixed system harzard θ, we first analyze the accepted ratio of schedulability tests with respect to set utilization U_Γ. Concrete experimental process is shown in Algorithm 1.

We take $\theta = 0.5$ and $N = 2$ for example. Firstly, one hundred types of task sets are generated, and their set utilizations uniformly locate in the field $[0,1]$.

For each U_Γ, N tasks are created. Each task utilization u_i distributed uniformly $U(0,1)$, and their sum equals U_Γ. Other parameters are configured as Table 2. Then we let the task set pass Peng's and Masrur's schedulability tests, and note the result

Table 2. User Characteristics

Characteristics	Parameters
set utilization U_Γ,	uniform distribution [0,1]
system hazard θ	uniform distribution [0,1]
user number N	2, 20
task utilization u_i	uniform distribution [0, 1]
task number	50
arrival interval T_i	uniform distribution [10, 100]
MapTask length	$10000 u_i T_i$ (MI)
ReduceTask length	$10000 u_i T_i$ (MI)

Algorithm 1. Accepted ratio w.r.t U_Γ

1: $\theta = 0.5$
2: $N = 2$
3: $numU = 100$
4: $numExp = 10000$
5: **for** $i = 1 \rightarrow numU$ **do**
6:    generate U_Γ
7:    **for** $i = 1 \rightarrow numExp$ **do**
8:       generate $[u_1, \cdots, u_i, \cdots, u_N]$ randomly
9:       configure other parameters of task set
10:      Peng's schedulability test
11:      **if** pass **then**
12:         $nPeng + +$
13:      **end if**
14:      Masrur's schedulability test
15:      **if** pass **then**
16:         $nMasrur + +$
17:      **end if**
18:   **end for**
19:   Peng's accepted ratio $pPeng = nPeng/numExp$
20:   Masrur's accepted ratio $pMasrur = nMasrur/numExp$
21: **end for**

---

whether this task set is accepted. We repeat this examination with the same hypothetical assumption 10000 times, so the accepted ratio can be calculated by a large number of task sets. In every loop, N tasks are randomly generated.

Schedulability curves are drawn under the condition that each task set contains 2 tasks in Fig. 3 and Fig. 4. Generally, $U_\Gamma < \theta$ is a necessary condition that a random task set can pass any schedulability test.

Fig. 3 deals with the functions of accepted ratio with respect to U_Γ, varying θ with the value of $0.5, 0.75$ and 1. Load test is beneficial to the tasks with a large set utilization, by offering more opportunities to be scheduled on a cluster. Take $\theta = 1$ for example,

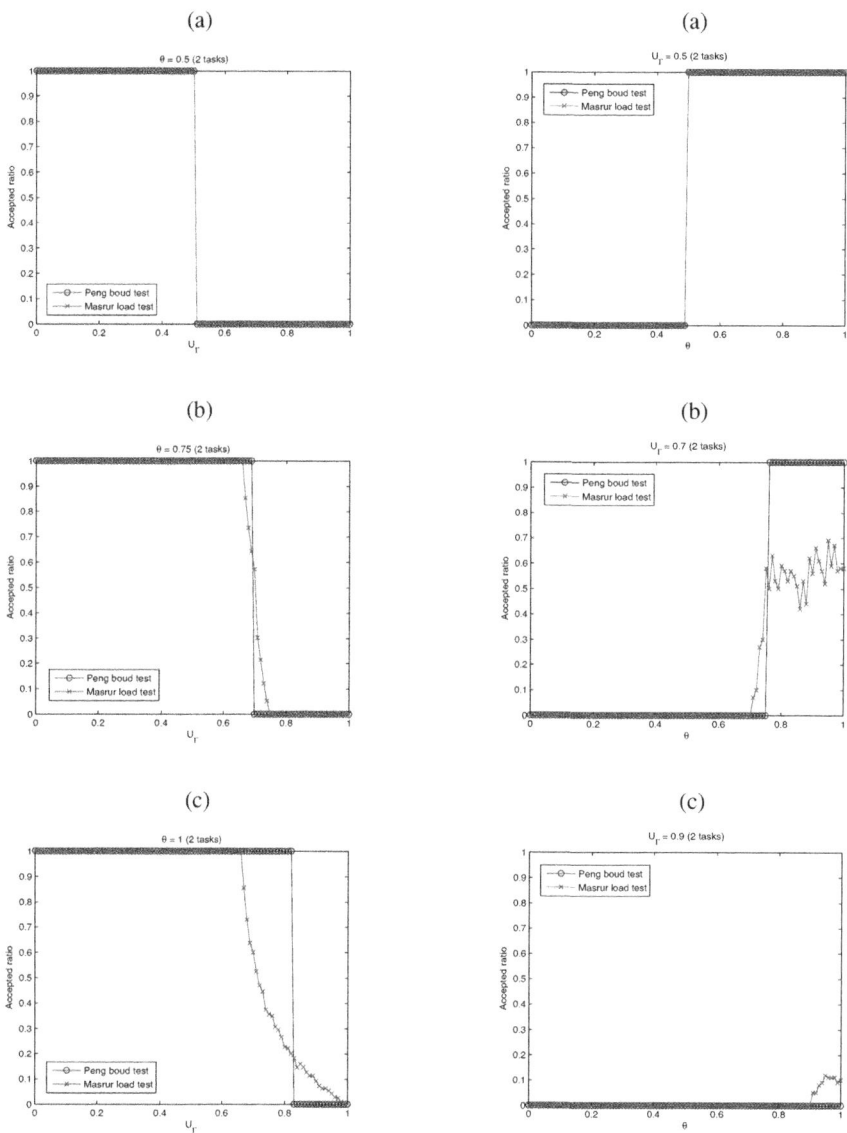

Fig. 3. Accepted ratio w.r.t. U_Γ (2 tasks)   **Fig. 4.** Accepted ratio w.r.t. θ (2 tasks)

task set with 90% utilization could be scheduled at 10% probability if system employs load schedulability test, but it certainly failed if bound test in applied. Observing three sub-figures in Fig. 3, the benefit from load test magnifies as the deadline is prolonged. However, this advantage is obtained at the cost of reducing schedulable possibility for the tasks with small set utilization.

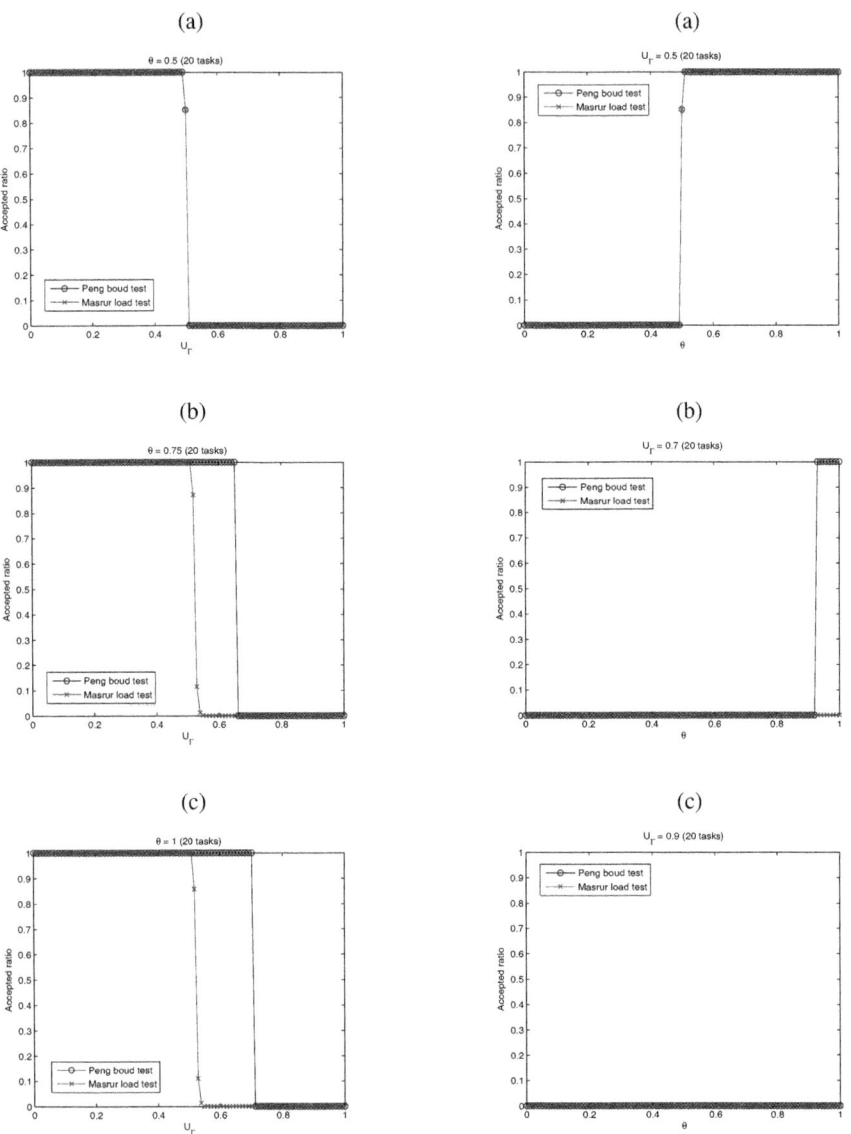

Fig. 5. Accepted ratio w.r.t. U_Γ (20 tasks)   **Fig. 6.** Accepted ratio w.r.t. θ (20 tasks)

Schedulable probability for a random task set is the area under accepted ratio curve. Shown in Fig. 4, each test has its own strength. For example, Peng's bound test allows more tasks to enter the cluster when U_Γ equals 0.7, while Masrur's load test still admits tasks when bound test refuses everything at $U_\Gamma = 0.9$.

The simulation results agree exactly with the conclusion deduced by reliability indicator. However, they are more intuitive than reliability analysis, and can not provide a practicable solution for system designers.

Next, we analyze the cases with 20 tasks per set in Fig. 5 and Fig. 6. Obviously, bound test outperforms load test in any case. When the deadline is relatively short ($\theta = 0.5$), two tests have the same reliability.

In Fig. 5, bound-based reliability keeps growing as U_Γ increases from 0.5 to 1, while the reliability of load test nearly remains unchanged. This phenomenon seems to go against that Masrur's test is always better than Peng's test when $\theta \in [0.5, u_l)$. That is actually caused by the small probability of preconditions. Assume that the possibility that task utilization u_i is less than u_l is $Pr(u_i < u_l)$. According to multiplication rule, for n independent tasks, the event that all utilizations are below u_l occurs with the possibility $\prod Pr(u_i < u_l)$. Since $0 < Pr(u_i < u_l) < 1$, the product decreases sharply with a large n. Besides that, $\theta < (1 + \min u_i)/2 < (1 + \frac{\theta}{n})/2$ must be met, so the value of θ falls into range $[0.5, n/(2n - 1))$. When the task number n increases, $n/(2n - 1)$ approaches 0.5 gradually.

These experimental results further validate our reliability analysis. Since it is rare that MapReduce cluster only deals with two tasks in reality, Peng's condition is more suitable for DM schedulability test than the Masrur's.

6 Summary

In this paper, we proposed a concept of test reliability to evaluate the accuracy of schedulability tests. Since the online schedulability tests are sufficient, a reliable test is concerned with that can admit as many tasks as possible. Two mostly used DM schedulability tests, bound test and load test, are investigated, through comparing their reliability indicators. Results show that the two tests perform the same when deadline is relatively short, less than half of the period. Otherwise, their test reliabilities depend on the parameters of task set. Load-based test only performs better than that based bound if there are a small number of tasks in set, so it is not recommended to system designers who deal with plenty of simultaneous tasks in ubiquitous computing cluster.

More improvement can be made by introducing practical system requirements such as dependent tasks, offsets, aperiodic tasks and distributed clusters. Consequently, schedulability tests will be more complicated and time consuming than before. Determining test reliability with a low time complexity and developing a general indication method are challenging issues to be addressed in the future.

Acknowledgement. The authors acknowledge financial support from the Chinese Science Council. The second author also acknowledge partial financial support form the Chinese Universities Scientific Fund of BUAA (Grant No.YWF1003020).

References

[1] Nguyen, T.-M.-H., Magoulès, F.: Autonomic data management system in grid environment. Journal of Algorithms and Computational Technologies 3, 155–178 (2009)
[2] Yu, L., Magoulès, F.: Service scheduling and rescheduling in an applications integration framework. Advances in Engineering Software 40(9), 941–946 (2009)

[3] Masrur, A., Chakraborty, S., Färber, G.: Constant-time admission control for deadline monotonic tasks. In: Proceedings of the Conference on Design, Automation and Test in Europe (DATE), pp. 220–225 (2010)

[4] Liu, C.L., Layland, J.W.: Scheduling algorithms for multiprogramming in a hard-real-time environment. Journal of the Association for Computing Machinery 20(1), 46–61 (1973)

[5] Peng, D.-T., Shin, K.G.: A new performance measure for scheduling independent real-time tasks. Journal of Parallel Distributed Computing 19, 11–26 (1993)

[6] Bini, E., Buttazzo, G.C., Buttazzo, G.: Rate monotonic analysis: The hyperbolic bound. IEEE Transactions on Computers 52(7), 933–942 (2003)

[7] Abdelzaher, T.F., Sharma, V., Lu, C.: A utilization bound for aperiodic tasks and priority driven scheduling. IEEE Transactions on Computers 53(3), 334–350 (2004)

[8] Leung, J.Y.T., Whitehead, J.: On the complexity of fixed-priority scheduling of periodic, real-time tasks. Performance Evaluation 2, 237–250 (1982)

[9] Buttazzo, G.C.: Rate monotonic vs. edf: judgment day. Real-Time Systems 29, 5–26 (2005)

[10] Joseph, M., Pandya, P.K.: Finding response times in a real-time system. The Computer Journal 29, 390–395 (1986)

[11] Audsley, N., Burns, A., Richardson, M., Tindell, K., Wellings, A.J.: Applying new scheduling theory to static priority pre-emptive scheduling. Software Engineering Journal 8, 284–292 (1993)

[12] Lehoczky, J.P.: Fixed priority scheduling of periodic task sets with arbitrary deadlines. In: Proceedings of the 11th Real-Time Systems Symposium, pp. 201–209 (1990)

[13] Sjodin, M., Hansson, H.: Improved response-time analysis calculations. In: Proceedings of IEEE Real-Time Systems Symposium, pp. 399–408 (1998)

[14] Abdelzaher, T.F., Lu, C.: Schedulability analysis and utilization bounds for highly scalable real-time service. In: Proceedings of IEEE Real Time Technology and Applications Symposium, pp. 15–25 (2001)

[15] Chen, D., Mok, A.K., Kuo, T.-W.: Utilization bound revisited. IEEE Transactions on Computers 52, 351–361 (2003)

[16] Bini, E., Buttazzo, G.C.: Schedulability analysis of periodic fixed priority systems. IEEE Transactions on Computers 53(11), 1462–1473 (2004)

[17] Fisher, N., Baruah, S.K.: A fully polynomial-time approximation scheme for feasibility analysis in static-priority systems with bounded relative deadlines. Journal of Embedded Computing 2(3-4), 291–299 (2006)

[18] Teng, F., Yu, L., Magoules, F.: SimMapReduce: a simulator for modeling MapReduce framework. In: Proceedings of International Conference on Multimedia and Ubiquitous Engineering, Loutraki, Greece, pp. 277–282 (June 2011)

[19] Bini, E., Buttazzo, G.C.: Measuring the performance of schedulability tests. Real-Time Systems 30(1-2), 129–154 (2005)

A Practice Probability Frequent Pattern Mining Method over Transactional Uncertain Data Streams

Guoqiong Liao[1,2], Linqing Wu[1,2], Changxuan Wan[1,2], and Naixue Xiong[3]

[1] School of Information Technology, Jiangxi University of Finance and Economics,
Nanchang 330013, China
[2] Jiangxi Key Laboratory of Data and Knowledge Engineering, Nanchang 330013, China
{liaoguoqiong,wlq0507}@163.com, wanchangxuan@263.net
[3] Department of Computer Science, Georgia State University, USA
naixue.xiong@gmail.com

Abstract. In recent years, large amounts of uncertain data are emerged with the widespread employment of the new technologies, such as wireless sensor networks, RFID and privacy protection. According to the features of the uncertain data streams such as incomplete, full of noisy, non-uniform and mutable, this paper presents a probability frequent pattern tree called PFP-tree and a method called PFP-growth, to mine probability frequent patterns based on probability damped windows. The main characteristics of the suggested method include: (1) adopting time-based probability damped window model to enhance the accuracy of mined frequent patterns; (2) setting an item index table and a transaction index table to speed up retrieval on the PFP-tree; and (3) pruning the tree to remove the items that cannot become frequent patterns;. The experimental results demonstrate that PFP-growth method has better performance than the main existing schemes in terms of accuracy, processing time and storage space.

1 Introduction

In recent years, large amounts of uncertain data are emerged due to the reasons including the inaccuracy of original data, rough granularity of data sets and missing of data values in ubiquitous computing environment[1]. The uncertain data is bringing new problems and challenges to database area, among which data mining technology over uncertain data streams has given rise to be concern in academic and industrial communities [2-5].

Mining frequent patterns has been one of the hottest research topics in the field of data streams mining from the beginning of this century. For instance, discovering frequent patterns from sensor data streams is useful for allocating sensor networks dynamically and flexibly; finding frequent patterns from RFID data streams can be used for solving the problems of missing-reads and cross-reads. However, because of the features of the uncertain data streams, such as incomplete, noisy, non-uniform distribution and mutable [6], there have already been frequent patterns mining methods for certain data streams which are no longer suitable for the uncertain data streams.

By now, there are some research results to mine frequent patterns over the uncertain data. A U-Aprior method is put forward in [7]. Similar to the traditional Aprior method, U-Aprior firstly scans databases twice to obtain candidate keys. Then, it

C.-H. Hsu et al. (Eds.): UIC 2011, LNCS 6905, pp. 563–575, 2011.

confirms the frequent patterns on the basis of a predetermined minimum threshold of exception supports. [8] improves the U-Aprior method further by using pruning technology to reduce the mining costs. To settle the problem of generating candidate keys, [9-10] come up with a mining method based on a tree structure for the uncertain data. A U-FPS method is discussed in [11] for the uncertain data, which allows to add constraint conditions by users' actual demands. [12] proposes new definitions based on the possible world semantics, trying to find all the items that are likely to be frequent in a randomly generated possible world. [13] shows how the broad classes of algorithms can be extended to the uncertain data setting. Nevertheless, these methods do not take the characteristics of data streams into account, so they cannot apply directly into mining frequent patterns of the uncertain data streams.

Based on the FP-stream method presented for the certain data streams in [14], two frequent patterns mining methods, UF-streaming and SUF-growth, for the uncertain data streams are proposed in [15]. The UF-streaming method will prune the items that may not become frequent patterns by setting a threshold, so as to reduce mining and calculating overhead, but the accuracy will decrease. In contrary, the SUF-growth method will keep all data items without pruning, so it can get a hundred percent frequent patterns, but as the number of windows increase, it needs much more storage space and processing time. Furthermore, both them have some shortages to process the uncertain data streams: (1) The fact that the importance of items in the uncertain data streams may differ as windows slide is not considered; (2) When calculating the projected database of itemsets, the whole tree has to be retrieved, which results in quite large retrieving costs; (3) They assume the probability of an item in the streams is the same, which doesn't correspond to practical applications since the probability of an item in different transactions should be also uncertain.

Aimed at above problems, this paper is going to study a probability frequent pattern mining method, called PFP-growth, for transactional uncertain data streams through adding a probability attribute to each item under a time-based probability damped window model.

The rest of the paper is organized as follows. In Section 2, the models of the uncertain data streams and windows are introduced. Section 3 describes the structure of a probability frequent pattern tree - PFP-tree in details. In Section 4, the maintenance and frequent pattern output algorithms for the PFP-tree are presented. The experimental performance analysis is discussed in Section 5. Finally, we conclude and discuss future works in Section 6.

2   Transactional Uncertain Data Streams and Windows Models

In the uncertain data streams, each item indicates its uncertainty by a probability attribute, which can be a concrete probability value or determined based on a probability density function. This section will introduce the models of transactional uncertain data streams and probability damped windows.

2.1   Transactional Uncertain Data Stream Model

A transactional data stream is a sequence of records that log interactions between entities. For example, a stream of stock market transactions consists of buy or sell orders for particular securities from individual investors[16].

Definition 1. Supposed I is a data item and its probability is P, then I is called a probability item, denoted as a two-tuple $<I, P>$.

Definition 2. Supposed X is a pattern consisting of λ probability items, that is, $X=\{<I_i, P_i>|1\le i\le\lambda\}$, then X is called a λ-probability pattern, and its probability is:

$$P_X=\prod_{i=1}^{\lambda} P_i \tag{1}$$

Definition 3. Supposed k is a sampling instant, then all v probability items produced in k is called an observation transaction, denoted as:

$$TR_k = \{< I_i, P_i^k >|1 \le i \le v\} \tag{2}$$

Of which, I_i is the ith probability item and P_i^k is the probability of I_i in transaction TR_k.

Definition 4. In a time interval of $[t_m, t_n]$ and $m<n$, the set made up of multiple mutual independent observation transactions is called a transactional uncertain data stream, denoted as $US=\{TR_k| t_m\le k\le t_n\}$.

Definition 5. The transactional uncertain data stream produced between m and n as an arbitrary transaction window, denoted as:

$$W[m, n]=\{TR_k \in US \mid m\le k\le n\} \tag{3}$$

Definition 6. Supposed the window size is w, and t_c is current instant, then the transaction window when $m=t_c-w+1$, $n=t_c$ is called the current transaction window, denoted as W_c.

Definition 7. Supposed the probability of item $x\in X$ in TR_k is P_x^k, then the expectation support of X in TR_k is:

$$\exp\_\sup(x,TR_k) = \prod_{x\in X} P_x^k \tag{4}$$

Definition 8. The expectation support of X in $W[m, n]$ is:

$$\exp\_\sup(X,W[m,n]) = \sum_{k=m}^{n}\exp\_\sup(X,TR_k)$$
$$= \sum_{k=m}^{n}(\prod_{x\in X} P_x^k) \tag{5}$$

2.2 Probability Damped Window Model

In order to obtain more accurate frequent patterns, the paper suggests a probability damped window model to weaken the contributions of the older transactions to the expectation supports gradually.

Definition 9. The damped ratio of expectation supports in a basic time unit is called a damped factor, denoted as f ($0<f\le 1$).

In the certain data streams, the damped factors are only related to time, that is, the older a transaction is, the smaller the damped factors of the patterns in the transaction is. Moreover, the damped factors of all patterns in the same transaction are identical. While in the uncertain data streams, because a pattern may have different probability values in different transactions, the damped factors for the probability patterns should reflect this characteristic.

Definition 10. Supposed f_x^k is the damped factor of x in TR_k, then f_x^k can be calculated as following formula:

$$f_x^k = f^{\frac{t_c-k}{P_x^k}} \tag{6}$$

From Definition 10, we can see:

• In the same window, the older of the transactions that an item belongs to is, the smaller its damped factor will be.

• In the same transaction, the smaller the probability of an item is, the smaller its damped factor will also be.

Definition 11. Considering the effects of the damped factors, the expectation support of X in W_c is:

$$\exp\_\sup(X,W_c) = \sum_{k-t_c-w+1}^{t_c} (\prod_{x \subset X} P_x^k f_x^k) \tag{7}$$

According to Formula 7, when calculating the expectation support of X, corresponding damped factors should be multiplied. Hence, the minimum threshold of the expectation supports for all patterns in a transaction window should also be damped synchronously.

Definition 12. Supposed θ ($0<\theta\leq1$) is the initial threshold of minimum expectation supports in a time window, then the threshold of minimum expectation supports in the window with size w can be calculated as following formula:

$$\theta*f^{w-1} + \theta*f^{w-2} + \cdots + \theta*f^1 + \theta*1 = \theta(f^{w-1} + f^{w-2} + \cdots + f^1 + f^0)$$
$$> \theta w \sqrt[w]{f^{w-1}*f^{w-2}*\cdots*1} = \theta w f^{\frac{w-1}{2}} \tag{8}$$

Definition 13. If following formula

$$\exp\_\sup(X, W_c) \geq \theta w f^{\frac{w-1}{2}} \tag{9}$$

holds, X is called a probability frequent pattern in W_c.

To reduce the calculating costs, non-frequent patterns in the uncertain data streams should be pruned. However, in order to guarantee that patterns which may become frequent patterns in next windows will not be pruned, we have following definition:

Definition 14. Supposed ε is a maximum permitted error, and $0<\varepsilon<\theta$ if following formula:

$$\exp\_ \sup(X, W_c) < (\theta - \varepsilon) wf^{\frac{w-1}{2}} \qquad (10)$$

holds, X is called a non-frequent pattern in current window.

3   Probability Frequent Pattern Mining Method

To overcome the shortcomings of the SUF-growth and UF-streaming methods, a novel probability frequent pattern tree, called PFP-tree, is designed to maintain pattern information in the uncertain data streams. This section will introduces the structure of PFP-tree and a practice mining method based the tree.

3.1   PFP-tree Structure and Construction

In the PFP-tree, all nodes are sorted according to a predetermined relation of a certain total order, such as the numbers of sensors or the unique codes of the tagged RFID objects. This is because that if the tree is established on the basis of expectation supports, although the height of the pattern tree can be guaranteed to be mimimum, the nodes will be realigned when new transactions arrive, which will result in high maintenance overhead. Considering the effects of transactions "ages" and the probabilities of items on expectation supports, the damped window model is used to calculate the frequent patterns in the tree.

PFP-tree is made up of three parts: a prefix pattern tree (PPT), an item index table (IIT) and a transaction index table (TIT):

- PPT is used to store the items and patterns in the streams. Each node in PPT contains following information:
  - *item*: the name of a specific item;
  - *child_node*: pointer pointing the child node of the item;
  - *same_node*: pointer pointing the next homonymy node;
  - *tran_list*: pointer pointing the transaction probability list (TPL) of the item.
- IIT is used to maintain an index of all items in PPT. Each row contains:
  - *item*: the name of a specific item;
  - *exp_sup*: the item's expectation support;
  - *first_node*: pointer pointing the first homonymy node of the item in PPT.
- TIT is used to store an index of all transactions in current window. Each row in the table contains:

  - *trid*: transaction identifier;
  - *pointer*: pointer pointing the first node of the transaction.

For instance, supposed $w=5$, $f=0.8$ and there are 5 transactions $TR_1 \sim TR_5$ in an uncertain data streams:

TR_1 : <$(I_1, 0.9), (I_2, 0.8), (I_3, 0.7), (I_4, 0.9)$>
TR_2 : <$(I_1, 0.8), (I_2, 0.6), (I_4, 0.8), (I_5, 0.9)$>
TR_3 : <$(I_1, 0.9), (I_2, 0.7), (I_3, 0.6), (I_4, 0.85)$>
TR_4 : <$(I_1, 0.8), (I_2, 0.6), (I_3, 0.8)$ >
TR_5 : <$(I_2, 0.8), (I_3, 0.75)$>

Figure 1 is the PFP-tree for this example. The figure only shows the TPL of I_4, and the TPL of I_1, I_2, I_3, and I_5 are omitted.

The construction of PFP-tree is to insert the nodes of new transactions into the tree. Firstly, the root node (R_NODE) is created when the PFP-tree initializes. Then, when any transaction TR_k arrives, all items it contains will be inserted into PFP-tree.

What should be illustrated here is that each item's expectation support (exp_sup) in IIT is calculated on the basis of Formula 7.

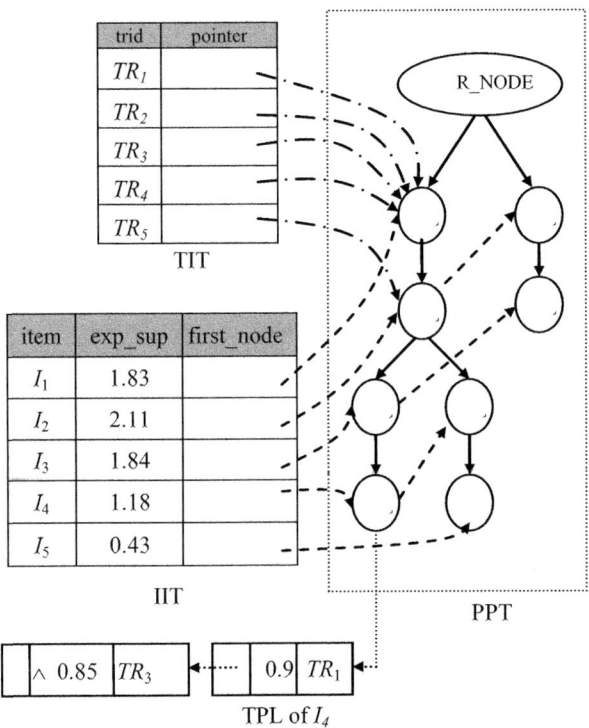

Fig. 1. An example of PFP-tree

3.2 PFP-tree Pruning

As the windows slide, many non-frequent patterns will be certainly contained in the tree. In order to reduce the space and time overhead to maintain PFP-tree, the tree should be pruned timely. Nonetheless, those nodes that may become frequent patterns cannot be pruned prematurely. Otherwise, some frequent patterns may be lost. Therefore, only the non-frequent patterns can be preserved.

Theorem 1. If x is a non-frequent item, then X is surely a non-frequent pattern.

Prove: Because x is a non-frequent item, exp_i.e., $sup(x, W_c) < (\theta - \varepsilon)wf^{\frac{w-1}{2}}$ (Formula 10), and because $x \in X$, exp_sup$(X, W_c) \leq$ exp_sup(x, W_c), so exp_sup$(X, W_c) < (\theta - \varepsilon)wf^{\frac{w-1}{2}}$, it means X is non-frequent pattern.

Therefore, if x is a non-frequent item, then all nodes involving x on the tree can be pruned. In general, the pruning procedure should include two parts: the nodes of the overdue transactions should be removed and the nodes that are not possible to be frequent patterns should also to be removed. The firs part is simple to remove the nodes of the overdue transactions from the tree using the index in TIT. Here we just discuss the procedure to remove the nodes which are not possible to be frequent patterns. The procedure can be described as follows (Algorithm 1).

```
Algorithm 1. PFP_Pruning
Input: θ, w, f
Output: pruned PFP-tree
1.  begin
2.      for (∀Iᵢ(exp_sup(Iᵢ,Wc)≠0))
3.          if exp_sup(Iᵢ)<(θ−ε)wf^{\frac{w-1}{2}}
            /*Initialize pointer Iᵢ's the homonymy nodes*/
4.              s_node:=NULL;
            /*Search the first node of Iᵢ */
5.              s_node:=FIRSTNODE_FIND(Iᵢ);
6.              while s_node!=NULL
7.                  if s_node points a leaf node
                    /* delete the node */
8.                      NODE_DETETE(s_node);
9.                  else
                    /*link s_node's father and child nodes*/
10.                     LINK_PARENT_CHILD(s_node);
11.                     ns_node:=s_node.same_node;
12.                     NODE_DETETE(s_node);
13.                     s_node:=ns_node;
14.                     if there exists the same path
                        /* merge the paths */
15.                         SAMEPATH_MERGE( );
16.                     end if;
17.                 end if;
18.             end while;
                /* upate the item index table */
19.             exp_sup(Iᵢ)=0
20.             Iᵢ.first_node= NULL
21.         end if
22.     end for;
23. end
```

3.3 Frequent Patterns Output

When the uncertain data arrives continuously, PFP-tree will maintain the frequent patterns in current window in time.

From the head of IIT, for each item, if its expectation support is greater than $\theta wf^{\frac{w-1}{2}}$, put it into a frequent pattern set, and put all of its offspring nodes into an offspring node set. For the item in the offspring node set, if the new pattern combining it with the frequent patterns is also a frequent pattern, also put it into a frequent pattern set. The procedure of frequent patterns output is presented as Algorithm 2.

```
Algorithm 2. PFP_OUTPUT
Input: θ, w, f;
Output: frequent patterns;
1. begin
2.     for (∀Iᵢ(exp_sup(Iᵢ,Wc)≠0))
           /* Initialize offspring node set */
3.         OFFSPRING_SET:=∅;
           /* Initialize frequent pattern set */
4.         PFP_SET:=∅;
5.         if exp_sup(Iᵢ,Wc)> θwf^(w-1/2)
6.             PFP_SET:=INSERT_PFP(Iᵢ);
               /* search all offspring items of Iᵢ*/
7.             OFFSPRING_SET:=FIND_OFFSPRING(Iᵢ);
8.             while (OFFSPRING_SET!=∅)
               /* get an item from OFFSPRING_SET */
9.                 Iₓ=Get_ITEM(OFFSPRING_SET);
10.                    for ∀Xⱼ∈PFP_SET
                   /*judge whether the frequent pattern com-
                      bining the offspring item is a frequent
                      pattern */
11.                        Y=Iₓ∪Xⱼ
12.                        if exp_sup(Y, Wc)> θwf^(w-1/2)
13.                            PFP_SET:= PFP_SET∪{Y}
14.                        end if;
15.                    end for;
                   /* remove Iₓ from OFFSPRING_SET */
16.                    OFFSPRING_SET:= OFFSPRING_SET-{Iₓ};
17.                end while;
18.            end if
           /* output all frequent patterns */
19.        OUTPUT_PFP(PFP_SET);
20.    end for;
21. end
```

4 Performance Analysis

4.1 Experimental Datasets and Parameters

The datasets in the experiments comes from IBM generator[17]: T10I4D100K, T15I5D100K, T20I6D100K, T25I7D100K and T30I8D100K. For each item in these data, a random probability value between 0 and 1 is attached. The corresponding datasets are called data1P10L, data1P15L, data1P20L, data1P25L and data1P30L, with different transaction item lengths 10, 15, 20, 25 and 30, respectively.

The method based on the PFP-tree suggested in the paper is called PFP-growth method. The main performance measures used are *memory size, average processing time* and *precision ratio*. The experimental parameters are listed in Table 1.

Table 1. Experimental Parameters

Parameter	Description	Value
w	Window size	1000~10000
θ	Minimum expectation support threshold	0.5%~2%
ε	Maximum permitted error	0. 1θ
f	Damped factor	0.98~1
trans_length	Transaction item length	10~30

4.2 Experimental Results and Analysis

Experiment 1. Testing the impact of window sizes on performance
This experiment is conducted on the datasets data1P10L, and set θ=1%, ε=0.1θ, f = 0.992 and w from 2000 to 10000.

As demonstrated in Figure 2, as the size of windows increases, the memory space needed by the three methods also increases. The reason is when w enlarges, the number of items to be deal with will also increase. But the increment ratio of memory space is smaller than that of window sizes, since there are much more transactions sharing prefix patterns when the size of windows becomes large.

We can also conclude from Figure 2 that the memory space SUF-growth method needs is the highest among the three methods. This is because SUF-growth has to preserve all items, but PFP-growth and UF-streaming methods may save storage space by pruning.

Figure 3 indicates that the average processing time of SUF-growth and UF-streaming methods are more than that of PFP-growth method, respectively. This is because PFP-growth uses an item and a transaction index tables bedsides pruning.

Experiment 2. Testing the impact of transaction item lengths on performance
This experiment is conducted on the datasets data1P10L, data1P15L, data1P20L, data1P25L and data1P30L, and set θ=1%, ε=0.1θ , w= 1000. The performances are shown as in Figures 4 and 5.

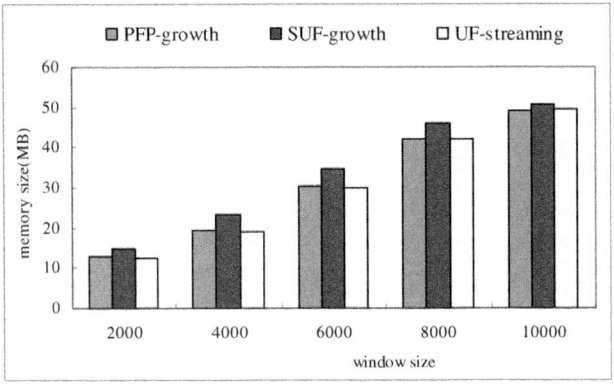

Fig. 2. The impact of *w* on memory space

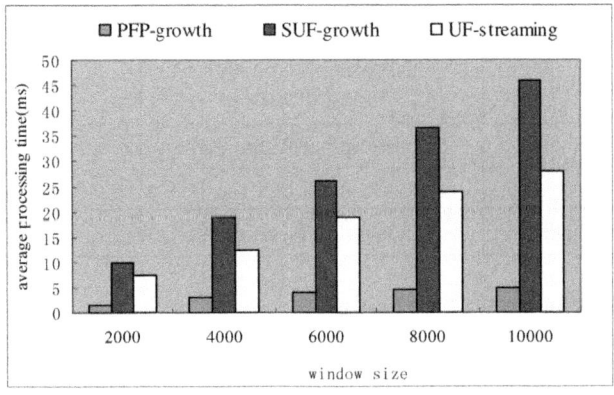

Fig. 3. The impact of *w* on average processing time

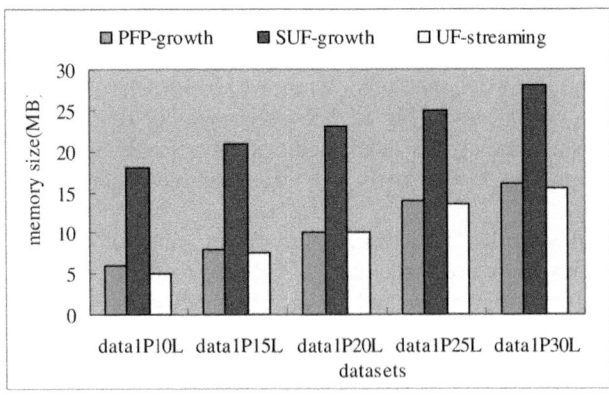

Fig. 4. The impact of transaction item lengths on memory space

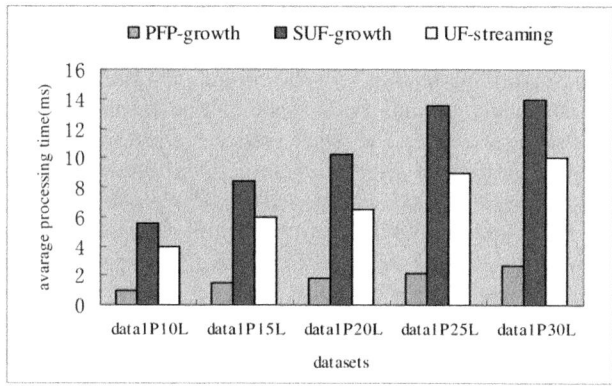

Fig. 5. The impact of transaction item lengths on average processing time

From Figures 4 and 5, we can know that as the lengths of transaction items increase, the memory space and processing time needed by the three methods increase as well, but they don't grow up in pace with the lengths. This is because the longer the length is, the more the patterns shared by transactions are.

Experiment 3. Testing precision ratios
This experiment is conducted in the dataset data1P10L, and set $w=1000$, $f=0.992$, $\theta=1\%$.

We can see from Figure 6 that the precision ratio of PFP-growth d is a little less than that of SUF-growth, but is more than UF-streaming. This is because SUF-growth uses all transaction items to calculate the frequent patterns, while PFP-growth will delete the items that are not critical frequent patterns by pruning. Compared with UF-streaming, because PFP-growth has taken the effects of transaction "ages" and probability on the expectation supports into account, and the damped window model is adopted to calculate the frequent patterns, its precision ratio is higher than that of UF-streaming.

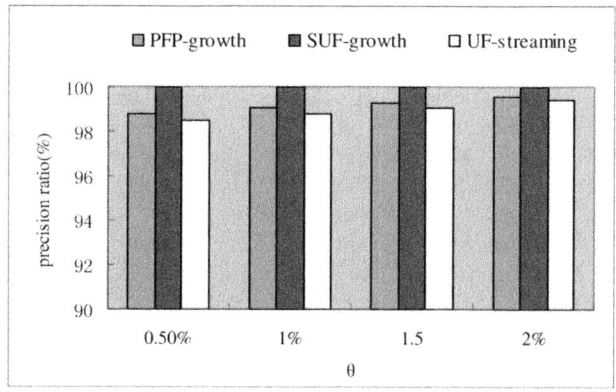

Fig. 6. Comparison of precision ratios

5 Conclusion and Future Works

The frequent patterns mining methods for the certain data streams are no longer suitable for the uncertain data streams because of unique features such as incomplete, noisy, non-uniform and mutable. The paper proposes a practice frequent pattern mining method called PFP-growth over the transactional uncertain data streams. The method uses a time-based probability damped window model to distinguish the contributions of the items taking both time and probability into account, and mines probability frequent patterns based on a novel PFP-tree. The experimental results demonstrate that PFP-growth method has better performance than the main existing schemes in term of higher accuracy, less processing time and storage space.

In the future, we will apply the method into the practice applications such as the transactional data streams in sensor networks and RFID application environment.

Acknowledgment. This work is supported by National Natural Science Foundation of China (No. 60863016), Natural Science Foundation of Jiangxi, China (No. 2008GQS0019) Science Foundation of Jiangxi Provincial Department of Education (GJJ10694).

References

1. Zhou, A., Jin, C., Wang, G., Li, J.: A Survey on the Management of Uncertain Data. Journal of Computer 32(1), 1–16 (2009)
2. Zhang, C., Jin, C., Zhou, A.: Clustering Algorithm over Uncertain Data Streams. Journal of Software 21(9), 2173–2182 (2010)
3. Aggarwal, C.C., Yu, P.S.: A framework for clustering uncertain data streams. In: Proc. of the 24th Int'l Conf. on Data Engineering, ICDE 2008, pp. 150–159 (2008)
4. Aggarwal, C.C.: On high dimension projected clustering of uncertain data streams. In: Proc. of the 25th Int'l Conf. on Data Engineering, ICDE 2009, pp. 1152–1154 (2009)
5. Zhang, C., Gao, M., Zhou, A.: Tracking high quality clusters over uncertain data streams. In: Proc. of the 1st Workshop on Management and Mining of Uncertain Data (MOUND 2009) Joint with ICDE 2009, pp. 1641–1648 (2009)
6. Li, J., Yu, G., Zhou, A.: Requirements and Challenges of Uncertain Data Management. Communication of China Computer Federation 5(4), 6–14 (2009)
7. Chui, C.-K., Kao, B., Hung, E.: Mining frequent itemsets from uncertain data. In: Proceedings of the 11th Pacific-Asia Conference on Knowledge Discovery Data Mining, IEEE ICDM Workshops, pp. 47–58 (2007)
8. Chui, C.K.-S., Kao, B.: A decremental approach for mining frequent itemsets from uncertain data. In: Washio, T., Suzuki, E., Ting, K.M., Inokuchi, A. (eds.) PAKDD 2008. LNCS (LNAI), vol. 5012, pp. 64–75. Springer, Heidelberg (2008)
9. Leung, C.K.-S., Mateo, M.A.F., Brajczuk, D.A.: A tree-based approach for frequent pattern mining from uncertain data. In: Washio, T., Suzuki, E., Ting, K.M., Inokuchi, A. (eds.) PAKDD 2008. LNCS (LNAI), vol. 5012, pp. 653–661. Springer, Heidelberg (2008)
10. Leung, C.K.-S., Carmichael, C.L., Hao, B.: Efficient mining of frequent patterns from uncertain data. In: Zhou, Z.-H., Li, H., Yang, Q. (eds.) PAKDD 2007. LNCS (LNAI), vol. 4426, pp. 489–494. Springer, Heidelberg (2007)

11. Leung, C.K.-S., Brajczuk, D.A.: Efficient algorithms for mining constrained frequent patterns from uncertain data. In: Proceedings of KDD Workshop on Knowledge Discovery from Uncertain Data, pp. 9–18 (2009)
12. Zhang, Q., Li, F., Yi, K.: Finding frequent items in probabilistic data. In: Proc. of 27th ACM International Conference on Management of Data, SIGMOD 2008, pp. 819–832 (2008)
13. Aggarwa, C.C., Li, Y., Wang, J., Wang, J.: Frequent Pattern Mining with Uncertain Data. In: Proc. of ACM KDD Conference, pp. 29–38 (2009)
14. Han, J., Pei, J., Yin, Y.: Mining frequent patterns without candidate generation. In: Proc. of 19th ACM International Conference on Management of Data, SIGMOD 2000, pp. 1–12 (2000)
15. Leung, C.K.-S., Hao, B.: Mining of Frequent Itemsets from Streams of Uncertain Data. In: Proc. of the 1st Workshop on Management and Mining of Uncertain Data (MOUND) Joint with ICDE 2009, pp. 1663–1670 (2009)
16. Cortes, C., Fisher, K., Pregibon, D., et al.: ACM Transactions on Programming Languages and Systems 26(2), 301–308 (2004)
17. Agrawal, R., Srikant, R.: Fast algorithms for mining association rules. In: Proc. of the 20th Int'l Conf. on Very Large Data Bases, VLDB 1994, pp. 487–499 (1994)

Reducing Total Energy for Reliability-Aware DVS Algorithms

Yongwen Pan, Man Lin, Laurence T. Yang

Department of Mathematics, Statistics and Computer Science
St. Francis Xavier University

Abstract. Power aware scheduling is of increasing importance in real-time system design, especially in this global warming era. Reliability is also very critical for real-time system design. In this paper, we aim at minimizing total energy while guaranteeing reliability constraints. Total energy refers to the sum of static and dynamic energy. (Dynamic Voltage Scaling) DVS is usually used for reducing dynamic energy consumption by reducing speed. Unfortunately, it has been shown that the transient faults of the system will be increased when the processor runs at reduced speed. To guarantee reliability be at least as high as that of without speed scaling, previous reliability aware DVS algorithms reserve recovery job for each of the scaled down tasks. However, these previous reliability aware DVS algorithms do not explore the shutdown technique to reduce static energy consumption. Static energy is consumed whenever the processor is on, and in modern processors, static energy consumption is comparable to the dynamic energy consumption and can not be ignored anymore. To lower total energy consumption, we integrate leakage control method and shared-recovery technique with reliability aware DVS algorithms. Experimental results show that our methods are effective.

1 Introduction

Power aware scheduling is of increasing importance in real-time system design, especially in this global warming era. In this paper, we study scheduling methods that take both total energy consumption and system reliability into account.

Total energy refers to the sum of static and dynamic energy. Dynamic power consumption is caused by the switching activities of transistors and has been previously considered as dominant part of total energy consumption. Static energy, also called leakage energy, is consumed whenever the CPU is on. According to [1], with processor size shrinking, supply voltages and threshold voltages of CMOS circuits shrink too, which results in exponential increases in sub-threshold leakage current. At and under $70\,nm$ processor technology, supply voltage is less than $1.0\,V$, the static power consumption occupies more than 50% of total energy, which is comparable to dynamic power consumption. In order to obtain minimal total energy consumption, static power consumption must be considered together with dynamic power consumption. Dynamic Voltage Scaling (DVS) technique can reduce dynamic energy consumption by scaling down the

C.-H. Hsu et al. (Eds.): UIC 2011, LNCS 6905, pp. 576–589, 2011.

voltage level. Shutdown method can reduce static energy consumption during idle period. DVS and shutdown methods can be combined to reduce total energy consumption.

Reliability is another major attribute of embedded system design. Reliability of a real-time job is defined as the probability of the job being correctly executed before its deadline [2]. Many embedded systems used in critical areas, such as defense and aerospace, require high-level reliability. For an embedded real-time system, faults occur unpredictably during run time due to various reasons, such as hardware failures, electromagnetic interferences as well as the effects of cosmic ray radiations [2]. If the faults are not dealt with in time, it may lead to a disaster. Faults usually can be classified as transient faults and permanent faults, and the transient faults occur much more frequently than permanent faults [3]. We only concentrate on transient faults in our work. It has been reported that when CPU is executed with a reduced speed, the transient faults of the system will be increased and thus the reliability of the system is reduced [4].

Our work considers a set of periodic tasks scheduled with (Earliest Deadline First) EDF policy, and aims at minimizing total energy consumption while guaranteeing reliability. Previous reliability aware DVS algorithms [4] guarantee reliability to be at least as high as that of without DVS by reserving recovery job for each scaled down task. However, these algorithms do not explore the shutdown technique to reduce static energy consumption. To lower total energy consumption, we integrate a few techniques such as leakage control method with existing reliability aware DVS algorithms.

2   Models

2.1   Task Model

The task model under consideration is periodic task set. Each task T_i is modelled as (a_i, e_i, d_i, p_i) where a_i is the arrival time, e_i is the worst case execution time (WCET) when the processor is executed with maximum speed (normalized to 1), d_i is the deadline, and p_i is the period of the task.

The tasks are scheduled with preemptive EDF policy. Schedulability test is a test that guarantees that all the tasks can be feasibly scheduled without missing any deadline. For periodic tasks scheduled by a preemptive EDF scheduler on a single processor, the schedulability test condition is that all the periodic task set's total utilization is equal to or less than 100% [5], that is, $U = \sum_{i=1}^{n} \left(\frac{e_i}{p_i} \right) \leq 1$, $0 < i \leq n$.

2.2   Power Model

We adopt the power model in [6]. The power consumption of the tasks can be divided into two parts: *dynamic power consumption (P_{dyn})* and *static power consumption (P_{stat})*. Dynamic power consumption consists of the switching power for charging and discharging the load capacitance, and is defined as: $P_{dyn(f)} = C_{eff} V_{dd}^2 f$, where C_{eff} is the effective switching capacity, V_{dd} is the supply voltage and f is the operating frequency/speed. Static power consumption consists of the power consumed by the subthreshold leakage and the reverse bias junction current [7]. The static power per CMOS circuit is defined as: $P_{stat(f)} = V_{dd} \times I_{subn} + |V_{bs}| \times I_j$, where V_{dd} is the supply voltage, I_{subn} is the subthreshold current, V_{bs} is the body bias voltage and I_j is the reverse bias junction. Thus, the total energy consumed during the active mode for time period t is

$$E_{(f)} = P_{dyn(f)} \times t + L_g \times P_{stat(f)} \times t \tag{1}$$

where L_g is the CMOS circuit number in each processor.

2.3   Critical Speed and Critical Interval

S_{cri}, the *critical speed* (or *threshold speed*), is defined as the speed to execute a cycle with the minimum total energy consumption [2,8,9,6]. When the processor is active (not idle), either increasing or decreasing the processor speed would consume more total energy than executing with S_{cri}. However, not all the jobs can be executed with S_{cri}, as it will cause some jobs missing deadlines. Therefore, the jobs of a system would be executed with the speeds between S_{cri} and the processor's maximum speed. In this paper, the maximum speed is normalized to be 1 and the speed of a processor is within the range (0,1].

Besides scaling down a processor, we can also shutdown a processor, when it is idle, to save energy. When a processor is shutdown/woken up, extra energy and timing overhead would be consumed to save/restore all the data from cache and buffers to/from the hard disk [6]. Such cost can not be ignored and is denoted by E_0 (E_0 is assumed to be a constant). When an idle interval is very short, it is not worth to shutdown the processor. *Critical interval* (t_{cri}) refers to a time interval which is used to judge if the idle interval from the current time to the execution time of next coming job is long enough such that it is worth to shut down the processor. The processor can be shutdown only if the idle interval is longer than critical interval. According to [8], the length of critical interval can be derived as follows: $P_{stat} \times t_{cri} = E_0 + P_{sleep} \times t_{cri}$, and $t_{cri} = \frac{E_0}{P_{stat} - P_{sleep}}$.

2.4   Fault Model

The transient fault of the system will be increased when the system runs at a reduced speed [4]. Assuming the transient faults follow Poisson Distribution [10], the average transient fault rate for a job running at frequency f and voltage V is [4]:

$$\lambda(f, V) = \lambda_0 \times g(f, V) \tag{2}$$

where λ_0 is the average fault rate corresponding to V_{max} and f_{max}. At the lowest frequency f_{min} and supply voltage V_{min}, the average fault rate is assumed to be [4]:

$$\lambda_{max} = \lambda_0 \times 10^d \tag{3}$$

$d(>0)$ is a constant. So for the job running at f and V where $V = f \times V_{max} = f$ (V_{max} is normalized to be 1), the average transient fault rate can be expressed as [4]:

$$\lambda(f,V) = \lambda(f) = \lambda_0 \times 10^{\frac{d(1-f)}{1-f_{min}}} \qquad (4)$$

From formula 4, we can easily derive that $g(f,v) = 10^{\frac{d(1-f)}{1-f_{min}}} > 1$ for $f < f_{max}$ and reducing the supply voltage for lower frequency results in exponentially increased fault rates.

3   Algorithms

Our approach guarantees reliability at least as high as that of without voltage scaling by reserving recovery job for each scaled down task. This way of guaranteeing reliability is based on the previous works SUF/LUF developed by Zhu [4]. In order to guarantee the reliability of every job after implementing DVS is no less than its original reliability, which means the probability of correctly completing the job at maximum speed, SUF/LUF arrange a recovery job after each scaled down primary job [4]. Although the leakage power has been considered in SUF/LUF, the processor is always active during the scheduling. Our approach is to extend these previous methods with leakage control method.

Leakage control method takes static power consumption into consideration. The main idea is to shutdown the processor when it is idle and then wake it up when the next job comes. The longer the idle interval, the more static power consumption can be saved with power shutdown. Shutting down and waking up a processor cost energy. Therefore, a leakage algorithm needs to check whether it is worth shutting down the processor or not via critical interval (see Section 2.3). *Procrastination* method is used to help avoid frequent shutdown. The idea is to delay the execution of an incoming job, so that small intervals can be merged for power shutdown to save more energy thanks to less shutdown overhead.

Fig. 1 shows a simple example [11] about processor shutdown and task procrastination strategy. Suppose there are two jobs J_1 ($a_1 = 0$, $d_1 = 3$, $e_1 = 2$) and J_2 ($a_2 = 4$, $d_2 = 8$, $e_2 = 2$), where a_i, d_i and e_i are the arrival time, deadline and worst-case execution time (WCET) of J_i respectively. In Fig. 1(a), the processor is shut down twice during the idle intervals. But if J_2 is not executed until time point 6, the processor only needs to be shutdown once and can get the same length of idle interval while meeting the deadlines, as shown in Fig. 1(b) (procrastination).

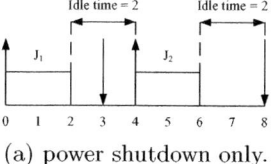

(a) power shutdown only.

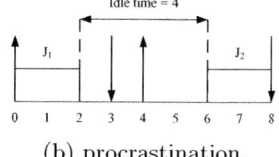

(b) procrastination.

Fig. 1. Leakage Control Method

Several algorithms which combine DVS and leakage control method for power management have been proposed [12,13,14,9,8]. However, none of the integrated DVS methods above is a reliability aware algorithm. And the reliability-aware DVS methods which consider both reliability and energy consumption [4,15] have not explored the shutdown technique. Our first algorithm SUF-L extends a reliability aware DVS algorithm SUF with leakage control method.

3.1   SUF-L: Integrate Leakage Control with SUF

SUF-L first applies SUF which chooses the first m smallest utilization tasks to scale down and reserve time slot for each scaled down task. After SUF completes, every task would be assigned with an initial speed. SUF-L then pre-computes procrastination length for each task. The execution speed and procrastination length of every job generated by the same task would be the same. The procrastination length calculation (See Theorem 1) is based on an existing procrastination algorithm CS-DVSP [6]. The difference is that in our calculation, in order to guarantee the reliability of the system, we must reserve some slacks for potential recovery job tolerance.

Algorithm 1. SUF-L: The Leakage Control Algorithm

1: Calculate initial speed for each task by SUF;
2: Calculate procrastination length for each task;
3: **During the scheduling**:
4: **if** (Processor is not idle) **then**
5:    Schedule jobs according to EDF policy;
6: **else**
7:    Calculate next coming job J_i's arrival time a_i;
8:    Judge if there is any job J_j's arrival time a_j is between a_i and $(a_i + L_i)$;
9:    Set the wake up time to be $min(a_i + L_i, a_j + L_j)$;
10:    **if** (sleep time interval is longer than critical interval) **then**
11:       shutdown the processor until wake up time;
12:    **else**
13:       Keep processor in idle state until next job arrives;
14:    **end if**
15: **end if**

The following is an example of an application that applies SUF-L.

Suppose we have a periodic task set $\{T_1(p_1 = 12, e_1 = 2), T_2(p_2 = 17, e_2 = 1), T_3(p_3 = 18, e_3 = 4)\}$ with $U = 0.45$. After applying SUF algorithm, T_1 and T_2's initial speed is 0.58, T_3's initial speed is 1 and the new utilization is 0.61. Then we can calculate the procrastination length (L_i) of every task according to Theorem 1, resulting in $L_1 = L_2 = L_3 = 3$. Different from the SUF scheduling, job J_{12} is not executed until time 15 in SUF-L, and the start execution times of job J_{22}, J_{32} and J_{13} are delayed accordingly. J_{23} is also not executed until time 37. Since the execution speed of every job by SUF and SUF-L scheme is all the same, the reliability of the system is also guaranteed by SUF-L, which

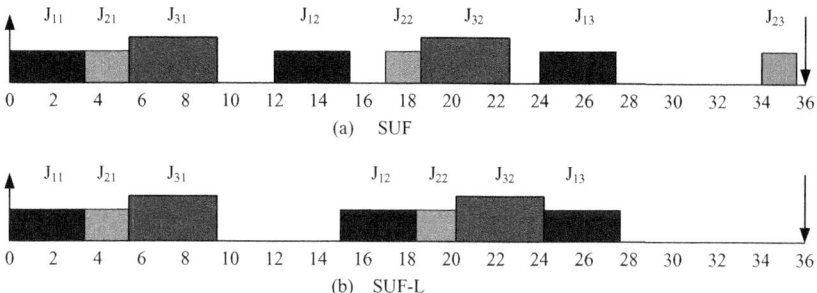

Fig. 2. SUF and SUF-L

means enough slacks have been allocated in advance for any potential recovery job during the run time, although we do not consider any fault in this example. After scheduling, the total energy consumed within 712 time units (the least common multiple of periods) is 648.84 by SUF-L compared with 696.90 by SUF. Our simulation results in Section 4 also show that SUF-L can save more than 10% energy on average compared with SUF.

Theorem 1. *For a periodic task set with non-decreasing order of task period (non-increasing priority), the procrastination algorithm guarantees all task deadlines if the procrastination interval L_i of task T_i where $i = 1, \ldots, N$, satisfies:*

$$\frac{L_i + e}{p_i} + \sum_{k=1}^{i} \frac{1}{s_k} \times \frac{e_k}{p_k} \leq 1, \quad i = 1, \ldots, N \tag{5}$$

$$L_k \leq L_i, \quad \forall_{k \leq i} \tag{6}$$

where e stands for the maximum execution time among non-higher priority tasks of T_i.

Proof. Suppose the processor is idle at current time, and the next coming job J_i would arrive at a_i with the procrastination length L_i. In [6], it has been proved that for any task's procrastination length Z_i, if it satisfies

$$\frac{Z_i}{p_i} + \sum_{k=1}^{i} \frac{1}{s_k} \times \frac{e_k}{p_k} \leq 1,$$

then the schedulability of system can be guaranteed. In our algorithm, the new procrastination length L_i satisfies $L_i + e = Z_i$. Considering only single fault tolerance, there will be two situations after the procrastination:

1. J_i or a lower priority job J_j arrives after a_i:
   Without considering the slack reserved for recovery job, the schedulability can be guaranteed after J_i is procrastinated with a length Z_i. Even if a fault occurs during J_i or J_j, the recovery job can use the reserved slack $e = Z_i - L_i$ for re-execution. So the schedulability is not violated.

2. A higher priority job J_j arrives after a_i:
   Since J_j's priority is higher, it would be executed as soon as it is available, even before J_i. The slack of R_j has been considered in advance after implementing SUF, thus the execution of J_j and R_j has no bad effect on the execution of lower priority jobs.

Note that, in SUF-L, we calculate the initial speed and the procrastination length for every task in advance before scheduling, with the time complexities $O(N)$ and $O(N^2)$, respectively. During scheduling, the time complexity is $O(N)$. Here, N is the number of periodic tasks in the task set.

3.2   SUF-S: Shared-Recovery Static Algorithm

SUF is a conservative algorithm and a lot of slacks have to be reserved for potential recovery jobs. Since the fault ratio is extremely low, it is very unlikely that two faults occur during the execution of one job. Thus, we can make two primary jobs share one recovery job and the extra time reserved for the other recovery job can be used to further slow down the primary job. SHR proposed by Zhao et. al. [15] used shared-recovery technique which is based on allocating a shared recovery block/slack that can be used by any faulty task at run-time. SHR is more efficient than SUF, and gets much better energy performance. However, SHR only works for a periodic task set of the same deadline/period. Our second method SUF-S is to extend the shared-recovery technique to the case where the periods of the tasks in the task set may be different.

As shown in Fig. 3, after applying SUF, two slacks $R1$ and $R2$ have been reserved for primary scaled jobs J_1 and J_2, respectively. With the shared-recovery technique, we only need to reserve one slack R to tolerate fault either from J_1 or J_2. Since we only consider tolerating at most one fault during every period, the reliability of the system is still guaranteed. Furthermore, the released slack which has been reserved for R_2 in SUF can be used to further reduce J_2's execution speed. Different from the leakage control method, the shared-recovery technique is used when the processor is busy. The following is an example.

We use the same task set as in Section 3.1. During the scheduling by SUF-S, after sharing recovery job with J_{21}, J_{11}'s speed is further slowed down from 0.58 to critical speed 0.41. If an fault occurs within J_{11} or J_{21}, there is still enough slack to schedule the recovery job without missing any deadline, shown in Fig. 4(c). So is J_{12}, which can share recovery job with J_{22}. The total energy consumed within 712 time units without any fault is 681.67 by SUF-S compared with 696.90 by SUF. Our simulation results in Section 4 also show that SUF-S can save more than 5% energy on average compared with SUF. The following theorem defines how to judge whether two primary jobs can share their recovery jobs.

The shared-recovery job can be found using the *shared-recovery job (SRJ) rule* as described below.

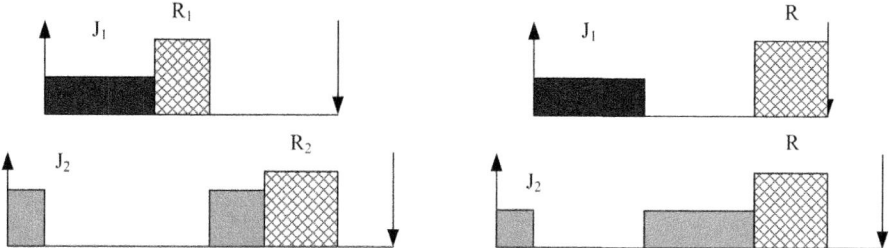

Fig. 3. Shared-Recovery Technique

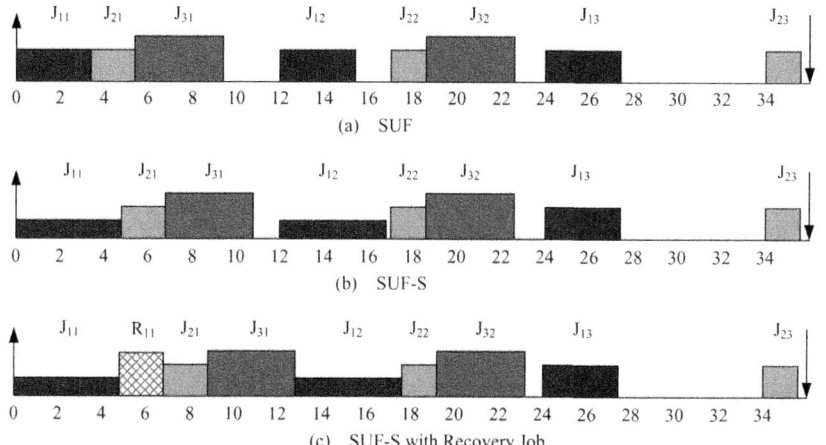

Fig. 4. SUF and SUF-S

SRJ rule: For primary job J_i, if another primary job J_j satisfies the following two constraints, then J_j can share its recovery job with J_i.

1. J_i and J_j's initial speeds are less than maximum speed.
2. J_j arrives no earlier than a_i and its recovery job finishes before d_i in pre-schedule.

Since only scaled down job is reserved enough slack for recovery job after implementing SUF, the first condition ensures that both J_i and J_j are scaled down jobs. Only if the second condition is satisfied, then J_i can use the slack reserved for J_j when necessary. In order to verify the second condition, a new job list should be constructed which consists of J_i and all the jobs arriving between a_i and d_i. In the worst case while scheduling the new job list, after every scaled down job, a recovery job would also be executed with the maximum speed. Then the first finished job other than J_i satisfying both two constraints above would be the job that can share recovery job with J_i.

Once we discover that J_i and J_j can share recovery jobs, we need to calculate the new execution speed for J_i. There are two situations to be considered:

- $e_i \leq e_j$ R_j can be shared by J_i and J_j, and the slack time reserved for R_i (which is e_i) can totally be used to scale down J_i's execution speed. For J_i, new execution speed $s'_i = \frac{e_i}{\frac{e_i}{s_i} + e_i} = \frac{s_i}{1 + s_i}$.
- $e_i > e_j$ R_i can be shared by J_i and J_j, and the slack time reserved for R_j (which is e_j) can totally be used to scale down J_i's execution speed. For J_i, new execution speed $s'_i = \frac{e_i}{\frac{e_i}{s_i} + e_j}$.

The same as SUF-L, time complexity of calculating initial speed in SUF-S for every task is $O(N)$. But during scheduling, since we need to pre-schedule to find out the shared recovery job, the time complexity is $O(N^2)$. N is the number of periodic tasks in the task set.

3.3   SUF-LS: Combined Static Algorithm

In Section 3.1, with leakage control method being able to extend the power down interval and reduce static power consumption, we explore to integrate the unused slacks in the existing system to minimize total energy consumption. In Section 3.2, with shared-recovery technique being able to further scale down execution speed when processor is busy to reduce dynamic power consumption, we explore to reduce the reserved recovery time and extend power management time to minimize total energy consumption. In this section, we combine these two different methods together and develop a new algorithm called SUF-LS. In SUF-LS, we try to share recovery jobs whenever possible during scheduling and delay the start executing time of next coming job as long as possible if processor is idle.

In Fig. 5, the same task set is used as Section 3.1. In SUF-LS, J_{12} and J_{23} are delayed to execute in order to merge small intervals. J_{11} and J_{12}'s execution speeds are lower than initial speeds after sharing recovery jobs. If a fault occurs within J_{11} or J_{21}, the recovery job can also be executed without missing any deadlines, shown in Fig. 5(c). The total energy consumed within 712 time units without any fault is 640.16 by SUF-LS compared with 696.90 by SUF. Our simulation results in Section 4 also show that SUF-LS can save more than 12% energy on average compared with SUF.

Different from SUF-S, when we pre-schedule in SUF-LS, we must take the leakage control method into consideration as well. If we do not, suppose we can find J_i and J_j to share recovery job in pre-scheduling, then in the actual scheduling, J_j would be procrastinated and if a fault occurs, the recovery job of J_j would miss deadline. After considering the leakage control method in pre-scheduling, once J_j is procrastinated, enough slack to tolerate a recovery job in the period has been reserved, in both pre-scheduling and actual scheduling. Meanwhile, after sharing recovery job, the two primary jobs only require one slack for one error, which has been met by the procrastination algorithm. So

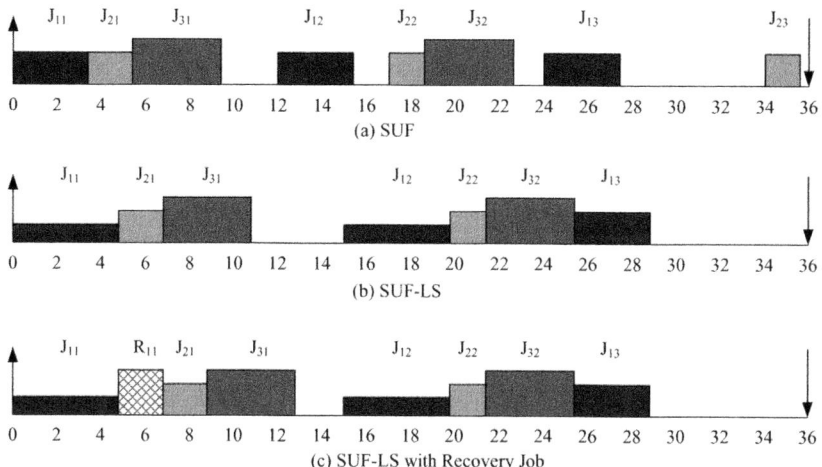

Fig. 5. SUF and SUF-LS

Algorithm 2. SUF-LS: The Combined Algorithm

1: Calculate initial speed for each task by SUF;
2: Calculate procrastination length by Theorem 1 for each task;
3: **During the scheduling:**
4: **if** (Processor is not idle) **then**
5:     **On execution of a new job** J_i:
6:     Find if there is an incoming job that can share recovery job with J_i following
        Algorithm 3.
7:     Schedule J_i with speed s_i under EDF policy
8: **else**
9:     Judge whether to shutdown processor or not according to Algorithm 1.
10: **end if**

Algorithm 3. Pre-Schedule in SUF-LS

1: **On execution of a new job** J_i:
2: **if** $(s_i < s_{max}$ and R_i has not been shared) **then**
3:     Construct a job list with the primary job and the recovery job arriving between
        a_i and d_i:
4:     Pre-Schedule each primary job with recovery job under EDF policy
5:     **if** (There is idle interval in the pre-schedule) **then**
6:         Judge whether to shutdown processor or not according to Algorithm 1
7:     **else**
8:         **if** (a job can share recovery job with J_i according to the SRJ $rule$) **then**
9:             Update s_i
10:        **end if**
11:    **end if**
12: **end if**

---

even if an error occurs in actual scheduling, the recovery job can still be executed successfully. In this way, both the schedulability and reliability of the system are guaranteed.

In SUF-LS, before scheduling, the time complexity is the same as that in SUF-L, which is $O(N^2)$. During scheduling, we also need to pre-schedule to find out shared-recovery jobs, so the time complexity is $O(N^2)$ as well. N is the number of periodic tasks in the task set.

4   Simulation Results and Analysis

In this section, the following algorithms are simulated in a discrete single processor simulator to evaluate energy and reliability performance. LUF-based algorithms work the same as the SUF-based algorithms except that the first m tasks selected for scaling are the m largest utilization tasks.

- NPM: all jobs are executed with the maximum speed, and processor is always on.
- UTI: all jobs are executed with $max(U, s_{cri})$, and the processor is always on. This is supposed to be optimal if only dynamic power is considered.
- CS-DVSP: a task-level oriented leakage control method [6].
- SUF/LUF: reliability guaranteed task-level algorithm which uses recovery job to make up for the descending reliability because of power management.
- SUF-L/LUF-L: the heuristic leakage control method combined with SUF/LUF task-level algorithm.
- SUF-S/LUF-S: the heuristic shared-recovery technique combined with SUF/LUF job-level algorithm.
- SUF-LS/LUF-LS: the heuristic leakage and reliability well balanced job-level algorithm.

In our simulation, the power settings are the same as those in [8]. The power model and technology parameters of the processor used in the simulation are

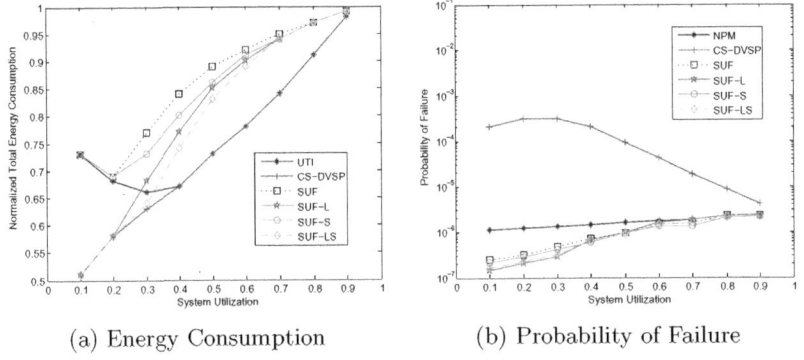

(a) Energy Consumption   (b) Probability of Failure

Fig. 6. Simulation Results of the SUF-Based Static Algorithms

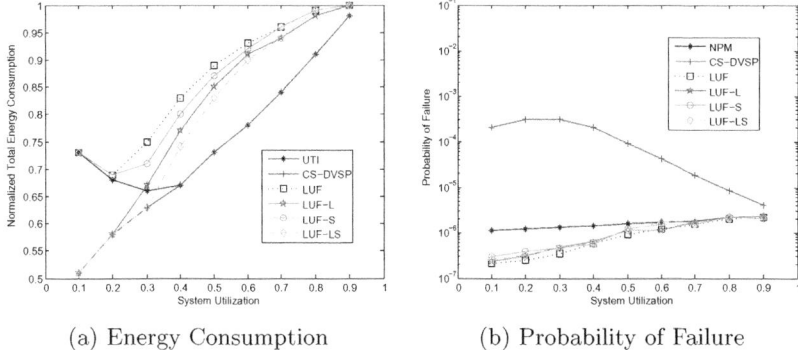

(a) Energy Consumption   (b) Probability of Failure

Fig. 7. Simulation Results of the LUF-Based Static Algorithms

from [7] (The s_{cri} for this model is around 0.4 [6]). The overhead of processor power down/up is the same as that used in [6], where $P_{idle} = 240mW$, $E_0 = 483\mu J$, $t_0 = 2ms$, $L_g = 4000000$. To evaluate energy consumptions, we set up system utilizations from 0.1 to 0.9 for each algorithm. For each point in the chart, we generate 20 task sets and each task set is executed with five million time units. Every task set includes 20 periodic tasks. The periods and the WCETs in each task set are randomly chosen in the range of $[10, 200]$ and $[1, 10]$, respectively. Transient faults are assumed to follow the Poisson Distribution with an average fault rate of $\lambda_0 = 10^{-6}$ at f_{max} per megabit [4]. The same as [2], in order to take the effects of DVS into consideration, the exponent in the fault model $d = 2$, which means the average fault rate with s_{min} is assumed to be 100 times higher than that of s_{max}. The energy consumptions by every algorithm are normalized to that by NPM, and the probability of failure is calculated through dividing faulty job number by total executed job number.

Figs. 6 and 7 show the simulation results of different algorithms. Figs. 6(a) and (b) are about the performance of SUF based algorithms while Figs. 7(a) and 7(b) are about the LUF based. The results clearly confirm that SUF and LUF based algorithms perform roughly the same. We take the SUF based algorithms as an example. Fig. 6(a) first shows the total energy consumption with different algorithms. CS-DVSP consumes the least energy while SUF consumes the most. At $U \leq 0.3$, the power performances of UTI, SUF and SUF-S are almost the same. That's because almost every task's initial speed is less than s_{cri} after implementing SUF. All jobs would execute with s_{cri} during scheduling so that even with shared-recovery technique, jobs still execute with the same speed in different algorithms without considering leakage control method. For SUF-S, when utilization is higher, more tasks would be initialized to execute with maximum speed to guarantee the reliability. At $U = 0.3$, nearly all tasks are initialized with speeds between s_{cri} and s_{max} while only half tasks initialized with scaled down speeds at $U = 0.6$. Meanwhile, with shared-recovery technique, job's execution time is extended and more static power is also consumed. The energy consumption of SUF-L is much better than SUF-S. Especially when utilization is low, a lot of slack can be merged and processor is shutdown to save static power. Under $U = 0.3$, almost every job can execute with s_{cri}, the energy consumed is the same as that consumed by CS-DVSP. At higher utilization, more jobs would execute with s_{max} to guarantee reliability so that more energy would be consumed. After combining shared-recovery technique, SUF-LS enhances the energy performance more. Generally, SUF-S can save at most 5% energy and SUF-L and SUF-LS can reach more than 10% energy saving on average compared with SUF.

Figs. 6(b) and 7(b) show the probability of failure of different algorithms. For NPM, it increases slightly since more workload would be finished while system utilization is growing up. CS-DVSP does not consider reliability, so the probability of failure proves to be 1000 times more than NPM. With recovery jobs arranged in advance, our proposed schemes all have lower probability of failure than NPM, which shows that the reliability of the system is guaranteed.

5   Conclusions and Future Work

After taking both static power management and system reliability aspects into consideration, energy saving algorithm design is more complicated. In this work, we propose algorithms to approach total energy and reliability codesign problem from two different aspects. The first is to integrate the leakage control method with reliability aware DVS technique and the second is to use the shared-recovery technique. The proposed algorithms are evaluated through simulations. The results show that, with our proposed algorithms, the system reliability can be guaranteed, and total energy consumption is reduced compared with existing algorithms. All these algorithms proposed are static algorithms. Our future work will extend the algorithms to dynamic algorithms to consider the case when the tasks do not run with worst case execution time.

Acknowledgements. The authors would like to thank NSERC (National Science Engineering Research Council, Canada) for supporting this research. The authors also want to thank Dakai Zhu and Baoxian Zhao for their kind help during the work.

References

1. Reed, D.: Keeping leakage current under control (2003),
   http://www.eetimes.com/design/communications-design/4137563/
   Keeping-leakage-current-under-control
2. Zhu, D., Aydin, H.: Reliability-aware energy management for periodic real-time tasks. In: RTAS 2007: Proceedings of the 13th IEEE Real Time and Embedded Technology and Applications Symposium, pp. 225–235. IEEE Computer Society, Washington, DC (2007)
3. Castillo, X., McConnel, S., Siewiorek, D.: Derivation and caliberation of a transient error reliability model. IEEE Transactions on Computers, 658–671 (1982)

4. Zhu, D., Melhem, R., Mosse, D.: The effects of energy management on reliability in real-time embedded systems. In: ICCAD 2004: Proceedings of the 2004 IEEE/ACM International Conference on Computer-Aided Design, pp. 35–40. IEEE Computer Society, Washington, DC (2004)
5. Liu, J. (ed.): Real-Time Systems. Prentice-Hall, Englewood Cliffs (2000)
6. Jejurikar, R., Pereira, C., Gupta, R.K.: Leakage aware dynamic voltage scaling for real-time embedded systems. In: Proceedings of the Design Automation Conference, pp. 275–280. ACM Press, New York (2004)
7. Martin, S.M., Flautner, K., Mudge, T., Blaauw, D.: Combined dynamic voltage scaling and adaptive body biasing for lower power microprocessors under dynamic workloads. In: ICCAD 2002: Proceedings of the 2002 IEEE/ACM International Conference on Computer-Aided Design, pp. 721–725. ACM, New York (2002)
8. Niu, L., Quan, G.: Reducing both dynamic and leakage energy consumption for hard real-time systems. In: CASES 2004: Proceedings of the 2004 International Conference on Compilers, Architecture, and Synthesis for Embedded Systems, pp. 140–148. ACM, New York (2004)
9. Chen, J.J., Kuo, T.W.: Procrastination determination for periodic real-time tasks in leakage-aware dynamic voltage scaling systems. In: ICCAD 2007: Proceedings of the 2007 IEEE/ACM International Conference on Computer-Aided Design, pp. 289–294. IEEE Press, Piscataway (2007)
10. Zhang, Y., Chakrabarty, K.: Energy-aware adaptive checkpointing in embedded real-time systems. In: DATE 2003: Proceedings of the Conference on Design, Automation and Test in Europe, p. 10918. IEEE Computer Society, Washington, DC (2003)
11. Pan, Y., Lin, M.: Dynamic leakage aware power management with procrastination method. In: John's, S. (ed.) CCECE 2009, pp. 247–251. IEEE CS Press, Newfoundland (2009)
12. Lee, Y.H., Reddy, K.P., Krishna, C.M.: Scheduling techniques for reducing leakage power in hard real-time systems. In: Proceedings of 15th Euromicro Conference Real-Time Systems, pp. 105–112 (2003)
13. Jejurikar, R., Gupta, R.: Dynamic voltage scaling for systemwide energy minimization in real-time embedded systems. In: ISLPED 2004: Proceedings of the 2004 International Symposium on Low Power Electronics and Design, pp. 78–81. ACM, New York (2004)
14. Jejurikar, R., Gupta, R.: Dynamic slack reclamation with procrastination scheduling in real-time embedded systems. In: DAC 2005: Proceedings of the 42nd Annual Conference on Design Automation, pp. 111–116. ACM, New York (2005)
15. Zhao, B., Aydin, H., Zhu, D.: Enhanced reliability-aware power management through shared recovery technique. In: IEEE/ACM International Conference on Computer-Aided Design, ICCAD 2009, pp. 63–70 (2009)

Author Index